United Kingdoms

United Kingdoms

*Multinational Union States in Europe
and Beyond, 1800–1925*

ALVIN JACKSON

OXFORD
UNIVERSITY PRESS

Great Clarendon Street, Oxford, OX2 6DP,
United Kingdom

Oxford University Press is a department of the University of Oxford.
It furthers the University's objective of excellence in research, scholarship,
and education by publishing worldwide. Oxford is a registered trade mark of
Oxford University Press in the UK and in certain other countries

© Alvin Jackson 2023

The moral rights of the author have been asserted

All rights reserved. No part of this publication may be reproduced, stored in
a retrieval system, or transmitted, in any form or by any means, without the
prior permission in writing of Oxford University Press, or as expressly permitted
by law, by licence or under terms agreed with the appropriate reprographics
rights organization. Enquiries concerning reproduction outside the scope of the
above should be sent to the Rights Department, Oxford University Press, at the
address above

You must not circulate this work in any other form
and you must impose this same condition on any acquirer

Published in the United States of America by Oxford University Press
198 Madison Avenue, New York, NY 10016, United States of America

British Library Cataloguing in Publication Data
Data available

Library of Congress Control Number: 2023932340

ISBN 978–0–19–288374–2

DOI: 10.1093/oso/9780192883742.001.0001

Printed and bound in the UK by
Clays Ltd, Elcograf S.p.A.

Links to third party websites are provided by Oxford in good faith and
for information only. Oxford disclaims any responsibility for the materials
contained in any third party website referenced in this work.

For Joyce, once again

Acknowledgements

The origins of this book date back over 30 years. When, in 1987, as a callow postdoctoral student I was presenting work on Irish history at Brasenose College, Oxford, Robert Evans broached some of the possible analogies between Ireland and central Europe. From this exchange arose—very gradually—various interests which are now developed within the structure of the present volume. The book is entirely free-standing, but its concerns are also closely linked with two of my earlier works, *Home Rule: An Irish History* (2003/4) and *The Two Unions: Ireland, Scotland and the Survival of the United Kingdom* (2012/13). In essence these three volumes constitute an informal trilogy: they apply an ever-widening perspective onto the politics and workings of the union state, first in Ireland alone, and then comparatively, in both Scotland and Ireland. This volume addresses the functioning of multinational union states of different types, including several varieties of professed 'united kingdom', across 19th- and 20th-century Europe: these unions were generally linked by the circumstances of the Napoleonic wars, and by the imperatives of British policy. The book takes the theme of survival and longevity, and seeks—on the basis of a wide range of historical experience—to move towards establishing a taxonomy of success and failure. However, the starting point and the end point remain determinedly the unions of the United Kingdom; and (as I hope will be clear) I make no claim to offer anything other than a perspective and an interpretation stemming from my work as an Irish (and British) historian.

I am deeply grateful to the Leverhulme Trust for awarding me a Major Research Fellowship, thereby permitting the freedom to research, think about, and write this current volume. I am also grateful to my colleagues in the School of History, Classics, and Archaeology at the University of Edinburgh for supporting the project through the award of some additional leave, and through constant intellectual debate and stimulus. My fourth-year students on my 'Disunited kingdoms' special subject at Edinburgh have, over several years, allowed me to test and debate ideas—and have offered argument and insight.

Earlier, and different, drafts of some individual sections of the book have appeared elsewhere. A version of section 2.2 has appeared as a contribution to a festschrift for my mentor and friend, Brian Harrison; also, a version of section 5.2 has appeared within Robert Schütze and Stephen Tierney (eds), *The United Kingdom and the Federal Idea* (London, 2018). Similarly, an earlier draft of section 4.8 has been published as 'Union States, Civil Society and National Symbols in the Nineteenth Century: Comparing United Kingdoms', in *Scandinavica: An International Journal of Scandinavian Studies*, 58/2 (2019).

Other sections were delivered as lectures or talks at numerous locations between 2015 and the onset of lockdown in 2020: at Aberdeen University, Boston College (the Lowell Lecture in the Humanities), Cambridge University, Concordia University, Montréal, the Collège d'Europe at Natolin, Warsaw, Durham University, the Graduate Institute (Geneva), Groningen, the University of Helsinki, the Institute of Historical Research, London, Notre Dame University, the University of Oslo, Oxford University, Princeton (the Fund for Irish Studies Lecture), Queen's University Belfast, the University of Salzburg, and University College London (the Ecclesiastical History Society). I am very grateful to all my hosts for the opportunity to air ideas and for their feedback: Robert Frost at Aberdeen, Rob Savage and Jim Smith at Boston, Barry Colfer, Eamon Duffy, and John Kerrigan at the Cambridge Group for Irish Studies, Eugenio Biagini, Niamh Gallagher, and Charles Read at the Cambridge Modern Irish History seminar, Richard Butterwick at the Collège d'Europe, Michael Kenneally at Concordia, Robert Schütze and Stephen Tierney at Durham, Emmanuel Dalle Mulle, Mona Bieling, and Davide Rodogno at Geneva, Raingard Esser at Groningen, Jani Pekke Marjanen, Jussi Kurunmaki, and Maren Jonasson at Helsinki, Rosamond McKitterick at the Institute of Historical Research (the Ecclesiastical History Society conference), Patrick Griffin at Notre Dame, Roy Foster and Ian McBride at Oxford, Ruth Solveig Hemstad and Dag Michalsen at Oslo and UCL, Fintan O'Toole at Princeton, Richard English at Queen's Belfast, and Laurence Cole at Salzburg. In 2019–20 I was invited to speak to a range of academic audiences in France on some of the themes broached within this volume—at the universities of Caen Normandie, Clermont Auvergne, Paris 3 (Sorbonne Nouvelle) and 4 (Sorbonne), Rouen, Toulouse Capitole. I am very grateful to my friends Anne-Catherine de Bouvier (Caen), Tim Whitton (Clermont), Yann Béliard (Paris), Geraldine Vaughan (Rouen), Marie-Violaine Louvet (Toulouse) for their invitations, hospitality, and stimulating conversation. Some of the material relevant to Ireland and Austria-Hungary was aired at a seminar hosted in February 2021 by the President of Ireland, Michael D Higgins: I am very grateful accordingly to Uachtarán na hÉireann for his invitation to contribute to this Machnamh 100 reflection on commemoration.

In addition some friends kindly read and commented upon sections or—occasionally—all of the text: I should like to record my warm thanks to Brian Harrison, Ruth Hemstad, Paul O'Leary, and Jill Stephenson. Maurice Bric kindly allowed me to read the manuscript of his forthcoming work on O'Connell and Papineau. John Gilmour, Calum Maciver and Donncha O'Rourke generously provided advice and support on linguistic and historical issues. None of these bears any responsibility whatever for any errors, of omission or commission, in the final text. The dedication acknowledges once again my greatest debt of all.

Alvin Jackson,
Edinburgh.

Contents

List of Illustrations   xi
A Note on Terminology   xiii

1. Introduction: The United Kingdom and Its Analogues   1
    1.1 Structures   2
    1.2 Choices   4
    1.3 Definitions   8
    1.4 The Longevity of Union   14
    1.5 Exporting Union: Viscount Castlereagh and His Circle   19
    1.6 Importing Union: Continental European Exemplars in the Age of Gladstone and After   29

2. The Unions of the United Kingdom of Great Britain and Ireland (1535–1922): Case Studies   39
    2.1 The First United Kingdom: Scotland and Ireland (1707/1801–1922)   39
    2.2 Wales (1535–1922)   55

3. European Unions and Beyond: Case Studies   90
    3.1 Introduction   90
    3.2 The United Kingdom of the Netherlands (1814/15–30)   90
    3.3 The United Kingdoms of Sweden-Norway (1814–1905)   102
    3.4 The United Province of Canada (the United Canadas) (1841–67)   121
    3.5 Austria-Hungary (1867–1918)   134
    3.6 Conclusion: After Union   158

4. Centripede: The Institutional Bolsters of Union   164
    4.1 Introduction   164
    4.2 Monarchy   166
    4.3 Aristocracy   174
    4.4 Armies and Security   180
    4.5 Bureaucracy   185
    4.6 'Kneeling Armies': Church and Faith   192
    4.7 Parliament   205
    4.8 Civil Society, Space, and Symbols   210
    4.9 Trade and Infrastructure   219
    4.10 Class Politics and Union   228
    4.11 Imperial Dark Arts: Crushing, Cosseting, and Dividing   233

5. Alternative Unions: Federalism   247
    5.1 The Historiography of Federalism   247
    5.2 Failed Panacea? Federalizing Britain and Its Empire   250

5.3	Federalizing Canada	268
5.4	Federalizing Austria and Austria-Hungary	279
5.5	Unions, Federations, and Beyond	285

6. Centrifuge: Why Do Unions Fail? — 294
    6.1 Defining Failure — 294
    6.2 Union Creation Myths and Visions — 301
    6.3 The Symmetry Problem in the Union State — 306
    6.4 *Kulturpessimismus:* Unionist Identities and Organizations — 311
    6.5 National Difference, Small Difference, and Indifference — 320
    6.6 Foreign Affairs — 328
    6.7 The War Against Union and Empire, 1914–18 — 334

7. Untied Kingdoms: Past Politics and Present History — 349

Select Union Chronology — 366
Bibliography (including Reference Lists) — 377
   Manuscript Sources — 377
   Newspaper and Journal Sources — 377
   Printed Primary Sources — 377
   Secondary Sources — 388
Index — 421

List of Illustrations

1. Castlereagh and his union circle
1.1. Robert Stewart, Viscount Castlereagh (1769–1822) (watercolour portrait: National Portrait Gallery, London).   34
1.2. Richard Le Poer Trench, second Earl of Clancarty (1767–1837) (oil portrait: National Portrait Gallery, London).   35
1.3. Percy Smythe, sixth Viscount Strangford (1780–1855) (portrait on ivory: National Portrait Gallery, London).   36
1.4. Charles Stewart, later third Marquess of Londonderry (1778–1854) (oil portrait: National Portrait Gallery, London).   37
1.5. Edward Cooke (1755–1820) (mezzotint: National Portrait Gallery, London).   38
2. Architect of union
2.1. William Pitt the Younger (1759–1806) (mezzotint: National Portrait Gallery, London).   87
2.2. Carl XIV Johan of the United Kingdoms of Sweden-Norway (1763–1844) (oil portrait: Swedish Royal Collections Department).   88
2.3. Willem I of the United Kingdom of the Netherlands (1772–1843) (oil portrait: Amsterdam Museum).   89
3. Monarchy and union
3.1. Queen Victoria and her people—the Diamond Jubilee Service, St Paul's Cathedral, London, June 1897 (photograph: National Portrait Gallery, London).   162
3.2. The Emperor-King Franz Joseph visits Sarajevo in the recently annexed Bosnia, May—June 1910 (photograph: Bildarchiv der Österreichischen Nationalbibliothek).   162
3.3. The Emperor-King Karl (Károly) publicly taking his coronation oath as King of Hungary, Budapest, December 1916 (photograph: Bildarchiv der Österreichischen Nationalbibliothek).   163
3.4. The Emperor-King Karl (Károly), Crown Prince Otto and the Empress-Queen Zita installed as Apostolic rulers of Hungary, Budapest, December 1916 (bilingual postcard: private possession).   163

4. Faith, church and union state

4.1. King George V, Supreme Governor of the Church of England, the Duke and Duchess of York (later King George VI and Queen Elizabeth) together with Princess Elizabeth (later Queen Elizabeth II) after worship at Crathie Church of Scotland, Balmoral, Aberdeenshire, c.1935 (cigarette card: National Portrait Gallery, London). 245

4.2. Queen Mary, Monsignor Daniel Mannix (President, Maynooth College), and Archbishop William Walsh of Dublin, Maynooth Seminary, July 1911 (postcard: private possession). 245

4.3. The Empress-Queen Zita and the Emperor-King Karl receive a blessing at a Pressburg/Bratislava synagogue, 1917 (photograph: Bildarchiv der Österreichischen Nationalbibliothek). 246

4.4. The Empress-Queen Zita, Capuchin friar and Emperor-King Karl at the Marco d'Aviano celebration, Vienna, 1918 (photograph: Bildarchiv der Österreichischen Nationalbibliothek). 246

5. Theorist of union

5.1. Georg Jellinek (1851–1911), jurist (photograph: Universitätsbibliothek Heidelberg). 289

5.2. Oszkár Jászi (1875–1957), civil servant, minister, academic (photograph: Calliope 777). 290

5.3. A. V. Dicey (1835–1922), jurist (photograph: Harvard Law School Library Collections). 291

5.4. F. S. Oliver (1864–1934), businessman, historian, and ideologue (photograph: private possession). 292

5.5. R. W. Seton-Watson (1879–1951), scholar, civil servant, and activist (postcard: private possession). 293

I am grateful to the institutions above for permission to reproduce images in their care. Images 5.1, 5.2 and 5.3 are reproduced under Creative Commons Attribution Share-Alike Licence (https://creativecommons.org/licenses/by-sa/4.0/deed.en). To owners of copyright whom I have been unable to identify or whom I have inadvertently omitted, I offer my apologies.

A Note on Terminology

Difficulties with naming and designation are a recognized issue in any treatment of multinational union states—and it is a common contention within the literature that the ambiguities over the title of several such polities reflect more profoundly on their cultures and indeed their general robustness.

There are some particular challenges, however, which require elucidation from the start: several of these relate to Austria-Hungary after the Ausgleich (compromise) of 1867. I refer to Austria-Hungary as the 'Dual Monarchy' and also as the 'Habsburg empire'. But I also describe Austria-Hungary as a 'union', since it was indeed a personal union of the imperial crown of Austria with the royal and apostolic crown of Hungary, the crown of Bohemia, and with the various other royal and ducal domains presided over by the Habsburgs. In addition, I occasionally refer to Austria-Hungary as a 'state', although I acknowledge that there has been a long discussion on this issue, and that 'states' or 'dual state' might do just as well: at the very least, though after 1867 Austria and Hungary were separate in many ways (and certainly, from the point of view of Hungary, wholly so), under the terms of the compromise a range of common concerns and activities was specifically identified (and see Deak 2015, pp. 2–3). However, as the early 20th-century English commentator Henry Wickham Steed remarked, 'strictly speaking, there is no Hapsburg [sic] state save in the sense that a Hapsburg monarch can, without serious exaggeration, say: "L'État c'est moi!". There is an Austrian State, a Hungarian State, and there are joint Austro-Hungarian Departments of State' (Steed 1919, p. 59).

With the United Kingdoms of Sweden-Norway, the difficulty with the name is one of precedence: which of the two constituent kingdoms comes first in naming the polity? Contemporaries and later commentators often altered the name according the context of usage: in Sweden the united kingdoms were Sweden-Norway, while in Norway they were Norway-Sweden. In general I have used Sweden-Norway, given the greater size and influence of Sweden; but the precedence could just as easily have been reversed. It is worth noting—in terms of the issue of names and precedence, dignity and sensitivity—that on Swedish coins the king was described as (taking one example) 'Oscar II, Sveriges och Norges Konung', while on Norwegian coins he was 'Oscar II Norges og Sver. Konge', with 'Sweden' invariably being abbreviated on the latter—although there was also sometimes an additional inscription, *Brödrafolkens väl/Broderfolkenes Vel* (the well-being of the fraternal peoples).

With Canada, the issue is that the eponymous dominion created in 1867 was a federation which encompassed more than the United Province of Canada of 1841–67. Like contemporaries, I use 'British North America' to refer to British possessions on that continent in the years before confederation. Similarly, any reference to 'Canada' at this (pre-1867) time is an allusion specifically to the United Province, or the 'United Canadas', created by the act of union of 1840.

The United Kingdom of Great Britain and Ireland presents its own range of difficulties and national sensitivities in these areas. A century ago Scotland was routinely rendered as 'North Britain', abbreviated as 'N.B.', for postal and other purposes. Since then 'England' has been deployed as a synonym for 'Britain' or the 'United Kingdom'—not least (ironically) in the writing on home rule of the constitutional scholar, Albert Venn Dicey (1835–1922), and in the reflections of the Scottish unionist historian and polemicist, Frederick Scott Oliver (1864–1934), for whom 'the word "Britain" we tolerate as a convenient term of denotation; but it lacks both bouquet and after-taste. One can love or hate England, but not so easily Britain' (Oliver 1930–5, vol. 1, p. 42). Similarly, 'the British isles' have often been rendered as a shorthand elsewhere for the islands of Britain and Ireland. Various (sometimes clunky) formulations have been deployed within cultural and diplomatic contexts to circumnavigate these treacherous waters—neologisms such as 'islands of the north Atlantic' (IONA) or 'the Atlantic archipelago' have been proffered at different times and in different quarters. On the whole I have stuck with 'Britain and Ireland', or 'Ireland and Britain', which (while not perfect) are, arguably, least worst options.

More generally, the specific title of 'united kingdom' has been commonly applied to a range of the multinational polities considered within this volume; but not always in an official or uniform way. The legal title of the union polity created by acts of the Irish and British parliaments in 1801 was indeed the United Kingdom of Great Britain and Ireland. Similarly, the legal title of another (distinctively pluri-continental) union which is invoked occasionally in the book was the United Kingdom of Portugal, Brazil, and the Algarves (1815). The official title of the limited union of Sweden and Norway was the United Kingdoms of Sweden and Norway, with a patriotic emphasis on the plural. However, the union of the northern and southern Netherlands and Luxembourg was officially designated as the 'kingdom of the Netherlands' or more colloquially the 'united Netherlands', though it has also been called the 'United Kingdom of the Netherlands' in common usage ever since (Marteel 2018, p. 1 n. 2). Equally, though a specific 'act of union' brought together the provinces of Upper and Lower Canada, the resulting polity was (officially and legally) the 'Province of Canada'; though it was also commonly designated as the 'United Province' or the 'United Canadas'.

Finally, the focus of the work is on union states which embraced either several pre-existing polities, or several nationalities or ethnicities. However, there has been a marked push-back within some recent scholarship on 19th-century

Europe against the suppositions and vocabulary of nationalism and nationality (see e.g. Judson 2016). On the other hand, this has had a much greater influence on (for example) the research on Austria-Hungary than on that relating to the United Kingdom. In practice, therefore, I have used the terms 'multinational' and 'multi-ethnic' interchangeably throughout the work.

1
Introduction
The United Kingdom and Its Analogues

We are not, however, the first country, or the first dominant portion of a country, which has been asked, from a conjoined and incorporated section of its territory, to concede Home Rule, and has refused that request. Holland was asked for Home Rule by Belgium, and refused it. Belgium is now independent of Holland...But Home Rule has often been conceded; and, as the denial has in no case been attended with success, so the concession has in no case been attended with failure. Through the establishment of Home Rule in Norway, at a time when she was on the verge of an armed conflict with Sweden, they have been enabled to work peacefully together; and not only the sentiment of friendship, but even the sense of unity has made extraordinary progress...the relations of Austria and Hungary forty years ago were not only difficult but sanguinary, and they constituted not simply a local, but an European danger. Since Home Rule was granted, profound peace and union have prevailed.

(Gladstone 1892, pp. 364–5)

There are many examples in history, and some in very recent history, to show how hard it is for one nation to fuse another nation's life into its own, unless indeed the fusion be mutual and voluntary. For nationality is at root a spiritual thing and difficult to kill...Forcible fusion, in fact, must have proved, if it had ever been adopted, a futile policy. A futile and—let it be frankly said—a vicious policy.

(Coupland 1925, pp. 194–5)

It must never be thought that the infamous fog in the English channel which left the continent isolated from time to time was a permanent blanket that separated Britain from the rest of Europe for the century after 1815, and created two distinct and rival historical experiences.

(Brockliss and Eastwood 1997, p. 208)

1.1. Structures

This book is about a group of 'united kingdoms' of the 19th and early 20th centuries, about their performance and survival, their fate (in so far as this is decipherable), and the explanations for this fate. All of these polities were created, or substantially overhauled, at roughly the same time: the United Kingdom of Great Britain and Ireland (1800–1), the United Kingdoms of Sweden-Norway (1814–15), and the United Kingdom of the Netherlands (1814–15), with the Canadian union and confederation (1840, 1867) and the Austrian empire (1804)—reformulated as Austria-Hungary (1867)—as slight outliers. While all these provide the case studies which are at the core of the work, it also broaches other unions which date from the early 19th century, and specifically the era of the Napoleonic global wars, including the Grand Duchy of Finland (1809) and the short-lived United Kingdom of Portugal, Brazil, and the Algarves (1815).

The book is concerned with comparisons, and with venturing thereby towards some overarching and general reflections on the success and failure of union states. These polities sometimes had their roots as composite monarchies in the medieval or early modern eras, but they were dramatically reimagined and partly 'modernized' in the revolutionary circumstances of the early 19th century: indeed, union itself may be seen as an effort to reinvigorate some of the institutions of the *ancien régime* for a new age of revolution and nationhood. In essence, however, the work deals with the good health of these rejuvenated constitutional organisms, as well as with their ultimate epidemiology, morbidity, and pathology. It deals, too, with the many interlinkages between these unions, and especially between them and the United Kingdom of Great Britain and Ireland.

Here, at the start, some navigational guidance may be offered concerning not just the subject matter of the volume, but also its particular shape and structure. This, first, chapter sets out to explain the geographical focus of the work—to illuminate the choice of the particular case studies of union which serve to inform its central arguments. Here, too, some consideration is given to definitions and an understanding of the wider multinational union state—as well as to the (still) counter-intuitive theme of the longevity of such states. While the work deals with a closely related group of adapted composite monarchies or personal unions, it also accepts the diversity of their adaptation, as well as the shared lineage and resemblances characterizing these different polities. And, while the work is concerned with the ways in which such polities end, it also seeks to avoid any teleology of inevitable decline and fall.

At the heart of the work are several chapters offering a set of case studies, beginning with the unions of the United Kingdom. This is complemented by studies of European and wider union polities, often varying in constitution, but united by an association with British and Irish policy makers, or by deep linkages with British and Irish constitutional reform, or by chronological and wartime context. In developing these case studies, several unifying themes are adduced—including not only the particular linkages between these European and other unions with Britain and Ireland, but also the complex array of agencies and institutions which served to support and maintain union. Acknowledging the distinctions between these polities, the work also aims to deliver some generic conclusions on the shared histories of multinational union states across the long 19th century.

Complementing the case studies, and picking up and collating their concerns, are two comparative and thematic chapters, focusing on the bolsters and solvents of union, or those centripetal and centrifugal forces and agencies playing upon the structures of the multinational union state. It will become clear that these discussions have been partly influenced by a range of contemporary observations and taxonomies, including work by the Irish-born constitutionalist and statesman, James Bryce (1838–1922), and by the Hungarian-born statesman and historian, Oszkár Jászi (1875–1957). But it will also become clear that, while (in the interests of the work's structure) the centripetal is separated from the centrifugal, in reality the two were often interchangeable, and the centrifugal could readily become the centripetal (and vice versa). In essence, unions were malleable political entities; and the forces and institutions supporting or subverting them were also highly fluid.

Linking these two discussions is a discussion of a mediating theme—the reform of union polities, and in particular the application of federal reform ideas and initiatives. Federalism has been conventionally (and often unsuccessfully) deployed as a nostrum for the ailments of troubled multinational polities, whether with the Dual Monarchy or with Britain and Ireland. Indeed, federalism remains very much in play as a potential means of balancing countervailing demands within the troubled United Kingdom state.

Given that most of the unions considered in the volume were born in the context of the Napoleonic global conflict, some consideration is given towards the end of the work to the devastating impact of a later global conflagration, the First World War, on two of the study's central chosen unions, Austria-Hungary and the United Kingdom. The final chapter seeks not simply to summarize, but also to link the historical concerns of the work with where we are now, in the 21st century.

Finally, here at the outset it should once again be emphasized that this is a work of political history—and a work which in particular seeks to link the history of Ireland and Britain with a set of wider spatial and thematic horizons. Readers can expect due weight to be given to change and contingency and to the frequent untidiness or ambiguity of evidence and definition. But they should also come away from the book with a clear sense of how the United Kingdom was related to other contemporary union polities, how all these polities worked—and when and why they failed.

1.2. Choices

This book focuses, then, on the fortunes of several union states—with the United Kingdom of Great Britain and Ireland very clearly at the heart of the analysis. But the study also encompasses other polities, of different shapes and sizes and locations, while sharing some fundamental features in common. All were multinational or composite monarchies, and indeed several of them boasted of being 'united kingdoms': several were either empires or were associated with empire, and indeed (as will become clear) there is a wider elision between the concepts of 'union' and 'empire' (see e.g. Armitage 2000, p. 23). Thus, while the United Kingdom of Great Britain and Ireland is both the starting point and centre of the analysis, the study also embraces the short-lived (1815–30/39) united kingdom of the Netherlands (since then often called the *Verenigd Koninkrijk der Nederlanden/ Royaume uni des Pays-Bas*) as well as one of its successor states, the Kingdom of Belgium. Attention is also paid to a third 'UK'—the United Kingdoms of Sweden and Norway (the United Kingdoms/*Förenade konungarikena Sverige och Norge/ De forenede Kongeriger Norge og Sverige*). A further major focus of the work is comparison between Britain and Ireland and the major European power which most 19th- and early 20th-century British and Irish contemporaries invoked in terms of analogy and comparison (and whose interests were long seen as most closely aligned with those of the British): the reformulated composite monarchy that was the Austro-Hungarian empire (Anon. 1870, p. 70). Finally, British and Irish reformers paid close attention to an ailing and revised union within the empire—namely Canada, which had been bound by an Act of Union in 1840, but then (in 1867) federated alongside other provinces under the terms of the British North America Act. Moreover, as will be shown, the Scots and Irish unions were not only exemplars for Canadians, but Irish and Scots statesmen were disproportionately significant influences in the shaping of Canadian union and confederation.

Not all of these polities were alike, and the distinctions should be carefully recognized from the outset. The challenges (and the benefits) of comparative history are indeed well-known, and have been aptly summarized many times, whether in terms of the risks of decontextualization or of the fudging of difference—or, alternatively, the risks of determinism, universalism, and exceptionalism (see Kocka 2003; Cohen 2004, pp. 60–4; Levine 2014, p. 341; Butterwick-Pawlikowski et al. 2017, p. 47; for the 'distinctiveness of Austrian history' see Ingrao 1994, pp. 1–22). England and Scotland formed a parliamentary union after 1707, as did Britain and Ireland after 1801: at the same time, however, none of the 'British' unions was wholly complete, for very substantial vestiges of national distinctiveness remained within the political and administrative structures of both Ireland and Scotland, and by the late 19th century the distinctiveness even of Wales was gaining increasing legislative recognition. The United Kingdom of the Netherlands was also a (short-lived) parliamentary union—at least in the particular sense of having a single parliament for the union. However, both Austria-Hungary and Sweden-Norway were modified or reinforced personal rather than parliamentary unions though, since there were formal legal foundations in each case, they were also 'real unions'; moreover, with each there were political structures or institutions beyond the crown which helped to unite the distinct parts of the composite monarchy. In each, too, there were periodic efforts to create a more united government. It is perhaps best to see these different multinational states as all originating in traditions of composite monarchy, but with different intensities of subsequent amalgamation—Britain and Ireland being clearly a more thoroughgoing union than (say) Sweden-Norway, though with neither of these being complete or 'perfect' in their unity and with each sharing some points of similarity in terms of origins.

Why, then, choose this particular set of polities for comparison, given the bewildering array of possibilities? Aside from a general union *Familienähnlichkeit*, there are a number of specific explanations which are relevant here.

First, although these unions developed in some distinctive ways, they were indeed all either rooted in the model of composite monarchy, a combining (or union) of crowns in one ruler, or were very strongly influenced and shaped by that model. England and Ireland formed a type of composite monarchy between 1542 and 1801 (the 'kingdom of Ireland' had been proclaimed by Henry VIII): England and Scotland were a composite monarchy between 1603 and 1707, while Britain and Hanover were united in a similar way between 1714 and 1837. Norway graduated from being part of a composite monarchy with Denmark to being part of a (type of) composite monarchy with Sweden between 1814 and 1905. The United Kingdom of the Netherlands had a single union legislature, but had historic links with composite monarchy and was distinguished by a relatively powerful crown which linked the new throne of the Netherlands with the Grand Duchy of Luxembourg. The Dual Monarchy remained a complex composite monarchy until its fall in 1918. The provinces of British North America between 1841 and 1867, and beyond, sat in a clearly colonial relationship with London; but (as has been said) the definitional frontier between empire and union is sometimes blurred, and it was certainly the case that these different British colonies were for long principally interconnected through a shared monarch.

Second, and linked with this, these case studies were all complex multinational union polities. Though a few of the unions, and in particular the United Kingdom, sometimes acted like, and were even casually seen as, nation states, and though some were bound by an overarching dynastic or imperial identity, akin to nationality, in reality there were clear differences between (on the one hand) these polities and (on the other) nation states like France, Italy, or Germany. Each of the latter had of course strong regional identities, and each had both linguistic variations and differences. Even after unification, Germany remained a decentralized state with component identities and some clear national and linguistic minorities (Polish and Masurian in Posen, Silesia, and East Prussia, French in Alsace Lorraine, Danish in Schleswig-Holstein). But in each there was an overwhelmingly dominant language and identity, which was not always the case elsewhere: on the whole the German empire was successfully united by Germanness, and the French empire and republic by Frenchness, where on the whole the United Kingdom was (certainly so far as Ireland was concerned) *divided* by Britishness. Of course there may be a case for defining multinational union polities as in fact unsuccessful nation states (that is to say, treating France and Germany as the product of successful if sometimes brutal assimilation, while treating the United Kingdom as the product of *unsuccessful*, if sometimes brutal, assimilation). But this is a separate issue; and in any event, posing the question in such terms is to treat the nation state as normative, which the evidence of 19th-century Europe (and beyond), with its proliferation of empires and union, does not entirely justify.

Third (in terms of explaining the choice of polities), and as has been mentioned already, is the issue of chronology. Most of these unions (Britain and Ireland, the Netherlands, Sweden-Norway, Canada) were created at roughly the same time and for broadly similar reasons, rooted in the warfare and the wider geo-politics of the revolutionary and Napoleonic era. Some other union arrangements which are broached in the book—for example, the Grand Duchy of Finland, and the United Kingdom of Portugal, Brazil, and the Algarves—were also products of this global conflict in the first two decades of the 19th century. It is, indeed, one of the key contentions of this book that there was an age of unions in the early 19th century, of which Britain and Ireland formed only part—though a decisive part (cf. Parent 2011, p. 27). It is also one of the contentions of the work that unions may be seen as an *ancien régime* effort to adapt old structures of rule to new revolutionary circumstances (see e.g. Schultz 2001, pp. 2–4).

Indeed, a fourth key explanation for the choice of these particular case studies and comparisons is that a number—the Netherlands, Sweden-Norway—either generally, unofficially or officially, came to be called 'united kingdoms', or were created by discrete 'acts of union', as were the British and Irish exemplars (though see Marteel 2018, p. 1 n. 2). There were often direct and personal linkages between the unions, as exemplified by the role of Viscount Castlereagh, who (as will shortly be shown) was an advocate of the United Kingdom of Great Britain and Ireland and was later a promoter, too, of both the United Kingdom of the Netherlands and of the United Kingdoms of Sweden-Norway. British policy played a central role, too, in the attainment of the United Kingdom of Portugal, Brazil, and the Algarves in 1807–15. In fact, if the French may be said to have exported the idea of the centralized nation state throughout Europe, then—for their part—the British exported the idea of the multinational union state (see below, section 1.6).

Fifth, even though some (generally unionist) advocates of the British constitution sometimes complained about the elisions involved, all these polities were routinely identified by British and Irish contemporaries as comparators or models for the United Kingdom and its reform, particularly in terms of home rule in 1886, 1893, and 1912. It must be emphasized (once again) that the argument here is not that the various unions which are discussed in this book embodied exactly the same constitutional architecture, or that the notions of 'union' or 'home rule' meant exactly the same thing for each of these complex polities: definitions and terminology within even the confines of late 19th-century British political debate were (as has already been pointed out) notoriously slippery, despite some efforts towards greater precision (see the discussion below, section 5.2). The argument is rather that contemporaries themselves saw close 'family resemblances'; and they frequently invoked these polities, often (as with liberals and nationalists) to present a preferred exemplar, and sometimes (as with unionists) to counter the nationalist case by emphasizing difference as well as British 'uniqueness'.

This case has already been introduced, and indeed will be elaborated more fully later in the volume (see section 1.6). But, to take quickly the example of Austria-Hungary, Irish and British home rulers—and indeed British imperial federalists—very often looked to the Dual Monarchy as a model for what Great Britain, Ireland, and the empire might become (see, most famously, Griffith 1918; but also Labilliere 1894, p. 10; Reid 1886, pp. 161–76; Zách 2021, pp. 23–73; see also below, Chapter 5). On the other hand, a unionist constitutionalist like A. V. Dicey, simultaneously invoked Austria-Hungary only to emphasize its distinctiveness, as did the home ruler and historian, E. A. Freeman (1823–92); while yet another home rule scholar and Gladstonian, R. W. Seton-Watson (1879–1951), argued both that Austria-Hungary presented issues which were deeply relevant to the home rule debate of 1912, and that Britain as a whole constituted a possible constitutional export model for central Europe—both before and after the First World War (Figures 5.3, 5.5; Dicey 1887, pp. 48ff.; Dicey 1893, p. 161; Freeman 1888, pp. 189–94; Seton-Watson 1911a, 1924). Similarly, the Austrian Gladstonian sympathizer, F. L. Weinmann, writing in a liberal home rule tract in 1886, acknowledged both similarities and differences between the Irish and Hungarian cases, but argued tendentiously (in fact like Gladstone himself) that dualism had deepened 'the firm foundation of loyalty to the Crown, a circumstance which affords a sufficient guarantee for the future of the Hungarian State and the indissoluble union of the [Habsburg] empire' (Weinmann in Reid 1886, pp. 161, 176). The implications for the beneficent effects of a dualist home rule reform of the union were clear.

In short, this work invokes a range of case studies, not because these countries were exactly the same, but because they were similar, because they were often closely interconnected, and because contemporaries were preoccupied by the similarities and links (Cohen 2004, p. 65). These preoccupations will be revisited at greater length in later sections of the book. But, above all, the work aspires to attain one recent definition of comparative history—through 'an attentiveness to the interplay of local and global, to the meaning of rupture as well as commonality, and always with an eye to the teleologies of essentialism that plague not just comparative but all forms of historical endeavour' (Levine 2014, p. 347).

1.3. Definitions

The history of Europe's several union states has been conceptualized in different ways, with different categorizations—all mostly derived from long-standing debates upon the fundamental nature of political sovereignty, as well as from late 19th-century jurists, seeking (in an age of rapid and complex state formation) clarity on state and international legal personality. The foremost of the latter was perhaps Georg Jellinek (1851–1911), who in his *Lehre von den Staatenverbindungen* (Doctrine of the connections between states) (1882), offered a complex but influential typology of the interlinkages between and within states, emphasizing the distinction between unorganized and formally organized associations (*organisierte Verwaltungsbündnisse*), and between unions based on personal-historical contingency ('personal unions') and those based on formal treaties or other juridical foundations ('real unions') (Figure 5.1). 'Unorganized' associations of states could be created or compelled through, for example, non-union treaties or military annexations such as the occupation of Bosnia by Austria-Hungary (discussed below); but the category also embraced a range of polities including protectorates, and *der Staatenstaat* (subordinate, tributary, or 'vassal' states). Organized associations between states might include international commissions, *der Staatenbund* (the confederation of states), *der Bundestaat* (or federal state), and—generally—'real' unions (as distinct from personal unions) (Jellinek 1882; see also Forsyth 1981; Frost 2015). More recently, H. G. Koenigsberger (1918–2014) and Sir John Elliott (1930–2022) have each focused upon early modern monarchical unions, drawing a distinction between those composite monarchies, or personal unions, which were accessory (where governance and laws were wholly shared) and those which were *aeque principaliter* (where traditions of legal and other distinctiveness were preserved in polities otherwise connected through a shared monarchy) (Koenigsberger 1978, p. 202; Elliott 1992; Elliott 2018).

Historians and their conceptualization of union are an abiding and central concern throughout the work; and this is first and foremost (and for better or worse) a work of history. But any history of union necessarily intersects with the definitions and taxonomies provided by other scholarly disciplines. There is of course a great and stimulating political science literature on 'why nations rise', on the formation and death of states, and inferentially the formation and death of different union states, all of which is occasionally invoked here (most recently Miller 2021; also e.g. Lehning 1998; Burgess 2006; Parent 2011). More specifically, there is a distinguished body of political science and international relations scholarship on particular forms of union, and especially both federal and 'voluntary' (as opposed to enforced) unions (the literature on federalism is extensive, but see the work of Michael Burgess: for specifically 'voluntary' unions see e.g. Parent 2011). There is also a relatively recent, and gradually consolidating, literature on secession from established states: this has tended to concentrate on the ethical and legal conditions for secession, and in particular on secession from federations, but it certainly has a bearing on some of the concerns developed here (Hicks 1978; Buchanan 1991; Moore 1998; Lehning 1998; Bartkus 1999).

But, unions still present clear and complex challenges, whether for political scientists, scholars of international relations—or for historians. Some arise from the fluidity and complexity of the polities themselves: these are discussed shortly. Yet other challenges emerge from language—and partly from the fact that not all contemporary politicians or even campaigners were as precise in their conceptualization and expression as the 19th-century jurist Jellinek, or the distinguished contemporary academic, Elliott. A further fundamental difficulty, however, relates to shifts and variations in meaning from historic usage, even as 'recently' as the early 19th century, through to the present day. In some ways, these shifts are in fact the more dangerous for the modern period, where the social, cultural, and political landscapes are apparently more accessible than (say) for those studying the late medieval era. However, as the later chapters of the book reaffirm, some of the basic vocabulary of union has evolved in complex ways over the last century and a half, and more.

While federal unions are not the principal concern of the current study, both of the points just made may readily be illustrated by historic slippage and imprecision over the definition of 'federalists', 'federations' or 'federalism', and of federal unions. Thus, as is well known, 'federalists' in the United States at the beginning of the 19th century were generally those who favoured a strong central authority in the union state, rather than an over-mighty 'periphery' (see below, section 5.2). Equally, and famously, 'confederation' was the label applied by contemporaries, and thus by posterity, to the creation of the dominion of Canada in 1867: that is to say, 'confederation' was the description given to the creation of, in fact, a federation (see below, sections 3.4, 5.3).

On the other hand British 'federalists' like the influential Scot, F. S. Oliver, cheerfully (and repeatedly) conceded that there was an absence of precision in their debates on 'federalism' (figure 5.4): 'federalism' was, in effect, a useful shorthand for a scheme of asymmetric devolution or variegated home rule all round (Oliver 1910, p. 50; Oliver 1914, p. viii; Oliver 1918, pp. 11, 22). Similarly the Irish national leader, Isaac Butt, in promoting legislative autonomy for Ireland, initially cast his ideas in the—professedly—indefinite language of federalism, before reframing them in the context of the cosy new notion of 'home government', and then, finally, 'home rule' (Butt 1870, pp. 21, 29). In a sense this was to replace one form of imprecision with yet others, and the useful opaqueness of home rule (which helped to generate unity while relegating divisions for a later day of reckoning) would soon become palpable (Jackson 2004). Moreover, the attractiveness of the notion of 'home rule' ensured that, however porous and open-ended, it has had an astonishingly long life, returning to simultaneously uplift and blur British political debate in the early 21st century, well over a century after its initial outing.

Part of the challenge to any crisp taxonomy of union relates not just to the ambiguities of political language, whether through determined imprecision or variations over time: there was also the fluidity and complexity of the union polities themselves. Thus, taking the best-known cases, England, Wales, Scotland, Ireland, and Hanover, which are all at the centre of this study, for long constituted a composite monarchy, but with manifold variations: Wales, conquered and assimilated, was an accessory union under the incorporating legislation of 1535 and 1542, while Ireland and Scotland were originally (from 1542 and 1603 respectively) forms of personal union, notionally (at least in the Scottish case) *aeque principaliter*. Personal unions might be distinguished from 'real' unions; but, looking elsewhere, unions such as the United Kingdoms of Sweden and Norway or the Austro-Hungarian empire, while clearly being 'personal' in certain respects, could also have some of the features of real unions, since their interconnectedness went beyond merely the identity of the monarch or ruling family. Equally, the personal unions of England, Scotland, and Ireland graduated into the parliamentary or real unions of 1707 and 1801, with the creation of Great Britain and the United Kingdom (though, as has been noted, the United Kingdom monarchy remained in personal union with Hanover until 1837). And, in contemporary terms, while the United Kingdom remains formally a single state with some marked unitary and metropolitan cultures, the reality is that the incremental growth of devolution has produced a federalizing tendency; and while it is true that Westminster remains sovereign, and while a distinction between federal states and decentralized unitary states has long been recognized, it is also true that—given the political difficulties of challenging devolved authorities or recouping their powers—this may increasingly be a distinction without a difference (see e.g. Hicks 1978, p. 5). The overall difficulty, therefore, is not the differentiation of constitutional 'apples' and 'oranges': it rests with comparing different forms of hybrid fruit, which (at the same time) were continually evolving (cf. Cohen and O'Connor 2004, p. 27).

There are many other taxonomic challenges with the notion of union. Were, for example, these unions of 19th- and 20th-century Europe—unions such as the United Kingdom of Great Britain and Ireland with one overwhelmingly predominant partner—essentially 'empires' in flimsy constitutional disguise? There were (again) unquestionably overlaps, as the definition of empire proffered by Ulrike von Hirschhausen and Jörn Leonhard in their important collection, *Comparing Empires* (2011), readily suggests: 'empires', they have written, 'were characterised by huge size, ethnic diversity, a multitude of composite territories as a result of historic cession or conquest, by specific forms of supranational rule, by shifting boundaries and fluid border-lands, and finally by a complex and interactive relationship between imperial centres and peripheries' (Leonhard and von Hirschhausen 2011, p. 12). To this list might be added economic and/or military asymmetry, exploitation, and disparity as well as contemporary, usually nationalist, definitions and verdicts (that is to say, empires may be partly identified following contemporary vocabulary and judgements).

Each of the components of this carefully structured definition might equally apply to some, at least, of the union polities under consideration throughout this volume. And (more generally) there is at least a case for seeing a genetic constitutional relationship—another family resemblance, perhaps—between union polities and empires, while allowing for some slippage within each category of definition. The United Kingdom has of course been defined as an empire because of its overseas colonies and related imperialist ideologies; but it was also an empire because of the complex historic, economic and military relationships between England and Wales, Scotland, and Ireland. Moreover, as David Armitage has eloquently underlined, the formation of the Stuart composite monarchy was closely associated, and synchronous, with the foundation of an overseas empire (Armitage 2000, p. 23). The United Kingdom was both a union and an empire, just as Austria-Hungary was both a union and an empire—and just as the complex successor states of central Europe after 1918 were 'multinational empires in miniature' (Gerwarth 2016, p. 14).

In fact this imperial dimension has been routinely recognized within Irish (and Scottish) nationalist discourse, and effectively within some branches of Irish scholarship (for Scots nationalist thought see Jackson 2020). Colonial and postcolonial theorists have been active in Irish literature and political science, but (at the same time) they have so far achieved less traction within modern (as opposed to medieval and early modern) Irish historiography on the union state. The colonial paradigm which is uniformly applied in the Irish and British case relates to the overseas British empire, and in particular (though by no means exclusively) India. Much of the Indian experience of British rule chimes with that of the Irish, and much of the conceptual framework thrown up by those theorists working primarily from Indian evidence has a clear resonance for Ireland (that is, the ideas generated through the work of, say, Homi Bhabha (b. 1949)). On the other hand, of course, substantial voluntary Irish participation in the union state and in its wider colonial empire, together with Irish political assimilation within metropolitan political culture, have all tended to complicate the picture, and to stimulate a degree of caution among some historians of Ireland, union, and empire (see e.g. Howe 2002).

Moreover, notions of internal colonization, popularized in the 1970s within the British context by scholars such as Michael Hechter, together with comparative European evidence of conquest and colonization, are just as relevant to the Irish and Scottish cases—the United Kingdom—as wider, global, comparisons or analogies (Hechter 1975; Kumar 2003, p. 85). Migration, military settlement, and colonization within the Habsburg empire (e.g. involving the movement and cultural ascendancy of German-speaking settlers) all created complex ethnic, linguistic, and/or religious frontiers which chimed with the experience of similar English settlement within Britain and Ireland (cf. Healy 2017). In essence, postcolonial theorists working on Ireland have tended to neglect continental European evidence which might (in some ways) have effectively served their conceptual goals (cf. Zách 2021, pp. 5–6).

Yet, despite this recent effloresence of interest in the comparative study of empire, and despite some well-established and long-standing investigation into the formation and bonding of states, little attention has been given to many aspects of the taxonomy of modern union states. This is partly because, as has been said, the language and categories of analysis have been extremely challenging—and partly because the polities themselves were often complex and fluid: indeed as the argument of the book is developed it will be suggested that fluidity and malleability are essential qualities for union states (see also e.g. Jackson 2013). But it is also the case that the drive to define and understand union as a concept has been largely consumed within anglophone scholarship by federalism. The considerable political science literature on federal unions, dominated in turn by consideration of the United States, has itself been diverted by long-standing disputes about definition, which have only recently been superseded by a kind of exegetical peace born from exhaustion. On the whole, however, federal unions have been distinguished from other forms of union state through the clearly delineated divisions of sovereignty which they characteristically embrace (though, again, it would be wrong to pretend that this distinction is uncontested).

As has been said, however, this present work is not primarily concerned with federal unions, except in particular circumstances (see Chapter 5). These include the occasions when federation was identified (and sometimes applied) as a salve within failing union polities of other types (such as Canada in 1867, Austria-Hungary in the last 20 years or so of its constitutional life, the United Kingdom in the 1870s, 1910–14, and again after 2014). But it is also the case (and this was one of the central ambiguities of federal constitutions) that federations were seen simultaneously as a balm for the ailing, as well as a mechanism to create new union states out of separate components. This, in fact, was the nub of A. V. Dicey's complaint about the potential federalization of the United Kingdom which (as he saw it) was threatened by home rule after 1886. For Dicey, the central problem with federalism was that, while it had been hitherto deployed (notably in the USA) as a means of creating new unions, Gladstone and Charles Stewart Parnell

(1846–91) each proposed to apply it to redesign (what Dicey regarded as) a broadly healthy and functioning existing union.

As a (formally) unfederated multinational monarchy with numerous 'composite' legacies, the United Kingdom (despite some refits over time) might well be viewed instead as a rare survivor from the early modern era. Indeed the UK of the late 20th century and before has been seen by opponents (even, sometimes, by exasperated friends) as a kind of living constitutional fossil, just as the Habsburg empire of the 19th century (with the centrality of its governing dynasty and some other feudal vestiges especially in its eastern, Transleithanian, half) was often regarded—from Hegel onwards—as a curious relic from an earlier, medieval, era of governance or, worse, as an organism from the more distant past (Rudolf Kjellén, quoted in Jászi 1929, p. 239; Deak 2015, p. 3). Like Austria-Hungary in the early 20th century, where the great constitutional compromise of 1867 provided some passably modern political clothing, the United Kingdom has concealed its fundamental constitutional antiquity underneath some convincing later tailoring, including (as has been suggested) the union of 1801 itself.

The modern United Kingdom has been variously defined as both a unitary state, and increasingly now (with its incrementally developing devolution settlements) as a union state or rather a state of unions—all this despite the complex ancestry outlined above (McLean and McMillan 2005; Jackson 2013; Mitchell 2014). The institution of devolution in 1921 (through the creation of the parliament in Northern Ireland) and its reapplication in a radically reformed manner to Belfast in the aftermath of the Good Friday Agreement of 1998, as well as to Scotland and Wales, has not yet formally altered the United Kingdom's standing as a unitary state; but in practice there is now an increasing tension between unionist constitutional theory at the centre and nationalist or devolutionist political practice at the 'periphery', with the latter gradually winning out at present, particularly in Scotland and Northern Ireland. At the time of writing (2016–22), the United Kingdom (much like the Habsburg empire in its last years) appears to be moving gradually in the direction of either a federalized constitution or (even) disaggregation: like the Habsburg empire in its later years, the UK resonates with the cries of visionary nationalists, trenchant unionists, and those (generally former unionists) who seek a mediating third way through the formal federation of the state. As with the Habsburg empire of 1914, it is hard to overlook the presence of those, profoundly dissatisfied with the condition of the polity, and motivated in part by a sense of nostalgia for an imagined golden age, who are willing to take potentially serious political risks to achieve its recovery.

In short, therefore, unions were and remain conceptually elusive entities; and their slipperiness was fully recognized by contemporary observers. Union polities have often been constitutionally fluid, rather than wholly static; and individual unions may therefore develop across several different definitional categories within a relatively short lifespan. These categories themselves have sometimes assumed different meanings with the passage of time. Voluntary decentralized unions often share some similarities with federal unions: unions often share some similarities with empires (Armitage 2000).

But there is light at the end of this taxonomic tunnel. The unions embraced by this volume were generally ultimately rooted in composite monarchy, and they generally had a clear 'union' moment—often a formal legislative act or treaty of union. They were therefore personal unions which had been modernized as real unions of different kinds. Differences there certainly were; but these unions were all further connected either through the pressures of war or of British diplomacy. Their genetic similarities, their *Familienähnlichkeiten*, were real; and a subsequent section of this chapter makes the case for the remarkable closeness of their shared ancestry (see below, section 1.5).

Moreover, ambiguity should not simply be seen as a challenge to understanding union, and fundamentally as a problem; instead it should be accepted and understood as an essential part of the definition of union. Unions were often created as pragmatic bargains wherein ambiguity was a mechanism for securing the deal: the fudging of some difficult issues, their elision or (just as often) their postponement, were all needed. For example, the Swedes, and certainly Carl XIV Johan (1763–1844), saw the agreement with Norway as the foundation for ever closer union, while the Norwegians saw it as a loose arrangement between two sovereign states (Figure 2.2): both, divergent, interpretations were central to the securing of agreement. The English and the Scots emerged from 1707 with fundamentally different views of the union parliament and of the nature of political sovereignty; and the radical revision of the union between Britain and Ireland which occurred through the Treaty of 1921 was made possible through several central wheezes and dodges, of which the most significant was the effective postponement of the Irish border question through the device of a boundary commission. The Austrians and Hungarians viewed the Ausgleich of 1867 in quite different ways, certainly in the view of Albert Graf Apponyi (1846–1933)—with the Austrians thinking of Austria-Hungary as a federation and the Hungarians seeing it as a confederation ('im ungarischen Bewußtsein war Österreich-Ungarn ein Staatenbund, im österreichischen ein Bundesstaat': quoted in Haslinger 1996, p. 5). In short, union and ambiguity are inextricably interconnected: union should in fact be seen as inherently ambiguous.

1.4. The Longevity of Union

This book contains a lengthy reflection on the weakness and endings of unions, but this does not mean that it is grounded in any teleology of inescapable failure or in the inevitability of the nation state. The United Kingdom and the Habsburg monarchy may eventually have come to seem antique formulations, but this is not necessarily to deny that they were for long viably antique—or that antiquity should be equated with inevitable disintegration. My own earlier work, on the unions—Scots and Irish—of the United Kingdom, was a sustained reflection on the longevity of each of those bonds; and to some extent this present volume is preoccupied with similar themes (Jackson 2013; see also e.g. Cole and Unowsky 2007, p. 2; Berg 2014).

The elephant in the room of union historiography in the United Kingdom—certainly with regards to the Irish union—has been the issue of its lengthy survival: the inherent paradox within a great deal of Irish, Scots, and Welsh political historiography, which focuses on national consolidation, and (in the Irish case) the achievement of independence, is the stubborn (sometimes burdensome, sometimes oppressive) presence of the supranational union. My work on *The Two Unions* (2013) was in part an attempt to disentangle this paradox (in terms of Ireland and Scotland) through looking at the ways in which the union state infiltrated everyday lives and negotiated the challenge of nationalist opposition—sometimes through concession and malleability, and sometimes through bloody suppression (Jackson 2013). This approach to the unions of the United Kingdom broadly chimes with the most recent scholarship on Austria-Hungary, which (again) emphasizes the factors supporting the state, interrogates any overdetermined declinology, and maintains a scepticism with regard to overly rigid teleologies of all kinds (one key starting point is Cohen 1998; see also Judson 2016).

These historiographical symmetries suggest even wider possibilities, however. Recent work (which recalibrates our understanding of the Habsburg empire) simultaneously reflects but also challenges some aspects of our settled outlook on the British and Irish unions. This is partly a matter of sharing approaches to identifying the institutional bolsters of union; it is also about revisiting the role of empire within the history of the union states, and building upon the insights of the theorists of internal colonialism (like, in the British and Irish case, Michael Hechter) as well as of post-colonialism (like, in the Irish case, Seamus Deane (1940–2021) or Luke Gibbons) (Cohen 1998; Cornwall 2002, pp. 6–7). But it is also about achieving a more sophisticated understanding of the fluidity and contingency of national affiliation in the (ostensibly) crisply nationalizing environments of both the Dual Monarchy and the United Kingdom. In essence, we may now have to look not only to comparative or 'four nations' approaches within the United Kingdom, but also to consider a possible additional 'non-nation': those whose primary identities were not fixed with any individual national identity, but were local, contingent, negotiable—or 'situational'. The possibility of 'national indifference' now needs to be written into the history of the United Kingdom (cf. Zahra 2010, p. 105, for a discussion of the term).

Here one can scarcely do better than to look to the reflection on this question offered by Pieter Judson and Tara Zahra in thinking about the Habsburg empire. In 'studying nationalism in this period', Judson has argued,

> it helps to avoid seeing people as consistently belonging to one or another defined nation in the way that nationalists did. Instead, we might think more fruitfully in terms of the situations or events that drove people to identify with one national group or another... it helps to approach questions of identification by thinking more in terms of particular practices that expressed feelings of loyalty or commitment rather than in terms of people's fixed identities.
> (Judson 2016, p. 312; see also Zahra 2008; Zahra 2010, p. 103)

While it is clearly possible to take these insights too far, it is also the case that they quietly chime with (for example) a disparate array of existing Irish historical scholarship, embracing work on Irish local electoral politics in the 19th century, and work, based partly on the (relatively) new releases from the Bureau of Military History, which reflects both on the 1916 Rising as well as on the revolution. Unsurprisingly not everyone, it seems, was a hero either of the struggle for union or of the Irish revolution; and only the most convinced and impassioned of contemporaries could have expected otherwise (see e.g. Hoppen 1984; McGarry 2017; Hughes 2016; see also below, section 6.5).

In highlighting new approaches to the understanding of the Dual Monarchy and other 19th-century multinational unions, this work implicitly broaches the case for the reconceptualization of the United Kingdom. In essence (and amongst other matters) this involves introducing into the history of this (and other) unions the notion of the citizen who (in the context of seismic political or economic events) was primarily concerned with their own survival and wellbeing rather than with the apotheosis of either the British empire or the Irish republic. It involves, too, a reconsideration of Britishness as a supranational dynastic identity, rather than wholly as a national affiliation like Englishness (or Scottishness, Irishness, and Welshness). In short, both the Habsburg empire—as well as the United Kingdom—may have survived, not because each was associated with its own vibrant state nationalism, but rather because in each case it presented an alternative to nationalism in the form of a supranational dynasticism and loyalism (and imperialism).

Several additional observations about the theme of longevity need to be reaffirmed at this point—particularly in terms of the comparative perspectives and their value. There is the—in some ways obvious, if underappreciated—point that the historiography of union states (as of every other polity) is itself historically situated, and that periods of political instability have generally nurtured the hermeneutics and literatures of crisis. Much reflection on the Irish and Scottish unions has been undertaken in the context of the early 21st-century disruption or threatened disruption of the United Kingdom state—which in turn may be said to date back to the challenges mounted (in very different ways) by constitutional nationalism in Scotland (and Wales) and separatist republicanism in Northern Ireland from the late 1960s onwards. Particular periods of intensification within the wider British constitutional debate—as with (for example) the electoral consolidation of the SNP under the leadership of Alex Salmond and then Nicola Sturgeon—have had an historiographical dimension in terms of an intensified reflection on the union and its component parts. Similarly, the push for Irish and, to a lesser extent, Scottish home rule in the late 19th and early 20th centuries stimulated greater historiographical interest and reflection. This earlier work was often (as with Dicey and Rait, writing in 1920 on the Scottish union) clearly tendentious; but equally it would be wrong to ignore the presentist influences and contexts within much more modern reflections on the unions of the United Kingdom (Dicey and Rait 1920).

In general these nationalist contexts and pressures have helped to encourage the development of a genuinely all-encompassing 'British'—though certainly not 'union'—history, in contradistinction to the markedly anglo-centric definitions predominant in an earlier generation. From the mid-1970s, and in the context of the wider crisis of the British state, J. G. A. Pocock (1924–) argued for a more integrative British history, led by the 'periphery' rather than the metropolitan 'centre' (again in ways which resonate within contemporary Habsburg scholarship, with its emphases upon provincial case studies); and an effort has recently been made by some to apply Pocock's (early modern) insights within a set of late modern historical contexts (see e.g. Lloyd Jones and Scull 2018). The distinction between British history and United Kingdom or union history remains an extremely sensitive one, however, and has perhaps not yet fully been resolved within this historiographical initiative—not least because the United Kingdom state itself remains a contested phenomenon. By way of contrast, the same levels of sensitivity do not affect the history of the Dual Monarchy—partly because Austria-Hungary (whatever its long-standing signs of vitality before 1918) is now incontrovertibly dead, partly because the nationalist activists who vigorously sought to awaken and shape the identities of their compatriots have long been demobilized, and partly because the idea of multiple identities within an overarching supranational framework has a renewed accessibility or even 'relevance'.

Indeed, following on from this point, it is clear that the historiography of the Dual Monarchy has been susceptible to revisionist assessment which in turn has been linked to wider intellectual and political conditions. After 1918, Austria-Hungary's reputation as the 'prison of nations' tended to be reaffirmed, as the successor states sought appropriate historical narratives for their own liberation, birth, and survival. There has always been, however, what might be described as a legitimist nostalgia within certain sections of the historiography of the Dual Monarchy (advanced sometimes by those writers with strong familial links to imperial and royal service); and in some ways this has been reinforced—though for quite different reasons—in the combined contexts of the consolidation of the European Union project and the redrawing of parts of the central and south-east map of the continent after the fall of the Berlin Wall in November 1989 (see e.g.

Deak 2015, pp. 4–5; Leisse 2012; see also Zách 2021, p. 167, for Habsburg nostalgia in Ireland).

The European Union has been historically situated and contextualized in different ways, but in general historians have been interested in examining the interconnections between it and other great supranational European polities—even sometimes heading back to the history of the later Roman republic in this quest for contextualization (see e.g. Engels 2013). However, the relative strengthening of the EU and of European identities has also, directly and indirectly, encouraged research which has transcended the nation state—or, at any rate, it has encouraged a more precise and rigorous historiographical treatment of the language of nationality and nationhood. Indeed a key strain within recent work on the Dual Monarchy, for example, has been the setting aside of older narratives of terminal decline and the emergence of a picture which emphasizes the institutions and ideas which bound the empire together, the extent to which the successor states in fact inherited many of the features of the former empire—and the contingency and negotiability of national identity itself. In this, revisionist, analysis, which has had numerous advocates but which has received its fullest synthesis in Pieter Judson's work, traditional readings of a dichotomy between the Habsburg state and its component nationalities have been replaced with an emphasis upon other forms of identity, as well as a stress upon the extent to which nationalist activists had to strive in order to mobilize support which was sometimes not naturally forthcoming (designated members of the 'nation' could be lamentably slow in recognizing their good fortune) (Cohen 1998; Judson 2016). Equally, teleologies of decline have been replaced with an emphasis upon survival and relative longevity.

As has been said already, in all of this the direction of work on the Dual Monarchy bears comparison with recent examinations of the unions of the United Kingdom where attention has turned to understanding the longevity of union as well as of the struggle of nationalist activists to address the often ambiguous loyalties of local people (compare Jackson 2013; Cole and Unowsky 2007; Hughes 2016). But there are also, however, similarities with the direction of scholarship in other union states, such as Sweden-Norway. Here a century of cooperation on economic and defence questions, and a softening of some of the nationalistic passions which delivered the breaking of union in 1905, have also produced a more measured set of reflections which do not dwell exclusively on the ultimate breakdown of relationships: as one distinguished historian of Scandinavia has observed, 'might [the union] not with at least equal justification be regarded as a reasonable solution that in time outlived its usefulness?...while much scholarly attention has been devoted to its [the union's] negative aspects and ultimate demise, relatively little and only sporadic attention has thus far been given to the credit side of the ledger' (Barton 2003, p. 167).

Moreover, the great Hungarian scholar and statesman, Oszkár Jászi (1875–1957), argued wisely in the 1920s that the two sides of the 'ledger' on union, debit and credit, and the two sets of forces strengthening or diffusing union, centripetal and centrifugal, were very far from being discrete (Jászi 1929; see Figure 5.2). Other have rightly complained that 'comparatively little attention has been devoted to the centripetal forces identified by Jászi' (Cole and Unowsky 2007, p. 2). Similarly, the current volume, while certainly interested in understanding and defining the failure of union states, is also concerned to highlight their successes and (where appropriate) their longevity—and to underline that the forces working for union might (in certain circumstances, and with other contingencies in play) become agents of subversion.

1.5. Exporting Union: Viscount Castlereagh and His Circle

Understanding these unions of early 19th-century Europe, their connectedness, their survival and longevity, and (sometimes) their endings, means understanding in detail the ideas and networks which delivered first, the United Kingdom of Great Britain and Ireland, and then a succession of other cognate states. The personal and macropolitical connections between the first of these 'united kingdoms' and several of its successors have never fully been excavated and explained; and yet they are central to understanding the shape of—in particular—northern Europe after 1814–15. Much less important, except for the particular purposes of the current work, is the fact that this connectedness in the early 19th century also helps to further illuminate some of the choices of case study for the pursuit of comparison (see also above, section 1.2).

The creation of the United Kingdom, finally attained in 1801, was principally the work of William Pitt (1759–1806), the British Prime Minister, alongside a group of talented protégés, chief amongst whom was Robert Stewart (1769–1822), Viscount Castlereagh (from April 1821 until his death in August 1822 marquess of Londonderry) (Figures 1.1, 2.1). Pitt's perspectives were imperial and anglocentric; and—while he had long desired a closer relationship between Britain and Ireland, his will had been thwarted by a stubbornly patriotic, while also narrowly constituted, Irish parliament in Dublin. The war with France after 1793, and the increasing likelihood that Ireland would be used by the French as a springboard into England, heightened the desirability of union: already by the late summer of 1797 Pitt had put out feelers in Dublin as to its viability. The firing of a republican rebellion—with French assistance—on 23 May 1798 determined the matter; and within days of its outbreak, on 28 May, Pitt was moving towards the activation of his goal. Bills for the parliamentary union of the two countries were eventually passed in both the British and Irish houses of commons in July and August 1800 respectively (Geoghegan 1999, pp. 1–24).

Lord Castlereagh, as Pitt's Chief Secretary for Ireland (he was also MP for County Down in the Irish parliament), and Edward Cooke (1755–1820), the

Under Secretary for Ireland (and MP for Old Leighlin, Carlow), were each central to the difficult and grubby task both of defining union and of securing its successful passage in Dublin (Figure 1.5). Castlereagh's half-brother, Charles Stewart, later third Marquess of Londonderry (1778–1854), was foisted upon the borough of Thomastown, Kilkenny, as MP in the Irish parliament, though he was soon translated to the representation of County Londonderry: he of course followed Castlereagh in voting for union (Figure 1.4). Among those others (eventually) persuaded to support the measure in the Irish parliament was the MP for County Galway, Richard Le Poer Trench (1767–1837), who succeeded as second Earl of Clancarty in 1805 (Figure 1.2). Among those caught up in the intense debates over union in Dublin was Percy Smythe (1780–1855), who graduated from Trinity College Dublin in 1800, and who the following year succeeded as the sixth Viscount Strangford (Figure 1.3). Along with Edward Cooke, Stewart, Clancarty, and Strangford would each subsequently play an important role in Castlereagh's later career as Foreign Secretary (1812–22)—as well as in his wider plans while occupying that office.

Why union? For both Pitt, an Englishman, and Castlereagh, who was Irish, union was fundamentally about imperial security at a time of domestic and international instability (Geoghegan 1999, p. 7; cf. the emphasis on security in voluntary unions in Parent 2011). The precedent of the Scottish union, which was laid down in 1707, was an active consideration—the successful stabilization of (from the metropolitan perspective) a difficult and potentially dangerous neighbour in the context of a threatening European conflict. There was also some Welsh input into the debate, in so far as the most famous published unionist statement of the period, one widely regarded as being an authentic exposition of the thinking of Castlereagh and Pitt, was prefaced by the reflections of Josiah Tucker (1712–99), a Carmarthenshire divine who had become Dean of Gloucester: the pamphlet itself, *Arguments for and against an union between Great Britain and Ireland* (1798), was published anonymously, but certainly came from the pen of Edward Cooke (Cooke 1798; Geoghegan 1999, pp. 50–1). Cooke pointed trenchantly to the comprehensive challenge posed by France, and effectively argued that French conquests and ambition posed an existential threat to the constitution of Great Britain and Ireland. Imperial security could only realistically be obtained through a comprehensive union of the two countries—and only then if the acquiescence of the majority Catholic interest in Ireland could be secured through an augmentation of civil and political rights. The fundamental argument, however, was not focused on the Catholic question, but rather on the notion (to retrospectively apply di Lampedusa's famous dictum) that 'everything must change so that everything can stay the same' (di Lampedusa 1960). In essence, Cooke, Pitt, and Castlereagh were seeking a modification of Protestant ascendancy in Ireland so that the existing order could be sustained broadly intact. Union, therefore, was a radical constitutional device for the purposes of stability and security—and for the revamping of monarchy and empire (see e.g. Hilton 2006, p. 97; Schultz 2001, pp. 3–4).

Pitt died in January 1806; but his political project was sustained through the ongoing careers of his key lieutenants. A year before, in January 1805, he had crystallized his foreign policy objectives in a famous memorandum which encompassed the rescuing of those countries which had fallen under French dominion; and in particular he looked forward to the creation of 'such an arrangement with respect to the territories recovered from France, as may provide for their security and happiness, and may at the same time constitute a more effectual barrier in future against encroachments on the part of France' (quoted in Hilton 2006, p. 235). 'Effectual barriers' against French encroachment and mutual security (and indeed 'happiness') were emphatically all part of the rhetoric of union; and it should come as no surprise that the broad principles of Pitt's thinking on Ireland and internationally should have coincided, since each was anchored in the defence of Britain, its interests, and its empire. Moreover, Pitt's reflections on international relations were largely shared by Castlereagh (as they had been on union); and in March 1812 this harmony assumed a greater than ever practical significance, when Castlereagh was appointed as Secretary of State for Foreign Affairs (Tangeraas 1983, p. 194; Marteel 2018, p. 22).

But it was not just Castlereagh's (inherited and Pittite) principles of foreign policy which invoked union: it was also his networks of support. Edward Cooke, a key architect of union (he drew up the relevant legislation and was, as has been shown, a critical propagandist), followed Castlereagh in his ministerial progression, and eventually to the Foreign Office in 1812: Cooke remained indispensable to his superior throughout the last years of the war, and the subsequent period of international reconstruction, until his retirement in 1817 (Jupp 2004; Figure 1.5). Castlereagh's half-brother, Charles Stewart, voted for the Irish union; and when his military career stalled in 1813, he was appointed, on Castlereagh's recommendation, to be British minister plenipotentiary in Berlin and then (in 1814) ambassador in Vienna, where he assiduously pursued his half-brother's diplomatic strategies. Much later, in the 1840s, Stewart gathered Castlereagh's letters and papers in a published celebration of the latter's political achievements, stretching across three series and twelve volumes, and beginning with the Irish union (Stewart 1849–53). Lord Clancarty, who (as Richard Le Poer Trench) had voted for union in 1800, subsequently emerged as 'one of Castlereagh's greatest friends and admirers' as well as 'the most faithful and assiduous of all his assistants during these years [1812–15]': Clancarty (who was central 'in formulating a plan for the incorporation of the Belgian and Dutch provinces into the new state of Netherlands') served as in substance the first British ambassador to the United Kingdom of the Netherlands between 1816 and 1823 (Webster 1925, p. 40; Webster 1931, p. 181; Yonge 1868, ii, p. 514).

Other younger Irish peers reflected Castlereagh's landed background, values, and outlook, as well as his unionism: Viscount Strangford was British minister plenipoteniary to Portugal at the time of its effective union with Brazil (1806–8); and he was later minister plenipotentiary to the United Kingdoms of Sweden-Norway between 1817 and 1820. Finally, between 1817 and 1819 Castlereagh was served as private secretary by yet another young Irish Protestant aristocrat, Richard Meade, third Earl of Clanwilliam: Lord Clanwilliam subsequently became acting Under Secretary at the Foreign Office under Castlereagh (1819–22), before graduating into the substantive role in the months before the latter's suicide (on 12 August 1822). Castlereagh relied heavily upon Clanwilliam, to the extent that he appears to have confided to his protégé some of the secret personal history which preceded his breakdown and death (Hyde 1959, pp. 187–8).

Castlereagh's diplomatic team therefore disproportionately comprised those who shared his own background and his view of union—sometimes to the extent of having worked with him in the delivery of union in Ireland. Did this matter? What, if any, were the consequences for the direction of British foreign policy after 1812?

Sir Charles Webster, writing in 1931, described the United Kingdom of the Netherlands, formed in 1814–15, as being 'of course the special creation of Britain, and in particular of Castlereagh' (Webster 1931, p. 387). Ultra-Protestants in Ireland, whose outlook was often defensive and self-referential, subsequently interpreted Castlereagh's union-building in the low countries as an offspring of his desire to return to Catholic emancipation in Ireland: an anonymous conservative reviewer in the *Dublin University Magazine* (possibly Isaac Butt (1813–79)) opined that:

> Lord Castlereagh had long been the advocate of what was called Catholic emancipation, and there is nothing exaggerated in the notion that he was desirous of furnishing a practical proof of the compatibility between the profession of the Roman Catholic religion, and the fullest enjoyment of constitutional privileges under a Protestant government. If he could successfully point to Holland and Belgium, and say, see how beautifully these people get on together...he was of opinion that a material point would be gained in advocating his favourite measure, and that the promotion of this Roman Catholic people into an incorporation with that Protestant state would be but the precursor to the removal of the civil disabilities which at that time it was the fashion to say paralysed the energies of the Catholics of Ireland.   (Anon. 1835, pp. 572–3)

This was clearly a (prolix) expression of Orange Protestant suspicion; but it is still likely that Castlereagh was seeking to enact in the United Kingdom of the Netherlands that which had been politically unattainable in Ireland in 1801—namely Catholic civil liberty within an essentially Protestant union state. Certainly a heightened concern for equity—'that each party after the annexation shall enjoy equal benefits and each share their proportion of all the incumbrances'—as well as for the sensitive treatment of the southern Catholic clergy characterized much of Castlereagh's Dutch correspondence during early 1814 (see e.g. Londonderry 1848–53, 3rd series, ii, p. 40: Clancarty to Castlereagh, 19 May 1814).

More immediately, and just as the union of Ireland with Britain was designed in part to strengthen those islands against any form of French threat, so Castlereagh saw the union of the former Dutch republic with the former Austrian Netherlands as an essential barrier to any future French aggression in the low countries of north-west Europe (see e.g. Londonderry 1848–53, 3rd series, ii, p. 51: Castlereagh to Clancarty, 30 May 1814). With Napoleon's defeat at Leipzig in October 1813, French forces were in continental retreat, and the Netherlands (both north and south) were finally liberated from their rule: accordingly, the challenge of reconstruction came more fully into focus, both for the Dutch themselves as well as for the victorious allies. Castlereagh's agent for his Dutch plans was Clancarty, who accompanied Willem Frederik, Prince of Orange (1772–1843), from the latter's exile in England back to The Hague in November 1813 in preparation for accepting the new title of 'sovereign prince of the Netherlands' and for rule over the eponymous 'sovereign principality' (1813–15) (Figure 2.3).

In addition, Clancarty had been seeking to advance the possibility of the marriage of Willem Frederik's eldest son, the later King Willem II (1792–1849), to Princess Charlotte of Wales, who at that time was likely to inherit the throne of the United Kingdom (in fact his efforts towards marital diplomacy, and indeed towards a yet greater union of united kingdoms, ultimately failed). Castlereagh and Clancarty were each central to the scheme for the unification of the northern and southern Netherlands under the rule of Prince Willem Frederik; and this idea was a keystone both of the allies' Treaty of Chaumont (March 1814)—largely drafted by Castlereagh, and regarded by him proprietorially as 'my treaty'—and of the subsequent Treaty of Paris (May 1814) between the allies and France. Unification was also a central notion within the allies' London Protocol (or the Eight Articles of London) (June 1814), which famously called for a union both 'intime et complète' (Bew 2011, pp. 346, 370; Marteel 2018, p. 23).

Napoleon's escape from Elba and the subsequent 'Hundred Days' campaign added urgency to Castlereagh's ambition for a strong northern buffer to contain the French; and, pressed by the great powers gathered in congress in Vienna, Willem Frederik announced the creation of the new united kingdom under his own rule (as King Willem I) in March 1815 in a speech which invoked the united Burgundian realms of Charles V, as well as the strategic ambitions of William the Silent (Marteel 2018, p. 25). This new union was confirmed by the final act of the Congress of Vienna, signed in June 1815. Castlereagh, and (to a lesser extent) Clancarty, were (as Webster had pointed out) central to this achievement (see also e.g. Kennedy 2017, p. 285).

All this, of course, is emphatically not to say that the idea of the binding of north and south in the Netherlands was the unique property of Castlereagh and his close-knit circle of Irish and other subordinates. Still less is it to suggest that they had invented the notion: the long and complex history of the low countries is discussed later in the book in terms of the issue of unity. In any event, Willem Frederik had independently harboured plans for territorial acquisition in the south (and indeed elsewhere). But Castlereagh's sense of British and wider interests trumped any particularist ambition: 'more important than William's [territorial] aspirations', it has been said, 'were the interests of Britain which wanted a strong buffer state to the north of France' (Wielenga 2015, p. 149). Having designed a union state in the 'British isles' for clear reasons, Castlereagh and his lieutenants sought a related form of construction in the Netherlands—and for much the same reasons.

This was also true in Scandinavia where the end of the war left an, if possible, even more complex set of diplomatic challenges. Here Denmark had been in union with Norway since the early 16th century, while Sweden held sway over its (then) eastern province of Finland. Denmark-Norway's effort to remain neutral during the revolutionary and Napoleonic wars took it into the League of Armed Neutrality (1800–1), which was interpreted by the British government as a threat; and, after British attacks on Copenhagen in 1801 and 1807 (the British feared, amongst other matters, that the Danish fleet might be used for an Irish landing), Denmark-Norway was pushed towards an outright alliance with the French (Glenthøj and Ottosen 2014, p. 27). British naval action not only eliminated the Danish fleet: it also brought a maritime blockade of Denmark and Norway, which had the effect of cutting Norway off from its predominant partner, and thereby of augmenting both Norwegian autonomy and national feeling at this critical historical juncture. Moreover, as will shortly be shown, the mounting failures of the French after Leipzig in 1813 also ultimately spelt disaster for their Danish allies— with the looming prospect of the dismemberment of the Danish-Norwegian union.

Sweden, too, was squeezed within the rapidly morphing diplomatic politics of the period—and squeezed in particular between, on the one hand, the threat of France, and on the other hand, that of Russia. The *rapprochement* between these two powers, formalized in the treaties of Tilsit (1807), rendered the Swedes vulnerable; and they soon faced invasion from Russia, which (after Tilsit) was also now at war with the British (1807–12). Conflict between Sweden and Russia (1808–9) culminated in Swedish failure, and the loss of the eastern province of the kingdom, which was duly absorbed into the Russian empire as the semi-autonomous Grand Duchy of Finland. However, though defeated and humiliated, Swedish support for the British and the wider coalition against Napoleon remained a valuable commodity, which was fully and shrewdly exploited. From 1810 the heir to the Swedish throne was Crown Prince Carl Johan (the former Napoleonic marshal, Bernadotte) (1763–1844); and since, given the shifting geo-politics, the recovery of Finland was now out of the question, Carl Johan pursued another territorial ambition, the acquisition of Norway from Denmark, as his price for Sweden's military support (Tangeraas 1983, p. 197; Figure 2.2).

Napoleon's seizure of Swedish Pomerania and then his invasion of Russia (in March 1812) pushed the British towards the 'implicit' acceptance of Carl Johan's claims (Lucas 1990, p. 271). Castlereagh (and the Russians) explicitly agreed to these at the Treaty of Stockholm in March 1813 (described by the Scots radical journalist and traveller, Samuel Laing (1780–1868), as 'the foulest blot perhaps in British history'); and this agreement was then confirmed and augmented through the Treaties of Kiel (January 1814) (Laing 1836, i, p. iv; Tangeraas 1983, p. 203). Kiel, in turn, provided a form of diplomatic and legal foundation for the complex personal union ultimately forged between Sweden and Norway in and after October 1814.

At the same time it should be underlined that the subsequent pressure on Castlereagh and the British to backtrack on this question of union was immense, for the Norwegians not only now wanted independence, they also pressed their case extremely cogently in London at the beginning of 1814 (Carsten Anker (1747–1824) was their leading advocate) (see Frydenlund 2015, p. 34; Tangeraas 1983, pp. 215–16). Moreover, Bernadotte, though a British ally, was also an exceedingly slippery one, whom Castlereagh did not wholly like or trust; and in addition there was some sympathy for the patriotic Norwegian cause in the press and amongst the opposition forces in parliament, where Earl Grey (1764–1845) was calling for an independent Norway (Tangeraas 1983, p. 206; Lucas 1990, p. 273). Castlereagh's chief, the Prime Minister, Lord Liverpool (1770–1827), hinted at the countervailing tensions within British politics in admitting at this time (May 1814) that 'though our policy respecting the union of Norway to Sweden has always appeared to me right, I confess I felt for some time that the question was the most awkward and embarrassing of any in our European politics' (quoted in Webster 1931, p. 308; Tangeraas 1983, p. 222; Mestad 2015, p. 2). In the end Norwegian eloquence did not prevail, and Castlereagh vigorously adhered to the policy of union: as he emphasized in March 1814, nothing can 'be further from the truth than any notion that the British government feels the slightest inclination to support or connive at the independence of Norway'—words which were reinforced through a breaking of communications with the Norwegians (Londonderry 1848–53, 3rd series, i, p. 314: Castlereagh to Thornton, 7 March 1814; Webster 1931, p. 495). And as a thoroughly relieved Edward Cooke reported to Castlereagh in May 1814, 'there is [now] not much danger of trouble on the Norway question, nor much disposition in opposition to collect' (Londonderry 1848-53, 3rd series, ii, p. 39: Cooke to Castlereagh, 16 May 1814; Lucas 1990, p. 273).

Why, then, did union between Sweden and Norway appear to Castlereagh and his ministerial colleagues as (in Liverpool's description) 'right'? In essence the post-war problems posed in the Baltic were similar to those which had characterized Britain and Ireland between 1798 and 1800: France was the major expansionist power promising universal disruption in 1800, where in 1814 Russia threatened to deliver similar turmoil amongst its neighbours. In each case the bonds of union offered consolidation and strength—whether for Britain and Ireland in the face of the French threat in 1800 or for (in particular) Sweden and eastern Europe in the context of the Russian challenge after 1814 (see e.g. Alison 1861, ii, p. 500; Tangeraas 1983, p. 220). But circumscribing the French threat remained wholly relevant even to the construction of the Swedish-Norwegian union in 1814 (Lucas, 1990, p. 273 n. 12). As in Ireland, so in Norway, it was critical for the success of union that it should ultimately be agreed and in neither case should union simply be a conquest after the style of the French: the Treaty of Stockholm (1813) had expressly deprecated union by force (article 2). As in Ireland, so in Norway it was desirable to hold out concessions to the key parties, and if these had ultimately failed with the Irish (in terms of the crushing of Catholic emancipation), then Castlereagh was quick to affirm Carl Johan's parallel efforts to reach out to the Norwegians (Webster 1931, p. 497). More generally, Carl Johan himself shrewdly identified the required language and arguments when he wrote to his British allies, urging that 'the union of the whole northern peninsula under one monarchy gave to it at once a sort of insular security against any invasion with military force alone... it would impose upon them [in Sweden] the agreeable obligation of cultivating a constant union with Great Britain, whose maritime superiority was the sole guarantor of their safety by sea' (quoted in Webster 1931, p. 95). Carl Johan's emphases on the geographical integrity of 'the whole northern peninsula', and the related logic of its political union, were part of a wider propaganda on these themes (Hemstad 2015, p. 110; Hemstad 2019, pp. 88–9; Berg 2014, p. 272). The allusion to the United Kingdom ('a sort of insular security') was oblique, but clear enough; while the stress on the future ties between the new Scandinavian union and their British protector, defined tellingly as 'a constant union', was no less well-judged. Indeed, from its genesis, the idea of Sweden's acquisition of Norway was formulated in terms which an architect of the Irish union was likely to understand and accept.

As with the Netherlands, so with Sweden-Norway, the connections to Ireland and its union were to be found not only in terms of arguments, but also in terms of people. Castlereagh himself, the architect of the Irish union, essentially pursued in Norway in 1814 a variant of his earlier policy regarding Ireland. That is to say, just as he had quelled Irish independence in 1798, so in 1814 Castlereagh and his agent in Norway, John Philip Morier (1778–1853), ultimately resisted the Norwegian claim to independence, while seeking (as Castlereagh had originally sought in Ireland) to advocate relatively generous terms of union. As in 1707 and 1801, so with Norway, British military action reinforced the diplomatic campaign—in the Norwegian case, in the form of a naval blockade of Norway, sustained between February and September 1814. It is sometimes said that, while Norway was compelled into union with Sweden, it was also able—through military defiance culminating in the Convention of Moss (August 1814)—to determine its form; or, alternatively, that the Convention embodied an 'incompatible commitment to Norwegian independence and union' (Parent 2011, p. 96). It is also true, however, that both the fact of union, as well as its content, broadly reflected Castlereagh's settled outlook—and his abiding faith in agreed union polities.

In addition, as in the Netherlands, Castlereagh eventually drew upon his circle of Irish Protestant and unionist gentry to sustain British diplomatic interests with, and to offer support to, the newly minted United Kingdoms of Sweden-Norway. It should be said, though, that the first minister plenipotentiary to Stockholm after the union with Norway was Edward Thornton, an Englishman and self-made senior diplomat, who had long experience of negotiation with the Swedes and who was profoundly sympathetic to Bernadotte and his ambitions (Tangeraas 1983, p. 211). In 1817 Thornton was translated by Castlereagh from one union state, Sweden-Norway, to serve as minister and later ambassador to yet another, the very short-lived United Kingdom of Portugal, Brazil, and the Algarves (Schultz 2001). Thornton was replaced in Stockholm by the Irish peer, Lord Strangford, who (as has been noted) was British minister plenipoteniary between 1817 and 1820: Strangford's successor in Stockholm was William Vesey Fitzgerald (1783–1843), later Lord Fitzgerald and Vesey, who served until 1823, and who was a scion of a leading Protestant landed family in county Clare (he is firmly lodged in the footnotes of Irish history as Daniel O'Connell's ill-fated opponent in the critical Clare election of 1828). The first appointment to Stockholm after Castlereagh's death was Lieutenant General Benjamin Bloomfield, Lord Bloomfield (1768–1846), a Protestant landed gentleman from King's County (Offaly) in Ireland: Bloomfield, who was greatly liked by Carl XIV Johan, served in Sweden from 1823 to 1832 (Barton 1925, p. 196). In essence, thus, British interests in the United Kingdoms of Sweden-Norway after Thornton's departure were largely superintended by landed Irish unionists who were drawn directly from Castlereagh's circle of protégés and clients, or who were otherwise of precisely the same class.

This was partly the case, too, with a final united kingdom of the Napoleonic era, which was created with the support of the British: that of Portugal, Brazil, and the Algarves. The British had long been an influence within Portugal—and indeed, through the Methuen Treaties (1703), effectively exercised control over its key (port wine) industry: the Duc de Choiseul (1719–85) went so far as to claim that 'Portugal must be regarded as an English colony' (Schultz 2001, p. 19). In late 1807 Portugal was threatened by Napoleonic conquest and subjugation; and on 29 November the royal family set sail from Lisbon, bound for their Brazilian colonies. Some eight years later, and despite the defeat of Napoleon, this effective union of Portugal and Brazil was formalized through a royal decree creating a new United Kingdom: in fact the notion of a united kingdom of Portugal and Brazil had already been deployed at the earlier Congress of Vienna (Schultz 2001, p. 190). The monarch of the new United Kingdom, João VI (John VI), was duly acclaimed at a public ceremonial in Rio in 1818 (for a first-hand description by an Englishman see Luccock 1820, pp. 571–3).

The British had of course little control over the circumstances which forced the flight of the House of Braganza from Lisbon to Rio; and it was also the case that Castlereagh's fellow Irish unionist (and rival), George Canning (1770–1827), was in office as Foreign Secretary. But there was still strong and influential British support for the action, and Portuguese supporters of the move tended to be those most sympathetic to the British alliance (Schultz 2001, pp. 28–9; Luccock 1820, p. 569). Indeed, Pitt was invoked in contemporary polemic as a posthumous supporter of the new union arrangement (Schultz 2001, p. 29). The British minister plenipotentiary in Lisbon at the time of the departure of the Braganzas was the Irish unionist, Lord Strangford; and the royal family was escorted to Brazil by a Royal Navy squadron under the command of Admiral Sir Sidney Smith (1764–1840). The British government (with Castlereagh now as Foreign Secretary) supported the formal promulgation of union in 1815. Moreover Canning, who succeeded Castlereagh as Foreign Secretary on the latter's death in September 1822, simultaneously recognized the independence of the several new republics of south America while seeking to maintain a form of union between Brazil and Portugal. The declaration of an independent 'constitutional empire' of Brazil in September 1822 created the possibility of rupture; but Canning strove both to persuade João VI of Portugal to recognize Brazilian independence, while advising that the new constitutional emperor, Pedro, be acknowledged as the heir apparent to the Portuguese throne (Armitage 1836, i, p. 190). In essence, and whatever their rivalries, Canning may be seen as an heir to Castlereagh's Pittite strategies of sustaining union.

More generally, of course, the post-war settlements forged in 1814–15, in which Castlereagh and the British played so prominent a part, brought a restoration or consolidation of empire (Austria, Russia) as well as other forms of multinational or supranational polity (the new German Confederation). But, as the book makes clear, this was also an age of union: four multinational (and sometimes self-styled) 'united kingdoms' were created in the course of less than 15 years, and with strong British support—the United Kingdom of Great Britain and Ireland (1801), the United Kingdom of the Netherlands (1814), the United Kingdoms of Sweden-Norway (1814–15), and the United Kingdom of Portugal, Brazil, and the Algarves (1815). All four shared some degree of consanguinity; but (as has been argued) three of the four were especially closely linked.

The United Kingdom of Great Britain and Ireland was created for the purposes of security and stability and as a bulwark against France. The United Kingdom of the Netherlands was created for the purposes of security and stability and as a bulwark against France. The United Kingdoms of Sweden-Norway were created for the purposes of security and stability and as a bulwark against France and Russia. In effect, Castlereagh and his lieutenants (primarily Edward Cooke) took their template for the Irish union and adapted it elsewhere in northern Europe. They did not always invent the idea of union in these territories; nor were they its only advocates: but they did make these unions possible, where (without their sustained support) this might not otherwise have been the case. And there remains a clear sense in which the British exported the idea of the multi-national union.

1.6. Importing Union: Continental European Exemplars in the Age of Gladstone and After

If (as has just been argued) Castlereagh and his circle were connected to the creation and advancement of union in Ireland and subsequently in both the united kingdoms of the Netherlands and Sweden-Norway, and to that extent 'exported' the multinational union state, then throughout the later 19th century, there was a reciprocal set of European influences upon constitutional thought within the United Kingdom (see above, section 1.5). In other words, if the establishment of the United Kingdom has to be understood in the context of a wider set of continental European developments, then the increasingly pressing issue of its reform, from the 1870s onwards, has similarly to be understood within this wider framework. Different configurations of union elsewhere in Europe played a role in the imagining of home rule at this time, first and foremost for Ireland, but shortly afterwards for both Scotland and Wales as well. British and Irish contemporaries, especially nationalist contemporaries, not only anticipated the kinds of comparison which are sustained throughout this book—they also looked to complex union polities like Sweden-Norway or Austria or, within the British empire, Canada for active inspiration and guidance (see e.g. Loughlin 1986; Hoppen 2016; Rosland 2017; Zách 2021).

By the last decades of the 19th century there were numerous alternative models available for the construction of a complex multinational state, beyond that of the parliamentary union instituted in 1707 and 1801. The United Kingdom of the Netherlands, in fact a form of parliamentary union (or, at any rate, a single-parliament union), was not one of these models: as will be shown shortly (section 3.2), this had swiftly disintegrated in the context of the Belgian revolution in 1830. However, the United Kingdoms of Sweden-Norway were at this time—the second third of the 19th century—evidently well-established and generally flourishing, and seemed to present a workable, if clearly loose and sometimes fractious, model of personal union and association. The revamping of the Austrian empire through the compromise, or Ausgleich, of 1867 created a dual monarchy, Austria-Hungary, which equally appeared to offer possibilities for others, including the British and Irish. And, lastly, there were North American exemplars, both in terms of the reconstructed United States after the Civil War as well as (in particular) Canada, newly reconstituted after the British North America Act (Constitution Act) of 1867. Each of these alternative models of union—personal (Sweden-Norway), dualist (Austria-Hungary), federal (Canada)—presented liberal reformers and nationalists with an apparently more attractive set of possibilities than the asymmetries and incorporation of the British practice.

The great Irish activist and reformer, Daniel O'Connell (1775–1847), was sympathetic to the Norwegian cause from as early as 1813–14, while he subsequently held up the United Kingdoms of Sweden-Norway as a potential model for a reformed constitutional relationship binding Ireland and Britain. So, too, did his followers in the Repeal Association, who in fact organized a national essay competition in 1844 around this broad theme (the competition specifically required its contributing essayists to 'illustrate the international relations which they propose shall hereafter subsist between Great Britain and Ireland, by examples taken from the history and existing institutions of other countries, and in particular that they should examine how far the constitution of Norway, and its connexion with Sweden, may serve as a model for the new constitution of Ireland') (Anon. 1845, pp. iii–iv; Rosland 2017, p. 126; see e.g. Daunt 1848, ii, p. 301). The relationship between O'Connell's repeal campaign and the Swedish-Norwegian union was perceived in Scandinavia itself: Count Magnus Björnsterna, writing in 1840, referred ironically to the possibility of 'uniting Norway and Sweden at least "by the golden link of the crown", as Daniel O'Connell expresses himself in speaking of his scheme, the repeal of the union, [also] called, in Sweden, the Union' (Anon. 1840, p. 56; Barton 2003, pp. 51–3).

Later in the century all of these international paradigms were researched and lauded by a new generation of Irish nationalist, including Isaac Butt (1813–79) and his ally, Thaddeus O'Malley (1796–1877), though it is also true that the succeeding leader of the Irish home rule movement, the great Charles Stewart Parnell, was not distinguished by any marked geographical breadth of outlook, still less any specific engagement with Sweden-Norway (Rosland 2017, p. 130). On the other hand, O'Connell, Butt, and O'Malley in turn helped to influence key British sympathizers like the Liberal leader, William Ewart Gladstone (1809–98). Butt's manifesto, *Home government for Ireland* (1874 edition), was (eventually) perused by Gladstone in January 1876: but, even more strikingly, the work of O'Malley, *Home rule on the basis of federalism* (1873), which was particularly strong in its use of international models for Ireland and Britain, was read by Gladstone immediately on publication—and reread in September 1885 as he was earnestly researching the possibility of Irish home rule (Foot and Matthew 1968–94, xiv, pp. 323, 505).

Indeed, the clearest and best-known evidence for the cumulative impact of external, continental, analogy within the reform of the British state rests with Gladstone and his circle of advisers and confidants in 1885–6 (Rosland 2017, p. 131; Shannon 1999, pp. 372–3; Loughlin 1986). Gladstone and the scholar and statesman James Bryce investigated the constitutions of Austria-Hungary, Sweden-Norway, and Canada in formulating a home rule settlement for Ireland; and they and other contemporaries invoked not only all these polities, but others as well (Finland, the United States). For Gladstone this was not just a question of private study: his keen interest in Sweden-Norway was partly stimulated by tourism, for in 1883 and again in 1885 he famously sought escape from the rigours of office through sailing holidays in the Norwegian fjords (e.g. Shannon 1999, p. 374; Rosland 2017, p.133). Moreover, given his didactic bent, he was also predictably keen to encourage cabinet colleagues to follow his own researches: for example, in the late summer of 1885 he was cajoling ('in headmasterly style') his cabinet colleague, Lord Hartington, to lift his gaze and consider the question of Irish self-government and reform of the union in a truly international and historical light: 'the general development since then [the 1840s debates on repeal of the Union], the prolonged experience of Norway (I might perhaps mention Finland) and the altogether new experience of Austro-Hungary along with them the great power placed in the hands of the Irish people require the reconsideration of the whole position' (Gladstone to Hartington, 8 Sept. 1885, Gladstone Mss, British Library (hereafter BL), Add.MS. 44148, f. 127; Shannon 1999, p. 378; Jackson 2017b, pp. 163–5). At around the same time Gladstone and his Foreign Secretary, Granville, were exchanging material on the Austro-Hungarian Ausgleich and its institutions—including Arthur Patterson's essay on 'Dualism in Austria-Hungary', recently published in the *Fortnightly Review* (Granville to Gladstone, 6 August 1885, Gladstone Mss, Add.MS.44178, f. 185; Ramm 1962, ii, p. 391). In the following spring, March 1886, Gladstone was distributing with approval an account of the conduct of foreign affairs in the United Kingdoms of Sweden-Norway (Morley to Gladstone, 28 Feb. 1886, Gladstone Mss, Add.MS.44255, f. 59). On the other hand, it is significant that Joseph Chamberlain (1836–1914) (who visited Sweden—rather than Norway—in 1882) formed a quite different view of the United Kingdoms—one more favourable to Swedish interests and to union; and, by extension, his experience came to shape his overall opposition to home rule in Ireland (Knaplund 1952, p. 42).

Foreign correspondents urged detailed evidence and exemplars upon Gladstone in his researches: the Viennese lawyer, Dr Jacques Fischer (1858–96), highlighted the connection between Hungary and Croatia-Slavonia 'als Vorbild', and subsequently pointed out (rather as a warning) that Galicia had been given 'full' autonomy, and that the dominant Poles of Galicia 'have ruled Austria by selling themselves to the party which most wanted their support' (Fischer to Gladstone, 15 Mar. 1886, Gladstone Mss, Add.MS.44495; Fischer to Gladstone,

15 Apr. 1886, Gladstone Mss, Add.MS.44496, f. 247; cf. Markovits and Sysyn 1982, p. 91). At around the same time Alexander Grönberg, a student working in Helsingfors (Helsinki), lamented Gladstone's emphases on Sweden-Norway and Austria-Hungary as models of self-government rather than the case of the Grand Duchy of Finland within the Russian empire (Grönberg to Gladstone, 16 Apr. 1886, Gladstone Mss, Add.MS 44496, f. 254; Jackson 2017b, p. 163). As Grönberg pointed out, Finns in the 1880s (before the onset of 'russification' and oppression at the turn of the century) enjoyed the dual benefits of a relatively large degree of autonomy as well as easy access to the economic and professional opportunities offered by the Russian empire; and in consequence they looked to Russia 'with feelings of the deepest loyalty'.

In addition to these continental European analogies, Gladstone also actively sought evidence on the American and (in particular) the Canadian constitutions: he wrote to a recent (Liberal) governor general of Canada, Lord Lorne (later the ninth Duke of Argyll) (1845–1914), to this effect in September 1885; and he discussed the American exemplar with Andrew Carnegie as well as Lorne's father, the (highly cerebral though also deeply antagonistic) eighth Duke of Argyll (1823–1900) (Gladstone to Lorne, 17 Sept. 1885, Gladstone Mss, Add.MS 44492, f. 94; Carnegie to Gladstone, 25 Jan. 1886, Gladstone Mss, Add.MS. 44494, f. 71; Argyll to Gladstone, 29 Jan. 1886, Gladstone Mss, Add.MS. 44106, f. 89). The wider British empire was also eagerly scanned in search for practical solutions to the various challenges posed by home rule, such as the constitution of an upper house in any potential legislature (Description of elective houses in colonial legislatures, 15 Feb. 1886, Gladstone Mss, Add.MS. 44632, f. 36).

It is indeed possible that Gladstone, given his untrammelled enthusiasms and numerous blindspots, was unaware 'that the Austro-Hungarian and Swedish-Norwegian cases were [largely] dualistic in character'. At least one of Gladstone's biographers has considered that this was likely; and that the GOM chose not to recognize either that 'the parties were on a footing of absolute constitutional equality in relation to one another' or that (in the case of Sweden-Norway) their relationship was increasingly characterized by acrimony and instability in advance of their separation in 1905 (Shannon 1999, p. 373). It is certainly true that Gladstone could sometimes be extraordinarily perverse and wrong-headed, as is illustrated by his sympathies for the West Indian plantation owners, and by his very deeply problematic views on slavery (Quinault 2009). He was also adept at selectively deploying (not to say massaging) complex evidence to document his own preferred conclusions; and he was much happier to receive corroboration of his preconceived opinions than to have these jolted in any way. Thus, though Gladstone travelled to Norway in August 1885, he appears to have determinedly turned his gaze away from any indication that there were difficulties in its relationship with Sweden (Shannon 1999, p. 373). Equally, the hapless British consul general in Christiania who ventured to provide a despatch (accurately) suggesting that there were ongoing commercial tensions between Norway and Sweden was (after vigorous interrogation) effectively dismissed as inadequate and negligent (Gladstone to Bryce, 4 June 1886, Gladstone Mss, Add.MS.44548, f. 89; Knaplund 1952, pp. 150–2). In short, despite his voracious reading and intellectual thirst, Gladstone was deeply susceptible to confirmation bias.

At the same time, however, it is unlikely either that he entirely misunderstood, or was entirely misinformed. It would have taken an unusually languid inspection of these constitutional analogies, as well as an unusually blunt intellect, to have misread their fundamental content; and, whatever else, Gladstone was of course neither indolent nor stupid. Moreover, he also kept a keen eye on both polities, and in particular the United Kingdoms of Sweden-Norway (see e.g. Ramm 1962, ii, p. 191; Knaplund 1952). In addition it is worth remembering that he was approaching these exemplars at a time when they were seemingly more persuasive than they were shortly to become: Sweden-Norway and Austria-Hungary (and Finland) were all in a relatively settled and flourishing condition in the early 1880s, though they were certainly experiencing significant problems by the mid and/or late 1890s.

In any event, this evidence, and these conversations, fed into both Gladstone's final embrace of home rule, as well as into the construction of the first home rule bill itself. Much more might be said about the impact of these European and north American analogues upon Gladstone and other British and Irish contemporaries in the era of home rule; and indeed fuller explorations are offered in the later sections of the book. It is sufficient at this stage to underline that Gladstone and his Irish nationalist allies (and indeed an earlier generation of Irish nationalist) defined repeal, home rule, and union in terms of a set of wider continental European and north American analogies.

For Gladstone both Norway and Hungary enjoyed what he never failed to define as 'home rule'; and it was an article of faith (doubtless in both actual and metaphorical senses, given his providentialist outlook) that this 'home rule' had provided the foundations for friendship, peace, and (true) union (see e.g. Gladstone 1892, pp. 365–6, quoted as the chapter epigraph). Moreover, his political heirs within Liberalism loyally shared these readings; and when the Eighty Club (formed in 1880 to commemorate Gladstone's great electoral victory of that year) visited Hungary in 1906, the analogies between English oppression in Ireland and Austrian oppression in Hungary were still keenly felt (Anon. 1907, pp. 399, 409). Expressing these points in a narrower and more instrumentalist manner, the comparisons which are a central feature of this book originate, not in casual choice, but rather in the outlook and argument of key contemporaries themselves (Cohen 2004, p. 65).

Figure 1.1 Castlereagh and his union circle: Robert Stewart, Viscount Castlereagh (1769–1822). Watercolour portrait by George Dance (1794) (National Portrait Gallery, London).

Figure 1.2 Castlereagh and his union circle: Richard Le Poer Trench, second Earl of Clancarty (1767–1837). Portrait in oils by Joseph Paelinck (National Portrait Gallery, London).

Figure 1.3 Castlereagh and his union circle: Percy Smythe, sixth Viscount Strangford (1780–1855). Portrait on ivory (National Portrait Gallery, London).

Figure 1.4 Castlereagh and his union circle: Charles Stewart, later third Marquess of Londonderry (1778–1854). Portrait in oils by Thomas Lawrence (National Portrait Gallery, London).

Figure 1.5 Castlereagh and his union circle: Edward Cooke (1755–1820). Mezzotint (National Portrait Gallery, London).

2
The Unions of the United Kingdom of Great Britain and Ireland (1535–1922)

Case Studies

2.1. The First United Kingdom: Scotland and Ireland (1707/1801–1922)

In the first decades of the 21st century the United Kingdom of Great Britain and Northern Ireland often appeared in a weak and threatened state, with constitutional drift across the kingdom, deepening nationalist feeling in Scotland and in Northern Ireland, profound divisions over Brexit and the response to the Covid pandemic, and the consequent looming possibility of disintegration. These forces were now associated with the growth of an English (rather than a British) national sentiment which seemed likely to further accelerate the disintegrative tendency (Kenny 2014; Henderson and Wyn Jones 2021).

The comparison between this and the late 19th century is illuminating. In the last quarter of the 19th century there were similar centrifugal forces at play in the union, with the consolidation of Irish nationalism through the home rule movement, the emergence of a highly patriotic nonconformist Welsh radicalism, and mounting (if still small-scale) interest in Scots home rule. Some key centripetal institutions of the state—such as the monarchy—appeared, in the 1870s, to be wavering. But many of these apparent trends or growths were ultimately cut off through the emergence of a unifying popular imperialism and a reinvigorated Britishness which peaked in the 1890s, and which fed into (and diverted) both Welsh and Scottish radical patriotism and even—to an extent—Irish constitutional nationalism, at least in terms of its Redmondite formulation (see e.g. Jackson 2018b, pp. 136–44).

The gap between the cultural resources of the United Kingdom state in the early 20th century and its successor in the early 21st century is stark. Those institutions and agencies which once exercised a unifying function in the context of threatened disintegration have been characterized by a long-term weakening or (in some cases) a thorough discrediting. On the other hand, the forms of political identity which have been consolidating, and which have evidently contributed to these centrifugal tendencies, have in many cases originated amongst the unionists themselves. In the early 20th century, the union state held together because it possessed a variety of resources which either no longer exist in quite the same form, or (where they do) have been substantially undermined (Jackson 2013; Keating 2021, pp. 194–5).

How, then, has this situation arisen? This chapter of the book seeks to provide some answers, to address both the historic longevity and the later faltering of the unions of the United Kingdom, by looking (in the first section) at the two parliamentary unions, the Scots and the Irish, and then turning (in the next section) to consider an accessory union, the Welsh. The three 'unions' were of course interconnected, and the two sections of the chapter have been constructed with an eye to their links and complementarity. Readers will find that, given the comparative mode of the chapter (and of the book as a whole), the ideas and themes in the first section are consolidated in the second, where the Welsh union is contextualized in terms of the Irish and Scots experience.

There was indeed a determined effort by some Welsh unionist radicals in the first years of the 20th century to retrospectively define the 'laws in Wales acts', the assimilationist legislation of 1535 and 1542, as 'acts of union' and then to equate these measures with the unions of 1707 and 1801 (Williams 1909, p. 110; Edwards 1901). However, the Welsh connection with England was distinctive, not least because at the time of 'union', in the 1530s, there was so very little state structure to 'unite' with England: in particular there was no Welsh parliament to unite with Westminster, as there was a Scots parliament and an Irish parliament (Jackson 2013, pp. 26–7). There was thus no negotiation between parliamentary commissioners, such as was the case with the Scots in 1706, or amongst parliamentary representatives, as (in however constricted a manner) with the Irish case in 1799–1800: the Welsh 'union' (whatever its beneficent or other influences) was achieved by English parliamentary *fiat* (Jackson 2013, p. 27). Moreover, the interconnections generally between Scotland and Ireland for the period from the 17th century were indisputably denser and more intimate than those binding Wales and Ireland. Accordingly, the chapter considers Scotland and Ireland together, and the Welsh discretely (for a fuller argument and analysis of this, and of the Scots and Irish unions generally, see Jackson 2013).

It should also be reiterated now, and by way of caution, that discussion of the unions of the United Kingdom is by no means confined to the different sections of this chapter, and that the rest of the book invokes these unions in many and different ways. What follows in this, and the following section, is designed therefore to introduce a range of relevant themes in the history of these unions, which are then developed comparatively and in other ways. This section, and the next, harbour no ambition whatever to be the last word. But, if not the last, then certainly very many later words on the unions of the United Kingdom are to be found throughout subsequent chapters of the work. For those who are interested in a yet longer exegesis on the theme, there are the arguments offered in my earlier *Two Unions* work (Jackson 2013).

Just as successful unions elsewhere in Europe depended upon the internal unity of each of the preceding composite polities, so the forging of the kingdoms of both England and Scotland in the early medieval period—particularly in the 9th and early 10th centuries—was simultaneously a crucial precursor to a wider political unity within the island as well as a major counterweight to this epiphany. A form of English kingdom was forged through the military and diplomatic thrusts of monarchs of the house of Wessex such as Athelstan (894–939), who also briefly appears to have extended his overlordship into Scotland (and he certainly claimed on his coinage to be 'rex totius Britanniae'). In the contemporary north Constantine II (c.879–952) is seen as a central figure in the assimilation or melding of Gaelic and Pictish cultures which underlay the formation of the medieval kingdom of Alba or Scotland; though like his successors on the Scottish throne, Constantine also had to face the militarily powerful and ambitious southern neighbour. He briefly features as a mere *subregulus* in a legal document of Athelstan's reign (dated 934), and his forces were certainly vanquished at the epic bloodletting of Brunanburh, 'the Great Battle', fought at (perhaps) Bromborough, in the Wirral in 937.

However, it has been argued that one key reason that 'Britain' failed to coalesce lastingly in the medieval period was because confident and assertive Scots rulers 'increasingly saw themselves as the equal of English kings rather than as their clients'—a confidence expressed in their names (Constantine, Alexander, David) as well as, often, in ambitious building programmes (discussed in Mackillop and Ó Siochrú 2008, p. 38). Under their royal houses of Bruce and Stuart, the Scots successfully fended off the English invasions associated with the two 'wars of independence' (1296–1328 and 1332–57); and they maintained their hard-won national autonomy until the death of the childless Elizabeth I of England in 1603, when James VI of Scotland inherited her throne and thereby finally cemented the union of the island's two ancient crowns. Even allowing for this 'union of the crowns', the distinctive Scottish state remained largely in place until the parliamentary union attained in 1707.

In contrast to Scotland, while there were sometimes dominant rulers in both medieval Wales and Ireland (the titular princes of Wales, or high kings of Ireland), there was no single, sustained and unified, monarchy in either of these polities; and English military subjugation, though never wholly complete, particularly in Ireland, was nevertheless relatively more sustained and effective than in contemporary Scotland. This, combined with the economic and demographic dominance of England, and the migration and 'plantation', or colonization, of English settlers, has led some sociologists (like Michael Hechter or, later, Krishan Kumar) to apply the notion of an 'internal [English] colonialism' within the Atlantic archipelago. This is a concept which, while not without relevance to the Scots, has a clear bearing on the relationship between the English and Irish, and also (as will be shown) some relevance to the health of the constitutional relationships which were eventually forged between the different nations of the two islands (Hechter 1975; Kumar 2003).

In any event, with the Scots, a combination of sustained military vigour, royal and aristocratic alliances and ties with England, together with the heavy English cultural influence in the lowlands, all meant that they were generally better able to sustain their political independence than the Welsh or Irish. Paradoxically, this may also have meant that the Scots were ultimately able to enjoy a more effective, because more equitable, form of union with England than that experienced either by the Welsh or Irish. It was certainly the view of later patriotic Scots Tories such as Walter Elliot (1888–1958), successively Financial Secretary to the Treasury (1931–2), Minister of Agriculture (1932–6), Secretary of State for Scotland (1936–8), and Minister of Health (1938–40), that the historic military defiance sustained by the Scots had produced a better because more equal and balanced union than would otherwise have been the case ('how thankful we should be to our forefathers who fought Bannockburn (and indeed who held the border)!') (Elliot to Dugdale, 24 August 1938, Walter Elliot Papers, NLS, Acc.12198/8). In Elliot's taxonomy a robust patriotism was essential to successful union.

Despite these links and influences, Britain in the 17th and 18th centuries and after was a complex constitutional formation, which defied easy categorization. The 'union of the crowns' achieved in 1603 between England and Scotland created a composite monarchy familiar enough elsewhere in Europe—but this was only a start. The revolution of 1688, and the arrival of William of Orange as joint monarch of England, Scotland, and Ireland, together with his wife Mary, created in effect a yet more complex composite, since William was both hereditary Prince of Orange and also (after 1672) the stadtholder of Holland and other Dutch provinces (an effectively monarchical role, though within what was in principle a republican constitution). Smouldering English patriotic resentment at the Dutch connection and its personal and practical implications hinted at tensions and jealousies to come within the future iterations of the unions of the 'British isles'. William died in 1702 and was succeeded by his Stuart sister-in-law, Anne; with her death, childless, in 1714, the throne passed in turn to a great grandson of James VI and I, George, elector of Hanover.

The agreed accession of George revitalized the notion of a personal union binding disparate territories—though now Britain and Hanover, rather than (as before 1707) England and Scotland, or (between 1688 and 1702) England and the Netherlands. For a century after this (1714–1814) the kings of Great Britain were also *Kurfürsten*, electors, of Hanover and rulers of the territories acquired by Hanover—Bremen, Land Hadeln, Osnabrück: after 1814 (and with the earlier demise of the Holy Roman Empire and the concomitant role of elector) Hanover was ruled by kings. George III, George IV, and William IV were not only monarchs of Great Britain and Ireland, they were also simultaneously Georg III, Georg IV, and Wilhelm, *Könige von Hannover* (see Ward 1899; Dann 1991; Rexheuser 2005; Simms and Riotte 2009).

The significance of all of this is easy to miss: the United Kingdom may indeed (as its Whig celebrants claimed) have been moving seamlessly and swiftly towards a settled unitary condition, but it had deep—and lasting—roots as a composite monarchy, and indeed it remained such (in terms of the Hanoverian connection) until the death of William IV, in 1837. In other words, composite monarchy and its associated political cultures were a long time in dying within the Atlantic archipelago. A key part of this legacy was the retention of strong and jealous national identities, characterized (as has been seen) by English elite antagonism towards the role of the Dutch within the court of William III, or by similarly deep-seated suspicions of Hanover, or by recurrent jealousies or animus—from the time of the earl of Bute to that of Gordon Brown—towards 'excessive' Scottish influence over government.

In addition to the legacies of composite monarchy, Britain and Ireland were of course also characterized by parliamentary unions—the union of the English and Scottish parliaments, launched in 1707, and that binding the British and Irish parliaments, operative from 1 January 1801. There were certainly distinctive inflections to the nature of the British unions; but, as Andrew Mackillop and Micheál Ó Siochrú have each rightly observed, 'the extinction of Scotland's parliament was far from unique and corresponds to a broader pattern of pressure upon representative assemblies through the continent' (Mackillop and Ó Siochrú 2008, p. 7). Mackillop and Ó Siochrú have also usefully pointed out that 'the dominant model of state formation in early modern Europe remained the composite, conglomerate or multiple monarchy beneath which there existed a wide variety of provincial kingdoms, city states, republics, commonwealths and confederations': moreover, Scotland conforms to 'a wider European pattern whereby assimilative pressures operating from the provinces towards the metropole proved a persistent feature of early modern state formation' (Mackillop and Ó Siochrú 2008, pp. 13, 20). Parliamentary unions were therefore neither distinctively British nor Protestant nor northern European, as Victorian Whigs and other British exceptionalists might once have proposed, but were instead recognizably part of a wider type of early modern European state formation. It was in fact not so much the unions that were distinctive or indeed distinctively British as the carefully negotiated and formally voluntary nature of their attainment. And, looking ahead to 1815 and beyond, the extent to which British politicians and diplomats were associated with an 'export' of union, the external propping of its structures and values, was also distinctive (see above, section 1.5).

This negotiated and voluntary status of union, ostensibly an explanation for survival and longevity, begs the questions—how and why did the two parliamentary unions work (Jackson 2013)? The question of the 'success' of the British unions is rather less clear cut than for most of the other polities under consideration, or otherwise broached, in this study: after all the United Kingdom of Portugal, Brazil, and the Algarves was broken apart in 1822, the United Kingdom of the Netherlands came to grief in 1830, the United Province of Canada effectively foundered after the late 1850s, Sweden-Norway followed in 1905, while the Grand Duchy of Finland and Austria-Hungary dissolved in 1917 and 1918 respectively. For its part the British state was rocked by serious revolt in 1715 and particularly in 1745–6 when the Stuart legitimists again sought to reclaim the throne lost to them in 1688: these two Jacobite revolts drew upon anti-union sentiment, and, certainly in the case of the '45, shook the Hanoverian establishment to its foundations. In Ireland, the union state was challenged by separatist insurgency in 1803, 1848, 1867, and through the revolutionaries of the Irish Republican Brotherhood (formed originally in 1858) and the not-so-revolutionary but trenchant parliamentary action of the home rulers at Westminster: British rule in the 26 southern counties of Ireland was eventually ended in 1921, though the extent of the failure was masked by the theological intricacies of 'dominion' status, by the divisions within the separatist camp over the details of independence, and in particular by the absence of the desired republic (it has been convincingly suggested that Irish republicans, in emphasizing—like the British—the importance of symbols, threatened to pull defeat from the jaws of victory) (Garvin 1987, 1996). On the other hand, Great Britain and a truncated or revised United Kingdom are (at the time of writing) still with us, albeit in an occasionally shaky condition; and any political configuration which has survived for over 300 years (as in the case of Great Britain), or for over 200 years (as with the United Kingdom) has to be defined in terms of some measure of 'success' or at least of resilience.

How has this been achieved? Each of the two unions, Scots and Irish, was usefully incomplete in so far as many of the distinctive national institutions of the old composite monarchy remained in place. In Scotland the aristocracy, as well as professional elites—ecclesiastical, legal, and educational—were largely untouched by parliamentary union. Scotland retained its own autonomous church, and its own independent universities: the separateness of its legal system (drawing more heavily on Roman law traditions than the English, and recently rationalized by James Dalrymple, Viscount Stair, 1619–95) was confirmed (by article 19 of the 1707 treaty of union). The whole gamut of local privilege—heritable offices, jurisdictions, lifetime offices and jurisdictions, were all specifically protected (article 20) (see e.g. Ferguson 1977). The rights and privileges of the main Scottish towns, or burghs, were similarly protected (article 21). Civil society was scarcely touched, at least directly, by union; and it served to foster a space for the encouragement of (what has been described as) a 'unionist nationalism' (see section 4.8) (Morton 1999; cf. Lloyd Jones 2014). In other words, the very limitations of the Scottish union worked to ensure its survival and longevity.

In Ireland the union of 1800 was similarly incomplete. Here, too, there were elites and institutions which survived union largely unscathed. The monarchy continued to be directly represented through a viceroy or lord lieutenant, sometimes an Irish Protestant aristocrat, though more often English, whose nominal chief secretary, frequently in cabinet, was thereby often the most important British minister with responsibility for Ireland; but there was in fact a semi-detached Irish government, comprising the lord lieutenant, the chief secretary, the lord chancellor of Ireland, the two Irish law officers, and—after 1899—the vice-president of the department of agriculture and technical instruction (in effect the Irish minister for agriculture) (McDowell 1964; Hoppen 2016). The landed aristocracy, though cashiered from their doomed Dublin parliament in 1800, were generously compensated by the new United Kingdom's taxpayers, and retained their position at the head of Irish society until the end of the 19th century. The Irish judicial system was largely untouched by union, and key legal and other professional elites functioned as before (see Campbell 2009). Ireland retained a central and separate administration, based in Dublin Castle. The country's banking system (led by the Bank of Ireland), its currency (the Irish pound, quite separate from its English counterpart), and its tariff structures were certainly addressed by union, but remained in place during a very lengthy transition period: the Irish pound, for example, was only finally abandoned a quarter of a century after union (in 1826).

There were, however, critical differences between the position in Ireland and that in Scotland. The social and economic elites in Scotland which were unscathed by union were accepted within Scottish society as national elites, and were broadly representative (not least in terms of religious faith) of that society. The social and economic elites in Ireland which retained their position and autonomy after the union were primarily representative merely of one (albeit diverse) social class—the Anglican landed elite, or (as it was known after the 1780s) the 'Protestant ascendancy'. This effectively meant that the national social and physical spaces in post-union Scottish society which were so critical to the flexible and effective functioning of the 'unitary' state did not exist in the same way in Ireland. Moreover, the civil society which functioned as a means of containing and managing a 'safe' patriotism in Scotland again did not exist in the same form in Ireland, where (in the analysis of James Livesey) the civil society of the enlightenment era had been largely razed through the sectarianization and violence of Irish society at the end of the 18th century (Livesey 2009). In short, distinctive Irish institutions remained or were recreated under the union, but they did not work in harmony with the union state, as in Scotland. In fact they ultimately constituted a form of counter-state, or state within the state (for a fuller discussion see section 4.8).

The British and Irish unions survived, not only because (paradoxically) they were incomplete, but also because (paradoxically) they were unrobust. More specifically, the unions (like some of their relatively successful continental European counterparts) were characterized by a persistent malleability or flexibility:

expressing this in more positive terms, the unions developed organically. This partly arose because, while each of the two unions was enshrined within separate legislation (the English parliament's Act of Union with Scotland (1706), the Scottish parliament's Union with England Act (1707) together with the Irish and British parliaments' Acts for the Union of Great Britain and Ireland (1800)), the overall constitution of the union state was—famously, or notoriously—'unwritten' or uncodified, and based upon usage, precedent, and tradition, invented or otherwise (see e.g. McLean 2010). This has remained so to the present day, though the speed of change under the Blair governments and since has increasingly stimulated calls for an overarching codified constitution (for example, by the distinguished British historian, Linda Colley) (Colley 2014a, 2021). But, in essence, there has been no central codified constitution for the United Kingdom; and one of the key implications of this has been, arguably, the existence of a much greater degree of adaptability, flexibility, and invention (or, alternatively, incoherence, inconsistency, and moral vacuity) in the governance of the union than might otherwise have been the case (for the positive version of this argument see Dicey 1887).

Flexibility, as with other—continental—European unions, generally (and on balance) encouraged longevity, however. In Scotland and Ireland and Wales, there have certainly been periods of determined integrationist government, especially in the early 19th century; but the flexibility of (for example) the Scots union has been demonstrated through the growth of administrative devolution beginning with the creation of the Scottish Office in 1885, and gaining ever greater momentum in the inter-war years. As in Ireland, so in Scotland the plight of the rural poor was addressed through distinctive reform legislation—in the case of the Scots through a succession of Crofters' Acts between 1886 and 1891. The capacity of the union state and its main agents to respond to national protest was further demonstrated through (for example) the Liberals' movement towards Scottish home rule, and through the successful second reading of a home rule bill for Scotland in June 1914 (even if this measure was in the end scuppered by the outbreak of the First World War) (Lloyd Jones 2014, pp. 862–87). Looking ahead, the mounting challenge of the Scottish National Party in the 1960s and 1970s was met by the Scotland Act (1978), by the (unsuccessful) referendum on devolution in March 1979—and ultimately by a second referendum in September 1997 which brought the restoration of a Scottish parliament. A broadly comparable trajectory in Wales is discussed more fully in the book's next section.

Similarly, the union between Ireland and Great Britain survived partly on the basis of a degree of malleability, and the linked capacity to disarm at least some opposition (although neither feature should be exaggerated). The Irish union originally made provision for a united state church binding the two islands, supported by tithe payments levied on almost all, including Catholics, who of course were in an overwhelming majority in Ireland (around 80 per cent in 1834) (Brown

2001). But the union government was still able to deliver an equalization of civil rights for Catholics, albeit conspicuously late—29 years after the idea had originally been mooted in association with the union itself. From the 1830s onwards the privileges of the unnecessarily elaborate and over-endowed Church of Ireland were cut back through measures such as the Church Temporalities Act (1833) and the Tithe Rent Charge Act (1838), culminating in the complete disestablishment of the Church (and the consequent amendment of the union settlement itself) by the Liberal Prime Minister, W. E. Gladstone, in 1869.

The flexibility of union was further demonstrated by the increasing centrality of the notion of Irish legislative independence, or home rule, embraced publicly by Gladstone from December 1885 onwards. Home rule for Ireland was ultimately enacted by the British parliament in September 1914, though—like both its Scottish counterpart and Welsh disestablishment, which were also being debated at this time—its further consideration was fatally delayed by the outbreak of the First World War.

In addition to all of this, London governments across the 19th and 20th centuries experimented with both notions of integration and differentiation in their treatment of Ireland and Scotland; and they experimented, too, with their choice of local allies—certainly in the government of Ireland (Hoppen 2016). Throughout the 18th century successive administrations subcontracted much of the government of Ireland to chosen 'undertakers' (those who 'undertook' the work) within the landed elite—a class akin to the Argyll-Campbell nexus in Scotland in the early and mid-18th century or the 'Dundas despotism' of the late 18th century; though from the last quarter of the century British ministers worked more directly to sustain the government of Ireland, and subcontracted less (Fry 2004; Bartlett 1979). With Catholic popular mobilization in the 1820s and after, the position of the 'ascendancy' became much more vulnerable, and—particularly after the calamitous Great Famine (1845–51)—their usefulness rapidly waned. While English Conservatives never wholly severed their ties with Irish land, the trend of land reform ran decidedly in favour of the tenant interest; and even Tories, when they were in power (from the 1890s onwards), sometimes looked—like their Liberal counterparts—towards the Catholic Church and the home rule leadership. George Wyndham (1863–1913), Chief Secretary of Ireland (1900–5), communicated much more happily and confidentially with home rulers like John Redmond (1856–1918), William O'Brien (1852–1928), and T. M. Healy (1855–1931) than with Edward Saunderson (1837–1906) or the other Irish unionist leaders. By 1914 the Home Rule party was widely seen as the government of Ireland in waiting.

Why, then, did this 'first edition' of the United Kingdom fail, as it clearly did in 1921? Does this failure shed any light on the vulnerability of (what might be called) the later iterations of the United Kingdom? The proximate cause, or at any rate context, illuminating the demise of the first union was of course the First

World War: this had the effect, not so much of creating the problems with union, as of radically concentrating them into one highly destructive constitutional laser beam (as will be discussed in greater detail in section 6.7). The dark side of the main themes of union government was ruthless exposed. The abiding tendency for the London government to relegate its geographical periphery was further encouraged by the pressure of the war: the opportunities for enflaming the volatile national sensitivities of the Irish grew ever greater. Home rule was promised, enacted, postponed, and then subverted. The union had always involved (by British standards) exceptional or extraordinary levels of policing, and the Royal Irish Constabulary (armed and centralized) was itself, by British standards, exceptional. The military presence in Ireland was unusually strong by the standards of Wales and Scotland. All of these features were intensified by the war—even allowing for the blanket application across the United Kingdom of restrictive wartime measures such as the Defence of the Realm Act (1914) (Palmer 1988; Muenger 1991). Moreover, the malleability of the union had involved a studied responsiveness to Irish militancy (expressed through strategic reform or movement in the face of militant Irish pressure)—and the evident success of the latest and (in some ways) most radical expression of Irish militancy, the Ulster unionist mobilization of 1912–14, created an immediate inspiration and opportunities for those separatists who delivered the Easter Rising in April 1916.

Equally, these uncertain pendulum swings of union government from integration to differentiation were exposed during the war. This was especially clear between 1916 and 1918, when Irish expectations of exceptionalism and malleability (based securely on past ministerial performance) were brusquely challenged by British ministers' successive integrationist efforts to extend military conscription to Ireland. In several respects, therefore, the key drivers of the radicalization of Irish nationalist opinion during the war were ultimately rooted in some of the long-standing features of union government, albeit now magnified by the bloodletting on the western front.

In fact, this point may be extended by looking beyond these patterns of union government, towards the institutional bolsters of the union in the years before and during the First World War: in a clear sense the union failed partly because some of its key supports either failed or were seriously compromised at this time. The institutions which are now generally identified as key props of the union of the 19th and early 20th centuries (and identified by others, like Jászi, as performing the same strengthening function in other union polities) included the monarchy, empire, the army, religion—and, where relevant, parliament (Jászi 1929; Jackson 2013; Hennessy 2015; see also Chapter 4). Of these the standing of the crown in Ireland and Scotland varied considerably according to the interests and reputation of individual monarchs—with Queen Victoria (for example) playing considerably more effectively in Scotland than in Ireland, and her successor, Edward VII, occupying precisely the reverse position (Finlay 2002, 2005; Murphy 2001; see Figure 3.1).

George V had an exceptionally well-developed instinct for survival in this era of toppling thrones, and (whatever his private sympathies) he bestowed his favours with reasonable equity in both Ireland and Scotland, and on nationalists as well as unionists (see Figures 4.1, 4.2; Jackson 2018b, pp. 141–2, 149).

Similarly the empire was deployed with increasingly marked effect by John Redmond, who (at this acme of colonialism) was keen to remove one of the key arguments in the unionist arsenal, and to demonstrate that the cause of home rule was wholly compatible with the health and welfare of Britain's imperial standing. Political leaders across the empire queued up to endorse Irish home rule, while Carson and the unionists found themselves with little effective colonial support (whatever their own imperialist aspirations) (Jackson 2018b, pp. 144–7). In these circumstances, it became increasingly difficult for the unionists to argue convincingly that home rule would bring imperial disintegration.

On the other hand, several props of union conspicuously wobbled or failed at this time. The army, which admittedly had for long occupied an ambivalent position within the affections of Irish nationalism, recruited substantially amongst Irish Catholics, who often fought with marked gallantry throughout Britain's many wars across the 'long' 19th century (see also section 4.4). But the outbreak of global war in August 1914 effectively forced a resolution of what had been these useful ambiguities within Irish nationalism's stand on the British army: John Redmond abandoned the traditional janus-faced approaches, and in September precipitated a formal split within Irish nationalism, and the formation of a more radical and separatist splinter-group, when he directly and unequivocally encouraged Irish recruitment to the British army. This splinter-group became the engine of violent insurgency both in 1916 and again in 1919.

There were other flies in the martial ointment of 1914 and afterwards. First, the Curragh 'incident' of March 1914 (when British cavalry officers indicated that, given the option, they would resign rather than march against Ulster unionists), whatever its complexities (and whether or not it was technically a 'mutiny') lastingly persuaded many Irish people that the British army favoured unionists. Second, the successful landing by the Ulster Volunteers of their cache of weapons at Larne and other ports in the north of Ireland in April 1914 was accomplished without effective interference by the crown forces: this stood in apparent contrast to the Irish Volunteers' landing of weapons at Howth in July 1914, which culminated in a confrontation between the King's Own Scottish Borderers and a crowd of protesting civilians, four of whom were killed and 38 wounded when the soldiers opened fire (the determination of the Irish Volunteers to put on a public display in contrast to their northern counterparts was immaterial in terms of popular perceptions of unfairness). Lastly, the apparently preferential treatment of the Ulster Volunteers and the 36th (Ulster) Division within the British army—in contrast to the shabbier treatment of the Irish Volunteers and Irish military units within the army—served to underline to Irish nationalism the extent to which the institutions of the union state were no longer fit for purpose (if, indeed, they ever had really been so, from an Irish perspective; though see Jackson 2018b, pp. 183–5).

One other key institution that increasingly fell into this 'now not fit for purpose' category was Westminster. Parliament has sometimes been seen as a key binding agent in the unions of the United Kingdom (the Scots and Irish unions were, after all, fundamentally parliamentary unions); and it certainly served, broadly, to keep both Irish and Scottish political opinion accommodated within the United Kingdom for most of the 19th century. Irish home rulers expressed their contempt for Britain and its institutions—but they did so for nearly half a century within the confines of Westminster itself (Lubenow 1988). At the same time, however, one of the central traits of the government of union was the tendency of successive British governments to institute reforms for Ireland only when it was too late, or when constitutional agitation had turned despairingly to militancy, or threatened militancy: this was true in the O'Connellite era, in the era of the Irish Republican Brotherhood and the Land League, when some of the most substantial reforms (Catholic emancipation, disestablishment, successive land acts) were achieved only in the face of Irish nationalist militancy. It was certainly possible to move British governments through constitutional action (as was broadly the case with the reforms instituted after 1906 by the Campbell-Bannerman and Asquith administrations); and this was also true of the parliamentary horse-trading which delivered a home rule bill in 1912. But the fundamental problem with home rule after 1912 was ultimately that popular expectations, including among separatists, were sky-high—while at the same time unionists were dramatically adapting the Irish tradition of violently forcing the British parliament to pay attention. It is frequently said that the great irony of Ulster unionist militancy in 1912–14 was that it helped to provide an inspiration and an exemplar for the radicalization of nationalists. But a surely greater irony lay in the fact that unionists fought to defend the union in 1912–14 by effectively subverting one of its key institutional foundations—Westminster (see also section 4.7).

This radicalization of nationalism fed ultimately into support for the creation of a separate Irish parliament (Dáil Éireann) (in January 1919) and into the military campaign of the Irish Republican Army against the crown forces, fought between January 1919 and July 1921, when a truce was declared which created the space for negotiations and a treaty (6 December 1921). The Irish experience, in fact, has in some ways served as a paradigm for Scottish nationalists, and especially the historically alert Alex Salmond (First Minister of Scotland between 2007 and 2014); but it also offered a set of more general parameters or guidelines for the debate on Scottish independence (Jackson 2016). One striking and still pertinent feature of the settlement of 1921 was the extent of the independence on offer from the British, provided that the symbolism of their monarchy remained in place. Ultimately this reflected not only the military situation in Ireland, which was improving for the British by 1921, but rather both the global politics of Ireland's struggle for independence, and the malleability—even at the end—of Ireland's long union with Britain. Ultimately, too, the emphasis on monarchy reflected the lasting (if seemingly skewed) institutional priorities of the union state.

The bolsters of this state have been more securely in place in Scotland than in Ireland, though latterly these, too, have weakened under stress. Following through with the Irish comparison requires a glance forward, towards the later 20th century and indeed beyond. Scotland's integration into the industrial economy of 19th- and 20th-century Britain was more robust than that of Ireland (where only the north-east was heavily industrialized); and the Scottish union was supported by the wider economic success of the British state in a way that was not the case for most of Ireland, as the experience of the Great Famine painfully underlined for most Irish people (see also section 4.9). For the Scots relative economic as well as imperial decline were counterbalanced by the post-war expansion of the union state, by widespread nationalization, and the growth of uniform standards of health and social welfare provision (Ireland had not only left the union by this time, it had also formally become a republic and had left the Commonwealth (1949)). But the reversal of the post-war Butskellite consensus under Margaret Thatcher and the elevation of neo-liberal economic values and policies on the whole played badly in Scotland, where dependence on the state for welfare support and upon nationalized industries for employment was disproportionately strong. The retreat of the large British state, and of British manufacturing and heavy industry, all fed into the heightened vulnerability of union.

Constitutional unions have also sometimes rested upon active and organized movements of support—though there is a question here as to the distinctions between symptoms and causes (that is to say, whether unionism was a bolster of union, or a symptom of its health, or a combination of both, or indeed neither). However, while many of the union states under discussion in this volume clearly suffered from the lack of a strong and widely based union party, the United Kingdom was a qualified exception. Indeed until 1885–6 the entire party machinery of the United Kingdom parliament was dedicated to the survival of the Irish and Scottish unions; and after Gladstone's embrace of home rule at that time the central purpose of the Conservative party—and indeed, ultimately, its name—became unionist.

But it would be wrong to exaggerate the effectiveness of unionism even within the United Kingdom. It is obviously true that the Conservative party, with its Liberal Unionist allies, dominated government between 1886 and 1905, as it did (now rebranded as the Conservative and Unionist party) for most of the inter-war years. But its effectiveness varied between the different constituent polities of the kingdom, and there were significant issues in Ireland, Scotland, and Wales. It should be said immediately that the professedly 'Unionist' party of the United Kingdom was not always the main or the most effective proponent of union, even though it claimed that role for itself: there is a strong case to be made for the Labour party as the most important agency for union throughout much of the mid-20th century (see Jackson 2013).

In fact unionism itself has been a central part of the story of the retreat of union. Labour was indeed a long-standing bulwark of union, with flinty Presbyterian patriarchs like Tom Johnston (1881–1965) or Willie Ross (1911–88) acting as the party's viceroys in Scotland in the manner of the Argethelian or Dundas regimes of the 18th century. But by the Blair era (from 1997 onwards) almost all of the party's calculations in relation to the union proved to be wrongheaded. Devolution was seen by Blair and his Scots lieutenant Donald Dewar (1937–2000) as a means of defusing and containing separatist pressures, much as Gladstone had viewed Irish home rule in the 1880s; but in fact (as Tory unionists had then correctly predicted with home rule) the devolved parliament's swift popularity and success encouraged and fired patriotic aspirations, rather than sating them. Westminster's nominal sovereignty is (as, once again, Edwardian unionists predicted with home rule) proving hard to sustain in the light of the settled opinion of the Scottish government and parliament: this might also have been foreseen on the basis of Westminster's reluctance to interfere with the affairs of the devolved parliament in Northern Ireland (1921–72). Moreover, it was Tony Blair's Labour governments which embarked upon highly divisive wars in Iraq and Afghanistan and which finally obliterated the identities of various historic Scottish regiments. Equally, Blair and his successor, Gordon Brown, were both respectful of Mrs Thatcher and (sometimes) her policies, despite the intense unpopularity of her legacies in Scotland. Finally, one ostensible hallmark of Labour's unionism—the extent to which the party's frontbench in the Blair and Brown eras was infiltrated by Scots—has in fact served to subvert the case for union. For the transfer market in Scots of first-class ability to the government of the United Kingdom often left Labour fielding its second eleven within the Scottish parliament; and, given both the increasing importance of Holyrood as well as the skills of its SNP strikers (especially Salmond and Sturgeon), the consequences seemed dire for the party's (once) beautiful game of union.

Tory unionism in Scotland, for much of the 20th century a dominant political creed, was virtually annihilated during the tenure of Thatcher and her immediate successors. Many Conservative leaders of the early and mid-20th century had strong family connections with Scotland and with Scottish Toryism and were (accordingly) relatively sensitive to the demands of union: Arthur Balfour (1848–1930) (from Whittingehame, North Berwick), Andrew Bonar Law (1858–1923) (from Helensburgh), Stanley Baldwin (1867–1947) (notable as a celebrant of Englishness, but in fact scarcely less lyrical about his maternal—Macdonald—Scottish ancestry), Harold Macmillan (with family roots on Arran),

Alec Douglas-Home (from Coldstream in the Borders) (for Baldwin see Ward-Smith 2001). Winston Churchill, essentially an English aristocrat, nevertheless represented Dundee (between 1908 and 1922) during his Liberal incarnation. In these supranational contexts Heath and Thatcher were unusual in the comprehensiveness of their southern Englishness; and both rode rough-shod over the sensitivities of their Scottish party (Pentland 2015). Thatcher in particular was, at root, an assimilationist unionist, yet with very little knowledge of life north of the English midlands; she was tone-deaf to the peculiar resonances of Scottish unionism, and inclined to deal with Scotland (and to lecture the Scots) in the language of Smilesian cliché. Her legacy was a Tory party much stronger on the rhetoric of union than on its comprehension—a party much less concerned than its precursors to prioritize the effective maintenance of the union, and much more overtly ideological on issues of political economy. Again, this combination of assimilationist sympathies and neo-liberal economics proved relatively unpopular with the Scots electorate (despite eloquent Scottish advocacy in the shape of—for example—Michael Gove and Fraser Nelson) (cf. Torrance 2009).

Only the attempted reinvention of the Scottish party under Ruth Davidson (born in 1978, and leader between 2011 and 2019) offered (temporary) hopes for a recovery. And it was scarcely surprising that the essence of Davidson's vision for a resurrected unionism involved going 'back to the future'—looking ahead on the basis of the kind of patriotic one-nation convictions which would have been instantly recognized and endorsed by distinguished early 20th-century Scots Baldwinians like Walter Elliot.

At the same time it is hard to escape the conviction that one of the central problems of union has been, and remains, unionism itself. Edwardian unionists like Carson and Bonar Law were willing to overturn the institutions of the union in order to sustain its defence. And the paradoxes are no less striking now, in the early 21st century, than hitherto. Conservative unionists have often believed in a small British state but a big British union; and over Brexit they eloquently deployed arguments for escaping from one (European) union alongside arguments for sticking with another (British) union. But occasionally between 2016 and 2020 it appeared that some disliked the EU more fervently than they loved the unions of the UK (Keating 2021).

Other institutional supports of the Scottish union have faltered or may yet falter. The monarchy has dutifully maintained its summer anchorage in Balmoral, its high profile in Scotland generally, and its embrace of tartanry in particular; but the future is uncertain, given recurrent scandal, the death of Queen Elizabeth II, and also given the effective embrace of monarchy by the Scottish National Party in the form of the reactivation of notions of a renewed 'union of the crowns' in the event of independence. The army has been similarly embraced by successive SNP governments, who have identified themselves strongly with the Scottish regiments; but, equally, defence cuts, the blurring of some historic Scottish regimental identities within the overarching Royal Regiment of Scotland, and a succession of unpopular wars (Iraq, Afghanistan) have weakened the impact of the army as a force for union.

There remains the issue of religion (see also section 4.6). One key distinction between the Irish and Scottish unions was the initial (and lasting) alienation of much of Irish Catholicism from the union where (on the other hand) the state had endeavoured to reach a settlement with the Kirk, the Presbyterian church in Scotland. In Ireland, as has been shown, the state worked in cooperation with the then dominant 'Protestant ascendancy' interest, though with the latter's increasingly weak and embattled condition, official attention eventually shifted towards the Catholic hierarchy. In Scotland the state has for long been closely associated with the Kirk, whose annually elected moderators serve as a kind of transient equivalent of the archbishops of Canterbury in England—in terms of embodying the relationship between spiritual and secular powers.

But the increasing secularization of Scotland in the last quarter of the 20th century has had an impact upon the effective command of the Kirk, and therefore indirectly of unionism. Moreover, while secularization has affected all of the churches, Catholicism's retreat has been relatively slower than that of Presbyterianism—and indeed, the Catholic Church (especially with immigration from eastern Europe until Brexit) has strengthened its position slightly at the beginning of the 21st century (2001–11), holding its own in term of overall 'market share', while the Kirk's number of professed adherents has fallen by 10 per cent, from 42 to 32 per cent of the population (a fall almost exactly balanced by the growth in the numbers claiming 'no religion'). The rapid growth of the Scottish National Party under (in particular) Alex Salmond has been linked to its promotion of a more inclusive and civic nationalist faith, as well as to a vision of nationality which refers respectfully to the achievements of Irish nationalism and of the Irish revolution: Scotland's Catholics, substantially of Irish descent, once locked within the embrace of Labour and thus of a soft unionism, have now been eloquently and successfully courted by successive SNP leaders (Jackson 2016)

In short, the Scottish union has survived longer than its Irish counterpart because (whatever its obvious limitations) it was the more consensual and equal relationship of the two and because it was generally seen as a voluntary partnership rather than an imperial conquest. Moreover, the institutions and networks which upheld the union in Scotland functioned more effectively than their Irish counterparts—not least because those institutions and networks generally had a more representative basis. Religion was certainly one of the factors bolstering the union and Britishness; and it is a striking irony that, while the demise of the Irish union has commonly been ascribed to an excess of religious zeal, the retreat of its Scottish counterpart may well now be linked to its absence.

2.2. Wales (1535–1922)

Why did Wales continue to embrace union in the late 19th and early 20th centuries, while the majority of the Irish pursued, and attained, independence? Why did Cymru Fydd, the Young Wales movement (1886–96), succumb ultimately to the allure of empire, while the Young Scots and their allies helped to push home rule for Scotland through the critical initial stages of its parliamentary journey in 1914, before the Great War intervened? How can we explain both the longevity and the tenacity of the Welsh union?

It should be said immediately that these are not, at root, new questions (see e.g. Morgan 1981, pp. 121–2). But in the past they have generally been approached through the interrogation of Welsh nationalism and its contours, rather than looking directly at the less prominent (but no less important) relationship between Wales, the union state, and unionism (Brooks 2017). Of course there have been some important exceptions here (see e.g. Johnnes 2011). But on the whole the Welsh union and its associated unionisms remain (even more than has usually been the case) starkly underwritten phenomena.

Nor have these questions generally been approached through the kind of sustained comparative methodology which is deployed throughout this book. Detailed comparisons between the Welsh experience of union and unionism, and those of the Scots and Irish, are rare (though, it is true, not wholly unknown) (see e.g. Davies 1992; Ward 2005; O'Leary 2016; Evans and Pryce 2017). More generally, however, as in Ireland, so in Wales and Scotland, the emphasis has—quite reasonably, given the success of the Irish revolution and the growth of the SNP—been upon the evolution of nationalism. Indeed, the comparison of Welsh, Scottish, and Irish nationalism has occasionally been broached, either explicitly or implicitly, though not always in a sustained manner, by a range of scholars spanning from Sir Reginald Coupland in the 1950s through K. O. Morgan and Christopher Harvie to the compelling contemporary Marxian perspectives of Simon Brooks (Coupland 1954; Morgan 1980; Harvie 2008; Brooks 2017).

Setting aside the issue of union for a moment, the wider comparative dimension to Welsh social and political history has already produced some important and suggestive conclusions. This is especially marked in terms of the work of distinguished Welsh historians of central Europe such as R. J. W. Evans or Robin Okey, but also in the occasional, stimulating evocation of Habsburg analogies in the great surveys of Welsh history written by K. O. Morgan or in the scholarly polemic of Brooks (Evans 1998, 2006, 2010; Okey 2010, 2015; Morgan 1981, pp. 91–2; Brooks 2017). But much of this work on *Mitteleuropa* has naturally started from the perspective of the component nationalities, and particularly their associated linguistic identities, rather than from that of the Habsburg state and those 'centripetal' forces holding it together (to invoke once again the language of Oszkár Jászi) (Jászi 1929).

However, recent political and intellectual emphases—the debates on Brexit and union, the effort to revive 'four nations' history through a late modern initiative and inflection—have each underlined the importance and resonance of understanding the traction and longevity of the several unions of the United Kingdom (see e.g. Lloyd Jones and Scull 2018). And a wide range of new work on the unions and unionism now permits a revisiting of the key issue of Wales's location within the complex politics of the longevity and survival of the United Kingdom.

The central question of survival also has to be interrogated in at least one other sense. For, in seeking to understand why Wales has remained in the union, there is a normative presumption about the political trajectory of clearly defined nations and their national territories. Viewed from the perspectives of Irish independence, and of the growth of the Scottish National Party, and of the constitutional uncertainty generated by Brexit, this again is an entirely reasonable presumption; but it is a presumption nevertheless. Yet, as recent work on Austria-Hungary eloquently underlines, it is important not to regard the supranational or the non-national as inherently 'abnormal'—at any rate in the context of the late 19th century (Judson 2016). It is equally important, in terms of the Habsburg exemplar, not to presume an automatic equation between strong linguistic and cultural identities and a desire for political independence. As a range of scholarship has long recognized, the centralized nation state was not the sole, or even the predominant feature of 19th-century European political geography; it was instead empire which was dominant, and indeed its close relative, the multinational union state. In a sense, then, one initial, but fundamental, answer to why the Welsh union survived is to be found in the fact that long-lasting and complex union states (whatever their defects or difficulties) have been a much more common part of the European and global landscape than narratives associated with the self-interest of burgeoning nation states would otherwise suggest.

Wales and union is of course a huge and complex issue. In what follows, therefore, and as in the previous section, several subsidiary themes are highlighted: union and Britishness; labour, land, and class; religious faith; monarchy, army, and empire; and finally unionism (see also Chapter 4). The central purpose of the section is to introduce these themes in comparative perspective with a view to establishing their influence (if any) over Wales's place within the unions of the United Kingdom.

As a starting point, it is indeed worth re-emphasizing that the United Kingdom has been historically less a union state than a state of unions; and that any comparative approach to Wales and the union has to recognize immediately that Wales was bound to a different form of 'union' than Ireland and Scotland (see e.g. Mitchell 2010b, pp. 98–116; Keating 2021). As has been said, there was (and is) a taxonomy of union, ranging in intensity and type from federal union or personal union through to incorporating union—and Wales, Ireland, and Scotland sat (and still sit, in terms of the different devolution settlements) in separate places upon this span. In short, applying John Elliott's distinction between accessory unions and unions *aeque principali*, Wales adhered to union partly because its union with England, and its experience of union, were distinctively 'accessory' (Elliott 1992). The Welsh union was, as William Rees of the (then) University College Cardiff bluntly wrote in 1938, 'an annexation' (Rees 1938, p. 52).

Indeed the popular idea of a Welsh union, or 'acts of union' (in reference to the assimilating legislation of 1535 and 1542) was largely invented in the late 19th and early 20th centuries, and in the light not only of its Scots and (especially) Irish counterparts but also of the values of contemporary liberalism (Rees 1938, p. 29; Davies 1993, p. 232). The great Welsh educationalist, Sir Owen Morgan Edwards (1858-1920), who combined liberalism, unionism, nonconformity, and an intense devotion to Wales and its language, was in fact among the first to deploy the notion of a Welsh 'act of union'—writing in 1901 (Edwards 1901). Equally, William Llewellyn Williams (1867-1922), radical, patriotic—a veteran of Cymru Fydd—nonconformist and unionist, defined the legislation of 1535 and 1542 as both union and 'the grant of a free constitution' (Williams 1909, p. 110). For Williams, this 'union' transformed Wales (as it would do Scotland)—but not because of the fear of punishment and oppression; rather because 'the grant of free institutions [through "union"] had removed the causes which had led to the growth of evils' (Williams 1909, p. 112). Union was about these free institutions, greater opportunities, and greater legal equality for the Welsh—but it was certainly not about assimilation; and indeed Williams, in his concluding peroration, argued that the achievement of union had survived 'in spite of the dangers which the influx of strangers [ie English migrant workers] has wrought in the social condition of the industrial districts of south Wales' (Williams 1909, p. 117). The Welsh union, in short, had provided not only an exemplar for future generations but also (in fact) the very foundations of empire itself: union was no less than 'a precedent and inspiration, and on the principles upon which Henry VIII proceeded in his pacification of Wales has been based the mighty fabric of the British empire' (Williams 1909, p. 117). This outlook was complemented by an enthusiastically patriotic view, articulated by Thomas Edward Ellis (1859-99) and many others, which attributed Magna Carta, the establishment of an English parliamentary tradition, and the 'blessings' of Tudor government (both the dynasty and its key servants, the Cecils, were of course Welsh) to the principality and its citizens (see e.g. Ellis and Ellis 1912, pp. 103-5; Nicholson and Williams [1919], pp. 233-5).

The further stretches of 'blue water' between the experience of Wales, and that of both Ireland and Scotland, are obvious, do not require much rehearsal, yet help (as a starting point) to illuminate Wales's historic commitment to union. Unlike Scotland, Wales was decisively conquered. It did not have a national parliament or national structures of governance such as existed in pre-union Scotland and Ireland; and there was at first little institutional (as distinct from cultural) counterweight to those many cross-border structures which 'continued to bind Wales into greater English frameworks of organisation' (Bowen 2011, p. 10; Morgan 1981, p. 92). By contrast, and as has been shown, Scottish unionists were fond of emphasizing not only that historic military resistance to English dominance made possible Scots distinctiveness—but that it also facilitated, paradoxically, an effective because equal and dignified union partnership (Jackson 2013, p. 257).

Wales accepted the Protestant Reformation—there were early Welsh translations of the Book of Common Prayer (1567), the New Testament (1567), and of the whole Bible (1588): like England, it was predominantly Anglican (until the flight to nonconformity of the 19th century). In contrast, Ireland (where Protestants were slower to undertake the critical work of translation) remained largely devoted to Roman Catholicism, while Scotland embraced a different, and more radical, religious Reformation. Where both Ireland and Scotland were long used to separate legislative and administrative treatment, Wales had to wait until the 1880s for the first specifically Welsh legislation since the Commonwealth, achieved (like Irish disestablishment) on the back of vigorous denominational mobilization—the Sunday Closing (Wales) Act (1881) and the Wales Intermediate Education Act (1889) (see e.g. Ellis and Ellis 1912, pp. 205–24). As a remarkable comment on the tenacity of the unitary state, it had to wait until 1964–5 for the creation of a distinctive Welsh Office (the Scottish Office had been created back in 1885 and the Irish Office in 1801).

However, this is not to overlook the shared aspects of Welsh, Irish, and Scots history (Jackson 2013). All three were subject to Norman and English military conquest, though (as noted) with varying degrees of completeness: each experienced English or English-sponsored migration and settlement, though none encountered the successive waves of formal expropriation, colonization, and plantation which were applied to Ireland during the reigns of Elizabeth I and James VI and I. In each there were areas, usually characterized by English (or, in the Irish case, English and Scots) settlement or influence, which were distinct from the rest of the country: the north-east of Ireland, the 'Pale' around Dublin, and (for example) the 'little England', the *Anglia Transwalliana*, of Pembroke in Wales. In each there were areas (south Wales, central Scotland, the north of England) characterized by subsequent economic or other forms of migration, especially from Ireland (see e.g. O'Leary 2000). The 'Celtic' highlands of Scotland were long differentiated from the 'Germanic' lowlands, while south ('industrial') and north ('agricultural') Wales have also long been treated separately (and sometimes in too absolute a manner) (Kidd 1993). In both Wales and Ireland recent work has sought to revisit and reinvigorate the notion of 'internal colonialism', the economic and other inequalities separating a metropolitan core and its (in this case, Celtic) periphery, a notion originally applied to the 'British isles' by the sociologist Michael Hechter in the 1970s (as noted above) (O'Leary 2019; Brooks 2017; see also Hechter 1975 and Kumar 2003, pp. xi, 85). Indeed, the concept has been taken a step further, in distinguishing between an anglophone 'centre' within Wales itself, and economically and culturally disadvantaged areas such as the Llŷn peninsula in the north-west of the country (Brooks 2017).

However, Wales was generally well integrated into the industrial economy of the English midlands and beyond, deploying English capital and addressing English and imperial markets, whether in terms of goods or people. As in Scotland in the 18th century, so in Wales a combination of external (English) capital and local natural resource led to the development of substantial ore mining and smelting businesses as well as to the excavation of coal and (in north Wales) slate. As in Scotland, heavy industry was regionally concentrated in Wales (largely, though by no means exclusively in the south); but unlike Ireland, where the Protestant north-east was the island's industrial heartland, this differentiation did not coincide with substantial ethnic, religious, or cultural fractures. Unlike Scotland, Wales lacked both a long-distance merchant fleet and (before the development of Swansea in the late 18th century) a major port: each of these deficits reinforced dependence on English resource (Bowen 2011, p. 10). On the whole, however, the economic experience of Wales (and Scotland) within the context of union was growth, and on the whole socio-economic unrest in Wales was not associated with ethnic or nationalist grievance (one well-known exception being the Mold riots of 1869, which arose out of nationally inflected tensions between Welsh miners and their English management). But in Ireland the economic history of the 19th century was dominated by the Great Famine, which very rapidly acquired an ethnic and national dimension as a cataclysmic example of the failure of the union, and of the evident malevolence of British rule.

Each union—Scottish, Welsh, Irish—was distinctive, but there were also shared symmetries and asymmetries. The Scots union was (as has been shown) delivered by negotiation between the representatives of two parliaments: the Irish union was delivered by the negotiation between the British parliament and the Anglican ascendancy interest; the Welsh union was, as has been observed, 'an annexation' (Rees 1938, p. 52). However there was some similarity in the context to each union. Each was launched in the context of domestic unrest. Each was launched, too, against the backdrop of real or potential existential threats to the English or British state in the form of external enemies. In Wales there was, in the mid-1530s, the possibility of revolt in the wake of the execution of Rhys ap Gruffydd in 1531 as there was also the possibility of continental invasion—just as domestic unrest and continental warfare were critical backdrops to the unions of 1707 and 1801. In 1535, and in 1707, and (to some extent) in 1801, the 'need for a unified system of defence...had become urgent' (Rees 1938, p. 51). None of the unions could, given the inescapably gritty realpolitik of their origins, be convincingly presented as great visionary enterprises (though the effort was sometimes earnestly made by later unionist historians in Wales and the other nations).

Each—Scotland, Wales, and Ireland—remained in the shadow of the dominant nationality, England. As with the Irish and the Scots, and as in other contemporary European multinational polities, so there were clear metropolitan prejudices against these minority partners. These prejudices were expressed in cartoons, satire, and other forms: they often took the form of demeaning ethnic characterization against 'Taffy', 'Jock', and 'Paddy'. Nancy Wingfield has pointed out that 'since the Enlightenment there has been a western European discourse on a lesser-developed, lesser-civilised eastern Europe' (Wingfield 2003, p. 1). It might also be remembered, however, that, since the Enlightenment—and indeed before the Enlightenment—there has been a western European discourse on a 'lesser-developed', 'lesser-civilised' north-west European seaboard. Stereotyped metropolitan images of the Celtic 'Other', whether in an Irish or Scots or Welsh formulation, have chimed with similarly pejorative Austrian or Hungarian images of outgroups within the wider Habsburg lands.

On the face of it, at any rate, the particular parallels between Irish nationalism and the Welsh experience in the 19th century were also close. Each was a riven society, with religious, cultural, and political divisions increasingly separating the landed interest from farmers and labourers. In the second half of the 19th century it has been said that Wales and Welshness came to signify 'celebrating a distinct heritage of opposition to the dominance of England and the Anglican church': in particular 'Welsh meant Welsh-speaking nonconformist and Liberal' (Cragoe 2004, p. 276). In similar ways after the Great Famine Ireland and Irishness came increasingly to signify celebrating a distinct heritage of opposition to the dominance of England and the Anglican Church: and by 1900, for some influential nationalist ideologues within the Irish Ireland movement, being Irish meant being a *gaeilgeoir*, and being both Catholic and Gaelic. In Wales and in Ireland protests against harsh, evicting landlords, and campaigns for disestablishment and (ultimately) home rule communicated with each other, and gathered momentum in the last quarter of the 19th century, though defenders of Welsh landlordism like J. E. Vincent were simultaneously anxious to stress the differences separating Welsh and Irish conditions (Vincent 1897, pp. 54ff.; cf. Howell 2013, p. 83). Welsh patriots certainly found particular inspiration in those Irish nationalists with identifiable Welsh heritage of whom perhaps the most important was Thomas Davis, whose thought exercised an influence over T. E. Ellis ('while his [Davis's] life's work was given to Ireland, yet he loved and understood Wales far better than did most of her political leaders in the 19th century...[and] his ideas have affected in no small measure the Welsh National Movement of our time') (J. Arthur Price (1861–1942) in Morgan 1908, pp. 353–72).

Yet, despite these congruities between the two nations, Ireland graduated after 1914 from home rule to revolutionary nationalism and independence, while

Wales (though influenced by Irish nationalism, and flirting with notions of self-government through Cymru Fydd and other agencies in the 1880s and early and mid-1890s and again in 1910–14) continued largely within the embrace of union, empire, and Britishness. It is the central purpose of this section of the book to revisit these continuities within Welsh experience, and to seek explanations in the context of a sustained comparative approach—primarily within the United Kingdom but also, given the reach of the book, more widely. The contention is that the different trajectories of Wales (and Ireland andScotland) in relation to the union may best be illuminated, not simply by narratives rooted in national distinctiveness, or in patriotic teleologies, but rather by understanding the ways in which the supranational cultures and institutions of the union state played out in each of its component polities.

The relationship with Britain and Britishness must be at the centre of any interrogation of Wales, the notion of the Welsh people (the *Gwerin*), and the union (Ward 2005, p. 73). A minor counterpoint to the recent national narratives in modern Welsh history emphasizes the importance of Britishness within both Wales and Welshness: Gwyn Alf Williams has suggested provocatively that 'what is immediately clear, from even a cursory survey of our broken-backed history, is that the tiny Welsh people...have survived by being British. Welsh identity has constantly renewed itself by anchoring itself in variant forms of Britishness' (Williams, 1982, p. 194). In this argument, an otherwise vulnerable Welshness has navigated the significant challenges of the English-dominated union state by adapting within an overarching if flexible British identity. This of course is a very similar narrative to that detailing the construction of mainstream Scottishness in the 19th century, with the 'safe' reconciliation of potentially combustible Stuart and Jacobite histories alongside the romantic literary narratives of Sir Walter Scott (1771–1832) and the 'Balmorality' of Queen Victoria. The monarchy and other 'British' institutions and agencies all played significant roles, as will be explored elsewhere in this chapter section. Equally, many Irish republicans were continuingly frustrated by the British imperial dimension to the parliamentary nationalism and identity of a John Redmond (though recent research on the evolving home rule movement of the late 1870s has also stressed its anti-imperial credentials) (e.g. Townend 2016). Britishness is habitually interpreted in the language of national identity, but it may also helpfully be compared with the overarching dynastic loyalties of other multinational union states or empires such as *die Habsburgtreue* binding Austria-Hungary (see Judson 2016; Judson 2017).

Strikingly, indeed, many of the Welsh patriots of 1880s, in Cymru Fydd and elsewhere, complemented (or indeed upturned) some of these notions by instead emphasizing the contribution of Wales—and 'the Celt' more generally—to Britain and Britishness (see e.g. Ellis and Ellis 1912, pp. 85–105). T. E. Ellis argued, in an address given in Manchester in January 1889, and working with the racialized language of the period, that Britishness was neither coequal with Anglo-Saxon, nor was it the antonym of Welshness; it was rather an amalgam of each of these. Indeed, in Ellis's analysis, the distinctiveness of the British—the characteristics which separated them from (for example) Germany—were the result of the critical admixture of the Celtic nations to the Germanic chemistry supplied by the Saxons, Jutes, and Angles:

> is it not this very Celticism which gives to Britain that special power and genius that distinctive gift which distinguishes Britain from Germany, and which gives it the pre-eminence? Is it not this which makes the religion of Britain more emotional, devout and ardent than that of Germany, which makes British oratory more passionate and effective than German, which makes Britain's language more strenuous, limpid and rapid than that of Germany, and which has helped to make Britain's contribution to the abiding wealth of the world weightier than that of Germany? (Ellis and Ellis 1912, pp. 92–3)

For Ellis the Welsh and wider Celtic contribution to British ethnicity, culture, institutions, and laws was central: here again, he emphasized the Welshness of the Tudors as well as (ultimately) of Oliver Cromwell, and thus the Welsh contribution to Britishness ('so much for Welsh Celtic infusion in the nature of the makers of Britain in the sixteenth and seventeenth centuries') (Ellis and Ellis 1912, p. 105). The demand for self-government, articulated by Welsh patriots like Ellis—and later by the likes of 'the earnest plodding' E. T. John and his lieutenant, Gwilym Griffith—was not rooted in the perceived antagonism between Welshness and Britishness: Welshness was rather a critical element of Britishness, and any distinction lay instead with the Anglo-Saxon tradition (Morgan 1981, p. 178). The demand for land reform and ultimately home rule in Wales was about the realization of this Britishness—'the awakening of Britain', rather than its suffocation (Ellis and Ellis 1912, p. 108; see also e.g. Morgan 1981, pp. 33–4).

Welshness and Scottishness were therefore, broadly, reconcilable with both Britishness and at least a reformed union, where Irishness ultimately was not: or at any rate the reconciliation was much more vitiated (Ward 2005, p. 73). Welsh Calvinist Methodism and the Calvinism of the Scots Kirk were of course utterly different from the Church of England, but there was still a shared basis of Protestantism, or rather anti-Catholicism, upon which to build a cohesive British identity. There is a basic point of chronology here. The Britishness identified and dissected by Linda Colley, and focusing on war, king, and empire, and the Catholic 'Other', was constructed in the 18th century well before the acts of union between Ireland and Britain of 1800—but after the Scottish union of 1707, and of course long after the laws in Wales acts of 1535 and 1542 (Colley 1992). It also had a Protestant religious foundation and focus which served to unite England, Scotland, and Wales, but which of course was always likely to pose difficulties for Catholic Ireland. Much learned effort (particularly within recent nationalist historiography) has been expended in seeking to distinguish colonial from national from religious identities and to assign them a proper agency and place in the history of the Atlantic archipelago; but in reality religion was often scarcely distinguishable from both Britishness as well as the identities which defined themselves in relation to Britishness. Equally, the supposedly binding identity of the United Kingdom, Britishness, was not fit for purpose; because, while it successfully accommodated Wales and Scotland, it did not do so for Ireland.

A full understanding of the wider relationship between Welshness and the British union state in the 19th and 20th century requires detailed exegesis; and only a start may be made here and in the rest of this section. But one central issue is that Welsh historians have tended to see national institutions in terms of nationalism rather than within the mediating context of Britishness and the British state: there is perhaps a distinction here between some mainstream approaches of Welsh historians and those of the Scots and Irish (Johnnes 2011, pp. 605–6). With Scotland it is generally argued that the many Scottish national institutions which survived union in 1707, together with those associated with Scottish civil society in the 19th century, all served as escape valves for the expression of a 'safe' Scottish patriotism—a 'unionist nationalism', in fact—within the clear parameters of the union state (Morton 1999). With Ireland, the distinctive national institutions and arrangements which survived union in 1801 did not fulfil this function as 'escape valves', because they were generally controlled by the ascendancy interest; and thus the only means of expressing a popular Catholic national identity were outside the confines of the state (Jackson 2013, p. 113; Hutchinson 1987).

With Wales the situation appears to have been different still—but closer to the Scots experience than the Irish. The assimilation of Wales into union with England meant that the kinds of national institution which distinguished Scotland or Ireland did not, on the whole exist for Wales: the Courts of Great Session are, as is well known, one partial exception to this, in so far as they helped to provide Wales with a separate legal identity between 1542 and 1830—while another was the Council of Wales, created in 1472, but given statutory recognition through 'union' in 1542, and surviving until 1689. Otherwise, in the 19th century, it was Welsh nonconformity and the Welsh language which were critical badges of identity, and each of these, like their Scottish cultural counterparts, proved to be entirely compatible with an overarching Britishness—this despite the notorious 'bluebook' criticisms of Welsh and of nonconformist education proferred by the official commission of enquiry into education in Wales pursued in 1846-7 (much discussed but see e.g. Coupland 1954, pp. 185–95; Morgan 1981, pp. 22–3). The gradual creation, from the late 19th century onwards, of a swathe of grand national institutions—the University of Wales (1893), the National Museum of Wales in Cardiff (1905–7), the National Library of Wales in Aberystwyth (1907), together with democratized Welsh local government (1889), the Central Welsh

(Education) Board (1896), the Welsh Department of the Board of Education (1907)—sent mixed messages; since these were simultaneously props of a Welsh national infrastructure, while also (as in Scotland) signalling the extent to which the consolidation of a Welsh national identity was bound in with the British state (Morgan 1981, pp. 110–12). Certainly one of the key advocates of each of these enterprises was David Lloyd George, who had securely anchored Welshness, indeed Welsh nonconformist radicalism, at the very heart of the British establishment (Harrison 1996, p. 112).

Some further comparative comment is necessary in terms of the consolidation of national consciousness in Wales and Ireland across the 19th century. Welsh historians speak of the formation of the *Gwerin* at this time—the bonding of the Welsh people, both the working and in particular the middle classes, and their identification with nonconformity and the Welsh language. In a similar sense a view of the Irish 'people' was propagated in the 19th century, united by Catholicism, as well as a Gaelic (if not specifically Irish-speaking) identity and a strong historical consciousness. It has often been suggested that the *Gwerin* disintegrated in the economic and social turmoil of the inter-war years, though recent work has relocated the timing of this fall, pushing it back to the class tensions and industrial unrest in the coalfields of the Rhondda in and after 1910 (Ellis 1996, p. 294).

What is the significance of these formations and their disintegration? The *Gwerin* of Wales, allied with political radicalism, had patriotic potential, but was ultimately associated more completely with nonconformist denominational rather than nationalist aspirations. It was partly captured by the popular imperialism of the 1890s and afterwards, and partly weakened by the upward mobility of aspects of middle-class nonconformist society. The investiture of Edward, Prince of Wales, at Caernarfon in 1911, which took place in the context of the south Wales miners' strike and the Tonypandy riots, has been depicted as an occasion showcasing the critical alignment of bourgeois Welsh nonconformity with the British royal and Anglican establishment (Ellis 1996, 1998, 2008; though cf. Morgan 1981, p. 124). The striking miners, who were partly ranged against the Cambrian Combine and its chairman, D. A. Thomas (1856–1918) (Welsh, Liberal, and originally a Baptist), looked to the wider British labour movement for organizational support (the South Wales Miners' Federation was the largest and 'ideologically the most aggressive' section within the Miners' Federation of Great Britain); and they subsequently advocated, and participated in, the national miners' strike of March–April 1912 (Davies 1993, p. 491; Rhondda 1921; Morgan 1918; Morgan 1981, p. 78). Equally, the Welsh railwaymen were significant participants in the national rail strike of July–August 1911, whose most bloody episode was the Llanelli riot of 19 August. However, nonconformist sensibility constituted a brake upon the most radical or violent activity, which (in any event) was largely defined within a wider British labour context (Edwards 2011).

By contrast, in Ireland, there was no decisive parallel movement—no realignment of the Irish Catholic middle classes alongside the ascendancy interest—the Anglican aristocratic and landed classes (although Charles Stewart Parnell perhaps envisioned such an epiphany—and the great agrarian leader, William O'Brien, certainly sought a reconciliation through his successive 'conference plus business' initiatives) (Bew 1980; Jackson 2004). Nor was there (or could there be) any public event like the investiture to effect such a reconciliation. Upwardly mobile middle-class Irish Catholics did not embrace Anglicanism at this time, and while they did sometimes accept honours, this was not a given. This is not to say, however, that Irish nationalism was either wholly united or markedly radical before 1914. Though the Irish were profoundly divided over Parnell and his legacy in the 1890s, a similar disintegration to that ascribed to Wales only really occurred in the aftermath of Irish independence, and with the civil war fought over the Anglo-Irish Treaty in 1922–3. Irish nationalism under the leadership of Redmond *could* potentially have followed Welsh nonconformist radical patriotism in some respects—in so far as Redmond had (like some Welsh radicals) a vision of nationality in an imperial and monarchical context, and also in so far as nationalism under his command was a relatively conservative enterprise. But at the end of the day, when the *Gwerin* split, the disputants looked naturally to British allies for support; where in Ireland, when Irish nationalism fragmented—as it did after 1891, or (with the Dublin lockout) in 1913—the disputants pursued their antagonisms largely without British aid, and within a set of Irish organizational frameworks.

Thus, for example, the industrial unrest in Dublin of 1913, which pitted Irish-organized unions, led by the Irish Transport and General Workers' Union (ITGWU), against Irish-organized employers, may be said to have led—through James Connolly and the Irish Citizens' Army—to revolution and independence. The strikers received financial aid from their British comrades, but no sympathetic British strike action was sanctioned by the TUC, and a variety of social and religious fears prevented the strikers accepting some British social and welfare support. By way of contrast, the industrial unrest of 1910–12 in Wales in a sense looked forward, not to separatist insurgency, but rather to Labourite unionism. In short, Welshness, Britishness, and union have been compatible in ways in which Irishness, Britishness, and union have not. A more detailed and comparative examination of the themes of class, labour, and Welshness offers further insight into why this should have been so.

Other cognate debates focus on the (supposed) ties of working-class solidarity and the bonds of union (see also section 4.10). This is linked, in turn, to work on the stability of modern Britain—on the absence of sustained radical protest in 18th-century Scotland and 20th-century Britain (see Jackson 2013, p. 25). Numerous Scots historians have examined the relative tranquillity of Scotland during the economic and political convulsions of the 18th and 19th centuries, emphasizing the evidence for limited disturbance (with the significant exceptions of the two Jacobite uprisings), the strengths of the *ancien régime*, and the great capacity of Scots Presbyterianism to simultaneously stimulate, express, and (yet) contain social resentments (see e.g. Devine 1990). British historians such as Brian Harrison have written on the centripetal tendencies within British politics, while others (Crossick, Gray), working from the theorization of labour aristocracy, have looked to divisions and gradations as well as mediating influences within the working classes in order to understand the relative tranquillity of the Victorian state (Harrison 1982, pp. 309-77; Gray 1976; Crossick 1978). Ross McKibbin has elaborated the case for understanding why there was no significant rejectionist political tradition in late 19th- and early 20th-century Britain (McKibbin 1990, pp. 24-5).

Working-class political organization within the union state is of course a subset of this wider argument. And, broadly—and as in so much else of this narrative—it is possible to identify a gradation of state assimilation, with the Welsh labour movement at one end of the spectrum and the Irish at the other end, and the Scots in the middle. Welsh historians frequently argue that the radical nonconformity of late 19th-century Wales, which ultimately fed into the labour movement, was circumscribed by its religious preoccupations and sensibilities, and was also (or rather consequently) susceptible to the popular imperialism of the 1890s and after. Moreover, Wales was comparatively well assimilated within the wider British labour movement, whether in terms of leadership or union and party organization (Ward 2005, p. 123; Ward 2011; Morgan 1981, pp. 297-8). There was, famously, an importation of Scots representation into Welsh labour, with Keir Hardie and Ramsay Macdonald each sitting for Welsh constituencies (Keir Hardie was MP for Merthyr between 1900 and 1915; Ramsay MacDonald was MP for Aberavon between 1922 and 1929). Equally, there was an export of Welsh talent to the Labour party's national leadership (Aneurin Bevan, James Callaghan, James Griffiths, Roy Jenkins, Neil Kinnock)—just as the Liberal party in Wales, but not in Ireland, had offered access to the top rank of the union state's political elite for an earlier generation (Morgan 1981, p. 344). A distinct Welsh regional council of the Labour party emerged only in 1947, followed by the Welsh Trades Union Congress—a subsidiary of the mainstream TUC—in 1974. On the other hand, the Scots TUC was formed in 1897 and, though a wholly separate body, has worked closely with its metropolitan counterpart. There were several efforts to launch a Scottish Labour party—the eponymous SLP in 1888, the Scottish Workers' Representation Committee (1899-1909)—but these were also eventually subsumed within the British Labour party, which from 1915 onwards offered Scotland merely a regional council (Jackson 2013, pp. 268-80).

Labour in Scotland and Wales was (some flirtation with home rule notwithstanding) essentially unionist (see e.g. Davies 1993, p. 543; Morgan 1981, pp. 297-8; Ward 2005; Ward 2011). Qualification is, admittedly, necessary. In the early 20th century there was certainly a perceived gap between the socialist and patriotic leanings of the south Wales mining community: two broadly sympathetic (if sometimes condescending) commentators, Ivor Nicholson and Lloyd Williams, still thought, however, that the 'Silurian' colliers had responded well to the call for enlistment in 1914–15, despite the countervailing 'socialistic and syndicalistic spirits' in their midst (Nicholson and Williams [1919], pp. 73–4). More generally, the Welsh labour movement struggled against a liberalism which was closely identified with a patriotic nonconformity, and it needed to counter accusations that it was an alien (maybe even an irreligious) import, and thus 'somehow foreign to Welsh culture' (Tanner et al. 2000, p. 243). It has accordingly been argued that, in embracing 'socialism in Welsh dress', Edwardian labour activists like the north Wales schoolmaster, David Thomas (1880–1967), were seeking both to advance Welsh national feeling, and also to establish the patriotic credentials of the labour movement in its contest with Liberalism. In this respect it was significant that the only Welsh-language defence of socialism ever published—by Thomas in 1910—did not directly address Welsh issues, but was instead 'a Welsh-language version of propaganda available and current in English' (Tanner et al. 2000, p. 244). Equally, debates on home rule in 1918 and after forefronted a range of qualifying issues which were also relevant within Scottish labour—namely the extent to which devolution, however attractive in principle, might serve to divide and divert Labour's support base. With the dramatic retreat in the inter-war years of both the Welsh and Scottish industrial economies, the labour movement in each polity had other preoccupations beyond the national question; and in terms of Wales, the latter tended to be expressed within the comparatively modest terms of a demand for a Welsh secretaryship of state—to belatedly complement its Scottish equivalent, which dated to 1926 (and, as a distinct ministerial role, back to 1885) (Morgan 1981, p. 298).

But Ireland was different—and the differences are instructive. From early on, the Irish had both a separate TUC (1894) and a separate Labour party, founded in 1912 by James Connolly, James Larkin, and William O'Brien. Here the mainstream labour movement in the Edwardian era was in competition, not (as in Wales) with patriotic and often imperialist nonconformists, but rather with a fully fledged nationalist movement which, by the eve of the First World War, was looking set to achieve its long-term ambition of home rule for all or most of the island of Ireland. As in Wales and Scotland, there were certainly debates about the extent to which the interests of the working classes would best be served either by national organization—or by organizing within a United Kingdom context, and seeking influence and ultimately control over the political institutions of the United Kingdom state. In Ireland the critical distinction was that these debates swiftly acquired a regional and sectarian inflection, with northern Protestant workers, represented by William Walker (1874–1918), arguing for mobilization within a UK context, and the rest of the island, led by Connolly and Larkin, looking to national and anti-imperial mobilization. Walker, who was a founder of the Independent Labour party in 1893, and a friend of Keir Hardie, stood for parliament in both Ireland and Scotland; and in actions and conviction was a recognizably British and unionist labour activist, in common with many Scots and Welsh contemporaries. But, familiar enough within British contexts, Walker was a minority phenomenon in Edwardian Ireland (see Mecham 2019).

Welsh labour grew from much the same foundations as Welsh liberalism, drawing on a nonconformist and radical set of heritages. But while 'socialism in Welsh dress' for both pragmatic and principled reasons at least broached the possibility of administrative or political devolution for Wales, it had ultimately inherited a set of British and imperial sympathies which sat comfortably within the politics of the union. This situation chimed with Scotland—but not with Ireland. Welsh (and Scottish) labour soon won a place on the government benches of the House of Commons overseeing union and empire; Irish labour, on the other hand, took up arms in 1916 and again in 1919 in order to subvert union and empire.

As with Scotland, so Wales was linked in terms of class bonds with England and Britain more generally (see also sections 4.3, 4.10). The Welsh landed aristocracy, at least in terms of its upper reaches, was part of a wider British territorial elite, with pan-British families like the Irish Londonderrys (Vane-Tempest-Stewart) or the Scots Butes (Crichton-Stewart) possessing Welsh estates: the Londonderrys owned Plas Machynlleth, Montgomeryshire (Powys), and 10,100 acres, while the Butes owned vast estates in south Wales, centred on Cardiff, and amounting to 21,600 acres (see e.g. Morgan 1981, p. 9; Londonderry 1938, p. 94). The Wyndham-Quin family, earls of Dunraven, were prominent in Irish and British politics, and owned substantial estates in Limerick and Glamorgan (23,750 acres in the latter): members of the family represented both Limerick and later Glamorgan in the House of Commons until 1906, with the fourth earl (1841–1926) being both a prominent Irish unionist as well as a member of Glamorgan county council for three years (Dunraven 1922, vol. 1, p. 30n.). The Earls Cawdor owned huge estates in Carmarthen and Pembroke (51,500 acres) as well as in Inverness, and successive members of the family sat in the Commons for south Wales constituencies (as well as holding office associated with their Scots properties) (see e.g. Davies 2020). As with the Irish landed elite in and after the era of land purchase, so many of the Welsh aristocracy withdrew from the principality in the early years of the 20th century—though in the Irish case land purchase legislation after 1885 ensured that the departure would be relatively more complete as well as permanent (Cragoe 1996, p. 254).

Below these major 'pan-British' landed aristocrats were middling landowners—those Welsh gentry who had been the particular objects of Tudor strategizing in 1535 and 1542. Thomas Cromwell, in launching 'union' in 1535, was intent upon bestowing responsibility for the administration of Wales upon its gentry; and since the administration of Wales was emphatically to be conducted in the English language, the corollary was a native, but now increasingly anglophone, class (Davies 1993, p. 235; Rees 1938, p. 79). A further consequence of Cromwell's legal architecture was the closer bonding of the landowning classes of Wales with both the monarchy and the wider English state.

But, in illuminating the bonds of union, the distinctions between Welsh landed society and its Irish and Scots counterparts are no less striking than the similarities (Howell 2013, p. 83). In at least two respects the Welsh landed aristocracy were different from their counterparts elsewhere in the United Kingdom. First, though their title to their property was certainly questioned (and in particular in the last quarter of the 19th century, with the definition and growth of a patriotic and nonconformist radicalism), and though there were some episodes characterized by great bitterness (such as the political evictions which followed the 1868 elections in Wales), still withal there was no indelible historical or indeed moral taint to compare with that afflicting the Irish landed classes: these last were, in the popular Irish nationalist reading, the alien beneficiaries of comparatively recent conquest and expropriation, and their (at times) selfish and even callous behaviour during the Great Famine had been a recent and telling reminder of their origins (Morgan 1981, pp. 81–2). In Scotland, while the gulf separating landlord and tenant was less profound, there remained comparable types of original sin in their relationship—in terms (for example) of the clearances afflicting both the Scottish highlands and lowlands in the late 18th through to the mid-19th centuries (see e.g. Devine 2018). Second, the Welsh aristocracy—until the popular Welsh embrace of nonconformity in the 19th century—mostly shared the same church and perceived ethnicity as the tenantry and labourers: as K. O. Morgan has said, 'unlike the Irish gentry, Welsh landlords were usually not alien in race. They lived on their home farms and preserved customarily good relations with their tenants' (Morgan 1980, p. 5; Morgan 1981, p. 13; Coupland 1954, pp. 184–5). This was broadly true, too, of Scotland, though the Protestant episcopal tradition was strong among the landlords where the tenantry was disproportionately Presbyterian, except for islands (sometimes literally so, as in Barra and South Uist) of Catholicism. Only in Ireland, however, was the landed class distinguished by generally an (Anglican) faith which was different from the bulk of the farming interest both in the north-east of the island (Presbyterian) and in the south and west (Catholic).

It is true, of course, that there was a 'parting of the ways' between the landed interest and the tenantry in both Wales and Ireland, though the timing and importance of this was different in each of the two polities. In Ireland, in some senses, given the colonial origins of landownership and corresponding religious differences, the 'ways' had been permanently apart. But the mobilization of popular Catholic opinion by Daniel O'Connell in the 1820s and afterwards effectively subverted landlord electoral control for the first time, while the anti-tithe agitations of the 1830s simultaneously directed popular anger against (what was seen as) the landlords' church, the Church of Ireland, while delivering a legislative denouement, the Tithe Rent Charge Act (1838), which transferred the focus of agrarian hostility on this issue from the Church to the landed classes (see also section 2.1). The Famine and agrarian downturn in the second half of the 19th century furthered the alienation which had been advancing in its first decades. Moreover, the circumstances of the union state in Ireland, which were sometimes dire and which often necessitated the application of policies which would not have been deployed elsewhere, meant that the government-funded liquidation of the landed interest was pursued from 1885 onwards, and reached an apogee with the Wyndham and Birrell land acts of 1903 and 1909. This Tory-driven revolution in landed proprietorship was complemented by a tenurial revolution pursued by Gladstone through legislation in 1870 and 1881; and, while this had an influence in Scotland through the Crofters' Holdings Act (1886) and the Crofters' Commission, its parallel impact within the more settled conditions of Wales was limited (see e.g. Cameron 1996).

Wales was indeed different. An older generation of scholar, such as Reginald Coupland, could confidently affirm that 'Wales had no real politics until the 1860s [and] no national politics until the 1880s'—arguments which in a limited sense chime with some interpretations of 19th-century Scotland, and indeed with K. T. Hoppen's emphasis on the local dimensions of Irish politics until the second half of the 19th century (Coupland 1954, p. 214; Hoppen 1984). But new work has shed light on the complex participatory politics of Wales well before the 1870s and 1880s, arguing for a more critical approach to those readings of modern Welsh history which have accepted the assumptions of the (from the 1880s onwards) dominant radical nonconformist tradition in Wales. The emergence of 'a new "national" rhetoric' in Welsh politics as early as the 1850s and 1860s has been highlighted—one which identified Wales and Welshness with nonconformity, Liberalism, and the Welsh language; but these fresh arguments also stress the patriotic (and indeed continuing) contribution of those Anglican and Tory landlords, often committed patrons of the Welsh language and culture, who had hitherto exercised great influence (Cragoe 1998a; Cragoe 2004, p. 276). Not the least of the merits of these insights is that they re-emphasize the contingency and negotiability of national identity—its often 'situational' quality; but they are also complemented by a revisionist view of conservative landlordism which emphasizes its deeply ingrained and lasting influence, and indeed its more benign qualities (in contradistinction to the unlovely images of an evicting and rackrenting and, above all, an Anglican landlordism invoked by nonconformist radicals). Indeed, in the most recent—and coruscating—analysis of the radical nonconformist traditions of late 19th-century Wales—the patriotic credentials of conservative landlordism are similarly upheld (Brooks 2017). Thus what in Irish historiography is seen as exceptional—namely a tradition of benign Anglican

Protestant landed nationalism—has in fact been mainstreamed in recent Welsh historiography.

What all this meant in practice, however, was that in Wales (and indeed in Scotland) the land question did not effectively connect with 'the' national question in the way that was thoroughly achieved in Ireland—and looked at least to be a possibility in parts of late 19th-century Scotland. Land, in fact, did not drive the national question in Wales. Nor did it drive violent agitation, as was clearly the case elsewhere, in both Ireland and parts of highland Scotland (Howell 2013, p. 110).

Turning directly now to issues of faith and belief—Robert Evans has asked, acutely, whether 'in the age of empire, had Welsh national ideas sublimated into religious ones, as their social and political goals were incorporated into the British Liberal and then Labour movements?' And he has also asked 'whether chapel-based religion, for the Welsh of that day, constituted an end in itself, or should be read primarily as a statement of something else' (Evans 2010, pp. 233, 238; see also section 4.6). The 19th century brought a considerable Welsh embrace of Protestant nonconformity, and especially Calvinistic Methodism; though the Established Church remained the single market leader in Wales in 1851 (at least in the admittedly limited sense of provision of church sittings), followed by the Calvinistic Methodists, the Congregationalists, the Baptists, and Wesleyans. This emerging nonconformist dominance may be identified with the consolidation of Irish Catholicism—and with nonconformist ministers playing the same kind of influential social and political role in 19th-century Welsh society as did Catholic priests in Irish society.

Welsh nonconformity, especially Welsh Calvinism, supplied the basis—as with Scots Calvinism—for a limited national or patriotic differentiation from England. The chapels of Wales provided a form of popular structure which, like the parochial organization and hierarchy of the Catholic Church in Ireland, was largely beyond the grasp of the British state (though there were also distinctions, some of which are discussed below). At the same time, however, Welsh nonconformism 'allowed for an alliance between Welsh and English liberals within the larger British system that undermined other forms of identity, especially conservative linguistic Welsh nationalism, that could have been used to articulate Welsh cultural and political distinctiveness' (Haesly 2018, pp. 1215–17).

Indeed, there is a sense in which, both within Scotland and Wales, the judgement of the Orcadian poet, Edwin Muir (1887–1959), writing in his poem, 'Scotland 1941', is more widely true—namely that Calvinism 'made us a nation; [but also] robbed us of a nation' (quoted often—but see e.g. Harvie 2008, p. 129). While Ireland at the end of the union remained very largely Catholic (at just under 74 per cent of the population), and while Catholicism provided a clear basis for a national identity distinct from Britishness, none of these factors was entirely relevant for Scottish and Welsh religion. In both polities Presbyterianism, whether of the Kirk or Free Church or Calvinistic Methodist varieties, was a shared badge of difference; but this was mitigated in various ways—not least in Scotland because, while the Kirk was clearly not the Church of England, it was nonetheless effectively an established church and thus culturally and politically entangled within the British union state. Moreover, in general terms Protestantism and Britishness were co-related; and thus, while Welsh nonconformism and the Kirk might not have been part of the union church, the United Church of England and Ireland (established in 1801), they were emphatically embraced within a broad British identity.

However, there were also additional complications. In both Scotland and Wales the fissiparous nature of the Protestant churches meant that, while they could (and did) provide a basis for Scots or Welsh difference, they were (unlike Irish Catholicism) a relatively ineffective organizational foundation for national mobilization. It is true that both Scots and Welsh Presbyterianism had their key institutions and citadels—Edinburgh and its university, for example, in the case of the Kirk, and Bala and its college in Merioneth (Gwynedd) in the case of Calvinistic Methodism. It is true, too, that a degree of nonconformist unity of purpose was provided by the shared call for Anglican disestablishment, originating with the Church of Ireland, and spreading then to the Church in Wales. On the other hand in Scotland the Great Disruption of 1843, and the break-away of the Free Church from the 'Auld Kirk', precipitated nearly 90 years of internal Presbyterian competition and wrangling; while in Wales, though there were indeed vital shared nonconformist cultures and sensibilities, in reality those who were not members of the Established Church were (in 1851) spread across four other churches—the Calvinistic Methodists (with around 25 per cent of worshippers recorded at the largest service on census day), Congregationalists (23 per cent), Baptists (18 per cent), and Wesleyans (13 per cent). Moreover, different types of nonconformity appealed to different parts of Wales (with the Welsh-speaking rural areas, for example, leaning markedly towards Calvinist Methodism) (Davies 1993, p. 423). A wider point of comparison has been suggested by Robert Evans, who (in making a plea for the international contextualization of the 19th-century Welsh nonconformist experience) has pointed to some parallels not just between the Welsh flight from Anglicanism into a fissiparous nonconformity and the Scots Great Disruption (1843) but also between the Welsh experience and the Dutch Reformed Church *Afscheiding* (or 'split') of 1834 and the later split or *Doleantie* (grieving) of 1886, which was associated with Abraham Kuyper (1837–1920) (Evans 2010, p. 237)). In any event, just as land and national questions might be associated in Wales (as over disestablishment and the associated tithes question in the 1880s and beyond) but were never formally bound (as they were in Ireland), so religion and national identity might be linked but could never be wholly mobilized (as in Ireland). As Coupland crisply commented in 1954, 'the [Welsh] nonconformists were seeking freedom from a predominantly English Church, not from a predominantly English parliament' (Coupland 1954, p. 221; see also e.g. Morgan 1981, pp. 40–1).

Moreover, a tentative final point (in terms of religion) might be proffered. Edwin Muir, as has been seen, accused Scots Calvinism 'with the destruction of the Scottish sense of community and humane belief' (Harvie 2008, p. 129). Welsh Calvinism, and indeed Welsh nonconformity more generally, have faced a related, though slightly different indictment. Here the long-standing suggestion has been that the chapels simultaneously commanded formidable loyalty, while helping to shape a political and electoral agenda which emphasized their own spiritual, sectional, and—sometimes—sectarian preoccupations. In other words, through the influence of the chapel, the evolution of a civic Welsh identity was impeded, while the fight against Anglicanism—and, indeed, the fight to demonstrate a distinctive moral purity to England and beyond—was given pre-eminence in public life. Welsh nonconformity may have sought 'a virtuous nation'—but the emphasis was emphatically on the 'virtuous' rather than the 'national' (cf. Davies 1993, p. 392). In similar vein, Rowan Williams has referred to the 'cultural Puritan national identity' of the Welsh and the associated claim that 'Welsh Dissenters were wholly loyal citizens of Queen Victoria's realm, distinguished only by exceptional piety, honesty, thrift, and sobriety, non-conformists perhaps, and political liberals, but very much a *loyal* opposition' (Williams 2019: my italics).

More generally, it might be said that nonconformism's cultures of economic as well as spiritual individualism militated against a sense of national cohesiveness (Okey 2010, p. 209; Brooks 2017). And, it may be worth hypothesizing that Irish Catholic nationalism was founded upon a relatively strong sense of community, where the evangelical and liberal cultures of Wales and Scotland (which of course did have strong communitarian aspects) in the end emphasized an intensely individual relationship with both God and Mammon at the expense of the national. If this has in fact been the case, then perhaps the secularization of both Scotland and Wales (with, for example, the rapid retreat of the Kirk) has in fact not so much weakened the bolsters of unionism—as removed some of the brakes which have hitherto been applied to nationalism.

The Welsh, like the Scots, but on the whole unlike the Irish, had shared ownership of the British monarchy and its associated institutions (see also section 4.2). Wales was associated with a British loyalism, which was in part linked to the Welsh origins of the Tudor dynasty. Llewellyn Williams, who wrote extensively on Tudor Wales at the beginning of the 20th century, emphasized the Welshness of Henry VII—his use of the red dragon standard at Bosworth and on his royal coat of arms, and his claimed descent from Cadwaladr, the 7th-century king of Gwynedd; and the Welshness of the Tudors provided a theme (and, in a sense, a constraint) for patriots and advocates of home rule like T. E. Ellis (Williams 1909, pp. 70–2; see also Nicholson and Williams [1919], p. 234; Ellis and Ellis 1912, p. 103). William Rees, no unionist partisan, argued that only the monarchy supplied the basis for the consolidation of any Welsh state: there was, he observed, 'little tradition of political unity in the country, and indeed little had survived which could serve as a nucleus for the building up of a united state, except perhaps the English king, himself the greatest holder of land in Wales and a member of a Welsh royal line' (Rees 1938, p. 80; Rees is discussed in Morgan 1981, pp. 102, 248). As has been noted, the circumstances and content of 'union' in 1535 and 1542 bound at least the landed classes to the crown.

In a similar manner, the Scots had a share of the British monarchy, both through the Stuarts, as well as through more recent familial interlinkages, such as the marriage connection between Queen Victoria's daughter, Louisa, and the future ninth duke of Argyll—and of course the marriage of Lady Elizabeth Bowes-Lyon, daughter of the fourteenth earl of Strathmore, to the Duke of York, the future George VI. For the Irish, however, there was no visceral sense of ownership to counterbalance these Welsh and Scottish claims; and indeed those Irish connections which the monarchy actually possessed were uniformly with senior members of the Irish ascendancy interest, such as the dukes of Abercorn. For example, senior Irish unionists have tended to be disproportionately favoured by the highest levels of royal patronage (four of the five dukes of Abercorn have been knights of the Garter, while two of the three viscounts Brookeborough have held the same honour).

On the other hand, it would be wrong to suggest that an uncomplicatedly rosy set of relationships prevailed between the Welsh and Scots and monarchy, and an uncomplicatedly bleak set of relationships between it and the Irish. The royal coat of arms, for example, incorporated heraldic references to Scotland and Ireland, but not (after the demise of the Tudors) to Wales; and the disputes within other European multinational monarchies on perceived heraldic slights—in Sweden-Norway and Austria-Hungary—forcefully illustrate the power of such apparently arcane issues (see e.g. Jackson 2019 and below, section 4.8). It is notable, too, that while there were distinctive Scots and Irish orders of chivalry (the orders of the Thistle and St Patrick respectively), there was no Welsh equivalent (though it is true, of course that the Order of St Patrick was yet another Irish national institution which exclusively served the interests of the ascendancy elite in the years of union).

Moreover, judged purely from the perspective of Victoria's reign, the Welsh came off worse, in terms of royal handling, than even the Irish. Victoria famously embraced Scotland and the Stuarts, while barely doing her duty in Ireland, and scarcely setting foot at all in Wales: the calculation is that, through her long reign, she spent a total of seven years in Scotland, spent very much less than seven weeks in Ireland, and managed seven days only in Wales (adapted from Loughlin 2013, p. 383). The Balmoral estate became, famously, a key locus of the British monarchy, which steadfastly resisted any Irish or Welsh equivalents. Victoria, Supreme Governor of the Church of England, enthusiastically embraced Presbyterianism while in Scotland, and took communion at Crathie Kirk; but she regarded the nonconformity of her Welsh subjects and the Catholicism of the Irish with much less comprehension or sympathy (see also Figures 3.1, 4.1). Her son, Edward VII, generally played well in Ireland (he visited three times, was fond of horseracing, and was rumoured to be sympathetic to home rule); but his otherwise louche reputation had very little appeal for Welsh dissent (Jackson 2013, p. 157).

In terms of the Welsh, however, there was a critical counterweight: the Welsh had ownership of monarchy, not simply through dynastic antiquity, but also through the princes of Wales. The designation of the heir apparent to the monarch as 'prince of Wales' from the time of Edward I ultimately created a direct association between Wales and the crown; and this of course was augmented by the invention of the tradition of investiture at Caernarfon Castle in 1911, and its renewal for Prince Charles, promised in 1958 at the Empire Games at Cardiff, and eventually fulfilled in 1969. As has been observed, the ceremony at Caernarfon in 1911 has been seen as cementing an alliance between middle-class Welsh nonconformity and the British royal establishment. Indeed, as in Scotland, so in Wales, contentious and divisive national histories were reframed in more ecumenical terms by successive monarchs: just as the House of Hanover annexed and detoxified its Stuart heritage, so its successors performed a similar function in Wales, turning (what was) an appropriated historical title into an agency of national unity. Even Prince Edward, later Edward VIII, otherwise known as a playboy, generally did his patriotic duty in Wales, and was effectively marketed there both for the monarchy and union (the first essay in the popular celebratory volume, *Wales: Its Part in the War* (1919), was devoted to an oleaginous consideration of 'The Prince of Wales in the War', while the volume as a whole bore a letter from the Prince as a frontispiece) (Nicholson and Williams [1919], pp. 3–21).

In short, if Scotland and Wales were effectively bound within Britishness, then they were also effectively bound within, and possessed part ownership of, key institutions of Britishness such as the monarchy. This was less true for Ireland. The problem was not simply that the British monarchy was wholly neglectful of Ireland; for this was not the case. In the end the challenge which the British monarchy faced in Ireland (as opposed to Wales and Scotland) reflected less on the performance of individual monarchs (though this was indeed pretty woeful so far as Victoria was concerned) than on the constraints of 'Britishness' itself. As it was, the monarchy was capable of generating some dynastic loyalty; and just as a widespread attachment to the Habsburg monarchy, or *Habsburgtreue*, constituted a key supranational bond within Austria-Hungary, so there was always a similar potential with the House of Saxe-Coburg-Gotha throughout all of the Celtic nations of the Atlantic archipelago (Judson 2016). But only in Wales and Scotland, and with sections of Irish unionism, was this potential realized.

The Welsh, like the Scots and (to a certain extent) the Irish, had part-ownership not just of the monarchy, but also of some of its associated and subsidiary institutions such as the British army (see also section 4.4). Unlike the Irish, however, there were few ambiguities in this possession. As in Ireland and Scotland, the strongly territorial and regional nature of the late Victorian army appealed both to local as well as more general patriotic identities in Wales. Ireland had its Connaught Rangers, its Munster Fusiliers; Scotland had its Argyll and Sutherland Highlanders, its King's Own Scottish Borderers; but Wales had the South Wales Borderers (1689), the Royal Welsh Fusiliers (1689), and the Welsh Regiment (1881), as well as a cluster of units with local roots which simultaneously proclaimed their wider Welshness (the Pembroke Yeomanry (1794) and the Glamorgan Yeomanry (1797), the Welsh Horse Yeomanry (1914)) (see e.g. Nicholson and Williams [1919], pp. 34–5). The extent of the Welshness of Welsh regiments certainly varied markedly; but, unlike in Ireland, where (as has been discussed) there were ongoing tensions between private and public attitudes towards the army, there was little evidence of serious political ambivalence in Wales. The deployment of these regiments in some of the most conspicuous episodes of the 19th-century empire was generally a source of patriotic and imperialist enthuasiasm—as with the South Wales Borderers' heroic but disastrous engagement at Isandlwana and at Rorke's Drift in 1879, during the Anglo-Zulu war. The Welsh Regiment were deployed effectively at the battle of Suakin (1885) during the Anglo-Egyptian war, and again in south Africa at Driefontein (1900) and on the Tujela during the Anglo-Boer war: the actions of the Royal Welsh Fusiliers at Paardeberg in South Africa (1900) were equally acclaimed (Morgan 1980, p. 179). It is true, of course, that there was some sympathy for the Boers in Wales—stronger, it has been observed, than in any other part of the United Kingdom except for Ireland (Davies 1993, p. 478). However, those sympathizers were still a minority of the Welsh, concentrated in nonconformist and Welsh-speaking areas, and motivated at least as much by religious as by any secular preoccupations (Morgan 1980, pp. 178–80; Morgan 1981, p. 30).

Unlike in Ireland, domestic encounters with the army did little to dent this patriotic pride. Since the most significant episodes of Welsh protest in the 19th century were not primarily driven by nationality, then any subsequent military action has not generally been interpreted through a nationalist lens. Thus the Newport rising of 1839, which resulted in the death of 22 Chartist protesters at the hands of the 45th (Nottinghamshire) regiment, has not been seen as an example of 'English' military oppression—and not least because one of the principal casualties amongst the government wounded was Thomas Phillips (1801–67), mayor of Newport, and subsequently knighted, who was a Welsh-speaking patriot (Coupland 1954, pp. 178–9). The Tonypandy riots of November 1910 and those at Llanelli in August 1911 brought bloody confrontations between soldiers (including in fact Munster Fusiliers) and local striking miners and railwaymen respectively, the troops being deployed at the orders of Winston Churchill; and, again, though there were casualties, including deaths, on each occasion, and though

Churchill and local officials and police were bitterly criticized, the episodes have not generally been interpreted as acts of English military oppression (see e.g. Morgan 1981, p. 147). Comparisons between events of this kind and near-contemporary Irish affrays are never likely to be exact, but the clear nationalist freighting of the Mitchelstown Massacre (1887), or the Bachelor's Walk Massacre (1914) strongly suggest the existence of two quite different levels of nationalist consciousness and engagement in Ireland and Wales.

By extension, the outbreak of war in August 1914 had different resonances in Wales (and Scotland), as compared with Ireland. Like Scotland, Wales wholeheartedly embraced the British war effort in 1914, even though—like Ireland—the Welsh initially faced official scepticism and resistance to their claims upon a national army unit (eventually formed as the 38th Welsh Division) (cf. Ward 2005, p. 79). Indeed in this particular respect, and in some others, the Welsh had nearly as much cause to complain at the actions of the union state as the Irish. Where Scotland and Ireland each possessed an elite national regiment of guards (created in 1642 and 1900 respectively), the Welsh Guards were only belatedly formed in 1915. Moreover, conscription was applied in Wales, as in the rest of Britain, but not Ireland, from 1916; so there was at least the opportunity for a patriotic resistance to enforced involvement in England's war. But the opportunity was largely untouched, not least because one of those ultimately responsible for its enforcement was David Lloyd George, Secretary of State for War (July to December 1916) and, from December 1916, Prime Minister. In a sense Lloyd George's ministerial ascent not only signalled Welsh ownership of the war effort; the emphatically Welsh character of his premiership, flanked in office (as he was) by scores of his fellow-countrymen, indicated the extent and effectiveness of the principality's conquest of the inner circles of the United Kingdom itself (Morgan 1981, p. 167). For a time (it might be said) Wales owned the union: this was very occasionally true, too, for Scotland—but it was certainly never the case for Ireland.

In short, the army and warfare presented a set of challenges and opportunities to the Welsh which chimed with those supplied to the Irish: both Welsh disestablishment and Irish home rule had been placed on the statute books in September 1914, and Redmondite nationalists in Ireland and Welsh patriots now each felt the need to demonstrate that Irish Catholics and Welsh nonconformists could support the British empire no less than Protestant unionists and English and Welsh Anglicans (see e.g. Matthews 2017). But, beyond this shared narrow ground, there were several fundamental distinctions. First, though both Irish nationalists and Welsh patriots like John Redmond and Revd John Williams of Brynsiencyn (1854–1921) energetically endorsed recruitment to the British war effort after 1914, the Irish (until 1916) remained deeply conflicted in their approach to England's armies, while the corresponding Welsh divisions were relatively slight (O'Leary 2017, p. 601). Second, Irish divisions (such as those between the Irish and National Volunteers) were precipitated by nationality, while those of the Welsh (where they existed) tended to arise from religious scruples—from the deep pacifist strains within Welsh nonconformity and within the growing socialist cause. Third and finally, the war focused and clarified the problems of union government for the Irish, and in doing so consolidated Irish nationality—both amongst those fighting in the ranks of the British army and with those who stayed behind. In 1914–18, and again in 1939–45, the experience of war certainly underpinned Welsh (and Scots) distinctiveness—but generally within a clear set of British contexts.

Despite the forefronting of anti-imperial traditions, in fact the Welsh, like the Scots, and—in a more limited way—the Irish, bought into empire, and especially in the 1890s. Welsh historians still routinely bemoan the underdeveloped literature on Wales and empire, and many of the long-standing arguments and explanations for this paucity remain in place (discussed in Bowen 2011, pp. 1–13; Ward 2005, pp. 79–80). However, there is now arguably a sufficient body of research to venture some provisional reflections on the comparative interaction of union and empire in Scots, Irish, and Welsh history (see Jackson 2013, pp. 132–6, 211–12; Bowen 2011; Jones and Jones 2003). Unsophisticated ideas of empire producing a homogeneous Britishness out of Welsh, Scots, and Irish engagement have certainly now been superseded; and on the whole it seems clear that the growth of empire in the 18th and 19th centuries, and concomitant Welsh participation, encouraged not simply a one-size-fits-all Britishness, but rather different forms of Welsh distinctiveness within a complex set of British and imperial contexts (Bowen 2011, pp. 11–12).

All three 'Celtic' nations engaged thoroughly with empire in the 19th century— the Scots (perhaps) most completely and unequivocally. In the case of Irish nationalism, while there was a strong tradition of anti-imperialism, evident in the 1870s and beyond, there was also a subdued history of nationalist engagement or accommodation with empire, most obviously with John Redmond—but perceptible also with Parnell (who accepted financial support from Cecil Rhodes), and even with the youthful Wolfe Tone (who flirted with the idea of service in the East India Company, and with the creation of overseas military colonies). If there was a spectrum of imperial engagement, then the Welsh perhaps fell short of the Scots position (for reasons which are explored below), while not buying into the ultimately dominant anti-imperial strains within Irish nationalism (Townend 2016).

As in both Scotland and Ireland, so in Wales the intensity of imperial engagement possessed a regional inflection. The development in the 19th century of an industrial economy in south Wales mirrored that of the north-east of Ireland. Thus, Scotland had its industrial 'central belt', with Glasgow as the 'second city of the empire', while Ulster unionists boasted of Ulster as 'the Imperial Province'— and the Welsh possessed their 'imperial Rhondda' (identified famously by H. J. W. Edwards, with Gwyn Alf Williams subsequently delineating an 'imperial

South Wales'—imperial both in formation and engagement) (Edwards 1938, chapter 12; Williams 1982, pp. 183–4). In each case there developed regional export-driven economies, exponential—migrant-led—demographic growth, and related social, economic, and cultural links within union and empire.

As in both Scotland and Ireland, so empire supplied Wales, too, with not just economic but also spiritual opportunities. For both nonconformist Wales and Catholic Ireland the empire provided a set of evangelizing opportunities within a global mission-field (Evans 2010, p. 235). The shift to evangelical religion in 18th- and 19th-century Wales was intrinsically linked with a widening and deepening sense of an international Christian community and concomitant spiritual opportunities (Bowen 2011, p. 108). It should be said as well that evangelical religion, especially evangelical nonconformity, possessed not only a global empire, but also archipelagic networks: evangelical spirituality provided some shared ground (in terms of experience, practice, and theology) for the many and fissiparous Protestant churches across Britain and Ireland, and to that extent supplied an implicit (and sometimes overt) bolster for union. In these contexts, religious revivalism spanned both the Atlantic Ocean—and also the Irish Sea, binding Welsh and Irish evangelicals both in 1859 and again (to a lesser extent) in 1904–5.

If Cymru Fydd was the fullest expression of late 19th-century Welsh national feeling, then its protagonists—T. E. Ellis, David Lloyd George—ultimately each embraced Britishness *and* empire (Rowland Hughes 2006; see Ellis and Ellis, 1912, pp. 85–118; Morgan 1981, pp. 33–4). It has for long been recognized that Welsh patriotic radicals were disarmed by the growing popular imperialism in the 1890s, not so much because they abjectly surrendered to an assimilationist Britishness, but rather because—as with Redmondite nationalism in Ireland— they saw empire as a vehicle for nationality. Most Welsh people—Lloyd George, famously, was an exception—supported the British struggle in South Africa (1899–1902); but, as in Ireland, there were divisions on the issue. However, a telling overall distinction between the Irish stand and the Welsh was that, while the former emphasized nationality and opposition to empire, the latter emphasized religious principle—and in particular that the empire was engaged in the suppression of good Calvinists in the shape of the Boers (Morgan 1980, p. 180). Recent research into the growth of St David's Day celebrations within Welsh schools after the Boer War has emphasized the extent to which patriotic and imperial themes now became closely interwoven, and especially of course during the struggle of 1914–18 (Grigg 2018, p. 115).

Empire worked for Redmondite nationalists, not because it necessarily imposed Britishness, but rather because it provided openings for the Irish. In the end, empire bound Wales to union because it facilitated the exercise of a distinctive Welshness on a global stage. Empire worked for Wales, not because it imposed Britishness, but rather because it identified, defined and liberated Welshness. Indeed, on the eve of the First World War Welsh patriots like Gwilym Griffith echoed, and elaborated, Redmond's attempt to locate home rule within a wider imperial framework. For Griffith, an associate of E. T. John, the essence of the British empire was the cultivation of liberty through nationality within a global supranational framework: 'to be Welsh is not to be anti-English' (Griffith 1913, p. 32). Griffith argued that on the whole Britain had recognized that 'loyalty is fostered by liberty'; and he developed his theme by suggesting that, since this recognition had been accorded to South Africa and was in the process of being extended to Ireland through self-government in each case, Wales had great claims to be next on the list. Welsh home rule was required, not because the Welsh hated Britain, but rather because the Welsh had contributed so extensively to the empire, and because 'her national ideals are consonant with the highest ideals of British statesmanship'. In this sense, 'the development of Welsh nationality means the enrichment, not the impoverishment, of the collective life of the Imperial Union' (Griffith 1913, pp. 32–3).

Finally, it may seem superfluous or circular to argue that the condition of unionism in Wales has been an important resource for the survival of the union—in so far as it might be thought that a buoyant unionism was not only a precondition for a healthy union, but also symptomatic of that health: 'a union state without unionism can survive a long time. But not perhaps for ever' (McLean and McMillan 2005, p. 256). But the condition and contours of unionism are of central importance in so far as the condition of a constitutional union may be affected not only by the absence of a unionism, but also by the nature of its presence (see e.g. section 6.4; Jackson 2013, pp. 219–333).

There was of course no single unionist party in late 19th-century Wales. Unionism instead was the implicit or default condition of much of Welsh electoral politics (as was the case in Ireland before the creation of the Home Government Association in 1870). As is well known, Welsh radical Liberalism, increasingly influential from the general election of 1868, took on a strongly patriotic inflection; but this had peaked in the mid-1890s, and had then subsided into an undertone because of internal and strategic divisions, as well as the diversion of some of its protagonists—Lloyd George, Ellis—into Westminster and eventually ministerial politics (Ellis, often seen as emblematic of the wider fate of Welsh radicalism, accepted office as deputy chief whip in 1892, and then chief whip and parliamentary secretary to the Treasury in 1894). The impact of leading Welsh Liberals within United Kingdom and imperial politics, especially from the mid-1880s onwards, has been seen as helping to 'ensure that Wales did not go the same violent way as Ireland: [and that] perhaps Welsh home rule was indeed killed by kindness' (Morgan 1981, pp. 56–8). But, in any case, it is hard to escape the impression that earlier Liberal calls for self-government (Ellis, speaking at various locations, including Bala in September 1890, demanded a Welsh legislative assembly) were fundamentally part of a wider conversation on how to make the union work better for Welsh interests—in much the same way that Daniel

O'Connell had originally sought the reform of the union in the interests of Irish Catholics, and with the threat of repeal in the background (see generally Ellis and Ellis, 1912, especially pp. 187–93).

Irish Liberalism, which—until the 1870s—successfully united Irish Catholics together with some northern Presbyterians (and Anglicans) has occasionally been seen by some (perhaps) generous counter-factualists as a great failed opportunity in late 19th-century Irish politics (Walker 1989; see also Thompson 2001). It is certainly the case that Liberalism for a time seemed partly responsive to Irish popular opinion, at least in so far as the disestablishment of the Church of Ireland and land reform were concerned; but ultimately it either could not deliver, or could not speedily deliver, an array of key popular reforms—and, moreover, the party functioned very ineffectively as a conduit for Irish Catholic access to the highest political office (there were admittedly one or two success stories, such as Sir Charles Russell, Lord Russell of Killowen (1832–1900)) (O'Brien 1901). Welsh Liberalism was different: it was different because (unlike its Irish counterpart) it successfully operated as a medium of assimilation or apparent assimilation (Gladstone had, after all, his Flintshire base at Hawarden, and his Welsh in-laws and networks, while numerous Welsh rose in the updraught created by Lloyd George's ministerial ascent). Irish Liberalism ultimately did not effectively represent Irish Catholics: Welsh Liberalism, on the other hand, became synonymous with Welsh dissent. Different Welsh historians have expressed this fundamental point in different ways. Robert Evans has rightly said that 'emergent British liberalism proved able to embody or at least accommodate almost all Welsh political aspirations. That would lead to the electoral breakthrough of 1868 being perceived as a patriotic triumph, as were the later careers of Tom Ellis and Lloyd George' (Evans 2010, p. 232). This insight has been elaborated more radically by Simon Brooks in his stimulating and provocative *Why Wales Never was* (2017), where he has argued that Welsh radicalism's 'guiding philosophy of liberal individualism contained within it the seeds of national destruction' (Brooks 2017, p. 53). Elsewhere Brooks asserts that 'there is no greater error in the study of Welsh political history than to assume that liberalism was of benefit to Wales. Liberal politics, so at tune with the Welsh in theological matters, was less threatening to the British establishment than the conservative ethnolinguistic activism that it had replaced' (Brooks 2017, p. 72). In other words, Welsh Liberalism functioned successfully as an essentially unionist enterprise, because (unlike its Irish counterpart) it effectively responded to the aspirations and ambitions of a mass constituency.

Formal Liberal Unionism—those Liberals who defected from the Gladstonian party over home rule—fared poorly in Wales (see e.g. Morgan 1981, pp. 43–4; Lloyd Jones 2015, pp. 482–507). Equally, their Welsh Conservative allies were on the electoral defensive between 1885 and 1935, weakly organized (at least until 1906), performing especially badly in the counties, and wrong-footed by the reforms of 1884–5: they sustained an average of only about 37.7 per cent of the total votes cast (Aubel 1996, pp. 97, 103–5; Morgan 1981, pp. 28, 45ff.). Here in Wales, as elsewhere, Conservatism was associated explicitly after 1886 with the defence of the union and empire: in Wales, as in Ireland, it failed at this time to articulate a local patriotic case, and was thus often damned as an alien phenomenon—too closely associated with English interests and the 'English', Anglican, Church (see Aubel 1996, pp. 108–10). Indeed, David Melding, perhaps the most deeply reflective and thoughtful of contemporary Welsh Tories, has suggested that 'it is little exaggeration to say that in defending the established church, the Conservative party disestablished itself as an indigenous force in Wales' (Melding 2009, p. 140).

However, several recent discussions of early and mid-19th-century Welsh conservatism have laid stress on its communitarian and patriotic content and its wider potential in these respects—and in fact these features were also echoed within both Scottish and even (quietly and counterintuitively) within aspects of Irish conservatism (Cragoe 1996; Brooks 2017). By way of comparison, Scots Tories frequently invoked patriotic and sometimes Jacobite themes, and even (some) Irish Tories flirted briefly with the possibility of home rule in and after 1870 (there has indeed been a *sotto voce* dialogue between Irish conservatism and Irish self-government from the time of home rule to the present). However, at the end of the day Conservatism in Wales and the rest of the United Kingdom was the party of union and empire, and while it is valuable to be reminded of its undoubted patriotic credentials, there are clear dangers of throwing out some unionist and imperialist babies with the constitutional bath water.

In fact, while in the post-1918 era Scots Conservatives developed strong forms of local patriotic identity and appeal, their Welsh partners conspicuously failed in this respect. It is also the case that (while—perhaps because—Wales had been incorporated much longer within a predominantly English state than had Scotland) Conservative administration in Wales tended to be more anglo-centric and heedless of local sensitivities than was the case in Scotland (Morgan 1981, pp. 379–80). Indeed, it has been said that 'the years of Conservative government between 1979 and 1997 emphasised an intransigent unionism and saw substantial damage to the party's already limited support in Wales'—and while this perhaps embodies an over-simplification, it is surely not an unfair characterization (Ward 2005, p. 124). As in 19th-century Ireland, so in 20th-century Wales, ministerial offices were routinely held by English politicians, and not by local representatives: indeed it was only in 1951 that a minister for Welsh affairs was nominated, and even then the appointees were mostly Englishmen (of the five holders of the office between 1951 and 1964, three were English, one was a Scot, one—Gwilym Lloyd George—was Welsh, and none of the five had Welsh constituencies) (Melding 2009, p. 144). While this record markedly improved with the creation of the Secretaryship of State for Wales in 1964 (of the 18 different ministers, 11 have been Welsh-born), the Thatcher years were characterized by what David Melding has called a 'disregard' for Wales—though it is not altogether clear whether Thatcher's 'disregard' had a more detrimental impact on the union than her professed (if condescending) 'regard' for Scotland and the Scots (Melding 2009, p. 122).

The 'intransigent unionism' of the Conservative rule in the 1990s in fact bears comparison with the apparently 'intransigent unionism' of Balfourian conservatism in Ireland a century earlier (Melding 2009, p. 123). Indeed, much more than the constructive unionists of the 1890s, the Tories of the 1990s showed some sensitivity in their pursuit of cultural policies, which culminated in the Welsh Language Act of 1993 (wherein Welsh and English were effectively made co-equal within the public sector). But, just as constructive unionism in Ireland did not convert the Irish to English Toryism, so a more constructive unionism in Wales could not wholly compensate for the relentless 'anglicisation of Welsh affairs' otherwise conducted by successive Conservative governments until the general election of 1997 (Melding 2009, p. 170).

Further comparisons of Welsh unionism, broadly envisioned, with Scotland and Ireland are, however, instructive. Irish unionism was partly defined by a variety of qualities which have repeatedly proved to be damaging to its stated goals, and which contrast with the condition of Welsh unionism. Irish unionism was ultimately a single party and movement (even though the distinction between Liberal Unionist and Conservative was only finally resolved after 1911). Irish unionism as a popular enterprise was also associated with the north-east of the island; and while there were some, especially urban or suburban, pockets of support elsewhere on the island, these only really functioned under the still restrictive electoral conditions of 1885–1918 (Dublin Rathmines, prosperous and relatively Protestant, was an exception). Irish unionism struggled, by and large fruitlessly, to lay claim to an Irish patriotism.

In all of these areas Welsh unionism was different, and more successful. It pervaded the party system as a given—at least until the creation of Plaid Cymru in 1925: unlike in Ireland, in Wales 'unionism' was always much more than 'Unionism' (cf. Aubel 1996, p. 108). It pervaded all of Wales—though it is true that there were slight regional variations—between north and south, between urban and rural, between regions like Pembroke and the marchlands of the east with other areas of the country. Above all, however, Welsh unionism was seen to be both Welsh and patriotic; and to that extent it served to channel national sentiment within a Britannic framework in ways which ultimately lay beyond the capacity of its Irish counterpart (see Hechter 1975; Davies 1993, p. 544).

Why then, finally, *did* Wales (and Scotland) stay in the union (thus far, at any rate)—and Ireland leave in 1921–2? One answer to this question lies in taxonomy—namely the varying types of union which have constituted the ostensibly unitary state of Great Britain and then of the United Kingdom. Different types of union were associated with different histories and different relationships with England: the Scottish union was the closest to being a coequal partnership, the union *aeque principali* defined by John Elliott and others, the Irish closest to a form of colonial relationship, and the Welsh was a distinctively assimilationist (or 'accessory') union (Elliott 1992). Wales has stayed within 'the' union—partly because its union was different (despite later, 19th-century, efforts to define the legislation of 1535 and 1542 as, in Scots and Irish terms, 'acts of union') (Edwards 1901, 1906; Williams 1909). At the risk of provocation, there is a clear sense in which modern Wales was in part defined by its form of 'union' (see even Rees 1938, pp. 78–80).

Expressing this in another way, while Irish nationalism has provided a model for its Welsh counterpart, Wales has provided a model for the governance of the union as envisioned by successive British governments: cultural in terms of its national expression, socially cohesive, largely integrated in its party politics, and wholly peaceful in its condition. Wales was the first of the unions; and, on the current available evidence, it may well survive to be the last.

Similarly, Wales's relationship with Britishness has, like that of the Scots, been close. The Welsh and the Scots to some extent were partners in the construction of Britishness in the 18th century, in ways which were not applicable to the Irish. Accordingly, the Welsh have had a purchase over some of the central historic institutions of Britishness, including the Protestant monarchy, its army, and empire. Much more than in Ireland, the very limited interest in Welsh home rule before the First World War was defined very firmly in the context of Britishness and empire: home rule could and should be granted, because Welsh loyalty was unquestioned, because home rule would therefore bolster empire—and because (implicitly) the principality deserved it more than the Irish who at the time were apparently well on the way to securing a similar concession (Griffith 1913, pp. 32–3).

Though an effort is sometimes made to define Welsh history in colonial and postcolonial terms, as with Irish history, on the whole the evidence for the Irish case is more convincing (O'Leary 2019). Thus, while Wales had a land question, and while Welsh landlordism by the end of the 19th century was increasingly alienated from the wider rural population, not least through religion, there was no recent history of catastrophic colonial intervention to mirror that of the Irish. The Irish landed classes of the 19th century, whatever their actual origins, were almost uniformly associated with the conquests and expropriations of the Tudor, Stuart, and Commonwealth eras; and they were separated from their tenantry not only through the scale of their wealth, but often through their Anglican Protestantism and sometimes through language. Food shortages and evictions were features of 19th-century rural Wales; but the scale of hunger, eviction, and emigration in Ireland was completely different. The consequence of this was that, while Welsh landlordism was increasingly perceived as distant and oppressive, the dimensions of the parallel Irish antagonism were much greater.

In Wales, as in Scotland, the dominance of class politics was simultaneously the dominance of unionist politics. Class, certainly in the particular sense of labour and its organization, bound both Wales and Scotland into the union and unionism, though the situation in Ireland was (yet again) both different and more complex. On the whole, though there were distinct Welsh labour organizations, these (like their counterparts in Scotland) were generally either subservient to British masters, or ultimately (as with the Scottish Labour party) became so. Welsh and Scottish Labour both advocated home rule for a time, before moving to the view that the working classes could best be protected and advanced through the institutions of a centralized British state. Indeed, this drift, particularly after 1945, created the superficially paradoxical position wherein the Labour party became in essence a defender of union, while the Conservative and Unionist party pragmatically played Welsh and Scottish patriotic cards when electorally appropriate. The able Scots Tory, Walter Elliot, famously remarked that (for the Scots) nationalization spelt denationalization (in the sense that the larger British state shaped under Attlee threatened local Scottish institutions and distinctiveness): the same might have been said of Wales (Jackson 2013, p. 275).

Welsh religion has decisively fed into union, albeit in complex ways. The Welsh were emphatically part of 19th-century Protestant Britishness and (more equivocally, given the Anglican church establishment) of the Protestant British state. But Welsh nonconformity, heavily inflected through Calvinism and evangelicalism, and heavily fissiparous, was associated at the same time with an ostensibly unified nonconformist culture, and an individualistic evangelical spirituality (together with considerable denominational in-fighting). Though nonconformity was in part a symbol of late 19th-century Welshness in the way that Catholicism was of Irishness, the similarities were more apparent than real: Irish Catholicism, whatever its own divisions, was ultimately a relatively more unified religious enterprise than Welsh nonconformity. Thus, Welsh nonconformity was both a symbol of Welshness as well as a symbol of its limitations. In the same way, Scots Presbyterianism was both a symbol of Scots distinctiveness, as well as of the limitations of that distinctiveness (given the schisms within the 19th-century Kirk, and in particular that of 1843).

It should be said that Welsh liberalism has been seen in similar terms—certainly within recent conservative nationalist critiques—as a creed which was simultaneously individualistic as well as assimilationist (Brooks 2017, p. 144). In addition, there is a sense in which late Victorian Welsh liberalism invented the very notion of a Welsh 'act of union' and of the principality's equal partnership within that union. All this of course chimes with the old paradox that liberalism has provided a much more effective force for union than the nominal party of union, Toryism; and indeed there has been a trend in recent scholarship (over the last 20 years) which has emphasized the local patriotic integrity and enthusiasms of Scots, Irish, and Welsh conservatives (Cragoe 1996; Brooks 2017, pp. 49–57;

Jackson 2013). This has been complemented by some imaginative reflection from Welsh conservative intellectuals such as (pre-eminently) David Melding ('I believe that all unionists in Wales should be patriotic Welsh nationalists') (Melding 2007, p. 33; Melding 2009, p. 227).

Possibly, then, Gladstone was indeed the most effective or the most profound unionist of his era (see e.g. Vincent 1977). And certainly Lord Randolph Churchill (1849–95) and F. E. Smith (1872–1930) (and indeed Boris Johnson), while playing their Orange cards in 1886 and 1912 (and in 2019), seem to have had quite different political decks discreetly tucked up their sleeves. So Wales may yet be driven from the union—but perhaps through the force of Conservative revolution, rather than of nationalist insurgency. As Sir Chartres Biron once said of Edward Carson, 'there is no revolutionary like a Tory on the run' (Biron 1936; for an earlier version of this section see Jackson 2022).

Figure 2.1 Architect of union: William Pitt the Younger (1759–1806). Mezzotint (original portrait by John Hoppner, engraved by George Clint (c.1806), National Portrait Gallery, London).

Figure 2.2 Architect of union: Carl XIV Johan of the United Kingdoms of Sweden-Norway (1763–1844). Portrait in oils by François Gérard (1811) (Swedish Royal Collections Department).

UNIONS OF THE UNITED KINGDOM (1535–1922) 89

Figure 2.3 Architect of union: Willem I of the United Kingdom of the Netherlands (1772–1843). Portrait in oils by Charles Howard Hodges (1816) (Amsterdam Museum).

3
European Unions and Beyond
Case Studies

3.1. Introduction

If the United Kingdom of Great Britain and Ireland held together on the basis of several very different types of union, how did other contemporary multinational polities perform the same feat? This chapter takes an array of complex, though ostensibly 'united', kingdoms, each closely linked and intercommunicating in a variety of ways, and presents their histories largely (though not only) from the point of view of their gelling and their longevity. Several, like Britain and Ireland, discussed in the previous chapter, experimented with different forms of governance or constitution: assimilation and centralism, divide and rule, devolution, federalism, or consociationalism. Most, in making these pitches, did so diachronically: one, Austria-Hungary, was able (after 1867, and with its complex new dualist structure) to do so synchronically. All were effectively seeking new ways of living together by constructing new ways of living apart (cf. Beller 2018, p. 127).

The chapter introduces a sequence of case studies in the form of analytical narratives. Each of these case studies follows a broadly similar structure, exploring first the prehistory and contexts of union, then examining its initial construction as well as its bolstering agencies and institutions, before finally broaching the themes of secession and disintegration. Each case study focuses on the comparisons and bonds with the unions of Britain and Ireland, introduced earlier in the work. Though at this stage, in the interests of clarity, each of the studies is presented as a separate section of the chapter, the linkages between them, as well as the interconnecting themes, are identified and introduced. These links and interconnections are then developed more fully and comparatively in the later, thematic, chapters of the book.

3.2. The United Kingdom of the Netherlands (1814/15–30)

The history of the low countries—the modern Dutch state, Belgium, Luxembourg—is (as with the other polities discussed in this chapter) a complex of unifying and fracturing centripetal and centrifugal tensions. Its links with the other case studies are clear: the southern low countries were for long in the hands of first the

Spanish and later the Austrian Habsburgs, while the eventual creation (in 1815) of the United Kingdom of the Netherlands owed a great deal to the geopolitical strategizing of the Irish patriarch of union, Viscount Castlereagh, together with his lieutenants, and deploying too the ideas of William Pitt, his mentor and patron (see above, section 1.5; Figures 1.1, 2.1). Just as the new United Kingdom was forged in a critical set of international contexts, so the shifting of the tectonic plates of European politics in 1830 created some, at least, of the forces for its dismantling (though cf. White 1835, vol. 1, pp. 18, 43, 172). Broken by the Belgian revolution and independence, the United Kingdom of the Netherlands and its fate were invoked by contemporary Irish unionists, and pre-eminently by the Belfast-born politician and traveller, James Emerson Tennent (1804–69), as a warning to the Irish and British of the dire economic consequences of repealing a valuable union (Tennent 1841, pp. vi, x, 174, 234).

As with the other case studies in this chapter, it should be said immediately that there is no desire here to produce an over-engineered or an overly deterministic history of the theme of union in the low countries (such as those eventually favoured by the House of Orange). Nor, for that matter, is there any countervailing desire to produce arguments for the primordial distinctiveness of Belgium and for the 'inevitable' failure of the United Kingdom (such as those favoured by later nationalists). The intention here (as with the other case studies explored) is rather to offer an analysis of the region's centripetal and centrifugal tensions with a view to understanding why it coalesced, and why it ultimately fractured (for some of the historiographical background see Marteel 2018, pp. 2–3).

British and Irish contemporaries, whether supporters of Belgian independence (like the author and former soldier, Charles White (1793–1861)) or supporters of union (like Sir Walter Scott) did, however, often point to the ancient unity of the low countries in broaching the politics of union; and this to some extent reflected the narratives of the new king, Willem (White 1835, vol. 1, p. 28; Anon./Scott 1816, p. 228). The low countries had been broadly interlinked in the late middle ages under the Valois dukes of Burgundy, who provided a buffer between the kingdom of France and the Habsburg domains until the death of duke Charles the Bold at the battle of Nancy in 1477. After 1477 the Burgundian Netherlands were inherited by Charles's Habsburg son-in-law, the future Holy Roman Emperor, Maximilian I (see Marteel 2018, p. 69). Bound for a time both by linguistic ties (the region was mostly Dutch or Flemish-speaking, though with some French in the south and south-east), and by the shared Burgundian and Habsburg legacies, the divisions within the region were reopened during the Eighty Years' War (1566–1648). The relative success of the Protestant Reformation in the region precipitated tensions between religious reformers and the Habsburg monarchy, with the many advocates of peaceful coexistence eventually being crushed between the ferocious policies of Philip II of Spain and his viceroy, Alba, and the parallel zeal of the Calvinist reformers. As a counterweight to the pull of any overly tendentious protonational analysis, it is worth remembering, however, that 'the religious, social and political factors determining the outbreak of the Revolt manifested themselves first in the most advanced provinces of the southern Netherlands' (Kossman 1978, p. 11; Marteel 2018, p. 5).

Geography as much as piety may have helped to determine the outcome of these struggles (see, famously, Pirenne 1899-1932). The divisions within the low countries were dramatically reinforced through the greater success of the Spanish military action in the more accessible south, as evidenced (for example) by their recapture of Antwerp in 1585. The peace of Münster in 1648 left the seven united provinces of the northern Netherlands (which had proved more difficult territory for Spanish arms) as an independent Dutch republic, with the southern provinces of the Netherlands remaining in the hands of Habsburg Spain. These provinces stayed with the Spanish until 1700, when they were transferred to the Habsburgs of Austria. Though the role of religion in the Dutch revolt has often been oversimplified (as it has been in Ireland and other conflicts), the 1648 settlement ultimately helped to deliver a primarily Protestant, Calvinist, north and an emphatically Catholic southern Netherlands. Indeed, these divisions in the low countries were interconnected and intercommunicating with those in the 'British isles': Scots Presbyterians commonly looked to the universities and trading opportunities presented by the Dutch republic, while Irish Catholics looked to the Habsburg south—and primarily to centres of Catholic learning such as Leuven/Louvain, where in 1607 an Irish College (dedicated to St Anthony) was established by the Franciscans.

However, despite these now formal diplomatic and territorial divisions, the subsequent history of the Netherlands was not wholly a matter of separate political, cultural, and religious development. After the battle of Ramillies (1706) Dutch rule was briefly extended over the southern Netherlands; and though these provinces were handed back to the Austrians in 1714, the Barrier Treaty of 1715 allowed the Dutch to maintain a line of fortresses in the south, which they duly did until 1782—and in fact at the expense of the southerners. The revolution in France helped to focus opposition to the reforming Joseph II in the Austrian Netherlands and also to encourage (in a highly volatile and complex political environment) some reappraisal of attitudes towards the north: the formation of the Belgian Patriot Army in 1789, the creation of a short-lived United States of Belgium in January 1790 (with a constitution looking back to the Dutch Union of Utrecht (1579) as well as to the American Articles of Confederation (1776)), produced some interest in union with the north in the early months of 1790—aspirations which were cut off by the Habsburg reconquest of late 1790 (discussed in e.g. White 1835, vol. 1, pp. 15-17). But, after the Habsburg and then the French conquests of the 1790s, ideas of a confederate or otherwise unified low countries were pursued by some émigré Belgians and Dutch Orangists seeking ways of envisioning the liberation of their homelands (Kossman 1978, p. 102). It is important, once again, not to overplay this narrative of the prehistory of union: there is a telling paradox in the fact that many of those 'Belgians' identifying with a common heritage of revolt against the Habsburgs, and thus alongside the north, would re-emerge in 1830 as heroes of the revolt against the United Kingdom of the Netherlands itself (Kossman 1978, p. 62). But, on the whole, the significance of the politics of the 1780s, of the 'Brabant revolution' and of the United States of Belgium, has been given more serious appraisal than hitherto within recent scholarship (see e.g. Marteel 2018, pp. 8–9; Judge 2016).

On the other hand, the narrative of union was not just a matter of some exploratory conversations between northerners and southerners, Dutch and Belgians—it was also (as in the Austrian empire and elsewhere) a question first of the internal unity of each of these separate components, which—until the 1790s, and scarcely even then—were far from being unified polities. The French conquest of the former Austrian Netherlands, culminating at Fleurus in June 1794, led to the formal incorporation of the whole territory, combined with the prince bishopric of Liège and the duchy of Bouillon (separate entities for a millennium), into France by October 1795—and there they remained until the final set of French defeats in 1813–14 (Blom and Lamberts 2006, p. 297). By that time the Austrians did not want to reacquire their former provinces in the southern Netherlands; and, with the neighbouring superpower, Britain, together with its Irish unionist foreign secretary, Viscount Castlereagh, keen to ensure a buffer against any resurgent France, the 'orphaned' provinces were nudged towards unity with the north (see above, section 1.5).

Equally in the north, one legacy of reform, revolution, and French conquest was now a unity that had not hitherto existed. The French invasion of the Dutch republic in 1795 had delivered what has been described as 'a Dutch revolution within French parameters', with a milestone constitution in April 1798 (after a false start in 1797) (Wielenga 2015, p. 136). This, the constitution for the 'Batavian people', created a unitary Dutch state with the people as sovereign; but thereafter the French 'parameters' of the Dutch revolution were more clearly asserted, with the imposition in 1805–6 of Rutger Jan Schimmelpenninck (1761–1825) as (in the event) the last Grand Pensionary of the Republic, and then the formal establishment of a monarchy under Louis Bonaparte (1778–1846) between 1806 and 1810. The united north suffered, albeit briefly, the same fate which had befallen the south—namely full incorporation into France. Nonetheless, the impact of the revolutionary and Napoleonic era was central in terms of the future constitutional shape of the low countries: it has been rightly said that 'the federal [Dutch] republic with its autonomous towns and cities and sovereign provinces had been replaced by a unitary state in which government taxation, legislation, culture and education were centralised...the result of the French period was the foundations on which the new kingdoms would be constructed' (Wielenga 2015, p. 143). These foundations included, of course, acclimatizing the republican Dutch to the institutions of monarchy (Marteel 2018, pp. 18–19).

The contexts for the creation of the new united kingdom of the Netherlands were economic freefall during the years of French occupation, and (as already noted) the triumphant allies' (and especially the British) desire in 1814–15 to create a strong northern buffer to the defeated France. As Charles White, a veteran of the Napoleonic wars, wrote in 1835:

> the reunion of the Netherlands of Charles V into one kingdom was a measure strictly and essentially European. A barrier was required: and that barrier could only be obtained by giving such strength and extent to the Netherlands as would convert them into a *tête-de-pont*, sufficiently powerful to resist the first shocks of French ambition. (White 1835, vol. 1, p. 29)

Or, as Castlereagh defined the matter, it was vital that the House of Orange 'be looked up to in Europe as the effectual guardian of its liberties in one of its most international frontiers' (Londonderry 1848–53, 3rd ser., vol. 2, p. 51: Castlereagh to Clancarty, 30 May 1814).

These geopolitical considerations of course chimed with the personal and dynastic goals of Willem Frederik, the ambitious Prince of Orange, who, already in late 1813, was noisily and tactlessly trying to drum up support in the southern Netherlands for his prospective rule. Lord Clancarty grumbled that 'his ambition seems to get the better of his judgement in this respect' (Londonderry 1848–53, 3rd ser., vol. 1, pp. 100, 255, 300: Clancarty to Castlereagh, 14 Dec. 1813, 11 Feb. 1814, 1 Mar. 1814). On 3 March 1814 Willem Frederik was proclaimed as King Willem I, accepting authority over the south later that year: he was finally declared ruler of the united kingdom of the Netherlands on 16 March 1815 (see Figure 2.3). The new united kingdom's military forces played a small but symbolically resonant part in the final defeat of Napoleon in June at Waterloo, where the new crown prince (later Willem II) was wounded ('it may almost be said fortunately', as Walter Scott commented); and indeed Waterloo was subsequently important in shaping the wider celebration of the union enterprise (Anon./Scott 1816, p. 235). It encouraged some otherwise ambivalent Belgians to give the new union state the benefit of the doubt; and it also provided it with a form of foundation narrative, which (as Joep Leerssen has observed) 'was assiduously exploited by the Orange-Nassau dynasty' (in Dunthorne and Wintle 2013, p. 117; Kennedy 2017, p. 287). But this narrative also signalled some pretensions to a much greater antiquity than Waterloo: the new union state was occasionally cast as the legatee of the medieval Burgundian realm, while the French defeat at the hands of the Dutch (amongst others) at Waterloo was linked to their defeat at the hands of the Flemish at Courtrai/Kortrijk in 1302 (Dunthorne and Wintle 2013, p. 119; Marteel 2018, pp. 22, 25; section 1.5).

From the start the new United Kingdom faced considerable (but certainly not overwhelming) obstacles. The general principle of union was not markedly unpopular in so far as it served as a blank canvas upon which numerous different, including southern Catholic, visions and aspirations were projected (Marteel 2018, p. 28). However, it was virtually unique in the history of unions in so far as a numerically dominant polity, Belgium, with 3.34 million inhabitants, was given as 'an extension of territory' to a much smaller (2.05 million) but politically dominant neighbour, the northern Netherlands (White 1835, vol. 1, pp. 34–6). Despite this asymmetry, the new union's constitution (1815) made provision for a bicameral States General, with (controversially) equal numbers of representatives from north and south in the lower, elective, chamber (this 'equality', in the light of the overwhelming demographic pre-eminence of one of the two components of the new united kingdom, looked forward to a similar sleight with the United Canadas in 1840; for a contemporary British critique see Londonderry 1848–53, 3rd ser., vol. 3, p. 165: James to Castlereagh, 10 Feb. 1816).

As with the other union settlements considered here, so the activation of the newly united Netherlands was beset with animosity and opposition. Like the francophone Catholics of Lower Canada and the union of 1840, the southerners resented the assigning of seats within the States General (what Stefaan Marteel has called the *vitium originis*), as well as the method of combining the national debts (that is to say, they resented both equality of representation, given the numerical preponderance of the south, and the linking of the very heavily burdened north with the less indebted south) (Marteel 2018, pp. 42–3). Many devoutly Catholic southerners thought that the principles of religious equality enunciated by Willem and the new union constitution in 1815 were an endorsement of error and heresy; and indeed the English poet and traveller, Robert Southey, was astonished to encounter a popular rumour at Waterloo that the new union with the Calvinist north would shortly be followed by the proscription of the Catholic mass ('the people here asked us if it were true that there was to be no more mass': Southey 1902, pp. 99, 115). The forced passage of the constitution—the suspect calculations according to what was termed the *arithmétique hollandaise*—created consternation (Marteel 2018, p. 61). All of this is highly evocative of the difficult and controversial passage of union in Dublin in 1799–1800 and in Edinburgh in 1706: in common with other union states, the new United Kingdom of the Netherlands (despite Waterloo, Courtrai/Kortrijk, and Burgundy) ultimately lacked a morally compelling birth narrative—except, perhaps, at the rarified heights of continental geopolitics.

The union state, which lasted between 1814 and 1830 focused significantly on the monarch, Willem I, who had a vision for the new kingdom based in part upon the centralizing initiatives pursued by the preceding Batavian and French regimes. Moreover, he had the capacity to realize this vision, and not least because the complex finances of the new state were partly designed to give him very considerable authority. On the face of it, epic levels of debt after the wars meant both that the official finances were racked, and that Willem's room for manoeuvre was limited; but he looked to sidestep these problems through what was in effect a set of institutional wheezes and dodges (Wintle 2000, pp. 138–9). There was the Amortisatie Syndicaat/Amortization Syndicate (1822), a sinking fund, whose functions were taken over in 1830 by the Nederlandsche Handel-Maatschappij (NHM)/Netherlands Trading Company (1824)—enterprises which each in essence permitted Willem to raise new loans, to intervene in the economy, and in particular to spend huge amounts on infrastructure and subsidies largely free from any regular form of accountability or responsibility (the NHM was treated 'as an instrument of royal policy rather than as a commercial enterprise': Wright 2013, pp. 201–2; White 1835, vol. 1, p. 59).

However, Willem certainly did have an overall 'policy', and (though no ideologue) there was also a perceptible Williamite 'economic system' (Wright 2013, pp. x, 214–21). In particular he sought to integrate the three key components of his new domain—the Dutch provinces, distinguished by their international staples market, the relatively industrialized Belgian provinces, together with the Dutch colonies, restored to the Netherlands by the British at the end of the war (Wright 2013, p. ix). In Willem's grand scheme of things the industrial south would be complemented by the mercantile north, with southern goods being exported through northern ports, and with Java and the other colonies economically integrated and playing their part in boosting the kingdom's prosperity (not least through the infamous 'culture' or 'cultivation' system of taxation) (Wintle 2000, p. 217).

Towards these ends he pursued both a unified tariff (laid down in 1816 and revisited in 1821–2), which was originally designed to support Belgian manufacturing in the embattled post-war years, as well as a consolidated and unifying transport infrastructure (Wright 2013, pp. 94–111, 112–45). Willem was thus the 'Canal King', keen to forge his united kingdom through new waterways such as that giving the major Flemish city of Ghent access to the North Sea, by connecting it with Terneuzen, 32 kilometres away on the Scheldt estuary (1823–7). Similarly Willem was keen to see the development of roads and steam power, both of which were already serving as powerful binding agents in other contemporary union states (Kennedy 2017, p. 290). There are indeed some parallels here with the infrastructural improvements (canals, roads, steam power in terms of ships and rail) which helped so much to realize the unions of the United Kingdom of Great Britain and Ireland (Jackson 2013).

Union had cultural dimensions. There was a new (Dutch-language) national anthem, 'Wien Neerlands Bloed', unveiled in 1816 (and with French lyrics added—eventually, in 1824) (Hemstad 2019, p. 90). More generally, the Dutch language was supported, the overall official aim being to install it as the 'exclusive public language' of the Flemish provinces, while encouraging its adoption in Wallonia: Dutch was now the first language of the reformed primary school system in the Flemish provinces (though not of the secondary), while after 1819 it was designated as the exclusive language of the courts and local administration (Marteel 2018, p. 70). The great Dutch historian, Pieter Geyl (1887–1966), was keen to emphasize (in the face of more reductionist narratives) that Willem was seeking to 'undo' the gallicizing measures of the French, but that he had *not* uniformly 'imposed' Dutch; and indeed the most recent (not otherwise friendly) interpretations stress the gradualist and incremental approaches adopted by Willem, as well as relatively high levels of public acceptance (Geyl 1964, pp. 194–7; see Marteel 2018, pp. 70ff., 72 n. 3). The language issue arose not so much from what Willem planned, or even enacted, as from his autocratic and arbitrary methods of proceeding. Still, it has been rightly said that 'the grievances over language not only became integrated in a broader discourse of opposition, they were in fact the first issue in which this discourse became recognisable' (Marteel 2018, p. 71).

Willem's unifying, controlling, and centralizing impulses applied elsewhere in his realm, and certainly to the churches. The churches and religious faith were, for Willem, potential instruments of state-building; and his ultimate ideal seems to have been a unified state church, going beyond even the model of parliamentary and church union represented by the United Kingdom of Great Britain and Ireland and its associated United (Anglican) Church (Marteel 2018, pp. 176ff; section 4.6). But there were the revolutionary legacies with which to contend—and principally (so far as the north was concerned) the dethroning of the Dutch Reformed faith in 1798 from its privileged standing. The new constitution of August 1815 made no allowance for any restored state church—nor could it, given that the majority of the new United Kingdom of the Netherlands was now Catholic, while their king was a Calvinist. Instead, Willem sought to control the churches through two central Departments of Worship (created in September 1814) (Wintle 1987, pp. 12–13). On the whole this seemed to work for Dutch Protestants (though in fact it may have fed into some of their later schisms); but for Dutch Catholics the formal equality of the churches, constraints on religious orders and on the return of monasteries, and interference both in religious curricula in schools and indeed in the formation of the priesthood itself—all were extremely difficult pills to swallow from a state where Calvinism may not have been legally pre-eminent, but was certainly otherwise so (White 1835, vol. 1, pp. 66, 70).

The problems with all of this were therefore clear, and were in some ways replicated in the other polities considered in this book. Willem, as lynch-pin of the union, lacked the personal responsiveness and flexibility required to fully deliver on his ideals. He was paternalistic, but also authoritarian: much of the apparatus of the Napoleonic policing regime was left in place, including informants, spies, and press censorship, and indeed he favoured a range of other Napoleonic legacies, including in terms of personnel (see e.g. Kennedy 2017, p. 289). He was often able to strategize for union—especially in terms of the economic Big Picture and its associated institutions; but he had numerous blind spots. There was no effective or meaningful union government, for example—at least in the sense that Willem favoured Dutch ministers, preferred to deal with them individually rather than in council, and rejected the notion of ministerial responsibility (even as late as his infamous Royal Declaration of December 1829) (Wright 2013, pp. 94–5; Marteel 2018, pp. 255ff.). At the end, even an overseas—Irish—supporter of the united Netherlands and its promoters, James Emerson Tennent, thought that Willem was often 'manifestly wrong' (Tennent 1841, pp. 233, 242; White 1835, vol. 1, p. 83).

He believed in union; but it was not altogether clear who else did. There was no overwhelming evidence of unionist feeling in 1815, at the creation of the new United Kingdom, in either of its two component polities: the southern Netherlands were of course generally unenthused, but so too, in fact, was the north. Some effort was made to create unitary institutions; but in the end it might be said that the United Kingdom failed not simply because of southern alienation, but because of northern indifference. Northerners' anger at the eventual Belgian insurgency of 1830, their dented pride at southern 'ingratitude', should not be mistaken for deep-seated unionist conviction. And indeed in other union polities, while there has generally been a focus on 'subordinate' powers and their nationalisms, it has frequently been the politics of the dominant partners which have ultimately loosened bonds and eventually delivered disintegration.

Aspects of the fiscal system were deeply contested, as they were in Ireland. The southern provinces believed themselves to be, and in fact were, 'over-taxed' from the beginning of the union (see e.g. White 1835, vol. 1, p. 56). Calculations vary a little, but it is generally thought that about 45 per cent of the taxation of the new realm was raised in the south, as against a spend of only around 20 per cent of the total.

A range of cultural issues, especially those relating to language and faith, proved to be even more incendiary. The suspected imposition of language and related schooling policies were resented in the south, as indeed were similar British practices and policies in nineteenth-century Ireland (White 1835, vol. 1, p. 45). The Counter-Reformation cultures of the south, which had generated opposition even to a reforming and centralizing Habsburg in the shape of Joseph II, were not likely to cut much slack to an interfering and centralizing Calvinist in the form of Willem I (Kossman 1978, p. 54). Catholic opposition lingered from the beginning, and was articulated by the Bishop of Ghent, Maurice-Jean de Broglie (1766–1821), and his allies, who demanded that the Catholic character of the south be fully guaranteed, and who rejected any notion of the legal equality of the different churches (Wintle 1987, p. 16).

By 1828 Catholic and liberal opposition to the Dutch-dominated union was beginning to coalesce within a petition movement; and even northerners were now growing impatient of the state's opaque and antique budgetary arrangements, as became clear during debate on the decennial budget plan in 1829 (for reflections on this Catholic-liberal alliance see Marteel 2018, pp. 149ff.). The overthrow of the restored Bourbon monarchy in France in July 1830 provided an overspill both of revolutionary ardour as well as economic dislocation into its northern neighbour: the continental settlement which had helped to deliver the United Kingdom of the Netherlands in 1814–15 was also now changing dramatically. By the late summer of 1830 resistance to the union government was beginning to grow in the south, and this was given focus in October, when the southern, Belgian, insurgents, established their provisional government (Marteel 2018, pp. 266ff.). The London conference of December 1830 recognized Belgian independence, which was crystallized through the constitution promulgated in early 1831. As with the other unions which are considered here, the frontiers of the new successor state, the kingdom of Belgium, included groups—such as the merchant and manufacturing communities of Antwerp and Ghent—which generally had done well out of the old regime (Tennent 1841, vol. 1, pp. 172–3). But, as was the often the case with unionism or related dynastic loyalties elsewhere, so the Orangist sympathies of these communities was seen by contemporaries as a matter of advantage rather than passion or conviction; and with the realignment of interests after 1830, so they melted away (White 1835, vol. 2, p. 99; see also Wright 2013, p. 223).

Was, then, the new united kingdom in fact fatally burdened from the beginning? As with the other unions under consideration, it is important to be aware of the lure of presentism—and of teleologies of irresistible failure. Charles White, a well-informed contemporary, and writing in the immediate aftermath of 1830, was certainly downbeat, but even he (as a thoughtful Belgian sympathizer) repeatedly conceded that there were circumstances in which union might well have worked. Indeed, one of the central motifs of White's work on 'the Belgic revolution' is the ongoing reformability of union, until even very late in the day. For White 'in 1829 there was [still] ample time' to recover the union, while until August 1830 'there were not 20 persons in the capital [Brussels] who dreamed of the possibility of ever affecting even an administrative separation between the two countries': in the end 'absolute separation' only came about because of the Dutch military failures of September 1830 and after (White 1835, vol. 1, pp. 34, 83, 172, 211; Marteel 2018, pp. 269ff.). In terms of more recent comment, Friso Wielenga, chiming with cognate work on both Britain and Austria-Hungary, has also warned against overly reductionist arguments: portraying a foredoomed union is, in this argument 'too hasty because in the mid-1820s integration of the north and south had progressed to such an extent that stable national unity did not appear unthinkable' (Wielenga 2015, p. 151; see section 3.1). Catholic opinion, so influential ultimately in the overthrow of the union, was in fact *not* wholly irreconcilable; and there were mediating influences among the clergy and bishops, including the archbishop of Mechelen, François Antoine de Méan (1756–1831), and the priests of north Brabant, who were keen to maintain the religious freedoms inaugurated under the Batavian republic (cf. Blom and Lamberts 2006, p. 307).

Despite earlier opposition, it seemed by the early 1820s that the Catholic Church within the new united kingdom had broadly accepted the principles of religious freedom enunciated by Willem. But it is certainly true that religious issues remained highly sensitive in this doctrinally divided polity, and Willem's effort to regulate the training for the priesthood (evocative of Joseph II's controversial reforms of the 1780s), through the closure of colleges and seminaries and by the creation in 1825 of the Collegium Philosophicum at Leuven/Louvain, brought consternation to southern Catholics (Marteel 2018, pp. 171-2).

Equally, however, simple taxonomies of failure do not do justice to complex economic data. With the United Kingdom of the Netherlands, there is no evidence of comprehensive and calculated economic discrimination against the south; and in fact several of the key economic institutions of the new state played much better within the south than the north. Examples of this would be the Netherlands Trading Company, which was well-liked in Belgium, but less so in the north, or the Société Générale, established in Brussels in 1822, and envisioned by Willem (who deployed his own capital and gave personal guarantees) as a state bank (Wright 2013, pp. 138, 220). Moreover, the kingdom's unified tariff structure of 1816 was launched specifically to deal with the troubled condition of Belgian industry. The revised tariff of 1821-2 certainly moved a little towards recognizing northern complaints, but in general (despite some small-scale sores) 'there were now few major fiscal issues which could be presented as a direct conflict of interest between Holland and Belgium, and few economic grievances about which Belgian opinion was sufficiently united for an appeal to national feeling to be possible' (Wright 2013, p. 209).

Nor was the new union overwhelmed by the nationalisms of its component parts. Dutch and Belgian national sentiments were certainly nascent, but they were by no means substantial forces until very late in the 1820s and beyond (see Marteel 2018, esp. pp. 275, 301ff.). Each grew in the course of the 19th century, Dutch nationalism drawing upon a range of linguistic, historical, and imperial analogies, while the Belgians freely traced their nationhood back to the 'Belgae' and 'Gallia Belgica' of the iron age and Roman eras. Ultimately a robust Belgian nationalist historiography emerged, represented most thoroughly in the scholarship of the great Henri Pirenne (1862-1935), whose monumental *Histoire de Belgique*, published in seven volumes between 1899 and 1932, set out this 'primordialist', unified and unifying, vision of Belgian history and civilization (see also e.g. Pirenne 1915). But these were largely late 19th-century phenomena.

In the end, however, there was collapse. Union polities are often held together in part by a handful of key institutions such as the monarchy, and indeed by the skills, real or imagined, of key individual rulers (as with Franz Joseph in Austria-Hungary). The failings of the critical central actor of the United Kingdom of the Netherlands, Willem I, were clear. He was not a persuader: he helped to build some of the institutions of a united kingdom, but not a unified spirit (White 1835, vol. 1, p. 83). And, as Michael Wintle has commented, 'neither state nor empire is likely to be imposed permanently if there is no successful campaign of persuasion that the imposed values are acceptable and bear some relationship to reality' (Wintle 2000, p. 281). This diagnosis is strikingly similar to that offered by Oszkár Jászi in anatomizing the ultimate failure of the Dual Monarchy (see section 3.5; Jászi 1929).

Moreover, asymmetrical unions (as with Austria-Hungary) are generally characterized by resistance to—especially heavy-handed—centralizing projects associated with the dominant partner. The Belgians (despite their numerical preponderance) were effectively a subordinate grouping within the northern-dominated United Kingdom of the Netherlands. Indeed, traditional interpretations of the debacle of 1830 conventionally emphasize these imbalances and their consequences: as, for example, Joep Leerssen has pithily remarked, 'the break-up of the united Netherlands (marked by the 1830 Belgian secession) has often been traced and analysed, and is generally blamed on the thoughtless way in which the Dutch (northern) elite imposed its Dutch-speaking Orangist protestant stamp on what was in fact a linguistically and religiously heterogeneous society' (in Dunthorne and Wintle 2013, p. 116). But the lack of a deep-seated unionist conviction in the north is scarcely less striking than these perceived and actual impositions. The possibility of a reformulated, looser, and relatively more equitable union, such as that binding Norway and Sweden, was rejected out of hand when it might have provided the basis for preservation: even one of the insurgent leaders in Brussels in September 1830, Major Moyard, told Prince Frederick of the Netherlands (1797–1881) that, when he and the other protesting burghers asked for 'separation', 'I mean such a separation as exists between Sweden and Norway—between Austria and Hungary' (White 1835, vol. 1, pp. 248–9; see also e.g. Reid 1906, p. 223).

Finally, with other multinational unions there has often been an emphasis upon the ultimate, seemingly inevitable, 'fall' rather than upon (sometimes striking) issues of longevity. With the United Kingdom of Great Britain and Ireland, much attention has been paid to the effective, and long-anticipated, end of the Irish union—the revolution of 1916–21; with Austria-Hungary, especially with an older literature, the story of the Monarchy has been one focusing upon a cancerous set of nationality disputes which delivered an apparently preordained denouement in 1918 (see e.g. Steed 1937). To interrogate these narratives is not necessarily to subvert overall judgements upon the effectiveness or justice of these polities; but it is to question the application of post-hoc or presentist teleologies on often complex evidence. One of the thoroughly fundamental challenges in understanding the overthrow of the United Kingdom of the Netherlands, it has been well said, involves an appreciation of 'how the turn to Belgian nationalism emerged from different political movements that until very later in the day made no point of questioning the [unionist] constitutional order itself'

(Marteel 2018, p. 16). In a sense nationalism was as much a product of the Belgian revolution, and of the fall of the United Kingdom of the Netherlands, as a driver. More generally, perhaps, union states of the 19th century should be seen as, effectively, incubators of nationalism, as much as its enemies.

With the United Kingdom of the Netherlands there is clearly no need to call for greater reflection on the 'longevity' of a union that survived for barely 15 years. It was a uniquely asymmetrical union in so far as, like other unions, its components were dramatically imbalanced, while, unlike others, it encompassed the domination of a minority polity over a majority. But it *is* worth making the case for its possibilities—and it *is* worth remembering that, despite the shortness of its tenure, contemporaries saw such possibilities. There may never have been any union of hearts or minds, and there were certainly manifold problems; but in the mid-1820s a stable and lasting union was a not unreasonable prognosis. Failure came indeed in 1830, but it came as a surprise—except, that is, to later celebrants of the primordial nation (Wielenga 2015, p. 157; Kennedy 2017, p. 289; White 1835).

3.3. The United Kingdoms of Sweden-Norway (1814–1905)

The union of Sweden-Norway, like those of the 'British isles' and of the Netherlands, had some identifiable medieval roots, with the dynastic union of the two Scandinavian kingdoms in 1319, and with their (Kalmar) union with Denmark in 1397. Gustavus Vasa's (1496–1560) successful rebellion in Sweden against the 'centralising and anti-aristocratic policies' of the Danish regent, Christian II (1481–1559), culminated in the Treaty of Malmö (1524), Swedish secession from the union and its consequent demise; thereafter Denmark and Norway were bound through the ongoing personal union of an elective monarchy (Barton 2003, p. 5). After 1661, however, Norway was tied to Denmark in a more integrated union of 'Two Kingdoms', each enjoying an equal citizenship but (now, with Frederik III's *Lex Regia* of 1665) under the authority of an absolutist monarchy ruling from Copenhagen. This union was finally broken only in 1814, when Denmark, an ally of Napoleonic France, was compelled to cede Norway to the king of Sweden under the terms of the Danish-Swedish Treaty of Kiel (the emphasis on compulsion lastingly rankled Norwegian patriots, while the cession of Norway to the Swedish crown, and not kingdom, was of lasting interpretative significance for the same patriots) (Jorgenson 1935, p. 306). From Kiel came the acts of union of 1815, passed in both the Norwegian Storting and the Swedish Riksdag, and creating the United Kingdoms of Sweden-Norway (cf Parent 2011, pp. 93–108; see section 1.5).

There are clear similarities between the birth of the new Sweden-Norway and other unions across 19th-century Europe. The union occurred in the context of heightened national (as distinct from nationalist) feeling in one of the consenting parties, Norway. Britain and Denmark were militarily opposed during much of the Napoleonic era, and the British naval blockade of Norway (1807–14) simultaneously cut that polity off from its union partner as well as precipitating considerable economic hardship. Norwegians were effectively left to fend for themselves both politically and economically; and these experiences produced both more self-reliance in terms of governance (with a Commission of Government), self-help (there was a national Welfare Society during these 'Hunger Years', functioning as the '*de facto* Norwegian government'), as well as across the economy as a whole (by 1813 impoverishment and bankruptcy were generating some of the momentum for a national bank) (Berg 2019, p. 104). There was, in addition, a range of other national institutions created by the Norwegians in these years either immediately preceding or following the enactment of union: the Eidsvoll constitution (1814), a parliament (the Storting) (1814), a national government (1814), a supreme court (1815), a university (1811), and the nomination of a capital city, Christiania (1814) (Kouri and Olesen 2016, pp. 968–9).

As in Ireland, so in Norway the late 18th and early 19th centuries also provided some early evidence of national cultural formation: in Ireland there was aristocratic and patriot interest in the Irish language and history, while in Norway a national Literary Society was formed in 1771, a 'Society for the publication of manuscripts relating to the history of Scandinavia' was created in 1815, followed in 1818 with the foundation of the Gothic Society. Later still, in 1833, the first anthology of Norse myths was published amidst a wider scholarly effort to collect, transcribe, translate, and publish old Norse texts (Langholm 2016, p. 983; Barton 2003, p. 8).

In essence, therefore, the union with Sweden was launched against the unpromising circumstances of Norwegian nation-building or national revival—just as Great Britain and Ireland were united in the context of the birth and early consolidation of Irish republicanism, and in the immediate aftermath of an armed republican uprising (in 1798) against British authority. Equally, the contemporaneous United Kingdom of the Netherlands was created in the context of greater and relatively more unified Dutch sentiment as well as some parallel nascent nationalism within the southern Netherlands. In 1867 the Ausgleich reflected and indeed sought to harness the demands of a voluble Hungarian nationalism. So, while these various supranational unions were not always solely designed to deal with national challenges, and while (in turn) they were not always wholly subverted by national feeling, there is an apparent paradox here: most of the unions discussed in this book were launched against evidently unpropitious intellectual and ideological contexts. Perhaps these unions should be seen, not as antitheses of nationalism, but rather as complements or symbiotic dependants.

Linked with this, Sweden-Norway, like most of the other unions under review, was an unequal polity: Sweden in 1815 had a population of around 2.3 million while Norway had only around 885,000. These imbalances were also reflected in the United Kingdom of the Netherlands (with its northern political and cultural dominance, though demographic inferiority), the United Kingdom of Great Britain and Ireland (with English dominance), and in Austria-Hungary (where German Austria was predominant, at least until the succession of military humiliations from Magenta and Solferino (1859) to Sadowa/Königgrätz (1866), the last of which in fact forced the Ausgleich).

The implications of this asymmetry, which are discussed in greater length later in the volume, were many and varied; but in terms of the immediate creation of union, the issue was often in effect that the predominant partner had a veiled—and sometimes not-so-veiled—military advantage. In 1706–7, with the conclusion of the Scots union, the reality of a threatening English military dominance within Britain was clear, as it was in 1800 with the Irish union, which was concluded shortly after the bloody suppression of the 1798 Rising. Sweden had certainly been defeated at the hands of both Norway (or rather Denmark-Norway) and Russia in 1808–9, losing its Finnish lands to the latter; but Swedish armies acted to threaten the Norwegians in July–August 1814; and while the brief conflict was by no means one-sided, it certainly did indicate where the balance of military power lay. The Swedish military edge, as with that of the English and Dutch in their respective unions, remained a reality (though one that Norwegian patriots like Nansen tried hard to downplay) in the United Kingdoms of Sweden-Norway throughout their long, if sometimes tenuous, life (Nansen 1905, pp. 8–9, 16–17).

Sweden-Norway—like other unions—was also emphatically the creature of international power-play (as was underlined in section 1.5; see also Parent 2011, p. 101). The United Kingdom of the Netherlands had reflected the victorious powers', and particularly (yet again) the British, desire to have a relatively powerful buffer state on France's northern borders. The Scottish and Irish unions had reflected, in turn, the English and British governments' military embroilment in the war of the Spanish Succession and against revolutionary and Napoleonic France. The creation of Sweden-Norway was in part about the weakening of Napoleon's ally, Denmark; but it also spoke both to the diplomatic impossibility of returning Finland to Sweden (lost to Russia after the war of 1808–9) as well as the perceived need to compensate the Swedes and their crown prince, Carl Johan (King Carl XIV Johan from 1818), for their participation in the closing stages of the struggle against Napoleon (see Figure 2.2). Both Britain and Russia wanted a robust, but emphatically not an overmighty, Sweden; and both were also concerned, as in the Netherlands, with the future possibility of renewed French power. The British wanted, too, a buffer against further Russian influence in Scandinavia and the Baltic. It is also clear that, since the key British agent in the creation of Sweden-Norway was Viscount Castlereagh (one of the architects of the Irish union in 1800), the new polity reflected at some level a British susceptibility to the export and proliferation of union states. It will be recalled that Castlereagh had also backed the emergent United Kingdom of the Netherlands (see section 1.5; Webster 1931, pp. 306–9).

What type of union was in place between 1815 and 1905? There was of course a shared monarch. In addition Norway had a resident senior minister, or statsminister, in Stockholm, who acted with two junior ministers, while there was a ministerial council, chaired by a cabinet president, or first minister, in Oslo: only in 1873 were the statsminister (hitherto pre-eminent) and the cabinet president given equal weighting. Joint meetings of the Norwegian and Swedish cabinets were, however, rare. Norwegian ministers gained a 'muffled voice' in the definition of foreign policy in 1834–5, and from the 1840s onwards they were consulted about the appointment of their fellow ministers (Jorgenson 1935, p. 53; Derry 1973, pp. 22, 70). Of course this was not a parliamentary union, as with Britain and Ireland, since the Storting was essentially created to deal with the crisis precipitated by the failure of one union, with Denmark, and the promulgation of another, with Sweden: Sweden had its Riksdag. Each parliament had quite distinct electorates and structures (the Storting was formally unicameral, though it had two divisions; it was elected by a broad male electorate, and was constrained only by the king's suspensory veto, while the Riksdag comprised four corporate estates before 1866, and was governed by an absolute royal veto). It was not a religious union, since (like England and Scotland) there were effectively separate state churches in the different component parts of the union—but (unlike the United Kingdom) there was no overarching union church (for a fuller discussion see section 4.6).

Nor was it an economic union, since Norway and Sweden had originally their own currency (and always had their own coinage), their own central bank, and their own tariff structures. Scots and Irish (and other) travellers in the 1830s and 1840s such as Samuel Laing were frequently surprised to encounter customs inspections in travelling (in Laing's case from Gothenburg to Christiania) within an ostensibly 'united' polity: indeed Laing also noted on his travels the complete absence of Swedish currency in circulation in Norwegian markets and fairs (Laing 1836, pp. 13, 292). There was, however, cooperation over tariffs, and joint tariff laws were in place between 1825 and 1897 (Lindgren 1959, p. 38). Moreover some more general cooperation came—slowly and slightly—with time: a trade treaty in 1874 created free trade by land and extended the scope of sea-borne free trade; adherence to the Scandinavian currency union in 1875 eased some of the complexities created by formerly separate currencies.

But for almost every unionist action there was an equal but opposite patriotic Norwegian reaction. The joint agreement on tariffs lapsed in 1897 and was not renewed: as Raymond Lindgren commented, 'when the tariff union binding the united kingdoms' economic relations was eventually removed, the foundation itself for the political union was thrown away' (Lindgren 1959, p. 38). And there are of course clear distinctions here between the condition of Sweden-Norway and the lasting fiscal and/or tariff unions established in the United Kingdom of Great Britain and Ireland (effective from the mid-1820s), the United Kingdom of the Netherlands (1816), and in the Austrian empire and Austria-Hungary (1850, 1867).

Linked with this, but more fundamentally, the two national economies were largely separate, with little of the complex interconnectedness which characterized (for example) Britain and Ireland and Scotland in the 19th century. The economic consequences of union for the Irish in particular have been much debated, with arguments heavily inflected with national sentiment: the most recent and authoritative assessments have tended to stress a close but complex relationship, with Irish access to markets, capital, and technology being counterbalanced by the damaging effects of cheap English competition and political dominance (see e.g. Bielenberg 2009). The economic history of Ireland under the union was overshadowed by the cataclysmic famine of 1845–51. In the Scots case, the presence of a massive array of raw materials—coal, ironstone, and other metal ores—meant that the balance of advantages in the relationship was rather more clearcut and favourable. In both the British and the Netherlands cases, the economic linkages of union were associated with resentments arising from perceived or actual injustices in the balance of regional taxation: both the southern Netherlands and Ireland complained of being overtaxed within the union regime. With Sweden-Norway, however, the two national economies remained relatively discrete, and indeed looked outwards to Germany and England respectively for economic or technical aid, rather than to each other (Lindgren 1959, p. 37). Consequently, while there was little continuing sense in Norway of Swedish fiscal oppression (apart, perhaps, from specific episodes), there was also little perception of economic benefit from the union, such as experienced or felt by many in Scotland or in Ulster (Derry 1973, p. 60).

Norway and Sweden were not militarily unified. Unlike Austria-Hungary, the United Kingdom of the Netherlands, and the United Kingdom of Great Britain and Ireland, both Sweden and Norway each had their own separate army and navy, though in the Norwegian case these (especially the navy) were both relatively small. There can be no question that the relationship between the 'union' army and the constituent polities of these several states was at best cautious and ambiguous, and could be fraught (especially when the 'union' army was seen in effect as an agency of the dominant union partner). But—while scholars increasingly emphasize the complexities—these united armies have generally been seen as, on balance, forces for assimilation; whereas with Sweden-Norway the military cultures, though ostensibly bound by the king, were ultimately a force for disunion, though also perhaps for peaceful disunion (for a fuller discussion see section 4.4; see also Parent 2011, p. 103). Efforts to achieve a greater coordination of military effort were repeatedly made—as in 1856, when the viceroy Carl (who had a predilection for strong monarchy and strong armies) presided over a joint defence coordination committee, or in 1865, with the second joint committee on the Union (1865–7), when defence coordination was once again on the agenda (Jorgenson 1935, pp. 252–3; Lindgren 1959, p. 51). On each occasion, however, the Storting treated movement towards a unified approach to defence as 'an insidious advance towards political amalgamation' (Derry 1973, p. 87).

It was not just a question, though, of resistance to cooperation. The original union was formulated in the context of a Swedish show of strength in the summer of 1814; and Sweden more generally used (or seriously considered using) military mobilization or manoeuvres throughout the history of the union as a means of applying pressure to the Norwegians—as in the early summer of 1884, with a defiant Liberal-dominated Storting, and in June 1895, when the recurrent dispute over a distinct Norwegian consular service was in full spate. Even when the representatives of two polities were negotiating the termination of union in the masonic hall of Karlstad in September 1905, a backdrop was provided both by Swedish troop movements and Norwegian mobilization (Lindgren 1959, p. 189). A degree of military decommissioning—the creation of a neutral zone between the two countries, the razing of military forts—formed a critical part of the eventual Karlstad agreement, signed on 23 September 1905 (Lindgren 1959, p. 193).

The consolidation and modernization of communications systems are routinely identified as mechanisms for the strengthening of nation and (less routinely) union states, and they played a role in both Austria-Hungary and the Netherlands; but with Sweden-Norway the relative lack of interconnectedness throughout the 19th century was one significant brake upon union. Rail and road networks even within each of the two nations certainly grew, but at a much more modest pace than was the case in and between (say) either Britain and Ireland or Austria and Hungary: the Norwegian road network grew from 11,000 km in 1814 to only 20,000 km by 1870, while the rail network expanded from around 68 km in 1854, when the 'Trunk Line' from Christiania to Eidsvoll was opened, to a still-modest 359 km in 1870 (Kouri and Olesen 2016, p. 970). The approval of the Storting was required until 1851 (after 35 years of 'union') for any new road which linked Norway with Sweden (Derry 1973, pp. 112–13). The first Norwegian railways were built only in the early 1850s, while the first connection between the two capitals, Christiania and Stockholm, opened only in 1871 (Barton 2003, p. 99). There was some growth in the steamship operations which were otherwise such an important mechanism for uniting the islands of Ireland and Britain in the 19th century, as well as for extending the reach of the union state throughout maritime Scotland: a state-supported steamship enterprise, in place between 1827 and 1870, was complemented by the expansion of private routes from the 1840s onwards (Kouri and Olesen 2016, p. 970).

Though there was also an expansion of the press in Sweden-Norway, it remained almost exclusively nationally specific—addressing separate Norwegian and Swedish readerships (see e.g. the comment in Parent 2011, p. 104). Equally, the post office, which was a key agent of the union state in Ireland and Britain, remained divided between Norwegian and Swedish operations: national postal systems (as opposed to a union system) developed in each of the two polities from the mid-1850s, and indeed the first postage stamp for all of Norway (as distinct from Sweden-Norway) was only introduced in 1855, 15 years after the launch of the 'penny black' and other stamps in the United Kingdom.

Finally, in terms of the condition of disunity, there were the issues of unionism and Swedish nationalism. Unionism is a relatively under-reported phenomenon in the history of the United Kingdoms of Sweden-Norway, and indeed (apart, perhaps, from Scandinavianism) there was no effective unionist movement spanning the two polities: moreover, unionism in Norway was clearly the preserve of an elite minority (the foundational text in English is Jorgenson 1935). But perhaps a quarter of the delegates at the Eidsvoll constitutional convention in April 1814 supported the idea of union with Sweden, and the leading advocate of this position was an influential nobleman, Johan Casper Herman, Count Wedel Jarlsberg (1779–1840), educated partly in England and susceptible to British constitutional influence, who later became Norwegian statholder (or governor general) (Jorgenson 1935, pp. 14ff.; Lindgren 1959, p. 11; Redvaldsen 2014, pp. 191–2). These 'unionists' (as was often, though not invariably, the case in other multinational polities) were essentially pragmatic, rather than visionary: union with Sweden would bring peace and trade with Britain, one of the promoters of union; and it would create military and economic cooperation with Sweden, which (in all probability) could not otherwise be easily resisted. Some evidence of local, regional, support for union has been found in (for example) Larvik and Jarlsberg (the latter being Wedel Jarlsberg's homeland): some evidence of farmer support has also been noted, though (again) rooted more in loyalty and royalism than in a considered or proactive unionism (Jorgenson 1935, pp. 27–8). 'Unionism' did not disappear with the creation of the United Kingdoms, but it was ultimately squeezed both by the growth of national feeling in each of its constituent polities as well as by the recurrent firing of a range of divisive issues (such as the divisions over the statholdership and especially the related political crisis of 1860–1) (Jorgenson 1935, p. 306). In Norway it lingered on, perceptible in the commemoration of Carl Johan and in the anniversaries of the union settlement (see e.g. Knaplund 1952, pp. 142–3); it was also a vestigial presence in Scandinavianism—the overarching (if ill-defined) northern movement which looked to greater forms of unity in Scandinavia, perhaps even under the authority of the Swedish royal house, but which had largely burnt itself out by the time of the second Schleswig war (1864) (Henrik Berker-Christensen in Kouri and Olesen 2016, p. 932; Jorgenson 1935; Hemstad 2018; for some of the origins see Barton 1970).

Sweden's relationship with both Scandinavianism and unionism more generally was deeply paradoxical. Swedish nation-building and the formation of a concomitant nationalism in the 19th century lagged behind parallel developments in other polities. As in other polities, so in Sweden, middle-class urban elites were critical to the development of a sense of national identity, and in particular to the elevation of the romantic 'cult' of the peasantry (Petterson 2016, pp. 980–1). In the countryside itself some sense of national identity had begun to achieve traction across the 19th century. This sense of nationhood was consolidated through improved communications (the first telegraph lines were laid in 1852, to be followed in 1855 by a Swedish national postal system, and in 1857 by plans for a national rail network): the growth of a local press from the 1850s onwards supplied an additional critical driver of national unification (Petterson 2016, p. 987). The expansion of voluntary associations and of civil society were equally central, as was the evolution at this time of a national school system: 'teaching in a common [Swedish] national language, combined with the expansion of the bourgeois public sphere and the press contributed to creating a unified national culture' (Petterson 2016, p. 988). All of this built upon a robust underlying patriotism—a strong sense of a once-glorious Swedish empire, dominating north-east Europe in the 17th and early 18th centuries. It expressed itself politically through a definition of union which automatically assumed Swedish supremacy; and which, in turn, pushed back against any proposed reforms (such as the abolition of the statholdership) which looked like either sleights upon Swedish national dignity, or unreasonable Norwegian bids for co-equality (see e.g. Jorgenson 1935, p. 303).

How, then, given all these impediments, did Sweden-Norway not only survive, but emerge as a paradigm of union and cooperation for others, including those in Britain and—especially—Ireland (*pace* Parent 2011)? There are several difficulties in disentangling this critical question. The historiographies of Sweden-Norway in the 19th century, as indeed with the historiography of Britain and Ireland, remain disproportionately national in focus, with relatively little writing on the supranational union state: thus, one leitmotif within the historiography of Sweden-Norway is the tension between a tradition of Swedish royal and aristocratic pragmatism and Norwegian constitutional legalism (Berg 2014, pp. 266–7). Indeed, there has been a long-standing tendency, noted (for example) in the work of Laing, and recognizable in the historiographies of other union states, to depict the two partners as largely distinct in history and culture, and thus emphasizing difference. For example, the constitutional scholar Dag Michalsen has observed that 'in Norwegian historiography, even when the approach is critical, the history of the Norwegian constitution is often portrayed teleologically...as a history of the steady rise of national and political freedom reaching its culmination in 1905 with the dissolution of the union with Sweden' (Grotke and Prutsch 2014, p. 213).

In fact faith in the viability of the union has oscillated with time, with early optimists looking forward to the prospect of ever greater closeness—while those writing in the wake of Norwegian secession in 1905, like the great historian of union, Raymond Lindgren, generally took a more bleakly deterministic line. Indeed, Lindgren argued uncompromisingly that 'the ties forging the union were not only fragile, at times they seemed hardly to exist...almost from the beginning the union distilled the poisons responsible for its ultimate demise' (Lindgren 1959, p. 28).

More recently, however, there has been some evidence of a swing back to more open-ended interpretations of union states with historians of the Irish and Scots unions, and of Austria-Hungary, focusing on longevity rather than overdetermined narratives of inevitable failure (scholars of international relations have tended still to be more strongly persuaded by the compelling force of the macropolitical) (Jackson 2013; Cole and Unowsky 2007; Judson 2016; *pace* Parent 2011). It would be foolhardly to pretend that there is much historiographical pressure to reconsider the prospects of the United Kingdoms of Sweden-Norway (and indeed it has been tellingly observed that 'the union period is practically completely neglected in Swedish historiography'); but within Norwegian historiography there has certainly been movement away from an older patriotic determinism (see e.g. Seip 1995; Neumann 2000; Berg 2014, p. 267). The fact remains that the union lasted for over 90 years; and, while there were certainly seemingly incurable resentments (discussed below), the end came swiftly, and to some extent surprisingly, even for contemporaries. As with Austria-Hungary, the Netherlands, and Great Britain and Ireland, there was emphatically no inexorable momentum towards dissolution: in Sweden-Norway (as in these other polities) there were indeed many periods when it looked as if a greater *rapprochement* was attainable (as during Carl XV's relatively brief reign, 1859-72: Jorgenson 1935).

Moreover, it is essential to grasp that often the ongoing tensions within Sweden-Norway—as in both the Scots and Irish unions—arose not so much (or not only) from nationalist activism, but rather from official efforts to redefine union in ways which were seen as threatening to its original conception and the status quo. In Sweden-Norway, as in Ireland and Scotland, the union authorities oscillated between policies of attempted consolidation or relative integration (for example, the efforts of Carl XIV Johan to bolster his own monarchical authority) and benign neglect (cf. Hoppen 2016). Just as with agreements between Irish nationalism and the British state, where ambiguity often played a critical part in negotiating otherwise intractable difficulties, so in Sweden-Norway efforts by (in particular) the monarchy to obtain clarity over issues such as the fudged mechanisms of foreign policy tended to produce furore. On the other hand, as in both Ireland (until 1916), and in Scotland (until the late 20th century), so in 19th-century Norway, while there was much evidence of nationalist conviction, there was as yet no mass mobilization for complete independence. In this sense, Norwegian nationalists in the 19th century, like Scottish nationalists, may reasonably be judged as much as the guardians of a particular—limited and loose—conception of union as of complete separation.

So the union survived, even if its weaknesses seem more obvious than its strengths. Ultimately it survived for as long as it did because the Swedes, though in several respects stronger, were also comparatively pragmatic, while the Norwegians, though constitutionally pugnacious, were also weaker (and again there are analogies here with England and Ireland) (cf. Parent 2011, p. 99). The union survived, too, perhaps, because (paradoxically) it was itself so very weak: there was, in the end, relatively little to fight over (though, at the same time, it is true that there were grievances which festered for nearly 91 years). In addition, the union survived because (as with Britain and Ireland) it was a relatively flexible instrument: indeed much more than even the British and Irish unions (which were loose enough in some respects), it offered considerable wriggle-room to its partners. Lastly, the union survived because—while most of the institutions which helped to bolster other unions in fact fed into Norwegian or Swedish nationalism rather than unionism—there were some which ultimately did serve to underpin union.

As with other unions, the monarchy was an important binding agent—indeed, given the nature of the Norwegian and Swedish acts of union (1815) the crown is often regarded as the only binding agent (Dag Michalsen has observed that 'the legal relationship between the two countries was defined only through the common king', while T. K. Derry has remarked, Norway was 'organically linked with Sweden by the monarch alone' (Grotke and Prutsch 2014, p. 213; Derry 1973, p. 18)). The monarchy had been a keystone of the union between Norway and Denmark ('the Norwegian peasants were proverbially loyal to the king in Copenhagen, regarding him as their protector against bureaucratic abuse') (Barton 2003, p. 7). The institutional binding of the monarchy with Norway was tightened by the fact that until 1891 the heir to the throne served conventionally as the Norwegian viceroy, while the king also appointed a governor general or statholder—a strategically significant office held originally by Swedish aristocrats but later by Norwegians (Herman Wedel Jarlsberg and Severin Løvenskiold) until its final abolition in 1872 (Berg 2014, p. 277). In addition the king exercised some influence over the armed forces of Norway, and some influence over the union's foreign policy: he had a right of veto over the Storting's legislation, though (unlike in Sweden) he could only delay rather than overturn the enactment of measures.

Successive union monarchs flexed and swayed, often (as with Carl XIV Johan, who reigned between 1818 and 1844) pushing a relatively more assertive and unitary agenda (and seeking to divert the Norwegian constitution away from its revolutionary origins and towards 'restoration norms'); but just as often he had to accept defeat at the hands of an ever-sensitive and vigilant Storting (Grotke and Prutsch 2014, pp. 214ff.; Berg 2014, p. 274). Carl XIV Johan disagreed with the Storting on the issue of his own veto (which in 1821 he pushed to make permanent in line with his Swedish powers), on the question of the nobility (which the Storting wished to abolish in Norway), and—a lasting slow-burn in the history of the union—on the crown and Sweden's predominance in the exercise of foreign policy (see e.g. Jorgenson 1935, p. 37; Parent 2011, p. 97). Subsequent monarchs did not always have Carl XIV Johan's slippery pragmatism (or indeed his general popularity); and indeed—as one Irish unionist student of Bernadotte admiringly and tactfully recorded—it was 'clear that if Bernadotte was successful in maintaining and consolidating his Norwegian throne, he did not accomplish his purpose by any servile courtship of popular favour' (Barton 1925, p. 185; for his popularity see Jorgenson 1935, p. 32).

In fact the popularity of the monarchy in Norway was repeatedly observed and noted, including (for example) by contemporary British commentators and travellers. It is true that Samuel Laing's own views of Carl XIV Johan grew more embittered as his experience of Scandinavia developed, but in 1836 he freely conceded that the Norwegians were 'unquestionably a loyal people, attached to the highest degree to their sovereign and his family' (Laing 1836, p. 197). In 1836 Laing still believed that Carl Johan's reign was 'the moral triumph of the constitutional over the legitimate principle', though by the end of the decade (and after another sojourn in Sweden) Laing was complaining that 'the character of his reign has been to oppose the spirit of the age; to govern by an aristocracy upon the ultra legitimate principles of kingly government, to extinguish in his Norwegian dominions the constitutional rights of the people in their legislation' (Laing 1836, p. 197; Laing 1839, p. 397). Other British travellers like R. G. Latham (writing in 1840 about a journey undertaken in 1833) observed that portraits of Carl XIV Johan and of his wife were displayed in many homes and that 'you would not do wrong in measuring the extent of his popularity by the ubiquity of the pictures of him' (though he also acknowledged the existence of 'personal disapprobation of the king's mode of procedure' (Latham 1840, vol. 1, pp. 100, 228-9; Jorgenson 1935, p. 75). H. D. Inglis, writing as Derwent Conway, noted that throughout his travels in Scandinavia 'Bernadotte [Carl Johan] is never named but in terms of respect' (Conway 1829, p. 42).

The periodic royal tours of Norway, which were a staple of British commentary, generally elicited impressive displays of support and loyalty. Latham witnessed the visit of Crown Prince Oscar, as viceroy, to Norway in 1833, and admiringly recorded the street decorations (triumphal arches of fir boughs and intertwined flowers), the public acclamation (a long, loud cheer followed by 'a succession of minor huzzas'), and the inevitable military review and grand ball (Latham 1840, vol. 1, pp. 101-3). Lord Dufferin, sailing in the north Atlantic in the summer of 1856, encountered Crown Prince Oscar (later King Oscar II) at Trondheim as well as similar evidence of popular esteem for the crown prince and the monarchy: Dufferin was impressed with 'the many windows filled with flowers, its [Trondheim's] bright fiord covered with vessels gaily dressed in flags' and the night-time illuminations, all in honour of Oscar's presence (Dufferin 1903, pp. 194, 214-16).

A striking feature of the British travel narratives of the 1820s and 1830s was that they often explicitly compared these royal visits to Norway to a critical epiphany in the history of the British monarchy's relations with the Celtic nations and with union—namely George IV's coronation tour in Scotland and Ireland of 1821-2. Thus Latham invoked Crown Prince Oscar, who 'was in the year 1833 taking a tour of his western dominions more especially Norway and the cities belonging thereto—just as George IV, ὁ μακαριτης [of blessed memory], visited Scotland and the sister isle of Erin' (Latham 1840, vol. 1, p. 98). Samuel Laing was present when Carl Johan visited Levanger in Norway in January 1835, but—while also deploying the comparison with George IV's coronation tour—he was keen to illustrate the easy and natural relationship between the Norwegians and the union monarchy, as distinct from the evidently pretentious, laboured, and theatrical efforts of the Hanoverian court in Scotland:

> Carl Johan's visit to Norway may well be compared to the visit of George IV to Scotland. It was in better taste both on the part of the monarch, and of the people. The king came over the frontier without military escort or guard and with the most simple attendance and retinue. In Scotland there was a little too much pretence and attempt at show. All were to appear what they were really not.
> (Laing 1836, p. 385; see also e.g. Jorgenson 1935, p. 54)

Of course it is important not to equate these British perceptions of Norwegian loyalism and monarchism with uncomplicated or impassioned unionist sentiment. Norwegians were loyal to the Bernadotte dynasty primarily as kings of Norway, and not as heads of the union state: for the Norwegian patriot, Fridtjof Nansen, the great antiquity of the monarchy in Norway meant that 'fidelity to their Royal House has therefore always been particularly characteristic of the Norwegian peasantry' (Nansen 1905, p. 5). Moreover, as with other multinational union states, popular endorsement hinged upon the personality and abilities of individual monarchs (as has been said of the Habsburgs, 'if one member of the...dynasty did not attract popular support, there was always another who might be chosen as a channel for maintaining a link with the monarchy and expressing loyalty' (Cole and Unowsky 2007, p. 5). Carl XIV Johan was generally respected because of his considerable battlefield prowess (like Crown Prince Willem in the United Kingdom of the Netherlands), and because—though he regularly chanced his arm in claiming enhanced powers—he was shrewd, well-advised, and basically loyal to the (Eidsvoll) constitution of 1814 and the wider union settlement. His legacy, as effective patriarch of the union, was commemorated in Norway in different ways: a Carl Johan society was founded in Norway in 1858 (ten years after the Swedish Karl Johans Förbundet) and it was followed by the planning and construction of an equestrian statue of the king at the royal palace, Christiania (1864–75) (Barton 2003, p. 65; Lindgren 1959, pp. 48–9).

Carl Johan's son, Oscar I (r. 1844–59), 'inherited little of his father's capacity for adroit compromises' but was nevertheless relatively liberal and sensitive to Norwegian claims (he gave Norway precedence in all Norwegian references to the union state, granted a half-share to Norway in the union coat of arms, and created a specifically Norwegian order of merit, the order of St Olav in 1847) (Derry 1973, pp. 19, 72). Oscar's eldest son, Carl XV (r. 1859–72) was generally popular, but died at the age of only 46; and in any case—bowing to Swedish and aristocratic pressure—he reneged upon a promise to abolish the increasingly contentious statholdership (seen by Norwegians as symbolic of Swedish ascendancy, and by Swedes as a symbol of their national dignity), with the consequence that 'the union as a slowly growing bond of sentiment had suffered the severest possible setback': Carl's hopes, as crown prince, for a union parliament, shared Swedish-Norwegian defence deployments, and other integrationist reforms, accordingly were given short shrift by the Storting in 1857 (Jorgenson 1935, pp. 242–6; Lindgren 1959, pp. 50–1; Derry 1973, p. 89; Langholm 2016, pp. 966–7). Still, his period of influence may be seen as the highpoint of the union ideal in Scandinavia (see e.g. Jorgenson 1935, pp. 206–50).

Carl's brother, Oscar II (who reigned over the United Kingdoms between 1872 and 1905), was (astonishingly) the only monarch of the United Kingdoms of Sweden-Norway who could speak Norwegian; and it was he who, in 1872, finally axed the hated statholdership (Derry 1973, p. 19; Barton 2003, p. 64). On the other hand, given the premature death of his brother, Oscar was never given the chance to serve as viceroy of Norway, and thus to learn about its politics at first hand; and, despite the general evidence of the popularity generated by official tours, he rarely visited Norway (Derry 1973, pp. 94–5). On one occasion when he did, he encountered R. A. Anderson, the Irish agrarian reformer and protégé of Sir Horace Plunkett, who later recalled that the king, enraged by their content, destroyed the Norwegian newspapers which were presented to him each morning (Anderson 1935, p. 53). These factors, together with Oscar's obligations to defend the union, did not help to ease his relationship (or indeed that of his son, Gustaf, a markedly unpopular regent in Norway) with his increasingly contumacious Norwegian subjects; and it was ultimately Oscar who was compelled to preside over the dissolution of the union in 1905.

Even then, however, and though the Storting may have been characterized by republican insolence, the Norwegian people ultimately voted—in November 1905—to retain the institution of monarchy. Moreover, if the *arriviste* Bernadotte dynasty had embodied the triumph of pragmatism and invented tradition over historical legitimacy, then the new monarchy was just as artfully constructed: it simultaneously evoked the ancient tie with Denmark (the new king was a prince of the House of Oldenburg), as well as the ancient monarchy of Norway itself (the king smoothly took the title of Haakon VII, even though the last Haakon of Norway had died as far back as 1380: Barton 2003, p. 82). But above all the new

Norwegian monarchy (like the union monarchy of 1814–15) reflected some of the realities of the country's external relationships as well those of European power politics. Haakon VII was the nephew of the Queen of Great Britain and Ireland, Alexandra; and Haakon's wife, Maud, was the youngest daughter of Alexandra and Edward VII. Indeed the British in-laws tactfully supplied the new Norwegian royals with 'much wanted' plate as a coronation gift in 1906 (Murray of Elibank Papers, Ms.8801, f. 52: Knollys to Murray, 11 May 1906).

It should also be said at this point that support for the monarchy was complemented (especially in the third quarter of the 19th century) by some wider Norwegian interest in the union, and indeed in the possibility of its continuation. The union was popular with some Norwegians some of the time (just as its equivalent was popular—or at least tolerated—by some Irish some of the time). As has been shown, its central institution, the monarchy, was generally well-liked. While the two national economies were indeed very largely discrete, there was broad sympathy for improved, easy, and free trade between the two polities. All this even fed into a modest commemorative culture: it was certainly true that Union day (4 November), together with the significant anniversaries of the act of union—such as its 40th, in 1854, and its golden jubilee, in 1864—were celebrated in Norway by some, especially amongst the bourgeoisie and the influential class of civil servants (Jorgenson 1935, p. 194; Knaplund 1952, pp. 142–3; Lindgren 1959, p. 49; Derry 1973, p. 92). With the solidifying of political tensions in the 1870s, the Norwegian (unionist) conservatives named their first organization, 'the November Society' (Seip 1995, p. 40; Hemstad 2019, pp. 91–2).

Moreover, and critically, the dominant official political class in mid-19th-century Norway was much more unsettled by the European revolutions of 1848–9 and by the rising power of the small farmer class than it was by any threat posed by Sweden or the union: this increasingly conservative cadre was led for much of the third quarter of the 19th century by Frederik Stang (1808–84), who was successively the senior official at the Norwegian Domestic Ministry and first prime minister of Norway (1873–80) (Barton 2003, p. 65). By 1880 the radical patriot-poet, Bjørnstjerne Bjørnson (1832–1910), was writing that 'in Christiania they are now saying quite openly that it would be better to be Swedish than to submit to Norwegian peasant rule'; he was proclaiming, too, that he was 'unshakably opposed to a Swedish king's or Norwegian or Swedish reactionaries' attempts to make an England-Scotland out of Sweden-Norway, that "closer union" they speak of' (quoted in Barton 2003, pp. 66–7).

But, if successive unionists, especially in the early decades of union, thought that the then exiguous union of the two countries would become much more solid with the accretion of mutual trust and respect, then they were to be ultimately mistaken. An especially festering difficulty for the United Kingdoms of Sweden-Norway lay in the realm of foreign affairs—which were one of the few areas vested in the union government, or (more specifically) with the crown. Almost from the beginning of the union, while its monarchy was respected largely as a specifically Norwegian institution, the conduct of foreign affairs created profound difficulties. From the point of view of Norwegian patriots like Nansen the constitutional position after 1814–15 was that the king of Norway (who also happened to be simultaneously king of Sweden and of the union) had responsibility for foreign affairs, and might therefore choose to permit a Swedish-born foreign minister to administer Norway's foreign relations (Nansen 1905, p. 51). Matters improved after 1835, when a Norwegian minister of state was to be present whenever any diplomatic matter which concerned Norway was being aired before the ministerial council; but the drift towards greater democratization and ministerial accountability in Norway and even in Sweden itself meant that after 1885 it was no longer the king (whether of the union, Norway or Sweden) but rather his Swedish foreign minister who had control of all diplomatic matters (Barton 2003, p. 72). In this shift, this revision of relationships, claimed Nansen, 'lay the principal cause of the last twenty years of strife in the union' (Nansen 1905, p. 54).

In fact the conflicts over diplomacy in these final 20 years which culminated in the dissolution of the union were freighted with a longer history of commercial and constitutional (and threatened military) antagonisms between its two polities. In 1821 the Storting cavilled at the $3 million bill which Sweden had agreed with Denmark as the price of Norway's portion of the pre-1814 state debt of the union of Norway and Denmark: Norwegian acquiescence was compelled by the background threat of military force, registered by a controversial military review conducted in the summer of 1821 (Nansen 1905, pp. 33–4; Lindgren 1959, pp. 46–7). Equally, the contemporaneous Bodø affair caused consternation in Norway: this complex episode (1818–21) involved the Swedes paying (at Norwegian expense) compensation to a British trading company, which had been accused of illegality, and then prosecuted by the Norwegians. Each of these two cases fed suspicions that the Swedish foreign ministry had but slight regard for Norwegian national interests; and they contributed to a wider (though by no means continuous) campaign to establish Norwegian control over Norway's foreign and diplomatic concerns (Lindgren 1959, p. 47; Berg 2019, pp. 106–7).

In fact the issue of challenging foreign affairs, though present at the beginning of the union, and a precipitant of its demise, waxed and waned according to wider context. As in Ireland, ameliorative initiatives on other issues could take the steam out of the festering diplomatic question: thus concessions on the question of some key issues of national symbolism (the union flag, its coat of arms) helped to defuse tensions on the more substantive questions of foreign policy in the early 1840s (Lindgren 1959, p. 48). As in Ireland, however, though palliative measures created the space for potentially constructive conversations on the great constitutional questions of the union, this space was never effectively utilized. The union committee on foreign affairs (1839–44) had little impact (a new draft act of union was mothballed); nor did detailed proposals for a closer union (1857) or the later committee on the revision of the union (1865–7) effectively deliver (this last also produced a new draft union, which was eventually voted down in the Storting) (Jorgenson 1935, pp. 62–6, 242–7, 356–62; Lindgren 1959, pp. 48, 51; Derry 1973, pp. 72, 93). As in Ireland, so in Sweden-Norway, there is a sense in which these episodes simultaneously underlined the possibilities of union, as well as the extent of its lost opportunities. As Louis de Geer (1818–96), first prime minister of Sweden, mournfully commented after the failure of the union committee in 1867, 'from that moment I gave up hope that the union by some constitutional method might become something entirely different from what it was' (quoted in Lindgren 1959, pp. 51–2). On the Norwegian side, the liberal political leader, Johannes Steen (1827–1906), who had until recently been an ardent Scandinavianist, passionately repudiated the proposal for closer union in 1871, saying that:

> I know in reality not even a union king. I know only a Norwegian king and a Swedish king united in one person, representing through him and his dynasty the mutual interests of war and peace...but it is with dread and in agony that I envision a future in which the Norwegian and the Swedish people have through a unitary state's institutions become one social organism and that the names Norwegians and Swedes may yield to a common denominator...to the Scandinavian North the development would be fatal in its consequences; to our own country it is death itself.
> (*Stortingstidende* 1871, p. 394, quoted in Jorgenson 1935, pp. 360–1)

The conflict over foreign policy which finally fractured the union can be periodized in different ways, but three last phases may be identified between 1885 and 1905. In 1885, in the context of intensified ministerial accountability, control of foreign policy was effectively ceded by the king to the (invariably) Swedish foreign minister; and from this there arose increasing pressure in Norway for separate diplomatic representation (Nansen 1905, pp. 53–4). A proposed fudge (with linguistic ambiguity reminiscent of similar agreements between the British and the Irish throughout the history of the union) was offered by Oscar II to the effect that 'ministerial matters shall be exercised for the king by the minister for foreign affairs in the presence of two other members of the Swedish together with three members of the Norwegian council'. But even this attempt to square Swedish and Norwegian claims was given short shrift by the Storting in 1889, since the wording (which hinged on the word 'other') seemed to imply that the foreign minister would always be a Swede (Lindgren 1959, p. 63).

Norwegian national demands, which were articulated by the liberal Venstre (or 'Left') party and its increasingly nationalistic farming, or *bønder*, support, were met with a reciprocal Swedish nationalism and indeed belligerence. A particularly striking aspect of these conflicts in the late 1880s, early 1890s, and afterwards was the combination of rhetorical militancy and indeed threatening actions: 'throughout these two years [1892–4]', it has been said, 'public opinion reached an inflamed point where reason vanished and emotion reigned' (Lindgren 1959, p. 67). In 1891 Baron Gustaf Åkerhielm (1833–1900), Prime Minister of Sweden between 1888 and 1891, pronounced elliptically if ominously that 'Swedes should speak Swedish both east and west'—a dictum which was read in Norway as an implied threat. For his part, Johannes Steen, who was Venstre prime minister of Norway between 1891 and 1893 and again between 1898 and 1902, offered a retaliatory threat of secession from the union. The draining of Swedish patience was expressed in apparent preparations for war in the summer of 1895, in the appointment of an ardent unionist, Count Ludvig Douglas (1849–1916), as union foreign minister in June 1895, and in conversations between Oscar II and the Kaiser during the summer of 1895, wherein Germany promised Sweden its support in the event of an attempted Norwegian secession (Wilhelm paid a private visit to Sweden in July 1895) (Knaplund 1952, pp. 260–1). In the face of these obstacles, the Storting backed down from its threat to create its own consular network; but the Norwegians, too, were now beginning to turn from constitutional argument to military expenditure in order to augment their case.

The legacies from the crises of the early and mid-1890s were those of an embittered and belligerent rhetoric from both sides, and an increasing resort to threatened military action from each. There was certainly both a heightened Norwegian and Swedish nationalism which fed into hardline positions, and which underpinned both the demand for a separate Norwegian consular service as well as for Swedish supremacy within the union; but it is important to see as well that Norwegian unionism was, by now, largely exhausted. The conservative unionist Norwegian historian, Yngvar Nielsen (1843–1916) wrote that, during the last months of union, he had become increasingly disillusioned and had come to welcome its demise (Barton 2003, p. 82). Swedish nationalism was also increasingly associated (from at least the 1880s onwards) with the conviction that Sweden might do better if liberated from the relentless distractions of union politics and addressing Norwegian sensibilities (e.g. Knaplund 1952, pp. 141, 180; Lindgren 1959, p. 72). This viewpoint received a particularly full and thoughtful exegesis at the hands of Professor Harald Hjärne (1848–1922), a conservative member of the Riksdag, who in a series of articles published in early 1905 argued that 'it was better to end fruitless argument and to dissolve the union, substituting some form of defence union in which each country would be sovereign and equal' (Lindgren 1959, p. 98; Barton 2003, p. 81). Other leading Swedish conservative intellectuals, such as Rudolf Kjéllen, shared this analysis (Kirby 1995, p. 189). This combination within the dominant union partner of an intensified nationalism as well as a paradoxical mixture of an integrationist unionism together with a rejection of the tribulations of partnership has of course informed the politics of other union states—and not least those of Britain in the early 21st century.

In the last years of Sweden-Norway there were therefore apparently countervailing Swedish policies. On the one hand, there was a military build-up in Sweden and occasional hardline initiatives, associated especially with Erik Boström (1842–1907) as prime minister (1902–5): on the other hand, there were some conciliatory and pacific gestures, particularly with the moderate Alfred Lagerheim (1843–1924) as union foreign minister (1899–1904). In 1900 it was accepted that posts in the foreign service would be equally shared between Swedes and Norwegians: in 1902 it was agreed to form a fourth (and final) union committee of enquiry focusing on the consular service. There was some tentative reciprocity from the conservative (Høyre) prime minister of Norway between 1903 and 1905, Francis Hagerup (1853–1921), who led a coalition broadly in favour of negotiation and opposed to radical constitutional action. For a time—indeed until as late as the end of 1904 and early 1905—it looked as if an agreement might be possible (on the basis of separate consular services) between those relatively consensual elements in government in both Stockholm and Christiania; but the resignation of Lagerheim (largely at the hands of Boström) from the union foreign ministry on 4 December 1904 removed the keystone from the delicate architecture of trust and diplomacy. Fridtjof Nansen thought that with the Lagerheim debâcle there was 'lost an exceptional opportunity of bringing the two peoples to a better understanding' (Nansen 1905, p.82); Sigurd Ibsen (1859–1930), the son of the great dramatist, broadly agreed, believing that 'the affair presaged a break between Norway and Sweden' (Lindgren 1959, p. 92 n. 14).

In these circumstances the space for conciliation and for conciliators (which had existed until a very late hour in the life of the union) was squeezed shut: Hagerup was replaced as Norwegian prime minister on 11 March 1905 by the hardline liberal, Christian Michelsen (1857–1925), who pushed forward a revivified plan for a separate Norwegian consular service. A last-minute Swedish effort to revive negotiations, spear-headed by Crown Prince Gustaf, failed: even the replacement of Boström as Swedish prime minister on 13 April came too late to avert the dissolution. The Storting passed Michelsen's consular law on 18 May, and the king immediately exercised a veto: his Norwegian ministers resigned *en bloc* and Oscar was unable to find any replacements. On 7 June 1905 the Storting decided that in the circumstances the king was no longer able to exercise his constitutional functions; and these were accordingly ceded to the Norwegian ministers.

Norway, in effect, had declared that the union had ended. The extent of the popular support for independence, upon which Michelsen's consular strategy had hinged, was revealed by a plebiscite held on 13 August 1905, when 367,149 Norwegians voted for the ending of union, and only 184 could be mustered in its support (Lindgren 1959, p. 167). On 27 October 1905 Oscar II formally abdicated from the throne of Norway, and was efficiently replaced by Prince Carl of Denmark, the newly minted Haakon VII, who arrived to claim his crown on 25 November.

By 1905 the building blocks of union were no longer in place. The Swedish vision of union—one in which Sweden itself was dominant, and where the union functioned as a weapon of its foreign policy—had long since faded: former unionists now looked to salvage a workable relationship with Norway out of the remnants of the united kingdoms—just as many southern Irish and British unionists sought to rescue the vestiges of partnership with Irish nationalism in 1920 when the old order was clearly beyond recapture. Norwegians had been prepared to work within these united kingdoms, but it was evident throughout its long history that their conception of union differed fundamentally from that of their Swedish partners. Even the central institution of union, the monarchy, which had for long retained the respect of Norwegians, had ceased to exercise the kind of magic dispensed by Carl XIV Johan: Oscar II (who was 76 in 1905) was treated politely by his Norwegian subjects, but Crown Prince Gustaf was an object of frank suspicion (Lindgren 1959, p. 81). This, then, had become a union where the unionists had lost faith, and the bulwarks of union had lost efficacy. It had become a union whose original sense of purpose had been lost—and indeed where this seemed more likely to be attained through dissolution rather than survival (Parent 2011, p. 107).

But it was also a union which had lasted for nearly 91 years—maintained by Swedish military and financial predominance, comparative flexibility, and by the concomitant space and freedom given to Norwegian national institutions and sentiment. In general the union had been an effective mechanism for mutual strength and security, and for the negotiation of national difference. An escalation of belligerent rhetoric from the early 1890s onwards, the deployment of veiled or overt military threats, and the disrespect eventually shown to the royal family—all of these were powerful subversive influences: they may even have been inherent in lop-sided unions where one partner was dominant. But as late as 1904 it seemed likely that some form of recalibrated union settlement could be devised to further extend the life of the constitutional jalopy. And the calmness of dissolution—this most deep-pile of velvet revolutions—which is often seen as signalling the emptiness of union, also surely says something about the mature cultures of negotiation and accommodation which were nurtured under its aegis. It says something, too, about the critical differences between Scandinavia and the Balkans (and also perhaps something about Austria-Hungary) that the weakening and final dissolution of the United Kingdoms of Sweden-Norway did not (despite extensive Great Power engagement) trigger any wider dispute (Knaplund 1952, p. 53; Lindgren 1959, p. 133).

In the end, therefore, it is important to strike a realistic balance between the powerful teleologies of nationalist historiography and the clear possibilities of union: it is important to balance the powerful taxonomies of international relations theorization and the real contingencies evident in the history of the United Kingdoms of Sweden-Norway. It is often said that, while there were indeed resentments which long simmered between the two polities, the final dissolution between Norway and Sweden would have been difficult to predict in the years before 1905—as indeed was also the case with Britain and Ireland in the years before the separatist uprising of 1916. As with Britain and Ireland, so with Norway and Sweden, the demise of union was driven forward not only by legalistic and relentless nationalists but also by often insensitive and exhausted unionists: it was achieved both by the sores and the aspirations of the smaller nation as well as by the limitations and (ultimately) the indifference of the larger nation.

With the benefit of hindsight it is always possible—indeed it is usual—to construct narratives of the history of union which forefront the playing out of the consequences of fatal original problems. But in fact contemporaries sometimes dared to believe that the United Kingdoms of Sweden-Norway might survive, and (as in Ireland or central Europe under the Habsburgs) nationalism gained strength from the apparent expansiveness and energy of union rather than the reverse.

3.4. The United Province of Canada (the United Canadas) (1841–67)

The theme of union in British North America (the territorial concept came into usage, principally by Orangemen and outsiders, in the 1830s) was rather different from the other case studies discussed in this and the preceding chapters; because, unlike the European examples, the context here was principally colonial (Martin 1999, p. 523). The Austrian empire and Austria-Hungary were composite and (later) dual monarchies, comprising ancient crownlands, while Sweden-Norway was a personal union of ancient kingdoms with some additional shared (diplomatic) aspects: the United Kingdom of Great Britain and Ireland, and the United Kingdom of the Netherlands, were both parliamentary and wider unions with overseas empires (and indeed, as has been discussed, with Britain and Ireland there were also strong 'internal colonial' features). But the union of Upper and Lower Canada which was forged between the Durham report of 1839 and the enacting legislation of 1840 brought together two British colonies of settlement (or, more accurately, one colony of British settlement, Upper Canada, and one, Lower Canada, where there had been some British settlement within a long-established French, francophone, and Catholic, colony); and (while there were local supporters amongst the merchant classes) union was fundamentally driven by the overarching, British, imperial power. Similarly, the radical reconfiguration of British North America which occurred when the United Province of Canada was superseded by confederation in 1867 took place only with the formal approval of Westminster and the British government of Lord Derby. And indeed the

Dominion of Canada which emerged from all this remained for some decades yet in the shadow of the sovereign imperial power.

However, in several critical respects the Canadian union of 1841 was closely bound with at least some of these other case studies. Its attainment, like that of the other unions discussed earlier, was in effect yet another example of the British 'export' of union; but, as with the other unions, Canada also illustrated the reciprocity—the complex ebb and flow—of influences linking its constitutional experience with that of Britain and Ireland. The union of the Canadas was achieved in the aftermath and context of the establishment of the Irish union, and of discussion about its future (focusing on the issue of 'repeal' which was re-emerging in the later 1830s). Although the influence of Castlereagh and his circle was not directly felt here, as they were with other 'united kingdoms', debate on union in Canada *was* certainly influenced by Irish and Scots (and English) statesmen who brought to North America constitutional predilections which were vitally shaped by their respective homelands, or by their views of Ireland and Scotland: the principal architect of Canadian union, John George Lambton, first earl of Durham (1792–1840), imbued his task with strong influences from both the Irish and, especially, the Scots unions, and he had also engaged critically with other of the union polities discussed in this volume, including Sweden-Norway and the Netherlands (Reid 1906, vol. 2, p. 333; Coupland 1945, pp. lxi, 161). The Scots-born Canadian premier, Sir John A Macdonald (1815–91), and the Irish-born governor general, Charles, fourth Viscount Monck (1819–94), brought to confederation preferences for a British-style legislative union: the English-born colonial secretary, Lord Carnarvon (1831–90), and the Irish peer, Lord Dufferin, governor general (1872–8), each defined confederation and its institutions in terms of their readings of the Scottish and Irish unions (see e.g. Herbert 1902, pp. 118, 152, 178; de Kiewiet and Underhill 1955, pp. 159, 175). But by the end of the 19th century there was a counterflow: Canada's successful experience of confederation meant that it now served as a model to those in Ireland and Britain who sought home rule or some related mode of constitutional reform (see e.g. Martin 1999, p. 522; Stevenson 2006; Kennedy 2015).

The critical point of comparison between (on the one hand) Great Britain and Ireland and (on the other) Canada, acquired by the British through the Treaty of Paris (1763), lay in the fact that both the new colony and the old, Ireland, were overwhelmingly Catholic. Moreover British migration into both Ireland and Canada created complex multinational societies which were divided by culture, religion, and language: in the case of Canada (or Quebec) the defeat of British arms during the American War of Independence led to the flight north of around 70,000 United Empire Loyalists—those who had either been too closely associated with the *ancien régime* for comfort, or who did not otherwise want to accommodate themselves to the new republic. These migrants settled in what became in 1785 the province of New Brunswick, as well as in the western reaches of Quebec. Here they joined an existing Canadian population, which was francophone, Catholic, and which preserved distinctive French legal and tenurial regimes.

From the beginning there were clear lines of reciprocity binding Canada and Ireland. From early on, the experience of Scotland and Ireland (and eventually their respective unions) was relevant to Canada, generally in the dual sense that Scotland was seen as a precedent to be emulated while the Irish case was one to be avoided. The critical Quebec Act (1774) was the work of General Sir Guy Carleton (later Lord Dorchester) (1724–1808), an Irish Anglican, who had been born in Newry, in south Ulster, and who seems to have retained a vigorous suspicion of the pushy Presbyterian middle classes of his native province (Coupland 1925, pp. 41n., 65–6). In some senses his act supplied an antonym to the condition of Ireland: the overwhelming majority community, the French Catholics, unlike their Irish counterparts, were to enjoy the free exercise of their faith, and their priests were to receive their customary rights (including tithe payments); the civil law of Quebec was to reflect the traditional French practices rather than English common law (the latter was practised in Ireland); there was to be no assembly (the Irish parliament, dominated by landed Anglicans, had repeatedly caused grief to London); and in addition the boundaries of the province were to be substantially extended (Coupland 1925, pp. 91–2).

The act unquestionably further enflamed patriot opinion in Britain's unsettled Thirteen Colonies (an 18-year-old Alexander Hamilton (1757–1804) penned a condemnatory pamphlet); and it was read by opposition leaders at Westminster, such as Fox and Burke, as a repudiation of British freedoms (Coupland 1925, pp. 97, 121n.). But different views prevailed in the longer term; and in general the Quebec Act came to be seen as an essential foundation giving respect and protection to a key community in the complex union politics of the later Province and Dominion of Canada. The contrasts between this denouement and Ireland were inescapable: George III had happily signed off on the full protection of the rights of his far-off Catholic subjects in Quebec in 1774, while denying them to his Irish neighbours and subjects in 1800 (Coupland 1925, p. 104). The constitutional scholar, Reginald Coupland (1884–1952), writing in the aftermath of the Irish war of independence, and indeed himself possessing strong Irish interests, was clear that Canada survived within the empire only because British policy there was exactly the opposite to that applied in Ireland: 'if British statesmen had treated Canada as Ireland had been treated, torn up the Treaty of Paris like the Treaty of Limerick, and cynically applied the familiar doctrines of religious intolerance and race ascendancy, the British government of Canada would surely not have lasted long' (Coupland 1925, p. 122; see also Stevenson 2006, pp. 36, 46ff.). In fact, in Quebec the Catholic Church not only enjoyed legal protection, it swiftly emerged as the British administrations' favoured intermediary in the government of the province (Stevenson 2006, p. 52).

Coupland was also deeply interested in the politics of partition; and an early example of a territorial division of this kind came in 1791—with the application of an intercolonial, ethnic, and religious, boundary through Quebec, and the resulting creation of two new provinces, namely Lower Canada and Upper Canada (Stevenson 2006, p. 56; Coupland 1945, p. xiii). Lower Canada comprised the francophone and Catholic heartland of the old province, while Upper Canada was formed from its western reaches, which were now (in the aftermath of the American War of Independence) attracting anglophone Protestant loyalist settlers and other British migrants. In essence, British policy in North America at this time, as elsewhere in the empire, was to govern by means of division, and to strengthen the reach of central authority, and to lessen its problems, either by weakening the resources of the periphery, or by isolating potentially difficult communities (see e.g. Reid 1906, vol. 2, p. 320; see section 4.11). But there were other possible (and apparently countervailing) approaches, including—following the Irish example—the reconfiguration of awkward local majorities within new and ostensibly more manageable forms of political structure. In the light of the experience of Scotland and (to a lesser extent) Ireland, it came to be seen that union might be applied as a means of dealing with political and military challenge.

The Province of Canada (the United Province or the United Canadas) was formally inaugurated in 1841, after many years of discussion of the possibility of union, and with some consideration of the preceding Scottish and Irish models. As in Scotland and Ireland, so union in Canada was not simply a precipitate or isolated event, but was instead a protracted (if intermittent and sometimes lowkey) debate. As in Scotland and Ireland, so in Canada, union had an economic dimension, being designed to address not just issues of public order, but also those of economic growth and instability. As in Ireland, so in Canada, union was partly a response to existing, unpopular and ineffective, oligarchies. As in Scotland and Ireland, union was finally achieved in the context of warfare—and in the specific cases of Ireland and Canada, in the context of republican insurgency. Above all, Canadian union (whether in terms of its design or its execution) engaged those who had direct knowledge and experience of the Scottish and Irish cases. In short, and as a contemporary noted, 'the union of the Canadas is in some measure a sort of second edition of the Irish union' (*Quebec Mercury*, 23 March 1841).

Taking each of these contexts to union in turn, neither in Canada nor in Ireland nor Scotland were the respective acts of union *dei ex machina*, but fitted instead into longer conversations on the question. It will be recalled that Scottish union with England had been first broached in the sixteenth century, was forwarded by the union of the crowns in 1603, and developed during the Cromwellian era: union had been further discussed throughout the Restoration and revolutionary era, with different definitions supplied, 'federative' or incorporating, depending on the preference for local or central strength. In Ireland, similarly, a form of parliamentary union had been attained under Cromwell, while the Scottish union of 1707 had precipitated some Irish longings for a similar end: union had been considered by William Pitt long before its final attainment on 1 January 1801 (see section 2.1; Jackson 2013).

In Canada and in London different forms of union, whether federal or legislative, whether addressing all of British North America, or merely part, had been discussed from the 1780s onwards, and drew upon Tory and loyalist ideologies: William Smith (1728–93), an ally and protégé of Carleton, and Chief Justice both of Quebec and later Lower Canada (1786–93), argued for a form of defensive federal union of all those British colonies in North America which had survived the deluge of the American revolution (Kendle 1997, p. 20; Upton 2003). A successor as chief justice of Lower Canada, Jonathan Sewell (1766–1839), actively promoted the idea of various forms of union within Britain's North American colonies over a long judicial and political career (he was chief justice between 1808 and 1838). In seeking to achieve a greater British influence within Lower Canada, Sewell supported the kind of incorporating union which had been applied to Ireland and Scotland; but he met some initial resistance from Sir James Henry Craig (1748–1812), who was governor general of the Canadas between 1807 and 1811 (Martin 1990, p. 166). In the context of the American war of 1812–14, and the related need to strengthen Canadian defences, Sewell turned to the idea of a federal union of all of British North America, publishing his ideas as *A plan for the federal union of British provinces in North America* (1814) (Greenwood and Lambert 2003). In the early 1820s, when the idea of a legislative union of the Canadas alone was gaining traction amongst in particular Montreal's (disproportionately anglophone and Protestant) mercantile elite, together with some allied office holders, Sewell was opposed, preferring instead to disinter his earlier federalist proposals: his views on federal union were now broadly espoused by another, rising, and increasingly influential lawyer, John Beverley Robinson (1791–1866), chief justice of Upper Canada (1829–41) and of Canada West (1841–62) (Martin 1990, pp. 166–71; Saunders 2003). Once again, however, a British governor general, George Ramsay, ninth earl of Dalhousie (1770–1838), in office between 1820 and 1828, resisted the notion, preferring the possibility of legislative to that of federative union (or—in other words—the British model of union to that of the Americans). And in fact legislative union of the Canadas remained a feature of British policy from 1822 and 1823, when it was the centrepiece of two failed bills at Westminster, through to 1839–40, with (at last) the success of the earl of Durham's Act of Union.

The tension between incorporation and federation to some extent reflected the changing context and purpose of Canadian union. Those who sought wider strategic goals, in particular the defence of British North America against its ambitious southern neighbour, tended to look to federal union: this recognized the need to enlist the sympathy and active support of French Canada in any military endeavour, and to draw upon (what came to be seen as) the glorious legacies of the Quebec Act in delivering French Canadian support during the revolutionary war and again in the war of 1812 (Coupland 1925). On the other hand, those British Canadians who sought short-term sectional or wider economic advancement, or who were strategically concerned to weaken the overall influence of the French and Catholic traditions—to create a more thoroughly 'British' British North America—often looked instead to various forms of incorporating union. A key context, and driver for the union debate of the late 1830s, and the Act of Union of 1840, were the economic difficulties of Upper Canada, and the expectations that these might be alleviated through union with its relatively more prosperous neighbour. Equally, economic pressures had been one of the motor forces behind union for both Scotland in 1707 and Ireland in 1800: in each case the racked condition of the economy initially sweetened the prospect of union with a much wealthier neighbour, and helped in the formation of unionist conviction.

Union in Ireland and union in Canada were also (effectively) about the attainment, or rather the management, of political reform. In Ireland the United Irish movement, formed in 1791 in Belfast and Dublin, had been thwarted in their quests for parliamentary and constitutional reform and, harried by government, they had moved steadily by the mid-1790s towards more militant means and more radical ends. The Irish parliament and the Irish executive (despite the false dawn of Earl Fitzwilliam's brief viceroyalty in 1795) had resisted pressure for comprehensive reform; and in fact this only became more attainable in the context of the passage of union in 1800 (Jackson 2010). Similarly in the Canadas, especially in Lower Canada, the overwhelming authority exercised by the governor general, in association with the executive and legislative councils (each appointed by the crown), together with the almost complete powerlessness of the elected legislative assembly, soon presented a challenge for reformers. In both Ireland and the Canadas royal government was exercised through, or in association with, favoured allies or clients, who generally enjoyed a monopoly of patronage: in Ireland this was (broadly) the ascendancy interest, and in particular (until the 1770s) the 'undertaker' class, while in Upper Canada it was the patronage network known as the 'family compact' and in Lower Canada 'the château clique'. In the 19th century in both Lower Canada and Ireland royal government enjoyed a cautious but often mutually productive relationship with the Catholic Church.

Reform politics gained traction in Lower Canada from at least 1810, when the legislative assembly voted in favour of acquiring budgetary control; these gained further momentum after the war of 1812–14, and focused both on democratic reform within the province as well as on resisting British Canadian (and other) efforts at legislative union. The key agency for reform politics was the Parti Canadien, which was succeeded in 1826–7 by the Parti Patriote. The key leader of reform politics was Louis-Joseph Papineau (1786–1871), who in 1834 was partly responsible for the compilation and approval (by the legislative assembly) of a comprehensive manifesto known generally as the Ninety Two Resolutions. These resolutions called for responsible government—an elected legislative council and an executive council answerable to the legislative assembly—but, though couched in carefully loyal language, they were treated by the Whig government in London with apparent contempt. After fully three years' delay, the Whig Colonial Secretary, Lord John Russell, responded with his own set of (ten) resolutions, effectively dismissing the efforts of the Canadian reformers towards responsible government. The effect, as in Ireland in the mid-1790s, was to signal the apparent impossibility of achieving significant peaceful change within the existing order; and, as in Ireland, there was a swift radicalization of reform politics which ultimately delivered a republican insurgency—and, indirectly, union.

However, at this point it should be emphasized that the politics of the pre-union Canadas of the 1830s not only bear comparison with pre-union Ireland in the 1790s—there was also significant mutual political engagement (Stevenson 2006). The reformers of Lower Canada attracted considerable support at Westminster from the pre-eminent Irish political figure of the era, Daniel O'Connell, as well as from British radicals such as the Montrose-born Joseph Hume (1777–1855) and J. A. Roebuck (1802–79, who was also the parliamentary agent for Lower Canada's legislative assembly): in the prelude to rebellion O'Connell strongly supported Papineau and the Patriotes, pointing out in debate that the analogy between Canadian and Irish political conditions was 'in fact...complete' (quoted in Stevenson 2006, pp. 74–5). Indeed, O'Connell was himself compared by contemporaries and later commentators to both Papineau and (more accurately, perhaps) the latter's moderate successor, Louis-Hippolyte LaFontaine (1807–64): Roebuck observed that 'the persecutions of Ireland have produced O'Connell, the misgovernment of Canada...has produced its O'Connell in the person of M.Papineau' (Roebuck 1835). Moreover the governor general of Canada at this time (1835–8) was an Irish peer, Archibald Acheson, second earl of Gosford (1776–1849), who—though, as an Anglican landowner, was a representative of the ascendancy interest—was also for a time relatively sensitive to the Patriote party in the legislative assembly: he had been chosen for the governor generalship precisely because of his emollient track-record in Ireland, as lord lieutenant of the troubled and divided county of Armagh—and because he was viewed sympathetically by O'Connell at a time when the Whig government was dependent upon the latter's votes and influence (Buckner 2003). It should be said as well that one of the principal opponents of Gosford (as of his predecessor, the fifth Lord Aylmer, and another Irish peer) was a fellow Irishman, Edmund Bailey O'Callaghan (1797–1880). O'Callaghan, from Mallow, county Cork, was a medical doctor and the editor of the Montreal newspaper, the *Vindicator*; and he was successful in seeking to reconcile anglophone Catholics, often Irish, to support both for Papineau and more advanced Patriote politics.

Gosford not only brought to Canada a track-record as a conciliationist, an opponent of Orangeism in his home county, and a friend to moderate Catholic interests—he also brought a record of opposition to legislative union. Like the circle of Castlereagh, discussed earlier, Gosford (as Archibald Acheson) had been caught up in the debates over the Irish union, serving in the Dublin parliament (1798–1800) as member for county Armagh; but unlike most of Castlereagh's circle, Acheson opposed union, and for long afterwards sustained that opposition. Though his attitudes towards Patriote politics gradually hardened, and though his efforts to co-opt moderate Patriotes ultimately ended in failure, Gosford's stand on union remained broadly unchanged. Long after his departure from office (in February 1838), and his retirement to his Irish estates in Markethill, county Armagh, he maintained an interest in the governance of British North America; and in 1840 he opposed union in Canada, as he had done for Ireland 40 years earlier.

Union in Ireland and in Canada followed immediately upon insurgency and its suppression by the forces of the crown (or loyalist bodies such as, in each case, the Orange Order). In each case, too, the failure of constitutionalist reform action led to militancy, and in each this militancy was pursued by different communities. In Ireland the insurgency of 1798 was a feature of both the substantially Presbyterian counties of eastern Ulster as well as the overwhelmingly Catholic south-east and west of the island; while in 1837–8 there were uprisings in both Lower and Upper Canada, which were pursued by both francophone Catholics as well as anglophone Protestants. In each set of risings, Irish and Canadian, militancy was precipitated by the heavy-handed arrest of reformers (Stevenson 2006, p. 79). The two risings were linked in the minds of contemporaries, and with none more clearly than E. B. O'Callaghan: 'it was Castlereagh and the Irish union over again', he wrote in July 1852, 'Goad the people into violence and, when they fall victims to the snares, abolish their constitutional rights. Read the history of Ireland and its legislative union with England, and you will see as in a mirror the plot of 1836–7 against Canadian liberty' (quoted in Daley 1986, p. 1).

In Lower Canada angry support for the Ninety Two Resolutions was expressed in a series of mass meetings through 1837, in which the demands and rhetoric grew more extreme. All this fed into unrest on the streets of Montreal and soon (by 16 November) the government was moving against Patriote leaders such as Papineau and O'Callaghan. These now fled from Montreal to two key rural strongholds of Patriote politics, the Richelieu valley (east of the city), and Deux-Montagnes (just to the west): small-scale military actions led to the comprehensive victory of the crown forces in November–December 1837. A near-synchronous rising in Upper Canada, led by the Dundee-born radical editor, William Lyon Mackenzie (1795–1861) was also easily crushed, as was a renewed Patriote effort in November 1838, pursued through a new secret society, the Frères-chasseurs (or hunters' lodges), and culminating in two defeats at Napierville and Odelltown, just inside Lower Canada, at its border with New York and the United States.

In 1798 the rebels in eastern Ulster, in Wexford, and the west, had sought an Irish republic. In 1837–8 the insurgents, provoked by British truculence and inspired by the American model, sought a Canadian republic: Mackenzie proclaimed a republic in December 1837 on Navy Island in the Niagara river, while the Patriote leader, Robert Nelson (1794–1873), was declared president of the republic of Lower Canada in February 1838: a convention of hunters' lodges in Cleveland, Ohio, elected Abram Smith (1811–65) as the 'first' president of the Canadian republic (Stevenson 2006, p. 81). Pursuing a republic, in each case Irish and Canadian rebels inadvertently created instead the argument and opportunity for union. Indeed, in each there were (unsubstantiated) allegations that the crown had deliberately and cynically provoked insurgency with this ultimate end in view (Stevenson 2006, pp. 89–90).

The architect of Canadian union was, as has been said, the earl of Durham. Durham, sometimes described either a 'radical Whig' or as 'moderate radical', had been identified earlier in his career with a variety of reformist causes, including both Catholic emancipation and the parliamentary reform of 1832: he had long been interested in multinational union polities, and had hitherto been sensitive to the conditions of subsidiary nationalities such as the Norwegians (to whom he had devoted his maiden speech in the House of Commons) as well as the Belgians and indeed the Irish. However, even the sympathetic Reginald Coupland felt compelled to concede that Durham 'shared the general English belief in the superiority of the English way of life over that of any other nation in the world' (Coupland 1945, pp. lxi–lxii, 161).

In 1838 Durham was appointed to succeed Gosford as governor general, with a sweeping mandate to reconstruct the government of British North America in the wake of the catastrophic risings in Lower and Upper Canada (though in fact, as has been said, there was renewed violence on his watch). The parallels with Ireland in the aftermath of the 1798 rising are clear; but there were also critical distinctions, partly in terms of the horrendous scale of the Irish rising (where at least 30,000 died, as opposed to the 325 or so in Canada), and partly in so far as the Irish parliament needed to sanction its own demise, while the legislative assembly of Lower Canada (which had already been prorogued in 1838) was not required to do so. And of course though the interconnections between Irish and Canadian politics have preoccupied politicians and scholars from the 19th century onwards, these links have always needed to be cast in the light, shone at the beginning of the section, of colonialism. Ireland was closely embroiled with the configuration and survival of the neighbouring imperial superpower: Canada, 3,000 miles away, never posed an existential threat in the same way.

Each union had some prehistory and some local support—but each was essentially an example of an imposition from the imperial government and parliament in London: each, in other words, exemplified one of the themes discussed with the earlier case studies, namely the British export of the idea and practice of union. In each case union was a response to internal and external threat and insecurity (in 1837–8 the United States had remained wholly neutral—earning President Martin Van Buren a coruscating biography from E. B. O'Callaghan's pen—but it was still a potential adversary); in each case union was a response to economic and sectional pressures. Above all, however, the idea of union in each polity changed substantially as the ideal was adapted to the circumstances on the ground. In the Irish case this meant the rapid fading of Pitt's vision of an Ireland where Catholics would enjoy emancipation and the kinds of legal protection which were supplied in Canada through the Quebec Act; in the Canadian case it meant that, as his researches progressed, Durham moved away from a 'federal' model of union towards something more in keeping with the unions of the United Kingdom (Reid 1906, vol. 2, pp. 332–3; Ormsby 1969). Indeed, in a sense the union which finally emerged in Canada in 1840–1 was, whatever its manifold failings, a vision of the Irish union as it was meant to be— predominantly British and anglophone, certainly, but otherwise liberated from religious exclusivity.

Durham's tenure of the governor generalship was brief and controversial, and rapidly became entangled in the politics of the Whig high command in London; but his 'Report on the Affairs of British North America', laid before parliament in February 1839, had a lasting significance, and not least because it provided the basis for the subsequent British North America Act, or Act of Union, in 1840. Interpretations of Durham's report have varied hugely, with 19th-century imperialist commentators (and successors, like Reginald Coupland) seeing his work as the foundation of representative colonial government within the Victorian empire, while more modern Canadian nationalists have emphasized instead its ethno-centric purposes, and questioned its characterization of the profound divisions in Canada ('I expected to find a contest between a Government and a people; I found two nations warring in the bosom of a single State; I found a struggle not of principles, but of races; and I perceived that it would be idle to attempt any amelioration of laws or institutions until we could first succeed in terminating the deadly animosity that now separates the inhabitants of Lower Canada into the hostile divisions of French and English': see e.g. Reid 1906, vol. 2, pp. 315–16; Lyall 1905, vol. 1, pp. 205–6; Stevenson 2006, pp. 99–100; Coupland 1945). In essence Durham saw representative government as an emollient for the unrest in the two Canadian colonies; but he equally saw that the introduction of representative government into Lower Canada would be a politically fraught proceeding, given French ascendancy and likely British hostility. Like Pitt in 1799, Durham tried to solve the problem of a necessary but difficult concession by reframing its terms of reference; and, just as Pitt had wanted to introduce Catholic emancipation within the context of a new united kingdom, so Durham sought to establish representative government in Canada through the agency of a new United Province. But he also explicitly wanted to achieve the effective assimilation of francophone Canada within a thoroughly British North America; and, again, just as Pitt had reconciled the perceived challenge of Catholic Ireland by creating a Protestant United Kingdom, so Durham sought to reconcile the challenge of francophone Lower Canada within a predominantly anglophone United Province (Coupland 1945, pp. 161–2). Of course Durham was not in any sense chained to Pitt's legacies, not least given that the circumstances of the rising of 1837–8 were compelling him to overturn the Constitutional Act of 1791 (Stevenson 2006, p. 99). Moreover, the original Scottish union of 1707 was also an explicit model for Durham (as it had been for Pitt, too); and he believed that the existing legal structure of Lower Canada, as well as various interests (primarily the Catholic Church) could be protected through the devices of union no less than had been the case for the laws and faith of the Scots in 1707 (summarized in Reid 1906, vol. 2, pp. 333, 337).

Durham's recommendations were embodied in the union legislation introduced into the Commons in March 1840, and swiftly passed into law by July, with the only significant opposition coming from Daniel O'Connell and other Irish critics of (Irish) union: Durham, who died from tuberculosis at the age of 48 in July 1840, survived just long enough to see his recommendations enacted (Reid 1906, vol. 2, p. 367). Lower and Upper Canada were now bound together as the United Province (or the United Canadas): they retained, however, a lingering administrative significance as the two sections, 'Canada East' and 'Canada West'. The United Province possessed a governor general, based initially in Montreal, and in addition it was given a Legislative Council and a Legislative Assembly; but responsible government, as envisioned by Durham, had to wait a while (see e.g. Coupland 1945, pp. lxivff.). As in a range of other unions (such as the United Kingdom of the Netherlands, where the *arithmétique hollandaise* of the constitutional vote provoked outrage), some of the basic features of the new Canadian arrangements were deeply contested: the new Legislative Assembly of the United Canada had equal representation from each of the two former colonies, even though Canada East (the former Lower Canada) had at this time a substantially greater population (650,000) than Canada West/Upper Canada (450,000). As in the United Kingdom and the Netherlands, so union in Canada was also designed to advance the interests of a politically dominant partner; as in the United Kingdom and the Netherlands, this design had both religious and linguistic dimensions—in the case of the new United Province the effective dominance of anglophone and Protestant interests.

The economic and administrative unions in Canada were more complete than in Ireland (where distinctive institutions remained after union, and where there were cautiously transitional currency and tariff arrangements stretching over many years). But in Canada this effectively meant at first the subsidizing of the more impoverished west by the more prosperous east—just as in the Netherlands the indebted north was supported by the south: in each these arrangements stimulated unrest (see Stevenson 2006, pp. 100–1). However, there were also more effective emollients: as in Scotland, so in Canada East, the legal protection continued for churches which were distinct from the ecclesiastical establishment of the United Kingdom (the Catholic Church in Canada East, the Kirk in Scotland). And as in Scotland, so in Canada East, distinctive legal and tenurial regimes were relatively untouched by union: roman law traditions survived in different forms in both polities, as did different versions of seigneurial and feudal tenure.

As with all the unions discussed in this work, it is important to interrogate overly emphatic and presentist teleologies of failure—specifically, in the Canadian case, teleologies and histories which deliver the 'inevitable' denouement of confederation in 1867 (Martin 1990, p. 12). Indeed, even those who were amongst the most impatient and volatile critics of union, such as the Alloa-born publisher and 'Clear Grit' leader, George Brown (1818–80), were prepared to recognize that it was an honourable experiment which had produced much that was beneficial (see e.g. Morton 1999, p. 81). What, then, held the United Province together for the quarter century of its existence?

In a sense the union of 1841 survived not wholly because of the wisdom of its architects, but rather because much of their vision was swiftly overtaken by, and adapted to, political realities (Kennedy 2015, pp. 43–4). Canadian union survived for a time, not because the French-speakers of Canada East became (as Durham had expected) fully assimilated within a British anglophone and Protestant polity, but rather because they were divided in their attitudes. While *Canadiens* were broadly opposed to union, they were also split between those who sought *la survivance* within the possibilities of the new dispensation, and those who (like their contemporary O'Connellite counterparts in Ireland) looked to the repeal of union. However, it was the former grouping, led at first by Louis-Hippolyte LaFontaine (1807–64) and later by George-Étienne Cartier (1814–73), which prevailed. Just as in Ireland, so union survived in Canada because those whom it disadvantaged mostly sought to work within its structures rather than attempt its violent overthrow.

Related to this, union survived in Canada because, although the imperial authorities sought both to advance the ethno-centric ambitions of the Durham report as well as to delay the institution of responsible government, in practice these goals proved difficult to achieve: union survived because *all* of the communities of the United Canadas ultimately enjoyed a share in responsible government. In effect this happened quickly after the passage of union, thanks to the emergence of party leaders in both parts of Canada who were pragmatic, reforming, and understanding of wider interests and sensitivities: LaFontaine in Canada East and Robert Baldwin (1804–58) in Canada West. LaFontaine and Baldwin shared the leadership of the government of the United Province in 1842–3, before the principle of responsible government had been formally established:

this last had to wait until February 1848, when they jointly returned to office for a second time, appointed after a general election victory by the governor general, James Bruce, the eighth earl of Elgin (1811–63). But part of the reason for the experiment of 1842–3 lay in the fact that the then governor general, Sir Charles Bagot (1781–1843), clearly saw that the United Province could not be governed peaceably without the cooperation of its francophone citizens (Stevenson 2006, p. 127). Bagot's insight (which was not always shared by other governor generals of the 1840s) surely owed much to his experience, as a long-serving British ambassador (1824–9), in another complex union polity with an embattled francophone community—the United Kingdom of the Netherlands. Here, again, therefore, the experience and politics of complex multinational union polities in the early 19th century were interconnected, rather than discrete.

The union survived, then, because it embraced a form of power-sharing; and indeed it has been seen as evincing the first example of the kind of consociationalism which subsequently featured as a principle of government in other divided societies—most recently and conspicuously through the Good Friday peace settlement in Northern Ireland (Noel 1974, 1993). It is true that 'the distinctive system of intercultural elite cooperation' initiated by LaFontaine and Baldwin was not associated with any formal requirement for the kind of multiple majority sanction associated with (for example) the consociational administration in Northern Ireland (Stevenson 2009, p. 21). But in practice governments were headed by party leaders, as premier and deputy premier, from each section of the 'united' province: moreover, there were two attorney generals, representing the different legal regimes in each of the two sections, and (where appropriate) the legislation of the province was tailored to the particular circumstances of each of the sections (Stevenson 2009, pp. 21ff.). In practice (though not in legislative principle) an informal mutual veto existed, since it was widely expected that a government could only survive if it commanded majorities in both sections of Canada (Kennedy 2015, p. 44). When this mutuality began to falter, as it did from the late 1850s onwards, then so, too, did the union itself.

This of course highlighted a critical difference between Canada and Ireland under the union—and also a distinction, though less sharp, with the Scottish union. A fundamental problem with the union in Ireland was that the majority Catholic community, while represented in the House of Commons after 1829, had little direct influence over, or presence within, government: few Irish Catholics, in fact few Catholics of any nationality, made it to the ranks of government across the many years of union (Jackson 2013, p. 144). No institution of central government was fully representative of the Irish Catholic interest; and, on the contrary, the Irish Protestant interest exercised disproportionate sway at Westminster, not least in the House of Lords, and elsewhere. In the circumstances one of the lessons of union appeared to be that government would respond effectively to Irish Catholic dissatisfaction, not when it was expressed through normal constitutional pressure, but rather primarily through manifestations of threat or violence (see Jackson 2018b).

However, this is not to say that union was static or inflexible; and one of the key bolsters of union in Ireland and Canada (and even, to some extent, the Dual Monarchy) was in fact its malleability (Jackson 2013, pp. 188ff; cf. Steed 1919, pp. 125ff.). The Irish union was capable of delivering reform, albeit inefficiently and often in the context of militant threat: this was the case with Catholic emancipation, reform of the established church and indeed disestablishment, land reform, and ultimately with the possibility of home rule. The Canadian union was similarly flexible, delivering responsible government and bilingual union administration (in 1848), compensation to those *Canadiens* and others who had suffered through crown action during the 1837–8 rebellions (the Rebellion Losses Act of 1849), and major land reform (in the shape of the abolition of the seigneurial system in 1854). The numerous other glories of the union years included the negotiation of a major commercial treaty with the United States in 1854, and the authorization of the great legal codification project which, operating from 1857, ultimately delivered the *Code civil du Bas-Canada* in 1866 (described, by W. L. Morton, as 'one of the great achievements of the Canadian Union') (Morton 1999, p. 198).

But union also nurtured a set of political cultures of negotiation and accommodation which in turn facilitated a major constitutional redefinition—confederation, discussed in detail in a later section of the book (see section 5.3). In this sense, then, confederation in 1867 was ultimately not so much an expression of the failure of union, as of its strengths and possibilities (Morton 1999, p. 20).

3.5. Austria-Hungary (1867–1918)

Castlereagh and his allies may have enabled and shaped several of the union polities which are discussed in this book—the United Kingdom of Great Britain and Ireland, the United Kingdom of the Netherlands, the United Kingdoms of Sweden-Norway; but the territories of the Habsburgs had spanned Europe when Castlereagh's family, the Stewarts, were merely obscure Donegal gentry, and when the state that he came to represent had not even been envisioned, still less realized. However, the Austrian empire was central to British diplomacy after 1815, as an important agent in a wider European balance of power: for Castlereagh Austria was no less than 'the pivot of Europe, and our shoulder is always ready to support her. We are like a lover whom she will always find waiting for her' (quoted in Bew 2011, p. 522). Similarly, Baron Henry de Worms (1840–1903) in 1870 invoked 'those great powers whose interests in all important questions must of necessity run parallel with those of Austria—viz England and France. The traditions of Austria's foreign policy pointed to Great Britain as the power which should be placed foremost in this respect' (Anon. [An Englishman], 1870, p. 70). And, beyond diplomacy, there were some even more fundamental points of linkage between the lands of the Habsburgs and those of the Hanoverians.

Both the Austrian empire and, later, the Dual Monarchy, together with the United Kingdom of Great Britain and Ireland, were complex multinational polities bound by a variety of shared—in Oszkár Jászi's vocabulary, 'centripetal' or 'internationalist'—institutions such as the monarchy, the civil service, and the army (Jászi 1929; see also Bryce 1901, pp. 255–6; Burgess 2006, p. 16). Each polity had a degree of ethnic or national, linguistic and religious diversity, though this of course was especially marked in Austria-Hungary. Austria-Hungary in 1910 had a population of 51.4 million, of whom 28.6 million resided in Cisleithania (its western, predominantly Austrian, half): 20.9 million lived in Transleithania (Hungary and its territories) and 1.9 million in the recently annexed (1908) Bosnia-Herzegovina. The four main everyday languages (*Umgangssprachen*) recorded were German (23.4 per cent), Hungarian (19.6 per cent), Czech (12.5 per cent), and Polish (9.7 per cent); and there were also smaller populations speaking Croatian, Ruthenian, Romanian, Slovak, Slovene, and Italian. The overwhelming bulk of the empire's population was Roman Catholic (76.6 per cent), with Protestants (8.9 per cent, mostly Calvinists and Lutherans) and Orthodox (8.7 per cent) coming far behind in terms of numbers and proportions, together with an even smaller Jewish population (4.4 per cent): Protestantism, Orthodoxy, and Jewishness were proportionately more significant in the eastern, Hungarian, lands of the empire (see the figures for 1880 quoted in Jenks 1965, pp. 2ff.).

By way of comparison, in 1911 the United Kingdom had a population of 45.3 million: censuses were undertaken that year in England and Wales (where the population was recorded as totalling 36.1 million), Scotland (4.8 million), and Ireland (4.4 million). In terms of language, there was no category as subtle (or perhaps slippery, since it tended to favour German) as the *Umgangssprache* in the British taxonomy; but there was instead a distinction between mono- and bilingualism. Those using the Welsh language alone numbered 8.5 per cent of the Welsh population, while the proportions of Scots Gaelic and Irish Gaelic monoglots were as low as 0.4 per cent (those for bilingualism were somewhat higher, at 43.5 per cent (Welsh), 14 per cent (Irish), and 4.6 per cent (Scots Gaelic)). Religious practice was only recorded in the English and Welsh censuses in 1851 and 2001, and some of the relevant data for Wales were discussed in the preceding chapter (2.2); but the statisticians were more continuously interested in the religious breakdown of the Irish population which, in 1911, was recorded as predominantly Catholic (73.8 per cent), with significant minorities adhering to the Church of Ireland (13.1 per cent) and Presbyterianism (10 per cent).

In other words, the United Kingdom in 1911 had some ethnic, religious, and linguistic diversity, which (as has been shown) frequently fuelled comparisons with other complex polities; but at the same time the Habsburg empire was an especially multi-layered conglomerate. Each, however, was characterized by dominant national or linguistic identities—the English in the case of the United Kingdom and (after 1867) Germans and Magyars within the Habsburg empire. Each was also shaped by the ongoing restlessness of non-dominant nationalities and their associated diasporas—the Irish, and (to a lesser extent) Scots and Welsh with the United Kingdom, and the Hungarians (until 1867), northern and southern Slavs (Czech and Slovak speakers, Slavonians, Croats, Serbs), Poles, Ruthenians, and Italians in the case of the Habsburgs.

Just as Great Britain and the United Kingdom were each in turn forged in the context of challenging international warfare and/or dynastic change or uncertainty, so successive revisions of Habsburg rule were pursued against similar backdrops. The Pragmatic Sanction (1713) of the emperor Charles VI (1685–1740), last of the Habsburg males in the direct family descent, clarified lines of inheritance, and provided for 'the indivisible unity of the Hapsburg [sic] lands and their obligation of mutual defence': the Sanction was devised and promulgated against the context of European war and internal insurgency (Steed 1919, pp. 42–3; Deak 2015, pp. 9–10). The Austrian empire itself was unveiled in August 1804 against the exigencies of a world war: half a century later, in 1859, military defeat at the hands of the French and Piedmontese precipitated a speedy turn to constitutionalism, while renewed defeat, by Prussia in 1866, required some more drastic action in the form of the great Ausgleich of 1867 (Oszkár Jászi believed in fact that the 'dualistic system was born on the battlefield of Königgrätz': Jászi 1929, pp. 100, 106). This, though dealing only really with Hungarian disaffection, provided nationalists in the United Kingdom with a recurrent paradigm for its possible reconstruction (see section 1.6). But with Austria-Hungary, as with the other forms of 'union' state under examination, these influences were reciprocal; and British parliamentary and local government practice, together with the British model of union, were very closely inspected (in the former case by, for example, the great Austrian liberal, Josef Redlich (1869–1936): Redlich 1903, 1908). More specifically, the model of 'Scotland in Britain' was projected by (in particular) the Scots Slavophile, R. W. Seton-Watson onto Habsburg central Europe and indeed onto its successor states (Cornwall and Frame 2001, pp. xxi, 121; Seton-Watson 1924). For Arthur Griffith, the patriarch of Sinn Féin, the 'resurrection of Hungary' presaged the resurrection of Ireland: for Frano Supilo, the southern Slav patriot, the Habsburg successor state, Yugoslavia, promised to be 'our future Great Britain' (quoted in Cornwall and Frame 2001, p. 100).

As in Great Britain and Ireland, so with the Habsburgs, a form of territorial unification or regularization (in the shape of the new Austrian empire) came in the context of the global war against revolutionary France; but in each case unity was prefigured by earlier initiatives and earlier actors (see section 2.1). For the Habsburgs a central dynamic figure was Joseph II (1741–90), Holy Roman Emperor (1765–90) and sole ruler of Austria (1780–90). However, it is also now generally recognized that Joseph's work of state-building built upon the vital administrative experiments of his mother, Maria Theresa (1717–80); and that it was decisively complemented by his otherwise lacklustre nephew, Francis (1768–1835), who in 1804 finally turned the complex Habsburg domains into the one state, the Austrian empire, as well as promulgating an overarching civil law code, the *Allgemeines bürgerliches Gesetzbuch*, in 1811 (Judson 2016, p. 54; Deak 2015, pp. 15–16).

Frequently seen as the archetypal enlightenment ruler, Joseph pursued policies which unsettled the existing religious, aristocratic, and to some extent the ethnic allies of the Habsburg monarchy. He was an opponent of papal power, and of the 'unproductive' monastic orders: he promoted a vision of a reformed erastian faith, with a modernized and rationalized Catholicism working in close partnership with the state—'in effect a state-run church' (Judson 2016, p. 69). He promoted toleration of Jews and Protestants (Judson 2016, pp. 66–7). In consequence, he generated enmity amongst those traditional Catholics who had hitherto looked to the Habsburgs to supply both dynastic as well as a quasi-spiritual leadership across much of Europe. In areas such as the Austrian Netherlands, strongly influenced by Counter-Reformation cultures, Joseph's religious reforms fed into a growing political instability and indirectly contributed to the possibility of union with the north (see section 3.2).

But Joseph also sought to reform the vestigial feudal structures of the Austrian empire, extending some legal rights to the serf class in 1781–4, and attempting the abolition of serfdom itself in 1785: these initiatives went hand-in-hand with a wider revision of taxation, crystallized in a fresh Tax and Agrarian Regulation of 1789, and designed to create a uniform levy of 30 per cent on income arising from land (Judson 2016, p. 81). The key beneficiaries of the old order, the nobility, were directly threatened by these initiatives, both in terms of their local and regional authority, as well as (even more directly) their income. As a consequence, noble and aristocratic opposition to Joseph grew. In all of this there were premonitions of the late 19th-century reforms of the United Kingdom state which sought to broaden its support and foundations away from the Anglican landed aristocracy and gentry (or 'Protestant ascendancy') and from the minority Protestant Church of Ireland towards a greater embrace of Catholic Ireland (see section 2.1).

The paradox (familiar enough within Ireland in the 19th century) was, of course, that Joseph's apparently liberalising reforms were associated with a vision of a highly centralized and uniform state and with a militaristic outreach. Joseph pursued his agenda through an enhanced, centralized, and uniform bureaucracy as well as a (typically) rationalized secret police apparatus (not that Joseph himself had much faith in spies): it has been pointed out that 'a critical aspect of Joseph's bureaucracy was its growing cultural identification with the imperial center in Vienna and specifically with an *Austrian* state' (Judson 2016, p. 62; cf. Steed 1919, pp. 90ff.). Even more controversially, he sought uniformity in language through his lands, promoting (for example) German as the first language even in Hungary (1784); though, again, this was essentially an exercise in efficiency and uniformity, rather than a statement of national chauvinism (Judson 2016, p. 79). Here, as elsewhere with his complex agenda, Joseph's ambitions lay unfulfilled at the time of his early death, at the age of 49, in February 1790.

Joseph bequeathed a complex dual legacy to his Habsburg successors in terms of the management of their diverse territories, and this goes some way to explaining both the survival of the loose union of states under the dynasty's sway, as well as (simultaneously) its difficulties. On the one hand, he largely created a tradition of liberalizing reform (he was not a liberal) in the areas of land and religion: on the other hand, he also envisioned a centralized, vigorously policed, and German, Habsburg state. To some extent each of these rival impulses was in place and in conflict until the fall of the empire in 1918. And to some extent, too, while Ireland and the Habsburg lands were distinguished as much by their differences as their similarities, this combination of liberalizing reform as well as vigorous policing and centralization was a hallmark of union in the United Kingdom (Jackson 2013). In Joseph's Austria (as in that of the absolutist regime of the 1850s) and in British Ireland in the long 19th century, there is a clear sense in which a 'liberal' and a 'modernizing' agenda were often pursued by armed force (see section 4.11).

In the short term, Joseph's legacies of regularization, uniformity, and centralization provided some foundations for an emerging Habsburg state, which was given greater coherence and unity through the promulgation (by Francis) of a new Austrian empire in 1804. All of the established powers confronted an existential challenge posed by the French; and (while, again, the analogy clearly cannot be pushed too far) the further unification of the British composite monarchy, achieved through the Irish union of 1801, and the creation of a (more) unified Austrian empire in 1804 bear some comparison in terms of rational responses to a shared external threat. Moreover, in both supranational polities, some effort was invested in the consolidation of a related patriotism, in both cases linked very closely to dynastic loyalties. This upsurge in British and Irish loyalism and Austrian dynastic patriotism was associated (respectively) with the creation of the English volunteer regiments (yeomanry) in 1794, and the Austrian *Landwehr* (1809) (Blackstock and O'Gorman 2014; Judson 2016, p. 93). Of course France in each case was the defining 'Other' and the allied victory achieved in 1814–15 was a further spur to a unified patriotic fervour (even if the post-war economic recession provided a swift diminuendo) (Judson 2016, pp. 97–100).

The Austrian empire, like the British union, emerged from the revolutionary and Napoleonic wars with its conservative character reinforced and with its military and diplomatic reputation riding—in the Austrian case, unrealistically—high. Klemens, Prinz von Metternich (1773–1859) was chancellor of Austria (1821–8) and its foreign minister (1809–48) and has been routinely condemned for presiding over a regime characterized by both a determined social conservatism and a lengthy rearguard action against the liberal and nationalist tendencies of the era. In the years after 1815 Austria was central to the diplomatic calculations of the British foreign secretary and architect of union, Viscount Castlereagh, who—on the basis of overlapping global interests—worked well with Metternich (Bew 2011, p. 522; Bridge 1972, pp. 3–4). At home (and abroad) Metternich elaborated what has been dubbed 'a dubiously principled conservative tradition' using the secret funding and rigorous censorship of the press, the propagation of aristocratic conservative groupings, and some empty rhetorical gestures towards civil rights and nationality (Okey 2001, p. 126). It has certainly been possible to exaggerate this picture and to forget that Austria, thanks in large part to Joseph and Francis, was a Rechtsstaat, and that (even if this had not been the case) it had not the resources to pursue comprehensive repression (Judson 2016, p. 216). But, even so, the state's abnegation of reform—its shift from 'realising an ideal' under Joseph towards mere 'preservation' after 1815—ultimately played into the hands of those very national forces which it also sought to crush: as in Ireland, these now gained strength through the steady accession of social discontents (Judson 2016, p. 154). Little wonder, then, that the Austrian *Vormärz* period (like the years between 1815 and 1829 in Ireland and Britain) has been defined, with some metaphor mixing, both as a time 'when too much water was allowed to run under the bridge'—and as one characterized by 'long decades of ostrich-like government inactivity' (Okey 2001, pp. 119, 155–6).

In 1848 the Habsburg monarchy was, it was said, 'a multitude of Irelands'; like Ireland, the monarchy rose in revolt in 1848—an insurgency which provided certain long-term lessons to those interested in sustaining the complex composite union which it encompassed (Rudolf Kjellén quoted in Beller 1996, pp. 38–9). Though liberalism and nationalism were intertwined in the various revolts of these years, Germans, Slavs, and Magyars had their own conflicting and rival visions of the reformed future, just as with the Catholic and Protestant Irish (Judson 2016, p. 205). In most cases, as with Scots, Irish, and Welsh patriotism within the United Kingdom, these visions were not about separation and independence, but rather about greater autonomy and influence within the overarching structure of the Austrian empire. And, just as some Scots and Welsh (and even Irish) patriots occasionally conceded that their interests were best protected inside a supranational framework, so the ideologues of 1848—such as the great Moravian historian and 'father' of Czech nationalism, František Palacký (1798–1876)—argued not only in national but also often in supranational terms: for Palacký asserting a nationalism meant arguing not for the overthrow of empire, but rather for its (federalist) reformation and preservation (Koralka 2007; Judson 2016, p. 207),

If this were not sufficient evidence for the mediating and binding space available to the crown, then the insurgents were often loath to sever 'the umbilical cord to the [Habsburg] dynasty' (although it is true that in Hungary and

Lombardy this severance actually occurred for a time). Still, opportunities for an historic settlement were also available, with a reformed monarchy together with the equality of languages and nationalities on the table during constitutional discussions at Kremsier, Moravia, in early 1849. But the resurgent forces of the Habsburg state, led by Prince Felix von Schwarzenberg (Minister President 1848–52) crushed this delicate growth with a vengeance—and, while it is impossible to be certain about the precise extent of the opportunities lost, it has been reasonably claimed that these can 'hardly be over-stated' (Okey 2001, pp. 155–6). The history of the United Kingdom in the 19th century, like that of the Habsburg lands, was one characterized by missed opportunity and by an easily underestimated (if sometimes superficially perplexing) loyalty to the ruling house; though on the whole the drift which was so damaging to Austria was less marked and less damaging in Ireland and Scotland.

In many of the union states under review there are perceptible patterns encompassing the successful suppression of nationalist revolt, followed by (what might be described as) a reforming absolutism: there are also discernible patterns of military defeat (or sometimes exhausting and costly victory) followed in turn by major constitutional revision and reform. At the same time, however, it is important to recognize long-term continuities (Judson 2016, pp. 218–21). In Austria the successful (if bloody) struggle against insurgency in 1848–9 underpinned a dangerous tendency for the state to throw punches well above its slowly diminishing weight (even though victory was only really achieved with Russian support). The insurgents' final defeat in August 1849 also ushered in a decade of repressive rule under, first, Schwarzenberg (who died suddenly in 1852), and then Alexander Freiherr von Bach (1813–93). This era has traditionally been defined as 'neo-absolutist', although a more recent generation of scholarship has stressed instead that Bach in particular (who, remarkably, was a veteran of the 1848 rising in Vienna) pursued a partly liberal agenda which he combined with emphatically illiberal throwback policies on religion as well as authoritarian enforcement strategies (Judson 2016, p. 219).

As with Ireland, so across the Austrian empire there were pulses of assimilationist or integrationist activity (Theo Hoppen has identified an integrationist era of British policy in Ireland from the 1820s through to the 1860s: Hoppen 2016). Under Bach a 'unified, uniform and centralised administration' was pursued in the 1850s, with the complete integration of what he was wont to describe provocatively as 'the former kingdom of Hungary' being awarded special attention (Beller 2018, p. 94; Judson 2016, p. 223): 'the former kingdom of Hungary' evokes comparisons with the subtle relegation of Irish and Scots identities through the attempted application of the nomenclature of 'West Britain' and 'North Britain'— and indeed James Wilkie has gone further than this, provocatively suggesting that 'North Britain' was a sort of premonition of 'Ostmark', the nazified version of 'Austria' ('*eine Art Vorecho der 'Ostmark*') (Wilkie 1991, p. 334). As with English in the administration of Ireland, so German was reinforced as the language of imperial Habsburg bureaucracy—but (again, as in Ireland) not with any overtly nationalistic intent, but rather as an expression of 'efficiency' and 'modernity'. Where Ireland differed of course, was in the disproportionate presence of an (Anglican Protestant) religious minority across the administration, but especially in terms of its upper ranks (see e.g. Campbell 2009).

How much the centralization and expansion of the Austrian and British states in the mid and late 19th century mattered to local, rural, communities across central Europe and in the United Kingdom is difficult to gauge. In broad terms the 19th-century expansion of the union state in the United Kingdom has been associated with a sense of a renegotiated bargain over union, and ultimately therefore with different forms of national resistance or push-back (such as, in Scotland, the National Association for the Vindication of Scottish Rights (1853)) (Jackson 2013, pp. 137, 174; Coupland 1954, pp. 281–90). However, detailed work on mid-19th-century Ireland has emphasized the continuing importance of local issues to rural communities who were still often only loosely or inefficiently connected to wider horizons: in this sense the railways were both an agency of nation as well as of union (Hoppen 1984; Lecky 1908, vol. 8, p. 549). The same prioritization appears to be true for Scotland and particularly for Wales, where—though recent scholarship has tended to emphasize the strength of patriotism before the consolidation of radical nonconformist Welshness after 1868—political nationalism was much slower to gain traction than patriotic cultural identities (Cragoe 1996; Morgan 1980, 1981). Similarly, work on the language frontiers of late 19th-century imperial Austria, drawing on nationalist sources, has underlined 'the frequent irrelevance of nationalist identities to rural society', and equally has vigorously questioned whether, in Austria's numerous fluid cultural and language frontier areas, 'their inhabitants ever became national' (Judson 2006, pp. 11, 18; Kuzmany 2016).

In both Ireland and across the Austrian empire the 1850s and 1860s were years of relative economic growth, encouraged by *laissez-faire* strategies, freer trade policies, and infrastructural consolidation (though the fearful human devastation wrought by the Irish famine in the early 1850s and—to a much lesser extent—by Austria's successive wars also need to be kept firmly in mind). In November 1851 the tariff barrier between Austria and Hungary was removed, with general reductions in tariffs following in 1852 and 1856: in 1853 the Austrian empire, through its new commercial treaty with Prussia, was effectively associated with the German Zollverein. Banking and credit were expanded, notably through the creation in 1855 (by Karl Ludwig von Bruck, finance minister between 1855 and 1860) of the new Credit-Anstalt: this in turn fed into investment (or speculation) in infrastructure, and in particular of course the expanding rail network (see section 4.9 for a fuller discussion). Educational reform in the empire delivered secondary and tertiary systems which were primarily German-speaking: in

Ireland the creation of the national schools in 1831, followed by an expansion of university education in 1845 (the Queen's Colleges), created a primarily anglophone educational structure. The emancipation of the Austrian peasantry, which had been an achievement of the 1848 revolutionaries, was confirmed in the era of neo-absolutism; and, while its detailed ramifications varied (given the complexity of the empire) and are sometimes hard to decipher, it is clear that Austrian agriculture was now liberated from many of the restrictions of the *ancien régime*, and was consequently both more 'modern' and more market-driven (Beller 2018, p. 93). Irish agriculture was changing dramatically in the aftermath of the cataclysmic Great Famine: Austrian agriculture was changing in the relatively more benign circumstances of revolution and emancipation.

The key weaknesses in Austria's performance arose directly from those areas where the emperor, Franz Joseph, exercised a particular influence: the army and foreign affairs (Beller 2018, p. 100). The complex balance between the empire's interests and the delicate imperial sense of honour meant that, at the time of the Crimean war (1854–6), Franz Joseph repudiated his Russian friends (who had saved him and his dynasty in 1849), accepting instead what turned out to be a condition of diplomatic isolation. On the other hand, the emperor was quick to respond to perceived insults from (what were thought to be) more manageable neighbours; and in April 1859 he delivered an ultimatum to Piedmont (defeated by the Austrians in 1848), quickly following this up with a declaration of war. In fact the Piedmontese and their French allies achieved bloody victories over the Austrians at Magenta (4 June 1859) and Solferino (24 June); and with these came the loss of Habsburg territory (Lombardy), the wider weakening of the bonds of empire, and a massive diminution of monarchy (not least since Franz Joseph himself had been in command at the second of these battles: Beller 1996, p. 73).

These various disasters generated, in turn, an intense debate about the structure of the Austrian empire, since the centralist and absolutist regime of the 1850s was now militarily and financially (and otherwise) discredited. A provisional set of answers to the questions around the balance between centre and periphery in the empire emerged with the federalist October Diploma (1860) which was soon superseded by the more centralist February Patent (1861): together these delivered an enhanced imperial parliament, the Reichsrat, with powers over taxation, along with provincial assembles and the restitution of Hungarian rights and institutions (Steed 1919, p. 15; Okey 2001, p. 178; Judson 2016, p. 220). With the February Patent the effective constraints on the emperor were tightened. The authority of the Reichsrat was consolidated, though it was vested with the type of 'in' and 'out' arrangement of national representation which would later feature in various British reflections on the challenges of governing their multinational union state: the full Reichsrat, including its 120 Hungarian members, deliberated for the whole empire, while a narrower assembly considered only that business which affected the non-Hungarian half of the realm. In the event, this settlement did not survive the decade; but—however ephemeral in other respects—it marked the final end of the Josephinian attempt to create a more unitary Habsburg state (Beller 2018, p. 110).

It has been said that the constitutional settlement of 1860-1 was loved by German liberals in the empire, and by the empire's financiers, but by few others: it was certainly unloved by the emperor, who preferred a dualist strategy to the prospect of having his imperial and royal authority eroded by German liberal constitutionalism. Equally important, it was also unloved by the bulk of Hungarians, despite its concessions to national feeling. However, further military humiliation—by the Prussians at Königgrätz/Sadowa in 1866—once again raised the question of the shape of empire, and of the relationship between centre and 'periphery'; and it also gave space to those who (for whatever reason) had not fully bought into the earlier settlement. In fact the move towards change had begun before the war, which provided a stimulus rather than a point of origin: from December 1864 Franz Joseph had already been moving towards revising the constitution of 1860-1, not least through the suspension of the February Patent. By 1865 it was clear that the emperor favoured a divided empire and an enhanced monarchy over imperial unity and constricted imperial and royal authority.

The result of these imperial and Hungarian preferences, and of the bleak opportunity created by Königgräz/Sadowa, was the great and influential 'Ausgleich', or compromise, of 1867. This provided a bandage for the divisions of the empire by buying off Hungary through a substantial grant of autonomy, and distributing (and therefore diminishing) the challenges posed by the Slav nationalities between the two components of the redefined empire: Gyula Andrássy (1823-90), soon to be prime minister of Hungary, allegedly epitomized this central idea in saying, ominously, 'you look after your Slavs, and we will look after ours' (quoted often, but see e.g. Beller 2018, p. 120). The Ausgleich agreement identified shared areas between Austria and Hungary—the monarchy (the emperor of Austria was also king of Hungary, and soon to be crowned as such), and defence, finance, and foreign policy, all of which were managed by joint ministries and (somewhat less effectively) by a joint delegation (numbering 60) from the parliaments in Vienna and Budapest (often described, but see e.g. Steed 1919, p. 17; Beller 1996, pp. 94ff.). A crown council, or joint ministerial council, was not an explicit part of the deal, but arose out of its provisions and its operation (including the emperor's prerogatives together with the clunky workings of the delegations). An agreement on the shared ministries meant that Hungary, which was growing in wealth and influence, paid only 30 per cent of their costs, while 'Austria', or Cisleithania, paid the remainder: this quota was, however, subject to decennial revision by deputations from the two parliaments. These periodic negotiations, together (more generally) with the shared institutions of the state (especially the army), provided focuses for smouldering disagreement in the decades ahead. But, in essence, the two principals—the emperor and the Hungarians—had got what they each wanted.

Franz Joseph had effectively elevated the imperial precept of 'divide and rule' onto a continental scale, and not least given that there was now no overarching (and, for the emperor, constricting) Reichsrat for the entire Dual Monarchy; the Hungarians, on the other hand, had achieved a significant measure of autonomy, significant economic and military protection—and all on the cheap. Or, borrowing Steve Beller's pithy summation, 'the problem with the Austro-Hungarian compromise was that it was not so much that the circle was squared as that it was split in two' (Beller 2018, p. 127).

As has already been pointed out, the Ausgleich also provided a point of reference for successive advocates of the reform of the United Kingdom of Great Britain and Ireland, from Gladstone (who carefully perused the intricacies of the new constitution) to both Arthur Griffith and John Redmond (see section 1.6). Writing on the eve of the third Home Rule Bill for Ireland, and operating at a more profound analytical level, R. W. Seton-Watson proceeded somewhat more cautiously. He was a supporter, or rather a critical friend, both of Irish home rule and of the idea of Austria-Hungary; but at the same time he unhesitatingly indicted the legacy of the Ausgleich in the shape of Magyar political, economic, and cultural domination over the Slav peoples of Transleithania (Seton-Watson 1911a, 1912). Opponents of reform (at least in its home rule formulation), like A. V. Dicey, either denied the applicability of the Ausgleich to British and Irish conditions, or instead argued that the ostensible success of the overarching formula masked profound problems in (especially) the Transleithanian detail: that is to say, Hungary may have gotten a good deal from Austria, but Croatia-Slavonia had not fared so well in terms of its settlement with Hungary.

And indeed the Ausgleich did *not* equalize the nations of the Habsburg empire, nor did it end national dominance—and nor was it intended as a visionary document of this kind, any more than were the acts of union of 1707 or 1801. What the Ausgleich did instead was to spread the embrace of domination, which now included Germans, Hungarians, and (to a slighter extent) the Galician Poles and (even more equivocally) the Croats ('you look after your Slavs, and we'll look after ours') (Markovits and Sysyn 1982, p. 91). The 'subject' nationalities included the Czechs and Slovaks of Bohemia, Moravia, and Slovakia, the Ruthenians (Ukrainians) and Romanians of the east, and the Serbs and (the small numbers of) Italians in the south. Or, expressing this another way, 'the centre/periphery dynamic that had, after many decades, led to Compromise with Hungary was not solved; it was just divided in two like the division of a cell' (Beller 2018, p.127).

However, this cellular division of 1867 was not the end of the story; and there were subsequent efforts right through to 1918 either to turn two cells into three (Magyar dualism into Slav trialism), or to change the molecular composition of the Austrian cell altogether (through federalism or consociationalism). The history of the Dual Monarchy was for long defined in terms both of its role as a 'prison of the nations', and—to use the language of the English journalist, Wickham Steed—of its 'foredoomed' failure and collapse on the back of the nationalities question (Steed 1937, pp. vii–x; cf. Steed 1914). Scholars of the Monarchy now seek to achieve a history defined in its own terms—that is to say, divested of ahistorical nationalist presumptions or teleologies (see e.g. King 2002; Judson 2016). But, by extension, it is also possible to read the history of Austria-Hungary as one, not of political morbidity, but rather of a vitality of constitutional thought and experimentation which complemented the wider intellectual life of the empire, and which was on the cusp of success by 1914 (see e.g. Seton-Watson [Scotus viator] 1908, p. 399). The Ausgleich may indeed have multiplied the number of Habsburg 'cells'; but it also created the laboratory space wherein a healthier constitutional life form might well have emerged. This in fact was true, too, for other ostensibly failed unions, such as the United Province of Canada (see section 3.4).

However, this effort was not uniform throughout the two halves of the Monarchy and in Hungary the *idée fixe* was the magyarization of the peoples of Transleithania: if the chief tendency in Austria was towards national equality, then its counterpart in Hungary was towards a uniform national state (Jászi 1929, pp. 283, 298). There was certainly some early evidence of (relatively) generous intentions (expressed originally through leaders like Ferenc Deák and József Eötvös (1813–71) and through measures such as the Nationalities Act (1868) and the *Nagodba* (1868), which ostensibly provided special status for the Croats). However, the Liberal party in Hungary under Kálmán Tisza (1830–1902, and prime minister between 1875 and 1890) soon used the freedom created through the Ausgleich to pursue vigorous policies of magyarization, and to limit relations between Austria and Hungary as far as possible to a union of crowns, or personal union: magyarization encompassed not only nursery and primary schools, where the teaching of Magyar was made compulsory (in 1879 and 1881 respectively), but also local government throughout Transleithania (Steed 1919, pp. 29ff.). Nationalist activism was dealt with through vigorous policing and the no less energetic manipulation of the electoral process—malpractice patiently excavated by Seton-Watson for an anglophone audience through his series of influential studies published before the First World War (Seton-Watson 1908, 1911a, 1911b, 1912).

Comparisons were invoked by contemporaries between these assimilationist, and sometimes oppressive, Magyar nationality policies and those practised elsewhere: 'the policy of Russian tsarism against the Poles, the Finns and Ruthenians; the policy of Prussia against the Poles and Danes; and the policy of feudal England against the Irish reflects the same spirit and methods'—though Jászi (a Calvinist Hungarian of Jewish descent) also argued pointedly 'that they never reached the brutality of the English against the Irish or that of the Prussians against the Poles' (Jászi 1929, pp. 328, 337). But it is noteworthy, especially given the coverage of the present book, that the consolidation of Magyar nationalism in the 19th and early 20th century drew strength, not just from these robust assimilationist strategies, and from the wider political and economic consolidation of Transleithania, but also from outside exemplars of national divergence. Thus, the Irish repeal movement generally 'kindled the fantasy of the struggling nations of the monarchy' (Jászi 1929, pp. 260–1). And the separatist strain within Magyar nationalism looked to the fraught politics of the United Kingdoms of Sweden-Norway; and the final fracturing of this union in 1905 clearly had 'a great repercussion'—and brought great encouragement (Jászi 1929, pp. 181, 364; see section 3.3).

It should perhaps be said at this stage that part of the success of magyarization came not just from efficient enforcement, but also from unenforced assimilation. The economic growth of Transleithania was associated with the consolidation of the unitary Magyar ideal, with the expansion of towns and cities which were hotspots of voluntary magyarization (Okey 2001, p. 312). In general, too, there was much Jewish assimilation into the overarching Magyar identity (as illustrated in fact by Jászi and his family). But, above all, Transleithania was held together by a potent set of Magyar national myths (which the overarching Ausgleich could not match)—of an ancient and sanctified, or apostolic, monarchy, the crown of St Stephen, an ancient constitution (dating back to 1222), and of a relentless quest for freedom from the oppression of more powerful neighbours. Indeed, Magyars turned easily to the English for what was seen as an equivalent and robust history of libertarian struggle—an identification which had a physical manifestation in terms of the neo-gothic Hungarian parliament building (1885–1904) and its echoes of Westminster (Okey 2001, p. 314).

If there was a dominant ethnicity and related language community in Transleithania (analogous to Irish Protestants for part of the union period), then there was equally a dominant social caste—the upper gentry and nobility (just as there was in Ireland for much of the 19th century). One clear aspect of each of these dominations was that some of the key agencies for modernization and union within Transleithania—trade and transportation—were effectively harnessed by either the dominant nationality, or the dominant caste, or both. Thus, the developing rail networks were specifically designed to serve the economic needs of Hungary, rather than either those of the Croats and other non-dominant nations—or for that matter those of the wider Austro-Hungarian empire (Seton-Watson 1911a, pp. 329, 334). Equally skewing in its impact was the domination of agriculture by a 'feudal' coalition of gentry and nobles, together with a protectionist regime which boosted their incomes at the combined price of inflated living costs for the poor as well as an increasingly lop-sided economy (Jászi 1929, pp. 201, 417, 453). The destabilizing effects of this were clear (Jászi called these the *'morbus latifundii'* of the Dual Monarchy); and they were compounded (as in the Irish case) by growing emigration and the creation of diasporic communities and networks, particularly in North America, who were generally no friends to the existing dualist order.

The tendency, therefore, in Transleithania was towards a unitary Magyar state, with pressures urging conformity and assimilation. One partial exception, however, was the kingdom of Croatia-Slavonia—the 'Triune Kingdom'—which (despite Dicey's sneering dismissal) was widely seen as presenting clear lessons for the Irish and British home rulers of 1912–14 (Seton-Watson 1911a, pp. 66–71; Seton-Watson 1912, p. 68; Dicey 1911, p. 153). Croatia had a form of 'home rule' within Transleithania, embodied in the agreement, or *Nagodba*, of 1868. This allowed the kingdom (at least nominally) an enhanced autonomy over domestic matters through its diet (the *Sabor*), together with an 'in and out' arrangement of representatives in the parliament at Budapest (depending on the issues under discussion): it also served to relaunch the role of viceroy, or *Ban*. But the home rule settlement had in fact been vitiated from the start, based (as it was) upon acceptance by a diet 'which owed its composition to an illegal franchise and to gross electoral corruption', each of which delivered a majority for the local unionist party (that is to say, the party seeking greater alignment with Budapest) (Seton-Watson 1912, p. 68). Moreover, the Croatian *Ban* generally represented the interests both of the dominant nationality and of these unionists—and in the case of Count Károly Khuen-Hédérváry (1849–1918), in office between 1883 and 1903, this was done with a particular vigour. Comparisons have been invoked between Khuen-Hédérváry and the British Conservative party's administration of Wales: the *Ban* knew Croatian, 'but was otherwise barely more Croat in feeling that Conservative Secretaries of State for Wales have been Welsh' (Okey 2001, p. 328). Khuen-Hédérváry certainly pursued the kinds of imperial policy of *divide et impera* which were a marked feature of British government in Ireland (and also, allegedly, of royal government in Sweden-Norway), and indeed he was associated with 'horsewhip and oats' strategies which bear comparison (both in name and content) with the constructive unionism ('kicks and ha'pence') practised in Ireland by successive British administrations, but especially at the end of the 19th century (Jászi 1929, p. 370; Jorgenson 1935, pp. 270–1; Curtis 1963; Gailey 1987; Hoppen 2016). Just as the stability of British rule in Ireland depended upon (and often received) local support and local agency, and just as these were periodically threatened by broad coalitions of dissent, so the perennial fear of the Habsburgs and their agents was that 'if the Croats were driven by reactionary Magyar policy into the arms of Belgrade [Serbia], then the position of the monarchy would be one of real danger' (Seton-Watson [Scotus viator] 1908, p. 415). In sum, the suppurating problems of Croatian home rule demonstrated to a contemporary like R. W. Seton-Watson that any scheme of home rule required both the approval of the 'vast majority' of those affected as well as the 'strict' cooperation of the more powerful partner nation. Moreover, financial relationships had to be tightly nailed down from the start; and any governor or viceroy had to be much more than the agent of the dominant power. At the same time, however, the Croatian 'in and out' arrangement *had* in fact operated quite well; and a consequent lesson for the Irish and for the British was that, while there would be difficulties, Irish representation in an overarching federal-style parliament could be made to work—if it was carefully defined as part of a coherent wider scheme (Seton-Watson 1912, p. 68).

Cisleithania was the province of German Austrian domination and the non-dominant nationalities fared somewhat better here than their counterparts in the east. Indeed, Cisleithania and Transleithania are sometimes seen as complementary or opposite models of governance (even though bound together within—what at least the Austrians regarded as—the one *Kaiserreich*): certainly the centralist and assimilationist and oligarchic model pursued in the east was not systematically shared in the west. Here instead an array of sometimes radical reform proposals was broached—from informal autonomy (exercised by Galicia's Polish nobility), federalism and 'trialism' (sought for Bohemia), through occupation and annexation (Bosnia) to the partitionist and consociational models of the last years of the empire (Moravia, Bukovina, Galicia) (see e.g. Leslie 1991, p. 136; Stourzh 2007, pp. 277ff.). Indeed, it is tempting to suggest that, just as the freshly minted Ausgleich presented a model for (some) Britons at the height of their empire, so the autumn of the Dual Monarchy might yet provide (federal and consociational) models and stimulus for—what some have seen as—the 21st-century autumn of the United Kingdom.

Various wider perspectives on the centre/periphery relationship in Cisleithania are sustainable and represent a starting point for discussion, before the various models themselves are examined. There is certainly a theme of pragmatic, opportunistic management, as evidenced by the lengthy ascendancy of Count Eduard Taaffe, whose clericalist coalition or 'Iron Ring' dominated Austrian politics between 1879 and 1893 (see e.g. Jenks 1965, pp. 25, 304ff.; Deak 2015, pp. 198–9). Taaffe elevated the psychologies of partial reinforcement into a strategy of government, and indeed it has been said that he did not so much seek to appease his various nationalist partners as to keep them 'just interested enough' to garner their support: he himself famously talked about the task of ruling Austria as consisting of keeping its component nationalities in a condition of 'well-tempered discontent' (often quoted but see Cornwall 2002, p. 48). He certainly offered concessions to Czechs, Poles, Croats, Slovenes, and to the Catholic Right, and tolerated too the consolidation of a political anti-semitism (Beller 1996, p. 121; Okey 2001, p. 270; Deak 2015, pp. 204–5). This combination of pragmatic concession to nationalism, dependence upon nationalist votes, luck (in terms of timings), and general *fortwursteln* (or muddling along), are all reminiscent of certain types of British, especially British Liberal, approach to Ireland, and in particular those of the Asquith government, whose pragmatic and opportunistic—'wait and see'—tactics were in place in the years before 1914 (see e.g. Okey 2001, p. 276; Jackson 2004).

Taaffe, too—like Asquith with Ireland in 1914—was moving towards partition as a means of dealing with the particularly fraught national problems of Bohemia (which, it has rightly been said, 'bore some resemblance to Britain's Irish problem'):

Germans, who were roughly one-third of the population of Bohemia, wanted to divide Bohemia in two, but in 1890 Taaffe secured (what looked for a while like) an agreement—the *Punktace*—on the basis of apportioning the crownland into German and Czech administrative and judicial areas (Cornwall 2002, pp. 63, 79; Beller 2018, p. 185; Zách 2021, pp. 55ff.). Discussion over the division of Ireland on the eve of the First World War was part, therefore, of a much more complex array of similar discussions than the current literature fully acknowledges (including both Fraser 1984; Jackson 2004).

Another, and related, style of imperial government was pursued by the liberal Ernest von Koerber (1850–1919), who was Minister President of Cisleithania between 1900 and 1904 (and again briefly at the end of 1916) (see Deak 2015, pp. 232ff.). Koerber served mostly in the context of a suspended Reichsrat, and survived by doing deals in the Imperial Council: his 'system', which laid stress upon the initiative and centrality of the bureaucracy, was to encourage the different parties and interests to trade with the government rather than with each other—'a classic imperial model of "divide and rule"' (Beller 1996, pp. 161–4). Here again there are parallels to be drawn with Ireland under the union—where the British administration (as with Koerber) tended to act more as 'arbiter than mediator', and where the 'aim of the game was more to put one over on the opponent than to come to compromise with him' (Beller 1996, pp. 161–4). Under this model, as applied whether in Ireland or in Koerber's Cisleithania, there was little incentive for the parties to negotiate with each other.

Related to this is the wider picture of repeated well-intentioned and inventive, if utterly bungled, opportunities for agreement, rather than (as in the east) one of energetic—often ruthless—linguistic, cultural, and political homogenization. To that extent the pattern of opportunity and heightened expectation, together with the activity of key veto-players (sometimes, though not always, from the dominant ethnicity) are again reminiscent of the political culture of Ireland in the later decades of the union—when political initiatives designed to improve and bolster the existing constitutional relationships were either lost or otherwise vitiated by unionists who wanted things to stay the same, but who did not recognize that they had to change in order to do so. In these (and indeed other) respects, Irish unionists bear comparison to the German-Austrians of late 19th-century Bohemia (Wright 1988; Zách 2021, pp. 55ff.).

This was broadly true for the theme of trialism or federalism, which is the first of the great areas of constitutional experimentation which requires some consideration (see also section 5.4). Thus, the effort—pursued in 1871 by the Minister President of Cisleithania, Karl Graf von Hohenwart (1824–99), and his Commerce Minister, Albert Schäffle (1831–1903)—to redefine the position of Czechs within the government of the empire was shot down in flames very largely by an informal alliance of the empire's dominant nationalities (often discussed—see e.g. Deak 2015, p. 184). The core idea, contained in the Fundamental Articles (1871), was to grant Bohemia a measure of autonomy similar to that enjoyed by Hungary, and with the Czech language occupying an equivalent position to German. The reform has been seen as an attempted movement away from the dualism of the Ausgleich towards 'trialism' or a federalization of the Austro-Hungarian empire; and, as such, while Czechs saw it as a substantial restitution of their 'ancient liberties', it also threatened to undermine the key beneficiaries from that later compromise (Sked 1989, p. 219). Both Germans and Magyars responded with defensiveness and antagonism—just as the beneficiaries of the Irish union vigorously resisted its modification. It has been rightly argued that, with the failure of the Fundamental Articles and the Hohenwart-Schäffle ministry, there 'ended the most ambitious attempt between 1867 and 1918 to respond to the non-dominant peoples' dissatisfaction with the Dualist system' (Okey 2001, p. 222).

A second, and even more resonant, exercise of the veto by the dominant German communities of Cisleithania occurred in 1897, during the tenure of the Galician Pole, Kasimir Graf von Badeni (1846–1909) as Minister President (1895–7). Badeni's ministry sought through several radical initiatives to counterbalance the centrifugal forces affecting the Austro-Hungarian empire: the introduction of a cautious element of wider suffrage for the lower house of the Reichsrat (through the creation of a new, and open, electoral cohort or curia) helped to channel social and political grievances in ways which were not accepted in the Hungarian east (Cornwall 2002, pp. 79–83). Moreover, in April 1897 Badeni sought to address Czech national aspirations by placing the two languages, Czech and German, in a position of equality within the government service in Bohemia (not, in the first instance, Moravia)—a reform which threatened in effect to create an overwhelmingly Czech provincial bureaucracy since Germans were less likely to be bilingual and therefore more likely now to be excluded from government employment (Deak 2015, pp. 224–5). The Czechs were certainly hardline; but they were also seeking in the first instance (like many Irish home rulers) to reform the empire in their own interests, rather than to comprehensively overthrow it (Sked 1989, p.222; Beller 1996, p. 150). As with the failed Fundamental Articles of 1871, so with Badeni's language decrees, it was German mobilization which threatened more immediate instability than radical Czech grievance (just as, again, vigorous unionist mobilization against home rule often threatened more fundamental subversion than home rule itself): street protests, riots, parliamentary obstruction, and general mayhem in the Reichsrat—all served to underline the impossibility of reconciling a modernized vision of a multinational empire with local interests together with the still potent Josephinian model of monoglot centralism. But Badeni, who saw clearly the long-term military and other dangers of the empire's ethnic cauldron, now himself appeared to be one of the ingredients of instability; he was removed in November 1897, and was followed in 1899 by the revocation of his language decrees. His failure looms large in narratives of the later Habsburg empire (Okey 2001, p. 308; Cornwall 2002, pp. 82–3). Even those scholars who have otherwise been keen to emphasize the sturdiness of 'the Austrian idea' have conceded that 'the Badeni crisis constituted a critical point in Austrian parliamentary history'—while also ultimately demonstrating the malleability and negotiability of Austria's institutions (Deak 2015, pp. 225–6; Judson 2016, p. 314; Beller 2018, p. 191).

'What was left of political multinationalism' was briefly disinterred by Max Freiherr von Beck (1854–943), Minister President of Cisleithania (1906–8). Beck appointed German, Czech, and Polish deputies to his cabinet in what he called '*eine Ausgleichskonferenz in Permanenz*': he sought, too, to extend the achievement of Badeni and institute universal male suffrage for the Reichsrat. But, just as mediating between the fears and aspirations of Germans and Czechs in Bohemia had broken Hohenwart and Badeni, so too this negotiation proved too much for Beck, who was already balancing much else (Okey 2001, p. 352; Beller 2018, pp. 201–3).

The last dregs of 'multinationalism' may have been drained under Beck; but there was an additional theme of governance which characterized (what we now know were) the last years of the Dual Monarchy, and which offered (as in Canada in the 1840s) the possibility of further renewal and longevity: this was (broadly) consociationalism, or power-sharing and the construction of institutions which were designed to diminish the possibility of communal conflict (see section 3.4). These, it has to be said, often involved the institutionalization of different forms of social pillarization (as in the Dutch case in the 19th century) or even partition. But they also represented an imaginative effort to reconcile the demands of rival nationalities with those of the supranational state. The losers in each case were, perhaps, those who were left out of the reckoning—namely those citizens who did not see themselves primarily in national terms, or whose loyalties where fluid, multiple, or indeed dynastic.

The idea of using individuals rather than territories to shape the structures of governance had various points of origin within the Dual Monarchy, but the work of the Austro-Marxists, Karl Renner (1870–1950), who was a German Moravian, and Otto Bauer (1881–1938), a Viennese German, was of particular importance (Bauer 1907; Renner 1902, 1906; Burgess 2006, p. 142). These formed part of the intellectual background to three major experiments in non-territorial autonomy conducted in various parts of Cisleithania in the decade before the First World War: the Moravian compromise (1905), and the settlements in both Bukovina (1909) and Galicia (1914). In Moravia tensions between German and Czech speakers were mitigated through a new provincial constitution (in 1905) which allowed for nationally determined electoral rolls, with the members of the Moravian diet being assigned to one of three categories (noble, German, Czech). Every voter was defined, not just (as in the past) by his electoral curia, but now, in the aftermath of these reforms, by his nationality. Citizens initially had the right to decide their own nationality; but, after a decision by the Austrian Supreme

Court in 1910, in effect it was open to others as well to make this determination. The 'nation' now had the right to claim its own members (Kuzmany 2016).

Bukovina, on the eastern borders of the Monarchy, was widely regarded as its most linguistically mixed province, and the settlement of 1909–10 reflected this complexity. Here there were in fact five different national electoral rolls, and five different types of member of the local diet. Unlike in Moravia, nobles were 'nationalized'; unlike in Moravia, however, no proportionality was applied to public appointments (see the eulogistic assessment in Leslie 1991). The settlements in Moravia and Bukovina formed, in turn, the basis for a deal in Galicia between the dominant Poles and the Ruthenians, with the related creation of Polish and Ruthenian electoral districts and electoral rolls. But, though agreed, the settlement was not implemented, for the outbreak of war intervened (Kuzmany 2016). It was clear, however, that with these three agreements—together with three other attempts along the same lines in Bosnia (1910) (where religion was the critical arbiter of identity), Budejovice (1914), and Bohemia (1914)—the concepts of legal personality rather than territoriality were now being deployed as the favoured panacea for the ailments of the multinational state (Kuzmany 2016). This, in turn, gives some traction to the argument that (as with home rule and Redmondite nationalism in Ireland) the 'nationalities question' in the Dual Monarchy (and indeed in the United Kingdom) was capable of solution—even as late as 1914 (Stourzh 2007, p. 177).

Count Alois Lexa von Aehrenthal (1854–1912), the Monarchy's foreign minister (1906–12), once pointedly remarked to Josef Redlich that 'it is very difficult to improve the condition of the monarchy peacefully' (quoted in Beller 2018, p. 244). International relations and military action were of course vital to the formation and working of the different national relationships and settlements which comprised the Dual Monarchy—and this broaches one final set of means by which the Monarchy approached the management of its nationalities: diplomacy and warfare, and in particular the occupation and annexation of Bosnia. The ethnic tensions of the great Austro-Hungarian 'union' had profound implications within the global and diplomatic arena—which in turn ricocheted back on the empire itself: these connections were by no means unique to the Dual Monarchy—and indeed (as has been stressed) with all these great multinational 'unions', foreign affairs were intimately and reciprocally linked with their birth, survival, and (sometimes) their demise. In particular, however, problems were frequently either exacerbated by, or arose from, diasporic national communities, or—more specifically—irredenta, lands and communities within the Monarchy which were claimed by outside nation states. Defeat at the hands of the French and Piedmontese in 1859 had lost Austria the crownland of Lombardy and this, together with the subsequent loss of Venetia, facilitated the creation of the new kingdom of Italy and effectively ended Austrian influence on the Italian peninsula. But there remained an Italian irredenta in Istria, and in the Littoral, the *österreichisches Küstenland*, on the north-east shores of the Adriatic. Similarly, the empire had lost the leadership of the German states to Prussia even before Königgrätz/Sadowa—and there were now elements within the German population of Cisleithania (led by Georg von Schönerer) who increasingly looked, after 1871, to Berlin rather than Vienna. German Austria itself (or at any rate parts of it) was in danger of becoming another of the Monarchy's numerous and troublesome irredentas.

This left the Balkans, where the Monarchy (despite its best efforts at division) faced the increasing unity of Croats and Serbs in Croatia-Slavonia as well as (from 1903 onwards) an increasingly difficult relationship with Serbia itself. The troubled condition of Croatia-Slavonia, combined with the mounting threat posed by Serbia, encouraged the thought that diplomacy and war might be used to mitigate some of these challenges; and indeed Aehrenthal and the officials of the Ballhausplatz dreamt of thereby securing a form of trialism—a southern Slav territory, firmly under Habsburg suzerainty, and delivering the Monarchy's domination of the Balkans. These dreams were made easier by the fact that the former great power in the Balkans, the Ottoman empire, was in apparently terminal decline, and did not present the same kind of military or political threat as those supplied by the other European empires. The formal annexation of Bosnia Herzegovina in 1908, and its incorporation into the empire as an Austrian and Hungarian condominium, was a ruthless diplomatic coup, which simultaneously gave the impression of great power status while being in reality an expression of weakness and internal threat (see Figure 3.2). The annexation certainly destabilized some of the Monarchy's international relationships: the Russians believed that they had been conned, and British opinion was souring, partly because the annexation was followed by patently unfair treason trials in Agram/Zagreb in 1908–9, and partly because it was accompanied by a torrent of work from R. W. Seton-Watson heavily critical of Magyar policies against the Slavs (this in turn prepared the ground for an even more coruscating wartime literature) (see e.g. Seton-Watson 1908, 1911a; also e.g. Gayda 1915; Dickinson-Berry 1918). But, more immediately important even than these Great Power issues, the annexation accelerated an already decaying relationship with Serbia, which—in the aftermath of the two Balkan wars (1912, 1913)—was growing both in territory and clout: it also further challenged and enflamed the delicate condition of Croatia-Slavonia (since Croats and Serbs were simultaneously an important presence in the newly annexed provinces). And it was of course a Bosnian Serb, Gavrilo Princip (1894–1918), a Yugoslav nationalist seeking liberation from Austria, who fired the critical shots at Sarajevo on 28 June 1914 (see, generally, Okey 2007).

In a famously provocative assessment, Alan Sked has argued that the Habsburg monarchy deliberately started a world war in 1914 rather than compromise: 'starting or being prepared to start wars had become a Habsburg habit in the 19th century...and what failed [in 1914] was Habsburg statecraft' (Sked 1989, p. 269;

see also Sked 2014). While, in the immediate prelude to Sarajevo, it does not appear that the Ballhausplatz was focusing on plans for an offensive war against Serbia, such a conflict had clearly been on the cards during the Balkan wars; and in 1914 there were indisputably powerful hawks in the General Staff (distinguished by 'an unmitigated belief in the superiority of the offensive') and elsewhere at the apex of Habsburg society (see Günther Kronenbitter and Alma Hannig's view in Geppert et al. 2015, pp. 195, 246–7). Others have suggested that in the years before 1914 Habsburg strategists had come to the bleak conclusion that only the convincing threat of war made any impression within Europe, and that they therefore bought into a 'disturbing tendency to resort to militarised diplomacy' (F. R. Bridge's view in Cornwall 2002, p. 15). In any event, if the outbreak of the First World War was indeed a reflection of the failure of 'Habsburg statecraft', then this failure was further mirrored in its development and indeed its conclusion. If the empire started a war against Serbia in July 1914, fearing its increasing importance as a focus for southern Slav irredentism, then, as the conflict progressed, many of the other old national difficulties came home to roost (as indeed was the case in Ireland, and with Irish nationalism, when the United Kingdom and the British empire went to war) (see also section 6.7 for a fuller comparative discussion).

There are in fact wider debates among Habsburg historians, not so much about the overall contribution of the war to Austria-Hungary's fall (this is broadly accepted as decisive), as about the relative importance of internal and external factors during the conflict, and also, relatedly, about its critical tipping points (Cornwall 2002, pp. 167ff.). On the whole, however, it seems impossible to fully separate the 'internal' from the 'external', both since the 'nationalities' questions were tied up (as has been seen) with questions of diapora and irredenta and since the internal prestige of the dynasty itself had long been tied to external claims of dominance, and traditions of warfare within Italy and Germany. Historians also effectively look (as with their narratives of Ireland, the war, and the union) to different phases of the conflict, and in particular to its last year, as the last chance saloon of the Monarchy's survival. If the impact of war ultimately proved fatal for both Austria-Hungary and for the first iteration of the United Kingdom, then that terminal morbidity was only really apparent in each case after 1916–17.

The initial outings of the imperial and royal army in 1914–15 were certainly disastrous, with a humiliatingly unsuccessful invasion of Serbia in 1914, and successive defeats at the hands of the Russians in 1915, including at the battle of Lemberg/Lviv together with the surrender of the Galician stronghold of Premissel/Przemysl in March (Stone 1975; Watson 2019). The Italians, encouraged by these wobbles, entered the war against the Austrians in May 1915 and they too achieved some initial advances. The consequences of these early setbacks in terms of men and matériel were longlasting. But the Central Powers recovered their position in the summer of 1915: by the end of that year the Austro-Hungarian army had overrun Serbia, and in early 1916 they were pushing onwards towards the conquest of Montenegro and Albania. Another turning point ensued, however, in the summer of 1916. Feldmarschall Franz Graf Conrad von Hötzendorf (1852–1925), Chief of the General Staff (1906–17), whose preoccupation with Serbia in 1914 had facilitated the first Russian advances in Galicia, similarly focused now on the Italian front rather than the east, where the Russians achieved a second great breakthrough in Galicia in July 1916 (see e.g. Sondhaus 2000, pp. 188, 243–4). These renewed defeats pushed the Monarchy further into the hands of its predominant German partner, which in turn allowed for a recovery of the situation by the beginning of 1917.

Superficially the balance sheet of war now, in the winter of 1917–18, looked more encouraging. By late 1917 Russia was effectively out of the conflict (in the aftermath of the October revolution), as was Romania (which had joined the Allied cause in October 1916): on 24 October 1917 the Italians had been bloodily defeated at Caporetto. But the costs of transient success for the Monarchy by the beginning of 1918 were scarcely less than those of defeat. Temporary victory in these terms meant substituting the military threat of imperial Russia for the ideological threat posed by its revolutionary successor. It meant, too, accepting the overlordship of an ally rather than that threatened by its enemies. Austria-Hungary entered the last year of the war with its room for manoeuvre fatally limited, not just by familiar constraints like those applied by the Magyar elite, but also now by the intractability of its German master.

Issues of nationality had for long been a subterranean feature of the imperial and royal army, but they became ever more exposed as the war developed, and as its costs accrued, and—especially—as the numbers of conscripts grew. There was some variation across the provinces of the Monarchy. In Trentino patriotic Austrianism was in the ascendant, and it has been calculated that around 60,000 served in the Austro-Hungarian army, as opposed to the 687 who embraced the Italian cause: in the Littoral the comparable figures were around 60,000 who joined the Habsburg armies, with no more than 1,600 or 1,700 Italian volunteers (Cole 2014, pp. 314–15). Both northern and southern Slav conscripts in the imperial army often proved unreliable, though it is true that some caution is required in the light of later 'loyalist' readings and blame-games, and wilder narratives of mass desertion. Still, there were ten times more deserters from the Habsburg than from the Hohenzollern armies, and 40,000 fought in the Czech Brigade for the Entente and against the Monarchy and the other Central Powers—as at the battle of Zborov, in Galicia, in July 1917, their first significant outing: all this stands in contradistinction, say, to the overwhelming loyalty of the Catholic Irish troops in the United Kingdom army, very few of whom were lured to the German cause (Deák 1990, p. 195; Beller 2018, p. 264). The disproportionately high levels of casualty among certain of the empire's nationalities reopened ethnic jealousies, and stimulated both rage and allegations of deliberate strategic bias, as was also sometimes the case among the Irish, Scots, and Australians (one million in total died fighting for Austria-Hungary, and 1.7 million were missing or wounded) (Deák 1990, p. 193).

But the war was also eventually lost on the home fronts. The fundamental issue was that some of the historic saving graces of the Monarchy—its regional and liberal inflections—were now, as in the United Kingdom, largely eliminated with the onset of the conflict, to be replaced by centralism and (sometimes) by militarism (Cornwall 2002, p. 69). The assumption of military control in Cisleithania, where Conrad was 'virtual dictator of the Monarchy', brought the eclipse of the Rechtsstaat; and (as with similar British measures in Ireland) this tended to widen the distance between the state and its citizens, and especially where there was already a gulf created by nationality (Beller 2018, p. 250; Cole 2014, pp. 317–18). The Reichsrat lay in suspension until 1917: the Hungarian parliament continued to operate, but in much more restricted conditions. Large swathes of Cisleithania were designated as 'war zones', wherein the military authorities exercised overwhelming control. Some nationalities (Serbs, Ruthenes, Italians) were deemed to be unreliable in their loyalty or (as soldiers) in their determination to fight, and these tended to feel the weight of the military regime (whether in terms of arrests or—increasingly—executions). The infrastructure of the Monarchy was largely commandeered by the military, with an inevitable impact upon constitutional rights: a War Surveillance Department policed the civilian population in Cisleithania, with large numbers of arrests especially in those areas characterized by national unrest in the years before the war. There was also the commandeering and disruption of civilian supply chains: shortages and, as the war developed, starvation ensued. Scholarship on Vienna after 1914 has underlined the extent to which war precipitated a 'discrediting' of the Habsburgs at home, in the imperial capital, where the population looked locally (to government and national and ethnic rivals, rather than external enemies) for scapegoats at a time of threatened starvation. In particular these shortages reopened the animus between the two halves of the Dual Monarchy, with the Hungarians blamed by the Austrians for hostility and self-interest in the matter of critical food supplies (see e.g. Cornwall 2002, p. 186). Overall, it has been persuasively suggested that, for the Monarchy, 'the collapse was even more deeply internal than previously imagined' (Healy 2004, pp. 300–1).

The death of Franz Joseph in November 1916 simultaneously brought the removal of a central unifying factor in the Monarchy as well as the accession of a (relatively) more progressive and unstuffy emperor, Karl (1887–1922), who had greater federalist and peace-making sympathies (Cornwall 2002, pp. 169–70). But his youth (he was 29 when crowned), his inexperience, his indecisiveness, the wider dependence of his armies (and eventually the Monarchy itself) on German support, all subverted any substantial influence that he might have exercised (see e.g. Cornwall 2002, pp. 42, 169). Moreover, the challenges which Karl faced had for long confounded much more acute, slippery, and ruthless intelligences than his (as with the marmoreal opposition of the Magyar political classes to any programme of federalization) (see Figures 3.3, 3.4).

It was also the case that, with the apparent liberalization which characterized Karl's brief reign, the de Tocqueville paradox kicked in—namely that the regime became yet more vulnerable as it sought to reform itself (cf. de Tocqueville 1856). The demands of the different nationalities grew more strident, and were given increasing credibility both by the hardening attitude of the Allies and, ultimately, by the actions of the Monarchy itself. The Allies shifted ground in 1918 from considering a comprehensive rebooting of the Dual Monarchy to support for its thorough-going dismemberment—this partly in the light of growing Austro-Hungarian subservience to Germany (signalled in particular by a humiliating meeting between Karl and Kaiser Wilhelm II at Spa, Belgium, in May 1918). Already in June 1918 the Allies recognized the Czech National Council as a foundation for a Czechoslovak national government spanning northern Slavdom: they would soon extend a similar recognition to the Yugoslav national committee, representing the southern Slavs. On 9 August 1918 the British recognized that the Czechoslovaks were fellow 'Allies' in the struggle against the Central Powers (Cornwall 2002, p. 178).

As with British efforts to take control of a dizzyingly swift pace of reform in the Ireland of 1918–20, so Karl, similarly behind the curve, sought to offer a comprehensive federalization of Cisleithania (with autonomous Romanian and Ruthenian national councils) through his Manifesto of 16 October 1918 (see e.g. Herwig 1997, p. 436). But he was outpaced by the speed of events both on the military and domestic fronts—and in any event the Manifesto has been seen as much as a 'death warrant' as a remedy: it was certainly directed much more towards American opinion than to any internal constituency (again, as with successive British initiatives in Ireland during the war). The Austrian war effort was now disintegrating, while at home the grip of the regime was further loosening. Karl's Manifesto, which was accompanied by renewed efforts towards a negotiated peace, persuaded neither the Allies—nor indeed the different national councils (which were emerging partly out of the lower house of the Reichsrat). Amongst the wider nationalities of the Monarchy, those (particularly the Hungarians) who had historically been most invested in dualism were no less dismissive (Cornwall 2002, p. 69). On 21 October Woodrow Wilson responded to Karl by effectively sanctioning the dissolution of empire through his support for the creation of independent Czechoslovak and Yugoslav states (Cornwall 2002, p. 192). This, together with the collapse of the Monarchy's Italian front, supplied a final death sentence.

Revolution at the end of October brought independence and the creation of a Hungarian People's Republic; and with these came a formal repudiation of the Ausgleich. Similarly, on 28 October, a Czechoslovak republic was proclaimed in

Prague: on 29 October an autonomous State of the Slovenes, Croats, and Serbs was launched in Zagreb, soon to be followed by unification with Serbia (forming, from 1 December, the Kingdom of Serbs, Croats, and Slovenes, the precursor to Yugoslavia). On 30 October the German deputies of the Cisleithanian Reichsrat, acting as a provisional National Assembly for a new German Austria, passed a republican constitution. Once Karl had accepted the inevitable, renouncing his imperial powers on 11 November, the way was open for the formalization of the new republic of German Austria (on 12 November). Fundamentally, as Mark Cornwall has observed, 'during the war the Austro-Hungarian authorities [had] lost the battle for hearts and minds to those who believed in new state structures and new forms of government' (Cornwall 2000, p. 443). This was in fact the same fatal loss as that incurred by the otherwise victorious United Kingdom state in Ireland during the 1914–18 war.

However with the Dual Monarchy, as ever, there were paradoxes. As late as December 1917, whatever its crumbling political condition, and allowing for the critical support (in fact ascendancy) of the Germans, the Monarchy had achieved most of its war aims: Romania, Russia, and Serbia had all been defeated, and Italy looked for a time to be on its last legs (Deák 1990, p. 192; cf. Jászi 1929, p. 23). Even *very* late in the Habsburg day, the spring of 1918, there was still some support among some 'nationalities' for greater autonomy within an imperial and royal superstructure (see e.g. Cornwall 2002, pp. 189–90). In death, as in life, therefore, the Habsburgs put up a good show: but, then, this (and the ruthless desire to do so) had for long been a major part of their problems.

3.6. Conclusion: After Union

All of the unions considered within this chapter were closely interlinked with those of the United Kingdom of Great Britain and Ireland. The strength and survival of the Austrian empire after 1815 was, as has been shown, a diplomatic objective of the British foreign secretary and architect of the Irish union, Viscount Castlereagh, for whom Austria (and indeed the wider notion of composite monarchy or union) were central complements to his European and global strategies. Castlereagh and his lieutenants were also influences, sometimes critically so, within the construction of the United Kingdom of the Netherlands, and the United Kingdoms of Sweden-Norway. There were numerous personal interconnections between these polities and the shaping of union in Canada in 1838–40; and, here again, the influence of the Scottish and Irish unions had a bearing upon arguments for (and indeed occasionally against) the export of legislative union elsewhere. All of these unions, with the exception of the Netherlands, ultimately exercised a reciprocal influence upon the United Kingdom, in so far as their 'success' served as an exemplar for those at the end of the 19th century who sought its reform or, indeed, its overthrow. But even the failed Netherlands was hotly debated by Irish and British commentators in an age when the secession of the Belgians appeared to have an analogue in the interest of the Irish in secession through repeal.

Several of the unions considered within this, and the preceding, chapters ultimately collapsed in violence. The United Kingdom of the Netherlands ended in the wake of the Belgian revolution, while both the Dual Monarchy and the United Kingdom of Great Britain and Ireland dissolved either in the immediate context of the First World War or of associated military and paramilitary challenges thereafter. On the other hand, with the United Kingdoms of Sweden-Norway and the United Province of Canada there was a smooth transition towards, respectively, separation and fully sovereign statehood and a reformulated union in the shape of confederation.

The rest of the book, in moving away from the individual case studies, is devoted to a thematic reflection on the explanations for the fate of these various unions, and on the institutions and issues tending towards their survival and failure. But, for the moment, it is enough to observe that in all of these cases, with the possible exception of the Netherlands, there were cultures of mediation and arbitration, sometimes well-developed, which *could have* delivered peaceful endings or transitions, and which—in the case of Sweden-Norway and Canada—actually helped to do so. Even with the Netherlands contemporary observers, including those sympathetic to Belgium, were often careful to argue in favour of the contingencies which delivered secession late in the day—and to argue against any thought of a pre-ordained dissolution of the union (see e.g. White 1835). In Cisleithania, in the Dual Monarchy, numerous elaborate power-sharing settlements were activated or proposed in the last decade of its existence; while in the United Kingdom there were earnest discussions on federalization and on home rule, each of which was well advanced at the time of the Irish war of independence and the final dissolution of union. In Sweden-Norway the 90 years of union were characterized by periodic arbitration over a succession of questions, and—while there was occasional belligerence—the final divorce of the two kingdoms was, in consequence, relatively amicable. The Canadian act of union was associated with an early form of consociationalism, apparent both in ministerial power-sharing and in the double majority system; and the end of union, a diminuendo, was eased by an associated and powerful culture of arbitration.

All of these 'united kingdoms' bequeathed complex, sometimes bleak, legacies in the shape of their successor states. With the Dual Monarchy the dominant historiographical tone has often been inflected through sympathy and nostalgia—through a sense that, at the very least, the ambitions and claims of those who overturned the Monarchy produced a central and eastern European landscape which deeply aggravated its shortcomings without sustaining its merits. The dissolution of nearly all of the unions considered in this book was associated with the creation of successors which retained minority questions: big empires, it is sometimes observed, were replaced, especially (but not only) after 1918, with little empires. Equally, big unions were often superseded by smaller unions.

Thus, in the 19th century, the overthrow of the United Kingdom of the Netherlands delivered a successor polity, the kingdom of Belgium, which has been characterized throughout its long life by deep-seated cultural and linguistic divisions separating its francophone and Flemish citizens. Indeed some of the religious tensions of the former United Kingdom were reformulated in the new Belgium in terms of the gap between Catholics and liberals. Equally, some of the religious and cultural questions which bedevilled the United Province of Canada were bequeathed to confederation and the new dominion. In this sense an, at times, unstable United Province was succeeded by an, at times, unstable Canada; and an unstable United Kingdom of the Netherlands was succeeded by an, at times, unstable Belgium.

While the complex consociational experiments which have so far ensured Belgium's lengthy and peaceful survival are reminiscent of similar efforts within the crownlands of the Dual Monarchy, the Habsburg successor states themselves generally fared much less well than this. These were in fact often characterized by territorial frontiers which simultaneously addressed one set of questions posed by the old Monarchy, while creating others. An enlarged Italy now, after 1918, had more Slovenes and more German speakers (the Südtirol question dates from this time): an enlarged Romania now had greater communities of Hungarian and German speakers. The new Czechoslovakia also had significant Magyar and German, Sudeten, minorities (and contained both a substantial Czech majority as well as significant inequalities besetting the minority Slovaks). The composite monarchy of the Habsburgs was replaced in the Balkans by a composite monarchy of the Serbs, Croats, and Slovenes, dominated by the Serbs and (for a time) by their Karođorđević ruling dynasty; and indeed King Alexander I (1888–1934) assumed dictatorial powers over the renamed 'Yugoslavia' in 1929, suspending the democratic constitution and, in 1931, substituting an authoritarian replacement. Like the Habsburgs in the Balkans, Alexander found the management of his fissiparous and volatile kingdom profoundly difficult; and, like Franz Ferdinand (1863–1914) at Sarajevo in 1914, so Alexander fell victim to the region's bloody ethnic rivalries, assassinated in Marseilles in 1934.

On the other hand, even the United Kingdom of Great Britain and Ireland, a much vaunted model of constitutionalism and stability, descended into warfare, and was replaced by a union of Great Britain and a devolved Northern Ireland, together with an independent dominion, the Irish Free State, Saorstat Éireann. The national questions of the old union state were largely replaced in 1921 by reformulated questions affecting the Catholic minority of the new devolved Northern Ireland and (to a lesser extent) the small Protestant minority of the Irish Free State (Zách 2021, pp. 96ff.). At the time of writing (2016–22) the broaching in some quarters of the reunification of the island raises interesting questions about the possible supersession of a multinational United Kingdom by (amongst other polities) a new multinational united Ireland (though cf. Jackson 1997).

In short, these interconnected unions were replaced in various ways; but their often imperfect successor states frequently inherited, and in some cases amplified, old challenges. Lapidary or simplistic judgements on the defects of these 19th-century multinational unions, or on the natural 'progression' towards 'better' polities, are understandable; but they often reflect particular historical teleologies, and they are clearly not, therefore, the whole story. These unions and their successors certainly worked with (at best) variable success, judged (for example) from the particular perspective of inclusivity and representation. But multinational union states were certainly capable of adapting to challenge; and this adaptability often (as in the case of the United Kingdom or Austria-Hungary or Canada) helps to illuminate their survival. The next sections of the book move away from these case studies of individual polities, towards considering some wider comparative and thematic taxonomies of longevity and failure.

162 UNITED KINGDOMS

Figure 3.1 Monarchy and union: Queen Victoria and her people—the Diamond Jubilee Service, St Paul's Cathedral, London, June 1897. Photograph (National Portrait Gallery, London).

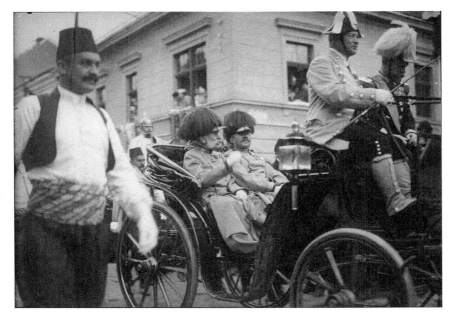

Figure 3.2 Monarchy and union: the Emperor-King Franz Joseph visits Sarajevo in the recently annexed Bosnia, May—June 1910. Photograph (Bildarchiv der Österreichischen Nationalbibliothek).

EUROPEAN UNIONS AND BEYOND: CASE STUDIES 163

Figure 3.3 Monarchy and union: the Emperor-King Karl (Károly) publicly taking his coronation oath as King of Hungary, Budapest, December 1916. Photograph (Bildarchiv der Österreichischen Nationalbibliothek).

Figure 3.4 Monarchy and union: the Emperor-King Karl (Károly), Crown Prince Otto and the Empress-Queen Zita installed as Apostolic rulers of Hungary, Budapest, December 1916. Bilingual postcard (private possession).

4
Centripede
The Institutional Bolsters of Union

4.1. Introduction

It has been famously suggested that the French state 'created' the French nation—and that it was the state and its institutions which were ultimately responsible for turning 'peasants into Frenchmen' (Sked 1989, p. 205; Weber 1979). By way of contrast, however, union states such as those reviewed in the previous chapter of this study have generally been seen as markedly less successful in delivering overarching and binding identities. Neither the United Kingdoms of Sweden-Norway nor the United Kingdom of the Netherlands were associated with lasting supranational identities fixing their citizens to the institutions of union; and even the United Kingdom of Great Britain and Ireland never developed a thoroughly inclusive identity, since it has been long recognized that the construction of 'Britishness' did not wholly embrace Ireland.

This was true, too, for Austria-Hungary. Both the enemies and friends of the Dual Monarchy, for example, alleged that (in the words of one wartime critic), and in contrast to the supposedly organic and spiritual qualities of the nation state, it was 'really only a system of government—a government with a central head and a network extending throughout the whole country' (Dickinson-Berry 1918, p. 28). For Oszkár Jászi, more nostalgic and sympathetic than this, the Dual Monarchy still represented 'a tragic failure in social cohesion [with] a fatal inability to develop a central political loyalty' (Jászi 1929, p. xiv). In fact more recent work has tended instead to emphasize the widespread traction achieved by an overarching dynastic patriotism (e.g. King 2002; Unowsky 2005). One highly influential scholar of the Dual Monarchy has indeed argued that its lengthy survival in the face of overwhelming obstacles was achieved by two institutional factors: 'the presence of [both] the multinational Habsburg army and the 68 year reign of the Emperor King Franz Joseph' (Deák 1990, pp. 3–4).

Contemporaries were of course fascinated by the tenacity of the Dual Monarchy; and even those, like Henry Wickham Steed, for whom (like other English commentators) 'the people exist for the [Habsburg] state, rather than the state for it', saw that there was a key set of central binding institutions: 'it may be said that the State consists of the Army, the Bureaucracy, the Police and the Church, for these are the main instruments of government' (Steed 1919, p. 59).

United Kingdoms: Multinational Union States in Europe and Beyond, 1800–1925. Alvin Jackson, Oxford University Press.
© Alvin Jackson 2023. DOI: 10.1093/oso/9780192883742.003.0004

For Jászi, too, as we have seen, there was also a dynamic within the Monarchy of countervailing centripetal and centrifugal forces: the former, which he dubbed 'the eight pillars of internationalism' included the Habsburg dynasty, the aristocracy and the army, the Catholic Church, the bureaucracy, free trade, and capitalism. Equally, he defined the centrifugal forces as being the *morbus latifundii* (the 'diseased' land system), the struggle between Austria and Hungary, and the national awakening (Jászi 1929, pp. 133–4). However, as he also shrewdly observed, 'almost all the centripetal forces developed in their later course centrifugal tendencies in one direction or another' (Jászi 1929, p. 133).

While, in much of the discussion which follows, Jászi's functionalist taxonomy of disintegration is deployed as a starting point and an effort is made to isolate both the centripetal and centrifugal, integrative and disruptive, forces in the united kingdoms under review, it is also abundantly clear that much of the operation of these forces was contingent, and that in particular circumstances the integrative might become disruptive and vice versa. In other words, simple interpretative binaries rarely suffice in what follows—and this, as it happens, chimes with a spectrum of work on the particular circumstances of the Dual Monarchy, including not just Jászi, writing in the late 1920s, but also more contemporary scholars (see e.g. Judson 2016, p. 368). These binaries do, however, provide a set of starting points in helping to understand the cohesion and survival of the various multinational union states under review.

Other approaches and influences are deployed, aside from those supplied by Jászi. As the opening sentence indicates, there is of course an extensive literature on state formation which has cognate concerns to those explored in this work. In particular, work on specific forms of complex state, whether federal or 'voluntary' unions, has been useful—at least in terms of identifying potential areas of relevance for the analysis pursed here. However, while the argument here accepts (for example) the important roles of external threat, and in particular warfare, in creating and sustaining states, and applies this insight to multinational unions, it will also be clear that the latter have often their own specific cultures and chemistries (Parent 2011, pp. 21, 23, 25). Other work has sometimes bravely attempted to identify 'purer' forms of union, but the focus here has been on a range of polities, bound together by shared ancestry and sometimes even by shared parentage, and linked in the imaginations of contemporaries, but still variegated, and therefore resistant to monocausal, or otherwise simple, taxonomies.

The purpose, then, of the following chapter is to look at a range of integrative institutions and agencies, generally (though not always) those identified by contemporaries like Jászi—but to do so in comparative context, using in each of the several sections evidence drawn from at least some of the case studies of union laid down earlier in the work. The chapter title itself is adapted from Franck 2008. The demands of the comparative approach, together with wider constraints of space, have meant that none of these sections aspires to provide anything other than an introduction to their respective subjects: they certainly do not claim to be exhaustive.

Nor does the organization of the sections reflect any analytical ranking assigned to their theme and its importance. The initial sections address a group of institutions associated with monarchy, and linked together in the arguments of some contemporaries. Later sections move away to consider other, relatively more abstract, but no less valuable, aspects of the unity of unions.

The ultimate purpose, then, is to move towards developing an overarching analysis of these union polities which, while allowing for their differences and contingencies, identifies some of their commonalities, and the features which they shared both in life and in death. But, again, the effort here is necessarily introductory, syncretic, and suggestive rather than lapidary or definitive.

4.2. Monarchy

Monarchy throughout modern Europe has had a central role—and generally (though not consistently) a unifying function—in the survival of multinational states. In both the United Kingdom and the Dual Monarchy the crown acted as an important binding mechanism, supplying critical dimensions both to British and, of course, Habsburg identities: indeed the importance of this in the British case is such that 'Britishness' might well be seen as a dynastic identity parallel to that associated with the Habsburgs. In Sweden-Norway and the Netherlands the crown helped both first to bind—and then to dissolve the union polities. In other complex unions (and, indeed their successor states) in Europe monarchy has been seen in similar terms: scholars have emphasized, for example, the importance of the monarchy as a bolster of the fissiparous Belgian state, and in particular while other key unifying institutions went into decline (White 1835; Conway 2012, p. 371).

However, as a starting point, much in terms of the survival of the 'united kingdoms' under consideration hinged upon contingency—and in particular upon the performance and personality of individual rulers, as well as upon the memory and adaptability of their legacy (see e.g. Cole and Unowsky 2007, p. 5). Distinctions have to be made, therefore, between the immediate impact of individual monarchs, and their longer term achievements; distinctions have to be made, too, between popular intellectual and political engagement with a monarch, and more sentimental or emotive attachments. In Austria Joseph II (r. 1765–90), whose reputation has varied over the years, looked to centralize and laicize and germanize, and came to be seen as a key figure in the maturation of the Habsburg realms from a dynastic and feudal domain into a Rechtsstaat: he came to be viewed (and memorialized) by late 19th-century German liberals as one of the architects of the survival of a reformed and centralized (and German) Habsburg state (see e.g. Nancy Wingfield's essay in Cole and Unowsky 2007, pp. 62–85; Steed 1919, pp. 84ff.). However, there was no automatic equation between reformist energy and either popular loyalty or (therefore) the consolidation of dynastic identity; and at the time Joseph II's disruptive reforms unsettled many, and especially conservative Catholics, throughout his empire—not least in the Austrian Netherlands. In other words, there was a distinction here between the immediately divisive impact of Joseph's reforms, and later liberal readings of his reign as a springboard for the modern Habsburg monarchy.

The Habsburgs, who were deeply associated with Catholic piety, did not need to be energetic or reforming rulers to generate support either for the dynasty or its associated institutions (see e.g. Figure 4.4). Deference and loyalty (and perhaps human sympathy) were shown to the Emperor Ferdinand (r. 1835–48), who was epileptic and hydrocephalic, who was deemed to be incapable of sole rule, and who was eventually persuaded to abdicate: this loyalty was widely evidenced even in 1848. Indeed, the masochistic unwillingness of the revolutionaries of 1848 in both Vienna and Hungary to 'break the umbilical cord to the [Habsburg] dynasty' has been identified as 'a constant refrain' in that year of revolutions (Okey 2001, pp. 138, 149).

The contingencies and complexities—and indeed the counter-intuitiveness—of popular dynastic loyalty were strikingly embodied in the protracted rule of Franz Joseph (r. 1848–1916) (see Figure 3.2). Nominally bound by constitutions after 1860–1, and with the Ausgleich, Franz Joseph in fact retained great power within Austria-Hungary, not least over military matters (see Beller 1996, p. 59; Judson 2016, p. 247). His limitations, however, were palpable, and have sometimes been linked to the ultimate collapse of the Dual Monarchy: it was certainly Jászi's view that Franz Joseph himself was a key part of the difficulties with his regime (Jászi 1929, pp. 116–18). Wickham Steed, the most prominent anglophone journalist commenting on the Dual Monarchy before 1913–14, saw the emperor-king and his dynasty as both a bolster and a source of vulnerability:

> the power of the Habsburg dynasty is still the strongest element in the Monarchy—stronger in the last resort than the influence of the Austrian Germans, the Austrian Slavs, the Magyars, the Church or the Jews. Its power is still, to all intents and purposes, absolute; but it is exposed to the danger that threatens all absolutisms...the danger of regarding their own existence as an end in itself; and of allowing their conduct to be guided solely by considerations of short-term expediency.   (Steed 1919, p. 295; Steed 1937 p. viii)

In the end, however, in this (as in so much else) Franz Joseph stands as a metaphor for his broader empire—in so far as (like the empire itself) he cannot be forced into any crude teleology of collapse. In fact Franz Joseph appears (rather like the limited and truculent but ultimately revered Queen Victoria in Britain) to have defied political gravity, managing to act as an effective binding agent within the Dual Monarchy, despite an array of countervailing pressures: like successive British monarchs, Franz Joseph won popular favour because he was apparently removed from grubby self-interest, and because he was evidently willing to be identified with 'his' peoples 'even at the cost, or perhaps with the object, of curtailing dominant parties and castes' (McKibbin 1990; Steed 1919, pp. xxiv–xxv). Franz Joseph was welcomed as king of Hungary after 1867, even though he had been partly responsible for its brutal subjugation in 1848-9: his patronage was sought by many faith communities across the empire (Jewish, Orthodox, Greek Catholic), even though full legal emancipation for some of these was a long time in coming, and though he had sought to restore the Habsburgs' role as the traditional defenders of a triumphant Catholicism (Judson 2016, p. 234). He preserved an almost medieval sense of personal and dynastic honour, yet he was personally responsible for the—almost routine—military humiliation of the empire between 1848 and 1878.

But these failings and complexities mattered less because, as the years passed, and the emperor's personal sorrows mounted, he was judged not so much for his (on the whole miserable) personal record of achievement and more as a benign and fallible *'pater patriae'*—buffeted by fate, yet remaining faithfully on duty at his desk in the Hofburg while most of his subjects slept in their beds. As with a range of late 19th-century popular leaders, so Franz Joseph acquired a variety of identifying hallmarks which eased their way into the popular consciousness: his supposedly spartan lifestyle was symbolized by his iron bed and simple washstand; and his benign features, sporting mutton-chop whiskers 40 years after the fashion had faded, were of course omnipresent across the Monarchy, and instantly recognizable throughout Europe (though cf. Murad 1968, pp. 74–5). Those features still beam down from shops and restaurants across the successor states of the Dual Monarchy (see the discussion of legacy in Kozuchowski 2013, pp. 149ff.).

Indeed, whatever the difficulties, even sceptical contemporary British observers like Wickham Steed, writing on the eve of the First World War, tended to see the Habsburg monarchy as ultimately a dynamic and successful institution, if also one fundamentally characterized by an icy formality:

> despite a statecraft frequently 'soulless', the Emperor Franz Joseph has cultivated and succeeded in maintaining throughout the greater part of his reign such a relationship between the dynasty and most of its peoples that the crown has come to be regarded as a personal possession of its subjects to an extent hardly to be paralleled in Germany, in Italy, or perhaps even in England.
> (Wickham Steed 1919, pp. xviii–xix)

Franz Joseph's dutiful competence was also a reassuring (if scarcely uplifting) part of his success: he was an accomplished master of the technicalities of the Ausgleich and indeed (as Pieter Judson has observed) 'he eventually learned the intricate rules of each constitutional system far better than did most of his cabinet ministers...[and] his behaviour tended in the long run to strengthen constitutional practice in both Hungary and Austria rather than to weaken it' (Judson 2016, p. 262). By contrast, his well-meaning but youthful and undertrained successor, Karl (r. 1916–18), was ignorant of much of the subtlety required to successfully navigate the dual system—to the extent that he found himself on the receiving end of unwelcome lectures on the subject from the likes of his Hungarian premier, István Tisza (1861–1918). It is hard to envision Tisza venturing to offer the same pedagogy to Franz Joseph—or indeed Franz Joseph deigning to receive it. Indeed, Albert von Margutti (1869–1940), a former general in the Austro-Hungarian army (and of maternal Irish descent), argued in 1921 that the empire was only held together at the end by 'the personality of the old emperor after whose death it would fall asunder "like an old barrel robbed of its hoops"' (von Margutti 1921 quoted in Jászi 1929, p. 12; see also Steed 1937, pp. 15–19; and Christiane Wolf's essay in Cole and Unowsky 2007, pp. 199–222). But, within his limitations, Karl still did his best to maintain the unifying function of the monarchy as defined by his great-uncle and predecessor, Franz Joseph (see e.g. Figures 3.3, 4.3).

The exceptional exclusivism and deliberate mystique of the Habsburg court helped to create an impression of monarchy which was (even) more elevated than that pertaining in the United Kingdom and the German empire (Beller 1996, p. 133). It seems likely that the elaboration of court ceremonial, especially in terms of its Catholic dimensions (for example, with the restoration and elaboration of the annual Corpus Christi celebrations, discussed later in this chapter), helped to promote the visibility of the monarch, dynastic patriotism, and also a degree of transferred loyalty to the wider Habsburg state (Judson and Rozenblit 2005, p. 142; see also Bucur and Wingfield 2001, pp. 24–5, 34; section 4.6). However, the ceremonial and commemorations associated with the monarchy extended far beyond the Viennese court; and, as with the British monarchy, so widespread celebration and engagement were associated with the various anniversaries of Franz Joseph's long reign. Focusing on the Emperor's golden jubilee celebrations in 1898, Daniel Unowsky has argued that 'the Monarchy did not seek to supplant nationality with state identity, but to project dynastic loyalty as an essential aspect of ethnic identity within a harmonious Austria' (Judson and Rozenblit 2005, p. 147). Instead, 'the court, army and Cisleithanian government presented Franz Joseph as the symbol of an ideal Austria yet to be achieved...through a shared devotion to the aging Emperor and a common Austrian patriotism, assumed to exist above and beyond nationalism' (Judson and Rozenblit 2005, p. 152).

On the other hand, it is important to recognize that even this dynastic patriotism and loyalty were uneven and had limits: if they were concerned with an idealized Austria, then they were still ultimately about Austria and Austrianness. Hungarians had some attachment to Franz Joseph and (rather more so) to his consort, the Empress Elisabeth (1833–98); but they also were keenly aware of the limited extent to which this was reciprocated by their apostolic king or his eventual heir, Archduke Franz Ferdinand (Haslinger 1996, pp. 40–4). English Liberal visitors to

Transleithania in 1906 noted the widespread perception 'that Francis Joseph has very little interest in Hungary, and he certainly does not go out of his way to acquire popularity in his kingdom' (Anon./Eighty Club 1907, p. 398). One galling expression of this indifference was Franz Joseph's reluctance to dwell in Hungary, despite the construction of a new royal palace overlooking the Danube: he was generally in residence for only three days a year. Following on from this, and in contrast to the celebrations in Cisleithania, it has been said that Hungarians treated Franz Joseph's golden jubilee celebrations of 1898 'as a holiday occurring in a neighbouring state' rather than as an event wholly owned by themselves; or alternatively that they marked the jubilee through a form of cognitive dissonance which simultaneously invoked the monarch's accession as well as the fiftieth anniversary of the uprising against Habsburg governance (Judson and Rozenblit 2005, p. 151; Cole and Unowsky 2007, pp. 2–3). This notion of royal celebrations as 'a holiday in a neighbouring state' has some occasional relevance elsewhere—including within the constituent nations of the United Kingdom (as was suggested, for example, by the somewhat patchy observance of Queen Elizabeth's Platinum Jubilee in Scotland in 2022).

Moreover, these ambiguities (or 'parallel realities') were encouraged by lingering suspicions that dynastic loyalty had no transactional value. While there was little mass opposition to the monarchy amongst the southern Slavs, or in Dalmatia, or Slovakia, Croats and others who were more overtly loyal to the dynasty were certainly poorly repaid for their devotion, with the partial consequence that they ultimately looked elsewhere for allies—to the Serbs and the Resolution of Fiume (1905) (Beller 1996, p. 191; Jászi 1929, p. 372). A wider point may be made in terms of the First World War, where despite the huge popular sacrifices across the Habsburg lands, there was a resounding failure (until it was too late) to offer concessions to loyal minorities—a failure 'which exposed ever more starkly a lack of genuine reciprocity in the loyalty relationship' (Cole 2014, p. 322). In the end the Habsburgs and their monarchy survived in spite of themselves, and certainly in spite of their legendary ingratitude (whether at a national or individual level)—which of course had gained an ironic currency as *der Dank vom Hause Habsburg* (see e.g. Steed 1919, pp. 8ff., pp. 71–3).

Similar arguments might be made on the basis of the commemorative events associated with the British monarchy in the 19th and 20th centuries. It has been argued that, in comparison with continental European monarchies such as the Habsburgs, the advancing commercialization of English public life in the 18th century created such an important, diverse, and compelling public sphere that the royal court was in danger of being wholly eclipsed (Rexheuser 2005, p. 465). Indeed, this aspect of the Hanoverian monarchy highlighted a perennial feature of the British and United Kingdom states, which were continuingly overshadowed by the marketplace. However, the suffocation of the monarchy in the public life of the state was ultimately prevented by George III, who grasped that the crown had to be positioned more closely in alignment with the British nation, and that (what Tim Blanning has called) 'a representational court of the continental variety' would not be fit for British purposes (Rexheuser 2005, p. 481). On the whole, therefore, the British monarchy, unlike many of its continental European counterparts in the 18th and 19th centuries, was characterized by an ongoing adaptability. Tradition was blithely invented and reinvented with successive coronations, from that of George IV (1821) onwards, as well as with royal jubilees, and in particular those of Queen Victoria in 1887 and 1897. These, together with the coronations of 1902 and 1911, and the welter of royal visits (again beginning with George IV in 1821-2) and investitures (as at Caernarfon in 1911), were associated with an expansive imperial and dynastic celebration which could generally be reconciled with the component national identities of Great Britain, and which served therefore as unifying 'national' (in reality supranational) events (Lant 1980; though cf. Beller's characterization of Franz Joseph's diamond jubilee as a missed opportunity for state-building: in Bucur and Wingfield 2001, pp. 68-9).

The Scottish dimension of the success of monarchy is well-known, and is variously dated. Here a combination of union, with the military defeats of the recusant Stuart challenge in both 1715 and again in 1745-6, and the final dying out of the main legitimist line, all played their part. Peter Davidson and Daniel MacCannell have argued that 'if one is looking for events which precipitated change in 18th century Scotland, the death of James Francis Edward [the Old Pretender] in 1766 can in many respects look like a more significant date than 1707' (in Mackillop and Ó Siochrú 2008, p. 179). The subsequent deaths of Charles Edward Stuart, 'Bonnie Prince Charlie', in 1788, and of his brother, Henry Stuart, Cardinal York, in 1807 also facilitated the realignment of 'soft' Jacobite sentiment behind the Hanoverian monarchy. Sir Walter Scott's bold incorporation of the complex traditions and loyalties of highland Scotland into the celebration of George IV's visit to Edinburgh in 1822 is well-known, as is Queen Victoria's elaboration of this comfortable version of Scottishness after her purchase of Balmoral in 1848-52. While the affection for Scotland of individual monarchs has waxed and waned, together with their own popularity, the more or less fixed association of the royal family with the highlands has unquestionably generated a set of institutions and anniversaries which have helped bind the Scots to the crown and to a wider British and imperial identity (see Figure 4.1). Similarly, with Wales, the investiture of George V's eldest son, Edward, at Caernarfon Castle in 1911 (again an invented tradition) reflected a version of Welshness which, rather than being exclusivist, was an important component within a wider Britishness (Ward 2005, p. 74).

However, if the British monarchy's relationship with Scotland and Wales reinforced loyalism and sometimes Britishness, if not always unionism, then Ireland presented a largely different picture (Murphy 2001; Loughlin 2007). It has been argued elsewhere that Queen Victoria sustained a complex relationship with the Irish, which was reciprocated in equal measure. It was of course fully possible to be patriotically Irish and 'loyal', as Daniel O'Connell (with Victoria) and John Redmond (who had a cordial relationship with George V) clearly demonstrated (Jackson 2018b). However, Victoria's general retreat from public life after Albert's death, and her particular upset at the refusal of Dublin Corporation to sanction a prime-site location (College Green) for a monument to her late husband, Prince Albert, brought a souring of relations. But the pivotal issue was ultimately the possibility of a permanent royal residence in Ireland to match Balmoral, and on this Victoria was immovably hostile (there was, as has been mentioned, a parallel Hungarian grievance concerning the reluctance of Franz Joseph to live in Budapest) (Anon./Eighty Club 1907, p. 398). There were royal visits, including four by Victoria herself, lastly in 1900: Edward VII visited in 1903 and twice subsequently, while George V paid an entirely successful visit in July 1911, as part of his coronation tour. But, though Edward VII in particular was well-liked (his enthusiasm for horses and his supposed home rule sympathies were useful), there was no royal embrace of Irish culture, the Celtic revival, or an Irish property. To this extent, Ireland always looked like the relatively unloved offspring of the Houses of Hanover and of Saxe-Coburg-Gotha.

Yet it was perfectly possible for a British monarch, supreme Governor of the Church of England, and communicant Presbyterian, to command the loyalty of a primarily Catholic polity within the empire. The *Canadiens* of Lower Canada and of the United Province had, on the whole, shown little interest in republicanism, even when a relatively small number of their compatriots proclaimed a republic during the uprising of 1837–8. Republicanism was in fact associated with the anti-clericalism and secularism of the revolution, and with its attacks on the Church, as during the suppression of the Vendée revolt: republicanism was associated, too, with the anti-Catholicism that was a feature of American public life in the early 19th century. The British monarchy, on the other hand, had guaranteed Catholic rights through the Quebec Act and in subsequent measures; and, though a 'semi-confessional' Protestant state, Britain had acted in defence of the papacy and of great Catholic powers such as Austria during the revolutionary and Napoleonic conflicts. Moreover, as was shown in the preceding chapter, the British crown cultivated a close relationship with the Catholic hierarchy in Lower Canada/Canada East, and to some extent came to work with its clergy in seeking to deliver stable government. The leaders of francophone Canada routinely expressed their loyalty, and they proudly accepted honours and office from the crown: four who held the joint premiership of the United Province were knighted by the Queen (LaFontaine, Taché, Cartier, Belleau) and two of these four (LaFontaine, Cartier) subsequently received the additional and hereditary honour of baronetcy. All of this points simultaneously to the reasonable possibilities for the crown in relation to Ireland: as in Canada, so in Ireland there was some suspicion of the legacies of the French revolution, some willingness to acknowledge an anointed monarch, and some cautious willingness on the part of the Church to work with government. But in the end, French Canada's historical relationship with the crown, and its current standing in terms of government, were each closer and better than the parallel conditions of the Catholic Irish. And it was ultimately too big an ask for the all-too-fallible institution of monarchy to generate the same unruffled loyalty in Ireland that characterized French Canada.

There are also some comparisons to be made here with the ambiguous track-record of the House of Orange within the short-lived United Kingdom of the Netherlands. On the one hand, the dynasty was associated with the glorious military action—Waterloo—which effectively underpinned the independence of the new kingdom and region: the crown prince, later Willem II, was heroically wounded in the action. Walter Scott, writing in 1816, argued that the crown prince's 'whole behaviour during the actions of Quatre Bras and Waterloo, and the wound which (it may almost be said fortunately) he received upon the latter occasion, have already formed the strongest bond of union between his family and their new subjects' (Anon./Scott 1816, p. 235). Scott later observed that he had listened to the ballad-singers of Brussels proclaiming the gallantry of the young prince, and that he had subsequently acquired published examples of this minstrelsy ('in which, by the way, there is no more mention of the Duke of Wellington or of John Bull, than if John Bull and his general had had nothing to do with the illustrious battle of Waterloo') (Anon./Scott 1816, p. 236). Robert Southey, who was travelling in the southern Netherlands at about the same time as Scott, recorded similar affection for the crown prince, though with some associated and unflattering reflections on his father: 'the Prince of Orange has won the hearts of the people [of Ghent] by the part he bore at Waterloo', Southey observed, 'he is a brave garçon, they say, and they frankly add that they care not how soon his father may care to die and make way for him...his wound tells greatly in his favour. The wish here is that he may marry an English princess, and not a Russian as is now talked of' (Southey 1902, p. 43). The site at Waterloo where the crown prince sustained his wound was subsequently memorialized (at the behest of his father, the king) through the creation of the Lion Mound on the battlefield (1820–6), a focus for Orangist and wider veneration (Marteel 2018, p. 25).

On the other hand, as in Ireland and Canada, so the Catholic southern provinces of the new United Kingdom of the Netherlands found themselves as (in effect) junior partners within a primarily Protestant polity, with (in the case of the Netherlands) an energetic and unresponsive Calvinist monarch in the shape of Willem I (see Figure 2.3). The House of Orange eventually emerged to act as a focal point for a specifically Dutch national feeling after the revolution of 1830 (just as the House of Saxe-Coburg-Gotha came to fulfil a similar function in Belgium). But this was only really achieved by the end of the 19th century, with (for example) the institution of Princess's Day (31 August) as a national holiday from 1885 onwards (Wielenga 2015, p. 190).

In short, monarchy tended to create supranational bonds in some multinational union states; but this was indeed a tendency, rather than a rule. Loyalty to the crown and the dynasty proved to be (on the whole) a unifying sentiment in Austria-Hungary, Britain, and Canada: there were unrequited possibilities in Ireland, the Netherlands—and in the United Kingdoms of Sweden-Norway, where Carl XIV Johan commanded widespread respect, and where the brief reign of the short-lived Carl XV constituted the highpoint of union within the United Kingdoms (Jorgenson 1935, pp. 206–50; Figure 2.2). But the loyalist cultures which were thereby generated naturally focused on the person of the monarch— and particularly so in the cases of the long-reigning Franz Joseph and Victoria. Moreover, the complex and composite nature of each crown meant that there was no automatic equation between a unifying loyalism and a unifying national sentiment: loyalty to the dynasty was not quite the same as loyalty to the union state, and Austro-Hungarianness or United Kingdomness were not the obvious by-products of these royal and dynastic sympathies for Habsburg or Hanover (see e.g. Beller in Bucur and Wingfield 2001, pp. 46–71).

Oszkár Jászi pointed out nearly a century ago that there could not always be a neat taxonomy of union, since centripetal forces might also function in a centrifugal manner; and in fact in both the Habsburg empire and in the United Kingdom, the respective monarchies have served simultaneously to bind *and* subvert the two states. On the one hand, as Pieter Judson has observed in relation to the Dual Monarchy, 'the symbolic language of monarchy often cloaked new forms of governance and government obligation in reassuringly familiar terms' (Judson 2016, p. 41). On the other hand, the symbolic language of monarchy might well (as with the Netherlands and Sweden-Norway) exercise little of this magic—if the symbols, the language, and individual monarchs failed to persuade. Even settled dynasties could be subverted with the departure of trusted, long-serving rulers and the succession of callow or untrusted replacements. This was the fate of the Habsburgs and their monarchy—and it may yet be that of the House of Windsor and the United Kingdom.

4.3. Aristocracy

It is clear that aristocratic elites could be critical to the formulation as well as the upholding of union (and other) states. It was certainly the case that in the domains of the Habsburgs, as well as those of the Stuart and Hanoverian dynasties, aristocracies served as a bolster of union and as partners in royal or union government. Recent scholarship has emphasized the importance of the Habsburgs' long-standing relationship with the Catholic landed elites of Hungary in creating a key foundation for the success and survival of their complex multiple union (Ó hAnnracháin 2015). Other work on the lower nobility, and specifically the Free Imperial

Knights of the Holy Roman Empire, has convincingly posited that, in the aftermath of the French revolutionary wars, those who were driven from the defunct empire into the Habsburg lands brought with them 'still lively traditions of universalism and cosmopolitanism that were later to feed into noble supranationalism': indeed, in this sense Habsburg 'supranationalism' was originally not so much a response to constituent nationalisms which (in the early 19th century) did not yet exist in a fully formed condition, as a response to 'new conditions and a recognition of the profound problems associated with aristocratic "naturalisation" there', in the Austrian empire (Godsey 2004, p. 254). Similarly, many others have pointed to the foundational role of the upper aristocracy in the maintenance of Great Britain and the subsequent United Kingdom (with all of the implications for the unity of the kingdom which were carried by the decline of that class from the late 19th century onwards) (see e.g. Colley 1992).

There were clearly similarities as well between the modern landed aristocracies of Ireland and of Bohemia—each being originally and for the most part *condottieri* imported into their respective polities in the aftermath of the wholesale expropriation and removal of existing local elites in the 17th century. In each case, and also in that of Wales, it has to be said that there was an early 'emotive identification' between some within these new aristocracies and the cultures and traditions of the landscape where they were now anchored: the 'colonial nationalism' of much of the 18th-century Irish landed interest—the strength of the propertied 'patriot' tradition in 18th-century Ireland—has been frequently discussed, alongside its related antiquarian and historical interests (Simms 1976). In addition, Matthew Cragoe's work emphasizes the role of the conservative landed classes in early 19th-century Wales in promoting national interests, while Rita Krueger has highlighted the intellectual engagements of 18th- and early 19th-century Bohemian conservative aristocrats, who in developing their cultural enthusiasms and institutions, simultaneously promoted the structures and language of Czech nationality (Cragoe 2004; Krueger 2009). But in each (though for different reasons) this activity also tended to be complicated by other, supranational and imperial, loyalties and identities before 1914 (see Godsey 1999, p. 152; Krueger 2009, pp. 7–8). In each, in the aftermath of this key foundational work, the leadership of the 'nation' was taken over by other, bourgeois, interests in the mid and later 19th century.

But there were also of course distinctions between the British and Irish nobility and their Habsburg and other contemporaries. Despite the much-vaunted mobility and fluidity of British society, and despite the possibility of access (through the acquisition of great wealth) to noble rank and title, these classes were often larger in other continental European countries (and beyond), and ease of access could be proportionately much greater. The ubiquity of nobility in (for example) Hungary and Poland was well known; but there were other examples, such as the United Kingdom of Portugal, Brazil, and the Algarves. Here the challenges of warfare and establishing a new union polity after 1808 meant that the prince regent, Dom João (later King João VI), created more noble titles in eight years than in the preceding 150 years of Braganza rule: 20 marquesses, eight counts, 16 viscounts, and 21 barons emerged from this bonanza (Schultz 2001, pp. 83, 96 n. 85; Armitage 1836, p. 16).

Precise definitions, comparisons, and 'rates of exchange' are, admittedly, notoriously difficult (given, for example, that the lowest titles within several of the polities considered were hereditary, where the British knighthood was not). There were certainly 322 English and Scottish hereditary peers in 1707, which—given that the combined population of the two countries was around 8.5 million—suggests that (at least in its very tightest definition) the titled hereditary nobility constituted merely around 0.004 per cent of the population. If the immediate families of these peers are included in the calculations, then the relevant proportions appear broadly equivalent to those within the German lands (0.01 per cent) though falling considerably short of the proportions in Sweden (0.5 per cent), Poland, and in the Dual Monarchy (see Cannadine, 1990).

In fact in Habsburg central Europe the traditions of a more extensive noble class were deeply entrenched: here, and especially in Hungary, the nobility constituted around 5 per cent of the population. Maria Theresa alone ennobled 430 Hungarians, and founded the Order of St Stephen for the Hungarian nobles at court: her successor, Joseph II, created a further new array of nobility (Jászi 1929, p. 61; Okey 2001, p. 37). Moreover, ongoing access to noble rank was also more readily achievable in the later Austrian empire and Austria-Hungary. In the United Kingdom, between 1849 and 1914 approximately 470 peerages were created, a figure which of course does not include the lowest form of hereditary title, the baronetcy: but in the Habsburg lands (where the population was only slightly larger than that of the UK) the comparable figure was at least twelve times greater, with 5,761 patents of nobility being issued between 1849 and 1914. The lavish application of honours, it was said, was critical in bringing the more able and ambitious sections of Habsburg society into 'a species of moral vassalage to the feudal classes'; and indeed the torrent of titles in the late Habsburg empire had become so furious that it even assumed a bleakly comedic dimension (Jászi 1929, p. 153; Jackson 2013; Unowsky in Bucur and Wingfield 2001, p. 40 n. 32).

Of course, the nobility was itself a diverse and unequal class, differentiated not just by grade, but also by antiquity and wealth. The idea of *Uradel*, ancient nobility, characterized by extended aristocratic pedigree, came into use in the Holy Roman Empire at the end of the 18th century (Godsey 2004, p. 10). The accession of Franz Joseph in 1848 brought a tightening and further formalization of the degrees of access at the imperial court: it was a cadre of older noble families—300 or 400 strong—who alone had access to the Habsburg court (and who thus, by definition, possessed the requisite *Hoffähigkeit*), and who were otherwise predominant in Habsburg society (Unowsky in Bucur and Wingfield 2001, pp. 18–20).

These included some fabulously wealthy clans; and in fact the leading aristocrats of Habsburg Austria were, in the late 19th century, still 'alone in Europe in matching the wealth of their British counterparts' (Okey 2001, p. 253).

However, despite this and the subsequent replenishings of the noble ranks under Franz Joseph, Jászi and others saw the late Habsburg aristocracy as characterized by 'apathy and lack of talent' (Jászi 1929, p. 152). By the first years of the 20th century, it was also clear that some of the great noble families of the empire were becoming progressively indifferent to the Habsburg cause, and indeed 'had begun to abandon their emperor' (Deák 1990, p. 157). More specifically, work on the Bohemian nobility in the last decades of the empire has depicted a class which was divided between feudal conservatives who looked to a more federalist or decentralized politics and the larger landowners who for the moment remained relatively loyal—*Verfassungstreu*—to the dynasty and to the Ausgleich constitution (Glassheim in Judson and Rozenblit 2005, p. 69). However, their particular position was becoming more widely embattled—caught between 'an ungrateful and uncreative Emperor [who] did little to build the imperial identity they hoped for' and the several insurgent non-German nationalisms. Just like many of their Irish landed counterparts in the era of cultural and political nationalism, Bohemian nobles, uncertain about their location in a swiftly developing new order, increasingly 'employed a nationalist vocabulary in the late 19th century, sensing that without it they could be doomed to political impotence' (Glassheim in Judson and Rozenblit 2005, p. 83). Here, as elsewhere in union states, subjects (even aristocratic subjects) tacked, flexed, and swayed in looking after their own interests.

The wealth and influence of these classes (both in Austria and Ireland) had certainly for long been formidable. Even in the west, Cisleithania, where the aristocracy was more immediately vulnerable, its significance remained clear. Indeed, recent research confirms a picture of a class which was convincingly united (and uniting) through a range of ties—endogamy, friendship, and the shared veneration of lineage, honour, and country house lifestyles (Judson and Rozenblit 2005, p. 65). Political influence continued through different media, including their control of one of the four curiae represented in the Reichsrat since the electoral reform of 1873. But it was also the case that the creation of a fifth curia in 1896 brought a shifting of power towards more democratic forces in Austrian society (Deak 2015, pp. 182–3). It has been been memorably observed that, for the nobility of Bohemia in particular, now facing multiple social, cultural, and economic challenges, the 1890s came to seem like 'a centennial *Götterdämmerung*' (Judson and Rozenblit 2005, p. 74).

This twilight was perceived in different ways and in different areas of the Monarchy. István Deák has pointed to a marked noble retreat 'in the western province of the monarchy as well as in the Austrian bureaucracy and the Austro-Hungarian army'—even though in 'Hungary, Croatia, Slavonia and Galicia the great landowning aristocracy and in Hungary in particular the gentry preserved much of its influence and power' (Deák 1990, p. 157). Moreover, by this stage, even the social leadership role of the western aristocracy had begun to wane, while other classes (such as the *petite bourgeoisie*) had begun to assume ever greater significance, filling the aristocratic vacuum. In the last decades of the 19th century the *petite bourgeoisie* began (what has been described as) their 'reactionary Odyssey'—taking them away from the challenges of modernization towards (what has been briskly described as) 'a mix of anti-capitalist nostalgia, cultural philistinism and racial prejudice—and leading eventually to fascism' (Okey 2001, p. 260).

Like the Habsburg nobility and the Dual Monarchy, it has long been recognized that the British and Irish aristocracy represented a key binding agent within Great Britain and ultimately the United Kingdom of Great Britain and Ireland. As has been said, the size and accessibility of the British and Irish aristocracy were not especially great by some continental European standards. On the other hand, part of the social and political architecture of union was, after 1707, a new British peerage, with the abandonment of the old national peerages of England and Scotland. Ireland, as always, was slightly different, reflecting the disproportionate leverage of its ascendancy interest; and after the union of 1801, an Irish peerage (just about) survived, though in practice the overwhelming majority of Irish-born ennoblements were to a new United Kingdom nobility. Orders of nobility were created, or developed, in the context of union—these binding the national aristocracies of Scotland and Ireland to the crown: the Order of the Thistle was founded in 1687 by James VII and II, followed just under a century later (1783) by the Order of St Patrick, a creation associated with the turbulent state of the British-Irish constitutional relationship at the beginning of the 1780s. Each was, in essence, a highly exclusive and highly coveted device for tightening the ties of senior Scots and Irish notables to London.

Moreover, the major landholding dynasties of Britain and Ireland possessed property empires which frequently spanned the different polities of the two islands, and exercised great influence both at the centre and periphery of power in Britain: mention has already been made of clans such as the Londonderrys, whose holdings in the late 19th century embraced England, Ireland, and Wales (see section 2.2). The union monarchy, a union aristocracy, and a union parliament generally worked together to ferocious effect. There were of course periodic challenges to the integrity of the landed elite and its generally close relationship with the united monarchy: some of the ancient English noble families privately looked down upon a monarchy which (at least in its post-1714 iteration) was decidedly *arriviste*. But there were also more specific issues in play. The problem for the 18th-century British aristocracy with the Hanoverian monarchy was that it was indeed Hanoverian, and there was now a personal union with Hanover; and it has been argued that this 'gravely weakened Britain as an international force because like its counterparts in Poland and Sweden it was unpopular and challenged the practice of crown-elite cooperation on which successful politics depended' (Rexheuser 2005, p. 454). But any permanent fracture was avoided since the later Hanoverian monarchs had less interest in their ancestral polity; and in any case the Salic legal traditions of Hanover meant that there was a split between it and the throne of the United Kingdom when, in June 1837, Victoria succeeded her uncle, William IV (r. 1830–7).

As in the Habsburg empire, so this aristocratic heyday was ending by the last decades of the 19th century. In the British case extensive land reform in Ireland (especially progressive land purchase measures from 1885 onwards), and to a lesser extent in Scotland, combined with more aggressively targeted forms of taxation on wealth, began to erode the once impregnable economic and political might of the landed interest. In the end landed power had created not only a political class which (at its peak) spanned and bound the United Kingdom, but also a profound strategic challenge in the context of an imperilled union. Convinced Tories such as Robert Cecil, third marquess of Salisbury (1830–1903, and prime minister 1885, 1886–92, 1895–1902), continued to regard the Irish landed interest (whatever its inadequacies and demerits) as a fulcrum of union, while his more pragmatic colleagues (and indeed relatives like Arthur and Gerald Balfour (1853–1945)) came to view this interest as so politically toxic—in the context of popular land agitation—that it ultimately subverted rather than bolstered union (that is to say, in Jászi's terms, it was a centripetal force which had gradually become centrifugal). These Tory pragmatists calculated that, by democratizing the principle of landownership, they could renew the link between proprietorship, union, and crown for a modern age: but they were, in fact, soon proved wrong.

However, established landed elites were also important to the functioning of different forms of royal and union government throughout the British worlds. In both Ireland and Scotland successive royal and union governments had exercised authority through in effect co-opting members of the aristocracy or gentry; and in Ireland a section of the ascendancy interest, the 'undertakers', 'undertook' government until the l770s in return for patronage, while in Scotland similar arrangements were in place with successive managers of government business—first, the ducal Argyll (or Argethelian) connection and later that of the Dundas (Melville) clan. A broadly similar relationship was in place between royal, later union, government in British North America and the seigneurial class of Lower Canada (Canada East). This privileged landed cadre had for long been effective allies of the crown, and they retained many of their semi-feudal rights until 1854, when the seigneurial system was finally abolished.

The position was, however, quite different both in the Netherlands and in Scandinavia. Here the creation of united kingdoms, while similar in timing to the Irish and Canadian unions, in fact built upon different foundations, given the recent and deep-seated associations between the southern Netherlands and the Habsburg crown, and between Norway and the Danish crown. Unlike

Austria-Hungary, where there were German-speaking and *Verfassungstreu* landed elites which connected different crownlands, and unlike the United Kingdom, where there was a landed class which transcended the component nations, neither the Netherlands nor Sweden-Norway possessed a unifying aristocratic or landed class. In the southern Netherlands the nobility generally held their titles from the House of Habsburg, and not that of Orange-Nassau; and indeed the British ambassador, Lord Clancarty, wondered in 1814 'whether the nobility who hold their titles neither from the Prince [of Orange] nor from those whom he represents will ever be brought to think their interests so intimately connected with his as to work the desired [unifying] effect' (Londonderry 1848–53, 3rd ser., vol. 2, p. 78: Clancarty to Castlereagh, 8 August 1814). Similarly, while Sweden had a strong aristocratic tradition which continued into the 19th century and beyond, the handful of Norwegian noble titles (12 in 1814) originated instead with the (now irrelevant) Danish crown; and in any case (and much to the annoyance of King Carl XIV Johan) the Storting finally abolished aristocracy in Norway in 1821 (Redvaldsen 2014, p. 199). In other words, aristocracy had once served as a unifying agency—during the Danish-Norwegian union and indeed earlier, in the middle ages, when the wealthiest nobles held land throughout the three kingdoms of Scandinavia; but this was no longer the case with the new United Kingdoms after 1814–15 (Jorgenson 1935, p. 5). Nor was it the case for the new United Kingdom of the Netherlands.

In short, in some union polities, even where the institutions of government were relatively weak, there were still strong social structures which transcended and which helped to unify the different component polities: this was true for the Dual Monarchy and for the United Kingdom, in each of which there was a cluster of unifying agencies and institutions. But elsewhere, as in the United Netherlands and Sweden-Norway, union government had fewer complementary resources; and here there was no supranational aristocracy to support the union monarchy. In fact, in Norway there was ultimately not even a national aristocracy to offer the required support.

Supranational aristocracies were not the sole, or even the principal, bolsters of complex union polities. The United Kingdoms of Sweden-Norway long survived in the absence of a supranational nobility—and, indeed, in the Norwegian case, in the absence of a national nobility. But it is still striking and suggestive that the demise both of Austria-Hungary and of the United Kingdom of Great Britain and Ireland was immediately preceded by the retreat of those powerful aristocratic interests which, in association with monarchy, had once served to bind their respective states.

4.4. Armies and Security

The army—and (sometimes) war—have each long been seen as exercising a unifying function in various of the union states under consideration in this volume (see also section 6.7). In several senses this should come as no surprise: armies in united kingdoms were often very closely associated with another key integrative force, the monarchy. But unions also frequently originated in the context of external military challenge—as defined either by one or other of the partners in union, or by one or other of its external architects (cf. Parent 2011). Security, it will be recalled, was a key consideration for both the English and the Scots in 1707; and security remained a key consideration for the British and Irish proponents of union both within and beyond the Atlantic archipelago, and both during and after the revolutionary and Napoleonic conflict. Maintaining the security of the partners to union meant, in turn, in many cases, maintaining an overarching union army.

Reflecting first, and briefly, on the theme of security—this was historically a central argument both for the British union in 1707 and for the Irish union in 1801, and indeed it remains part of the overall case for sustaining the unions of the United Kingdom in the 21st century. In 1707 union with Scotland protected England's northern frontier at a time of intense continental warfare: at the same time for the Scots union with England effectively demilitarized a border which had been unsettled and unstable—and it also reduced the threat of military incursion from their much more powerful southern neighbour. For the Norwegians and Swedes, though union was in part an external geopolitical imposition, and though (as will shortly be seen) the two nations were never unified militarily, union did help to consolidate a lasting peace within (what unionists termed) the Scandinavian peninsula (Hemstad 2018). Elsewhere, the Ausgleich of 1867 created a relatively more stable relationship between Austria and Hungary, and therefore a relatively more settled and stable central and eastern Europe.

Before proceeding further, it should be said that, while the security arguments for the Irish union remained in place until the signing of the Anglo-Irish Treaty in December 1921 (and were in fact addressed within that treaty), these arguments were not always straightforward; and on the whole they illustrate, once again, the porousness of the distinction between integrative and disruptive forces working within union. First, security could in fact be an asymmetrical argument, relevant for some union partners but not for others: security in terms of the Irish union worked for the ascendancy elite in Ireland and for the English government more fully than for Irish nationalists, as evidenced by their stands during the First World War and (after Irish independence) during the Second World War (though cf. Robinson 2020). Similarly, security (in the sense of the perceived threat represented by Russia in the 19th century) played relatively more strongly in Sweden, which had lost Finland to Russia in 1808–9, than in Norway. Second, unions in the short term could proactively subvert local security: aggrieved 'subsidiary' partners within complex union states were sometimes subject to the threat—or indeed the reality—of union force (this was true for Norway, for Belgium, and for Ireland). Moreover, government in unstable unions has sometimes looked to external conflict as a means of bolstering internal unity—and, in so doing, it has effectively gambled with the entire edifice of union: this was the case both with the Dual Monarchy in 1914 and (it has been sometimes argued) the United Kingdom over its relationship with the European Union. Third, it should be said that, with the growth of supranational security unions in the aftermath of global warfare in the 20th century, the case for locating security exclusively within the protective institutions of union states has been diminished, if not wholly eradicated. Some of these ideas are reconsidered later in the work, in the contexts of discussing both the violence of union (section 4.11), as well as of global war (section 6.7).

Turning from union security to the cognate issue of union armies, it is clear that successive scholars have perceived close interconnections between these and supranational political identity: for Linda Colley, the army and war were key constituents in the aggregation of Britishness in the 18th century, while for the Edinburgh sociologist David McCrone, war (and the welfare state) have supplied additional centripetal force to the British union state of the 20th century. Habsburg scholars and commentators, as has been noted, have routinely identified the army and the longevity of its commander-in-chief, the emperor-king Franz Joseph, as key binding agents within Austria-Hungary: 'the army', Wickham Steed opined in 1913, 'is a nursery of dynastic feeling' (e.g. Steed 1919, pp. xxv, 60; see also Deák 1990; Cole et al. 2011, pp. 27–8). Albert Graf Apponyi thought in turn that the army embodied the critical last blast of Franz Joseph's conception of a unified Austrianness ('*stets intransigent, dahin mochte sich der letzte Rest seines gesamtösterreichischen Bewußtseins geflüchtet haben*': quoted in Haslinger 1996, p. 36).

However, such insights are necessarily founded upon a normative correlation between union states and overarching union armies; and in both the United Kingdom and the Dual Monarchy there were indeed overarching union armies (though of course the latter had—in addition to the imperial and royal army— also the *Landwehr* and the *Honvéd*, the Austrian and Hungarian national guards; for the latter see the excellent survey in Cole 2014, pp. 4–11). But in the United Kingdoms of Sweden-Norway the particularly loose nature of the union meant that, while there was a shared monarchy and a shared foreign policy, there remained two distinct parliaments and two distinct national armies within each of the union's constituent polities. Command of the two armies was theoretically united in the person of the king; but in practice the two were entirely separate. This separation was indeed more than a formality: there was no coordinated command or strategy, nor—remarkably—was there any coordination even in the matter of logistics and armaments, still less uniforms. In the early years of union there were some desultory efforts at joint military, army and navy, exercises—there were, for example, joint army exercises from the time of union until the 1850s. But these petered out, largely due to an absence of any Norwegian enthusiasm (cost was cited as an issue). Indeed, in general, defence issues, rather than being (as in other union states) an agency for exploring common ground and common concerns, tended to be deployed as a means of advertising Norwegian difference. Thus, not only was there a separate Norwegian army, and separate Norwegian logistical policies, there were also separate Norwegian strategic perspectives, focusing on the construction of coastal forts and on the country's navy (the Norwegians were much less afraid of a land-based Russian invasion than the Swedes, who remained scarred by the war of 1808–9). Little wonder, then, that, while the ultimate dissolution of union was entirely a juridical and constitutional affair, Norwegian army officers should have been questioning the essential purpose and usefulness of union by the 1890s. In short, the nature of the Scandinavian union was such that the balance between integrative and disruptive forces in a key institution like the army was entirely distinctive; and the looseness of union meant that, while there was very little shared—union—ground over which to fight, there were also very few unifying agencies or institutions. Thus was it possible for an exiguous union to last for a remarkably long time—that is to say because, rather than in spite of, its exiguousness.

The Norwegian and Swedish armies were not only separate and national institutions—each was also mono-ethnic and mono-lingual. By contrast, both the Habsburg and British armies were multi-ethnic institutions. In the early years of the 20th century approximately 85 per cent of officers in the Habsburg army were German, while the rank and file comprised 400,000 Slavs, 227,000 Germans, 220,000 Magyars, 48,000 Romanians, and 14,000 Italians. Catholics were enormously overrepresented among Habsburg career officers, a reflection of the army's particular appeal to the empire's Catholic aristocracies: the small Calvinist elites, relatively more closely associated with Magyar nationalism, preferred the *Honvéd* to the joint army of the empire (Deák 1990, pp. 171–2).

There are in fact some analogies here with the British army of the 19th and 20th centuries where Irish Catholics and the Scots were overrepresented among the rank and file (greatly so in the early 19th century); while the English, as the dominant ethnicity, as well as dominant social castes such as the Irish Protestant landed elite (or 'Protestant ascendancy'), were overrepresented among the officer ranks. The highlands of Scotland made a particular contribution to the union army: during the Napoleonic wars it is thought that the region supplied as many as 74,000 recruits at a time when its total population was around 300,000 (Devine 1999, pp. 184–5; Henderson 1989, p. 5). Ireland was similarly overrepresented in the army of the United Kingdom throughout the 19th century: it has been variously calculated that in 1810 there were 200,000 Irishmen who has served in the ranks, while by 1830 around 42 per cent of the army was Irish (at a time when the Irish proportion of the United Kingdom population was less than one-third) (McBride 2009, p. 353; Spiers 1996, pp. 336, 340; Cookson 1997, pp. 180–1).

Unlike the United Kingdom, however, universal military service had been a feature of the Dual Monarchy from 1868 onwards, with a requirement of three years of active engagement. What did this mean in terms of the inculcation of a supranational identity or values? Some calibration is certainly necessary. In István

Deák's opinion this was 'too little time to shed an ethnic identity for a supranational one'—and it was thus the long-serving officer and non-commissioned (NCO) classes upon whom the Habsburgs particularly depended for continuity and unity (Deák 1990, p. 4). However, he has also acknowledged that officer cadets 'were never taught—either from the standpoint of grasping the complexities of the Habsburg realm, or from the standpoint of cultural enrichment—the folklore, customs, problems and aspirations of the monarchy's many peoples' (Deák 1990, pp. 91–2). More recent scholarship on the Dual Monarchy has elaborated this verdict: Pieter Judson has argued that 'military service constituted the most influential point of contact between the Habsburg state and its male citizens of all classes… [and that it] played a major role in inculcating male citizens from every region with a defined set of common practices and imperial ideologies' (Judson 2016, p. 365). Others have persuasively suggested that the Habsburg army had 'a strongly denationalised vision of the world that was extremely vigorous even late into the Empire' and that it sustained 'an unapologetically centralist vision of the Empire' (Cole 2014, p. 321). Laurence Cole has pointed to a network of veterans' associations, which expanded rapidly in the last years of the 19th century, and which also consolidated the experience of compulsory service in so far as these bodies were interlinked with a wider spread and 'popular appropriation' of military culture across Cisleithania and beyond: he also reiterates the telling suggestion that the veterans' bodies created 'a ritualised "festive" framework through which loyalty and acceptance of patriotic duty were internalised' (Cole 2014, pp. 3, 314, 317). However, the failure of the idea of an overarching veterans' organization, in addition to the complex linguistic policies pursued across the armed forces of the empire, simultaneously points to the continuing importance of local and regional cultures for the soldiers of the Dual Monarchy. Thus, while the army did indeed bolster imperial loyalties, then these have to be understood—not as the simple antithesis of nationalism or regionalism—but rather as a complex set of identities binding the supranational with the national (Cole 2014). All this in fact chimes closely with what is known about the complex relationship between Irishness (and Scottishness and Welshness) and service in the British army—and the possible cohabitation of strongly patriotic Irish (and Scots and Welsh) identities within the context of British and imperial military service.

There was, of course, no universal military service across the entire United Kingdom state, not even during the First World War. There was certainly much earnest discussion on this theme, particularly in the aftermath of the South African war (1899–1902) when it formed part of a wider debate on (what the radical right-wing journalist, Arnold White (1848–1925) dubbed) 'efficiency and empire': a National Service League was created in 1902, and was led from 1905 by Earl Roberts (1832–1914) (White 1901; Searle 1971). During the First World War conscription was instituted in Great Britain in 1916, and redeployed again at the beginning of the Second World War. But this was neither extended to Ireland nor again, in 1939, to Northern Ireland. In fact, if (whatever the precise calibration) universal military service served as a dynastic cement in the Dual Monarchy, then the threat of its application—very deeply unpopular in nationalist Ireland—acted as a solvent within the wartime United Kingdom.

While there is no evidence to suggest that universal military service brought a 'shedding' of ethnic identity and the robust acquisition of a 'supranational' or loyalist substitute, whether in Britain or in Austria-Hungary, it does seem that recruitment to the army generally encouraged the softening or even reconciliation of ethnic or national identities with the overarching union state. This was certainly not always or simply the case, as is illustrated by the examples of those Irish soldiers who turned to republican activism in 1919–21 and again during the Northern Ireland 'Troubles'—or indeed by the rumours of (rather than actual) mass desertions of Czech and other Slav recruits to the Austro-Hungarian army during the Great War. But the armies of union states such as these *did* enforce a uniform discipline, uniform imagery, a uniform dynastic loyalty; and they also created the circumstances wherein the different nationalities of empire cooperated together for their mutual well-being or indeed (sometimes) mutual survival. The protection of linguistic sensitivities within the Habsburg ranks, or (on the whole) of religious and regional loyalties within the British army, contributed to these processes of acclimatization, or even—sometimes— reconciliation.

Still, it would be wrong to imply that the paths towards these ends ran smoothly, as lasting tensions over the use of German within the Austro-Hungarian army indicate. Indeed the possibility of religio-political jealousies always existed within complex union states, as with southern accusations that northerners were privileged in the royal army of the Netherlands in the 1820s, or the strong sense after 1914 that Irish Catholic and nationalist soldiers were receiving a rougher deal at the hands of the British War Office than their Protestant unionist counterparts. The armies of union, and the wars that they fought, and the issues of security that they addressed, were never uncomplicated centripetal forces. But, however imperfect, and however incomplete, there was emphatically a process of acculturation and assimilation with the armies of union. Paradoxically, though, this was entirely compatible on occasion with the existence, even the consolidation, of national sentiment (see section 6.7; Jackson 2013, pp. 163–72, 196–9).

4.5. Bureaucracy

In Oszkár Jászi's elaborate taxonomy of Habsburg integration 'bureaucracy' features as one additional and critical form of institutional cement. Indeed, according to Adolf Fischof (1816–93), physician and 1848 revolutionary, the bureaucratic 'sitting army' came second only after the regular imperial army itself as a prop to the Dual Monarchy. The irredentist Italian journalist, Virginio Gayda (1885–1944), already on the first steps of a journey which took him to fascism, observed caustically in 1915 that 'the army of state employees was really Austrian before anything else...he [the bureaucrat] might be a Czech or Pole, but he spoke German, he submitted himself completely to the Austrian principle, and became a being without nationalism' (Gayda 1915, p. 279; cf. Zách 2021, p. 38). This idea of the non-national, so alien and incomprehensible (and yet also so visible) to a full-blooded nationalist like Gayda, will be revisited later in the work (see section 6.5).

As a starting point, it is worth remembering that the late 19th century saw a rapid expansion in both the responsibilities of the British and Austro-Hungarian union states, with a concomitant expansion in both the numbers of officials as well as the ways in which the state intruded in the lives of its citizens: this expansion was related to the growth of political participation and representative institutions in both polities (for the Dual Monarchy see Deak 2015, pp. 198–9). In Austria-Hungary the postal and telegraph systems (for example) expanded exponentially at this time, as did the railways: compulsory primary school education in both parts of the empire together with compulsory health and accident insurance for workers added to the burgeoning state sector. In addition to all of this was the army (discussed in the previous section), and mandatory military service. All of these initiatives, excepting universal military service, were echoed within the United Kingdom state. In each polity, but especially the Dual Monarchy, the 1880s and after saw particularly marked growth: for Austria-Hungary this meant that from 1890 to 1911 (when an imperial *Kommission zur Förderung der Verwaltungsreform* (Commission for the advancement of administrative reform) was inaugurated) the cost of domestic administration rose from 4 million to 18 million crowns, while the number of officials in the central administration tripled (Deak 2015, pp. 249ff.).

It was always likely that expanding and overarching supranational bureaucracies would supply a unifying focus and function to diverse union states (see e.g. Godsey 1999, p. 124). But was this in fact uniformly the case? And in what ways did officialdom interrelate with the unity of multinational union polities? Whatever else, it should be said immediately that, as with the other centripetal institutions which have been discussed, there was no easy correlation between union and its related bureaucracies.

In the first instance numerous union states were not characterized by wholly (or even substantially) unified bureaucracies. In the United Kingdoms of Sweden and Norway, and indeed in the neighbouring Grand Duchy of Finland, bound until 1917 to the Russian empire, there were very largely separate, national, bureaucratic establishments. In Austria-Hungary, as has been seen, there were three common Ausgleich ministries, which for long remained designated as 'imperial' but which eventually assumed an appropriate *kaiserlich und königlich* identity: these were foreign affairs (becoming explicitly 'k. und k.' in 1895), finance (1903), and war (1903). In the United Kingdom of Great Britain and Ireland there was indeed a substantially unified civil service, though the drift (long before political devolution or independence) was towards an incremental administrative devolution. Thus, in Scotland, the creation of a Scottish Office in 1885 brought in effect an agency for the increasing capture of administrative authority; and in Ireland the existence of a separate administrative focus—Dublin Castle—and the development of distinctive legislation in (primarily) land reform further encouraged a specifically Irish set of administrative institutions and initiatives, including controversially in 1904-5. England and Wales were closely bound in administrative terms, though even in Wales there was a slow drift towards administrative distinctiveness and devolution, beginning in the late 19th century with legislation explicitly designed for application in the principality alone.

However, separate bureaucracies did not always imply totally separate mindsets and a concomitant centrifuge. For example, with Sweden-Norway the years between 1836, when the first Norwegian statholder was appointed, through to the early 1880s have been identified as 'the high noon of the union' (Barton 2003, p. 58). Central to the attainment of this zenith was what has been defined as 'a *de facto* alliance between the Norwegian and Swedish official classes faced with the rise in both kingdoms of what appeared to be alarmingly radical and democratic forces' (Barton 2003, p. 58). The Norwegian official classes had not always thought in these terms; and indeed, educated in Denmark, and often bound by family ties to Denmark, they originally—in 1814-15—had hankered after the old union, and were correspondingly suspicious of the new: in 1814 they had even promoted the claims of the crown prince of Denmark to the throne of Norway (Jorgenson 1935, pp. 28, 37). But, with time, and by the early 1830s, they were increasingly unsettled by the growing power of the small farmers (or bønder) cohort, and were for a time interested in the possibility of achieving an easier working relationship with their Swedish counterparts (Jorgenson 1935, pp. 45, 48-9). This interest was reciprocated; and in turn the shared defensiveness helped to stabilize the wider union arrangement in Scandinavia. But the Norwegian bureaucracy had not always thought in these terms, and it worth emphasizing fluidity and contingency in any discussion of this kind.

So, while unified forms and structures were important and helpful, they were not essential for union—and indeed content was often more important than form: what bureaucracies did, and how they did it (as distinct from their organizational scope and shape), especially in terms of the gathering of knowledge, also mattered a great deal. Robin Okey has referred to how 'the spirit of conscientious public service that was the Austrian Enlightenment's main legacy came [ultimately] to be dubbed "Josephinian"' (Okey 2001, p. 67). Joseph's educational reforms had helped to lay the foundations for the trained bureaucracy for which 'the Enlightenment had striven' (Okey 2001, pp. 79-80). This spirit of mission and of conscientiousness was also, perhaps, present within the Scottish service. But it was perceived as lacking in Ireland's Castle administration (certainly by Irish nationalists and aloof Whitehall mandarins like Warren Fisher); and on the whole these perceptions came to be confirmed both by formal external review and also, ultimately, less formally but no less tellingly, by the insouciant memoirs of senior officials such as Maurice Headlam (1873–1956), enthusiastic socialite, angler, and also (incidentally) a senior Irish-based Treasury official (Headlam 1947; O'Halpin 1987). However in the cases both of the Habsburg empire, and those of Ireland, Scotland, and the British empire generally, the early and mid-19th century was characterized by the work of a 'new school of statisticians and ethnographers' whose purpose was to garner knowledge and to establish a more complete control over the territories under consideration (Okey 2001, p. 65). In both the British empire, including the unions of the United Kingdom, and the Habsburg empire the supposedly distinguishing features of individual ethnicities were identified with a view to establishing their military usefulness (or indeed threat).

Some further calibrations are necessary. Administrative expansion and embrace were not simply central, or top-down, initiatives and impositions from within the union state. It has been shrewdly observed that the impetus for some at least of the bureaucratic changes in the Dual Monarchy came from 'the margins of empire'; and to some extent this, too, was the case for the United Kingdom, within which the fresh demands (say) of administering relatively popular and technically complex land legislation from the early 1880s onwards created considerable fresh bureaucracies in both Ireland and (to a lesser extent) Scotland. In both Austria-Hungary—and the United Kingdom—'postal workers and elementary school teachers came to symbolise the empire for the general public, since they represented it in the most common daily life interactions' (Judson 2016, p. 337).

The expansion and tightening embrace of the union state were not by any means simple unifying forces. The growth of the state certainly meant that it touched the everyday lives of working people as never before. But it also (certainly in the Habsburg case) brought a greater squeeze on official budgets, and therefore enhanced instability. State growth also reflected and encouraged greater individual expectations as well as a wider democratization. Neither of these phenomena contributed straightforwardly (or at all) to the strengthening of the union state.

Moreover, state growth also tended to upset established relationships within the union state, and its perceived equilibrium. Expressing this point in a slightly different way, the relationship between union or imperial bureaucracies and those non-dominant nationalities within union states was complex and suggestive. This (for example) was the perception in Scotland in the 1850s and after, and it led to increasingly strident patriotic calls for redress. Similarly, the consolidation of a cultural and political nationalism in late 19th century Ireland may be read in part as a response to the expansion of the British state (see e.g. Hutchinson 1987). The growth of the British state in the late 19th century simultaneously provoked as well as ensnared Irish nationalists—in the sense both that the greater intrusion of British officialdom and of the English language (as the medium of an ever more meddling government) stimulated a nationalist push-back, as well as presenting ever greater opportunities for Irish people to gain 'respectable' employment and to reconcile themselves, however passively, to union and empire. As recent work has illustrated, the expanding British post office empire accommodated many Irish people within its ranks; and, while there was certainly a small cohort of burgeoning revolutionaries (the most prominent being of course Michael Collins), the overwhelming majority worked quietly within the embrace of the union and imperial state (see e.g. Maguire 2008; Joyce 2013; though cf. Campbell 2009).

There were some parallels here, again, with the Austro-Hungarian empire. Before 1914 Czechs comprised a comparatively great proportion of the Habsburg civil service; but, though they benefited thereby from the institutions of empire, and though 'in a way the latter fostered the acceptance of the [Habsburg] state', at the same time many Czechs (like many Irish) kept a cautious distance between themselves and the imperial or union enterprise (von Hirschhausen and Leonhard 2001, p. 506; Deak 2015, p. 218). Indeed, reflecting on the impact of the war on Austria's government and administration from the vantage point of 1925, Josef Redlich talked about the increasing 'nationalization' of officialdom in the last two decades of the monarchy ('*die Nationalisierung der altösterreichischen Beamtenschaft in den Provinzen während der beiden letzten Jahrzehnte des Reiches*') (Redlich 1925, pp. x, 284ff.). In other words, a supposedly unifying civil service (like the armies of union) encouraged passive acceptance, but not by any means uniform and enthusiastic acculturation. The civil service in several union polities, including Austria-Hungary, did not (or rather could not) crush national difference, but rather generated cultures of containment and competition: as Wickham Steed commented in 1913, 'the essence of the language struggle is that it is a struggle for bureaucratic influence' (Steed 1919, p. 77). Indeed, paradoxically, both the Habsburg administration and its challenges grew in parallel with the development of representation in, especially, Cisleithania: the administration was simultaneously a locus of mediation as well as of party conflict (Deak 2015, p. 217).

The growth of union state bureaucracies was problematic in other, related, respects. In Austria-Hungary the expansion of the civil service simultaneously reflected some of the dynamic aspects of the late Habsburg state, as well as its more sclerotic and masochistic features. Expanding bureaucracy reflected the state's reasonable efforts to address the work created both by greater social as well as national or linguistic representation; but it also produced overwhelming surges of paperwork and centralization. Expansion often meant the hiring of relatively large numbers of middle-ranking officials, rather than of the essential lower grades. Periodic efforts to further systematic reform by the Josephinian Ernest von Koerber (in 1904) and through the imperial *Kommision* (mentioned earlier) exemplified both the state's creativity as well as the problems which had to be overcome (see Deak 2015). Perhaps also there were fundamental problems with the vision of Koerber (and others of his ilk) who saw an enhanced role for the bureacracy in both central government as well as in mediating between the conflicting parties. At their best these were proposals for administrative efficiency; at worst they were an iteration of imperial 'divide and rule'—encouraging communication with the imperial metropole at the expense of (certainly more troublesome) communication with and between neighbours in the periphery.

Much, though not all, of this picture was replicated within parts of the United Kingdom. In Ireland and Scotland a degree of administrative devolution (especially from the 1880s on) effectively meant the mediation of powerful bureaucracies between citizens and the central state; and the overarching policies of 'constructive unionism' were certainly characterized by the application of financial and bureaucratic solutions to the demands of union government, certainly in Ireland (see Curtis 1963; Gailey 1987). In Ireland, too, the expansion of officialdom under the union became, as in the Dual Monarchy, Wickham Steed's perpetual 'struggle for bureaucratic influence', whether in terms of the village postmastership, or junior officials of the Irish Land Commission, or more senior ranks. And in Ireland, as in the Dual Monarchy, focusing upon the need to persuade the bureaucrats of the imperial metropole often meant paying less attention to negotiating with neighbours.

However, the correlation between officialdom and instability also had other, and distinctively Habsburg, inflections. As has been noted, foreign affairs in Austria-Hungary were an overarching *kaiserlich und königlich* enterprise. The foreign ministry, which was housed in the Ballhausplatz in Vienna, has frequently been seen as home to an aristocratic community of 'supranational patriots'—and indeed the 'young rebel' faction in the ministry (originally created and mentored by Count Alois Lexa von Aehrenthal (1854–1912), and then led by Count Alexander Hoyos (1876–1937)) pushed after 1912–13 for a more aggressive foreign policy as a means of averting the disintegration and restoring the 'great power' status of the Dual Monarchy (Godsey 1999, esp. pp. 102–23, 124–64; Tunstall 2012, p. 118; Cornwall 2002, p. 26; cf. Hannig in Geppert et al. 2015, p. 247).

This, together with the often labyrinthine structures and procedures—and consequent glacial pace—of later Habsburg bureaucracy raises once again the question of the elision between integrative and disruptive institutions, forces, and agencies within the Monarchy and beyond. Wickham Steed, who in fact saw the Habsburg bureaucracy as a key facet of the state, also believed that it possessed four fundamental and damning characteristics:

> the sense of authority and of superiority over those who are administered or governed, a sense formerly existing in the shape of a corporate bureaucratic consciousness, but now atomised and individualised; the dislike of responsibility and, consequently, a disposition to clothe administrative action in elusive forms

elaborated by the practice of generations; the hierarchical spirit which renders every official of a certain rank an object of respect for officials of lower rank and makes the attainment of higher rank the main object of bureaucratic endeavour; and the tendency to resent, as a sort of lèse-majesté, all attempts to criticise the working, to curtail the power, or to reform the organisation of the bureaucracy itself. (Steed 1919, p. 74)

Contemporary scholars have noticed the particularly intense bureaucratic cultures of the Habsburg foreign and war ministries respectively, and the ensuing inertia—especially damaging in terms of the drive (or rather lack of it) for modernization and augmentation within the armed forces of the Monarchy in the run-up to 1914. In short, there is an argument for seeing some of the key centripetal administrative institutions of the Dual Monarchy as functioning so ineffectively, so sclerotically, that they acted ultimately as disintegrative agencies rather than the reverse (see e.g. Steed 1919, pp. 74ff.).

Moreover, with the foreign ministry in particular, though there was indeed an overarching supranational vision of Austria, the parallel reality was that officials were drawn from different classes and ethnicities, and their work reflected—sometimes tendentiously or even disastrously—these particular origins. This was in fact paralleled in an extreme way within Sweden-Norway, where—while there was a shared (and thus potentially unifying) foreign and consular service—in reality Swedish personnel and Swedish interests predominated. In both the Austro-Hungarian and the Swedish-Norwegian cases what should have been a unitary and uniting institution, the foreign service, proved to be much more subversive: the theoretically centripetal became centrifugal in practice.

But in terms of the Dual Monarchy and the Ballhausplatz, the Magyar landed interest was well represented in the economic sections of the foreign ministry (as well as in the ambassadorial ranks); and detailed research has located some evidence to suggest that Aehrenthal's relatively conciliatory policies regarding Serbia were undermined by those within the ministry who believed that their own, and their class's, interests were thereby under threat: Leopold Graf Berchtold (1863–1942), ambassador at St Petersburg before succeeding Aehrenthal as foreign minister, and the owner of substantial Hungarian estates, effectively aligned himself with those Hungarians in the ministry who opposed Aehrenthal's more emollient economic approaches to Serbia after the Bosnian annexation of 1908 (e.g. Godsey 1999, p. 138). It need hardly be underlined that this subversion contributed to the ratcheting up of the ultimately disastrous tensions which characterized the relationship between Vienna, Serbia, and the wider Balkans.

The role of the foreign ministry, and its young rebels, in driving forward aggressive policies, especially after 1912–13, and the usefulness of war and conquest more generally as a means of 'salvation', point to unsettling aspects of the instability inherent in these union states (Herwig 1997, p. 8). Viewed from later perspectives, and in particular the blight of Nazi and Soviet dictatorship, the Habsburg empire has looked like a relatively benign community of nations (and this indeed was how some of its celebrants and apologists viewed matters even during the Monarchy's existence). But such interpretations may have downplayed both the Monarchy's unrelenting capacity to fight—and the presence of bureaucrats who sometimes sought to sustain internal unity through external conflict.

In short, union bureaucracies generally served to unite. But at the same time they often functioned as a battlefield for national rivalries. And in the end they may have harboured a tendency to seek unity in devastation—and even apocalypse.

4.6. 'Kneeling Armies': Church and Faith

The broad theme here, with this section, is the role of the churches, especially state or otherwise legally privileged churches, in bolstering the union state. The sectional title itself comes from a famous summary of the means by which Franz Joseph held his fissiparous multinational empire together. He ruled and maintained unity across the Habsburg lands (in Adolf Fischof's quip) through the agency of four armies—a standing army, a 'sitting army' (the bureaucracy), each discussed above: in addition to these there was a 'crawling army' (the secret police)—*and*, critically, a 'kneeling army' (the Catholic Church) (quoted often but see Beller 1996, p. 59; Judson 2016, p. 247; cf. Steed 1919, p. 90). Similarly, for Oszkár Jászi one of the key centripetal forces of the Dual Monarchy was the Catholic Church (he opined that 'aside from its army, the Roman Catholic church was the most solid pillar of the Habsburg dynasty') (Jászi 1929, pp. 133, 155).

More generally, the approach of this section complements the comparative methodologies pursued by Clark and Kaiser in addressing the European 'culture wars' of the 19th century between liberalism, secularism, and Catholicism (Clark and Kaiser 2003), by Hugh McLeod on religion and the decline of religion in western Europe (McLeod 1996, 1999, 2000), and by S. J. Brown on the established churches of 'these islands' and beyond (Brown 2001). Andrew Porter and Hilary Carey have each written comparatively on churches and empire, and in the particular context of the complex British empire (Carey 2008). Ulrike von Hirschhausen and Jörn Leonhard have, however, come closest to the concerns here through their pioneering scholarship on the different roles of churches and religion across a number of multinational empires—the British, Habsburg, Russian, and Ottoman (von Hirschhausen and Leonhard 2001, pp. 311–92). In each of these religious faith to some extent was intertwined with issues of unity and allegiance, whether in terms of Anglicanism, Catholicism, Orthodoxy, or—in the particular case of Abdul Hamid II (1842–1918), Sultan of the fracturing Ottoman empire—pan-Islamism.

In addition, the emphasis on the moral dimension of certain types of— federal—union venture, noticed by the late Michael Burgess and others, has supplied another related theme to (and point of reference for) the following discussion. For example, recent work on the making of the American federal union and its constitution emphasizes the influence of Christian theology, and in particular covenantal theory and theology (Burgess 2006, pp. 48–9).

Reviewing the different case studies as a starting point, the United Kingdom of Great Britain and Ireland embraced two established churches with divergent theologies and different relationships with the union state: the supranational United Church of England and Ireland (1801), which effectively included Wales and which was closely tied to the British state, and the presbyterian Church of Scotland, whose links with the state were somewhat looser (though of course still hotly debated). The two unions of Scotland and Ireland were intimately associated with church establishments (see e.g. Figure 4.1). The United Kingdom was therefore a parliamentary union which was associated both with a complementary church, but also with a wider theological diversity (Brown 2001, p. 92). As indeed S. J. Brown has sharply observed, this 'was a curious situation: the same state recognized two churches as established within its territories, while those two churches viewed each other as being in grave error' (Brown 2008, p. 19).

The curiousness of this 'curious situation' is compounded if aspects of the wider British empire are considered. The flexible Anglican ecclesiology of Britain's union establishment did not immediately stretch to embrace the majority faith, Catholicism, in Ireland; but on the whole it did manage, in an era of continuing European religious antagonisms, to locate an effective *modus vivendi* with the distant Catholicism of Quebec. As has been shown, the Quebec Act together with the avoidance of any minority Anglican establishment in Lower Canada, the re-establishment of a Catholic episcopal hierarchy, and the close relations between royal government and the Catholic clergy and seigneurial classes in both Lower Canada and the United Province—all stood in sharp contrast to the situation within Ireland at the beginning of the 19th century; and indeed all pointed to the broad outlook which royal government was striving for in Ireland by the end of the 19th century. In essence the Anglican union state of 1801 was not capable of embracing Irish Catholicism; but it *was* able to embrace the far-off French Catholics of Quebec. And the implications for the stability of royal government within each of these communities were strikingly distinctive: an alienated Catholic Ireland violently rejected union in 1919–21, while Catholic Canada peaceably worked out its forms of *survivance* and accommodation within both the United Province and the Dominion of Canada.

The United Kingdoms of Sweden-Norway constituted a still different form of union polity and embraced a different form of ecclesiastical establishment, or rather establishments. Unlike in Britain and Ireland there was no agreed supranational established church, even though Sweden and Norway each shared strong Lutheran identities. In essence, the United Kingdoms of Sweden-Norway had no unitary establishment, but had instead two individual national churches, the Church of Norway (*den norske kirke*, the state church in Norway from 1814, with the Eidsvoll constitution, to 2017) and the Church of Sweden (*Svenska kyrkan*, which survived as an established church in Sweden until 2000). In other words the state was associated with a strong moral and spiritual mission and with a firm church establishment; but the states concerned were the (still) evolving nation states of Norway and Sweden—and *not* the United Kingdoms of Sweden-Norway.

Turning to the case of the United Kingdom of the Netherlands—here, too, were variations on the structure of the union state and its associated church establishment. Here, too, the wider ambiguities of the post-1815 Restoration era were exposed, with the new polity looking back as much to the secularizing influence of revolution as to that of the *ancien régime* (Wintle 1987, pp. 14–15). Retaining some of the influence of the revolutionary era, the new polity lacked any overt form of church establishment or national church. Unlike Britain and Ireland, there was no supranational established church: unlike Sweden-Norway there were no individual national churches within the component territories of union. Unlike Austria-Hungary, discussed below, there was no single (legally) favoured dominant church. There were instead two pre-eminent Christian church traditions—the Dutch Reformed in the north, and Catholic in the south; but the north had housed no established church since the Batavian republic had, following the influence of the French, done away with such fripperies after 1795. Indeed, Catholic emancipation had been achieved in 1797, more than 30 years before the equivalent epiphany in the United Kingdom (Wintle 2000, p. 287). However, the creation of the new united kingdom meant, in effect, that—as in Ireland—a Protestant minority was now dominant in what was a primarily Catholic polity.

In 1814–15, with the creation of the new United Kingdom of the Netherlands, Protestantism and Catholicism were organized into two official departments of worship, while the new union constitution (again in contradistinction to Britain and Ireland) made no provision for a state church (Wintle 1987, pp. 12–13). The modern Dutch Reformed Church was greatly shaped by these changes imposed in 1816; and it was effectively officials from the new Department of Reformed Worship who came to run the Church (Wintle 1987, p. 19). These innovations (together with the influence of the Calvinist royal house of Orange) meant that, while there was formal religious equality, the state remained closely associated with a now tightly and centrally managed Reformed Church. So, if there was no state church as such, then the ethos and central institutions of the new United Kingdom of the Netherlands were certainly strongly Calvinist.

The Russian empire, though not a central concern of this book, has however been part of the burgeoning scholarly debate on the taxonomy of empire; and Austria-Hungary, which *has* been a significant concern here, has certainly long been compared with Russia, as one of the two great 'theocratic empires' of the 19th century (to borrow the description of Tomáš Masaryk (1850–1937)) (von Hirschhausen and Leonhard 2001, pp. 337–58). Moreover, there are several striking parallels between the complex ecclesiastical settlements within the United

Kingdom and those in Finland during its era as a grand duchy within the Russian empire (1809–1917). Here, too, with the Grand Duchy, was a multi-ethnic and multi-faith polity, where variable ecclesiastical geometries applied. Finland, after its annexation by Russia from Sweden in 1809, enjoyed considerable legislative autonomy within the Russian empire—the 'pax russica', which lasted until the damaging russification programmes of 1899 and after. There was a Finnish diet, a Finnish army, separate coins and stamps—and there was the established Finnish Lutheran Church: at the same time Finns (like the Irish and Scots in London) exercised a disproportionate influence in St Petersburg and Moscow. Finland was thus sometimes described (by, for example, the leading Finnish liberal statesman and lawyer, Leo Mechelin (1839–1914)) as being in a form of union relationship with the Russians: advocates of Irish home rule, and those who looked back to the pre-1800 Irish parliament, certainly saw analogies between the Grand Duchy of Finland and the condition of Ireland in its relations with Britain (Newby 2017).

But there were also links and parallels with the wider British union in an ecclesiastical sense—'a shared northern Protestant identity' has been identified, for example, along with diplomatic interests and commerce, as part of a robust British Fennophilia (Newby 2017). Similarly, the Lutheran Church of Finland, formed in 1809, when Finland was acquired by the Russian empire, was one of the two Finnish church establishments—the other being the Orthodox Church, the predominant faith of the wider empire and of the tsars. Russia, like the United Kingdom, sanctioned different official churches, and conflicting theologies, in its desire to reconcile the unity and spiritual direction of the wider polity. Indeed, because the Russian Tsar consciously sustained the Swedish law code with the annexation of Finland (as did the British with the Catholic Church and French legal practice in acquiring Quebec in 1763), and because the kings of Sweden had been heads of the Lutheran Church, the Orthodox Tsar now became the *de jure* head of Lutheranism in Finland, the nominator of bishops—a theological elision no less striking than the British monarch's mediation between Anglicanism and Presbyterianism, or the Anglican union state's mediation with Catholicism in (for example) Lower Canada and Malta. The Evangelical Lutheran cathedral of Helsinki, completed as the Church of St Nicholas in 1852, was built as a tribute to Tsar Nicholas I (1796–1855): it still has a statue of Tsar Alexander II (1818–81), erected in 1894, standing before it in the Senate Square. However, Finnish Lutherans, like many Scottish Presbyterians and Irish Anglicans, ultimately found it difficult to manage their relationships with secular authority, especially when that authority was theologically distant; and, like the Church of Ireland, the Lutheran Church of Finland was disestablished in 1869–70.

Finally there was the Austrian empire, redefined after the compromise of 1867 as Austria-Hungary or the Dual Monarchy. If union in the 'British Isles', both in terms of Scotland and Ireland, was associated both with Protestantism and with a religiously inflected English or British 'civilizing' mission, then of course unity in the Habsburg lands has been associated at different times with both Catholicism and German (and eventually Magyar) 'civilization'. If parts of the 'British Isles'—primarily and catastrophically Ireland—have been associated with the enforcement of the state faith, then the Habsburg empire, and primarily the Austrian lands and Bohemia, were associated with the comprehensive enforcement of the Catholic Counter-Reformation (particularly with the accession in 1619 of Ferdinand II as Holy Roman Emperor). Wickham Steed, drawing on an English Protestant tradition of anti-Catholicism, and in particular of anti-Jesuit feeling, emphasized in his classic study of *The Hapsburg Monarchy* (published originally in 1913) what he described as 'the permanent effects of the artificial but pitilessly effective standardisation of political and religious sentiment by Jesuit fathers and fanatical monarchs during and after the counter-reformation' (Steed 1919, pp. xxi, 105-19).

Christopher and Hugh Seton-Watson, in memorializing their eminent father, Robert, have pointed out that it was the apparently divinely ordained duty of the Habsburgs 'to uphold the true faith against the two threats of the infidel and heretic' (Seton Watson 1981, p. 23). The successful promotion of Catholic institutions and values was complemented by the vigorous suppression of (often) Protestant-led or influenced rebellion throughout the 17th and early 18th centuries, from the uprising of István Bocskai in 1604–6 through the Magnates' (or Wesselényi) conspiracy of 1670, the revolt of Imre Thököly (1690), to the revolt of Ferenc II Rákóczi (1703–11) (Ingrao 1994, pp. 40, 67–9, 111–17). What is noticeable about these revolts (amongst much else) is the familial interconnections of the leadership, the stimulus supplied by religious persecution, and the occasional resort of the insurgents to the most shocking of available tactical expedients—namely cooperation with the Habsburgs' Ottoman and Muslim opponents. The parallels between central Europe in the 17th and 18th centuries and contemporary Ireland need hardly be laboured—with persistent religious persecution melding with patriotic grievance to produce both a tradition of insurgency and indeed a tradition of resort to the Catholic enemies of the English and British states (including France and Austria itself).

Repressive legal frameworks designed to promote religious conformity were in place in Ireland until the last quarter of the 18th century, with something approaching an equalization of civil rights coming only in 1828–9 (when there was the combination of Catholic emancipation and the repeal of the Test and Corporations Acts). In the Habsburg lands legal frameworks compelling religious conformity were only gradually relaxed (with some marked ups and downs) from Joseph II's Patent of Toleration (1781) and his Edict of Tolerance for Jews (1782) through to the Protestantenpatent (1861) and the general liberalization encouraged with the Ausgleich of 1867. But this was emphatically not a seamless progression: the intimate relationship between dynasty and Church was renewed after 1848 and through the concordat of 1855—in what has been described as 'Vienna's response to the revolutionary upheavals of 1848' (Martin Schulze Wessel in von Hirschhausen and Leonhard 2001, p. 342). However, the 'clericalisation of politics'—this 'defensive ideology against modernity'—lasted in its latest and extreme iteration for only 20 years, being finally undermined by the three confessional laws of May 1868 and, more generally, through the period of liberal hegemony in Cisleithania, which ended in 1879 (Okey 2001, p. 256). Ultimately, by the era of the Ausgleich, Catholicism has been seen as 'less a State Church than an ecclesiastical department of the State, working like the army, the bureaucracy and the police in the interests of "government"' (Steed 1919, p. 103).

By the early 20th century what was left of this history of entanglement was (in both Austria-Hungary and the United Kingdom) a popular connection between the enforcement of union or empire and the enforcement of state-sanctioned religious practice: in Ireland union and British imperial supremacy were broadly associated with anglicization, Protestantism, and in particular the Church of Ireland, while in (for example) Bohemia and Bosnia Habsburg rule was linked with germanization and Catholicization. In each, therefore, the opportunity arose for an association between political and religious dissent, and the construction of ethnic nationalisms where religion was a contributing feature. In Ireland the 19th century saw the creation of a Gaelic Catholic nationalism defined in part against the union state and its church. In the Dual Monarchy Lutherans and Calvinists, though relatively small minorities, exercised a disproportionate influence within Slav and Magyar nationalism (Okey 2001, pp. 101, 108; Zách 2021, p. 160). Indeed, the historian Robert Nemes has described 'a clear hierarchy of confession in the [Hungarian] liberal nationalist imagination. Pride of place [he argues] belonged to Calvinists who, according to a well-established invented tradition, had repeatedly defended the liberties of the Hungarian nation against foreign absolutism' (Nemes 2003, p. 316). For František Palacký, the motor force of Czech nationalism sprang from 'the Hussite spirit of the Czech reformation' (Zách 2021, p. 32). In addition to all this, some German Austrians, led by Georg von Schönerer, also mediated their nationalism and opposition to the compromises of empire through religious opposition to the Catholic Church—in particular through the *los von Rom* movement (von Hirschhausen and Leonhard 2001, p. 25).

Connected with this, the protest against union, empire, and its imagery also became—in the context of the dying Dual Monarchy—protest against the memorialization of an imperial Catholicism. It has been tellingly observed that 'in Habsburg central Europe religious ritual, discourse and symbolism were never entirely divorced from nationalist practice'—and that 'the last decades of the 19th century and the first decades of the 20th century were an era of monument fever in Bohemia' (Cynthia Pares and Nancy Wingfield in Judson and Rozenblit 2005, pp. 107–8). While German liberals sought to commemorate Joseph II through the erection of numerous statues, Czech nationalists—Catholics and Lutherans—ultimately signified their repudiation of Habsburg dominance through the memorialization of the reformer Jan Hus (c.1372–1415), most significantly in the great statue erected in central Prague in 1915: Masaryk similarly chose the quincentenary of the martyrdom of Hus (6 July 1915) to declare war on the Habsburgs, on behalf of the people of Bohemia (Steed 1937, p. 94; Bucur and Wingfield 2001, pp. 178–205). The corollary of celebrating Hus was the overthrow of Catholic imagery specifically associated with the suppression of Bohemian autonomy, such as the Marian column in Prague, erected originally in 1650 at the end of the Thirty Years' War, and toppled in November 1918, or the statue of St John Nepomuk, toppled in the provincial city of Dobrovice in August 1920 (the Marian column of Prague was replaced in 2020). The government of the freshly created Czechoslovak state revived the national commemoration of Hus in 1925, though—in the aftermath of a spat with the Vatican over the celebration of 'heretics' in a still overwhelmingly Catholic state—there was also a counterbalancing festival in 1929 to mark the thousandth anniversary of the martyrdom of a more religiously orthodox Bohemian hero, St Wenceslas (see Cynthia Pares in Bucur and Wingfield 2001, pp. 209–35).

These case studies of church and union broach a further range of subsidiary themes. Of the several possibilities, only three may be briefly mentioned here, in the final parts of the section. They are: the moral basis of union, followed by monarchy, church, and union, and (last) union churches and the 'civilizing' mission of the union state.

The architects of unions, such as the United Kingdom of Great Britain and Ireland, or the Dual Monarchy, often sought to invest these new polities with a unifying sense of moral and spiritual purpose through the specific identification of a favoured or established church, or through the elaboration of religious ceremonial. Indeed, in the case of Britain and Ireland, the new United Kingdom of 1801 was (as both Geoffrey Best and Jay Brown have deemed it) 'a semi-confessional state', endowed with an ostensibly new enterprise, the United Church of England and Ireland (even if in practice the two Churches of England and Ireland continued pretty much as before).

But there were countervailing forces here, almost from the beginning. The effort to endow new unions with an ancestry and a unifying moral purpose, partly through church establishments or church ceremonial, was flawed often from the start, as the British case clearly demonstrates. With both the Scottish union (1706–7) and its Irish successor (1801) there were successful popular traditions critiquing the—evidently corrupt—means by which union had been enacted in each case. While these traditions have since been comprehensively interrogated by scholars, and often persuasively contextualized, the fact remains that—certainly for the British—the union church was launched not only in the face of massive Irish Catholic exclusion and scepticism, but also in the context of (what were widely seen as) a corrupt set of bargains (see e.g. Jackson 2013).

Advocates of union elsewhere in early 19th-century Europe and beyond sought with a similar lack of success for a unifying moral narrative—in, for example, the

United Kingdom of the Netherlands, where (as has been seen) the new union constitution was only clinched in 1815 using the unconvincing *arithmétique hollandaise* (that is to say counting some 'no' votes and abstentions as votes of support) (Marteel 2018, p. 61). This moral deficit was true, too, of Sweden-Norway, where union was agreed only in the context of military threat. Or, turning briefly to examples beyond the case studies, the United Kingdom of Portugal, Brazil, and the Algarves was effectively created partly through the enforced flight of the royal family from Lisbon in November 1807, and partly through the formal declaration of December 1815 (sometimes dismissed as 'little more than a paper measure') (Barman 1999, p. 3). With the case of Finland, too, the Grand Duchy was only established in the wake of the Russian military conquest of 1808.

Indeed, these corrupted birth narratives fed into wider moral critiques of union, or of the dominant partners within multinational union polities. This is an issue which may only be touched upon. But it takes us from the critiques of anti-unionists like the Scottish radical traveller Samuel Laing, commenting in the late 1830s upon the (supposed) moral decrepitude of Sweden in relation to democratic Norway, through to the famous sneer of James Joyce's 'citizen' in *Ulysses* at English 'syphilisation' (see Laing 1839; Joyce 1922, episode 12: Cyclops).

Turning briefly to the theme of monarchy and the churches—with each of the polities under review church and faith were associated with other key and interlinked agencies of union, and primarily the crown and its associated institutions. In Britain and Ireland the monarchy was of course intimately linked with the established church, as its supreme governor: loyalty to the Protestant monarchy became a significant binding agent within union, which also transcended unionism and had an impact upon national feeling within Scotland and Wales (and even, to a lesser extent, in Ireland). With British monarchs, however, while they were of course formally anointed, there was still no greatly sanctified tradition: though one English king, Edward the Confessor (1003–66), was recognized as a saint by the papacy, in general the English crown was distinguished by murderously creating saints and martyrs elsewhere (like Thomas Becket (1118–70) or Thomas More (1478–1535)) rather than itself sustaining a tradition of martyrdom and sanctity. The monarchs of the union period, faithful in their formal religious observance, have not always been distinguished by excessive personal piety or devotion (Victoria and Elizabeth II are exceptions to a rule which has been sustained, *inter alios*, by George IV, Edward VII, and Edward VIII) (see Figures 3.1, 4.1).

Recent research on the Dual Monarchy has increasingly recovered the importance of supranational dynastic loyalties, binding devotion to the emperor with Catholic conviction and local identities, as against more reductive notions of nationalism (Judson 2016; King 2002). But, much more than with the British ruling house, the religious devotion of the Habsburgs—the *pietas austriaca*—was of legendary standing, and drew upon a heritage of sanctity which was enfolded into the dukedom of Austria (through St Leopold) and the apostolic throne of Hungary (through St Stephen) as well as the throne of Bohemia (through St Wenceslas): it has been said that 'the symbolic origin of Christian rule in Austria' was the myth of Rudolf of Habsburg, who gave his horse to a priest carrying the sanctum and was thereafter elevated as king of Germany (Clark and Kaiser 2003, p.286; von Hirschhausen and Leonhard 2001, p. 346). Franz Joseph was certainly distinguished by a very clear public piety and religious observance; and indeed his long-serving minister and governor, Count Károly Khuen Hédervary, in mulling over the emperor-king's elusive personality with Henry Wickham Steed, ultimately came to the conclusion that faith and spirituality were at its roots:

> Behind the veil was the Monarch who decided everything by himself and took counsel of none save the Deity to whom alone he felt himself responsible. Thus I [Khuen Hédervary] have never known him; and nobody else has known or will know him. If you take this fact as the basis of your study and start with the conviction that you are dealing with a living embodiment of Divine Right you will not far go wrong... (Steed 1937, pp. 28–9; cf Steed 1924, vol. 1, p. 239)

Franz Joseph's great-nephew, Karl, the last Habsburg emperor, who relinquished the throne in 1918, and who died at the age of 34 in 1922, sustained this tradition of intense personal piety; and indeed he was ultimately beatified by Pope John Paul II in 2004 as Blessed Karl of Austria. Karl's widow, Zita, the last Habsburg empress-queen, who died in 1989, has also been the subject of a beatification cause (Figures 3.4, 4.3, 4.4).

In fact after the 1848 risings the Habsburg court revived a range of neglected religious (and other) ceremonial, including the Maundy footwashing and the elaborate Corpus Christi procession—the intention being (in Lawrence Cole's description) 'to demonstrate publicly the restored absolute power of the divinely ordained Christian ruler' (in Clark and Kaiser 2003, pp. 285–6; see also Unowsky 2005, pp. 26–32, Bucur and Wingfield 2001, pp. 24–5). This amalgam of faith and dynastic loyalty together with public assertions of divine ordination reached a peak with Franz Joseph's golden jubilee in 1898, when the Cardinal Archbishop of Prague (Franziskus Graf von Schönborn) and the complete Austrian episcopate endorsed a pastoral which implicitly compared the emperor to Christ (Unowsky 2005, pp. 94–7; Judson and Rozenblit 2005, p. 150).

It has also long been recognized that, as in the British Isles, so in the Dual Monarchy, the association of the monarchy with church and aristocracy (and the army) created a powerful binding agent. Elsewhere, however, these linkages were less clear. In Sweden-Norway there was (at least in theory) a shared Lutheranism which was headed by the monarch of the United Kingdoms. But the congruities were complicated: first, there were (as already noted) the two separate established Lutheran churches in Norway and Sweden, and (second) the monarch was head of the Church of Norway by virtue of being king of Norway, and not of the United Kingdoms. Moreover, unlike in Britain and Ireland and the Dual Monarchy, there was none of the powerful nexus of monarch, church, and aristocracy: as has been shown, there was no 'union' aristocracy spanning the United Kingdoms of Sweden-Norway, and there was no 'union' army.

In the Netherlands there were no state churches, given the impact of the French revolution and French military occupation. There was therefore no confessional or even 'semi-confessional' state in the Netherlands, as there was in the early 19th-century British Isles or Habsburg lands. But there was certainly a culturally and institutionally predominant Calvinism in a union polity which was predominantly Catholic, and whose southern components, the former Austrian Netherlands and Liège, were overwhelmingly Catholic.

All this, then, begs the question of the impact on 19th-century union states where political and economic asymmetries were associated with profound religious division. This leads to a consideration of the contentious interrelationship between union, religious faith, and 'civilizing' mission—the issues created by the intersection between the dominant nations of union, their associated churches, and the component polities where other faiths or churches prevailed. Here, in turn, there is an opportunity to briefly consider Catholic Ireland, predominantly Orthodox and Muslim Bosnia, Catholic Belgium and Lutheran Finland—all of which were in the shadow of dominant union powers and other faiths.

In both Ireland and Bosnia-Herzegovina the neighbouring imperial powers, Britain and Austria-Hungary, pursued policies of acquisition and 'civilization': Austria-Hungary had a self-proclaimed cultural mission in Bosnia after 1878, which bears comparison with the activities of the British state in Ireland in the decades before Irish independence (Okey 2007, pp. vii, 217). The Habsburg monarchy saw itself, in contradistinction to the other forms of European power-wielder, as being 'the only state experienced enough to handle the different ethno-linguistic and ethno-confessional cleavages while at the same time fulfilling the [necessary] civilising mission': the same self-regard might be said to have characterized the British union state's sense of its own 'mission' in Ireland (Gerwarth and Manela 2014, p. 75; Figure 3.2). The comparatively underdeveloped condition of Ireland at the time of the union (1801) chimed with that of Bosnia at the time of the occupation and annexation. Moreover, both Ireland and Bosnia's proximity to the metropolitan heartland of empire meant that the British and Habsburg states were operating in territories which 'could directly impact on [their]...domestic politics' (Okey 2007, p. 251): the small-scale and ferociously intimate divisions of Bosnian society have been convincingly compared with the fractured and volatile nature of Northern Irish life, not least because each sat on the doorstep of an imperial heartland (Okey 2007, p. 229).

As in Ireland, so in Bosnia, the state helped to develop a 'modernization' project which encompassed the transformation of towns and the consolidation of communications—post, telephone and telegraph, and railways: Robin Okey has summarized the 'mission' in Bosnia as amounting to the creation of a basic network of communications, a handful of secondary schools, a network of district commissioners, and a reconstruction of the Catholic religious hierarchy (Okey 2007, p. 251). As with Ireland's national school system (1831), so in Bosnia, the Habsburg state experimented with a multi-confessional school system. But perhaps a key distinction lay with the comparatively strong financial resources of the British state, as compared with its Habsburg contemporary: 'disinclined to find the full costs of cultural mission, the state tacitly shared the task with representatives of Austrian civil society in Bosnia. But instead of lubricating integration with the monarchy, increased multicultural contacts and the spread of the German language were seen as undermining the native society' (Okey 2007, pp. 221–2). In sum, the Habsburg cultural mission in Bosnia was 'conducted, as it were, on the cheap' (Okey 2007, p. 251).

Under the Habsburg occupation of Bosnia there was an effort to promote both an overarching provincial identity loyal to the dynasty as well as a recognition of the rights of the three main faith communities—Orthodox, Muslim, and Catholic (Figure 3.2). But on the whole 'civilization' was indeed done on the cheap with reliance on non-state actors such as (pre-eminently) the Catholic Church (Okey 2007, p. 251). The church hierarchy was restored in 1881, with the creation of four new dioceses, closely superintended by the emperor: and the proportions and visibility of Catholics within the province rose (from 18 to 23 per cent during the relatively brief period of Habsburg rule) through immigration from elsewhere in the empire. The occupation and annexation of Bosnia stimulated both Serb nationalism as well as Muslim retreat and migration—just as the growing anglicization of Ireland in the 19th century, allied with the legal privileging of the established Protestant church (until 1869), fed into both Irish nationalism and emigration. In each case an imperial cultural and military presence, associated with the effective consolidation of one church, contributed to an undermining of existing religious and political frontiers.

There are some links here, too, with the attempted russification of Finland between 1899 and 1905, and again between 1908 and 1914. For example, Tsar Nicholas II's February manifesto of 1899 was a move away from Finnish autonomy; and it included measures further advancing the Orthodox Church's legal standing in Finland. Russification, therefore, threatened to disrupt the established ecclesiastical balance in the country (amongst much else) (Polvinen 1995).

Religious ascendancy could also be expressed informally within union states, and beyond the confines of a legally privileged church. As has been seen, some Catholics were deeply suspicious in this regard of the new United Kingdom of the Netherlands—dominated by the Calvinist north and by the Calvinist monarch, Willem I, while at the same time nominally free from any state church. Could Willem successfully forge a united national identity on the basis of the very different histories of the component parts of his new kingdom? There was certainly a helpful legacy of religious toleration from the years of the Batavian republic—as noted, Catholic emancipation had been achieved in 1797. In 1814–15, with the creation of the new United Kingdom of the Netherlands, Protestantism and Catholicism were organized into two official departments of worship, while the new constitution of the union (again in contradistinction to Britain and Ireland) made no provision for a state church (Wintle 1987, pp. 12–13). The modern Dutch Reformed Church (*Nederlandse Hervormde Kerk*) was partly shaped by changes imposed in 1816, wherein the governance of the Church shifted from being largely 'bottom up', presbyterian and democratic, to 'top down', more centralized and hierarchical: it was effectively officials from the Department of Reformed Worship who ran the Church (Wintle 1987, p. 19). These innovations meant that, while there was formal religious equality, the state remained closely associated with a now tightly managed Reformed Church: if there was no state church as such, the ethos of the new United Kingdom of the Netherlands was Protestant Calvinist.

Some Catholics were therefore suspicious of the new union from its inception: Bishop Maurice-Jean de Broglie of Ghent (1766–1821) sought, in the early years of the new state, guarantees that the Catholic character of the south be upheld, while simultaneously rejecting any official move to enact equal legal status for all churches. While this was not by any means a universal Catholic view, even among the clergy, Willem I's educational initiatives trampled on other Catholic sensitivities: his effort to promote non-denominational education, and to organize the training of the Catholic clergy (including the creation of a Collegium Philosophicum at Leuven/Louvain in June 1825) were regarded with hostility, led to a clerical boycott, and helped to unite conservative Catholics with liberal dissidents against what was seen by both as a royal violation of the constitution (Marteel 2018, p. 184). Though Willem I softened some of his attitudes, and even managed—late in the day—to clinch a concordat with Rome (July 1827), it was this coalition of disaffection which in the end overthrew the short-lived United Kingdom of the Netherlands (White 1835; Marteel 2018, p. 178).

A preliminary set of conclusions may be proffered on the interrelationship between religion and the decline of union: did state churches, whose active purpose was unity and assimilation within disparate or complex union polities (or united kingdoms), fulfil their intended function? Generally, no. The United Church of England and Ireland came swiftly to grief in Ireland: the union state ultimately had to negotiate a relationship with Catholics in Ireland—as in fact it had already done in other British possessions with Catholic majorities (Quebec/Lower Canada, Malta). Even the relatively more dominant Catholicism of the Habsburg monarchy had ultimately—from 1860 onwards—to establish a *modus vivendi* with a range of religious minorities throughout central and southern Europe.

Linked with this—some of the potentially most damaging issues within these union polities were the pursuit of either a disruptive evangelism by churches tied to the union or an overturning of the settled legal relationships governing a 'union' church—especially in those areas where other faith majorities prevailed. Evangelism and/or other disruption of this kind were associated with Anglicanism in early 19th-century Ireland, Catholicism in late 19th-century Bosnia, and Orthodoxy in early 20th-century Finland. These were also threatened in early 19th-century Canada, where there was occasional pressure for the creation of an Anglican establishment—pressure which would have overturned any *modus vivendi* with the Catholic Church and Catholic society.

Did an association with union damage the related state church? This of course is linked to similar questions sometimes posed about the churches and establishment. It is possible that Anglicanism in England and the Kirk in Scotland have each ultimately been weakened through too close an association with the union state: equally, Catholicism's close relationship with the Habsburgs and the Dual Monarchy ultimately incurred some costs, as the Church came to be seen as 'an ecclesiastical department of state', and as imbued 'by the spirit of subservience to the dynasty' (Steed 1919, pp. 107, 108). Anglicanism in Ireland and Wales and Orthodoxy in Finland were lastingly associated with an intrusive and subjugating external power. By extension, the end of union—Finnish independence in 1917 and Irish independence in 1921—inflicted some damage on those churches, Anglican and Orthodox, associated with the old regime. The physical destruction inflicted after 1918 on many Russian Orthodox churches in another liberated province of the former tsarist empire, Poland, expressed popular national outrage at the former overlordship—and indeed it was drastically epitomized by the demolition in 1926 of the huge, new (1912) Alexander Nevsky Orthodox cathedral in central Warsaw.

Church theology mattered less, perhaps, than church organization in terms of the sustaining or subverting of union. This is worth emphasizing, given that a hiberno-centric perspective might superficially point in an alternative direction. The two established Lutheran churches of Norway and Sweden fed into individual national identities and consolidations rather than a shared supranational union sentiment. Catholics in the north and in the south generally took different stands on the United Kingdom of the Netherlands. Similarly, Catholicism in England and Catholicism in Ireland generally took distinctive approaches to the union. On the other hand, English Anglicanism and Scottish Presbyterianism on the whole established a rapport within the union state, as did Lutheranism and the Orthodox church within the Grand Duchy of Finland.

Where these multinational unions had controversial creation stories, their moral standing, and the challenges faced by any associated union church, became more complex. It was never going to be easy to build the new Jerusalem—whether in terms of a Protestant United Kingdom or a Catholic bulwark across central Europe—on foundations which were contested, if not by divinely ordained authority, then by contemporary opinion.

Monarchies, and their associated religious convictions, have been central (both positively and negatively) to the preservation and unification of complex union polities. This should scarcely surprise: most of these 'united kingdoms'—Britain and Ireland, Sweden-Norway, the Netherlands, Finland, Austria-Hungary—have developed from composite monarchies or personal unions.

Finally, a variable ecclesiastical geometry did, seemingly, work to support union polities. Thus, the complex religious circumstances of England and Scotland, or of Russia and Finland until the 1890s, or in the Dual Monarchy (outside of Bosnia) served on the whole to propagate union (Brown 2008, p. 62; Okey 2007, p. 257). The constitutions and churches of union states worked better as bespoke ensembles—rather than as 'one size fits all'.

In the 19th century the unity of these multinational unions was best achieved and sustained, not when they enforced or advantaged particular forms of belief. Indeed, the privileging of particular churches was too often controversially associated with the privileging of particular dominant nationalities or ethnicities. The unity of unions was best achieved when the union state recognized that unity could be secured through working with spiritual diversity rather than imposing uniformity.

There was certainly a cost in rigour or logic or perhaps sometimes in conscience to be paid: episcopal monarchs affirming presbyterian or Catholic governance, Orthodox tsars assuming Lutheran clothing, Catholic emperors deferring to Calvinist ministers. But in the end the price may well have been worth paying for the political benefits attained. If Paris had once been well worth a mass, then Edinburgh, Budapest (or Debrecen), and Helsinki were all surely worth their equivalent price in pragmatism.

4.7. Parliament

Most of the case studies considered in this work had, at least for a time, unified or single parliaments (the United Kingdom of Great Britain and Ireland, the Netherlands, the United Province and Dominion of Canada); and several— the Scots union (1707), the Irish (1801), the Canadian (1841)—involved the effective amalgamation of existing legislatures. One other contemporary union, the United Kingdom of Portugal, Brazil, and the Algarves, was briefly and disastrously associated (1820–1) with a restored national assembly, the Cortes (Armitage 1836, vol. 1, pp. 26, 52–3; Barman 1999, p. 3). While parliamentary unions are neither the only form of union polity nor the only form of union polity considered within this work, parliaments have certainly been closely associated with the binding of the disparate components of multinational states, and they have certainly been seen to function as bolsters of union.

Some emphasis, for example, has traditionally been placed by historians of 18th-century English politics upon the importance of parliament as an agency of the British union. But, if parliaments have been associated with the maintenance of union, then the corollary of this has been that the subversion of parliament (whether by nationalists, unionists, or others) has had a corresponding impact upon the stability of union. Again, as will be seen, there is some evidence for this proposition in terms of the political history of both the United Kingdom and the Austro-Hungarian empire in the immediate prelude to the Great War (see e.g. Brockliss and Eastwood 1997).

Aside from the celebration of parliament as an engine of union, there has been a more widespread (unifying and consensual) pride in the splendour of the ('unwritten') parliamentary constitution, which of course was closely associated with those liberties which were perceived as essential components of Britishness and thereby of union. For example, in the 18th century there was a renewed interest in, and celebration of, Magna Carta—fuelled by, amongst other writings, William Blackstone's *The Great Charter* of 1759 as well as by a gathering tidal wave of written constitutions. Indeed Linda Colley has also underlined the wider celebration in the 18th century and afterwards of 'Britain's own tradition of iconic texts'—Magna Carta, the Bill of Rights, the Treaty of Rights, the Treaty of Union. By the late 18th century British commentators were prepared to reinterpret the achievement of the United States constitution of 1787, not as the republican antonym to its British precursor, but rather as a natural derivative, with (for example) Tom Paine (1737–1809) linking the American constitution to the long English tradition of town and company charters (Colley 2014a, pp. 241–4). It has also been usefully observed that it was only late in the 19th century—from the 1870s onwards—'that British commentators became more unvaryingly and explicitly insistent on the quintessential non-writtenness of their own constitution' (Colley 2014a, p. 261).

In an obvious sense, too, the British parliament (whatever its many limitations in terms of representative embrace) served to unite, because it successfully contained and corralled an array of patriotic feeling from Wales, Scotland, and even Ireland. Westminster certainly provided an effective focus for successive generations of Irish nationalist protest, from the time of Daniel O'Connell and the creation of a parliamentary 'repeal of the union' grouping through to the home rule parties of Isaac Butt, C. S. Parnell, and John Redmond. Scholars routinely and fruitlessly search for an authentic 'bottom line' with complex, flexible, and pragmatic national leaders like O'Connell and Redmond; but, certainly for O'Connell in the 1820 and 1830s, his focuses were upon achieving full access to the Westminster parliament for his Catholic following, and then on a testing of its capacity to function in the interests of that following. While he judged that it ultimately failed this test (even before its deeply controversial handling of famine conditions in Ireland between 1845 and 1851), in the later 19th century Westminster responded with passable efficiency to the ongoing challenges presented by later Irish, Scottish, and Welsh nationalists, delivering administrative reform and devolution and at least the realistic promise of home rule.

It can be seen, however, that the undermining of the United Kingdom parliament was simultaneously a symptom and a cause of the wider subversion of union. For example, unionist militancy in 1912–14—while drawing upon older traditions of Irish pressure politics—effectively subverted the union, and not only in the well-known sense of having indirectly stimulated the rebirth of a popular separatist militancy which delivered the 1916 rising. Unionist militants deliberately defied the Liberal government and the Westminster parliament through clearly illegal acts such as the mass importation of weapons, and through the open creation of an alternative state in the north of Ireland, with the Ulster Provisional Government, armed forces (the Ulster Volunteer Force), and nursing and communications corps. This repudiation of the union parliament was simultaneously an effective repudiation of the existing union, and was thus (and not for the first or last time in the long history of Irish and Ulster unionism) a strategic choice which in the end effectively delivered exactly the opposite result to that which was intended. Looking far ahead, it might be suggested that the gradual dethroning of members of parliament from the generally high regard and respect which were the default positions of the late Victorian and Edwardian era to the sceptical and iconoclastic attitudes prevailing today, has been accompanied by a wider contemporary discrediting of the union parliament.

A similar narrative of threat is discernible within the parliamentary history of the later years of the Dual Monarchy (see e.g. Steed 1919, pp. 120–23). It should be remembered of course that, under the terms of the Ausgleich, there was no parliament for the entirety of Austria-Hungary, though there were overarching ministries in key areas as well as a joint ministerial council. There were, however, legislatures in each of the two parts of the Monarchy as well as provincial diets; and (in the absence of any equivalent of the vigorous drive towards magyarization which characterized Transleithania) the bicameral Reichsrat had some potential as a shared and binding focus for the complex multinational politics of Cisleithania. Wickham Steed, often a critical friend to Austria and institutions, thought in 1913 that the Reichsrat was 'an immense club where representatives of all nationalities meet, jostle and sometimes make acquaintance with each other...despite the particularist standpoints and individual interests frequently thrust into prominence, they gradually acquire a feeling of *Zusammengehörigkeit* [togetherness]...parliament, in this sense, is an institute for political education' (Steed 1919, pp. 120–1).

While the Reichsrat certainly moved towards the possibility of greater inclusivity and representativeness, with the addition of a working-class curia in 1896, and with universal male suffrage in December 1906, there was in the end little evidence that this potential had been fully realized. Wickham Steed complained (not unreasonably) that 'parliamentary institutions through which the "will of the people" is supposed to be expressed, fulfil, especially in Austria, functions ranging from those of a legislative registry office to those of a political market-place. They rarely serve as a means of imposing popular demands upon the Government, though they are sometimes valuable as a safety-valve' (Steed 1919, p. 59). It is true that the Reichsrat, like Westminster, for long provided a forum of sorts for, and thereby contained, different national divisions. However, its lower chamber, which embraced eight nationalities each split into a range of party camps, was highly fissiparous and unstable, and it was characterized by an aggressive gamesmanship, which had in turn been facilitated by a liberal standing orders regime from the 1870s: frequent resort had to be made to the 'silver bullet' of article 14 of the Ausgleich, which permitted the prorogation of parliament and government by emergency decree (Cornwall 2002, p. 48). It has been said, for example, that the aggressive (German) obstructionism which was generated by the Badeni crisis of 1897 'discredited not only Austrian parliamentarianism but what was left of political multinationalism': the scenes of obstructionist and other misbehaviour in the lower house of the Reichsrat 'lived on in the memory to tarnish the cause of parliamentarianism' (Okey 2001, p. 308). Similarly, Ernest von Koerber's system of government in Cisleithania (he was Minister President between 1900 and 1904), conducted partly under the article 14 arrangements, has been seen as paving 'the way for unbridled demagogy in Austria, both nationalistic and socialistic' (Beller 1996, p. 161; though for an alternative view see Deak 2015, p. 244). Equally, it has been argued that, with the fall of Max von Beck as Minister President (after 1907–8) 'the guts were torn out of Austrian parliamentarianism' (Okey 2001, p. 352; Beller 2018, pp. 201–3). On the outbreak of war in 1914, the Reichsrat was suspended (yet again) (Judson 2016, p. 378).

Hungarian parliamentarianism was ostensibly more stable than this, but for (even by contemporary Cisleithanian standards) all the wrong reasons. These were laid out by R. W. Seton-Watson in works such as his *Corruption and Reform in Hungary: A Study of Electoral Practice* (London, 1911), in which he detailed for his anglophone (and wider) audience the minority nationalities' case against the Hungarian electoral system (see Figure 5.5). The franchise of 1874 was, he argued, 'the most illiberal' in Europe': one-third of parliamentary deputies were elected by less than 100 voters, while two-thirds were elected by less than 1,000 voters (Seton-Watson 1911b, pp. 3, 5). Gerrymandering and bribery were 'wholesale': the need for universal, equal, and secret suffrage was palpable (Seton-Watson 1911b, pp. 8, 20, 158). Later scholars have described an electoral regime wherein only 6.5 per cent of the population was enfranchised, where there were 413 unequal single-member constituencies, and where open voting remained the norm (Cornwall 2002, pp. 100–1). The result of all this was the alienation of non-Magyars, their consequent and systematic boycott of elections, and a Hungarian parliament where (in 1910) there were 405 Magyar deputies, and only eight of other ethnicities or nationalities (Seton-Watson 1911b, p. 160; Cornwall 2002, p. 104).

However, even in this highly controlled and managed environment, there were episodes which were profoundly subversive of parliamentary culture, and which effectively illustrated its subjection to the threat of royal military violence: for example, in February 1906, in the context of the rising electoral influence of a coalition of Magyar nationalists, the Hungarian parliament was dissolved by an army unit headed by a general of the national guard, the *Honvéd* (Cornwall 2002, p. 102). Again, in June 1912, István Tisza, then Speaker of the Hungarian lower house, used troops to intimidate deputies into accepting the proscription of technical obstruction (see eg Cornwall 2002, p. 108).

Elsewhere parliaments and assemblies, ostensible institutions of union, and agencies of unity, had an equally powerful capacity to divide. In the United Kingdom of Portugal, Brazil, and the Algarves, the restored Cortes, which met in January 1821, nominally served the entire transcontinental union: 130 of its representatives came from Portugal while 70 were supplied by Brazil, though in fact only 50 of the latter ever made it to Lisbon. But the national resentments which had accumulated in Portugal during the years of French occupation, together with those created by an absent monarchy and royal government, combined to dominate and poison the proceedings of the assembly: as the contemporary British commentator, John Armitage, observed, the Brazilians 'were ever in the minority; and the demonstrations of contempt to which they were perpetually subjected were even more mortifying than their repeated defeats' (Armitage 1836, vol. 1, p. 77). The actions of the Portuguese majority in the Cortes in undoing the institutions of Brazilian government, in sanctioning the cession of Brazilian territory, and in recalling the regent, Dom Pedro—all of these effectively fed into the movement for Brazilian independence in 1822. The Cortes, a union parliament, had effectively served to break its associated United Kingdom.

In short, parliaments certainly had the potential to work as agencies of union, and in some cases and some of the time they effectively did so. The United Kingdom parliament provided a lasting (if not always easy forum) for the different nationalities of the 'British Isles', while the legislature of (for example) the United Province allowed the negotiation of the differences between British and French Canadians, and indeed has since been seen as a key starting point for consociationalism (Noel 1974, 1993). Even the Reichsrat for long provided space to the eight nationalities of Cisleithania to navigate their complex differences and affinities.

But there were of course challenges. Some union parliaments—in the United Kingdom, and in the Netherlands—had controversial origins which were never fully overcome: some were undermined by the exploitation, through obstruction and filibustering, of their own generous rules of procedure (Westminster, the Reichsrat). And there is evidence to suggest that union parliaments were ultimately undermined not only (or even primarily) by anti-unionists—but also by those privileged nationalities who were the nominal supporters and beneficiaries of union (German Austrians, Magyars, Irish unionists, the Portuguese). Here again the centripetal forces of union could so easily become agents of its disintegration.

4.8. Civil Society, Space, and Symbols

Some initial reflections may also be offered on the relationship between different multinational unions and civil society as well as their unifying symbols. In particular, these reflections are structured here, in this section, around several discrete but interlinked topics or questions. First, given that the relationship between associational cultures, civil society, and the democratic health of a polity has been debated since at least the time of de Tocqueville, should we not also consider more fully how union states have impacted upon the shape of civil society? And second, civil society (certainly in Gramscian terms) has been sometimes seen as the arena in which consent for the hegemony of the dominant class is achieved: any reflection on the process of consent broaches then the question of how unions are represented, especially symbolically, within civil society in different types of multinational polity. These, of course, are huge and—at least in terms of their comparative dimensions—very largely under-researched issues; once again, there is only really an opportunity (and space) here to open up analysis and debate (see also Jackson 2013, 2019).

Are the definition and nature of union states related to the shape of civil society—and vice versa? This key question is effectively an extension of the debate on the links between associational cultures, civil society, and a stable democratic polity. As R. J. Morris, the respected authority on British civil society, has argued, 'the nature of the state and its agencies was an enabling and limiting factor in all cases [of civil society]' (Morton et al. 2006, p. 15). He has also argued that 'the ability of an associational culture to contribute to a liberal pluralist civil society depended... upon the spatial and cultural context of the state' (Morton et al. 2006, p. 16). This section pursues these insights by making a start at examining the relationship between civil society and the union state.

The focus is primarily on several of the union case studies—English/Scottish, British/Irish, Swedish/Norwegian—though the section also considers the Dual Monarchy, the Netherlands, and indeed (looking beyond the main case studies of the book once again) the Grand Duchy of Finland. In essence the proposition here is that each of these unions was associated with a distinctive civil society and national symbolism; and that each of these was ultimately related to the condition and prospects of the union. In particular the suggestions are that, first, the origins of civil societies were critical to their relationship with union; second, the flexibility and representativeness of union settlements were related to the nature of civil society; and (last) the stability of union settlements was related to the symbols and spaces of the union state—especially royal symbolism—and its acceptability to civil society.

Looking briefly at Scotland first: this might now reasonably be characterized (on the basis of the earlier discussion) as an incomplete but also, comparatively, an inclusive union. Civil society was defined in several critical senses in 18th- and 19th-century Scotland. It was given a key textual exegesis by Adam Ferguson (1723–1816), who (writing in *An essay on the history of civil society* in 1767) was concerned with the problem of how the liberty of the individual might be sustained or reconciled within the context of an ordered society (Morton et al. 2006, p. 2). Samuel Smiles (1812–1904), born in Haddington, East Lothian, and an Edinburgh University graduate, published his hugely influential *Self-Help* in 1859, a work which was strongly associated with the promotion of self-improvement and associationalism—and which soon reached Scandinavia, being translated into Swedish by 1867 (and Danish by 1869).

Some scholars have gone further than all this, however. In particular Jim Livesey has offered the striking suggestion that the origins of civil society itself may be located in the efforts of those Scots and Irish within Britain's 18th-century Atlantic domain who sought to accommodate their loss of citizenship within the conditions of union and empire (Livesey 2009, p.7). In addition Livesey has highlighted the critical distinction between the success of Scots civil society in the later 18th century and the collapse of its Irish counterpart in the 1790s.

Some further expansion of these observations is clearly required. The Scottish union of 1707 certainly brought the loss of a separate Scottish citizenship with the emergence of the union or imperial state. But it was also inclusive of the major interests in Scottish society. It allowed an essential degree of flexibility within the new constitutional relationships—stemming in part from its incompleteness. As was explored earlier, Scotland preserved its legal system (based on Roman law), its royal burghs and their privileges, its heritable jurisdictions (until 1747), as well as its Presbyterian Church, its banking system, and its universities. All of these were distinctive national institutions which served as focuses for patriotic pride within the union state.

This particular type of incomplete and flexible union conditioned the forms of civil society which emerged in the 18th and 19th centuries. The relatively limited scope of union created the space for civil society and its associational cultures: the ultimately inclusive and accommodationist nature of union ensured that these cultures would augment rather than subvert union, and that they would work within civic space defined often by the symbolism of union. Indeed, by the mid-Victorian era Scotland's historic national institutions were complemented by a distinctive civic culture with a wide range of patriotically inclined voluntary associations, spanning philanthropy, religion, science, literature, and commerce (Morton 1999).

Mediating between this vibrant local culture and the relatively weak (though still expanding) British state were the politics and ideology of what has been called 'unionist nationalism'. 'Unionist nationalism' embodied a commitment to the union, and indeed an interest in closer union, but this was contingent upon patriotic fulfilment within local institutions and the continuing benefits and light touch of the union government: as Graeme Morton has argued, 'because of the way in which civil society was governed in the mid-19th century Scottish nationalism was loyal to the union of 1707' (see Morton 1999, p. 10; cf. Lloyd Jones 2014, Torrance 2020). The intrusion of the state or perceived inequalities within the governance of the union could certainly give rise to patriotic protest, such as with the National Association for the Vindication of Scottish Rights (of 1853). However, such protest accepted the principle and framework of union—even when it was opposed to innovations within its practice (Jackson 2013, p. 136).

In short, the inclusive and flexible nature of union was associated with the associational cultures of a civil society which was both patriotically Scottish and unionist. Scottish civil society, including (generally) the press, served to complement union. The Irish union, incomplete yet also (crucially) exclusive, shared some characteristics with its Scottish counterpart, but there were also decisive differences. Again, the layering of union needs to be seen and its importance appreciated.

In Ireland the parliamentary union of 1800–1, like its Scots precursor of 1707, preserved a set of distinctive national institutions—the administration (Dublin Castle), the viceregal court and executive, the courts and judiciary, and legal process. As in Scotland, there was an effort through union to connect the state to the forces of religion. But the specific intention of binding the union with concessions to the majority religious community (Catholicism) failed completely and with lasting consequences. In Scotland the Kirk was very largely bound to union; in Ireland the goal of connecting the Catholic Church to union was clearly on offer—but was ultimately spurned because of privileged, ascendancy, veto-players.

Union, therefore, acquired an exclusive, even sectarian, inflection almost from the moment of its promulgation. The distinctive Irish institutions which were retained after the union were in the hands of a dominant religious and social elite in Irish society—the Anglican (episcopal) landed class known from the 1780s as the 'Protestant ascendancy'. Unlike Scotland, the institutions of the union state in Ireland did not, therefore, fully accommodate a popular patriotic or national identity. This accordingly defined a different role and function for civil society in Ireland than in Scotland. Moreover, unlike Scotland, too, the chronology of the growth of civil society in Ireland was separate from that of the union state: it certainly preceded the acts of union in 1800.

In essence, economic growth and intellectual Enlightenment in the second half of the 18th century, in the decades before union, helped to generate new forms of sociability and civil society in Ireland. Michael Brown, for example, has defined the period between 1730 and 1780 as the 'apogee of the social Enlightenment': it 'saw the emergence of a literary public sphere marked by novel modes of communication (newspapers), changes in old mechanisms for divulging information (the culture of the theatre for instance) and new locations (the coffee house)' (Brown 2016, p. 210). Economic growth also simultaneously disrupted the precarious sectarian frontiers in a society where political authority was not only associated with propertied exclusivity, but also with religious exclusivity. Most Irish historians agree that civil society largely disintegrated in the 1790s in the context of the profound stresses created by the war. Insurgency in 1796–8 and the imposition of union in 1800 were in part expressions of that failure.

In Ireland neither the formation nor the consolidation of union were supported by civil society, therefore. It was rather the case that union was imposed upon a society where civil society had broken down, and that union helped to shape its radical and sectarianized restructuring. What re-emerged gradually in 19th-century Ireland was a civil society which, as in the later kingdom of the Netherlands, was fragmented or 'pillarized' along confessional lines. And, just as in the Austrian empire of the mid-19th century, so in Ireland, 'national and civic conflicts resulted in multiple – and riven – public spheres with contestation for dominance among competing interests, including conflicting concepts of national civil society'; although it was still possible, as was discussed earlier, to achieve a measure of unity in supporting external 'civilizing missions', as with the Irish and empire, or Austrian civil society and Bosnia (Wingfield 2003, p. 4; Okey 2007, pp. 221–2). Unlike in Scotland, where civil society functioned as a complement to union, in Ireland—as also in Norway—the civil society of the 19th century looked increasingly to alternative state formations.

Unlike in the Netherlands, where it has been said that 'the pillars and the pillarised voluntary associations articulated religious and political antagonisms in society but stabilised it also', this was not the case in Ireland (Morton et al. 2006, p. 116). In Ireland civil society was increasingly redefined in the mid/late 19th century in opposition to the union state—generating clashes between the two as well as a range of special restrictions on civil liberty, including upon the freedom of the press, which were not generally applied in Britain. In many ways, though, the Irish experience was not unique: as Stefan Ludwig Hoffmann has argued in his overview of contemporary European civil society, 'the [challenging] expansion, democratisation and politicisation of voluntary associations were [in fact]…a cause of the crisis of European civil societies before World War I' (Hoffmann 2006, p. 89).

Like the Scots and Irish unions, it will be recalled that the Swedish-Norwegian union was formulated in the context of the flexing of military muscle by the dominant partner. Like these earlier two unions, the Swedish-Norwegian union was partly anchored in the geopolitics of international warfare and its settlement. But, much more than the earlier unions, the Swedish-Norwegian union was limited and therefore offered an opportunity for the creation of distinctive associational cultures and the wider development of civil society. And, unlike the Scots and Irish unions, which were enacted by regular parliamentary legislation, the Norwegian was circumscribed both by a written national constitution (of 1814) and an act of the Storting which had constitutional status. Unlike these earlier unions, therefore, the Swedish-Norwegian union was a relatively constricted or tightly defined settlement (Michalsen 2014, pp. 214ff.).

Still, these constraints on union and on the state created space for civil society in Norway and in Sweden as well as for the nation state. Torkel Jansson of Uppsala has suggested that in the United Kingdoms 'the [union] state...dissociated itself from a number of functions it had previously fulfilled, and that society consequently had no choice but to associate itself': Norwegian society through the 19th century certainly came to be strongly marked by 'private civic associations' or, alternatively, by 'a new "association spirit"' (Jansson 2016, p. 687; Langholm 2016, p. 972). Most historians argue that the principles of voluntary association were spreading in Norway from the 1820s and 1830s, and that they were linked with economic growth—including the emergence of a newly commercialized agricultural economy in the 19th century. In addition, some scholarly emphasis has been laid upon the role of poor relief organization, Protestant revivalism, and temperance within these evolving associational cultures. Indeed, the period from the mid-19th century through to c.1930 has been defined as the 'pre-corporatist' heyday of autonomous associational activity (Götz and Hackmann 2003, pp. 42–3).

There were some differences in the forms of civil society and public sphere activity which flourished in contemporary Sweden. A trope of early 19th-century British comment was certainly the contrast between 'democratic' Norway and 'aristocratic' Sweden: for the radical Scots traveller, Samuel Laing, journeying in the later 1830s, 'Sweden [in the first decades of the union] is still under its *ancien régime*, while Norway is practically in advance of the age in its enjoyment of institutions favourable to political liberty' (Laing 1836, p. 134). In Sweden, Laing observed, 'the press is under a very strict censorship'; while in Norway 'the most entire freedom of discussion exists' (Laing 1836, p. 136). On the other hand, the associational cultures of Norway and Sweden (as of Ireland and Scotland) were each of course linked to improved communications (telegraphs, national postal system, rail networks)—and (from 1850, and despite Laing's gloomy prognostication) a rapidly expanding press. The 'growth of local [Swedish] newspapers in the 1850s turned the press into a major instrument of national unification'—but the unity related to Sweden, rather than the United Kingdoms of Sweden-Norway (Kouri and Olesen 2016, p.987). More than in Scotland or Ireland, the press in Sweden and Norway was characterized by a national rather than a supranational and union appeal. Even at times of political disturbance in Christiania, and consequent threats to the union (such as in the early and mid-1880s), British observers were astonished by the insouciance evident in the mainstream Swedish press (Knaplund 1952, p. 34).

Was there, then, any evidence of overarching union civic cultures or a union civil society in Sweden-Norway? It was certainly the case that up to the 1860s the growth of Scandinavianism, while by no means co-equal with unionism, and more widespread in Sweden than in Norway, was linked with some associational cultures which looked to the maintenance of the United Kingdoms (Jorgenson 1935; Hemstad 2010; Kouri and Olesen 2016, p. 989). Of these the 'unionist' rifle club movement was perhaps the most significant: this drew inspiration from Garibaldi and contemporary Italian nationalism, and has been described as the 'first autonomous mass organisation in Sweden' (Petterson 2016, p. 989). However, there were complexities here: the growth of Swedish national identity was associated with union sympathies, but (as with nationalisms in other dominant union partners) these sympathies were not straightforward. Swedish Scandinavianism tended to equate the notion of greater regional unity with the idea of a 'Greater Sweden' and with Swedish pre-eminence—as well as with the maintenance of the United Kingdoms. Similarly, the rifle clubs movement, supportive of union, was also, at the same time, an expression of Swedish national feeling: while it looked to greater Scandinavian unity and to unionism, it was simultaneously associated with nationalistic memorialization—commemorating (complex) patriotic figures such as King Carl XII of Sweden (r. 1697–1718), who was killed in action during an invasion of Norway, as well as Engelbrekt Engelbrektsson (c.1390–1436), widely seen by 19th-century Swedes as a national hero through his defiance of the Kalmar union. The rifles club movement, which sought military and parliamentary reform, faded after the attainment of the latter in 1865–6; but the paradoxical brand of dominant nation nationalism together with unionism and militarism which it embodied lived on as a strain within the politics of Sweden and of the United Kingdoms until their ultimate demise. Indeed, in a sense, here, once again, as elsewhere in the story of union, unionism fed directly into the death of union.

In short, the restrictive, constrained, light-touch union of Sweden and Norway created more space for the expansion of civil society. But it was a national civil society which was the result, rather than a supranational or multinational union version such as may be said to have existed in Scotland (Morton 1999). Moreover, given religious homogeneity, it was a coherent national civil society, unlike its pillarized equivalent in contemporary Ireland.

Turning briefly to the second of the questions posed at the beginning of the section—how much did civil society in these circumstances intersect with the different union states and their related symbolism? This, once again, is a potentially huge and certainly under-researched theme, which can only really be given a preliminary airing here. In Scotland an agreed and inclusive union permitted (on the whole) the infiltration throughout civil society of the symbolism of union, often casual or implicit (see Morton 1999). In Ireland, however, the exclusive, incomplete, and dynamic nature of union, which has been described above, created confrontations between the symbols of the United Kingdom and those of the growing national movement. In Norway, however, the limits of union were tightly and constitutionally defined; and the space for movement of any kind, whether in terms of symbolism or otherwise, was no less limited, and was certainly meticulously policed by Norwegian patriots.

Indeed what might be described as the narcissism of small national difference was still a feature of civic space in the variety of union polities discussed here (cf. Mitchell 2010b). This notion has a particular relevance for union states, which often (if not invariably) brought together neighbouring peoples and polities who were essentially similar in their cultures and experience. In these circumstances, the symbols of difference naturally acquired a much greater significance than might otherwise have been the case. There is in fact some overlap between Ireland and Norway in this respect: on the whole, however, the clash between Irish national and United Kingdom symbols was ultimately greater because the presence of the union state weighed much more heavily there than its counterpart in Norway.

Even with Sweden-Norway, however, tetchy disputes over flags, coats of arms, and royal titles all fed into a festering rancour with union. Norway underlined its constitutionally defined independent existence within the context of the union state through a separate national flag, which was devised in 1821. King Oscar I famously introduced a compromise arrangement for the flag in 1844, which remained in place in Norway until 1898–9 (and in Sweden until 1905)—but it was a continuing reminder to patriotic Norwegians of the fudges and compromises inherent in union (Seip 1995, p. 40). Alongside the flags question, coats of arms could accelerate resentments in an age when heraldic emblems mattered. Heraldry was not just a question of royal or aristocratic flummery, but (as Fridtjof Nansen observed in 1905) it was associated instead with a wide range of everyday official agencies and institutions, including (crucially) the coinage (Nansen 1905, p. 28 n. 1). The coat of arms of Sweden-Norway, which originally rendered the rampant Norwegian lion merely as a quartering of the Swedish arms, generated the same kind of patriotic animus as the flag question. This was only partly resolved with Oscar I's tactful uniting of the Norwegian and Swedish emblems on equal terms within the royal coat of arms (after 1844). Even then, Nansen complained that the Swedes had represented Norway in this way 'just as though Norway were actually a province of Sweden... [and that] it was only after considerable opposition from Norway that this [heraldry] was given up' (Nansen 1905, p. 28 n. 1). It should be said, too, that this issue was mirrored in Austria-Hungary: the representation of the kingdom of Hungary on (or alongside) the Austrian armorials was a bone of contention until 1915, when a solution of striking heraldic complexity was finally worked out in the context of the war (see e.g. Godsey 1999, pp. 145–6).

The stamp of the union monarchy certainly affected the 'pillarized' civil society of late 19th-century Ireland, but it did so primarily within its Protestant and middle-class aspects: Irish yachtsmen, golfers, musicians, and scholars all sought the patronage of the union monarchy for their disparate endeavours (Jackson 2013, pp. 207–8). For much of Catholic Ireland, however, the lack of any clear popular ownership of the union (in contrast to Scotland), together with its evident political and economic failures, created divisions over the institution and its symbolism. Royal visits and royal honours were contentious: in terms of civic space, royal statues and street-naming were equally contested. As was discussed earlier (section 4.2), British monarchs like Queen Victoria responded by showing an obvious preference for Scotland above Ireland. In short, the Scots had a clear ownership of the British monarchy and its symbolism, where the position of the Irish was much less certain (Jackson 2013, pp. 153–63, 199–207). The Irish had a weaker hold, though there were certainly efforts by some national leaders (pre-eminently John Redmond between 1900 and 1918) to redefine the monarchy as a national rather than exclusively a supranational (or union) asset—much as was the case in Norway, where the Bernadottes were accepted, not as monarchs of the United Kingdoms, but of Norway itself (Jackson 2018b).

Turning to civic space in the Dual Monarchy from c.1860 to 1900, the German bourgeoisie in Cisleithania propagated a range of 'cultural symbols', erecting monuments to favoured Habsburg rulers such as the unifying and centralizing Joseph II, or favoured military heroes, especially Field Marshal Graf Josef Radetsky (1766–1858), naming or renaming public space in celebration of such leaders, as well as 'deploying specific architectural styles to express [over-arching] liberal values in new public buildings' (Judson 2016, p. 280; see also Cole et al. 2011, pp. 243–68; Cole 2014, pp. 63–107; Bucur and Wingfield 2001, pp. 178–205). Here a liberal-nationalist neo-baroque architectural idiom competed with a Catholic conservative neo-gothic for the visual conquest of much of Cisleithania— just as the unionist architectural idioms of the neo-classical and, later, the Scots baronial came to dominate in parts of Scotland and the north of Ireland. In Cisleithania the function of buildings—and even the colour of the paintwork— denoted the imperial presence: buildings were commonly finished off in the imperial yellow of the Habsburgs. Ambitious city leaders across the empire identified particular recreational spaces—theatres and opera houses—as prestigious expressions of civic culture and metropolitan sophistication; and the Viennese architects, Fellner and Helmer, supplied around 50 of these throughout the Habsburg lands, all rendered in a broadly similar neo-baroque idiom. Even today, over a century after the demise of the empire, the physical legacies of the Habsburg monarchy are detectable throughout central, eastern, and southern Europe, in terms of the shape, style, and colourings of public architecture and civic space (to say nothing of the ongoing deployment of portraits of Franz Joseph I, the lasting personal embodiment of the Dual Monarchy).

Similarly, even in sceptical Norway, union had some lasting material presence in civic space, just as vestiges of the Grand Duchy and of its 'union' with the Russian empire have lived on in contemporary Finland. It is of course important not to exaggerate these legacies, which were disproportionately elite and metropolitan. The pre-eminent official class in mid-19th-century Norway, fearful of revolution and radicalization, looked with increasing sympathy towards the union with Sweden, as lesser challenges and indeed perhaps even as sources of stability. A society was founded in 1856 by Norwegian admirers of the effective founder of the union, Carl XIV Johan: this was followed by a public subscription which delivered, in 1875, an equestrian statue of the king, which still dominates the public space in front of the royal palace at Christiania/Oslo (Barton 2003, p. 65). Relics of the era of the Grand Duchy abound in modern Helsinki, from imposing places of Orthodox worship through the tsarist-era central railway station, with its imperial trappings, to various commemorations of popular tsars—whether through the tympanum (1903) of the House of Estates (1888–90) (later redeployed as a library) which depicts Alexander I (1777–1825) confirming the laws and rights of the Finnish people, or the famous statue of Alexander II in the nearby Senate square (1894). The 'Empress stone' in the Market Square of Helsinki, a popular social and recreational space, bears the tsarist double-headed eagle, and commemorates the visit of the empress Alexandra to the city in 1833. Above all, however, central Helsinki, like central Edinburgh, bears the prevailing imprint of union—in the Finnish case through the cool classical architectural idiom and pastel colouring of the tsarist era.

This section of the book has sought to pose some fresh questions about multinational civil society, civic space and union states. But if the questions are fresh, the answers are necessarily provisional. In particular, as with other aspects of the debate on civil society, these answers tend to be highly contingent: one-size taxonomies will not do.

Could a unifying civil society transcend the nation, developing within the parameters of the 19th-century multinational union state? The answer to this is a tentative 'yes'—but that possibility depended upon the nature of the union in question. In Scotland associational cultures and civil society developed after the union. The union, in turn, was linked to economic liberty, progress, and the consolidation of the Scottish nation. The relative flexibility and inclusivity and incompleteness of union in Scotland created space for associational cultures and a civil society which in turn worked to support union. Royal and union symbolism heavily infiltrated civil society and its spaces.

In Ireland union was instituted on the ruins of one form of civil society. As in Scotland, so in Ireland, union was incomplete and left space for associational cultures and civil society. But union was also associated with social and religious exclusivity. And it was therefore associated with the evolution of another, sectarianized and pillarized, form of civil society—one which was not only unsupportive of union but which represented a challenge and counter-state.

In Norway definitions of union were much tighter than in Ireland or Scotland, determined as they were by a national constitution. This gave space for associational cultures and the public sphere; but it also meant that the opportunities for the disruptive advance of union did not exist in quite the same way as in Scotland and Ireland. As in Ireland, though for different reasons, civil society was organized along largely national rather than union lines. A constitutionally limited union state also implied a spatially limited state; and in Norway the physical expressions of union, though real, were much less considerable than in relatively more elaborate union polities such as the United Kingdom or Austria-Hungary (where the memorialization, architectural shape, and colouring of union were manifest). But in Norway, as opposed to Ireland, civil society and the union state generally did not conflict—largely because at root there was so little of the union state with which to fight (see Jackson 2019 for an earlier version of this section).

4.9. Trade and Infrastructure

Unions have often been born out of economic calculation, and they have tended to wither and die on the same basis. The Scottish and Irish unions, and those in Sweden-Norway, and the Netherlands, were launched in the context of economic crisis, as were the parliamentary (1840) and federal (1867) unions of Canada; and they were all driven (at least in part) by the hope of relative material improvement. Each tottered for as long as the economic benefits of union remained unproven (or worse), though the Scots and Irish and Canadian unions (unlike, say, the United Kingdom of the Netherlands) were at least given the time to demonstrate their ultimate economic advantages, or otherwise. Equally, and in terms of contemporary history, as Britain's relationship with the confederation known as the European Economic Community, later the European Union, has demonstrated, the penalties of bad timing can be huge: the historian of British federalism, John Kendle, has argued that 'by remaining aloof from Europe for twenty years, the United Kingdom had done itself a disservice. Once it joined [the EEC], the world-wide economic down-turn ensured that no dramatic benefits were reaped' (Kendle 1997, p. 154). In essence, Britain's early experience of the European union coincided with a global recession and national economic crisis; and this, together with the subsequent absence of any dramatic gain, inevitably coloured some subsequent approaches to its utility and desirability. It is too early to say (at the time of writing) whether the timing of Britain's final departure from the EU on 31 January 2020 has been equally maladroit. But unions have certainly been shaped as a response to economic challenge; and, accordingly, they are more likely (though not bound) to fail if they do not serve this foundational purpose.

The unions of both Britain and Ireland, Austria-Hungary, Canada, and (for a time) of Sweden-Norway were each underpinned either by pre-existing 'free trade' arrangements, or by their establishment and consolidation alongside union;

and any subversion of this achievement was generally seen as an insidious assault on the unions themselves. In both Scotland (after 1707) and Ireland (after 1801) the coinage, currency, and taxation regimes were brought into line with those prevailing in the dominant partner, England, as part of the terms of the union settlements: in each a period of readjustment and acclimatization was allowed before the final attainment of uniformity (in the Irish case this period extended over the quarter century after union). Subsequent constitutional reform proposals (in particular for Ireland) were generally judged by both nationalists and unionists in terms of their threatened impact upon the integrity of the internal customs and fiscal union; and in fact none of the succession of home rule proposals for either Ireland or Scotland between 1886 and 1914 ultimately looked set to inflict any fundamental damage, certainly short-term damage, on the fiscal unity of the 'British Isles' (see Jackson 2004).

By comparison, the weakness of the United Kingdoms of Sweden-Norway was reflected in a relatively more hesitant and an ultimately more fragile equalization of tariffs—and in the absence of any pre-existing commercial alignment. Joint tariff legislation was certainly in place for the years between 1825 and 1897, and was associated with the heyday of union; but this did not prevent (often to the surprise of British travellers, accustomed to a different form of united kingdom) customs checks on the border between the two union partners (Lindgren 1959, p. 38; Laing 1836, pp. 13, 292). As was also observed earlier in the work, there was some more general if belated cooperation between the two polities, with a trade treaty in 1874 (which created free trade by land and extended the scope of sea-borne free trade) and the Scandinavian currency union of 1875 (creating a new shared currency of 100 øre to one krone). But alongside the increasing rift on consular services from the late 1880s onwards was a growing chasm between an increasingly protectionist Sweden and a robustly free trade Norway; and in fact when their joint agreement on tariffs finally lapsed in 1897, it was not renewed. Fridtjof Nansen, writing from a patriotic Norwegian perspective, saw this divergence as a critical loosening of the United Kingdoms as a whole, recording that,

> as time went on, Norway's and Sweden's commercial interests came more and more into conflict with one another and especially when in the eighties Sweden began to adopt a system of high tariffs, while Norway continued to remain as before...the free trade hitherto possible between the two countries was without doubt the strongest real bond between them, and by the breaking of it by Sweden a fatal injury was done to the commercial and industrial cooperation between the two countries.   (Nansen 1905, p. 68; Barton 2003, p. 72)

There seems little doubt that, just as political union (with both multinational polities as well as nation states) has often been anticipated by economic coalescence, here was an instance where the end of union was preceded by a radical divergence in trade policy.

To this may be added another case—that of the United Kingdom of Portugal, Brazil, and the Algarves. Here, too, union was subverted by a sharp divergence in trade policy separating the two principal partners, Portugal and Brazil. Until 1807–8 Brazil had sat in a relationship of economic and constitutional inferiority to its imperial metropole, Portugal; but the removal of the Braganza royals to Rio in early 1808 was accompanied (28 January 1808) by the opening of Brazil's ports, and the ending of three centuries of colonialist mercantilism (Armitage 1836, vol. 1, p. 13; Schultz 2001, p. 198; Manchester 1933). By way of contrast, the end of the Napoleonic warfare in 1815 and constitutionalist agitation in Portugal brought the return of the monarchy to Lisbon, and with it Portuguese demands for an abandonment of the new free trade regime (Armitage 1836, vol. 1, pp. 77–8). These differences did not in themselves end the united kingdom; but (as, later, with Sweden-Norway) they were certainly an important part of a landscape of increasing mutual divergence and resentment.

On the other hand, current orthodoxy has emphasized the economic consolidation of the Habsburg monarchy in association with its increasing economic and wider unity—including in the decades before the attainment of the Ausgleich (Good 1984; Sked 1989, p. 198). From the 1770s onwards there was a growing uniformity of customs duties across the empire which looked forward to the formal inauguration of a customs union in 1850–1: the customs union itself preceded the conclusion of the Ausgleich in 1867, and lasted until the very end of the Austro-Hungarian monarchy in 1918 (Jászi 1929, p. 58). Foreign trade was liberalized through a reform of tariffs, while the empire's customs union was in turn connected to the German Zollverein (customs union) through a trade treaty concluded in 1853 (Judson 2016, p. 230). Serfdom was abolished at roughly the same time—in both Austria (in 1849) and in Hungary (in 1853), with some important consequences for the development of agriculture in the empire (cf. Komlos 1983, p. 215). Parity in banking was achieved across the Monarchy in 1878, with the creation of the Austro-Hungarian bank (Cornwall 2002, p. 115 n. 1).

It should be briefly stressed, too, that this commercial unity across the different union polities was complemented by a shared range of infrastructural and cultural issues. As with other union states (most obviously the United Kingdom of Britain and Ireland), the rapid expansion of overarching banking institutions and of the rail network jointly underpinned the strengthening unity and integrity of the Dual Monarchy. It is clearly important, in making comparisons, to be alert to the presumptions regarding eastern Europe, legacies of the Cold War era, which have sometimes skewed discussions of the Monarchy's historic economic development (for a critique see Judson 2016, p. 119). In Austria, however, unlike Britain and the Netherlands, rail expansion *was* relatively slow in coming, with the decisive developments at last occurring under the 'neo-absolutist' rule of Alexander von Bach (who served as Austria's interior minister between 1849 and 1852): Bach and his ministerial colleagues facilitated the creation of new banks in order to widen the availability of credit. The most important of these was the Creditanstalt, created in 1855 as a bank for commerce and industry, and endowed with enormous capital reserves: the Creditsanstalt 'worked enormous effects on the lives' of ordinary Austrians, not least because it made possible the financing and ultimately the construction of rail lines throughout the empire, uniting local economies and peoples, and helping to consolidate the reality of the Habsburg state (Judson 2016, pp. 232–33).

However, a complementary set of reforms was needed before this happy consummation could be attained. It has been argued that 'the most striking feature of neo-absolutist economic policy was [in fact] the effort put into railway construction first under direct state auspices then from 1854 through generous state cash guarantees to private companies' (Okey 2001, p. 169). Until 1854 the Austrian state owned and managed almost three-quarters of the rail lines, but a combination of financial exigency and military and commercial pressures forced a radical rethink (one pressing issue was, as ever, Habsburg military spending—and in particular, at this time, the era of the Crimean war, an extremely expensive mobilization of the army). A railway concession act was promulgated in 1854, which allowed the state to privatize its rail holdings, while simultaneously underwriting generous rates of return for those who were tempted to invest in the new rail companies. This, in combination with the virtually simultaneous inauguration of the Creditanstalt, provided the opportunity and the means to effect a railway boom; and indeed it has been calculated that some 2,000 miles of rail line were built in this one decade alone, the 1850s (Judson 2016, p. 231). However, the great crash of May 1873 and after damaged not just this spectacular growth but also the wider liberal (and German) position within the Dual Monarchy—to the point that in 1879 the last liberal government of Cisleithania was ousted by a clericalist coalition under the conservative Count Taaffe.

Whatever the complex western presumptions about the supposed 'backwardness' of eastern Europe, in fact the spread of rail networks across the United Kingdoms of Sweden-Norway, in the north, was achieved even more tardily than in the Habsburg domains, and impeded communication as well as effective unification. Already in 1850 it was possible to travel by rail the 633 km between the two British capitals, London and Edinburgh, using (it is true) different companies. On the other hand, the first rail connection between the two capitals of the United Kingdoms of Sweden-Norway, Christiania and Stockholm (a distance of 417 km) was only opened in 1871. This tardiness reflected different circumstances, including disparities of wealth and industrial advance separating the different united kingdoms; but it was also an expression of the much looser union which characterized Sweden-Norway.

Economic unity was of course facilitated not just by infrastructural development (as with the railways), but also by cultural assimilation, and particularly in terms of language. This was true for Britain and Ireland, where the commercial and military domination of England within the union helped to underpin the rapid spread of the English language across Ireland and Scotland: some patriotic Irish leaders, including the *Gaeilgeoir* Daniel O'Connell, and the later commanders of the Irish parliamentary party, readily subordinated the Irish language to the challenge of achieving Catholic political and economic rights within an anglophone and Protestant union state. Similarly, one critical aspect of the 'expanding commercial framework' in the Habsburg empire was the widespread deployment of the German language, especially in Cisleithania—and it was this, rather than the common (imperial) identity and culture which Oszkár Jászi longed for in his work, which at first supplied a key unifying factor within the Habsburg empire (Jászi 1929; Okey 2001, p. 99). Language was of course readily challenged by nationalist activists in Ireland and throughout Cisleithania in the late 19th century; but in a sense this partly reflected the overpowering success of English and German as commercial *linguae francae*. By extension, however, it can be seen that union states like the United Kingdom and Austria-Hungary might well be destabilized, not simply by stagnation or decline, but rather by economic and cultural expansion: unions were often volatile entities whose very dynamism could be effectively subversive.

The corollary of this was that, neither in the Habsburg domains, nor in the other united kingdoms of northern and western Europe, did these unified trading environments represent any panacea—nor were they a substitute either for overall fiscal prudence or for fairness and equity. Expressing this point in another way, the economic success of multinational unions has generally been a necessary, but never a sufficient cause for their survival—since economic success has frequently been inadequately shared and has otherwise been associated with the growth of nationalism. It seems clear that social and economic advance in both the United Kingdom and the Dual Monarchy in the 19th century tended towards a relative but uneven democratization; and that this in turn 'fed into rival nationalisms and undermined non-dominant notables with whom the elite sought to do deals' (Okey 2001, pp. 360, 368). Thus, the political crises of the Habsburg monarchy, and also (it might be said) of the United Kingdom, were not in fact the by-products of economic stagnation, 'but [rather] of lop-sided development'—that is to say, of socially and spatially unequal development (Okey 2001, p. 335).

In essence, then, there has frequently been a tension between the overall evidence of economic growth, and perceptions of its impact and benefits. For example, pioneering work on the economics of the Habsburg monarchy has established that Hungary did relatively well out of its 'union' relationship with Austria, whether in terms of heightened access to Austrian markets for its agricultural produce, or the ready availability of Austrian capital for its wider economic development. These benefits were perceptible both before, but especially after the establishment of the customs union of 1850. Indeed, it is entirely likely that Austria may have been the marginal loser from the deal: it could readily have secured agricultural imports elsewhere, and the diversion of capital into Hungary effectively placed a brake upon its own recovery from the great crash of 1873. But these were not the perceptions which were forefronted in Hungary, where narratives of the kingdom's subjection to Austrian interests here (as elsewhere) more readily gained traction (see e.g. the conclusions of Komlos 1983).

Indeed, the Hungarians argued relentlessly that their kingdom was exploited economically, and thus they fought their corner bitterly in the decennial financial readjustments which took place under the terms of the Ausgleich (Cornwall 2002, p. 3). It was certainly the case that, with the 'reformed' tariff arrangements of 1775 and after, which favoured Austrian products, and which imposed heavy duties on exports outside the monarchy, Hungary's economic interests were subordinated to those of its dominant neighbour: Hungary's trade at this time was overwhelmingly directed towards Austria (with 86 per cent of total exports heading in this direction between 1760 and 1790), and, furthermore, no significant effort was spent in encouraging Hungarian manufactures (Okey 2001, p. 37). By the later 19th century many Hungarians (like many Irish, looking accusingly to England) were arguing for the notion of an historically underdeveloped Hungary kept in a semi-colonial position through the tariff union with Austria.

But, if Hungary complained about Austria, then Croatia-Slavonia (as a nominally semi-autonomous crownland within Transleithania) had in turn significant grounds for complaint against Hungary. Just as Magyars believed that they were being short-changed by Austria, so many in Croatia-Slavonia believed that they paid too great a quota of taxation to Budapest—a point made by Josip Frank (1844–1911) in his *Die Quote Kroatiens* (1879). Outside sympathizers like R. W. Seton-Watson argued as well that 'the railway policy which Budapest has advocated and enforced for many years past is the chief factor in checking Croatia's natural economic development and hence also the political development of the southern Slavs' (Seton-Watson 1911a, p. 329). Indeed, Seton-Watson believed more generally that 'the whole southern Slav world is at present the victim of a selfish policy of monopoly and favouritism directed from Budapest' (Seton-Watson 1911a, p. 334).

Similar internal resentments in the context of overall growth characterized the United Kingdom of the Netherlands; and the southern, Belgian, provinces of the kingdom certainly and fervently believed that they were more heavily taxed than their northern counterparts. The new union, like its Scottish and Irish counterparts, was forged in circumstances of great economic disruption—in the last months of a global war, and in the context of massive levels of public debt. It is calculated that King Willem I inherited 1.8 billion gulden of debt on assuming the crown of the new United Kingdom in 1814, and this burden meant both that he had comparatively limited room for manoeuvre, and that he was forced to adopt a range of wheezes and dodges to gather and dispense monies for the public good (Wintle 2000, pp. 138–9). Under the new union constitution, the national debt was equally shared between the two halves of the kingdom—and this generated great rancour in the south, which was less indebted than the north. The new union was also—in common with other union states—emphatically not a union of economic equals. The north relied on its colonial possessions, trade, and the service sector, while the south had both a flourishing agricultural base as well as mining and other industrial raw materials: it was also strong in manufacturing, and indeed the Belgian provinces of Ghent and Verviers contained what have been described as 'some of the most successful centres of mechanised spinning and weaving in the world' (Wintle 2000, pp. 131–2). The north (like Norway) therefore depended upon a greater openness of trade, while the interests of the south (like Sweden) on the whole lay with protectionism. Willem envisioned a complementarity in his new realm, whereby the south would manufacture the goods which the north would then export; and he worked hard to produce an equitable tariff regime (see Wright 2013). But in reality suspicions arose in the south that their Dutch king was pursuing secretive and shady economic policies which effectively delivered the subsidizing of the north through southern tax revenues. And in fact it has been calculated that in 1816 20 per cent of the new kingdom's spend was on the south, while 40 per cent of its taxation revenues were raised there (a proportion which rose to 50 per cent by the last years of the short-lived United Kingdom's existence).

It need hardly be emphasized that, no less than in the Netherlands or in the Dual Monarchy, contentious issues of taxation and benefit, and of asymmetric economic development, have also plagued the histories of Britain and Ireland since the formation of the two unions. Here, too, union has meant the controversial sharing of large national debts, disputes about the withholding of resource, and yet further disputes about the appropriate levels of taxation (most clearly during the Irish financial relations controversy of the 1890s). On the other hand, Irish perceptions of their economic relationship with the British were of course overwhelmingly framed by the uniquely disastrous Great Famine of 1845–51, and by the evidence of official British inadequacy or failure in its responses. As in Hungary, so in Ireland the perception arose that the interests of the economically dominant partner trumped all else, and gave rise to inequities in (for example) taxation and resource allocation. The formalization of a resource model in 1888—the Goschen formula—supplied evidence for this perception, since the algorithm gave Ireland, which had 12.5 per cent of the United Kingdom population, only 9 per cent of the available resource (the picture was in fact complicated by population decline—also blamed on the impact of union—and by specifically Irish legislation such as the land purchase acts) (Jackson 2013, pp. 173, 352–3). But in Hungary there was, through the Ausgleich, a parliament and other mechanisms through which to articulate and negotiate these grievances—where in Ireland they were weaponized against the union itself.

As with Hungary, so with Ireland there were also some complexities in (what was) a fluid and protracted economic relationship with Britain. If Ireland—or, in particular, Irish nationalism—complained about England, then Ulster unionists in turn pointed out that home rule and a reconfigured union threatened their sectional well-being. For these unionists the substitution of a nominally unitary British state with a home rule administration in Ireland implied the economic subjugation of their relatively industrialized heartland at the hands of a primarily agrarian nationalism. In essence, they feared the kind of tension between free trade and protectionist interests which characterized unrest in a range of the union polities under review—and including the Netherlands and Sweden-Norway.

Moreover, the British-Irish economic relationship (like that binding Austria and Hungary) brought a similar array of (at least) potential gains: these included for Ireland (as for Hungary with Austria) a large market for agricultural output, together with the ready availability of capital. As in Hungary, so in Ireland there was clear evidence of growth; but its effects were very uneven and were associated in particular with the regional—north-eastern—industrial hub of Belfast and its hinterland.

Equally, with the Scottish union, perceptions of economic benefit varied according to place and time. The union itself offered a financial package to reimburse those who had lost out through the mismanaged, epically expensive, and ultimately disastrous colonization effort in Darien, central America (1698–1700); but it also brought immediately heightened taxation and, in the short term, few compensatory gains. However, Scotland participated fully in the wider industrial and commercial growth of the later 18th century, though this was particularly concentrated in the central belt area of the country. There were also, as elsewhere, winners and losers from this growth: the introduction of commercial pastoral agriculture brought gains for proprietors at the expense of substantial and merciless clearances in both the highlands and lowlands, while rapid industrialization brought great wealth as well as the creation of oppressive factory cultures. Some of this union growth was tied in with Scottish participation in the cruelties and oppression of the British transatlantic slave trade and of slavery in general.

Scotland for long remained a well-integrated component within the British industrial economy, including the centrally directed nationalized industries of the post-war era; and indeed the corollary of this has been an association between deindustrialization, denationalization, and the weakening of union. Furthermore, issues of taxation and resource have also long simmered in Scotland. They were brought to the boil in the age of denationalization through the discovery and successful extraction of North Sea gas and oil from the mid and late 1960s—a mineral bonanza which, instead of being applied (as in Norway) to a sovereign wealth fund, was used by successive governments to pursue their various short-term ends, including the reallocation of domestic tax burdens (Harvie 1994).

On the other hand, it was also clear that economic inequality and constraint within union states could not simply be expressed in terms of national difference or the wiles of a dominant partner. In relation to the Dual Monarchy, Jászi and others have argued with conviction that the Hungarian landed classes were characterized by a remorseless economic self-interest which ultimately subverted the finances of the whole state: 'progress in agricultural production would have been the chief condition for raising the economic and cultural interdependence of its various nations and territories, By checking agricultural progress, the landed classes weakened the centripetal forces of the monarchy and increased the dissolving tendencies' (Jászi 1929, p. 201). Others on the whole have accepted and elaborated this analysis, arguing (for example) that in the late 19th century the Magyar landed elites became converts to agricultural protection, and embraced policies which 'meant high prices for the poor, subsidising of the well-off, and no hope of a breakthrough to a modern industrial democracy' (Okey 2001, p. 249). The last years of the Dual Monarchy were certainly not economically stagnant; but, at the same time, the effective failure of free trade in agricultural produce was not only a brake upon the economic modernization of the empire, it ultimately hastened its wider vulnerability and dissolution (Okey 2001, p. 233).

Moreover, the damage done by well-established vested landed interests, especially in Hungary, went even further than this: as Jászi argued, 'for the maintenance of their economic and political privileges, it was an outstanding interest of the feudal system to make national controversies more acute' (Jászi 1929, p. 238). For example, the relatively liberal commercial treaty between Hungary and Serbia signed in 1882 was opposed by the major Hungarian landowners, and was therefore not renewed: the consequence was a deteriorating relationship with Serbia, the strengthening of the latter's economic connections elsewhere (France, Germany), and a damaging commercial conflict—the 'Pig War' (1906-8). And, of course, the Monarchy's toxic relationship with Serbia was central to its descent into war in July-August 1914 (see e.g. Steed 1919, pp. 242-3).

In short, unions often coalesced in the contexts of economic challenge and with the clear hope of shared economic betterment through the institutions and agencies of greater political collaboration. They often came together constitutionally, while building on the foundations of earlier economic cooperation. The economic stalling of union often constituted, in a sense, a failure of its fundamental mission and purpose and mission; and (for example) the weakening of union has been convincingly linked both to industrial retreat in Scotland, as well as to the failures of the wartime Austrian economy in Cisleithania.

However, there has emphatically been no exact correlation between union and economic prosperity. The most that might be said is that prosperity is a necessary, but by no means a sufficient, underpinning for the success of union. On the contrary, relativities have been of the utmost significance. Unions which have prospered have often been judged, not on their overall health, but rather primarily on the effectiveness with which that prosperity has been distributed across their national components. Indeed, the combination of absolute economic prosperity and a ferocious sense of national injustice has proved to be an extraordinarily effective and combustible fuel for national sentiment and the subversion of union. Alex Salmond, it has been said, has foreseen that Scottish nationalism will attain its ultimate goal in conditions of prosperity rather than the reverse; and, on the basis of the available historical evidence across the case studies of this work, it is hard to disagree with his insight.

4.10. Class Politics and Union

While (as with the preceding example of Hungary) particular interest groups certainly did damage, then more generally class should be seen as much as a binding agent as a solvent of union; and the politics of class have certainly served as the politics of unionism. Turning briefly, therefore, to the issue of potentially unifying class alliances, much of the success of European union states hinged upon the binding power of dominant social groups whose interests spanned the polity in question. In the United Kingdom, as has been noted, a long-dominant landed class with interests often spanning all of the constituent polities of the state represented a key agency of union (Viscount Castlereagh and his family, the marquesses of Londonderry, are good examples of a unionist landed dynasty, indeed architects and agents of union, whose property and politics spanned the United Kingdom and indeed beyond: see section 4.3).

Other classes in other complex polities have fulfilled related unifying functions: it has been argued that much of the striking success of Belgium as a (complex and composite) state after the dissolution of the United Kingdom of the Netherlands in 1830 may be ascribed 'to the social ascendancy of a bourgeoisie, francophone in language but rooted as firmly in Flanders as in Brussels and Wallonia' (Conway 2012, p. 381). In Belgium the unifying power of the francophone bourgeoisie was replaced not by any national successor, but rather by variegated regional elites who helped to drive the federalization project between 1968 and the 1990s (Conway 2012, pp. 380–1).

In the United Kingdom, the power of the landed elites was under threat—especially in Ireland—by the end of the 19th and early 20th centuries; but, paradoxically, their function was to some extent inherited by a labour movement with (certainly so far as Scotland, Wales, and the north of Ireland were concerned) a strong sense that its interests were more likely to be realized through joint action in a United Kingdom rather than at 'local' level. Indeed, critical to the success of the United Kingdom in its heyday was the binding force of working-class solidarity across at least three of the four constituent polities (the partial exception being Ireland). In Scotland and in Wales the working classes tended to be organized ultimately into supranational, United Kingdom trades unions and a supranational political party, Labour. This meant that, certainly for so long as class was a critical determinant of voting choice, it served as a bolster of union (the corollary being, of course, that the relegation of class in electoral politics implied the relegation of union). The individual examples of Scots and Welsh Labour activists who combined patriotic local and class identities with a supranational 'Britishness' are many—and Paul Ward has done much to elucidate the histories of individuals such as Huw Edwards (1892–1970), who oscillated throughout his life between Plaid Cymru and Labour, ultimately settling with the latter: 'Edwards' Welshness was the central part of his political identity yet its expression came through the partnership of the Welsh with the English and Scottish working class inside the Union... his Welshness was combined with a sense of class identity which encouraged links to the rest of the United Kingdom through his activities for his trade union and within the Labour party' (Ward 2005, p. 123; see section 2.2).

In the Habsburg empire socialism had been temporarily crushed through the penal code of 1852; but there were organizational revivals in the 1870s, and a confluence of effort in 1889 finally produced the *Sozialdemokratische Arbeiterpartei Österreichs* (Social Democratic (Workers') Party of Austria), whose central tenet was the unity of the working classes (Okey 2001, p. 265; Cornwall 2002, p. 54). While the Social Democratic Party originally sustained what has been described as 'a highly centralised structure', in 1897 they accepted a more federalist constitution, and then proceeded to reorganize along national and linguistic lines (Cornwall 2002, p. 54; Judson 2016, p. 372). Henceforth the new individual national parties held their annual conferences while uniting every other year in a grand congress of the entire Austro-Hungarian party—but after 1911 the increasingly strained notion of an overarching identity was finally given up. It has been rightly said that the Social Democrats' 'multinational identity along with its commitment to suffrage reform made [them] in practical terms a mass party in support of a democratic vision of empire' (Judson 2016, p. 373).

Thus, the party and its intellectuals did much to generate creative thought about the possible future of the Dual Monarchy, and indeed in some senses its overarching constitutional vision swiftly came to reflect its own organizational choices. In 1899, at its Brünn/Brno conference, the now federalized Social Democrats called for the creation of a federalized and democratized Austria: they 'asserted their own, far more democratically inflected and highly oppositional concepts of nationhood' (Judson 2016, p. 373). The leading party members, Victor Adler (1852–1918), Otto Bauer, and Karl Renner—the patriarchs of Austro-Marxism—sought imaginatively to reconcile questions of class and national identity within the framework of the Habsburg empire by positing a scheme of federal government which hinged upon personal rather than territorial national identities (the key work here is Bauer's *Die Nationalitätenfrage und die Sozialdemokratie* (The nationalities' question and social democracy, 1907) (see Burgess 2006, p. 142; for a more cautious approach see Beneš 2017, p. 240). Nationality would be decoupled from the often toxic issue of territoriality: individuals would be free to choose their own national identity, rather than be subject to the imposition of (conceivably) an unwelcome identity through the accident of dwelling-place or language. National associations would be self-governing within an overall federated structure. This was not merely isolated utopian speculation. Rather, the importance of these views was related (albeit in complex ways) to the increasing electoral success of the Social Democrats: in May 1907, in the aftermath of the introduction of universal adult male suffrage and the simultaneous abandonment of the old curial franchise, they became the single largest party in Cisleithania's Reichsrat.

And indeed there was, it has to be said, complexity. Social democracy in east-central Europe at this time (as with the labour movement in the United Kingdom) was associated with some countervailing pulls. It certainly proffered a strong supra- and internationalism—a compelling sense of a class identity beyond the confines of the nation or even of the state. On the other hand, as the work of Jakub Beneš (focusing on the Czech lands) and others with different emphases has made clear, socialism could be simultaneously a nationalizing force, in that it 'empowered the growing ranks of industrial workers to lay claim to political rights as well as national culture' (see e.g. Beneš 2017). Moreover, this consolidation was only achieved with greater disruption and disorder (as with the street clashes between workers and authorities in Vienna, Prague, Brno, and elsewhere in November 1905) than has been frequently been conceded elsewhere (Beneš 2017, pp. 239–40). Czech socialists at this time (like James Connolly in Ireland) certainly saw no conflict in combining a ferocious nationalism with an internationalist class solidarity (Beneš 2017, p. 241).

Still, it remains true that the growing importance of the Social Democrats in (what we now know were) the last years of the empire, allied with the fertility of their thought on federalism, served to elevate a range of unifying forces within the empire at the relative expense of narrow regional nationalisms. In common with the British Labour party, which embraced the democratic reform of the constituent unions of the United Kingdom, and a democratic vision of union, the Social Democrats simultaneously engaged and melded strong national sympathies within a set of wider, transnational frameworks. Both parties effectively operated as agents of union—albeit reformed union: as a contemporary (if aggressively polemical) Italian commentator sarcastically complained, 'k.k. *Sozialdemokratie* [imperial and royal Social Democracy], the proletarian movement is called in Austria It is a fitting title of honour. Austrian socialism in truth is a good and meek subject, honours the emperor and no longer thinks seriously of rebelling against his laws' (Gayda 1915, p. 325). Indeed it has been suggested that even Franz Joseph himself offered some grudging reciprocation, seeing the Social Democrats as unifiers and internationalists (cf. Cornwall 2002, p. 50).

This conjunction of national or patriotic sympathies and transnational union cooperation was also a hallmark of the agrarian classes, and of the farmers' parties, in both Sweden and Norway in the last quarter of the 19th century, as representative politics across the United Kingdoms were increasingly characterized by popular mobilization and retreating conservative elites. Superficially, as with the rise of Labour in Britain, this implied the weakening of unionism and of the union; but in reality it created the possibility of a realignment of national relationships within a stronger if redefined union settlement: as the Norwegian patriot-poet, Bjørnstjerne Bjørnson, enunciated at Lilliestrøm in June 1881, 'the more independently and freely both [Norwegian and Swedish] peoples develop, the more firmly the union stands...long live Norway! Long live the union with Sweden!' (quoted in Barton 2003, p. 69). Bjørnson and the Norwegian liberal leader, Johan Sverdrup (1816–92) were important in forging a connection between the popular party within the Norwegian Storting, which was dominated by the small farmer interest, and the Swedish Lantmannaparti (Farmers' Party), which was growing rapidly after the Riksdag reform of 1865–6. Each of these shared the goals of constraining government expenditure and curbing the power of the old official and aristocratic elites; and from the early 1870s on there was cooperation between the two. The Lantmannaparti in the Riksdag gave support to the popular cause in the Storting at the time of the statholder crisis of 1871, and again with the Norwegian constitutional crisis of 1884, which compelled a highly reluctant king Oscar II to look to Sverdrup and the left-leaning (or Venstre) party to form a government (Barton 2003, p. 71; Knaplund 1952, pp. 34–5). In this debacle 'the role of the Swedish Farmers' Party would appear to have been crucial'; and indeed the coercion of the king was the apogee of its influence within the Riksdag (Barton 2003, p. 71). By the last years of the Swedish-Norwegian union, the left in Sweden and more conservative interests in Norway were each aligned—having 'found in the union reinforcement for their respective political objectives' (Barton 2003, p. 82). By way of contrast, Norwegian radical and—paradoxically—some Swedish conservatives now found a union which was becoming inimical to some of their core beliefs.

This raises the question for unions, also universally applicable to nation states, of their economic beneficiaries: *cui bono*? As has been argued, multinational unions (like unifying nation states) have often built upon pre-existing economic relationships, and they have often been designed to speak to particular economic challenges and particular economic interests. The Scottish union, for example, built upon close commercial relations with England, and it was launched in the economic and military turmoil of the first decade of the 18th century, and in particular with the existing vested interests of Scottish society in view: similarly, the

Irish union built upon existing 'free trade' arrangements with Britain, and it was launched in the economic and military turmoil of the 1790s, and in particular with the interests of the ascendancy elite in view (Jackson 2013). Other unions may have had slighter economic foundations than these, but they often came with similar expectations and with a similar range of favoured interests. Unions, in short, have generally been strongly pragmatic agreements, and have been shaped in the light of particular economic circumstances and interests.

What if these circumstances and audiences change? On the whole, trade and commerce, especially free trade and unified markets, have served to complement or even augment political union: on the whole, the era of class politics was (at the very least) often compatible with the politics of unionism and of the multinational union state. But the overall significance of class politics has diminished, certainly in the United Kingdom; and here, as across the other unions reviewed in this study, the structures of industry and trade have changed, and often dramatically. The structures of union were occasionally able to accommodate change: this was to some extent the case with the relative decline of landed elites in both the United Kingdom and in Cisleithania, in each of which there was evidence of adaptability in the early 20th century, when new forms of unifying economic and social agency emerged.

However, more significant or sudden structural (or other) change has been a different matter. The inability of the existing governance of British North America before 1867 to cope with the economic challenges posed either by the American civil war or the opening up of the west and north-west forced a redrawing of the union of the United Province and of its relations with the other British possessions. The ending of tariff alignment in Sweden-Norway in 1897 was seen by contemporaries as a catalyst for the break-up of union. The effective collapse of the wartime Austrian economy shortly preceded the demise of the Dual Monarchy itself. In both the United Kingdom and Belgium existing definitions of the union state have been undermined by shifts in patterns of economic growth and concomitant change within the class structure of the two states. In terms of recent history, it has been argued that the collapse of the heavy industries of Wallonia after the Second World War was a key point of departure 'for the crisis of the [Belgian] nation-state' (Conway 2012, p. 375). Similarly, the collapse of the heavy industries of Scotland and the north of England in the same era has been a key point of departure for some of the current difficulties of the United Kingdom state.

It would certainly be too simplistic to argue that there was a necessary connection between radical economic change, or even collapse, and the failure of union: unions may become more than the sum of their origins. But it is noticeable that those interests which were favoured by union, and which in turn have embraced union, have often shifted their outlook in accordance with economic and other changes within their home polity. Thus, the liberalizing influence of Norway and Norwegian politics within Sweden had created an economic and political situation by the 1890s where Swedish conservatives (who in the mid-19th century with their Norwegian counterparts had often been unionist) now increasingly saw the union as a liability rather than as an asset. And in Ireland and then Northern Ireland, unionists backed union because, they claimed, Irish nationalism was impoverished, isolationist, and clericalist. But a combination of the relatively anglocentric politics of Brexit together with the sustained liberalizing trajectory and economic growth of the Irish state has now produced a situation where these historic arguments for union no longer work: as elsewhere in the history of unions, it may no longer be in the interests of all unionists to be unionist. In short, unions fail, not always because of their enemies; but rather sometimes because they lose their social and economic purpose, and because (accordingly) their friends lose faith.

4.11. Imperial Dark Arts: Crushing, Cosseting, and Dividing

Multinational unions survived, therefore, because of agreed and (often) beneficent supranational (or, in Jászi's vocabulary, 'internationalist') institutions which have served to bind: they survived, too, because of the unifying impact of a range of social, economic, and cultural forces. But it would be wholly wrong to present union states solely as an expression of a range of essentially positive agencies. And it would also be wrong to present unions simply or solely as equal partnerships focused on mutual aid.

For these complex polities have also survived on the basis of more brutal interventions; and their longevity was sometimes as dependent upon the dark arts of realpolitik as it was upon the sunlit uplands of supranational unity and amity. Of these dark arts, three closely interlinked approaches in particular provide a focus for this concluding section of the chapter: *'divide et impera'* (divide and rule), partial reinforcement (the strategies variously described across Europe as constructive unionism, 'kicks and ha'pence' or 'horsewhips and oats'), and lastly (though also largely overlapping with 'partial reinforcement'), unmitigated armed repression.

As a starting point for this discussion it should be reiterated that, with the various multinational unions discussed throughout this volume, there have been asymmetries of economic and military power which have often had a marked imperial dimension. Asymmetry has played a key part in the theorization of federation and federal unions; but it has not been much considered in relation to the various composite monarchies, and their derivatives, which are the principal focus of this work. Political scientists have for long argued that there has been a correlation between symmetry and survival with federal unions, though it is true that there has been a more recent push-back for the opposite case, where asymmetry has come to be 'regarded very much in a positive vein, bordering on virtue'

(Tarlton 1965; cf. Burgess 2006, pp. 211-25). This issue is revisited later in the book, but on the whole it may be suggested now, in terms of the union polities considered here, that asymmetry worked, not necessarily because (as with federal unions) it was 'ultimately linked to fundamental issues of legitimacy, participation and political stability', but rather because it was connected with the effective domination of small partners by bigger and more powerful—and sometimes essentially different—partners (Burgess 2006, p. 225).

In other words, some of the unions reviewed here have been associated with empire, either as polities which were simultaneously both unions *and* empires (the United Kingdom, Austria-Hungary, both the Netherlands and, later, Belgium), or as polities which have been associated with internal colonialism (the United Kingdom, Austria-Hungary), or as polities which have had strong historic or other associations with empire (Canada, Sweden-Norway) (see e.g. Armitage 2000). Given these ties, which are also discussed later, it should come as no surprise to discover that unions functioned in some essential administrative and cultural respects as local empires.

Nor should it come as a surprise that united kingdoms which were also empires should have developed political cultures which applied both overseas as well as at home. All of the arts of union government which are reviewed in this section of the book were either derived from, or at least related to, overseas colonial precedents. And they were associated with a range of cultural attitudes (such as pseudo-scientific racial categorization and cultural stereotyping) which had similar links with the strategies applied in overseas imperial governance.

Taking first the motif of 'divide and rule', in Ireland and Scotland the crown and its ministers for long ruled using the agency of favoured aristocratic networks, favoured sections of society, and sometimes favoured institutions. In Scotland after the union the key agents of the Hanoverian crown were the clan Campbell, headed by the successive dukes of Argyll (the title was created for Archibald Campbell, tenth earl of Argyll (1658-1703), in 1701); where by the end of the century the critical managers of government business were Henry Dundas, first Viscount Melville (1742-1811) and his family (Fry 2004; Murdoch 1980). As has been observed earlier in the chapter, the reconciliation between the crown and the Kirk, between the Supreme Governor of the episcopal Church of England and the Calvinist elect of the Church of Scotland, was a particularly impressive feat of ecclesiological prestidigitation; and it ensured that the Kirk on the whole functioned, alongside key elements of the Scots elite, as loyal adjuncts to the monarchy in Scotland, as did the Church of England and the English landed elite south of the border (see sections 4.2, 4.6).

In Ireland, on the other hand, the religious divisions of the country were always more acute than this, and religious sensitivities and jealousies were correspondingly raw. Moreover, while there were of course profound social divisions in Scotland, and controversial socio-economic policies such as land clearance, these on the whole did not coincide with cultural and religious divisions, as was the case in Ireland (Devine 2018). In the era of the separate (but by no means 'independent') Irish parliament of the 18th century, the crown exercised political control through aristocratic clients, the 'undertakers', so-called because they 'undertook' the management of government business in return for a substantial cut of official patronage—though this arrangement shifted during the lord lieutenancy (1767–72) of George Viscount Townshend (1724–1807) (Bartlett 1979). In general the Protestant—Church of Ireland or episcopal—landowning classes were the key beneficiaries of British government in Ireland, at least until the era of the Great Famine (1845–51), when the calamitous condition of Ireland's landless labourers (or 'cottiers') was exposed for all to see, and blamed in part on the practices of the landlords. Thereafter successive British governments looked for other allies in terms of the management of Ireland, whether in the form of the Catholic Church, which was courted from at least the era of the Famine onwards, or (in the case of the Liberals) the Home Rule party, or (in the case of the Tories) the Irish and later Ulster unionists. By the end of the 19th and early 20th centuries in Ireland, as in the Habsburg domains, the rival cultures or nationalities generally looked to central government for the crushing of their local rivals (and for patronage) rather than to any proactive or responsible diplomacy amongst themselves.

Critics of the Dual Monarchy, like critics of the Irish union and of the wider British empire, alleged that the Habsburgs and their servants preferred 'to see the different nationalities at enmity one with another', and that they used divisions of this kind as a basis for imperial and royal government (Dickinson-Berry 1918, p. 31). German Austrians were certainly for long the effective *Staatsvolk* of the Monarchy, while in the east Galician Poles were routinely preferred over Ruthenians: Croatia-Slavonia had, in theory, a favoured position within Transleithania, though the Ballhausplatz was deeply suspicious of any coalescence between Croats and Serbs, and (as will be seen) sometimes intervened ruthlessly to subvert any tendency in this direction (Steed 1919, p. 124). But, above all, the Ausgleich itself was in some ways the ultimate expression of *divide et impera*, since it involved a carve-up of the Monarchy between (to begin with) Austrian Germans and Magyars. It was certainly the case that, with both the British governing elites and the Habsburgs, there was considerable scope for abandoning existing clients and identifying new ones; but ultimately this scope was restricted in the Habsburg case, because dualism was constitutionally enshrined within the Ausgleich, and because the Magyars were strikingly successful in resisting any significant change. In particular, the alluring possibility that 'divide and rule' might graduate from Austro-Magyar dualism to Austro-Magyar-Slav trialism was scuppered on a recurrent basis—beginning in 1871 with the ultimately failed effort of the Hohenwart-Schäffle ministry to cut through the problems of Bohemia by means of the Fundamental Articles (Okey 2001, p. 222). In short, dualism may well have simultaneously supported the Habsburg monarchy, while ultimately creating the seeds of its subversion.

But, while 'divide and rule' was an intrinsic element of the overarching architecture of the Ausgleich, it also subsequently prevailed in both the component parts of the Dual Monarchy. For example, in Cisleithania, the carefully calibrated rule of Count Eduard Taaffe (Minister President between 1879 and 1890) was the acme of partial reinforcement—since Taaffe aimed at keeping every national political partner not necessarily happy, but rather just interested enough in the possibility of happiness to support his government: Taaffe defined the challenge of governing Cisleithania as keeping its nationalities in a condition of 'well-tempered discontent' (Jászi's gloss was that 'all the nationalities should be maintained in the same well-tempered dissatisfaction') (Jászi 1929, pp. 114–15; Beller 1996, p. 121; Cornwall 2002, p. 48). Similarly, Ernest von Koerber (as Minister President between 1900 and 1904) sustained in government what has been described as an ever-more 'vertical hierarchical system—where the parties bargained with the government, that is to say the Habsburg officialdom rather than with each other as in a horizontal democratic system'. The result of this was that, as in Ireland, the government ended up dealing with different competing clients, whose interests lay in winning over ministers or senior officials rather than in carefully addressing their own differences. Thus, Koerber's system, whatever its original strategic purpose, 'became a classic imperial model of "divide and rule"', with sometimes dangerous implications in terms of communal antagonisms (Beller 1996, p. 161; Markovits and Sysyn 1982, p. 92; Steed 1919, pp. 121–2).

In Transleithania, on the other hand, the emperor, Franz Joseph, acted like an absentee landlord, allowing his effective middlemen—the Magyar nobility and gentry—considerable latitude, and granting them great authority over the minority nationalities (Beller 1996, p. 98). The Nationalities Act of 1868 was applied as an instrument of magyarization, with emphases on the wider cultural superiority of the Magyar nation, and on its 'civilising mission' (Sked 1989, p. 209). Contemporaries, even a (progressive) Hungarian like Jászi, increasingly saw that Magyar nationality policy could be deeply oppressive (Jászi 1929, p. 280).

Certainly the condition of Croats and other Slavs within Magyar Transleithania much exercised R. W. Seton-Watson in the years before 1914; but part of the great resonance of his widely debated research also lay in the fact that it appeared to highlight parallels between the divisive and destructive actions of the dominant nationalities in the Dual Monarchy, and those within the unions of the United Kingdom. For example, the anonymous reviewer of *The Irish Times*, in assessing Seton-Watson's *Southern Slav Question* (1911), saw (what the writer deemed to be) 'a parallel for Ireland' in the experience of Croats within the Austro-Hungarian empire: the home rule gained by Croatia-Slavonia through the *Nagodba* of 1868 was vitiated, because there were fundamentally different (Croat and Hungarian) readings of the settlement, because the governor (Ban) of Croatia was 'in no way responsible to the Croatian parliament', and—above all—because the dominant Magyars saw it as 'good policy to set the Roman Catholic Croat against the Orthodox Serb' ('A Parallel for Ireland', *Irish Times*, 18 Nov. 1911). Similarly, the *Daily News* reviewer, writing in May 1912, argued that 'the parallel between Croatia and Ireland is in some respects fairly close. There is in both an alien government which is out of sympathy with or hostile to nationality; in both religious divisions are exploited for the purposes of the alien government' ('Hungary's Ireland', *Daily News*, 2 May 1912).

In addition to these central European and British instances (or suspicions) of 'divide and rule', there were also the United Kingdoms of Sweden-Norway. Here there was a tradition of unrest amongst some Swedish conservatives concerning the union; irritation, above all, at the perceived provincialism and particularism of the Norwegians—but antagonism, too, towards the monarchy, including even the patriarch of union, Carl XIV Johan (see Figure 2.2). Carl Johan, whatever his military distinction, was seen by some influential Swedish aristocrats (such as Knut Bonde or Carl Anckarsvärd (1782–1865)) as less interested in the standing of Sweden than in that of the monarchy; and in particular Anckarsvärd firmly believed that the king had deliberately accepted a weak union so that he could exercise an enhanced influence through playing off one partner nation against the other: *divide et impera* (Jorgenson 1935, p. 271).

Part of the processes of 'divide and rule', and of harnessing the rivalries between different nationalities within the British and Austrian empires, involved ethnic calibration and stereotyping. It is now a well-established trope within the flourishing scholarship on the Habsburg monarchy, and beyond, that 'since the Enlightenment there has been a western European discourse on a lesser-developed, lesser-civilised eastern Europe'; but there has also been a western European discourse on a 'lesser-developed', 'lesser-civilised' north-west European littoral (see also section 2.2; Wingfield 2003, p. 1). Stereotyped images of the Celtic 'Other', whether in an Irish or Scots formulation, have chimed with similarly pejorative images of outgroups within the wider Habsburg lands (Jackson 2013, p. 150).

Moreover, 'influences from European colonialism meanwhile reinforced the vogue for ethnic and civilisational generalisation with disparaging force' (cf. Okey 2001, p. 292). Stereotyping by the dominant nationality of the 'British Isles', the English, of the 'junior' partners in union, the Scots and Irish, has been well-documented: the features of these caricatures included fecklessness and unreliability on the part of the Irish, as well as—particularly in the Victorian period—a racialized set of approaches which represented the Irish, especially those pursuing violent social and political protest, in crudely simian terms (the starting point remains Curtis 1971). But a paternalistic vocabulary which emphasized the 'ingratitude' and 'unreliability' of the non-dominant nation was part, not only of an English political discourse on Irish nationalism, but also of Dutch attitudes towards the Belgians, especially in the context of the revolution of 1830 which broke the United Kingdom of the Netherlands; and it was part, too, of a set of Swedish attitudes towards their Norwegian partners.

There are indeed parallels between 19th-century English attitudes towards the Scots (and indeed the Irish) and the Swedish perspective on Norwegians. It has been rightly said, for example, that 'the English infatuation with wild and romantic Scotland since [Walter] Scott's day offers perhaps the closest parallel to Swedish visions of Norway during the union, as do the mingled feelings of the English—admiration tinged with envy, tolerant amusement and aggravation—toward their dour, hardy, yet canny, and energetic northern neighbours' (Barton 2003, p. 182). But there were also symmetries binding these Scandinavian attitudes with those linking the English and Irish: Norwegians, observed a British diplomatic commentator in 1894, 'have a contempt for the Swedes, whom they look upon as indolent and luxurious, while the Swedes despise the Norwegians as a nation of rustics. The two people do not appear to have any feeling in common to bind them together' (Barton 2003, p. 150; see also e.g. Wollstonecraft 1889, p. 51). The themes of English decadence within some Irish discourse, and of Irish rural backwardness within some English discourse, have long been identified, and in some respects they have echoed the mutual disregard of the Swedes and Norwegians (or indeed of the Belgians and Dutch).

But there was also a more scientific set of approaches to culture and identity, though in each these approaches were associated with the project of 'union' itself: cultural historians of empire (and others) are of course well attuned to the links between imperial government and complex statistical assemblage. The growth of the civil service and of policing in both the United Kingdom and Austria-Hungary meant that ever more information was being gathered on the populations, and on their social, economic, cultural, and political characteristics (Jackson 2013, pp. 208–9). The Irish Ordnance Survey (1824) (whose work has famously been dissected by Brian Friel (1929–2015) in his play, 'Translations' (1980)) was followed by a succession of investigatory land commissions, which in turn chimed with initiatives in India such as the Great Trigonometrical Survey (1818) or the Geological Survey of India (1851). Both the United Kingdom and the Dual Monarchy (and indeed the United Kingdoms of Sweden-Norway) developed alongside advances in cartography and in the accessibility of map images—the latter being important not least in terms of a popular normalizing of the political frontiers of the 'British Isles' or of Scandinavia and Austria-Hungary (e.g. Hemstad 2018). And in the latter there were several ambitious and scientific efforts to capture the diversity of the empire, including the work of Karl von Czoörnig (1804–89) in his *Ethnographie der österreichischen Monarchie* (Ethnography of the Austrian monarchy) (1855–7) together with his *Oesterreichs Neugestaltung* (Austria's reshaping) (1858). But the acme of patriotic scholarly investigation came with the officially sponsored encyclopedia, *Die österreichisch-ungarische Monarchie in Wort und Bild* (The Austro-Hungarian monarchy in word and picture) published in 24 volumes between 1885 and 1907, and originally graced with an introduction from Crown Prince Rudolf (1858–89), who was credited with the inspiration for the project (and which therefore became known as the *Kronprinzenwerk*). As Pieter Judson has observed, the *Kronprinzenwerk* also underlined 'the degree to which scientists in several branches of the natural and human sciences in Austria-Hungary sought to demonstrate an underlying logic common to the far-flung and diverse territories ruled by the Habsburgs even as that territorial quality shaped their research' (Judson 2016, p. 328).

Associated with 'divide and rule', and with its related mixture of ethnic prejudice and taxonomy, were other—often more explicit—policies of partial reinforcement, and which were practised throughout the history of the British unions, and of the Austrian and Austro-Hungarian monarchy: these embraced the simultaneous application of measures of reform as well as (often together with) suppression, and were captured in the 'constructive unionism' which characterized so much of British policy in Ireland (and Scotland) in the 19th century, as well as in a variety of Habsburg stratagems. Expressing this in another way, the British applied both 'kicks and ha'pence' in Ireland, where the Habsburgs and the Magyars applied (what were called) 'horsewhips and oats' in Croatia-Slavonia. Unions survived because they demonstrated flexibility—and because they combined flexibility with the violent suppression of dissent.

Both the United Kingdom and the Dual Monarchy repeatedly showed themselves to be at least capable of reform and reinvention. With the United Kingdom and the Irish, Scots, and Welsh unions, land reform and church disestablishment and home rule were all broached; and substantial land reform was achieved in all three polities, the disestablishment of the Anglican Church was enacted for Ireland (1869) and Wales (1914–20), and home rule was passed for Ireland (in 1914 and again in 1920). Much of British policy in Ireland under the union might indeed be broadly described as 'constructive unionism', in the sense that it was based on a desire to make the union work across the 'British Isles'; but the label has become particularly associated with the years of Conservative and Unionist administration between 1885 and 1895, when a variety of reform policies were pursued with the view to 'killing home rule by kindness' (Curtis 1963; Gailey 1987; Jackson 1989).

The Balfour brothers, Arthur and Gerald, were especially associated with a reformist unionism in Ireland, and (though short-term tactical considerations also certainly played a part) its overall purposes were to demonstrate that Ireland could be governed in line with the norms prevailing in Britain, and that political discontent might be ameliorated through social and economic reform. In particular it was calculated that, if (as James Fintan Lalor (1807–49) and other Irish nationalists alleged) land was the 'engine' of the Irish national question, then comprehensive land reform, and in particular voluntary land purchase, would serve to detach the engine from its political carriages. Land purchase was a favoured principle, because it appeared to offer an intellectually, ideologically, and legally more coherent and therefore more desirable way of addressing the historic problems of the land question in Ireland; but it was also an exceedingly expensive stratagem, since it involved (especially the key act of 1903) supplying eye-watering levels of state credit to the Irish farming interest in order to permit them to buy out their landlords. Aside from the cost, however, the basic problem with this approach to Irish nationalism was its attempt to supply a spiritual question with a material answer.

There were, again, numerous parallels within the history of the Dual Monarchy. It is true of course that, unlike the United Kingdom, Austria-Hungary was not a parliamentary monarchy, and that the emperor retained huge powers over military and diplomatic matters. However, the Ausgleich itself illustrated that there were possibilities of reform: it has been rightly observed that the monarchy's metamorphosis in 1867 was 'a substantial achievement which enabled it to present itself as a "modern" European state' while at the same time 'the modernity was partial and the birthpangs of the new order traumatic and fateful' (Okey 2001, p.158). Moreover, the Ausgleich was followed (at least in Cisleithania) by an era of liberal hegemony wherein earlier clericalist policies were displaced, and with both the modernization of the army and the advancement of legal reform— all this despite an emperor who, while he generally got the ministers and policies that he wanted, had not done so on this rare occasion (Cornwall 2002, p. 47). Further evidence of progressive capacity came with the creation of a working-class curia (the fifth) in the Reichsrat in 1896–7, followed ten years later by the introduction of universal male suffrage in Cisleithania (Jenks 1950). More generally, it might be said that the Monarchy was capable of progressive reform in spite of itself; and others have identified the paradoxes and possibilities which were inherent in the idea of the 'liberal empire'—possibilities which existed not necessarily thanks to 'the tolerant spirit of its operators or to a scrupulous regard for legality, but because of a unique system of checks and balances which consisted of a finely tuned stand-off between an authoritarian bureaucracy, elitist liberals and anti-liberal mass-movements' (Cornwall 2002, p. 69).

But the, apparent or actual, complement of carefully calculated reform in both the United Kingdom and the Dual Monarchy was, frequently, violence. In Ireland union government was maintained by relatively high levels of police (an armed gendarmerie, the Irish Constabulary, was created in 1835) and army (the Curragh military base, strategically placed in the centre of Ireland, was built in 1855): union was maintained, too, by the subversion of (what for the rest of the United Kingdom constituted) 'normal' legal process. Moreover, and crucially, reform often came, not proactively, but only in the context of popular threat and military response.

In terms of the operation of the law, both unionist and nationalist contemporaries stressed that the government of Ireland under the union was sustained only through the periodic suspension of normal judicial process through a large number of coercion acts: calculations vary, but over one hundred of these measures were passed in the period of the union (1800–1921). There was a tailing off in this legislation before 1914, but only because of the presence on the statute books of the Criminal Law and Procedure (Ireland) Act of 1887, the so-called 'Jubilee Coercion Act', which was in effect a permanent measure of coercion, and which permitted the lord lieutenant to identify or 'proclaim' any disturbed district where trial by jury would be suspended. Similarly, the government of Northern Ireland (after 1921) under the union was sustained only through the (eventually) permanent presence on the statute books of the Civil Authorities (Special Powers) Act (1922). Moreover, in the past, where coercion acts were not in place, the legal business of the union government might be pursued by sharp practice such as jury-packing: Peter O'Brien, later Lord O'Brien of Kilfenora and Lord Chief Justice of Ireland (1842–1914), gained notoriety as a practitioner of this particular dark art while serving as a law officer of the crown in the troubled late 1880s (see O'Brien 1916).

The corollary of the notion of 'partial reinforcement' (or 'constructive unionism') was the apparently synchronous or sequential linkage of violence (both in terms of popular protest and state suppression) and substantial measures of reform. In Ireland the suppression of the 1867 rising and its aftermath gave rise to the controversial execution of the three 'Manchester martyrs' (in December 1867): the suppression of insurgency was swiftly followed, however, by a major reform of the union in the shape of the Irish Church Act (1869) as well as a symbolically important measure of land reform in 1870. The crown's campaign against the Land League and the National League was complemented by highly significant measures of tenurial reform in 1881, and of rent and arrears in 1882: ultimately the mobilization of national protest in the early years of the 1880s persuaded Gladstone that a complete recalibration of the union settlement along the lines of Sweden-Norway or Austria-Hungary was required, and this epiphany preceded his conversion to home rule in 1885. Actions arising from the Plan of Campaign, the agrarian protest of 1886–91, brought occasionally bloody clashes between protesters and the police—such as at Mitchelstown, county Cork, where three of the former were killed in what became known as the 'Mitchelstown Massacre' (September 1887); but the suppression of the 'Plan' was also interlaced with a succession of reform proposals, encompassing both land and local government. And the politics of brinkmanship which accompanied debate over the third home rule bill, the most convincing of the measures designed to create a subordinate Irish parliament, were the backdrop to a confrontation in central Dublin between an unarmed crowd and soldiers of the King's Own Scottish Borderers in July 1914, during which soldiers opened fire, killing four civilians: this became the 'Bachelor's Walk Massacre'. In short, it was entirely possible to interpret the malleability of union as essentially a function of popular challenge—an expression of the price which the political classes of the union were willing to pay for the maintenance of the existing order.

Reform and repression were also frequently interlinked within the contemporary Dual Monarchy. In Cisleithania in particular there was, as in the United Kingdom, the lingering possibility of flexibility and reform though here, too, as in the United Kingdom, there was a correlation between popular challenge and official malleability. As Wickham Steed noted originally in 1913, 'an Austrian people need never despair as long as it can find means, in case of need, to frighten the government. The impotent, or those for whom the State has "no use", are alone in a hopeless position' (Steed 1919, p. 125). As evidence of this proposition Steed noted the political relegation of the Italian communities of Cisleithanian Dalmatia in the aftermath of the loss of Lombardy (1859) and Venetia (1866), and the consequent transfer of imperial favour towards the politically more consequential and troublesome Slav peoples. Here, as elsewhere in the Monarchy, reform and change were driven by 'fear' (Steed 1919, pp. 126–8). Moreover, though there was evidence of generally 'amicable' and trusting relationships between citizens and the police across Cisleithania, and though reforms such as universal male suffrage were clearly attainable, there were still bloody confrontations between the police and military and (for example) socialist demonstrators (in 1905 and in 1911); and indeed, as in Ireland, it may have taken bloody confrontation to deliver reform (Steed 1919, pp. 96–7).

In Transleithania, Count Károly Khuen Héderváry, the long-serving Ban of Croatia-Slavonia (between 1883 and 1903), ruled his charge—applying (as it was said) both the 'horsewhip and oats' (Jászi 1929, p. 370). At a more considered level, perhaps, there were some strategic parallels between Balfourian constructive unionism and the mix of policies pursued in Cisleithania by Ernest von Koerber between 1900 and 1904. Like the Balfour brothers, Koerber sought to shift political debate away from questions of nationality towards economic questions; and like the Balfour brothers he pursued expensive infrastructure programmes, as well as attempting comprehensive administrative reform (Steed 1919, pp. 38, 121–2; Deak 2015, pp. 232–4; Beller 2018, pp. 194ff.). In some ways too, however, the ethical costs were the same in both the United Kingdom and the Dual Monarchy; and, while it is true that (unlike Koerber) the Balfours sought to expand representative local government institutions, it was also the case that in both polities interest politics became more deeply embedded, and the power of officialdom increased, while elected politicians were encouraged ever more to look to the government rather than to work at finding agreement amongst themselves.

As in Ireland, so in Transleithania, a liberal union and empire were associated not only with 'carrot and stick' reform strategies, interlinked reform and toughness, but also with violent repression *tout court*. As in Ireland, so in Transleithania, while there were numerous examples of military or police intrusion, a small number gained particular and great notoriety: Transleithania had its own versions of

Mitchelstown and Bachelor's Walk, and indeed on a larger and more bloody scale. On 24 April 1904, in the town of Élesd, in Bihor (in what is now Romania), the 'Hungarian' gendarmerie opened fire on a predominantly Romanian crowd supporting the Social Democratic Party: around 33 died as a result of the tragedy. On 27 October 1907, in the town of Černová (in modern Slovakia), 'Hungarian' gendarmerie opened fire on a Slovak crowd gathered to celebrate the consecration of a new church associated with a patriot priest, Father Andrej Hlinka (1864–1938): 15 people died as a consequence (and the affair was still resonating 15 years later, and despite the intervening carnage of the Great War, when the English traveller, C. J. C. Street—a former veteran of the British campaign in Ireland—visited) (Street 1924, pp. 117–19). As in Ireland, so in Transleithania, the complexities of individual episodes such as this perhaps mattered less to contemporaries than the meaning and significance which they rapidly acquired. In neither Élesd nor Černová were the killings a matter of Hungarian statists killing Romanian or Slovak dissidents (in the case of Černová the gendarmes were in fact mostly Slovak). However, each episode swiftly gained notoriety as (apparent and bloody) examples of the violent suppression of minority national protest by the state (Cornwall 2002, p. 166n.).

It should also be quickly observed that, as in Ireland, so in Austria-Hungary normal legal procedure could fall victim to the exigencies of state policy and be deployed in the interests of union and empire—even before the outbreak of the Great War (Judson 2016, p. 382; Cornwall 2015, 2017). Of the many examples of this, the mass prosecution in 1909 of south Slav activists, accused by the state, was particularly controversial. The prosecution, pursued in the Agram/Zagreb treason trial, complemented official anxiety over the Serb-Croat coalition in Croatia-Slavonia; but it all badly backfired on the government, partly because the cause of the defendants was widely publicized across Europe (and not least by Seton-Watson). More immediately significant, however, was the fact that a subsequent trial (for libel) of the historian and German nationalist, Heinrich Friedjung (1851–1920), eventually produced evidence that the case against the Agram defendants had been shaped by forged documents originating in Aehrenthal's foreign ministry (or at any rate in the Austro-Hungarian legation in Belgrade and thence back to the ministry) (Steed 1919, pp. 101–5, 245, 260–1). Southern Slav alienation from Budapest and from Franz Joseph gathered pace accordingly; but (thanks partly to Seton-Watson) a wider scepticism about Austria-Hungary's claims as a Rechtsstaat gained a simultaneous traction (Seton-Watson 1911a, 1912; Beller 2018, p. 232). And for observant Irish nationalists, the forgeries perpetrated by the agents of union at Agram were all too reminiscent of the faked letters, supplied by Richard Pigott (1835–89), and deployed enthusiastically (if unwittingly) by *The Times* and by the Irish Loyal and Patriotic Union, in their efforts to topple Charles Stewart Parnell and the leadership of the Irish home rule movement (O'Callaghan 1994).

At the end of the day, therefore, it has to be recognized that multinational unions survived—for a time—through both superior military fire-power and periodic judicial ruthlessness. The unions of the United Kingdom (both the Scots and the Irish), of the Netherlands, and of Sweden-Norway were all born with the dominant partner flexing military (or police) muscles; and these and the other unions considered in the work, including the Dual Monarchy, were subsequently upheld through continuing military, police, and judicial (or extra-judicial) intervention.

But this of course was not the whole story. Unions survived not simply because they were militarily repressive (though they sometimes were): military and judicial repression could, and did, sometimes backfire (as was the case, notoriously, with the British suppression of the 1916 uprising in Ireland). But, fundamentally, unions survived because there were both sticks *and* carrots, kicks *and* ha'pence, horsewhips *and* oats. Malleability was essential: so were inducements.

Unions survived, too, because they were bound by a range of shared overarching economic and social agencies, and by a range of key institutional bolsters, of which one of the most important was the crown. But, again, these only remained fit for purpose for as long as they remained adaptable to challenge. In the end a lack of sensitive adaptability almost always meant that the centripetal became the centrifugal.

CENTRIPEDE: THE INSTITUTIONAL BOLSTERS OF UNION   245

Figure 4.1 Faith, church and union state: King George V, Supreme Governor of the Church of England (second from right), the Duke and Duchess of York (later King George VI and Queen Elizabeth) together with Princess Elizabeth (later Queen Elizabeth II) after worship at Crathie Church of Scotland, Balmoral, Aberdeenshire, c.1935. Cigarette card (National Portrait Gallery, London).

Figure 4.2 Faith, church, and union state: Queen Mary (centre), Monsignor Daniel Mannix (President, Maynooth College) (left), and Archbishop William Walsh of Dublin (right), Maynooth Seminary, Kildare, Ireland, July 1911. Postcard (private possession).

246   UNITED KINGDOMS

Figure 4.3 Faith, church and union state: the Empress-Queen Zita and the Emperor-King Karl receive a blessing at a Pressburg/Bratislava synagogue, 1917. Photograph (Bildarchiv der Österreichischen Nationalbibliothek).

Figure 4.4 Faith, church and union state: the Empress-Queen Zita, Capuchin friar and Emperor-King Karl at the Marco d'Aviano celebration, Vienna, 1918. Photograph (Bildarchiv der Österreichischen Nationalbibliothek).

5
Alternative Unions
Federalism

5.1. The Historiography of Federalism

While there is an obvious set of theoretical distinctions between the types of union state considered in this study and their federal counterparts, the frontiers between the two are in reality generally blurred. For the unions which are considered here, federalism was often either an imagined or an actual reforming destination. It was, in essence, a silver bullet for ailing legislative and other unions—and indeed the sceptical A. V. Dicey wearily complained about the role ascribed to federalism as 'the panacea for all social evils, and all political perplexities' (Dicey 1887, p. 160; Figure 5.3). For these (and other) reasons, therefore, it seems appropriate to interpolate a reflection on federalism at this point in the work—between the discussions of the centripetal and centrifugal forces playing upon union. This chapter directly considers the federal theme in relation to several of the work's case studies.

For the United Province of Canada, the stalling and disaggregation of the legislative union of 1840 was followed by the application of federation in 1867, though it should now be clear that the political cultures fostered by legislative union no less than its failings helped to pave the way for the latter. For the Austrian empire a limited form of confederation was instituted in 1867 as a means of constitutional transfusion and resurrection; and later, when Austria-Hungary itself appeared to be at risk, alternative and more ambitious forms of federation were seen as a means of 'saving' the Monarchy, including even (as will be seen) the notion of a United States of Greater Austria. Similarly, the federal reform of the United Kingdom has been repeatedly broached over the past 150 years in times of constitutional difficulty; and indeed the UK's current trajectory has sometimes appeared to be towards that ultimate (or perhaps merely intermediate) condition. This chapter seeks to consider the debates on possible federation which took place within some of these (at times, ailing) union polities, and especially (given the other emphases of the study) in the United Kingdom. But a start is made with some brief historical reflections on the shape and concerns of the existing (political science) scholarship on the federal issue—as well as on their relevance to this book as a whole.

Despite this overlap between different forms of union, despite the (often) porous boundaries between federal and non-federal unions, as well as the great size of the theoretical and empirical literature on federalism and federations, it is worth re-emphasizing that the corresponding work on other union states is (in certain respects, at least) markedly constricted. Here, as elsewhere in the historiography of these islands, political scientists and early modern historians have been much more active and enterprising than their late modern counterparts (some exceptions amongst late modern historians include Barton 2006; Jackson 2013; Hemstad 2019). Thanks to the learned investigations of Sir John Elliott on Scotland and Catalunya, on the Habsburg and other domains, and thanks too to pioneering scholars such as Robert Frost (working on the Polish-Lithuanian commonwealth), the taxonomy of medieval and early modern monarchies has been much more precisely delineated than their later successors (Elliott 1992, 2018; Frost 2015). The literature on modern federalism is no less distinguished, with key scholars such as Michael Burgess making substantial contributions in terms of the history of the idea within British as well as wider, comparative and theoretical, contexts (Burgess 1995, 2006, 2012; Kendle 1997). Yet, despite these medieval, early modern, and federalist researches (and despite the interest in the constitutional future of the United Kingdom) we have already seen that there has been little wider comment on unfederated union polities in the late modern era. There has certainly been very little by way of definition, comparison, conceptualization, or abstraction.

The reasons for these disparities are complex. But they are partly rooted in the understandable preoccupation of scholars with American politics and government, and thus with the American model of federal union (e.g. Burgess 2006, p. 74; Dicey 1887, p. 160). However, while allowing for these imbalances, the burgeoning literature on American federalism also effectively offers some valuable insights into other forms of union state, including multinational composite polities such as the United Kingdom.

It is true that the study of federalism and federation has sometimes been seen as challenging or problematic, partly because it has been perceived as 'theoretically untidy' and partly because it has often been necessarily concerned with 'fundamental moral questions as well with amoral matters of fact' (Burgess 2006, pp. 1, 4; see also e.g. LaSelva 1996). Yet, these very 'problems' are often relevant to an understanding of the various types of union reflected in the case studies here: the 'untidiness' of theory and taxonomy is (for example) generally applicable, given the distinctions and contingencies of history and structure. But federalism's complex entanglement with the moral is no less useful as a starting point to consider the purpose and beneficiaries of this work's 'united kingdoms'—their 'vision thing', or (rather) often their lack of it.

On the other hand, the success of the American revolution and of American constitution-building has stimulated wide-ranging debates from the late 18th century and through the 19th century (despite the civil war) about the necessary conditions for (federal) union to flourish—whether in terms of the relative size of the linked polities, or shared issues of (for example) religion or language (Burgess 2006, p. 11). As Burgess has argued, it has been 'customary for scholars to identify a predominant motive in their quest to locate the origins of federations, namely defence and security goals on the one hand, and economic and commercial objectives on the other' (Burgess 2006, p. 76). This work on the origins of federation also has some very obvious implications for constitutional unions of other shapes and forms.

The great Belfast-born lawyer and constitutionalist, James Bryce, dwelt at length on the 'forces' making (and indeed unmaking) federal unions in his writings on the *American Commonwealth* (1888) and his *Studies in History and Jurisprudence* (1901). As will now be clear, this present study has been deploying elements of the (admittedly somewhat positivist) organizational schema used by Bryce, and inherited and adapted by Oszkár Jászi (see Figure 5.2). Each, Bryce and Jászi, sought to identify the 'centripetal' and 'centrifugal' (or 'aggregative' and 'internationalist' as opposed to the 'segregative') forces at play in the making and unmaking of, respectively, federal polities as well as the great composite monarchy of central Europe, that of the Habsburgs (e.g. Bryce 1901, pp. 255–6, 261; Jászi 1929, p. 133).

Thus the scholarly emphasis on specific binding and dissolving agents in individual federal polities has a particular relevance for this volume, given its sustained focus on the longevity of union. It is routinely suggested (to take one example) that the complex contemporary Belgian federal state has been kept alive by (principally) three unifying factors, namely 'the monarchy, membership of the European Union, and Brussels': as has already been argued, monarchy played a considerable role in all the unfederated unions discussed throughout this study (Burgess 2006, p. 116; see section 4.2). The emphasis on wider issues identified and explored within the scholarship on federalism, including the moral dimensions noticed by Burgess and others, supplies focuses for the reflections on unfederated unions pursued throughout the present study. For example, recent work on the American federal union emphasizes the influence of Christian theology, and in particular covenantal theory and theology (Burgess 2006, pp. 48–9; discussed in section 4.6). Related to this is the moral basis underlying the original Swiss confederation—the oath-bound fellowship, or *Eidgenossenschaft*, which evolved into the federated state of the 19th century. More generally, different scholars (like Charles Tarlton or Brian Galligan), reflecting on the failure of federal states and federations, have focused upon issues of imbalance or asymmetry in the formation of federal unions (see e.g. Tarlton 1965). Such work is complemented by a more recent, and wide-ranging, exploration of the pathology of federal failure (e.g. Franck 1968, Hicks 1978, Macedo and Buchanan 2003).

Perhaps the greatest (and most fundamental) stimulus supplied by the literature on federalism so far as the current study is concerned relates to the centrality of comparative approaches (Burgess 2006, pp. 135–6). This has produced a variety of thematic emphases (including on the moral dimensions) which in turn has created a greater conceptual clarity than has been attained hitherto. The comparative 'turn' in federal studies underlines the desirability of pursuing comparative work on other forms of constitutional union—and most obviously on the kind of composite union state represented by the United Kingdom (Burgess 2006, p. 283).

5.2. Failed Panacea? Federalizing Britain and Its Empire

On 19 April 2015, in the prelude to the United Kingdom general election, the then Prime Minister, David Cameron, told the presenter and historian Andrew Marr that—if the election produced a hung parliament with a minority Labour government and a substantial Scottish nationalist presence—SNP control over any Miliband administration would be the 'first time' that nationalists had ever exercised a sustained influence over a British government.

Mr Cameron had forgotten his history of the union. In fact many others were struck by the similarities between the constitutional debates over Scots independence and (later) Brexit and the last great crisis of the British union state, almost exactly a century earlier, over home rule and Irish independence—when (contrary to these assertions) nationalists did in fact exercise considerable influence over H. H. Asquith's Liberal government. Nor did Mr Cameron choose to recall the influence wielded by Irish and Ulster Unionists over the Conservative leadership at this time—an issue which would decisively re-emerge after his own departure from office, with the Democratic Unionists' strategic support for the governments of Theresa May and Boris Johnson. As the journalist and academic, Paul Gillespie, remarked, commenting on the 2014 debate on the Scots referendum—it was 'all uncannily reminiscent of the Home Rule dynamic that preoccupied British politics from the 1880s through to the First World War' (Gillespie 2014, p. 9; see also Mohr 2016, pp. 131–61).

A key part of that dynamic, and a key part of the ways in which home rule was addressed within British politics, was through the proposed federalist reform of the British constitution—or at any rate by what was then consistently defined as 'federalist' reform of the constitution. Thus, in 1914 a group of young unionist and imperialist ideologues pitched such a reform as a way of breaking the impasse over the third home rule bill. After 2014 several prominent unionists, impressed by the strength of Scottish nationalism, moved towards a tentative advocacy of federalism: these have included the members of the cross-party Constitution Reform Group at Westminster (Lords Salisbury, Peter Hain, and Menzies Campbell), the ex-Prime Minister, Gordon Brown, and the prominent Welsh Conservative, David Melding, a former Deputy Presiding Officer of the National Assembly for Wales (Brown 2014; Torrance 2014; Melding 2009).

Current debates on federalist reform are thus intimately connected with the lengthy historical roots of the issue—even though, clearly, not all within the political elite have had any strong sense of these antecedents. Just as the federal idea still touches British politics at both the national and transnational levels (in terms of Scotland and Europe), so in the 19th century federalism was a central part of debates on the British constitution (given Irish home rule), and on Britain's wider—global—relationships, in particular with the governance of the empire.

While each of these 19th-century debates illuminates its later counterparts, the emphasis in this section of the work is largely upon the United Kingdom and its unions, not least since the analogies here between the attempted reforms of the past, and those considered in the present, happen to be particularly close. In essence, British federalism in the 19th century was characterized by vigorous advocacy and eloquence, a mixture of ideological conviction and conceptual ambiguity, and some conservative and elite interest together with (certainly in Ireland) popular nationalist indifference: it was a response, in part, to the fear of 'disintegration', whether in terms of the empire or the union. Much, though not all, of this pathology remained in place in the early 21st century as well.

There are some initial challenges in terms of vocabulary and definition which need to be addressed immediately. Though the terms 'federalism', 'federal home rule', and 'home rule' were (and are) deployed frequently, their meaning and use were much less exact within British and Irish debate than contemporary political scientists, still less constitutional lawyers, would now find acceptable. This is not the place to revisit lengthy and essentialist disputes about the ultimate meaning of federalism, and in any event these have largely burnt themselves out (a key authority, Michael Burgess, has referred to the now 'tired' debates on definition: Burgess 2006, p. 9). However, it is all-too-rarely grasped that 19th- and early 20th-century advocates of federalism were both clearly aware of the ambiguities of their faith, and to some extent were deliberately more concerned with earnest evangelism than with rigorous taxonomy. It is also worth noting that, while political scientists and others have long since achieved precision, or at any rate equanimity, with this issue, the tradition of ambiguity in discussing federalist constitutional reform is deep-seated, and has a continuing relevance in contemporary debates, when federalist, devolutionist, and home rule vocabularies are still readily mixed (including for example by as subtle and thoughtful a commentator as Gordon Brown).

Isaac Butt, the Irish nationalist leader of the 1870s, and one of the patriarchs of federalist debate in the United Kingdom, pointed out in 1870 that 'it is not worthwhile to consider whether the word "federalism" *in its proper sense* be the most appropriate here to express what is proposed' (Butt 1870, pp. 21, 29). Equally, one of the foremost Edwardian advocates of a federal reconstruction of the British constitution—the Scots businessman, historian, and polemicist, F. S. Oliver—in propounding the cause admitted that 'there are...considerable difficulties at the outset; for, although the [federalist] idea has sprung up very vigorously in a great variety of quarters during the past few months, it is impossible to discover any authoritative explanation of the true doctrine' (Oliver 1910, p. 50; see also Oliver 1918, pp. 11, 22). Oliver also admitted later, in 1914, that:

> 'federalism' may possibly not be the best word to describe what is in the minds of some of us; but in any case, I am not responsible for it. I did not invent it, or dig it up...the term 'federal' is a loose designation, and is not to be subjected to fine academic tests. We can know roughly what it means and that is quite enough for any practical end. (Oliver 1914, p. viii)

Oliver and his contemporaries (like the other great Edwardian federalist, Lionel Curtis (1872–1955)) inherited some of these difficulties in terminology from the debates on the American constitution: indeed Oliver himself was an influential celebrant of Alexander Hamilton, one of the architects of the US constitution of 1787, and a leading 'federalist' at a time when the term implied support for a strong central executive at the expense of state powers rather than the distribution of power between the centre and the 'periphery' (Oliver 1906; Lavin 1996). An admirer of the US constitution, Oliver was more impressed by the nation-building that had occurred than in the autonomy of the component American states—and his advocacy of a federalist reform of the British constitution was driven by the desire both to consolidate the integrity of the government of the British empire as well as to sustain a unified and efficient United Kingdom government in the face of nationalist and other challenge—rather than through any wish to compromise the sovereignty of Westminster (see Figure 5.4).

There is no doubt, however, that, despite this awareness, ambiguities in terminology caused difficulty, partly because of different notions of what constituted federalism—and partly because at the end of the 19th and early 20th centuries federalism was entwined within two concurrent but discrete debates (on the reformed governance both of the wider empire and of the United Kingdom). The practice of 'federation' throughout the empire was so varied that colonial analogies to the United Kingdom tended to compound the confusion (for example, the Union of South Africa (1910) was clearly a much more centralized polity than either Canada (1867) or Australia (1901)—yet all three served, to a greater or lesser extent, as models for aspirant British and Irish reformers). Moreover, comparing Ireland (or Scotland) with Canada begged the question of whether Ireland constituted the federation as a whole, or was merely one of the component states of a federated union. Oliver himself defined the challenge, writing prophetically in 1917:

> It is hardly necessary to say that I entirely agree...about the false analogy between Ireland and a Dominion. For seven years at least I have been trying to get this into the heads of Unionists and Liberals alike, but it is extraordinarily

difficult to do so... we may drift into some kind of position where we shall find that we are pledged to give dominion status to Ireland or to all Ireland except the Six Counties instead of 'state' status. You can't possibly in my opinion give any kind of control over customs without landing yourself in Dominion status sooner or later.
(Oliver to Carson, 30 March 1917, Carson papers, D.1507/A/22/20)

A key irony here was that contemporary federalists pushed imperial analogies, in the hope and expectation that Ireland would emerge as a Quebec or even as an Ontario. But in fact Ireland emerged from British rule in 1921 as a Canada.

There were in essence three key determinants of the centrality (or otherwise) of federalism in 19th- and early 20th-century British politics: the challenges of closer and more efficient imperial governance, the seriousness of nationalist challenge especially in Ireland (and to a lesser extent, Scotland and Wales), and the apparently demonstrable success of federalism in other national contexts. A fourth aspect—the European or global federal ambitions of internationalists like Philip Kerr, Lord Lothian (1882–1940), in the 1930s—was swiftly overwhelmed by war in 1939, and was anyway often characterized by the 'shaky' thinking that vitiated so much federalist advocacy (and thus it cannot be regarded as a 'key' driver of the issue: Kendle 1997, p. 163). Taken together, and viewed over the *longue durée*, these first three themes constitute what has been described as 'the British tradition of federalism' (Burgess 1995). However, lest this discussion appear overly determined, the existence of an intellectually vigorous, and indeed often dominant, British tradition of opposition to federalism should be immediately flagged (and will indeed be discussed shortly).

Taking first the challenge of empire, Britain's external relationships constituted one set of roots for the federalist debate in the late 19th century (as, indeed, in the 21st). The successful federal unification of several major polities both inside and outwith the empire—including Canada and the USA—provided an exemplar to British politicians and ideologues who, writing in the last three decades of the 19th century, were ever more concerned with the threat of imperial disintegration. Such apprehensions, and their federal remedies, were reflected in the work of Sir John Seeley (1834–95), Sir Charles Dilke (1843–1911), and other, lesser, ideologues such as Francis de Labilliere (1840–95) and Thomas Spalding (Seeley 1883; Bell 2016, pp. 265–96; Labilliere 1894; Spalding 1896; Bell 2011; see also Mohr 2016). But the key agency for their evangelizing, the Imperial Federation League (1884–92), ultimately failed, partly because the complex and largely ad hoc structure of the British empire was simultaneously a stimulus to reformers, as well as a major obstacle in the way of any coherent reform. Furthermore, unlike a later generation of British federalists in the years between 1910 and 1920, those within the League largely failed to connect their cause with the pre-eminent constitutional question of the day, namely Irish home rule (see e.g. the neglect of the theme in Labilliere 1894). Ultimately, then, a combination of the intractability of the core issues, the dominance of other—primarily Irish—questions, as well as popular (and some elite) apathy, derailed the first comprehensive effort to apply federal principles to the governance of the empire.

A second, though sometimes entangled, strand of federalist thought was stimulated by the challenge of Irish nationalism, which in turn was related to both contemporary critiques of the Scottish (and Welsh) unions, as well as (ultimately) their continuing problems in the 21st century. Certainly in the mid–late 19th century Irish protest on national rights and on specific issues such as land reform and church disestablishment informed Scottish and Welsh protest. The pulses of federalist intellectual and political activity coincided with periods when Irish nationalist opinion was being successfully mobilized. Indeed, this highlighted a fundamental part of the problem with federalist advocacy in the 19th century: it often looked like (and indeed sometimes was) an alarmed conservative reaction to the challenge of more radical constitutional proposals.

Federalism, in other words, has frequently appeared to be both a reactive as well as an instrumentalist strategy rather than an ideal. Thus, 'federalism' won an early and important airing in the context of the popular campaign for the repeal of the Act of Union (1801), which developed from the 1830s, and flourished in the early and mid-1840s under the leadership of Daniel O'Connell. The federal idea was briefly and unsuccessfully promoted by conservative constitutional nationalists in Ireland in the 1870s partly as a device to soften British and unionist opposition to an Irish parliament. It was widely promoted by young Tory and imperialist intellectuals in the Edwardian era as a means of addressing several key problems of empire—but especially the challenges of Irish nationalism after 1910.

Third, while 'home rule' was (as A. V. Dicey memorably alleged, adapting the fourteenth earl of Derby (1799–1869) on parliamentary reform) 'a leap in the dark', and was thus readily susceptible to the catastrophizing of unionists (through a form of Edwardian 'project fear'), British and Irish federalists could point to a range of successful new or reformed federal—or confederal—states as inspiration (Dicey 1893, 1911). The US constitution of 1787 was a fundamental underlying influence. Both Irish nationalists and British unionists (with some exceptions) looked favourably on the American constitution, and both British and Irish federalist thinkers referred to its successes. For Irish Catholics, with a strong migrant presence in the USA, American models were often attractive—and (as has already been shown) both Daniel O'Connell and other, lesser, lights such as the Irish Catholic priest and political thinker, Father Thaddeus O'Malley, looked eagerly to the American federal exemplar (O'Malley 1873). The success of the federal or union cause in the American civil war tended to be interpreted as an international victory for the federal ideal. Edwardian English imperialists were interested in a range of federal models; but (as has been noted) perhaps the most well-connected and influential of these ideologues, F. S. Oliver, was also deeply interested (through his researches into Alexander Hamilton) in the origins of the American federal constitution (Oliver 1906). Oliver subsequently took on his subject's mantle and chosen pseudonym in his advocacy of federal reform during the British constitutional crisis of 1910 (Oliver ['Pacificus'] 1910).

Equally, the Canadian constitutions of 1840 and 1867 (discussed at length in sections 3.4 and 5.3) simultaneously reflected the politics of the British unions, and impacted in turn upon the British-Irish relationship—particularly through the British North America Act (1867) and its successful creation of a federal government overlying the three provinces of Canada, New Brunswick, and Nova Scotia. This was a perceptible influence both upon the Irish nationalist promotion of federalism in 1870 as a model for a reformulated relationship between Ireland and Britain, as well as upon later Scots patriots, such as William Mitchell, the treasurer of the Scottish Home Rule Association (Mitchell [1893], pp. 70–1). Isaac Butt argued in 1870 (following E. A. Freeman's earlier work) that there were different layers of precedent for his federalist proposals—ancient (the Achaean League), medieval (the Swiss cantons), and more modern—the United States, certainly, but also pre-eminently Canada: '[P]erhaps the most remarkable tribute to the principle of Federalism is to be found in the course taken by the British parliament in the year 1867 when it was thought to incorporate into one dominion all the north American provinces of the British crown' (Butt 1870, p. 23; Golden 2013, p. 1502; Reid 2014, p. 348).

The apparently successful creation of a strongly centralized union state in South Africa (by 1910) bringing together Cape Colony, Natal, Transvaal, and the Orange Free State supplied an even more direct model to more conservative constitutional reformers in Britain, including Welsh home rulers in 1913, since the union operated on a devolved rather than upon a strictly federal principle (see e.g. Griffith 1913, p. 32). Moreover, the idea of converting Boer insurgents into loyal citizens of a new British dominion was a strong influence on those imperialists who were seeking to bring Irish insurgents into a loyal constitutional relationship with the crown. North America appeared to offer a similarly encouraging narrative, wherein potentially (sometimes actually) dissident francophone Canadians had been disarmed by the successes of imperial statesmanship, including union and confederation.

Other continental European examples provided models and inspiration at different levels: the Swiss Confederation (1848), the United Kingdoms of Sweden and Norway (before its sudden collapse in 1905), Germany (with its federal constitution of 1870)—all of these were referenced in Irish and British federalist apologetics from the 1870s onwards (see e.g. Labilliere 1894, esp. pp. 72–85). Equally, even (very different) defunct states offered federalist lessons—such as the United Kingdom of Denmark-Norway (1536–1814), and especially the United Kingdom of the Netherlands (1815–30). Of course the United Kingdoms of Sweden-Norway ultimately proved an embarrassment to federalists, in so far as it was originally hailed as a 'confederal' success story, but by the 1890s this was less obviously the case (a point made in ironic vein by A. V. Dicey, commenting that 'the goodwill generated by a system of Home Rule is bringing these countries to the brink of civil war': Dicey 1911, p. 154; see also section 3.3).

But for its British and Irish proponents in the 19th and early 20th centuries, federalism was a constitutional wonder-drug: Thaddeus O'Malley gushingly called it 'the acme of the science of government; it is the eclecticism of political philosophy' (O'Malley 1873, p. 32). Brand-new polities had been made possible by federalism: nationalist federalists in Ireland like O'Malley pointed to the substantial success of the USA, temporarily disrupted (it was true) by civil war, but delivering an enormously wealthy and lasting federal union out of unpromising materials (O'Malley 1873, pp. 33–4, 77). German economic and social advances had been secured similarly by confederation and federalism ('we see the young German Empire, by this same federalism, springing up in a bound, into a gigantic colossus overshadowing and overawing all Europe') (O'Malley 1873, p. 33). For these true 'believers', complex established polities had been restored either by federalism or a reform of their federal constitutions: Switzerland had been refreshed in this way. Even the ancient and (it had once been thought) moribund empire of the Habsburgs had evidently been given (through the Ausgleich of 1867) a 'fresh lease of power' (O'Malley 1873, p. 33; cf. Labilliere 1894, p. 179).

Turning from these external inspirations for British, Irish and imperial federalists to their programmes of action—it should be immediately observed that from the end of the 18th century British, Irish, and American political elites were lengthily engaged in a political dialogue about the merits of federation. Indeed to some extent the federalism of the American constitution was defined and defended in relation to the perceived strengths and weaknesses of the British constitution. In the fifth *Federalist Paper*, published in November 1787, John Jay famously argued that America could learn from the problems encountered by the British before the union of 1707: 'the history of Great Britain is the one with which we are in general the best acquainted, and it gives us many useful lessons', Jay wrote:

> [W]e may profit by their experience without paying the price which it cost them. Although it seems obvious to common sense that the people of such an island should be but one nation, yet we find that they were for ages divided into three, and that those three were almost constantly embroiled in quarrels and wars with one another.

In fact Linda Colley has been able to point out that a key aspect of the British response to the American federal constitution of 1787 was an emphasis upon precisely those aspects which seemed essentially British; and she has also commented upon the interconnections (perceived by Thomas Paine and others) between that constitution and the British tradition of legal charters (Colley 2014a, pp. 237–66, 243, 247).

The growth (in the 1830s and afterwards) of a popular movement in Ireland in favour of repeal of the Act of Union (1801) helped to stimulate a debate about the range of constitutional alternatives available at that juncture—and in particular both the American constitution of 1787 and the new Canadian Act of Union (1840) were identified as possible influences which might be examined at Westminster. The intellectual protagonists of this debate in Ireland were (once again) Thaddeus O'Malley as well as the county Down landowner, William Sharman Crawford (1781–1861), and John Grey Vesey Porter, the son of a county Fermanagh landowner.

Sharman Crawford in February 1833 sought a constitutional *via media* in asking whether there was 'no intermediate course (between the existing union and its complete repeal) by which, at least, an attempt could be made to secure in some degree the benefits of local legislation without throwing off the beneficial control of imperial legislation in imperial concerns?' In October 1839 he was specifically arguing that the repeal of the union would create a parliament in Dublin which would be as powerless in contest with London as had the lately suppressed parliament of Lower Canada: in each case there was a need for a federal connection with Great Britain (Cronne et al. 1949, pp. 238, 241).

The development of the repeal movement into a thoroughly popular mobilization after 1841 brought with it increased interest in a federalist compromise, and in August 1843 Crawford enlarged upon his previous ideas, advocating parliaments not only for Ireland, but also for Scotland and England, each with powers of 'local' taxation. It has been quite rightly observed that 'Crawford's scheme was more devolutionary than federal in nature. There was no clear-cut division of sovereignty; [and] the imperial parliament retained veto powers in crucial areas' (Kendle 1989, pp. 9–10). But in fact Crawford's intellectual leadership stimulated others both within and beyond the repeal movement.

John Grey Vesey Porter, who was outside the movement at this time, published two influential pamphlets in 1843–4, the first praising the confederal United Kingdoms of Sweden-Norway, created (as will be recalled) in 1814 out of the old and heavily centralized union of Denmark-Norway, and with Norway and Sweden each united only by foreign policy concerns and a shared monarchy: '[until 1814] Norway was' he declared, 'a miserable backward out-farm; now a very flourishing kingdom' (Porter [1843], p. 82; see sections 1.5 and 3.3). Porter's later work lauded the American constitution, and proposed similar arrangements in the 'British isles': he called for a British and Irish parliament, each exercising sovereignty over its domestic affairs, and with an overarching imperial parliament with responsibility for external affairs (Porter 1844; Cronne et al. 1949, p. 247). He summarized his pitch in these terms:

[N]ow a federal union between Great Britain and Ireland, each island under one and the same king or queen, sovereign at home in its own affairs, over its own land, with an imperial congress or assembly or parliament (no matter what the name may be) of so many members for each island to settle all their common foreign and colonial affairs, is the only fair kind of union between them.

(Porter 1844, p. vii)

His argument was that 'free trade does not depend in any degree on a union of parliaments but on a union of the two nations which I hope and am sure will always continue between us' (Porter 1844, p. 70).

It would be wrong to dismiss either Porter or his initiative. Daniel O'Connell, famously, was briefly persuaded, announcing in October 1844 through a statement known as the 'Derrynane Manifesto' his preference for what he dubbed 'the federative plan' (Cronne et al. 1949, p. 248). Nearly 50 years later William Mitchell of the federally inclined Scottish Home Rule Association was still quoting Porter's homely metaphor that 'the table that stands strongest, and lasts longest, and that is best able to bear hard usage, is the table on four legs' (Mitchell [1893], p. 66). But in essence, while federalism appealed to pragmatists like O'Connell, it cut little ice with more fundamentalist nationalists, certainly in Ireland; and this in fact would emerge as a key feature of the political pathology of federalist debate over the next 150 years. Federalism was frequently posited as a compromise formula, which centrists and pragmatists could only accept at the risk of marginalization and rejection from more extremist (or purist) forces. And indeed this remains the case even in the early 21st century.

The federal idea re-emerged in the 1870s, again pitched as a compromise which would deliver an Irish parliament, while retaining an imperial or metropolitan connection. The international contexts here were the Canadian constitution of 1867 and also the reconstruction of the federal government of the United States after the civil war. The national contexts were the failed Irish Republican Brotherhood (or separatist) uprising of 1867, the mobilization of subsequent popular sympathy for the imprisoned or executed insurgents—and also the alienation of some Irish conservatives from the reformist strategies of the Liberal government in London. In addition federalism drew upon a tradition of nationally minded conservative and unionist thought in Ireland.

This set of influences delivered a proposal for Irish self-government, articulated through a body called the Home Government Association (1870), and led by Isaac Butt: Butt believed in federalism, but he also saw pragmatically that it might unite nationalists and conservatives within the one national cause. He called both for an Irish parliament with domestic autonomy and for a federated United Kingdom that would respect local needs while preserving the 'one great imperial state'. He fleshed out his ideas in the pamphlet *Home Government for Ireland* (1870), wherein he directly proposed Canada as a model for the constitutional relationship between Ireland and Britain. He envisioned an imperial parliament which would retain English, Scots, and Irish MPs and which would continue to legislate on military matters and foreign and imperial affairs (the latter to include relevant taxation) (Butt 1870, pp. 42–54; Reid 2014, pp. 332–61). The Irish parliament, by contrast, was to have complete control over Irish matters and was to comprise a House of Commons with some 250 members as well as a House of Lords.

However, Butt was wary of supplying too much detail, perhaps out of fear that this might divert attention away from the main thrust of his scheme and into the minutiae: there are certainly aspects of his federalist vision which are at best hazy. He did not tightly define the relationship between the proposed imperial and Irish parliaments, and he did not trouble to enlarge upon the crucial issue of customs and excise. In so far as Butt seems to have had in mind a division of sovereignty between the two assemblies, Irish and imperial, and in so far as the Irish parliament was to have had 'supreme control' over Irish affairs unless specifically reserved to London, it seems likely that he favoured local control of customs and thus a loose federation. But the evidence is ultimately unclear—in part because Butt probably wanted it that way (Jackson 2004, pp. 32–3). In any event, and even though he led the significant Irish home rule grouping at Westminster, his federalist pitch won little traction either in Ireland or in the House of Commons, where it was fruitlessly debated in June 1874 and again in 1876.

For Butt's ally, Thaddeus O'Malley, the 'best exemplar' of federalism remained unquestionably the United States (O'Malley 1873, p. 34). In essence O'Malley's own proposal for a federated United Kingdom was a direct adaptation of the US constitution. In this both the Scots and the Irish shared the same case for state parliaments, and there was the real possibility of adapting the model of the Supreme Court and other federal institutions for British and Irish use (O'Malley 1873, pp. 77, 85).

As has been seen, Gladstone, as Liberal leader and Prime Minister, sought to address the challenge of Irish national sentiment—looking (in August 1885) at the Austro-Hungarian model of the Ausgleich, and (in October) at the two key constitutional acts governing Canada (those of 1840 and 1867) (see section 1.6). His two home rule bills (1886, 1893) drew in particular upon the latter settlement, though it was also thought that the form of home rule (however unsatisfactorily) bestowed by Hungary upon Croatia through the Nagodba of 1868 had been an influence. Gladstone's successor as Liberal leader and Prime Minister, H. H. Asquith, essentially built upon these two earlier bills in launching his own home rule legislation in April 1912. None of these measures was strictly federal, but each had federal influences or (arguably) federal trajectories: A. V. Dicey certainly complained that the home rule bill of 1893 was 'at bottom a federalist or semi-federalist constitution; it introduces into English institutions many of the forms of federalism and still more of its spirit' (Dicey 1911, p. 13). The Gladstonian proposals for Ireland were also important stimulants for the home rule movement in Scotland, which (by the early 1890s) was expressing its vision in explicitly federalizing terms—this partly because 'it is the exceptional treatment proposed for Ireland which has created the greatest difficulty in obtaining Home Rule for that country' (see e.g. Mitchell 1892, [1893], p. 65).

The 1886 Bill provided (*inter alia*) for a unicameral Irish legislature, the abolition of Irish representation at Westminster, and wide-ranging powers for the Irish legislature over domestic issues. Westminster was to retain reserved (and residual) powers, control over domestic taxation, and over customs and excise. The 1893 Bill provided for the *explicit* supremacy of Westminster, an executive committee of the Irish Privy Council as a form of cabinet, a bicameral parliament, and (originally) the retention of Irish MPs on an 'in and out' basis—they would be excluded from specifically British debates and divisions, but admitted to all others (Jackson 2004, p. 94). The 'in and out'—a precursor of subsequent devices such as 'English votes for English laws' (2015–21)—was a feature of Croatian home rule, but was abandoned here because of criticism of its evident impracticality. In 1886 and 1893 it was proposed that Ireland should pay an 'imperial contribution' to London as a first charge on its revenue—this 'first charge' being ultimately equated with the yield from Ireland's customs duties.

Asquith's third home rule bill of 1912 also affirmed the supremacy of Westminster; and it provided for the retention of Irish members, albeit in much smaller numbers than proposed in 1893. As in 1893, there was to be a bicameral Irish legislature. As in the past, most domestic matters were ascribed to the proposed Irish parliament, but there remained a range of such matters (and imperial concerns) reserved to Westminster (e.g. land purchase, pensions, national insurance, tax collection, the Royal Irish Constabulary) (Jackson 2004, p. 127). The financial arrangements were complex—but in essence allowed for the transfer of all Irish revenue into the imperial exchequer which would then pay out the operating costs of those areas of administration under Irish control with an additional amount to provide a margin of error (this combined payment was termed the 'transferred sum'). The Irish government could levy new taxes, but not any that conflicted with imperial taxation. It could not levy customs duties. The Irish could raise existing taxes but not by more than 10 per cent.

Between 1910 and 1918 a group of imperialist unionists, but particularly F. S. Oliver and Lionel Curtis acting alongside the second Earl of Selborne (1859–1942), agitated to put a federalist reform of the British constitution at the centre of this debate on Irish home rule. They were essentially elite activists, and (on the strength of work by earlier bodies such as the Irish Reform Association) they looked to high-level conferencing and intricate published manifestos rather than mass mobilization. The Liberal home rule measures were, for them, very imperfectly federal, not so much because of the issue of indivisible sovereignty, but because they did not embrace the other constituent nations of the United

Kingdom. They dismissed the alternatives to federalism—a centralized union and independent dominion status. F. S. Oliver defined his version of federalism in 1914 in saying that:

> [W]hatever its [legislative] form, its effect should be to grant to Ireland powers of local government substantially similar to those exercised by local assemblies in Canada, Australia, and South Africa, while reserving to the Westminster parliament powers not substantially less than those reserved to the central governments of those three great self-governing dominions. (Oliver 1914, p. vii)

England, Ireland, and Scotland instead should get a legislature and responsible executive for their national concerns, while the common needs of the three kingdoms (and of the empire) would be treated within a supreme parliament. Each of these national parliaments would have wide powers, but the ultimate authority would lie with the central power, which would also control customs and excise. Unallotted powers should be retained by the central parliament. The detailed shape of the national legislatures would be left to separate national conventions: in a premonition of the 'asymmetric' devolution of the 21st century, Oliver decreed that it was 'not necessary that there should be uniformity in these constitutions. Their variety will not impair the unity, not threaten the security of the United Kingdom' (Jackson 2004, p. 219).

Wales, curiously, was relatively marginal to the concerns of Oliver and his circle (which tended to focus primarily on Ireland, England, and Scotland); and, accordingly, the principality featured little in the several reflections and manifestos which they produced at this time (there are perfunctory allusions in Oliver [Pacificus] 1910, pp. liv, 41, 56; see also Oliver 1913, 1914). But the drive for Irish home rule in 1912–14, together with the popularization of 'federal' notions of 'home rule all round', certainly fed into Welsh patriotic expression, and specifically into the proposals of E. T. John and his associate, Gwilym O Griffith (John 1912; Griffith 1913). Each of these argued that the seeming arrival of home rule for Ireland in 1913–14 'necessarily implied and involved', as John said, 'the grant of similar privileges and facilities to Scotland and Wales' (Griffith 1913, p. vi; Coupland 1954, pp. 240–1; Morgan 1981, p. 119). Griffith, indeed, went much further than this, envisioning home rule for Wales, not merely within a British and wider imperial federation, but as a first step towards a European (a 'united Europe') and global federal union (see e.g. Griffith 1913, p. 33). These aspirations of course were far in advance of the concerns of Oliver and his circle; though it is worth noting that some of those who were influenced by the group—including (as has been mentioned) Philip Kerr, Lord Lothian—would plot a similar internationalist trajectory amidst the challenges of the 1930s (Sayers 2011).

However, more immediately, and in so far as these federalist activists had any direct and immediate legislative legacies, then these lay with the last of the home rule measures, the Government of Ireland Act (1920). The legislation which created the partition settlement, a separate Northern Ireland, and a parliament and executive in Belfast, was a product of the home rule and federalist debates in British politics. The Government of Ireland Act did not create a strictly federal constitution: Westminster remained explicitly sovereign in all the circumstances envisioned by the 1920 Act. However the measure did create two bicameral parliaments in Ireland, in Belfast and Dublin, and created as well a Council of Ireland as a means of communication and cooperation between the two. While Westminster remained sovereign, the act did envision the possibility that authority over customs and excise might be granted to the Council of Ireland by agreement and in the future. More generally, because the convention was swiftly established at Westminster that the Northern Ireland parliament had autonomy within its own statutory areas of jurisdiction, an approximation of shared sovereignty was effectively put in place.

The act therefore embodied a settlement which, while nominally devolutionist, came very close to being federal in practice (much, in fact, as Dicey had predicted in relation to home rule in 1893). Certainly, before the fluid devolution settlements of 1998 and after, the Government of Ireland Act was the nearest federal-style encroachment that the British parliament was prepared to risk within the United Kingdom. While later parliamentarians and administrators were prepared to countenance elaborate federalist reforms for Malaya (1948–63), Rhodesia and Nyasaland (1953–63), the West Indies (1958–62), and Nigeria (1960–63), Northern Ireland was as close as it was allowed to threaten Britain itself (Kendle 1997, pp. 128, 136, 143, 146; Mohr 2016). Even then its unhappy denouement between 1969 and 1972, when the Stormont parliament was finally prorogued, served to reinforce British opposition to federalism.

Was there, in fact, a British *tradition* of opposition? Michael Burgess, writing in the mid-1990s, eloquently defined a British tradition of support for federalism, dating from the 1870s and surviving through to the end of the 20th century (Burgess 1995). Others, such as John Kendle, have defined a 'federal Britain' with an even greater longevity, spanning from the first theorizing at the time of the union of the English and Scottish crowns in 1603 (and before) through to the debates upon the British role within an evidently developing federal Europe (Kendle 1997, pp. 2–3). But in some ways a no less influential and striking tradition has been British opposition to federalism—those, often (not always) unionist, thinkers who have elaborated detailed critiques of the federalist idea, and whose arguments continue to present a challenge to federalist advocates. Paradoxically, these intellectuals have often found themselves in a tacit but effective alliance with radical nationalists, for whom federalism has always constituted a dangerous diversion from the true faith.

One of the key opponents of the application of federalist reform within a British and Irish context (as distinct from the federalist principle) was the historian and Gladstonian, E. A. Freeman (from 1884 Regius Professor of Modern History at Oxford). Writing in his epic but unfinished *History of Federal Government in Greece and Italy* (1863 and 2nd edition 1893) Freeman claimed that replacing the unions with a federated United Kingdom would be a poor substitution: 'no one could wish to cut up our United Kingdom into a federation, to invest English counties with the same rights as American states, or even to restore Scotland and Ireland to the quasi-federal position which they held before their respective Unions' (Freeman 1893, p. 70; see also Bremner and Conlin 2015; Bell 2016, pp. 327–33; Reid 2014, p. 357). Subsequently, in the context of Isaac Butt's advocacy of federal reform for Ireland, Freeman argued—in the *Fortnightly Review* of July 1874—that a federal system was to be supported if it tended to greater union, but not if (as in Ireland) it were a step towards separation: 'I am inclined to think that total separation would be a lesser evil than such a scheme of federation, or whatever it is to be called, as is now proposed' (quoted in Kendle 1989, p. 18). It has been convincingly suggested that the apogee of Freeman's assaults came in April 1885, when 'the most punishing criticism of imperial federation' was supplied by him in an essay published in the April edition of *Macmillan's Magazine* (Kendle 1997, p. 50).

A. V. Dicey built upon these foundations, arguing, like Freeman, that if 'the strict enforcement of ordinary law and strict protection for legal rights' was unworkable, 'then, tho' with the greatest regret, I should advocate separation' (quoted in Kendle 1989, p. 23). Dicey, Vinerian Professor of English Law at Oxford (1882–1909), and the most distinguished jurist of the age, was in fact the key critic of federalism—with his arguments first aired in a *Contemporary Review* essay in 1882, and later elaborated in his *Law of the Constitution* (1885) and in subsequent publications. Federalism, he wrote in 1882, 'revolutionises the whole constitution of the United Kingdom; by undermining the parliamentary sovereignty, it deprives English institutions of their elasticity, their strength, and their life; it weakens the Executive at home and lessens the power of the county to resist foreign attack' (see Kendle 1997, pp. 46ff.). Moreover, this would be a fundamentally unnecessary revolution since it

> holds out no hope of conciliation with Ireland. An attempt, in short, to impose on England and Scotland a constitution which they do not want, and which is quite unsuited to the historical traditions and to the genius of Great Britain, offers to Ireland a constitution which Ireland is certain to dislike which had none of the real or imaginary charms of independence, and ensures none of the solid benefits to be hoped for from a genuine union with England.
> (Dicey 1882; Kendle 1989, p. 23)

Dicey's great critique of Gladstone's home rule bill was embodied in his *England's Case Against Home Rule*, published originally in November 1886, wherein he argued famously that home rule would destroy parliamentary sovereignty and thereby weaken Britain and its empire. John Kendle's crisp analysis of Dicey's 1886 case is worth quoting at length:

> For Dicey the disadvantages of federalism were three fold: first, the sovereignty of parliament would be destroyed and all constitutional arrangements would be dislocated; second, the power of Great Britain would be diminished; and third, the chance of further disagreement with Ireland would be increased rather than lessened. As far as Dicey was concerned, parliamentary sovereignty provided the United Kingdom with more flexibility than would an American-style constitution. From the moment the United Kingdom became a federation the omnipotence of parliament would be gone, and the authority of central and local parliaments would be limited by articles of the constitution and by the Federal Court.
> (Kendle 1989, p. 55; also Kendle 1997, pp. 46-7).

Dicey's critique was further elaborated in his assault on the later iterations of Gladstonian home rule, published as *A Leap in the Dark* in 1893, and tweaked again for a new edition in advance of the third home rule bill, in 1911. Federalism, he repeated, would not satisfy nationalists: it would mean a division of powers which would undermine the strength of the country. It would mean government by the courts rather than parliament (there has been a remarkably hardy British self-image of minimal legal and constitutional regulation); and yet at the same time the rule of law would be subverted—because state authorities would not always enact imperial judgements. While Dicey was sometimes guilty of racist insensitivity, the example that he chose to illustrate this subversion of the rule of law was the brutal flouting of federal protection of the rights of African Americans in the southern, ex-confederate, states (Dicey 1911, p. 158; Mohr 2016, p. 159; Shinn and Cosgrove 1996, p. 149 n. 6).

Dicey also saw the practical political problems facing any federal reform as overwhelming. Despite the calls of some isolated evangelists (William Mitchell of the Scottish Home Rule Association, E. T. John of the Welsh National League), there was no substantial desire for federalization in Wales and Scotland. Moreover, the exclusion of Irish MPs from the federal (or rather) imperial parliament (as in the 1886 home rule bill) was tantamount to 'taxation without representation'. On the other hand, the 'in and out' arrangement for Irish MPs (as in the first draft of the bill of 1893) was wholly impractical. Nor could the unity of the empire, logically, be augmented by the disunity of the United Kingdom: federalism in fact would produce divided loyalties between state and centre. The international successes that federalists cited were inapplicable: 'all the conditions which make a federal constitution work successfully in the United States, in Switzerland, and possibly in Germany, are wanting in England and Ireland'. He pointedly denied the applicability of other analogies commonly deployed: he was unable (or unwilling) to take on board the contemporary arguments of R. W. Seton-Watson linking the experience of Transleithania to the debates over Ireland and Ulster ('of Hungary and its relation to the Empire of which it forms a part, nothing at all will be said. There is nothing in that relation analogous to Irish Home Rule') (Dicey 1911, pp. 153–4; cf. Seton-Watson 1911a).

Aspects of Dicey's critiques are unpalatable to a modern readership: his extreme unionist partisanship, especially in 1912–14, allied with his crude characterization and easy dismissal of Irish nationalism. While alert to English condescension towards the Irish, he was essentially anglo-centric, despite (or because of) his convinced unionism (Dicey 1887, p. 137). His identification of an indivisible parliamentary sovereignty is now commonly questioned. His occasionally patronizing and combative tones grate against modern susceptibilities. But at the same time his elaborate arguments have not always produced reasoned rebuttals; and indeed he is sometimes rebuffed, even by scholars, using the same polemical register which he himself increasingly adopted. Thus his influence—which was commanding during his lifetime—still resonates a century after his death (Burgess 1995, p. 21; Kendle 1997, p. 172; McLean 2010, p. 313).

One aspect of this resonance has become clear for the first time with the opening of the John Murray archive in the National Library of Scotland; and it may be briefly set out here. While it has long been recognized that federalist advocates like F. S. Oliver and Lionel Curtis were tireless and skilful publicists, it is now evident from the Murray archives that Dicey invested a great deal of care in tailoring his publications for the marketplace (Murray Papers, Ms.40331; see also Cosgrove 1980, pp. 126ff.). In other words, the considerable influence of his best-selling *England's Case Against Home Rule* (1886), which contained his core anti-federalist critique, was not accidental, but reflected considerable tactical thought and skill. It was Dicey who wrote to Murray in June 1886 proposing the idea of the work and recognizing the need to produce it quickly before the public's interest in home rule waned: it was Dicey who urged a cheaper price and second edition, since he wanted his arguments to circulate widely 'even at the cost of pecuniary sacrifice' (Murray Papers, Ms.40331, f. 27: Dicey to Murray, 20 Nov. 1886). Again, it was Dicey who was the driving force behind an abridged version of the volume (Murray Papers, Ms.40331, f. 70: Dicey to Murray, 21 Mar. 1887). Dicey repeatedly selected Murray to produce his key later unionist and anti-federal statements, including also *A Leap in the Dark* (1893)—but this was a carefully calibrated decision since he also used rival publishing houses such as Cassell for lesser tracts and pamphlets and Macmillan for more learned lecture and monographic material (though the original connection with Murray may have been secured only after an initial rebuff from Macmillan) (Cosgrove 1980, p. 126). In brief, Dicey was not only the most respected constitutional lawyer of his time, but also an extremely shrewd communicator. This combination of learning and strategy would help to create momentum for a lasting Diceyan tradition of unionist and anti-federal argument within British politics.

There clearly was no federalist reform of the British constitution in the 19th century, or in the first decades of the 20th century, and the obvious concluding questions arise: why not and what have been the legacies of this failure?

Federalism was almost always in effect a compromise idea, as was also the case in Austria and the Dual Monarchy (see section 5.4). Imperial federalists were seeking to reverse what they saw as a dangerous drift in empire, and to balance colonial autonomy with a central imperial structure and vision. The patriarchs of Irish federation, influenced by north American analogies, were consciously seeking to find a middle way between the restoration of a wholly autonomous Irish parliament under the crown—in effect Irish legislative independence—and the union settlement of 1800. Sharman Crawford and his supporters were seeking a balance between O'Connellite repeal and the status quo in the 1840s: Isaac Butt in the 1870s was proposing a moderate form of self-government which would unite different forms of Irish supporter, including Tories (even though he claimed that 'federal home rule was for him no mere tactical second-best; it was at once the thought-out expression of his own emotional view of the relationship between the two islands, and an offer of partnership to Irish protestantism') (Thornley 1964, p. 20). Federalists in the Edwardian era were seeking to cut through Irish nationalist concerns and to provide a more efficient imperial parliament.

In each of these cases federalism exercised a brief popularity, but failed partly because it did not ultimately satisfy deep-seated nationalist sentiment. Federalism in the 1840s, while interesting to O'Connell, did not appeal to the more radical Young Ireland movement. Federalism in the 1870s, while securing a fragile alliance between disenchanted Irish Tories and some nationalists, ultimately did not appeal to militants or indeed hardline constitutionalists led by Parnell. Federalism in the era of home rule was of no interest whatever to those who rose in 1916 to fight for an independent Irish republic.

Federalism, accordingly, was often seen in effect as a constitutionally conservative or unionist pitch. Even the home ruler Isaac Butt, originally a Tory and an Orangeman, argued that:

> [T]here is no people on earth less disposed to democracy than the Irish. The real danger of democratic or revolutionary violence is far more with the English people. The time may not be far distant when a separate Irish parliament might be in the best sense the Conservative element in the British constitution...I am not sure that one of the effects of a Federal Constitution would not be in many respects to strengthen the royal prerogatives out of the abeyance in which the system of governing by party has placed them. For myself I would not regret this...
> (Butt 1870, p. 64; Jackson 2004, p. 29; see also Reid 2014)

The key advocates of British federalism after 1910 were, however, usually conservative unionists motivated partly by wider ideas of imperial federation. Edward Carson, the militant leader of Ulster unionism, wrote in 1918 that (aside from Home Rule and partition):

> [T]he only other possible solution seems to me to lie in a system of federalism for the whole United Kingdom. Averse as I am from any change in the present constitution with its single parliament for all purposes, I do not deny that Union which I regard as the keystone of the British Commonwealth may nevertheless be preserved upon the principle of a true federation.
> (Carson to unidentified, 14 Feb. 1918, Carson Papers, D.1507/A/26/42)

But this identification of the federalist ideal with what was seen as hardline Ulster unionism was ultimately toxic so far as the possibilities of alluring Irish nationalism were concerned.

These federalist advocates were generally educationally or socially privileged and were characterized by a tendency to promote their cause *de haut en bas*. Federalist ideals were propagated uniformly by learned and elaborate essays and pamphlets, as distinct from mass campaigns. On this F. S. Oliver lamented in 1918, 'I have found...that the role of one who writes but does not talk in Parliament is necessarily limited. He finds the gate shut in his face at a certain point, a notice up that only practical statesmen are admitted beyond the barrier' (Jackson 2004, p. 224; see also Boyce and Stubbs 1976, pp. 53–81). While federalism had in fact colonized a substantial part of the House of Commons by the end of the First World War (there was an inconclusive Speaker's Conference on the theme in 1919–20), it never succeeded in gaining popular support (for reappraisals see Evans 2016, pp. 315–35; Evans 2017, pp. 366–83). The varieties and complexities of federalism proved harder to market than ostensibly simpler formulae such as 'union' or 'independence'—or even the somewhat more nebulous, but attractively packaged 'home rule'. Indeed, it would seem that some of these difficulties in communication have had a lengthy afterlife, in so far as much popular debate over Britain's complex relationship with a federalizing Europe has ultimately crystallized around the ostensibly unambiguous notions of 'remain' and 'leave' (or 'taking back control' or 'get Brexit done', the messages which helped to deliver election success for British Conservatives in 2016 and 2019) (Henderson and Wyn Jones 2021, p. 3).

The federal idea suffered, therefore, because it was characterized by lack of definition, by lack of conceptual clarity, and by division amongst its advocates. Federalism in the 19th and 20th centuries was used to designate a wide range of potential united kingdom constitutions—from in effect loose confederal arrangements, echoing the United Kingdoms of Sweden-Norway, favoured by 'nationalist unionists' like Butt, through to centralized devolutionist proposals offered by imperialist unionists like F. S. Oliver. Linked with this, it was being asked to carry too much political and conceptual weight. Irish nationalists saw federalism as (at best) a loosening of union, while imperialist federalists saw the reform as a means of attaining a more united United Kingdom, and indeed a more united empire.

Moreover, federalism was countered by a robust tradition of unitary unionism which (while its main features have sometimes been delineated) has never been comprehensively evaluated. The ideas of Freeman (in fact a heterodox home ruler) and Dicey dominated discussion of federalism in the era of Irish home rule and independence—and long afterwards; and while aspects of this dual critique were challenged, and while the polemical tones of Dicey increasingly grated, many features of the case remained standing.

Federal union, in the end, became an export product—a set of concepts which by 1950 were well-understood within important sections of the British political and administrative elite, which were freely adapted for colonial purposes, but which were not judged to be politically expedient for United Kingdom consumption (Kendle 1997, p. 149; Mohr 2016). In a sense the issue for federalist advocates has not been the sustained resistance of truculent elites, or indeed the deeply entrenched (but actually quite recent) cult of the 'unwritten' British constitution (see e.g. Colley 2014a). The British political classes have in fact flirted with federalist ideas for over a century, while the lengthy experience of decolonization (including federalist experiments in the West Indies, Malaya, Rhodesia, and Nyasaland) as well as of home rule and devolution endowed some British politicians and civil servants with a considerable experience of producing written constitutions. The problems, in the end, have not been lack of knowledge or lack of experience or the lack of debate: they have instead been anchored in popular British apathy and incomprehension as well as in the related difficulties of choreographing a deal (Kendle 1997, p. 149; Mohr 2016).

In essence, federalism was often too much of a compromise, and often too suspiciously unionist in origin and design: it was too elitist, too literary—and too slowly reactive to nationalism, in particular Irish nationalism. Whether federalism has now re-emerged too late in the day to engage Scots nationalists, and thus to provide a reform mechanism for the United Kingdom constitution, remains to be seen. But here, as elsewhere, there are clear symmetries between the British union state's last great constitutional crisis, arising from Irish home rule, and the current storms over Brexit and Scottish independence (see Jackson 2018a for an earlier version of this section).

5.3. Federalizing Canada

In 1840–41 Canadian union had been delivered by imperial policy and by clear and direct reference to the experience of union in Scotland and Ireland: the smooth transition to confederation in 1867, and its apparent success, ultimately constituted a reciprocal influence on the politics of reform within the British union. This peaceable and negotiated transition also reflected positively on at least some aspects of the institutions and cultures which had evolved under the union. But why, then, was federation, or (in the porous description and definition applied at the time) 'confederation', ultimately deemed to be necessary? And why was it successfully attained in Canada, and not in the other case studies reviewed here?

One issue was that the parliamentary union of 1840, as has been shown, was fundamentally an external imposition which ultimately satisfied few in Canada. The majority, and its leaders, in the francophone east worked grudgingly within the structures of the new United Province, seeking to adapt them to French and Catholic interests. But the majority in the anglophone west, having been relatively privileged by the original settlement in 1841, found themselves bound within a set of arrangements which progressively offered fewer political profits and eventually tipped into deficit. This was because Canada West grew significantly in size and wealth after 1841 to the point where it became the overwhelmingly dominant partner in the United Province. In essence this meant in turn that the forms of discrimination which had favoured their interests in 1841 (for example, enjoying equal parliamentary representation while their population was less than that of the east) now operated against them.

Expressing this another way, union in Canada was weakened by dynamic sectional change—but from within the burgeoning west rather than an alienated east. Again, there is a further comparison to be made here with Ireland and the economic and demographic growth of eastern Ulster in the 19th century. The decisive strengthening of both Ulster and Canada West in the 19th century overturned the conditions present at the creation of union in 1801 and 1841; and these radical changes in the end fed into the destabilization of union itself. That is to say, instability arose here (as has so often been the case with union polities) as much because of the dynamic condition of the union as because of external or oppositional forces.

In the short term, however, these developments certainly gave rise both to cultures of complex (and peaceable) negotiation and arbitration, as well as to consociational (or proto-consociational) institutions; but they also produced increasing difficulties in the formation and business of government. There was never any legal obligation for an executive to be supported by majorities in the Legislative Assembly of the United Province deriving from each of the two sections: there was never any formal requirement for 'double majorities'. Some (such as John Sandfield Macdonald (1812–72)) argued that this requirement had grown through convention, and it certainly was the case that between 1848 and 1856 an informal 'double majority' sanction was in place. But by 1857–8, with the rapid turnover of ministries, and in particular the complex creation, breakdown, and reconstruction of George-Étienne Cartier's (1814–73) shared ministry with John A. Macdonald (1811–91), maintaining respect for the 'double majority' convention was increasingly a challenge (Morton 1999, pp. 15, 19).

In each of the two sections of the United Province these difficulties, together with the more general sclerosis in government, fed into movements for alternative constitutional arrangements, including some which now looked beyond the Province to a reformed and widened union embracing all of the colonies of British North America. The notion of 'representation by population' ('rep by pop') was gaining traction in the, now more populous, west (where it was spearheaded by George Brown). In the east, however, 'rep by pop' stimulated deep-seated fears of the overwhelming of French and Catholic cultures; and here the long-standing preference was instead for a move away from centralism towards a restoration of greater provincial autonomy. The confluence, or (perhaps) lowest common denominator of these different pressures and aspirations became increasingly, from the late 1850s onwards, the notion of 'confederation'.

Why otherwise did confederation emerge at this time in Canada? It should be said immediately that the idea had been current from the era of American independence, rooted partly in the statist ideologies of the court party and in loyalist responses to the challenge of the American revolution: the ambitious federalist schemes of United Empire Loyalists such as William Smith and Jonathan Sewell have been discussed in the earlier Canadian case study of union (see section 3.4). There was, in addition, a long tradition of British radical reflection on federal reform, associated with such diverse proponents as the Fife-born Robert Gourlay (1778–1863), J. A. Roebuck, and Lord Durham (Martin 1990, pp. 16–17). In the United Province a federal union of all of British North America was pursued by visionaries such as Alexander Galt (1817–93), who tabled a resolution to this effect in the Legislative Assembly in July 1858. Galt's resolution was seized upon by pragmatists like Cartier and Macdonald as an escape chute from the constitutional impasse and instability of the time—as well as a means of addressing the sharpening challenges of westward expansion and defence. A reformulated and federalized union might, in these terms, facilitate the economic and territorial growth of British North America, as it had done for the colonies' southern neighbour, the United States. At the same time, a stronger union was seen, especially by those in the United Province (which had lengthy frontiers with the USA), as a means of warding off any southern territorial ambitions or depredations.

What did union, and specifically federal or 'confederal' union, mean in British North America in the late 1850s and beyond? Again, it is worth emphasizing that the road from the legislative union of the United Province to the 'confederation' known as the Dominion of Canada was by no means straightforward. There were, in the late 1850s and early 1860s, multiple expectations and definitions of a reformed union. These were, for the most part, clearly on show in the effort by the Cartier-Macdonald government to pursue federal union in 1858; and to some extent these differing goals and visions explain the failure of this first serious pitch at unifying British North America. Federation failed in 1858–9 because, strikingly, it was essentially about the interests of one province, the United Canadas: it was a United Canadian initiative designed to address primarily United Canadian problems, and indeed—even more narrowly—it was seen, in effect, as a 'proposal from one party in one colony' (Morton 1999, pp. 69, 77). The maritime provinces of British North America—New Brunswick, Nova Scotia, and Newfoundland—were physically distant and disconnected from the maelstrom of Canadian politics; and, generally speaking, the issues which fired debate in the United Province were much less combustible here. The stilted operation of representative government in the United Province was of limited interest to the maritimes: equally, the defence issues which came to preoccupy Canadians had less traction, even in New Brunswick which shared a (generally quiet) land border with the US state of Maine.

These maritime provinces experienced countervailing pulls, both westward towards Canada and eastward to London and empire, as well as towards greater cooperation amongst themselves. They were relatively unmoved by the Canadian enthusiasm for union: Prince Edward Island and Newfoundland were characterized by a merely 'detached interest' in the Canadian proposal of 1858, while New Brunswick and Nova Scotia were even 'less forthcoming and more critical' (Morton 1999, p. 63). For some or all of the maritimes there were shared interests in terms of fishing rights and an eastwards gaze towards the Atlantic fishing grounds and Britain. There were also distinctive concerns about railways; but, while New Brunswick and Nova Scotia might agitate about the possibility of an 'Intercolonial' rail link between the 'imperial fortress' of Halifax, Nova Scotia, and Quebec and Montreal, those in the United Province were somewhat less worried, since their principal rail concerns were increasingly westward looking (and in any case the Grand Trunk Railroad already had an Atlantic terminus in the United States, at Portland, Maine) (Morton 1999, p. 45). When, in the autumn of 1858, representatives went to London from British North America to discuss their hopes and concerns, there were in fact three delegations—one each from Canada, New Brunswick, and Nova Scotia; and there were different sets of interests—the Canadians worrying about union, the future of the west, and the Intercolonial railway, while the New Brunswickers and Nova Scotians were focused primarily upon the issue of the railroad alone. There were thus, for the moment, distinctive Canadian and maritime agendas. In practice this meant that, concurrent with the Canadian idea of a union of all of British North America, there was also increasingly the rival notion of a union of the maritime provinces alone.

In 1858–9 movement towards federation was stymied ultimately because, while there was no unity of approach amongst those who were the expected partners, the British government also refused to sanction its exploration. The British governing classes, constituting the overarching imperial authority, had their own, often very divergent, views of the future of their North American colonies; but for the moment (despite the variations) these did not encompass confederation. Some (like Gladstone) took an essentially 'little England' view of complex imperial challenges; and indeed Gladstone himself appears, in the context of the outbreak of the American civil war, to have coolly considered 'annexation'—a union of Canada with the northern states of the USA, if the latter 'thought fit to let the South go' (Goldwin Smith 1904, quoted in Jebb 1905, p. 4n.). Such views were linked to the desire, based on both strategic as well as economic calculations, to divest Britain of the responsibility for the defence of its North American possessions. Elsewhere at this time there was a broad suspicion of federation as smacking too much of the American republican model of government. There were prejudices in favour of the British version of union, as encompassing Ireland, Scotland, and Wales: that is to say, 'legislative' union rather than federation (these seem to have been shared by some Canadians, including John A. Macdonald). There were suspicions, too, that federation was merely a Canadian party tactic, rather than a strategy of national statecraft; and there was a belief that westward expansion could be sustained by the creation of new and autonomous colonies on the model of the existing structure of British North America.

Moreover, the British lieutenant governors of New Brunswick and Nova Scotia, John Manners-Sutton (1814–77) and George Phipps, Lord Mulgrave (1819–90), both thought that, from the point of view of their charges, legislative union of the maritime provinces was preferable to immediate federation. Successive British secretaries of state for the colonies, Sir Edward Bulwer-Lytton (1803–73) and the fifth duke of Newcastle (1811–64) shared this preference for maritime union, believing it might eventually provide a useful foundation for a wider initiative, but that the time had not yet come for this. Indeed, in January 1860, shortly after assuming office, Newcastle made clear in a despatch sent to all of the colonies of British North America that, while the British government would entertain any colonial proposal for union, it would not be taking the lead in the matter. This effectively ended the first sustained appraisal of federation (Morton 1999, pp. 63, 79). A failed attempt by the Canadians and maritimers in September 1862 at Quebec to pursue the idea of the Intercolonial railway on its own merely confirmed that British North America, both collectively and in terms of the individual colonies, faced a connected set of challenges which required an overarching set of trade-offs.

Major warfare, or insurgency, supplied a driver for all of the union polities under consideration in this volume; and the outbreak of the first great industrialized conflict, the American civil war, brought new emphasis to some of the old arguments for federation in British North America. In the prelude to war William Henry Seward (1801–72), the leader of the New York Republicans, and the party's rising star, had raised the possibility of uniting the divergent sections of the USA through looking to British North America and annexation. Once the conflict had begun, in April 1861, there was the sustained risk that it might spill across the Canadian border—whether through massive Northern resentment against British neutrality, and related incendiary naval episodes (such as those associated with the SS *Trent* and the SS *Alabama*), or through the isolated use of Canadian territory by Southern renegades to pursue their military objectives (as with the Johnson Island and St Albans raids in 1864) (Morton 1999, pp. 163-4). When the North finally triumphed in April 1865 there remained the possibility that its forces might now turn towards a war of conquest against British North America. Alongside this sabre-rattling was the possibility of economic warfare, expressed in particular through the US repudiation of the Reciprocity Treaty of 1854 (the Treaty required renewal after ten years).

The worst aspects of these threats were never realized. The (from the colonial perspective) more emollient Abraham Lincoln (1809-65) became leader of the Republicans and president in 1860-1, rather than Seward. Potentially combustible episodes did not in the end turn into a wholesale conflagration. After the cessation of hostilities, in August 1865 General Ulysses S. Grant (1822-85) and his staff certainly headed straight for Canada, and to Quebec—but for the purposes of holidaying rather than annexation or occupation. American military and diplomatic attention turned instead south, towards the task of undermining the French-sponsored Mexican regime of the emperor Maximilian (1832-67), brother to Franz Joseph of Austria; and their related concern, rather than fighting the British, was to persuade them to stay clear of Mexico. The US administration of Andrew Johnson (1808-75) reciprocated British neutrality when a group of Irish republicans, or Fenians, mostly veterans from the civil war, launched a number of (ultimately unsuccessful) raids on Campobello island, New Brunswick (April 1866), Ridgeway, Canada West (June 1866) and Pigeon Hill, Canada East (June 1866).

However, the combination of an at times very clear US threat, with the reality of Fenian violence, provided eloquent reinforcement for arguments for a wider union within British North America: confederation, like the other unions considered across this study, was forged partly in the context of war and the related need for security. In July 1861, with the outbreak of the civil war, the British had had to deploy three army battalions across the Atlantic—and in total some 14,000 imperial troops were posted to North America (Morton 1999, pp. 97, 100). This underlined the individual vulnerability of the different, often small, British colonies; and it also served to remind the metropolitan political classes that the current configuration of these colonies—one increasingly dysfunctional legislative union of the Canadas, together with a number of hard-pressed smaller maritime polities—was not likely to survive. In particular the rapid reinforcement of the British garrison highlighted both the importance of the ice-free seaport at Halifax, as well as its communications with the Canadian hinterland; and this in turn underlined the likely value of the projected Intercolonial scheme. Railroads (such as the Grand Trunk, which terminated at Portland, Maine) and telegraphs which used American territory or American operators were shown to be unreliable resources in the face of an existential threat.

The notion of reformulating union, which had been discussed and finally parked between 1858 and 1860, now, in the context of the US civil war, regained its old momentum. Much valuable preparation had been achieved in 1858, despite the disappointing immediate denouement; but not all of British North America, or the British themselves, had felt the pressure to reform as keenly as the United Province. This now gradually changed. In the short term, a key driver was the creation in June 1864 of the 'Great Coalition' government in the United Province, chaired nominally at first by Sir Étienne-Pascal Taché (1795–1865), but in reality controlled by Cartier and Macdonald, and now including old opponents such as George Brown: its principal purpose was to work for greater union within British North America, but its breadth and inclusivity effectively meant that union was now linked to 'rep by pop', provincial autonomy, the railroads questions (both Intercolonial and Pacific) and western and north-western expansion. Maritime union remained on the agenda for a conference at Charlottetown, Prince Edward Island, planned for September 1864; but the maritimers allowed the Canadian leaders to join their discussion, which delivered an agreement, if only as yet in principle, on confederation. Detail was supplied, drawing on the experience of 1858, in a reconvening of the conference at Quebec in October 1864.

During 1865, in the light of this wider agreement and of the ongoing US threat, the British at last came on board. Maritime support remained qualified and hesitant, however, and this remained a process driven primarily (if not now, exclusively) by the needs of the British and French populations of the two sections of the United Province. But at London in December 1866 a conference, chaired by Macdonald, secured a detailed agreement which was swiftly framed into legislation at Westminster, and passed into law in March 1867 as the British North America Act. On 1 July 1867 a new federal union came into being, the 'Dominion' of Canada, bringing together the former (and now disaggregated) United Province with New Brunswick and Nova Scotia. Maritime scepticism, however, was a long time in dissolving: Nova Scotia (having joined) swiftly turned against confederation, Prince Edward Island only embraced the new dominion in 1873, while Newfoundland belatedly made the leap in 1949, in the straitened aftermath of the Second World War.

The new constitution delineated in the Act provided for a relatively centralized federal union, with a bicameral dominion parliament at Ottawa: both the new senate and new House of Commons were constructed so as to make provision for further territorial expansion westwards, and the new Commons was effectively constituted on the basis of 'representation by population'. Legislatures were created for the new provinces of Ontario and Quebec (formerly Canadas West and East);

while those already in existence in New Brunswick and Nova Scotia were sustained. The balance of powers between the dominion and provincial parliaments was carefully calibrated with the advantage, including residuary powers, evidently assigned at first to the centre rather than the provinces (section 91 of the Act). The Act made explicit provision for the construction of the long-discussed Intercolonial railway to connect Halifax with the St Lawrence river. In general, the constitution was seen as enshrining a top-down approach to federation, in a conscious distancing from the republican American exemplar.

This broaches a central issue with confederation, namely the influence of the several British models of union. The historiography of confederation has shifted emphasis over the years, away from patriotic celebrations of nation and state-building, and from nationalist teleologies, towards high-political accounts of individual and sectional power-brokerage and, latterly, following the wider turn towards the history of ideas, examinations of the intellectual hinterland to the relevant debates: the geographical focus has shifted somewhat, away from Quebec and Ontario towards the maritimes and the west. In all of this the influence of the British union has been sometimes diminished, and reasonably so, given the understandable movement away from older colonialist and deferential readings. Yet the ultimate constitutional shift was still away from a British-style of legislative union in the United Province towards an (in the first instance) relatively British reading of federation.

The preamble to the British North America Act (1867) described the provinces coming together ('federally united') to form 'One Dominion under the Crown of the United Kingdom of Great Britain and Ireland, with a Constitution similar in Principle to that of the United Kingdom'. This in turn reflected a variety of pressures within constitution building, aimed at balancing the desire both of Quebec and the maritime provinces for heightened autonomy together with some unitary impulses coming in particular (but not exclusively) from John A. Macdonald. Durham had sought, through the Act of Union (1840), to recreate the achievements of the 'two Unions in the British Isles', especially the Scots, within a north American context; and in essence this is also what Macdonald, a Glasgow-born conservative and Orangeman, was seeking—in so far as it was attainable—through the agency of confederation. Lord Carnarvon, the British colonial secretary, was of a similar mind (Harding 1902, pp. 118, 152; Coupland 1945, pp. 161–2). Confederation in fact, for Macdonald, reflected 'in principle' the constitution of the United Kingdom, since it promised a strong central parliament and executive with the preservation of distinctive component polities, just as (in the British case) Scotland and many of its distinctive institutions had been maintained. The corollary of this was, of course, that Canadian confederation soon provided a paradigm for the reform of the United Kingdom constitution to British liberals such as Gladstone and even to a later generation of conservative nationalist in Ireland, not least John Redmond.

The Irish, indeed, exercised an influence over the formulation and consolidation of confederation. Thomas D'Arcy McGee (1825-68) foreshadowed the kind of imperially minded nationalism which Redmond later controversially espoused as leader of the home rule movement in Ireland. McGee, born into poverty in Carlingford, county Louth, migrated from Ireland to the USA and later to Canada; but he also migrated intellectually from support for militant Irish nationalism, through his allegiance to the Young Ireland movement and the 1848 rising in Ireland, towards an intensely Catholic and imperial conservatism and Canadian patriotism. McGee was a Canadian representative at Charlottestown and Quebec in 1864, and a strong supporter of the confederation of British North America, which he thought more likely to supply protection for minority rights (such as those of Irish Catholics) than the republican and WASP cultures of the USA. His disavowal of his own early militant career, gave him an influence over the early formulation of confederation; but it also seems to have inspired the Fenian rage which lay behind his assassination in April 1868 (Wilson 2008-11).

Scots and Irish unionists brought to Canada their native experience of union within the 'British isles'; and indeed the disproportionately large numbers of Scots and Irish who occupied the governor generalship suggests a deliberate policy, if not of consciously applying the experience of the British unions, then certainly of recognizing the significant proportions of Scots and Irish within the populations of British North America (this was still seen as an important factor as late as the selection of John Buchan, Lord Tweedsmuir (1875-1940) as governor general in 1935) (see e.g. Lownie 1995, p. 243). Scots like Lord Elgin or Lord Lorne (1845-1914) applied their knowledge of the complex relationships of the United Kingdom state to their roles as, respectively, Governor General of the Province of Canada (1847-54) and Governor General of the Dominion of Canada (1878-83) (see e.g. Argyll 1907). More strikingly, confederation was ushered into British North America by a trinity of Irish Protestant and unionist peers: Viscount Monck, John Young, first Lord Lisgar (1807-76), and Frederick Hamilton-Temple-Blackwood, first earl, later first marquess of Dufferin (1826-1902) (see e.g. Dufferin 1891). Of these Monck, a Tipperary-born landed proprietor, was perhaps the most influential, since his career as the last Governor General of British North America (1861-67) and the first Governor General of the Dominion of Canada (1867-68) spanned the attainment of confederation. It was an influence which was exercised in support of Macdonald (whose ability was equalled only at this time by his drunkenness); and it was an influence which was exercised not just in favour of union, but of a centralized union (Stevenson 2006, p. 147; Morton 1999, p. 99). But the others also viewed Canada through the lens of their homeland: Dufferin, for example, closely watched events in Ireland from his study in Rideau Hall, fretting about the activity of Isaac Butt, and seeking to frame reforms and institutions for Canada on the basis of the practice of union government in

Ireland: he was especially keen on deploying the model of the Royal Irish Constabulary as the template for a new Canadian police force, and invoked his own memories of the Belfast riots of 1864 in brooding over civil disturbance in Montreal (de Kiewiet and Underhill 1955, p. 46).

Ultimately, of course, these different Scots and Irish influences helped to ensure both the peaceable reconfiguration of a legislative union, the United Province, within a new federal union, the Dominion of Canada, as well as the robust construction of this new confederation. But within 20 years of the achievement of the latter, in 1885-6, Canada was being actively deployed as one of several models for the constitutional reform of the United Kingdom, with Gladstone closely questioning Lord Lorne, now returned from viceregal duties in Ottawa, about the possibilities: Lorne's experience of Canadian confederation had made him sympathetic to the notion of 'provincial' assembles across the United Kingdom and indeed to imperial federation ('the ghastly Irish mess becomes more terrible every hour', he wrote in Ottawa in December 1880, 'I am not at all sure that local Provincial Government would be a bad thing': Argyll 1907, vol. 2, pp. 461, 476-7, 518ff.; Gladstone to Lorne, 17 Sept. 1885, Gladstone Mss, Add.Ms.44492, f. 94). Despite different linguistic and religious traditions separating Quebec from the rest of the new dominion, and despite the growth of secessionist aspirations in the second half of the 20th century, Canada has held together peacefully in union in contradistinction to its former imperial motherland. Indeed, the first United Kingdom, the union of Great Britain and Ireland, was periodically threatened by insurrection throughout the 19th and early 20th centuries, tottered on the brink of civil war owing to unionist militancy in 1912-14, and effectively disintegrated through the revolutionary and counter-revolutionary violence of 1919-21. Why, then, did Canada arguably achieve greater success (through both unions, of 1840 and—especially—that of 1867) in building a form of multinational union than the former imperial power, and the original model of unions, the United Kingdom? Why, in particular, was federation successfully attained here, where in the other polities examined it so clearly languished?

Both the Irish union of 1801 and the Canadian union of 1841 were constructed with the idea of incorporating Catholic polities within new, and largely Protestant and British, political configurations. With Ireland, there was a burden of history—of bloodshed and broken promises—which was difficult, though not impossible, to overcome: this was less obviously the case with Quebec (the later Lower Canada), which was acquired from the French only in 1763. With Ireland, the historic targets of the British state, and of its traditional Irish allies (the ascendancy class), were the Catholic Church and Catholic landownership; but with Lower Canada the Church and the seigneurial classes were swiftly won over as allies, and served on the whole as advocates of the imperial connection (in contradistinction to the lure of godless republicanism either in its French or American formulations).

In essence Quebec and Canada supplied a model of Catholic subscription to monarchy and empire which both Daniel O'Connell and (especially) John Redmond tried for a time to adapt to Irish circumstances.

Under the union launched in 1840–1 francophone Canada was given a substantial share of parliamentary representation and of responsible government: Canada East, which included an influential anglophone minority, provided half of the membership of the United Provinces's representation, as well as one of its two political leaders. Under confederation francophone Canada had its own province, Quebec, and a substantial influence thereby within the parliament and government of the new Dominion. Under the union of 1801, however, Ireland returned a small minority of members of the United Kingdom legislature, and could only, in the rare conditions of a hung parliament (as in 1910), exercise a direct and decisive influence. Moreover Catholic Ireland was only effectively given access to parliament nearly 30 years after the passage of union; and neither Catholics nor Irish Catholics ever occupied a significant position within the central government of the union. Between 1801 and 1922 no Irish Catholic sat as British minister for Ireland (Chief Secretary): between 1801 and 1922 only one Catholic (who was not Irish) held the position of lord lieutenant or viceroy of Ireland (Lord Edmund Talbot, Viscount FitzAlan (1855–1947)) (Barry O'Brien 1912). In other words, Catholic and francophone Canada, whether under the Act of Union (1840) or under confederation (1867), could exercise a sometimes commanding influence through the structures of government: in Ireland under the union, the structures of power were stacked in such a way that decisive Irish Catholic influence could often only be exercised through extra-parliamentary mobilization.

The United Province was certainly divided between anglophone Protestants, generally of British descent, and francophone and Irish Catholics; and Lower (East) Canada also had distinctive anglophone and Protestant minorities, concentrated in Quebec and Montreal and characterized by relative wealth. But, while there were religious and cultural tensions in the United Province, and while the divisions of Ireland exercised an indirect influence (not least through the Orange Order), there was still nothing to compare with the intensity of the competition between Protestant unionist and Catholic nationalist (Stevenson 2006, p. 215; Houston and Smyth 1980). The successive unions of Canada were able to adapt and survive because of reasonably well developed cultures of accommodation: but these did not exist to the same extent in Ireland. The disproportionate strength of late 19th-century unionism in Ireland, and its evolving role as a key veto-player in British-Irish relations, meant, on the contrary, that reform of the union became ever more difficult; and ultimately in that sense Irish unionism effectively subverted its purpose.

In the end, while the contrasts are telling and important, the links between the unions of Canada and of the United Kingdom are no less striking. The unions of 1801 and 1841 were each shaped in the aftermath of insurgency, and against a longer background of political reflection. They were each designed for related purposes—namely the advancement of British political cultures. The unions of the United Kingdom exercised an influence over the formation of the United Province, not least through the Scottish and Irish statesmen who brought to Canada their home experience, a normative experience, of constitutional union. But here again, as so often in this book, the experience of union government was reciprocal, and Canada's success reverberated back to the United Kingdom.

Each union, the Irish and the Canadian, was fundamentally flawed in its operations, though each had (perhaps) more survival power than its ultimate fate might otherwise suggest. Each union, however, ended in the immediate context of bloody conflagration—because war (the US civil war, the Great War) decisively magnified a range of pre-existing arguments for change. But, in the end, the Canadian union, for all its many flaws, had nurtured an effective culture of arbitration and compromise; and it ended in a notably peaceable transition to confederation in 1867. In the United Kingdom these cultures ultimately failed; and—though federation was discussed among some within the British political class—the union ended between 1912 and 1922 with initially the threat, and then the reality of civil war.

5.4. Federalizing Austria and Austria-Hungary

One key aspect of federalism's significance for this study is that it has often been broached—whether in the Habsburg empire, Canada, or in the United Kingdom—as a miracle cure for ailing unions of other types. As a corollary of this, it has been a concept which has often been deployed either by pragmatic nationalists or by pragmatic unionists, depending upon the condition of the wider nationalities question in play, and upon the balance of advantage: unionists, for example, have tended to embrace federalism when the prospects of something 'worse' (from their perspective) have begun to coalesce, while nationalist interest in federalism has in turn tended to be associated with relatively more stable union polities where the possibilities of anything other than incremental advance have appeared remote. By extension, there has been (what might be defined as) a transient 'federalist moment', which has too often been lost, and when the calculations of gains over losses for the contracting parties have all-too-fleetingly appeared to be in strategic alignment.

Aside from timing, however, part of the challenge with federalism has been that the concept has had to do a great deal of work, in the sense that it has been freighted with the shared expectations of those whose convictions and outlook have often been fundamentally divergent. This has sometimes meant, in turn, that there have been ambiguities in conceptualization which have allowed debate to be carried a certain distance—before ultimate breakdown and failure.

Some of these issues are illustrated by the role of federalism within both the later Austrian empire and the Dual Monarchy. Here the notion was significantly advanced at the Kremsier/Kroměríz Reichstag and through the eponymous constitution of 1848–9 which offered a proposal for multi-layered representative institutions embracing a central parliament, parliaments for each of the historic provinces of the empire, and local assemblies within the constituent *Kreise* (circles or communities) of each province. Each nationality of the empire would have had its rights guaranteed under the constitution. Kremsier, which had never embraced Hungary or Lombardy-Venetia (because of the ongoing revolts there), was swiftly swept aside in March 1849 as the tide of reactionary absolutism gained momentum. But it had an afterlife, not only as a much-cited 'missed opportunity' in older pathologies of Habsburg failure, but also as useful source material for later prospective reformers of the monarchy.

In fact, though Hungary was not part of the failed Kremsier experiment, reformist Magyars such as Miklós Wesselényi (1796–1850) or Lajos Kossuth (1802–94) also looked to federal reform as a means of renegotiating Austrian centralism: Kossuth, the Hungarian statesman and hero of 1848, argued for the creation of a Danubian confederation. But with the eventual attainment of the Ausgleich and of dualism in 1867, and thereby of a full Hungarian partnership in empire, this patriotic interest in federalism melted away; and the federal ideal was instead redefined by the intellectuals of other nationalities as a means of renegotiating the dualist Austro-Hungarian union into a polity with a wider national embrace. More specifically, federalism tended to be embraced by these intellectuals as a *via media* between the seemingly inescapable presence of Habsburg rule and the vision of national self-government.

In terms of the 'nationalities' of the Dual Monarchy era, one of federalism's most conspicuous proponents was the Czech historian and patriot, František Palacký (1798–1876), who advocated the creation of eight national provinces within the empire (corresponding to its eight main perceived nationalities) (Seton-Watson 1908, p. 405). In Palacký's assessment there were essentially three possible arrangements for the governance and configuration of the Habsburg empire, each with their own characteristics and implications: 'centralism secures the hegemony to the Germans alone: dualism partitions it between two races, the Germans and Magyars: federalism alone guarantees those equal rights of all nationalities which it is the historic mission of Austria to achieve' (quoted in Seton-Watson 1908, p. 406). For Palacký, therefore, federalism was essentially a pragmatic and patriotic critique of the Ausgleich settlement, as well as being the optimal outcome of any reform effort.

This was largely true, too, for Aurel Popovici (1863–1917), a Transylvanian Romanian, who was a lawyer, journalist, and politician—and also one of the leaders of the Romanian National Party. In 1906 Popovici published his most important book, *Die Vereinigten Staaten von Groß-Österreich: Politische Studien zur Lösung der nationalen Fragen und staatsrechtlichen Krisen in Österreich-Ungarn* (1906) (The United States of Greater Austria: political studies towards the solution of the national questions and constitutional crises in Austria-Hungary)—a work which came to be associated with the 'Greater Austria' movement and with the political circle around the heir to the throne, the Archduke Franz Ferdinand. At the end of the 19th century, Transylvanian Romanians (as with other of the Habsburg nationalities) explored essentially two types of political discourse—the first focusing on national autonomy (and the possible union of Transylvania with Romania), while a second looked at federalist reform of the empire. In *Die Vereinigten Staaten von Groß-Österreich*, Popovici sought to reconcile two central, but ostensibly countervailing, allegiances—to the Romanian nation and to the Habsburg monarchy. In a sense his effort reflected, not just the obvious allure of Romanian nationality, but the simultaneous strengths of the supranational dynastic identity and ideal (see Seton-Watson 1981, pp. 36–7; also sections 3.5, 4.2).

Federalism was also in fact taken seriously by the political elite in Vienna, both in the discussions surrounding, and following the formation of Austria-Hungary. The heightened vulnerability of the empire after its defeat at Prussian hands in 1866 meant that the federalist reconstruction, which had been posited at Kremsier in 1849 (but ultimately crushed by Prince Felix von Schwarzenberg and Franz Joseph), came swiftly back on the agenda. Different models were suggested at this time both by Slav nationalists and, somewhat more cautiously, by Richard Graf Belcredi (1823--902), Minister President of the Austrian empire between 1865 and 1867: Belcredi proposed a federation of the crownlands to counter the dualism which was favoured by the emperor and his foreign minister, Friedrich Graf von Beust (1809–86). Given this patronage, dualism prevailed of course; but the challenges of Slav nationality did not go away, and indeed were enflamed by this privileging of the Hungarians at the likely expense of others. Subsequent ministers, in grappling with the problems of (in particular) Bohemia, where Czechs and Germans were in competition, turned again to a range of wider federal solutions. Karl Graf von Hohenwart (1824–99) sought, during his brief tenure as Minister-President (between February and October 1871), to address the position of Bohemia, and of the nationalities more widely, through the Fundamental Articles and the Nationalities Laws. The Fundamental Articles proposed a federalist relationship between the Austrian parliament and a Bohemian diet, as well as with Galicia; but they (and Hohenwart himself) were eventually overthrown by powerful opposition forces, which Franz Joseph himself eventually joined (Okey 2001, p. 222).

Indeed, turning to the monarchy, Franz Joseph remained stubbornly committed to the Ausgleich, which in fact has often been interpreted as essentially a deal between him and the Magyar elites. But the next generations of Habsburg had much less of a personal investment in the compromise. For example, while Archduke Franz Ferdinand's fundamental convictions are still the subject of some debate, he was at the very least a critic of Hungary and of dualism; and Berchtold, the Austro-Hungarian foreign minister between 1912 and 1915, certainly believed that the archduke wanted to rework the Ausgleich into a new and more inclusive federation (see e.g. Haslinger 1996, p. 43).

With Franz Joseph's death in December 1916, the key *kaiserlich und königlich* bolster of the Ausgleich went as well; and the new emperor, Karl, swiftly proposed an abandonment of dualism and the embrace of federalist reform from January 1917—that is to say almost as soon as he succeeded to the throne. Karl's choice as Minister President of Austria, Heinrich Graf Clam-Martinic (1863–1932), in office from December 1916 to May 1917, also talked generally about 'Austria as a federation of autonomous peoples', though in fact he (and Karl) only served thereby to encourage the thirst of the 'nationalities' within the monarchy at a time of growing vulnerability. In September–October 1918 Karl devised and launched a last ambitious scheme of federalization; but, with the military position of the Dual Monarchy in free-fall, and civil government now beginning to disintegrate, he was in effect (like many other unionist proponents of federalism in embattled conditions) trying to bargain without resource. In any event, throughout 1917–18, while Franz Joseph was certainly gone, the other historic partner to the Ausgleich, the Magyar political elites, were still very much in place; and to the very end they would not budge from their gains of 1867.

However, the most original, coherent, and timely thinking on the challenges of a federalist reconstruction of the later empire came, not from the Hofburg, but instead from within the Social Democratic party, which—at its biennial congress held in 1899 at Brno/Brünn—committed itself to the transformation of the Dual Monarchy into 'a federal state of nationalities' (Okey 2001, p. 308). At first the detailed exegesis was lacking; but this was soon provided by two rising stars within the party—Otto Bauer, whose key contribution has already been mentioned (*Die Sozialdemokratie und die Nationalitätenfrage* (1907) (Social democracy and the nationalities question)) (see sections 3.5, 4.10). R. W. Seton-Watson and some other contemporaries thought that 'a far more brilliant and original proposal' than this conventional type of territorially defined federalism was that provided by Karl Renner, writing as Rudolf Springer, wherein the government of the empire would have a dual basis, both national and territorial, with each nationality forming a corporation within the Habsburg state: Renner's most important works in this area were his *Der Kampf der österreichischen Nationen um den Staat* (1902) (The struggle of the Austrian nations for the state) and his *Grundlagen und Entwicklungsziele der österreichischen-ungarischen Monarchie* (1906) (The foundations and developmental goals of the Austro-Hungarian monarchy). This idea, certainly for Seton-Watson, who read the work with great approval, had the dual merits of addressing the injustices of dualism while preserving the essential unity of the empire, without which (he thought) there would be a meltdown of continental proportions (Seton-Watson 1908, p. 402; Figure 5.5).

Indeed, Seton-Watson was the most prominent of a range of outsiders, critical friends of the Dual Monarchy, who likewise saw in federalism a strategy for imperial survival—as well as lessons which might be applied closer to home. Reviewing the Habsburg empire more generally in 1908, Seton-Watson grouped the numerous proposals for its reform under four broad headings: assimilation, autonomy, separatism, and federalism (Seton-Watson 1908, p. 399). He swiftly dismissed the possibility of assimilation, certainly within Hungary, since there were 'too many non-Magyars'. But he was also impressed and influenced by the English failure in Ireland in this (and other) respects, since 'seven centuries of English occupation have failed to destroy the feeling of Irish nationality; and today, despite the gradual disappearance of linguistic differences and the support of a powerful anglophil minority we seem to be as far as ever from a solution to the problem' (Seton-Watson 1908, p. 400). Autonomy and separatism were equally impossible, though for different reasons: agreed autonomy depended upon an unshakeable Magyar elite, while separatism 'can only be regarded as a solution by those ignorant persons who believe in a dissolution of the Dual monarchy and the inevitable European conflagration which that would kindle' (Seton-Watson 1908, p. 402). This left federalism.

Seton-Watson would later, however, move to advocate a somewhat different reform of the dualist system, more modest than that devised by Renner/Springer, and one in which the southern Slavs would be elevated to a status equal to Cisleithania and Hungary in a 'trialist' or federalized monarchy (Seton-Watson 1911a, p. 337). More specifically, he saw that dualism, as practised in Transleithania, presented a comparative case study for those in Ireland and Britain preoccupied by the issue of home rule and the possible federalization of the 'British isles'. For Seton-Watson, 'the fact that Croatia provides the only continental instance of Home Rule (for neither Hungary nor Finland are parallel cases [in terms of the specific home rule proposals]) should render the affairs of that country of special interest at the present moment' (Seton-Watson 1912, p. 1). Croatia had (through the *Nagodba* of 1868) achieved a 'modest autonomy' from Budapest in non-economic matters, while Croatian was established as the official language in Croatia-Slavonia (Okey 2001, p. 189). Warming to his didactic theme, Seton-Watson argued that 'Croatia offers many valuable lessons alike to the Home Ruler and to the convinced Nationalist, or at least to all who place the interests of Ireland and of the sister isle higher than those of the party to which they may happen to belong' (Seton-Watson 1912, p. 68).

In fact Seton-Watson set out a number of 'chief lessons' from the example of Croatia and Hungary. He was clear that if the Irish adopted the policies of Sinn Féin, then they would be following—not their beloved Hungarian model, 'but rather the Czechs of Bohemia who, in abstaining from Vienna, had made possible the Magyar triumph... [and indeed] nowhere has the folly of abstention been more clearly demonstrated than in Austria-Hungary' (Seton-Watson 1912, p. 67;

Griffith 1918). More generally, he saw that any scheme of home rule, any revision of union, needed the approval of the 'vast majority' of its supposed beneficiaries, as well as the 'strict' cooperation of the more powerful sister-nation; the deal of 1868 which underpinned Croatian 'Home Rule' had been sanctioned by 'a Croatian diet which owed its composition to an illegal franchise and to gross electoral corruptions, and its validity was challenged from the outset' (Seton-Watson 1912, p. 68). Financial relations needed to be clearly defined: any viceroy or governor general should be more than the nominee and lickspittle of the dominant nation (again, the unlovely history of authoritarian Croatian 'Bans', following the commands of Budapest, was in his mind). The 'in and out' system of Croatian representation in the Hungarian parliament (which had been considered in principle by Gladstone for Ireland) only worked because of shared partisanship. Seton-Watson (who had expressed some cautious interest in federation in earlier work on Hungary) was now clear that the difficulties of reconciling the representation of the home rule polity in the central parliament 'can only be overcome by [a comprehensive] Federalism, not by any scheme of special treatment for Ireland': this, he was confident, 'is likely to be the conviction of any close student of the Croatian-Irish analogy' (Seton-Watson 1912, p. 68).

The benefits of hindsight ultimately did little to mitigate the attractiveness of this kind of reading. Looking back at the demise of the empire ten years after the event (and from the vantage point of his new academic refuge in Oberlin, Ohio), Oszkár Jászi accepted that, 'if instead of the Dual system, there had existed a large Danube federation several of the national irredentas could have been appeased inside of its frontiers' (Jászi 1929, p. 382; Figure 5.2). Jászi also drew a range of more wide-ranging lessons from the failure of the Habsburg empire. Writing in 1929, on the eve of the 'devil's decade', he thought that the demise of Austria-Hungary demonstrated the need for the revision of state frontiers to take account of ethnic and national minorities: he thought, too, that there should be separate bodies for the cultural and educational requirements and protection of minorities. Heavily overcentralized and bureaucratic states should be decentralized and made locally accountable. Greater economic and cultural cooperation brought dividends in terms of stability and harmony (Jászi 1929, p. 457). Much of this had been tantalizingly realizable under the Habsburgs—but had lain unattained by the time that the cataclysm of war had erupted.

In the end, however, federalism in the Austrian empire and in Austria-Hungary functioned very largely as it did across the other unions considered within this study. Federalism was a strategy which sprang from crisis within the union polity, whether the unified Austrian empire, or the 'union' of Austria and Hungary. In most cases (not all) it was a strategy which ultimately reflected either the lack, or the loss, or the losing of power. It was advocated by some Magyars until they obtained in 1867 what was, in effect, an even better deal than federalism, namely dualism and the Ausgleich. It was advocated by intellectuals from the other 'nationalities' (Palacký, Popovici) until they, too, sensed the possibility of better terms. By way of contrast, federalism was generally resisted by the Habsburg monarchy—until they too sought to use it as a bargaining chip in the context of a game which was already lost.

In the same way federalism was pursued by Irish nationalists from a position of weakness between the 1840s and the 1870s; and it was finally embraced by sections of the British and Irish political elite (including Seton-Watson) at a time, after 1910–14, when home rule for Ireland seemed inevitable. By extension, the *de facto* federalization—and sometimes even the disaggregation—of the United Kingdom in the early 21st century appeared to be proceeding apace; and yet proposals for a formal federation held little overt interest for Scottish nationalists, who (like their predecessors within the Dual Monarchy and within Irish nationalism) pubicly expressed higher aspirations. Instead the federal idea now principally attracted forlorn and embattled unionists—who sought thereby (again, like their predecessors in Ireland and elsewhere) to rescue the vestiges of union from the deluge.

5.5. Unions, Federations, and Beyond

For many of the complex, and stretched, 'united kingdoms' discussed in this study federation and federalism served as rescue plans or healing agents. Federation was posited, as has been discussed, as a means of reconciling the claims of nationality within the centralized United Kingdom at various periods of strain—during the repeal movement in the 1840s, in the era of imperial consolidation at the end of the 19th century, in the context of Irish home rule (before and during the First World War), and latterly, in the context of a resurgent Scots nationalism.

Equally, federalism was periodically broached in both the Austrian empire and Austria-Hungary as a means of reconciling the claims of nationality to the continuing existence of a (recalibrated) Habsburg monarchy. In Sweden-Norway tentative efforts towards greater centralism were occasionally proposed (by successive kings and by Swedish unionists), which (had they been successful) would have reconfigured the loose confederal style of the United Kingdoms into an effectively more federalized condition. Finally, so far as the scope of this book is concerned, federation was used as a device to safely disaggregate one failing union, the United Province, within the overall structure of a newly minted and wider federal successor, the Dominion of Canada. In all of these different forms of union, federalism was deployed, usually but not always forlornly, as a constitutional panacea. And indeed in the United Kingdom it continues to be so deployed.

It is important, however, to stress once again the limitations of the federalist medicine. In the weighty political science literature on federalism there have been disagreements over what the most stable foundations for a successful federal state might be; but, while opinions have varied on (for example) the role of similarity and difference between the component polities, it is broadly accepted (following Dicey's insight) that federal states succeed where there exists a visceral commitment among the consenting parties to that particular end (Dicey 1887, p. 161). The fundamental problem with federalism in most of the (at times) ailing multinational unions reviewed here has been that there has rarely been any form of shared consensus about a federal future. On the contrary, federalism has often tended to be deployed (in effect, if not in conscious intention) as a form of negotiating pitch by those in complex union polities who are disposed to bargain because they occupy either weak or weakening positions of authority. Thus the most considered federalist proposals in Austria-Hungary came either from parties (the Social Democrats) or nationalities (the Romanians or southern Slavs) who were arguing from relatively disadvantageous strategic positions; while in both Sweden-Norway and the United Kingdom (though in different ways and in different directions) federalism was pitched by unionists in the context of strengthening nationalisms. In the United Kingdom federalism has been deployed by both conservative and labour unionists as a means of trying to stem the rising tide of (in the early 20th century) Irish nationalism and (in the early 21st century) Scots nationalism.

In most of these cases the federal idea has failed because, while it has provided advantages to some of its promoters, it has not offered sufficient gains to its intended recipients: in other words, the required consensus of acceptance has not existed. Thus, in the Dual Monarchy, Hungarians—some of whose political leaders had once, before the Ausgleich, been prepared to countenance federal-style proposals—were not prepared to trade the ascendancy offered by dualism for the more modest position offered by trialism or some wider federal construction. In the United Kingdom, after 1911–12 (and indeed before), few Irish nationalists were prepared to exchange the possibilities of home rule (and the realizable promise of dominion status) for the more insipid gratification of a provincial assembly and British federalism. Similarly, there is no unambiguous evidence just now that Scottish nationalists will happily trade the vision of an independent, or substantially independent Scotland, for subsidiarity within a new, federalized, but still irremediably 'united' kingdom: circumstance and contingency may yet, of course, change all this.

Moreover, federalism has also often faced, and continues to face, one of the fundamental challenges confronting union polities. Multinational union monarchies were generally created as a result of pragmatism and contingency, and they rarely embodied any popular vision or passion: as has been shown, the first steps towards the formation of Great Britain, achieved with the personal union of 1603, were accompanied by some smart propagandizing (not least by James VI and I), but they were not attained by any widespread, uniform conviction, even within the political classes of the day. Similarly, the parliamentary or real unions of 1707 and 1801 were achieved in the context of much pamphleteering and propagandizing, but they reflected the pressing contingencies of war, insecurity, and economic disruption, rather than visceral passion. This was true, too, for the formation of the United Kingdom of the Netherlands, the United Kingdoms of Sweden-Norway, and the Ausgleich which created the Dual Monarchy: indeed, in one coruscating definition the latter was 'a bureaucracy with a supranational ideal' which by extension could 'not enthuse nations for it that feel removed from the decision-making process' (Okey 2001, p. 401). Related to this, the proposed modification of personal or parliamentary unions into federal unions has generally been pushed by political, economic, and/or cultural elites, and the related ideas and proposals have rarely gained widespread, popular, traction. As has been noted, British federalism failed partly because it was too elitist and too literary; and the same might be said for federal ideas elsewhere in early 20th-century Europe. This was especially the case given that, as has been noted, the federal pitch has generally been made by unionists endeavouring to respond to rising nationalist passions. In short, unions, including federal unions, have primarily sought to appeal to the 'head': nationalism has principally been about 'heart'.

This, however, leaves Canada and the confederation of 1867. Here the transition from a limited and failing parliamentary union in the form of the United Province to 'confederation' was successfully achieved because all (or most) of the partners to the negotiation were invested in a successful outcome: none was surrendering an obvious pre-eminence or ascendancy, and all had some objective to gain. The colonial context was important, as was (outside of much of Quebec) the shared sense of British heritage; but even francophone and Catholic Quebec had the prospect of gain through the creation of the new federal Dominion. There were certainly strong individual provincial identities which had an impact upon the smooth consolidation of 'confederation'; but these bore little comparison to the very deeply laid historic identities of the component polities of the multinational united kingdoms of Europe. Moreover—and this distinction was central to the critique of federalism offered by Dicey—in several of these continental union polities federalism was posited as a means of reconciling tensions between the central state and restless nationalities—as a (for Dicey, futile) means of preserving much of the social and political structure of the existing state albeit now within a looser union structure. This was a quite different role, as again Dicey observed, to that played by federation in Canada or the United States: here it was an agency of closer union rather than of negotiated disunion. However, it should of course be remembered that, even in Canada, though federalism has worked, it has not worked smoothly; and, as Michael Burgess has observed, 'clearly the largest obstacle to Canada becoming a genuine multinational federation would seem to be the dominant anglophone mindset with indelible preconceptions that remains stubbornly resilient about an overarching Canadian state nationalism' (Burgess 2006, p. 130).

Finally, the ongoing processes of constitutional change in the United Kingdom, driven in the long term by Scottish nationalist pressure as well as subsequently by Brexit, have produced a greater interest in both a federalist but also a 'written' reform of the constitution of the union state. Linda Colley has rightly warned of 'the need to develop more multistranded, less teleological perspectives, on the advent and meanings of written constitutions and of the age of revolutions itself'—and has helpfully disentangled some of the mythology surrounding Britain's 'unwritten constitution'—a phrase which, as she points out, only became embedded within political discourse from the 1870s (Colley 2014a, 251, 261; Colley 2021).

If the constitution of the union state may require codification, should that newly codified constitution be federal, then? Is a new, 'written', and federal constitution the requisite medicine for ailing union states? It may indeed be the case that, as one of the most distinguished and sympathetic scholars of the federal idea has observed, 'federation in the normal sense of a particular kind of liberal democratic state that embraces and celebrates social diversity via constitutional entrenchment together with federal type arrangements in formally non-federal states are likely to be the most successful institutional responses to nationality claims for recognition in multinational democracies' (Burgess 2006, p. 129). But such arguments also have a circular or tautological quality, in asserting that the polities most likely to respond successfully to nationality claims are those which are predisposed to respond successfully to diversity.

On the whole, the experience of the multinational united kingdoms of earlier generations provides grounds for further caution. Federalism was consistently aired in both the United Kingdom and Austria-Hungary at the beginning of the 20th century; but, though impressive political ingenuity was displayed in some of the arrangements instituted in, in particular, the Dual Monarchy, on the whole the challenges to effective federalization in both polities proved decisive (see e.g. Okey 2001, pp. 399–400). There was a sense in which federalism was an expression of weakness, and was treated as such. In the end, Norwegians were not interested in any federalizing turn: neither were Hungarians and the Irish. Nor, at the beginning of the 21st century, under the leadership of Alex Salmond and Nicola Sturgeon, were Scots nationalists.

ALTERNATIVE UNIONS: FEDERALISM 289

Figure 5.1 Theorist of union: Georg Jellinek (1851–1911), jurist. Photograph (Universitätsbibliothek Heidelberg).

Figure 5.2 Theorist of union: Oszkár Jászi (1875–1957), civil servant, minister, academic. Photograph (Calliope 777).

ALTERNATIVE UNIONS: FEDERALISM 291

Figure 5.3 Theorist of union: A. V. Dicey (1835–1922), jurist. Photograph (Harvard Law School Library Collections).

Figure 5.4 Theorist of union: F.S. Oliver (1864–1934), businessman, historian, and ideologue. Photograph (private possession).

ALTERNATIVE UNIONS: FEDERALISM 293

Figure 5.5 Theorist of union: R. W. Seton-Watson (1879–1951), scholar, civil servant, and activist ('author of "the Nationality Question and Hungary" [sic], sincere friend of the Slovak nation'). Postcard (private possession).

6
Centrifuge
Why Do Unions Fail?

6.1. Defining Failure

The variegated failure of unions has long been a feature of the political landscape of modern Europe, and of course continues to be pertinent to the United Kingdom in the era of Scottish independence and of Brexit. Yet, despite this ongoing contemporary relevance, and despite the work which has been undertaken on the demise of federations, wide-ranging investigation and reflection on the death of Europe's various united kingdoms remain disappointingly attenuated.

There are, however, many different navigational aids available for any discussion of failed unions (though, at the same time, there is only space to highlight a few of these in what follows). Lawyers, economists, political scientists, and some adventurous historians have extensively addressed an important array of cognate questions which have at least a bearing on the central themes of this volume. Scholarship of this kind raises a range of issues, but not least (so far as this study is concerned) the nature of failure, its categorization, and agency. Its focuses range from the wider demise of states and nations, through the collapse of specific types of state, including federations, to the lessons to be learned from the decline and fall of particular polities.

In terms of the first of these categories, this very diverse literature includes work such as Leopold Kohr's *The Breakdown of Nations* (1957; new edition 2001), Noam Chomsky's *Failed States* (2006), Daron Acemoglu and James Robinson's *Why Nations Fail* (2012), as well as Norman Davies's lyrical and perceptive spatial and temporal tour across his *Vanished Kingdoms* (2011). For Kohr (1909–94) and Chomsky (b. 1928), as well as those other commentators with sympathies on the left, state failure (and in particular the failure of big states) has often been essentially a moral category. Kohr, who is of particular relevance to this study, was born a subject of one vulnerable union, the Habsburg monarchy, and died as a subject of another, the United Kingdom: he lived through the fall of the Dual Monarchy and the subsequent rise of fascism and of the third Reich, moved to Wales in later life and embraced Welsh nationalism and Plaid Cymru, as well as the threatened disaggregation of the United Kingdom state. Kohr famously dismissed the notion that great union states were agencies of stability and peace, espousing instead the conviction that such polities 'failed' because they produced a host of social and political problems which small and weak states did not generate. Small states, in this calculus, were associated with greater virtue and greater happiness: small, in short, was 'beautiful'.

For Chomsky, on the other hand, writing during the 'war against terror', states which did not protect their citizens from violence and destruction, and which came to regard themselves as beyond the regulation of law, whether domestic or international, had *ipso facto* failed. In a general sense, and at the risk of censoriousness, what might be described as the moral condition of union polities, their origins and purpose, are focuses for reflection here, especially in the following section of the chapter, and indeed throughout the present study.

Other perspectives have emphasized either representative and libertarian values, or the importance of environment. Thus, for Acemoglu and Robinson, nations 'succeed' or fail as measured by their levels of economic growth and prosperity, and much of the driving force for success (in their schema) hinges upon the extent to which a nation embraces at least ostensibly representative institutions. In contrast, Jared Diamond's work has, over many years, laid great emphasis upon geography and environment in determining the relative longevity and prosperity (and 'success') of different polities and civilizations (though he has also highlighted the cultures of compromise within 'successful' societies, an observation which is particularly relevant to some of the ostensibly 'failed' unions under scrutiny here). There is thus a tension within the literature between work which pinpoints (inclusive) institutional and related economic explanations and that which favours environmental arguments for national success and failure—a tension which is sometimes reconciled through chronology: environmental circumstances have been seen as critical to the medieval and early modern periods, while inclusive institutions and their beneficent consequences have been seen as key agencies for success in the modern era (Acemoglu and Robinson 2012, pp. 51–4). The importance of representative institutions (parliament) and a range of economic circumstances (in terms of the various case studies here) have also been acknowledged at length within several earlier sections of this book (see sections 4.7–4.10).

Even more pertinent than the generic literature on failed states, however, is that which engages with secession, and specifically with the issue of failed federal unions, or federal states (Lehning 1998; see also Buchanan 1997; Hicks 1978). Given the consanguinity—the *Familienähnlichkeit*—of federal unions and the varieties of multinational 'united' kingdom under discussion within this study, the potential relevance and contribution of this work are considerable. One of the critical themes of this literature is the issue of symmetry in federal unions, which has traditionally been seen as a bolster of union ('federalism...is more likely to thrive in societies where regionally based societal differences are not extreme': Brian Galligan quoted in Burgess 2006, p. 225). Key scholars such as Charles Tarlton have stressed the correlation between high levels of symmetry and the survival of federation, although it is true that more recent literature has softened this emphasis somewhat; still, questions of symmetry are applied to the particular case studies of this work in the next section (Tarlton 1965; Franck 1968; Burgess 2006, p. 224). The influential scholarship of Thomas Franck has identified a shared commitment to the primary goals of federation as a key to success (and, by extension, he has suggested that its absence is a predictor of failure); and while, again, there is a hint of circularity in this and some cognate arguments (federations are successful when they succeed), they also, more fundamentally, chime with Ozskar Jászi's preoccupations with issues of civic education and unity in the Dual Monarchy (Franck 1968; Jászi 1929).

Also critically relevant to the condition of the mix of unions considered within this study is the broad consensus among federal scholars that 'probably the most common threat to federal values during the past century has been the insidious centralisation of federal government in virtually all public sectors in the federation' (see Burgess 2006, p. 282). Again, the energy and dynamism of union government have been identified as issues affecting the stability of the polities reviewed here: on the whole, when the expansion of the union has upset its previously accepted condition and balance, then push-back and weakening have ensued. But, above all, this is a literature which insists that failure with federal unions is a relative rather than an absolute condition; and even that failure, defined in terms of secession from federal union, is an oxymoron, in so far as secession, though desirable in certain circumstances, is theoretically inconsistent with the very concept of federation (Freeman 1893; Franck 1968; Burgess 2006, p. 270).

Thus if different scholars have posited rival explanations both as to 'why nations fail' and 'why federations fail', and have debated the circumstances under which break-ups are morally defensible, then, equally, there are also many forms and conditions of 'failure' itself. Norman Davies in particular has focused upon the different types of state 'death' or—as he prefers it 'dissolution', moving away from the traditional binaries (external and internal, voluntary and involuntary dissolutions) towards a somewhat more elaborate taxonomy: implosion, conquest, merger, (voluntary) liquidation, and 'infant mortality' (Davies 2011, p. 732). Thus, in terms of his chosen 'vanished kingdoms', Galicia, as part of Austria-Hungary, alongside the USSR, and the Yugoslav Federation all 'imploded', while Tolosa, Burgundy, the Byzantine empire, Poland-Lithuania, and Prussia were all finally destroyed through conquest. Ill-fated 'infants' include, in his taxonomy, the Napoleonic kingdom of Etruria and Kerensky's short-lived Russian republic of 1917 (Davies 2011, p. 738). More directly relevant to the present study is his observation that, since many states, and particularly dynastic states, are formed through the amalgamation, or merger, of pre-existing units, the likelihood of 'demerger' or 'of a collection breaking up into its original units' can therefore be considerable (Davies 2011, p. 737). Indeed Davies's pessimism regarding the future of that hardy dynastic amalgam, the United Kingdom of Great Britain and Northern Ireland, has been consistently enunciated from the 1990s onwards.

One can readily accept the general point—that Europe's 'united kingdoms' have been by their very composite nature vulnerable to dissolution or other forms of 'death'—without getting too entangled in the exegetical complexities of whether a de-merger is voluntary or involuntary (and—if the latter—whether 'involuntary de-merger' is really, for all practical purposes, tantamount to conquest and liquidation). Union states, especially the multinational united kingdoms which are the focus of this study, are inherently fissiparous and it is in fact (at least superficially) surprising that so many of them have defied political gravity for so long. This observation underpinned an earlier precursor to this volume, and its search for an understanding of the longevity of the two unions, the Scottish and Irish; and it has similarly underpinned the discussion in Chapter 4 (Jackson 2013; see also Cole and Unowsky 2007, p. 2).

Ultimately every single one of the united kingdoms discussed in this book 'failed' in some obvious and fundamental way; and, accordingly, it is the purpose of this penultimate chapter to suggest a pathology of 'dissolution' by identifying and briefly reviewing a range of relevant agencies and vectors. In terms of those union polities which are cited across the volume, but which do not form detailed case studies, the 'infant' United Kingdom of Portugal, Brazil, and the Algarves came to an end in 1822, felled by revolution and chauvinism in Portugal. Similarly, nearly a century later, in 1917, the somewhat more venerable Grand Duchy of Finland ended in the context of aggressive nationalistic interventions by Russia, followed by the latter's collapse into revolution.

Turning to the book's main case studies, the 'first' United Kingdom went into a form of partial and semi-voluntary liquidation with the agreed secession of the 26 counties of the Irish Free State in December 1921, after a protracted guerrilla war wherein neither side was able to achieve both absolute military *and* political ascendancy. The United Kingdoms of Sweden-Norway agreed (rather more peacefully) a voluntary liquidation and disaggregation through negotiation and plebiscite in 1905. The United Canadas agreed a liquidation and merger through the separation of Quebec and Ontario and their incorporation into the new federal dominion of Canada in 1867. The United Kingdom of the Netherlands imploded in 1830, though—given its relatively brief existence—there is also a case for seeing it is as an example of 'infant mortality'.

Lastly (in terms of the case studies), there is the Dual Monarchy, which (in the context of a dramatically strengthening external military crisis) effectively collapsed in the autumn of 1918. In Oszkár Jászi's famous assessment, which provides some points of navigation for the chapter as a whole, the Monarchy was weakened because growing national consciousness could not ultimately be accommodated, because the 'feudal' class, allied with the 'usurious kind of capitalism', exerted an intense and negative influence, and because the empire lacked any effective and binding kind of 'civic education'. Final failure came because there was a loss of confidence in the possibility of reform, and because of the 'irredentistic' propaganda of surrounding nations (by which he meant the nationalist propaganda of those neighbours which had overlapping or shared ethnicities with the empire). Ultimately it was the Great War which precipitated the final breakdown.

However, it is also worth positing that, while there have been highly charged individual episodes (such as the emperor Karl's renunciation of his throne), the failure of unions was rarely a single conclusive event; and it might instead be seen as a zone of transition between ostensibly different but in fact interrelated forms of polity. The failure of the first version of the United Kingdom, as has been said, can reasonably be dated to the Anglo-Irish Treaty of December 1921. On the other hand, the 26 counties of the south of Ireland emerged with 'dominion home rule' inside the British empire, retaining the king as head of state; and many within British politics (and indeed some within Irish republicanism) saw this as a victory for imperial statesmanship, and as standing in a tradition which had delivered the Union of South Africa and Canadian confederation out of the apparently unpromising materials of Dutch and French alienation. Ireland inched towards full-blown republican freedom through its constitution of 1937, finally breaking with the commonwealth only in 1949. In the United Kingdom, as with other of the unions under review, the issue of 'failure' is blurred because of protracted periods of transition and manifold continuities between the *ancien régime* and its successor polities in the Irish Free State and Northern Ireland.

This was partly true elsewhere, and even for Austria-Hungary. As Pieter Judson has argued, 'the breakup of the [Habsburg] empire in October 1918...did not create a radical break with imperial institutions, practices or legal systems...several [successor] states discreetly retained imperial laws, imperial structures of rule, imperial judicial systems, and even the same personnel in positions of authority' (Judson 2016, pp. 387–8). Furthermore, it is now widely accepted that 'many of the states that replaced Austria-Hungary could more usefully be considered little empires, given the ways they administered their populations, legitimated themselves, and conceptualised cultural difference' (Judson 2016, p. 388). This was clearly the case with (for example) inter-war Czechoslovakia which inherited the tensions between Czech and German Bohemians, the latter of whom were now redesignated as 'Sudeten' Germans; but Czechoslovakia also included Slovaks, Hungarians, and Ukrainians as well as a small Polish minority. Similarly, Yugoslavia incorporated dominant Orthodox Serb and Catholic Croat populations, together with Albanians, Hungarians, Macedonians, Montenegrins, Slovenes, and a significant Muslim religious minority. All this could conceivably have been the case with an imagined and unpartitioned Ireland after independence in 1921, which (like the successor states in continental Europe) would have been in effect a multinational unitary state—with a politically dominant Catholic and Gaelic Irish elite, the *Staatsvolk*, and a restless Protestant, planter and British minority in the northeast. As it was, with the partitioning of the island, Northern Ireland emerged as a form of micro-empire, with its dominant Protestant and unionist *Staatsvolk*, and a significant and disadvantaged Catholic and Irish minority (cf. Jackson 1997; Zách 2021, pp. 55ff., 96ff., 235).

Thus the passage of union and empire in central Europe often chimed with that of union and empire in Ireland. In both there was a remarkable contrast between widespread institutional continuities and highly charged symbolic changes. For example, in Ireland, as in the Czech lands, the memorialization of national heroes—and thus the reconquest of physical space hitherto dominated by state or union iconography—had begun long before independence, with (taking Dublin alone) the erection of statues to the patriots William Smith O'Brien (1870), Daniel O'Connell (1882), and Charles Stewart Parnell (1911): this continued apace after independence, when the memorials of the *ancien régime* were now removed (again in central Dublin): William III (erected in 1701, demolished in 1929), George II (erected in 1756, toppled in 1937) and Queen Victoria (1904, 1947). Royal coats of arms disappeared, postboxes were painted green and no longer carried the royal insignia, while stamps and coins soon carried the Irish harp rather than the portrait of the British monarch.

Similarly, in the Czech and Slovak lands, the memorialization of dissent began well before the fall of the Habsburg regime: it will be recalled that Jan Hus, who was martyred in 1415 for his dissenting religious convictions, and who was a symbol of Bohemian patriotic defiance, was commemorated in 1915, the quincentenary of his execution, through a massive statue in Old Town Square, Prague (for the 1925 Czechoslovak commemoration of Hus see also Cynthia Pares in Bucur and Wingfield 2001, pp. 210–21). Equally, the nearby Marian column, erected in 1650, and generally interpreted as a symbol of Habsburg ascendancy, was speedily demolished in November 1918. Thereafter the Habsburg *Doppeladler* was removed from official buildings, while other memorials associated with Habsburg ascendancy and oppression were toppled: thus, in addition to the monuments discussed earlier, the statue (1897) of the Empress Maria Theresa in Bratislava/Pressburg, commemorating her coronation there in 1741, and combining a particularly provocative set of Habsburg and Magyar allusions, was toppled by members of the Czech Legion in October 1921 against the backdrop of the rumoured restoration of the former emperor, Karl, to the throne of Hungary (see e.g. Street 1924, p. 80; Wingfield in Bucur and Wingfield 2001, pp. 193–9). In both the emergent Czechoslovakia and in Ireland the imagery of the new order was already partly in place long before that order had assumed a constitutional shape; but independence brought a final physical repudiation of union and empire through the thorough-going 'nationalizing' of public space.

However, other continuities were even more marked beneath the surface of state symbolism. While conditions varied considerably within the former crownlands of the Habsburgs, many state-builders (for example in the new Czechoslovakia), like their counterparts in the Irish Free State, were fundamentally uninterested in social revolution; and each looked to the old imperial institutions to provide a sure start to their respective polities. In Ireland there was a cross-over between service in the British army and recruitment to the National Army of the Irish Free State; equally, the Dublin Metropolitan Police, one of the two constabularies of the *ancien régime*, remained in place for the first years of Irish independence. The Irish currency, though different in design from 1928 onwards, was tied to British sterling until 1979: there was no central bank in Ireland until 1943. Similarly, it has been observed that with Czechoslovakia 'studies of the Interior Ministry, of the police force, and the military all demonstrate that a high degree of continuity in personnel characterised those institutions in the transition from empire to republic' (Judson 2016, p. 435). To paraphrase the settled scholarly verdict on the successor states in central Europe, the Czech—and Irish—nationalists who had just carried out their own revolutions did not want to see their new order upset by further revolution (cf. Judson 2016, p. 435).

In short, just as the supposed bolsters of union states might eventually become agents of subversion, just as the centripetal might become the centrifugal, so their 'failure' was (and is) a fluid concept (see Chapter 4). The unions considered here were different, and they 'failed' in different ways. Sometimes the fact of their failure (as with the United Kingdom in 1921) and the extent of their failure (as with continuities and legacies) has either been obscure—or has been for long difficult to discern. And in some cases (such as the United Canadas) the negotiation of the 'failure' of union in fact reflected in large measure its successes and achievements. The ends of union speak therefore to their quality and usefulness; and indeed, however paradoxically, a peacefully negotiated ending may well be seen as a fulfilment of purpose.

In what follows the weakening of union states, and their various endings, are considered in the light of several groups of themes. The first of these relates to the relative size of the different partners in union, and draws on debates amongst scholars of federal polities. Other thematic groupings which are considered include the foundation narratives and imagining of union states, together with the role of unionists and unionism in simultaneously upholding as well as subverting union. The chapter continues with a reflection on the role of externality—of foreign affairs, diasporic, and irredenta communities—in determining the condition of union. Finally, some attention is given to the role of war, so important in terms of the original emergence of the union states which are central to this book. War, it will be suggested, and in particular the First World War, served not only as a solvent of empire—but also as a solvent of union.

6.2. Union Creation Myths and Visions

Many scholars have emphasized that constitutions are not merely sets of rules, but also an embodiment of a nation or society's values: as the leading constitutional historian, Vernon Bogdanor, has remarked, 'almost all codified constitutions are enacted to mark a new beginning' (Bogdanor 2009; Loughlin 2013). The perennial problem with the constitutions of many union states is that, given their often contingent and opportunistic origins, they have lacked an expression of moral aspiration. Here, again, however much the union states under examination may have marked a new beginning, this was rarely associated with a compelling set of wider ideals or their robust articulation. Unions, in short, have lacked 'the vision thing'.

Origins are of course invariably a problem with complex union polities. With both Scotland and Ireland, the birth of their respective unions has been lastingly associated with bribery, corruption, the dark arts of political management, and culpable human weakness. The wider envisioning of Britishness by (in particular) Scots from the early 16th century onwards sometimes helped to mitigate this otherwise bleak reckoning of union; but on the whole (even allowing for some robust historical contextualization) the dubious nativity of in particular the Irish union has never been an inspiration, even for its most robust defenders.

This deficit, strikingly, was also a feature of the other unions under discussion. Just as the Scots and Irish unions were pragmatic deals, calculated in the context of war and economic disruption, and pushed through with some ruthlessness and even cynicism, so too the creation of the United Kingdom of the Netherlands in 1814–15 occurred in the context of war, economic dislocation, and international power-play. The establishment of Great Britain in 1707 and of the United Kingdom in 1801 each made sense in terms of wider international threats to England and its continental European allies; similarly, the creation of the United Kingdom of the Netherlands in 1814–15 made strategic sense in terms of the *Weltpolitik* of the day—in so far as a strengthened polity of this kind would be more likely to contain any renascent French ambition. In other words, a United Kingdom of Great Britain and Ireland in 1801 suited English strategic needs no less than a United Kingdom of the Netherlands in 1814, or (to a lesser extent) the United Kingdoms of Sweden and Norway in 1814–15.

Moreover, the new Netherlands polity, like the British unions of 1707 and 1801, had a representative deficit from the beginning—as a result of what has been called 'a huge dent in the [new] constitution's legitimacy' (Wielenga 2015, p. 151). The new union constitution made provision for a bicameral national legislature, the States General, with lower and upper houses, the latter being appointed by King Willem. Southern representatives, however rejected the constitution, being resentful at the allocation of seats between north and south, the combining of the two national debts, and (in the case of southern Catholic conservatives) the formal religious equality which the Dutch had embraced since the days of the Batavian republic. The somewhat dubious tradition, also a Batavian inheritance, of counting as 'yes' votes those who had in fact abstained, meant that the constitution was passed regardless of the opposition; and this suspect *arithmétique hollandaise* also created great rancour amongst southerners.

All this is not to say, any more than for Scotland or Ireland, that there were no other imagined ancestries for the new polity—or that a contentious creation narrative necessarily foredoomed the Netherlands union to failure. The Dutch cultural scholar Joep Leerssen (while emphasizing that the literary commemoration of Willem I's United Kingdom presents opportunities for more research) has eloquently pointed out that there were subtle literary efforts to locate the United Kingdom in the medieval past of the low countries—primarily by Prudens van Duyse (1804–59) who in his work linked the Flemish victory over the French at Courtrai (the battle of the Golden Spurs) in 1302 with the shared victory of the new United Kingdom of the Netherlands over the French at Waterloo in 1815. Leerssen also wryly observes Walter Scott's 'hollandising' of the Belgian provinces of the new Netherlands, and in particular of Liège in his *Quentin Durward* of 1823 ('the *cité ardente* is travestied into an uncongenial and plain wrong Flemish-Dutch character') (Dunthorne and Wintle 2013, p. 116). However wrong-headed these legitimizing efforts, they were also episodic and slight; and they effectively underlined the fact that from the beginning the new state had to grapple with deep-seated issues of acceptance and credibility.

Such, too, was the case with Sweden and Norway. Swedes and Norwegians would later sometimes acknowledge, even celebrate, shared Nordic cultural and other legacies; but there was ultimately no disguising the inglorious and largely involuntary origins of the United Kingdoms in the global political reordering at the end of the Napoleonic world war. Neither could there be any disguising of the initial Norwegian push-back, through the creation and early actions of the Storting; nor could Swedish aggression and (theoretically) superior fire-power be forgotten either. In short, the United Kingdoms of Sweden-Norway were shaped, not through a shared and voluntary Scandinavian vision, but rather through continental geopolitics, British foreign policy, and Swedish territorial ambition.

Bleakness also characterized the origins of Austria-Hungary. If the House of Orange-Nassau had at least the great victory of Waterloo as a form of creation myth for the United Kingdom of the Netherlands, then no amount of pride, relief, and self-congratulation could disguise the fact that the redesign of the Habsburg empire through the Ausgleich of 1867 was precipitated by the emphatically inglorious circumstances of the defeat by Prussia at Königgrätz/Sadowa in July 1866. As with the United Kingdom of Britain and Ireland, and that of the Netherlands, Austria-Hungary was born not only in the context of military challenge, but also concomitant financial threats (Judson 2016, p. 220). However, this nativity was also in a sense apposite: the relaunched empire was founded on a pragmatism born out of necessity, and in this way it was sustained for a further 50 years (and indeed it might have survived even longer, but for the carnage of the Great War). In the same spirit of negotiation and contract, the unions of the United Kingdom supplied no uplifting vision—but they did at least offer a workable model of horse-trading and compromise which (on the whole) kept the enterprise afloat, if not always shipshape, for over two centuries.

The inglorious origins of other contemporary complex union polities, not included amongst the case studies, may also be briefly mentioned. The Grand Duchy of Finland was effectively created through the Russian conquest of 1808, and the Swedish cession of the territory in 1808–9. The United Kingdom of Portugal, Brazil, and the Algarves was formally announced in December 1815— but it was fundamentally rooted in the flight of the Portuguese royal family, the Braganzas, from Lisbon in November 1807 in the wake of French invasion. With the defeat of Napoleon in 1814–15, the family elected to stay in Brazil; and the formal declaration of union followed on from this decision (Schultz 2001, pp. 192–5; Barman 1999, pp. 2–3).

Complementing these contested and unlovely creation narratives, it is also the case that, in contrast to national movements, union states have tended to lack a coherent and accessible vision. Alternatively, and equally problematic, they have sought to cling to a mission statement which has not been fit for purpose.

With both Britain and Ireland and the Dual Monarchy the problem was, perhaps, not so much the comprehensive absence of 'the vision thing' as its problematic construction—and ultimate unravelling—in both states. The unions of the United Kingdom were clearly formulated in the context of economic and military challenge, and while they drew upon an older vision of Britain and Britishness, this relationship—between Britishness and union—was always uncomfortable. Moreover, famously (or notoriously), there was never any coherent United Kingdom identity, though defenders of the union did—eventually—put in place a set of arguments in its defence (this particularly in association with the conflicts over Irish legislative autonomy, conducted between 1885 and the attainment of Irish independence in 1921). But the problem remained that the United Kingdom was essentially a pragmatic construct, which ultimately did not map exactly onto the notion of a British national identity (or even onto a British dynastic identity).

A similar set of observations might be applied to the Austrian empire and the later Dual Monarchy. A unified Austria was framed in 1804, like the United Kingdom of 1801, in the context of the revolutionary wars; but its rulers, including the Emperor Francis, benefited from an older vision of empire and of the dynasty—from a tradition of regularization and centralization, pursued in particular by Joseph II. However, after 1815 the vision of 'empire as it should be' gradually subsided: 'state building from above was often about preserving what could be saved, and no longer about realising an ideal' (Judson 2016, p. 154).

Again, as with the United Kingdom in 1801, so with Austria-Hungary in 1867, the union state was formed in the context of military challenges (the Habsburg defeat at Königgrätz/Sadowa) and the concomitant financial difficulties. As with the United Kingdom, so a sense of official purpose developed in the aftermath of the creation of the Ausgleich: defence of the United Kingdom was associated in part with an imperial and 'civilizing' mission, and drew upon a Britishness which had originally looked north and (in particular) west, to Ireland, in its 'civilizing' impulse. Britishness was historically associated with Protestantism—a great difficulty given the enfolding of Catholic Ireland within the union after 1801. With Austria-Hungary, there was a modified inheritance from the Austrian empire, of the state as a bulwark of Catholic civilization against threats from the Protestant north and (in particular) the Muslim east and south. After 1867 liberals and others saw that the state might have a continuing mission to spread the benefits of (German) civilization to the east, denoted pejoratively by the journalist and essayist, Karl Franzos (1848–1904), as 'Halbasien', as well as to Bosnia in the south, occupied in 1878 and annexed 30 years later.

Both the United Kingdom and Austria-Hungary sought to promote the idea that a multinational polity could better promote security, economic progress, and 'civilization' in general than a supposedly introspective ethnic nationalism. Both the UK and the Dual Monarchy sought, too, through various mechanisms to contain nationalism within the structures of the union state, whether through piecemeal legislative concessions or more substantial structural reform (as with land reform in Ireland or the various national compromises—Moravian, Bukovinan, Galician—in the Dual Monarchy).

Indeed for some contemporaries, such as Josef Redlich, Austria-Hungary was—above all—a tremendous ideal (Cornwall 2002, p. 2). For Oszkár Jászi, it was a great experiment in 'social cohesion' (Jászi 1929, p. xiv). In an impassioned counterfactual polemic in his influential treatise, *The Dissolution of the Habsburg Monarchy* (1929), Jászi argued that,

> if the Habsburgs had been able really to unite those ten nations [of the empire] through a supranational consciousness into an entirely free and spontaneous cooperation, the empire of the Habsburgs would have surpassed the narrow limits of the nation state, and would have proved to the world that it is possible to replace the consciousness of national unity by a consciousness of state communal unity. It would have proved that the same problem which Switzerland and Belgium have solved on a smaller scale under particular historical conditions should not be regarded as a historical accident. (Jászi 1929, p. 3)

There were, however, serious flaws within these various, British and Habsburg, visions for union. Although each nominally promoted the idea of an equal set of national communities enfolded within the one state or empire, or embraced within the one dynastic loyalism (whether Habsburg or Hanoverian), each polity—as the next section of the chapter explores—was upheld by nationalities who were dominant by virtue of numbers or the ubiquity of their language, or the favoured status bestowed upon their religion. By the late 19th and early 20th centuries it was still not entirely clear whether these dominant nationalities saw their compatriots—in Ireland, or Bosnia, or Bukovina—as essentially equal or as irredeemably unequal; but it was certainly the case that interested nationalists did not have to look very hard to find evidence for the latter proposition. In Ireland, for example, the failure of British policies during the cataclysmic Great Famine (1845–51) raised lasting questions over the equity and fundamental purpose of the union state—questions which were never truly resolved during the lifetime of the union, and which indeed have long tainted the wider British-Irish relationship. In Austria-Hungary, there were sharp distinctions between the two halves of the empire, with a thorough-going effort to embrace the nationalities being pursued in Cisleithania, while magyarization proceeded apace in the east. In neither half could it be said, however, that Habsburg rule dealt equitably with all its subjects.

All this raises the suspicion that the union states of the 20th century were essentially antique and outmoded constitutional survivals. But were they? Austria-Hungary, certainly in the view of the Swedish political scientist, Rudolf Kjellén, was a coelacanth-like survival in modern constitutional waters; or, rather, 'like an animal form of the tertiary period amidst the animal kingdom of the present day, so the Great Power of Austria-Hungary was a remnant of a previous stage of evolution, of the territorial state of the middle ages' (often quoted: see Jászi 1929, p. 239). More recently, William Godsey has adapted this notion, arguing that Austria-Hungary even after the Ausgleich should still be viewed primarily as (in John Elliott's terms) a 'composite monarchy' (see e.g. Godsey 2004). In some ways, the United Kingdom may be seen in a similar light—partly as an early modern dynastic 'union of the crowns', partly a top-down parliamentary union. Perhaps, then, the essential difficulty with the United Kingdom has been its failure (despite devolution) to achieve a fundamental constitutional modernization— whether through an effective federalism or an otherwise effectively reformed union.

It has certainly been the case that in early modern composite monarchies the primary focuses of attachment and loyalty were to the monarchy and to the immediate locality, rather than to any imagined or idealized nation state. Moreover, there is an argument for seeing this legacy as continuing to resonate within the Habsburg empire and the United Kingdom. In this, and in other senses, these states have indeed strong roots in different forms of pre-modern polity. They continue to harbour strong traditions of non-national loyalty and identity—loyalty to city and region, and to the ruling dynasty—all of which take the place of a strong overarching 'union' nationalism; but they also exist alongside, and are buffeted by, national loyalties.

The picture is, perhaps, even more complicated than this. It is indeed clear that union states such as the United Kingdom and Austria-Hungary, as personal unions or composite monarchies, retained vestiges of a pre-modern political landscape. On the other hand, it has been tellingly (and ironically) observed that early 1914 Austria-Hungary was 'remarkably modern in many respects', and that it was only really after its dissolution that it turned out that the Monarchy had been anachronistic after all (Kozuchowski 2013, p. 177). It is also possible that such polities, offering a supranational umbrella over national components, looked ahead to—what might loosely be described as—post-modern political and economic configurations which transcend and counterbalance the nation state. Here, despite some superficial differences, Oszkár Jászi and more recent commentators on the Dual Monarchy, such as Pieter Judson, share some unacknowledged common ground—in so far as Jászi argued that Austria-Hungary offered lessons for future supranational unions and in so far, too, as the silent presence of the European Union pervades much of Judson's eloquent and forceful analysis (Leisse 2012; Judson 2016).

While accepting all this, it should also be acknowledged that a further paradox linking several of these supposedly pre-modern polities such as the United Kingdom and the Dual Monarchy was that they served as conduits for 'modernity' across their territories. In Ireland, for example, most people encountered modernity—defined whether in educational, economic, or technological terms—through the agency of the hated union state, and indeed Irish (and other) nationalisms came to equate modernity with imperial oppression. Similarly, in the Dual Monarchy, 'most experienced modernity as imperial in nature'—while it was also the case that, as in Ireland, 'many worried that modernity came at a very high price' (Judson 2016, pp. 356, 363; see also the discussion in Kozuchowski 2013, p. 177).

In short, these union polities retained vestiges of their origins as composite or personal unions, and sometimes struggled to reinvent themselves within the modern world of the nation state. On the other hand, where they survived, they sometimes acted as harbingers of a post-modern constitutional architecture in the form of supranational unions such as the United Nations or the European Union. The complexities of this relationship with modernity were further evident in the extent to which successive union states served as agents for modernity within their constituent nations. Paradoxically, therefore, pre-modern union polities could be, and were, rejected by national movements on account of their very modernity.

6.3. The Symmetry Problem in the Union State

The issue of symmetry, or rather asymmetry, is generally discussed in relation to federal unions rather than the different (though uniformly non-federal) 'united kingdoms' examined within this book. As has been said, while asymmetry (at least in the senses of difference and diversity) has become an object of celebration, an older generation of federal scholarship has tended to see a correlation between it and dissolution. Expressing this another way, the presence of one predominant partner may create a set of imbalances within the governance, culture, and economy of the related union polity which ultimately contribute to its instability and failure.

However, there can be no fixed or simple connection between asymmetry and instability, and it is obviously, and famously, the case that carefully constructed federal unions, such as the United States, have successfully functioned while containing a spectrum of very different constituent polities—from California, Texas, and Florida at one end of the scale of demographic magnitude to (at the other end) Alaska, Vermont, and Wyoming. Moreover, the issue of asymmetry raises many subsidiary questions—and not least a 'chicken and egg' issue. In a union state like Great Britain and Ireland, one potential source of instability has been the imbalance between England, which with Wales (in the census of 1901) comprised 32 million people, and Scotland (comprising 4.47 millions) and Ireland (3.23 millions). On the other hand, this imbalance was not so much created by the union state as recalibrated within it: the economic and military predominance of England over its neighbours had been both a long-standing feature of the Atlantic archipelago as well as a precondition of union. Indeed, England's military conquests in Ireland, Scotland, and Wales, its economic ascendancy, and movement of population in the medieval period and after invite (as has been noted) the deployment of notions of an archipelagic English empire.

The problem with Britain and Ireland was that, after union, the predominance of England served both as a potentially integrating as well as a destabilizing element within the union state. In a sense England and the English served as the *Staatsvolk* of the United Kingdom in the same way as German Austrians saw themselves for a time as the *Staatsvolk* of the Habsburg empire—allegedly requiring each of them to 'pursue the interests of the whole state against the interests of any particular region or nation within the empire, including their own' (Judson 2016, p. 298). At best there were clear material benefits from the dominance of England and its (in the 18th and 19th centuries) buoyant economy: English wealth helped to improve the economic condition of the constituent elements of the state through the access to capital and markets that union offered to the Scots and later the Irish. Moreover, again at its best, the fiscal regime within the union state was ultimately shaped in ways which provided a uniform system of taxation and benefits—that is to say shaped in order to create (at least in theory) a redistributive mechanism throughout the union, from its richer components to its poorer. Indeed, the key formula for public service funding—supplied in 1888, as will be recalled, by the chancellor, George Goschen—ultimately came to function effectively as a means of subsidizing the Scots (though its short-term impact upon Ireland was, arguably, much less beneficial).

But there were of course counterbalancing disadvantages. England and English interests overwhelmingly dominated the parliament and government of union, to the continuing irritation of the Irish and Scots (see e.g. Waddie 1891). English dominance within the union state—whatever its possible material and other benefits—was also associated with an array of continuing national jealousies and sensitivities (very pale but recognizable variants of those prevailing in the Dual Monarchy) which ultimately fed into the dissolution of the first United Kingdom (in 1921). The English political elite was itself sensitive to disproportionate Scottish influence within the politics of the union—whether at the time of Lord Bute (in 1762) or, latterly, with the premiership and government of Gordon Brown (and to some extent even that of Tony Blair). The Scots, for their part, were—in the second half of the 19th century—sensitive to the amount of parliamentary time and legislative effort invested in addressing the many social and economic problems prevailing in Ireland (problems which existed, though unnoticed, in Scotland as well). For the Irish, in turn, the economic dividends of union were regionally and sectorally limited—confined in large part to the industrially thriving north-east of the island as well as to sections of the agrarian economy. In general patriotic Irish commentators (both nationalist as well as unionist) believed that the economic management of Ireland under the union was deeply flawed—and indeed unionists and nationalists combined at the end of the 19th century to urge a more generous fiscal relationship, arguing that Ireland had been for long overtaxed (Jackson 1989, pp. 152–3; Murray 1903, pp. 394ff.). Thus, in a union state such as Britain and Ireland economic realities were inflected through complex past histories—sometimes ancient histories—of subjugation and grievance; and these realities were also conditioned by entrenched national rivalries and jealousies concerning the equitable functioning of the union. In these circumstances, it was perfectly possible for national resentment to thrive despite—indeed because of—relatively strong economic data (see also section 4.9).

Moreover, English dominance within the—highly centralized—union state has been identified as a particular brake upon constructive constitutional reform. Writing in 1997, before Tony Blair's election victory and the onset of the extensive devolution programme, John Kendle argued strongly concerning the veto which England, as the overwhelmingly dominant nation within Britain and the United Kingdom, has historically imposed upon the constitutional reform of the union state: 'the British lack a tradition of open-ended public discussion of constitutional variables and as long as that is married to an overwhelming lack of interest in constitutional change in England, the largest of the UK nations, the federal idea will not receive the serious consideration it deserves' (Kendle 1997, p. 169). Kendle has also argued (strikingly) that the concentration of English power in London and its immediate area, the relative lack of any administratively strong or well-defined English regional units, the subjugation of the Irish, the incorporation of Wales into the English state, and the emasculation of the Scots political identity after the Act of Union of 1707 all reaffirmed the nature of state power in the British Isles, resting as it did on the highly centralised English state in existence since the thirteenth century.

(Kendle 1997, pp. 170–1)

This is a starkly rendered argument, which was (however) partly overtaken by the extensive devolution settlement inaugurated by Tony Blair's New Labour government in 1997–8; but it does emphasize well some continuing realities of the distribution of power in the United Kingdom, as well as (rightly) hinting at a centralizing or unitary mindset—which may in fact have not only survived devolution but be thriving still at Westminster and Whitehall.

The issue of the predominance of any one partner in union is also associated with what has variously been described as 'reverse asymmetry' or, alternatively (and in Wildean terms), the 'tyranny of the weak' (Wilde 1894, act 3). Here again this is an issue of imbalance within a union polity which could serve in both an integrative as well as a disintegrative manner. A smaller nation, such as Ireland or Scotland, could (through rigorously coherent organization and sustained pressure) exercise a relatively stronger influence over the politics of the union state than the disparate and unfocused political forces of larger component nations. This was, for example, clearly the case with the Irish land and home rule movements in the late 19th century, when (under the leadership of Charles Stewart Parnell) a highly disciplined and focused Irish parliamentary party helped to achieve a variety of legislative reforms which placed Irish tenant farmers in a much stronger legal position than their equivalents in most of Scotland, England, and Wales (despite, in particular, the bitter histories of eviction, dispossession, and enforced migration which characterized both highland and lowland Scotland) (Devine 2018). This pressure also, of course, delivered the real prospect of home rule, or legislative independence, for Ireland, with the conversion of Gladstone and the bulk of the British Liberal party to the cause in 1885–6. Similarly, at the end of the 20th century and the beginning of the 21st, the coherent and effective pressure of Scottish nationalists at Westminster and in the devolved parliament at Holyrood has delivered a range of legislative benefits—and a level of central government spend—not enjoyed within much of the rest of the union state.

However, it is clear that 'reverse asymmetry'—or 'the tyranny of the weak'—has served, no less than the predominance of any one national component, to undermine united kingdoms. This subversion may work in one of several ways: effective national pressure by one component polity may encourage parallel pressures in another part of the relevant union state (as Irish pressure stimulated

Scots resentments in the 19th-century United Kingdom). However, in all these cases the 'tyranny of the weak' within a union state has depended upon the willingness of the predominant partner in the union to show pliability and responsiveness. This in turn has hinged upon this partner's willingness to make sacrifices in the interests of preserving the wider union state. Thus, successive British governments were (eventually) prepared to amend the union settlement of 1801 in order to accommodate Irish national resentments; in particular they were willing to apply the financial resources of the United Kingdom state to subsidize the Irish farming interest, using the credit of the state to fund sweeping measures of tenant-led land purchase from 1885 onwards. In Scotland at the beginning of the 21st century successive British governments have—for a time—been willing to revisit and expand the definition of devolution in order to accommodate the demands of Scottish nationalists, and to preserve the structures of union.

In the end, however, there are at least three clear senses in which all this may be ultimately destructive of the union state. First, legislating in response to nationalist pressure may be in part a means of correcting deep-seated historic grievances and profound injustices; but by the same token this legislation may (as in the Irish and recent Scots cases) involve enhancing national exceptionalism and undermining some of the integrative agencies and institutions of the union state. Second, legislating in response to militant pressure from within the component nations may (as in the wider history of British government in Ireland) give rise to at least the suspicion that militancy is required in order for the voices of the 'small' nations to resonate at the heart of the union state (see Steed 1919, p. 125). It often took the threat of militant subversion for Irish voices to be heard during the course of the union, as with Catholic emancipation, Church disestablishment, and land reform: indeed the unionist minority in Ireland adapted the logic of this history in an extreme way in 1912–14 in organizing the cogent threat of paramilitary resistance to the third home rule bill. Third, in the end the 'tyranny of the weak' or 'reverse asymmetry' may provoke the tyranny of the powerful, or otherwise reinforce the regular asymmetries of a union state. Excessive pressure from the smaller nations of union may finally call into question the fundamental utility, desirability, and legitimacy of the union state itself—and particularly within the predominant partner. By 1905 (indeed long before) many influential Swedish unionists were weary of their high-maintenance union with Norway, and this fed into the dissolution of that year. There was some evidence in early 20th-century Britain of an English exhaustion with the Irish union; and, equally, there is some evidence at the beginning of the 21st century, of English exhaustion with the Scots and Northern Irish (Henderson and Wyn Jones 2021). It has at least been clear that, by the second decade of the 21st century, the historic defenders of the unions of the United Kingdom, the Conservatives, were often more driven by their desire for authority in London and England, and their antipathy towards Brussels, than by any affection for Edinburgh, still less Belfast.

6.4. *Kulturpessimismus:* Unionist Identities and Organizations

Union polities failed not only because they lacked an agreed narrative or vision, but because they either lacked a culture of union, or (alternatively) were associated with cultures which had lost a sense of purpose or direction. In other words unionist cultures, or—more specifically—unionist *Kulturpessimismus*—played a role in the dissolution of the union polities under review. Through adapting this notion of cultural pessimism, it is also possible to highlight connections between (on the one hand) wider conservative and other concerns at the advance of mass democracy, capitalism, and the *Industriestaat,* and (on the other hand) specific unionist concerns about, and disengagement from, the direction of travel of the multinational union state.

In both the United Kingdom of Great Britain and Ireland and the Habsburg empire there were some clear, enduring, and damaging cultural difficulties—starting even with contentions surrounding the very name and characterization of the state: these are intrinsic to any discussion of the limits of unionist confidence in union (Okey 2001, pp. 3, 193; Kumar 2003, p. 3). It is sometimes suggested that 'England' and 'English' have more emotional purchase than 'Britain' and 'British'—which in turn have more traction than the ostensibly more insipid 'United Kingdom' or 'UKer': 'one can love or hate England', F. S. Oliver once remarked, 'but not so easily Britain' (Oliver 1930–5, vol. 1, p. 42). England, as by far the dominant nation in 'these islands', has frequently lent its name to the archipelago as a whole; and it is well known that institutions and agencies properly described as 'British' have commonly been annexed as 'English'.

However, even 'Britain' and 'British' did not fully do justice to the complexity of the United Kingdom state with which they were conceptually associated. This is partly because of the close association between England (as the dominant component of the union state) and Britishness: as has been recently argued, 'it is more appropriate to view British nationalism as an extension of rather than a negation of English nationalism' (Henderson and Wyn Jones 2021, pp. 206–7). Aside from this, the 'Great Britain' formally established through the union of 1707 did not include Ireland, and even today (though it is casually and generally applied) 'Britain' does not cover Northern Ireland—an issue which routinely raises its head at sporting events, where Northern Irish or Irish contestants may still find themselves enfolded within a 'British' team. Tom Nairn has famously and teasingly proposed 'Ukania' as a short-hand for the 'United Kingdom of Great Britain and Northern Ireland', echoing the 'Kakania' of Robert Musil's *The Man Without Qualities* (1930–42)—and itself derived from the laborious 'kah und kah' formulations—*kaiserlich und königlich,* imperial and royal—of the Austro-Hungarian empire (Nairn 1990; Kumar 2003, p. 3). In both Austrian and British cases, as Kumar rightly argues, any discussion of this kind 'is of course more than simply about names. It reveals a history and a culture resonant with ambiguities and conflicts. It is a language of power and prejudice as much as it is a reflection of constitutional proprieties' (Kumar 2003, p. 3).

The same challenges prevailed in the new Dual Monarchy created through the Ausgleich of 1867. Here, even more than in Britain and Ireland, there were great difficulties both of nomenclature and iconography. The new polity of 1867 was of course a lineal descendant of the Austrian empire: but was the recommissioned Austria-Hungary *ein Kaiserreich* as had been unambiguously the case before the Ausgleich—and as had been accepted by the Hungarian leaders, Deák and Andrássy, at the time of the compromise (Steed 1919, p. 52)? Many German Austrians continued to see the state in these terms, while the Hungarians—highly sensitive to any suggestion of subjugation or Austrian dominance—ultimately demurred: with the ongoing consolidation of Magyar national sentiment in the later 19th century, many Hungarians objected even to the adjective 'Austro-Hungarian', preferring instead Austrian *and* Hungarian (Steed 1919, p. 52; Haslinger 1996, p. 5). In fact the institutions of the state only slowly adapted to the new circumstances of the 'duality' established in 1867: the imperial army became at last *kaiserlich und königlich* in 1889, while the shared ministries of foreign affairs, finance, and war only belatedly shed their imperial identities to become professedly '*k und k*' in 1895, 1903, and (again) 1903 respectively. The coat of arms of the Dual Monarchy continued to represent the kingdom of Hungary in a subordinate position until as late as 1915, when a new armorial device belatedly placed Austria and Hungary on an appropriately equal footing. Similarly, the issues of national flag and anthem created running difficulties throughout the existence of the Dual Monarchy (see e.g. Godsey 1999, pp. 145–6). In short, in the Dual Monarchy, as in the United Kingdom, many of the central institutions and cultures were painfully slow in adjusting to any sense of mutuality or partnership—painfully slow, in other words, in adjusting to the full implications of union.

In the United Kingdom the constituent nations were ostensibly bound together by (amongst other agencies) a British national sentiment which had developed from the 18th century onwards, and which acquired a potent imperial dimension in the 19th century. In Austria-Hungary the equivalent was a surprisingly robust dynastic patriotism. However, each of these supposedly unifying faiths had marked weaknesses; and in the case of the Habsburg empire it was clear that the entire educational system of the Cisleithanian and Hungarian polities was (beyond its dynastic loyalties to the Habsburgs) emphatically not concerned with the creation of any unifying state allegiance. Indeed, for Oszkár Jászi, one of the fundamental failures of the Habsburg monarchy lay with the undeveloped nature of civic education:

> we must seek the means and methods of such a civic education not only in the system of public teaching...in the collaboration of religious forces, in the

intellectual and moral training of the army, in the ideology of press literature and science influenced by the state, and in the social directives which the imperial court and the upper classes connected within it gave to the bourgeois society so appreciative of their favours... (Jászi 1929, p. 24)

Equally, 'the strangeness of the people to each other was the cause of the downfall of the old Austria, and our school system did nothing to prevent it' (Jászi 1929, p. 438).

For Jászi, and indeed for Wickham Steed too, 'the whole public instruction in Austria was permeated by the old dynastic and patrimonial conception of the state': 'the Austrian system was entirely incapable of establishing any kind of a popular state consciousness whereas the Hungarian civic education was overdoing Magyar national consciousness' (Jászi 1929, pp. 435, 447). Ultimately the dynastic patriotism of the Habsburg state proved to be 'powerless against the popular enthusiasm of the exuberant national individualities' (Jászi 1929, p. 449). There were clear contrasts between the Austrian/Cisleithanian school regime, where children had a constitutional guarantee that they would be taught in their own language, and the situation in Hungary which 'was the first European state to introduce a comprehensive civics curriculum, thanks to its distinctive conceptualisation of Hungarian nationhood'—and where the promotion of the Hungarian language was relentless (Judson 2016, pp. 303–4). Indeed, in 1907 radical nationalist parties in the Hungarian parliament enacted the Lex Apponyi which demanded that in the first four school years teaching be delivered exclusively in Hungarian (Judson 2016, pp. 304–5).

More widely, in both Ireland and the Habsburg empire attempts to unify through a binding liberal metropolitan culture ultimately failed: in Cisleithania any idea of a wider Austrianism ultimately 'lacked the energising power to override the [national] traditions of centuries'. The distinguished Welsh-born historian of Habsburg central Europe, Robin Okey, has sharply observed that 'liberal state traditions can work to counteract ethnic diversity, as was shown by 19th century Britain, France and Canada, if in less taxing circumstances, and with the Irish exception': but in this, and in other regards, the Habsburgs' 'aversion to new European [liberal] impulses was a strategic mistake' (Okey 2001, p. 127). Indeed, Okey has laid emphasis on the *Vormärz* period (before March 1848) as an era of missed opportunities in these respects for the Habsburg empire, arguing that the 'long decades of ostrich-like government inactivity after 1815' proved disastrous for its future potential. Okey stresses, in particular, that 'the folly of the state coup against Kremsier [parliament] and its constitutional settlement can hardly be over-stated' (Okey 2001, p. 156).

Similarly, for Christopher and Hugh Seton-Watson, reflecting on the life and writing of their father, Robert, there were recurrent missed opportunities to secure greater unity within at least part of the Habsburg empire. However, they ultimately focus on an era long before the *Vormärz*:

during three hundred years of common rule the people of the Austrian lands and Bohemia might perhaps with different policies by their rulers have been formed into a single nation with a single national consciousness but two languages. The history of France, Castile or Switzerland suggests various possibilities. However, the Habsburgs in the 16th and 17th centuries were concerned with wider problems than those of their home provinces. It was their task to uphold the true faith against the two threats of the infidel and heretic.

(Seton-Watson 1981, p. 23)

In fact, as has been discussed, no real attempt was made to unify the provinces into a centralized state until the reign of Joseph II, by which time it was too late, certainly for the successful forging of any widely assimilationist Austrian identity. On the whole, then, Jászi's insights (if not the strength of his emphasis) have been accepted by some later scholars (even where his wider conceptualization of a counterpoint between state and nations has been questioned): 'the late Empire was characterised by a remote, top-down, structure of power': there was 'precious little identification, trust or loyalty between the government and those governed... in such circumstances loyalty to another abstraction such as the nation could flourish as a counterweight to an alien all-inspiring state apparatus' (Beller 1996, p. 191).

As will shortly be discussed, this lack of a 'spiritual' underpinning to union ultimately counted, when (as with the pressures of war) the integrity of the union state and its purpose were seriously called into question: 'during the [Great] war the Austro-Hungarian authorities lost the battle for hearts and minds to those who believed in new state structures and new forms of government' (Cornwall 2000, p. 443; see section 6.7). Some scholars are disposed to question the overall part played by nationalist and other enemy propaganda in the ultimate collapse of the Habsburg empire, but even they accept that Austria-Hungary's resilience to propaganda was limited, and that this played a role, albeit 'a small role', in the end-game of empire (Cornwall 2000, p. 443).

In the same way, there was no robust unionist identity which bound together Norway and Sweden during the period of the United Kingdoms. The Scandinavianist movement (c.1840–64) for a period offered some possibilities, though it should be emphasized that its embrace was of course not confined to the nations of the United Kingdoms, but instead extended to Denmark and (even) Finland. Scandinavianism generally implied a belief in a shared ethnic descent, a shared linguistic tradition, and shared cultural values: it was driven forward by the students of the great Danish, Swedish, and—from 1844—Norwegian universities, and joint meetings (together with feasts in celebration of Nordic forebears) were held in the participating institutions, including Christiania in 1851, 1852, and 1869 (Jorgenson 1935, esp. pp. 67–118; Barton 1970; Barton 2003, p. 98). To some extent it originally embodied an assertion of Danish cultural pre-eminence in the midst of its political losses: to some extent, too, it reflected new Norwegian cultural institutions (Jorgenson 1935, p. 74). It was romantic and visionary; and it also embodied a practical response to the fear of Russian aggression (as evidenced, for example, by the suppression of the Polish insurgency of 1830) as well as, increasingly, German consolidation (Jorgenson 1935, p. 77).

But, while Scandinavianism encouraged the exploration of some of the ties binding Norway and Sweden (and Denmark), it was not the equivalent of a confident unionism. There was, it is true, something approaching a unionist inflection with a few Norwegian Scandinavianists: for example, the scholar and journalist Ludvig Kristensen Daa (1809–77) produced a Swedish-Norwegian dictionary in 1841 in which he argued that the time of the small state had now passed, and that the possibility of a union of Great Scandinavia, like that of Great Britain, offered small nations the necessary conditions and tools for further national development (Jorgenson 1935, p. 151). Indeed Daa argued that in contemporary Ireland the O'Connellite movement had gained traction and recognition precisely through the deployment of English (Daa 1841, p. vii). However, many other patriotic intellectuals like Peter Andreas Munch (1810–63 and uncle of the painter), Ivar Aasen (1813–96), and Bjørnstjerne Bjørnson (1832–1910), while similarly defining themselves as Norwegians and Scandinavians, and though fired (in the case of Munch) by the Prussian threat to Denmark in 1848, held much more ambivalent feelings about the union. Their views predominated; and in the round they have been seen as stimulating ('beyond calculation') liberal and national feeling, and (indirectly) the creation of the liberal nationalist, Venstre, party. In other words their Scandinavianism was limited and self-defeating, in so far as (despite airy aspirations) it worked against the union between Norway and Sweden, and thus effectively against any ultimate unity with Denmark (Jorgenson 1935, p. 144).

The heyday of political Scandinavianism ended with failure of the United Kingdoms to supply military aid to the beleaguered Danes during the second Schleswig war of 1864. But there was a lasting cultural afterglow from the glory days; and this, while it did not always generate unionist conviction, did tend towards a softening of some of the asperities in the relationship between Norway and Sweden. At the very least Scandinavianism provided an important counterbalance to the exceptionalist impulses of the most radical Norwegian nationalists, and in this way sustained a sense of Scandinavian commonality—even if this did not equate with union.

The United Kingdom of Great Britain and Ireland was somewhat different in so far as there were relatively more deep-seated cultures of union than in the continental European united kingdoms and unions which have been anatomized through this study. The unions of the United Kingdom were still pragmatic and contingent and imperfect creations like those in the Netherlands and Scandinavia; and indeed—just as later Habsburg loyalists sought, poignantly, to identify a mythical ideal moment for union in the distant past of the monarchy, so 20th-century British unionists were sometimes impelled to search for ancient lost opportunities for a more perfect British union. Thus, Richard Lodge of Edinburgh University wistfully suggested in 1907 that 'there will always be a lingering regret that the union was not accomplished rather earlier—either in the time of Edward I, when it might have resulted in a complete fusion, or in the time of Henry VIII, before the great divergence on ecclesiastical matters had begun' (in Hume Brown (1907), pp. 172–3).

On the other hand, the British union certainly drew upon much older intellectual traditions of reflection on the possibilities of union, and by the end of the 19th century they had generated popular movements of support, especially in Ireland and Scotland. The consolidation of a popular Irish nationalism in effect stimulated an equal and opposite unionist reaction both in Ireland and elsewhere in the United Kingdom: the home rule bills of 1886, 1893, and 1912 generated an efflorescence of popular unionist expression, whether in terms of formal politics, material culture, leisure, and recreation. Unionism and the union became enshrined within the British party system after 1885–6, being a central fracture line in distinguishing conservatism and liberalism. However, while in Wales and in Scotland unionism was well integrated within patriotic popular politics, this was less obviously the case both in Ireland and in England. In Ireland popular unionism was largely confined to the north-east of the island, though there were traces of primarily Protestant middle-class support in Dublin and elsewhere: in England, outside of areas associated with Irish immigration and political division (like Liverpool), the extent to which a popular unionism had an existence independent from an anglo-centric popular imperialism or Protestant chauvinism remained unclear. Moreover, the extent to which there was any fundamental appreciation of the complexities and diverse workings of the union state even at the level of the metropolitan elite was also wholly opaque. Certainly, recent work on popular expressions of support for Irish and Ulster unionism in Britain has tended to emphasize its geographic and other limitations (see e.g. Jackson 2009). And, certainly, too, supposedly fundamental unionist convictions remained negotiable for numerous leading conservatives throughout the home rule era— judged by the positions of Lord Randolph Churchill (1849–95) in 1885, George Wyndham in 1903–4, F. E. Smith in 1909–10, or larger swathes of the party during and after the Great War. William Harcourt (1827–1904) famously warned Edward Carson that 'the Conservative party...never yet took up a cause without betraying it in the end'; and this, while (at one level) perhaps an expression of a teasing partisanship, was also an entirely accurate reflection of the shallow or contingent nature of some metropolitan commitment to the enterprise of union (Hyde 1953, p. 120).

Following on from this, one closely related, though less tangible, factor uniting several of the vulnerable unions discussed within this study is what might be described as a collapse of unionist political confidence in the late 19th century—a waning of morale which ultimately sometimes preceded the collapse or (at the very least) the radical redefinition of the state itself. This was linked to several of the institutional and other factors discussed in this chapter, but it may also be treated as an independent vector of decline and ultimate failure. This wider exhaustion of social and political confidence and morale was defined in the late Habsburg empire as a *Kulturpessimismus*—but it was emphatically more than an exclusive Austro-Hungarian or German phenomenon, being part of the experience of other union states, including Britain and Ireland (see e.g. Kalberg 1987; Judson 2016, p. 382).

Fin de siècle Austria-Hungary was indeed famously characterized by a strain of *Kulturpessimismus* which infected (and indeed inspired) the intellectual life of the empire, but which was also associated with its fissiparous and unstable politics (Sked 1989, pp. 218, 230). The vacuum created by relentless political division and the, at best, staccato functioning of parliament was to some extent filled by cultural expression. For Oszkár Jászi, predictably perhaps, the pessimism underpinning Habsburg society and the empire was driven by a moral and cultural deficit: 'behind the dissolution of the monarchy there was a deep moral crisis which could have been avoided only by a civic education in the best sense. In the absence of this, the monarchy was doomed to perish' (Jászi 1929, p. 267). Most modern scholarship on the Dual Monarchy offers somewhat less didactic and deterministic arguments than this; but even here there has been a clear awareness of disillusion with the institutions of the Ausgleich in the mid and later 1890s, mounting Austrian antipathy towards Hungary, and a resigned acceptance that the supranational Austrian idea had failed to take root in the partner nation ('*das Großösterreichtum hat in Ungarn niemals Wurzeln fassen können*': quoted in Haslinger 1996, pp. 14–15).

There exists a parallel within late 19th-century Britain and Ireland to this Austrian phenomenon—and, indeed, there are (arguably) further analogies with the subsequent state of the United Kingdom in the context of referenda on Scottish independence and Brexit. The increasingly persuasive commercial and military challenges posed by the United States and Germany in the late 19th century, together with the difficult and protracted nature of the South African war (1899–1902), all helped (as is well known) to stimulate a crisis of confidence within British politics which fed into a wider debate, pursued (in particular) by conservative unionists, on 'national efficiency' (White 1901; Searle 1971). Out of this arose various initiatives to improve the health of the nation (which had been exposed as painfully wanting by the army recruitment campaigns), as well as other schemes for national regeneration, including universal military service and tariff reform. This crisis of confidence has also occasionally been seen as underpinning a movement towards a greater English national self-consciousness (Kumar 2003, p. 224). As with some of the political expressions of Habsburg *Kulturpessimismus*, so in England there was a strain of patriotic Toryism (represented within the thought of the likes of George Wyndham on the party's

Edwardian front bench, but drawing stimulus from Lord Salisbury's famous article on 'Disintegration' in the *Quarterly Review* of 1883) which embraced a nostalgic medievalism, and which elided anti-semitism and apprehensions concerning 'cosmopolitan finance'. While there were of course many other explanations, this pessimistic and nostalgic Toryism fed directly into the adamantine unionism and the high-risk strategizing of 1912–14. British party leaders, but especially the Conservatives, drew on their fears of national and imperial disintegration to pursue an exceptionally high-stakes political campaign which effectively put into jeopardy those very institutions—including the union itself—which it was ostensibly designed to protect.

Extending this argument somewhat, it might be suggested that the current condition of the United Kingdom constitution partly reflects the same elements of *Kulturpessimismus*—a fear of national retreat and decline, combined with (in the circumstances) a paradoxical nostalgia for the Victorian heyday of Lord Salisbury who was himself (as has been noted) nostalgic for a still earlier patriotic era. As in the Edwardian era, when Conservatives sought to advance the national interest through a redefined set of commercial relations with the empire and wider world (encapsulated within the tariff reform movement), so 21st-century Conservatives have sought a redefined set of relations with the wider world in the interests of national regeneration. As was the case a century ago, so too now they have sometimes been prepared to take risks with the constitution of the union state in order to realize this wider vision.

Thus, unions like the United Kingdom may be critically threatened by the diversion or distraction of long-standing unionists through other ideological commitments. With the dominant nationalities in the union state, there may indeed come a tipping point where they effectively disinvest from union, and develop in ways which are inimical to it. In Austria-Hungary, for example, a robust German identity re-emerged during the First World War, especially within the dominant military cultures in the western, Cisleithanian, half of the empire. These were of course much more interested in military victory than in the intricate balletic politics of the Ausgleich; and it seems clear that they contributed to the general weakening of trust and confidence in the empire which (in turn) ultimately hastened its demise.

In the United Kingdoms of Sweden-Norway one of the facilitators of Norwegian independence in June 1905 was the waning of Swedish unionist conviction. For Swedish unionists (as indeed for British and Irish unionists) a key function of union was the military defence of their polity; and in Sweden-Norway, from at least the mid-1890s onwards (just as was the case for Ireland and later Northern Ireland) the union was clearly becoming a defensive liability rather than an asset. From the time of the consular crisis of 1895, the Norwegian Venstre party realized that Norway had to develop its own national military capacity further in order to avoid the inevitable trumping of their political demands through the threat of Swedish military superiority. This meant the consolidation of the national army, together with (from 1900) the construction of fortifications along what was meant to be the peaceful, almost 'internal', border between Norway and Sweden. Thus, from the Swedish perspective, Norway was not only contributing its customary pittance to the common defence of the peninsula, it was now investing instead in a military threat which appeared to be directed as much against Sweden itself as any 'foreign' enemy (for Norwegian patriots, of course, Sweden was 'foreign', as much because of union as in spite of it). There was a growing Swedish disinvestment from union beginning at least in 1884, when ministerial responsibility had been established in Norway, and returning with the sabre-rattling and brinkmanship over the consular question in the 1890s and afterwards (Knaplund 1952, pp. 141, 158, 180). Swedish conservative intellectuals like Rudolf Kjéllen (who taught at Gothenburg and then Uppsala) and Harald Hjärne (Uppsala) each at different times began expressing an equanimity about the end of union: Kjéllen (writing in 1895) expected that an independent Norway would sooner or later seek readmission to union, while Hjärne argued in early 1905 that an effective and voluntary defensive alliance and union between Norway and Sweden now made more sense than the increasingly toxic personal union of the two kingdoms (Lindgren 1959, pp. 98–9; Barton 2003, p. 81). Clearly, part of the explanation for the ultimate dissolution of Sweden-Norway was that key interests within the dominant partner were coming to feel that the game of union was no longer worth the candle—and that union had now in fact come to work against its original functions.

Similarly, within the United Kingdom of Britain and Ireland at the end of the 19th century the once predominantly unionist parliamentary elite at Westminster became keen to divest itself of the burden of direct responsibility for Ireland, and sought (in the case of Gladstone and the Liberals) to devolve Irish affairs to a Dublin parliament through the agency of home rule. Even some Conservative unionists, like their Swedish counterparts, had privately come to understand (by around 1910) that an unreformed union was an increasing liability, and to consider either some direct deal over home rule, or reframing the challenge of Irish self-government through a wider federalist initiative. Ultimately a majority of British parliamentarians, Conservative, Liberal, and Labour, signed off on a treaty (in 1921) which gave most of Ireland dominion status and which devolved the entangled affairs of the north of Ireland to a parliament in Belfast.

Looking ahead, and to the 21st century, there has been a recrudescence of English national sentiment, 'entangled' within a rising populism, which has ultimately diverted the British Conservative party into a variety of policy positions more obviously designed to combat the rival United Kingdom Independence Party in English constituencies than to sustain the union in Scotland and Northern Ireland (see e.g. Kumar 2003; Kenny 2014, pp. 233–4; Henderson amd Wyn Jones 2021). English national feeling has had, in part, one form of expression in Brexit; and (regardless of the pros and cons of this stand) it has involved the traditional unionist party of the British state drawing on nationalist sentiment to attack one (European) union—while using language and arguments that are clearly relevant to Scots and Irish nationalism in their respective assault on the unions of the United Kingdom. In short the historic party of union may now be occasionally as much nationalist as unionist (cf. Henderson and Wyn Jones 2021, p. 215).

Moreover this embrace of English sentiment, sometimes nationalism, at the expense of British unionism, understandable in the context of hungrily assertive national assemblies in Belfast, Cardiff, and Edinburgh, as well as the comparative invisibility of Englishness in the culture, nomenclature, and institutions of the contemporary union state, has been linked with some even more fundamental ideological shifts within Conservatism. British Conservatism's increasingly firm attachment to a small-state, individualist neo-liberalism has arguably involved at best a realignment of the party's priorities and at worst a set of internal contradictions. Conservative unionism has scaled down assets of the United Kingdom state which have historically served as bolsters of union (Jackson 2013). An emphasis on the individual's economic and other freedoms may jar with the collectivist underpinnings of the union settlements: that is to say, the union state has traditionally been defended in collectivist and distributive language and using collectivist and distributive arguments which have not always chimed with some of the dominant ideological modes inside modern Conservativism. Subtracting the institutional and intellectual content from British unionism in these ways leaves at best a hazy collection of shared values—and at worst an all too clearly defined set of political, social, and religious prejudices. As in some other union states under consideration, the United Kingdom is wobbling—but as much because of disillusioned and distracted unionists as of disaffected nationalists (cf. Jackson 2013, p. 358). Or, alternatively, the UK is wobbling as much because of unionist *Pessimismus* as nationalist confidence.

6.5. National Difference, Small Difference, and Indifference

Nationalism has conventionally been seen as a simple solvent of union—as a key centrifugal agent within such polities. This section of the study does not seek to revisit those great national confrontations which have shaped traditional narratives of unions, and which have been discussed in each of the case studies provided earlier (see Chapters 2 and 3). It instead seeks to make the case that those great confrontations need now to be contextualized in relatively more sophisticated and nuanced ways. At the same time it suggests that, in understanding the ends of union, we also need to look at the cumulative and corrosive impact of small differences—as well as reconsider the role of national indifference.

While modern historians now commonly interrogate the application of the vocabulary and presuppositions of nationality, contemporaries like R. W. Seton-Watson, Wickham Steed, and Oszkár Jászi accepted that it was fundamentally the 'nations' question which brought the downfall of the Dual Monarchy (Seton-Watson 1911a; Steed 1919; Jászi 1929; Sked 1989, p. 208; cf. Judson 2016). For Seton-Watson, for example, Magyar national chauvinism came to endanger the entire future of the Dual Monarchy, not least because it was threatening to drive the Croats into the embrace of the Serb state and thus (for Vienna) a disastrous southern Slav alliance (Seton-Watson 1908, pp. 392, 415). The only available silver bullet (he thought) was the possibility of an extension of the franchise for the Hungarian parliament, following a similar democratization in Cisleithania, which would effectively permit the national diversification of parliamentary politics in Budapest. However, Seton-Watson also understood that this would not readily be conceded by the Magyars, and might only be attainable through the intervention of the emperor-king himself, since 'the historic mission of the House of Habsburg is the vindication of equal rights and liberties for all the races committed to its charge' (Seton-Watson 1908, p. 418).

For Jászi as well, 'the world war was not the cause but only the final liquidation of the deep inner [national] crises of the monarchy' (Jászi 1929, p. 23). Even Jászi, a Hungarian and a progressive, resignedly accepted that 'the empire collapsed because the historic tradition of each nation stood in a hostile and hateful way against the historical experiences of other nations' (Jászi 1929, p. 130). For him the Habsburg empire was ultimately in essence 'that race struggle'—a state of two contrasting halves, wherein one (Cisleithania) was moving towards national equality, while the other (Hungary) was moving towards 'a uniform national state' (Jászi 1929, pp. 134, 298, 337). But, while the trajectories were quite different, in each the story of the Dual Monarchy was essentially that of nation versus state.

However, it has become increasingly clear that this kind of analytical binary, which emphasizes difference, and which pits insurgent nationalities against recalcitrant union authorities, will not now suffice as a full characterization of the politics of multinational unions across the 'long' 19th century (see e.g. Seip 1995). Centrifugal forces within union polities often drew upon intensely patriotic identities which long predated the elaboration of modern nationalisms: this was clearly the case for Norway within the United Kingdoms, for the southern Netherlands/Belgium, for the Irish and Scots—and for the peoples of the Austrian empire and Austria-Hungary (see e.g. Seip 1995, p. 37). Moreover, as has already been observed, liberal influences and tendencies within union states or empires created the capacity to address and sometimes defuse ethnic and national diversity; and the examples of 19th-century Britain (excepting Ireland), France, and Canada are sometimes cited in this respect (Okey 2001, p. 127). Indeed, while there have been laments about the missed opportunities of the *Vormärz* era, it is quite clear that this union capacity to address and defuse diversity and division also characterized even the Dual Monarchy, and that by 1914 the 'national question' was arguably abating—in so far as sophisticated consociational political agreements had been worked out in Moravia (1905), Bukovina (1910), and Galicia (1914) (see section 3.5). Equally, looking even at Ireland, a combination of Gladstonian liberalism and constructive unionism more generally had seemingly helped to soften the asperities of the national division by the eve of the Great War.

Of course it is important not to push these arguments too far, and to overstate the liberalism of 'liberal' empires or of 'liberal' unions at the expense of either imperialism or unionism. Certainly in terms of Austria-Hungary, it is ultimately hard to overturn Steve Beller's verdict:

> there is much that is laudable about the economic performance, the level of civilisation, the relative rule of law, and the relative security which the Habsburg state had brought to central Europe by 1914, especially in today's retrospect; but the fact that it remained a dynastic empire led by a monarch and ruling elite intent first of all on maintaining imperial power and prestige and only secondarily tending to the national conflicts among its subjects meant that it could not channel the immense forces which nationalism had stirred up by then.
> (Beller 1996, p. 159)

Much of this verdict is in fact applicable to other unions, including even the United Kingdom of Great Britain and Ireland. Indeed this, though a parliamentary democracy with responsible government, still lacked a coherent codified constitution, possessed a monarchy and ruling elite which exercised disproportionate influence, and attended to national conflicts among its subjects 'only secondarily' and often only under duress.

All this is not to deny the existence of a serious 'channelling' effort, whether here, in Austria-Hungary, or in Ireland under the union. Indeed, in the most recent analyses of the Dual Monarchy the argument has been made that the nationalities' question was in fact encouraged by the empire, rather than existing in separation or permanent antagonism: the empire effectively assimilated (or, indeed, institutionalized) national questions within its structures in the last decades of its existence, and the three distinctive national compromises effected in Moravia, Bukovina, and Galicia 'threatened to remove the burning relevance of nationalism from daily life' (Leslie 1991, p. 136; Stourzh 2007, p. 177; Judson 2016, p. 316). On the other hand, in those provinces where compromises of this kind had been reached, the Habsburg state was effectively relegating the language rights of the individual and advancing those of the national community. Given that these legal and constitutional developments occurred so close to the demise of the monarchy, it is really impossible to say definitively whether the empire had effectively contained the nationalities question—or whether it remained (in the famous indictment) a 'prison of the nations', albeit one in which the inmates had now successfully taken over several of the wings (or, further still, whether the prison of the nations had in fact become the prisoner of the nations). At the very least it seems that, if the empire had indeed partly assimilated the nationalities' question, then the price of containment may have been the institutionalization and internalizing of that which had once been external and contingent. But, given that mainstream nationalists were generally willing to work within the union 'system', in neither the United Kingdom nor the Habsburg empire in the early 20th century was the challenge of nationalism necessarily a threat 'to the very existence of the state itself' (Judson 2016, p. 332).

Moreover, it has long been recognized that the Habsburg state wrestled with nationalist ideologies, while being itself an expression of a comparatively 'non-nationalised world' (Judson and Rozenblit 2005, p. 1). Pieter Judson and Marsha Rozenblit are only amongst the latest to point out that

> the Habsburg state did not itself attempt a nationalisation of its people in the ways that the self-proclaimed French, Italian or German states had. At least until 1867 the Habsburg state functioned as a collectivity where patriotism or loyalty to the dynasty rather than an ideology of shared nation-ness bound subjects and later citizens to the greater polity. (Judson and Rozenblit 2005, p. 2)

Other work has suggested (for example) that Habsburg dynastic patriotism long remained vital and important in a range of areas—amongst, for example, the Germans of the Tirol (Judson and Rozenblit 2005, p. 11). The most recent scholarship on Austria-Hungary in fact emphasizes 'both the contingency and diversity of specific forms of national identity in order to avoid relying on ahistorical prescriptions of eternal identities': this encompasses a formidably broad range of regional studies within the Dual Monarchy, from Bohemia to Istria and Dalmatia (Judson and Rozenblit 2005, p. 1; Zahra 2010, p. 100). And, as will be discussed shortly, this work is also relevant to an understanding of the United Kingdom in so far as it chimes with strains of interpretation which emphasize either the pre-eminence of local identities or the negotiability of identity as a whole.

Working from his study of the city of Budweis, later České Budějovice, in southern Bohemia, Jeremy King has similarly warned against overly nationalizing readings of complex historic issues of identity: he has stressed, too, that 'national indifference was an inconvenient fact that national leaders denied and minimised' (King 2002, pp. 3–4). Complementing King's urban emphases, Pieter Judson has studied the rural landscapes of Cisleithania in the late 19th century and concluded that (as occasionally in Ireland in the last years of the union) the accounts of nationalist activists 'betray a consistent disappointment with the apparent failure of their rural compatriots to become nationalist or nationalist enough... they consistently despair of integrating rural populations successfully into the national community' (Wingfield 2003, p. 146).

King has drawn a striking distinction between the language differences which 'divided a population vertically into protonational columns' and 'corporative and socioeconomic solidarities [which] divided it into Habsburg layers—and [which] had far more institutional anchoring and sociological significance' (King 2002, p. 7). He has also emphasized the contingent nature of ethnic and national identification, the extent to which ostensibly coherent 'nationhoods' were in fact 'rich amalgams'—as well as the fact that Budweis's key political conflicts were not nationally driven (between Czechs and Germans) but were to be found instead 'among burghers, unprivileged town dwellers, peasants and nobles as well as among Catholics, Protestants and Jews—in other words among Budweisers and other varieties of Habsburg loyalist' (King 2002, p. 22). The city's population was *not* German-speaking *or* Czech-speaking, but was instead overwhelmingly bilingual in German *and* in Czech; while there was also 'a significant minority' which exploited the ambiguities of ethnic and national identification 'to switch to the more powerful national side, in some cases more than once' (King 2002, p. 210). For King, Budweis, '*die allzeit getreue*', ever loyal, illustrates emphatically that 'historians must pull the Habsburg state into their narratives, and push supposedly ancient ethnic groups out' (King 2002, p. 210).

Moreover, a corollary of the non-national worlds which scholars of the Habsburg empire are excavating is the issue of multiple or overlapping national and other identities. For example, Marsha Rozenblit has argued that Jews in the Habsburg empire (who were in some places categorized as 'national' but in other place not so) embraced a tripartite identity: they were politically loyal to Austria, often had an affinity for German culture, but also nurtured a Jewish ethnic identity (Judson and Rozenblit 2005, p. 188).

There are some echoes of this work on the last decades of the Habsburg empire within Martin Conway's anatomization of 20th-century Belgium. For Conway, as for the scholars of the Austro-Hungarian empire, there are dangers in underestimating the resilience of an overarching and unifying identity for the Belgian state: 'in fact', he has argued, an overarching 'Belgian nationalism was never as weak nor the ethnic and linguistic bonds of Walloon or Flemish identity as strong as retrospective simplification might suggest...local regional linguistic and national loyalties intersected with each other in different ways at different times' (Conway 2012, p. 369).

More pertinently, in terms of the current study's preoccupations, this wider sense of a 'non-nationalized', or of an overarching supranational, world is also strongly relevant to Britain and Ireland, at least in so far as the constituent national identities—English, Welsh, Scots, and Irish—complemented a relatively weak but still vital and unitary British identity. Cisleithania, Judson and Rozenblit have each argued, presents us with a powerful example of modern state-building not linked to nation-building: similarly, the United Kingdom presents us with a powerful example of modern state-building not linked to any effective national consolidation. Consequently, and by critical extension, the shrinking of the British state has had a disproportionately damaging impact on the union itself (Jackson 2013).

In addition the recent work on Cisleithanian Austria-Hungary, with its emphases on the fluidity and negotiability of national identity, chimes with a range of work relating to Ireland under the union in the 19th century. Just as the history of Austria-Hungary cannot now be exclusively or simply defined by the tension between the nations and the Habsburg state, so, too, the history of Ireland (or Scotland) under their respective unions cannot be rendered simply as a set of crude binaries (unionist versus nationalist, nationalist versus the union state). In neither the British nor the Austrian case is this to ignore the vital importance of national mobilization across the 19th century, or to sidestep the (sometimes) critical conflicts between nationalists and their opponents. It is, however, to suggest that in both Ireland and Austria-Hungary nationalist activists faced similar challenges in mobilizing their respective populations.

In the former case, in work which strikingly prefigures that of King and Judson on Cisleithania, scholars such as Theo Hoppen have pointed to the prevailing importance of regional (rather than national) political priorities and horizons in mid-19th-century Ireland (Hoppen 1984). The growth of scholarly interest in the Irish contributions to the British army and empire underlines (at the very least) the compatibility for many of an Irish patriotism with the opportunities created by British imperialism. The close study of the Irish revolution which has emerged since David Fitzpatrick's pioneering work on county Clare has from the beginning underlined the fluidity of political identity—one of the strengths of this approach being a closer understanding and anatomization of the dizzyingly swift regrouping of nationalism away from home rule towards separatist loyalties (Fitzpatrick 1977). More recent work on the 1916 rising and the revolution, drawing on the rich archival resources of the Bureau of Military History in Dublin, has pointed repeatedly both to the limited impact of the revolutionary struggle on the lives of the majority as well as to the impatience of activists with the (often) determinedly tepid national loyalties of their compatriots: there was, in fact, a robust vocabulary of abuse reserved for these laggards ('shoneens', West Britons, Castle Catholics)—as there was for their counterparts in central Europe (McGarry 2017; Wingfield 2003, p. 146; Zahra 2010, pp. 104–5).

Brian Hughes's study of the ways in which the Irish Republican Army sought to enforce its authority between 1919 and 1921 usefully underlines the 'indifference, indecision or cynicism' that often prevailed beyond the community of separatist activism. Indeed, Hughes presents case studies which chime remarkably with King's work on Budweis/Budějovice in terms of the contingent—or 'situational'—nature of political choices: particularly striking in this respect is (to take one detailed example) Hughes's evocation of an egg-dealer from Arva, county Cavan—James McCabe (b. 1861)—who simultaneously applied to both the Irish Free State and the British authorities for compensation arising out of the struggle of 1919–21. McCabe, a (long) retired officer of the Royal Irish Constabulary, looked to the British Treasury-funded Irish Grants Committee for financial relief on the grounds of his service to the crown; but he was also an Irish nationalist, who had a son active in the IRA, and he turned too to the Irish Free State authorities for financial redress, citing the family's record in the revolution. Few were as brassnecked as McCabe in seeking to milk the two competing jurisdictions for personal benefit; but his actions do clearly connect with the Bohemian worker, cited by Zahra, who, when asked about his national loyalties in 1948, replied simply that 'it is a matter of who is giving more' (Zahra 2010, p. 100). And McCabe's story does crisply illustrate the kind of ambiguous, alternate, or sequential loyalties which characterized many as the first Irish union came to an end. Disappointingly, these have not yet been comprehensively addressed by Irish historians; and yet the full story of the Irish revolution needs not only its heroes and visionaries, its villains and 'baddies', but also its pragmatists and quietists, and even its selfpreserving chancers.

Linked with this ongoing and radical reconceptualization of difference within multinational polities is the Freudian insight, *der Narzissmus der kleinen Differenzen*, the narcissism of small differences: this, too, has a particular relevance for union states, which often (if not invariably) brought together peoples and polities who were essentially similar (cf. Mitchell 2010b, pp. 98–116; Parent 2011, p. 105). In these circumstances of intimacy and similarity, symbols of difference were often invested with a much greater significance than might otherwise have been the case. Flags, party, and national colours, nuances of language and dialect, have all conventionally been linked with larger disputes inside contested union states; but it is clear that these symbolic issues could—and did—attain an independent life and importance. Union states were weakened not just by sometimes destructive dialogues between minority or non-dominant nationalisms and the supranational institutions and ideologies of union: they were also subverted by the independent force and aggression which coalesced around these symbols of difference. R. W. Seton-Watson observed that 'the desperate quarrels so frequently kindled in Austria-Hungary by such apparent trifles as the inscription over an office, the address of a post-bag, or the coloured ribbon worn by a child, seem merely ludicrous to the foreigner who is unaware of the importance of external trappings in a country where each race upholds a rival theory of constitutional law' (Seton-Watson 1911a, p. 329). But in fact, far from seeming ludicrous to 'the foreigner', Seton-Watson could well have applied each of these detailed illustrations to his own country, the United Kingdom, where all were very readily applicable. In Ireland, Wales, and in Scotland postal addresses (for example) readily signalled political preferences (Derry/Londonderry, Caernarfon/Carnarvon, North Britain/Scotland), the use of Irish and Welsh within the postal service was for a time contentious, party colours were spectacularly incendiary, and children were routinely drawn into political rivalries (whether the Protestant Sunday School children of Castledawson in June 1912, the child-victims of the fighting in 1916, or—latterly—the Catholic schoolchildren of Holy Cross School, Ardoyne, in 2001–2) (see e.g. Duffy 2015).

With Sweden-Norway, even at the mid-19th-century zenith of the United Kingdoms, flags, coats of arms, and royal titles and uniforms all fed into a festering rancour with union (Seip 1995, p. 40). The radical Scottish traveller, Samuel Laing, observed in 1836 that 'there is, however, an excessive jealousy among all ranks of the slightest independence by the sister kingdom of Sweden. The spirit, which was probably excited by the weak and abortive attempts to amalgamate the two countries displays itself sometimes *on the most trifling occasions*' (Laing 1836, p. 197: my emphasis). Norway underlined its independent existence within the context of the union state through a separate national flag, which was devised by Fredrik Meltzer in 1821. The acceptance of this was, however, resisted by the king, Carl XIV Johan; and in addition there was a practical problem for Norwegian merchant vessels operating south of Cape Finisterre, where Norway (unlike Sweden) had no protection against the Barbary pirates. Oscar I introduced a compromise arrangement in 1844, whereby each of the two national flags, Norwegian and Swedish, carried (in their top left corner) a badge of union, comprising a red, blue, gold, and white mixing of the respective national colours. This, the much-derided 'herring salad', remained contentiously in place until 1898–9, a continuing irritant—and an upbraiding reminder to patriotic Norwegians of the compromises inherent in union (Parent 2011, p. 105).

Equally, as has been discussed in section 4.8, in an age when heraldic emblems mattered, and when they had a ubiquity in citizens' lives through their presence in public spaces and on the coinage, the detail on coats of arms could accelerate resentments. The coat of arms of Sweden-Norway, which originally rendered the rampant Norwegian lion merely as a quartering of the Swedish arms, generated the same kind of animus as the flag question (Nansen 1905, p. 28 n. 1). Coats of arms mattered within Austria-Hungary, too, where the Habsburg insignia were a recurrent source of grievance for, in particular, the Hungarian half of the Dual Monarchy. Just as in Sweden-Norway, where the Norwegian lion was heraldically caged by the Swedes until 1844, so with the Habsburgs the Hungarian arms featured merely as one of eleven shields decorating the imperial *Doppeladler* after the Ausgleich of 1867. Only very late in the history of the Dual Monarchy—in 1915—was the issue addressed through the invention of a new imperial armorial, which depicted (in strikingly grandiloquent style) the arms of the two halves of the empire, Cisleithania and Transleithania, resting side-by-side under the imperial and royal crowns.

The regnal numbers of union monarchs characteristically caused similarly disproportionate grievance. In Austria-Hungary, for the most of the decades after the Ausgleich, there was little difficulty, since Franz Joseph I (he was invariably, and optimistically, rendered as Franz Joseph 'I') was indeed the first ruler of his name for both Austria and Hungary: his short-lived successor, by way of contrast, was simultaneously Karl I of Austria, Karl IV of Hungary, and Karl III of Bohemia. When Carl XIII of Sweden assumed the throne of Norway in 1814, he was not the thirteenth of his name to hold the Norwegian throne, but rather only the second: equally, his successor, though officially Carl XIV Johan of Sweden was also in fact Carl III Johan of Norway. Similarly, the nomenclature of the British monarchy after the union of 1707 generated resentments in Scotland, which in turn fed into national feeling: while the Georges and Victoria created no particular difficulties (there had been no Scottish or English monarchs with these names before 1707), more controversy was generated by William IV (or III of Scotland), Edward VII (or I of Scotland, and tactlessly redolent of the medieval 'hammer of the Scots'), and Elizabeth II (or I of Scotland). The accession of Elizabeth II (and I) was greeted with loyal enthusiasm through much of Scotland, though there was an undercurrent of patriotic irritation which fed into isolated assaults on window displays and postboxes which carried the offending English-only royal insignia.

In short, nationalism and its symbols mattered as subverters of unions: but, beyond this, careful calibration is urgently required. Union states became adept at assimilating nationalist grievance, even at the cost of empowering the institutions and language of nationalism in the governance of union. Nationalists, on the other hand, were often prepared to work pragmatically within the contours of the union state. Difference—especially small symbolic difference—could, and did, assume disproportionate significance in the politics of nationalism and union. But, on the other hand, the fetishization of small differences should not divert from the reality that citizens were often characterized by contingent, sequential, and negotiable identities. Just as often, they were distinguished by plain indifference, as they sought meaning for their lives through other forms of agency and activity. So, yes, nations and nationalisms mattered in the fall of united kingdoms; but it is not enough to pit nationalism against union in any simply binary or crude teleology of decline (see e.g. Seip 1995).

6.6. Foreign Affairs

Foreign affairs (where indeed they have been considered at all in these contexts) have generally been seen as centripetal forces within the histories of multinational union polities: foreign enemies, foreign wars, foreign churches, have all seemingly provided a unifying 'Other' for a complex polity such as Great Britain or the United Kingdom. Yet in reality foreign affairs illustrate once again the deeply porous border between the centripetal and the centrifugal, originally delineated in 1929 by Ozskár Jászi, and invoking Austria-Hungary.

Foreign affairs in fact have more often proved to be a stress-point than a unifier in terms of the coherence and integrity of union states, whether personal unions or the more comprehensive parliamentary unions embodied ultimately in the United Kingdom. The explanation for this is not hard to find: foreign affairs have tended to act as a focus for a variety of economic, cultural, and historic distinctions between the constituent polities of a union, not least because these polities often have quite different diplomatic prehistories (as, famously, with Scotland's 'auld alliance' with France). In contemporary terms, this has been seen most obviously with the various calibrations of response to the European Union and 'Brexit' across the different nations of the United Kingdom in 2016 and afterwards. The substantial endorsement of Brexit obtained in England was of course not echoed in Scotland (62 per cent in favour of Remain) or in Northern Ireland (55.8 per cent Remain), or even in Wales, where the majority in favour of Brexit (52.5 per cent) was slightly less than in England (53.4 per cent). And the apparent centrifugal impact of Brexit was particularly evident in Scotland, where it seemed to strengthen the forces of nationalism.

Successive British governments, and the political classes of the United Kingdom, have for long fretted about their international connections; and during the debate on Brexit various historical analogies were uncovered in order to document the adamantine nature of (in particular) the European challenge. However, while much attention was focused upon the free trade and tariff reform disputes within English Conservatism of the 1840s and the Edwardian era, an equally pertinent debate concerns the value (or otherwise) of the link between Britain and the German state to which it was bound for over 120 years in personal union—Hanover. Just as (at different stages) Ireland and Scotland have been seen as threatening the security of England (and thus requiring constitutional 'fixing'), so the Hanoverian realm also impacted upon English security and foreign policy—though of course in distinctive and much-debated ways. Brendan Simms has regarded Hanoverian and British interests as broadly overlapping, arguing that the former 'was in fact a net contributor to British security and imperial success through the 18th century' (Rexheuser 1995, p. 334). But the most convinced exponent of the idea that Hanover was instead a strategic liability has been Jeremy Black, for whom Hanover did not so much 'save' Britain in its wars with France as it did Austria (1741) and Prussia (1757): for Black the Hanoverian link instead 'gravely weakened Britain as an international force because...it was unpopular and challenged the practice of crown-elite cooperation on which successful politics depended' (in Rexheuser 2005, p. 451). In other words the strategic vulnerability of Hanover together with the wider obligations arising from the personal union created a source of weakness for the British state—since they tended to generate a tension between the monarchy and the governing elite in London, and thus a further subversion of the union government.

What was true of the personal union of Hanover and Britain, and their (perhaps) divergent diplomatic interests, was also true for other, later, unions.

Sweden and Norway had a supposedly united foreign policy, superintended until 1885 by the king; but in reality each of the two constituent polities had very different histories and different traditions of foreign engagement; and just as the English believed that (their link with) Hanover might embroil them in an unwanted continental conflict, so too the Norwegians believed that Swedish interests might similarly ensnare them. Sweden looked fearfully eastward to the threat posed by the Russian empire—an apprehension founded upon the all-too-vivid reality of the loss of its one-time Finnish province to Russia in 1809. Sweden, too, had a presence in western Pomerania until 1815, and it tended to turn to Germany in the later 19th century for financial, technical, and diplomatic support: Norway, on the other hand, generally looked instead to Britain and France. Control of foreign policy in Sweden-Norway was theoretically in the hands of the union king; so in Norwegian legal principle, therefore, its foreign policy was devised by the king of Norway. But in practice the predominant Swedish influence was clear, and especially after 1885 when (with growing ministerial accountability) the responsibility of the foreign minister to the Swedish Riksdag was more explicitly defined. This meant that, when the interests of the individual nations of the union diverged, as was the case increasingly with trade, then the limitations of the foreign ministry were clearly exposed: it meant in effect that by the end of the 19th century in Sweden-Norway the foreign ministry, ostensibly a key institutional bolster of the union, had become a critical point of weakness.

Indeed the history connecting Sweden and Norway over the last 20 years of union was essentially the history of clashes over the administration of diplomatic and consular business. The establishment of the Riksdag's control over foreign affairs in 1885 was, for patriots like Fridtjof Nansen, 'the principal cause of the last twenty years strife in the union' (Nansen 1905, p. 54). In 1890 negotiations began between Sweden and Norway to establish a joint ministerial council on foreign affairs; but these soon broke down in acrimony, with the veiled threats of force which had become customary in such contexts. By 1892 a definite proposal for a separate Norwegian foreign minister had been tabled in the Storting, only to be vetoed by Oscar II. Military preparations were, once again, the backdrop to the crisis of 1895, when (given the scale of threat) the Norwegians agreed at last to deal. But the Norwegian strategy combined not only negotiation, but also intensive military preparation, including now (from 1900) the fortification of the frontier, not with Russia (which is what the Swedes were doing), but rather with Sweden itself. Further talks, on the basis of separate consular services and a single diplomatic staff, were pursued in the context of a last joint union commission—but these, too, came to grief, in 1904, though this time at the hands of the Swedish conservative prime minister, Erik Boström. Boström's crude intervention allowed a new coalition government in Norway, led by the separatist, Christian Michelsen, to create the conditions for (effectively) a declaration of independence on 7 June 1905. In essence, entirely differing priorities had first destroyed the possibility of a fully integrated diplomatic and consular service, and then overturned the union itself. At the end, even unionist Swedes came to recognize that their defence and diplomatic interests might best be served by the dissolution of union and its replacement by a new set of political and strategic relationships with their Norwegian neighbour. In the same way even (many) unionist Britons came to recognize by 1921 that their global interests might now best be served by a self-governing Ireland.

Control of foreign affairs in asymmetrical union states like Sweden-Norway or Britain and Ireland became particularly divisive in the context of the threat of war (unions and the actuality of global war are discussed more fully in the next section of the book, 6.7). Both England and Sweden were moved by threats, which were not felt with the same immediacy or clarity by (respectively) Ireland or by Norway. Both English and Swedish priorities overwhelmingly dominated the diplomatic strategies of their respective union states, which meant that there was a real possibility that Irish (or Scots or Welsh) and Norwegian lives would ultimately be lost in wars that were not of Irish (or Scots or Welsh) or Norwegian making. Though in both 1900, with South Africa, and again in 1914, with the outbreak of the Great War, Irish nationalists joined the union army, heavy casualties and (in particular) the threat of conscription swiftly brought disillusion and provided a critical mobilizing issue for separatist republicans. The United Kingdoms of Sweden-Norway had dissolved long before 1914; but the prospect of Norwegians fighting and dying for essentially Swedish interests—perhaps in a Russian war—had for long been a potent fear for liberal patriots in Norway like Bjørnstjerne Bjørnson. Just as Irish separatists emphatically had no desire to die for England, so Bjørnson—writing in 1894—underlined that 'we [Norwegians] have no desire to become Swedish cannon fodder' (quoted in Barton 2003, p. 74). Indeed, much of modern Ireland's relationship with the United Kingdom has turned upon the Irish desire never again to be English cannon fodder.

The cracks within united kingdoms may also be shaped by the national and international complexities arising from the particular areas of emigration and diaspora. Indeed, questions of nationality in the Dual Monarchy, and with the other unions considered here, were threatening precisely because they were often much more than matters of domestic politics: on the contrary, they could, and did, seep into the realm of diplomatic and foreign affairs. On the one hand, emigration, especially to the United States, appeared to be a 'real safety valve for the [Habsburg] monarchy'—as it was for the union state in Ireland as well as Sweden-Norway (Jászi 1929, p. 238). However, there was an obvious flip-side to migrant cultures. For example, emigration from Norway to America gained momentum in the 1830s and afterwards, with the bulk of those departing comprising well-to-do peasant farmers and even some members of the intelligentsia: it has been observed that 'their letters home and published accounts of America not only describe its material abundance but emphasise the social and political equality that prevailed there, thus highlighting existing inequities in the homeland' and stimulating dissatisfaction with the political status quo (Barton 2003, pp. 32–3). Elsewhere, southern

Slav/Jugoslav and Czech emigrants to the USA provided vital political and financial support for the different nationalist movements of the Dual Monarchy, including the important Jugoslav Committee (1915) (Dickinson-Berry 1918, p. 36). This Slavic diaspora was a political resource which far outweighed that of the Magyars (who dominated Transleithania). Equally, of course, an Irish migrant community in North America developed exponentially (both in terms of numbers and social embrace) during and after the Great Famine, and was vital in providing cash and political support for the national cause in Ireland itself. In other words, mass migration sometimes brought a temporary political respite within multinational union states, and therefore its suspension (as during the First World War in Ireland and elsewhere) created huge difficulties and pressures. But in the mid term mass migration delivered increasingly prosperous and alienated diasporic communities who in turn came to represent a global external challenge to the union state.

Related to issues of migration and diaspora was the question of the irredenta—those linguistic and ethnic communities divided by existing frontiers between unions and empires and their neighbours. For example, the explosive potential of Austro-Hungarian diplomacy was augmented because it had both its own Serb population (in Bosnia) and Serbia itself as a neighbour, because it had Italians (in the Littoral) and Italy as a neighbour, and because it had a substantial Romanian population in Siebenbürgen/Transylvania and Bukovina as well as the kingdom of Romania as a neighbour. The possibilities of creating internal instability through ill-advised, or simply unfortunate, international endeavour were therefore huge.

The fissures within united kingdoms were also shaped by external relationships, not just with the transnational and the diasporic, but also with supranational polities and structures well beyond the union state—whether cultural, commercial, or imperial. Swedish and Norwegian responses to the pan-Scandinavian cultural movement of (in particular) the mid-19th century varied, partly depending upon the extent to which Scandinavianism was likely to acquire a predominantly Swedish inflection (see Jorgenson 1935; Hemstad 2010, 2018). At this time Swedes, and in particular the Swedish monarchy, looked to Scandinavianism as a means by which either the lost Finnish provinces might be reacquired, or the entire region united under Swedish dynastic leadership (e.g. Jorgenson 1935, p. 241). Norwegians, however sympathetic to Scandinavianism as a cultural phenomenon, were suspicious of its political and constitutional resonances—and in particular of the possibility that it might either weaken Norwegian autonomy in relation to Sweden (or indeed its former union partner, Denmark) or involve Norway in unnecessary foreign warfare. However, a few Norwegian liberals embraced a Scandinavianism which looked to the inclusion of Denmark in a confederation with Norway and Sweden—this in the belief that Danish participation would counterbalance that of Sweden, and thus (paradoxically) augment Norwegian equality and autonomy (Jorgenson 1935, p. 325).

The high-point of Scandinavianism came, arguably, in 1848, when the Storting agreed (in an extremely dilatory way) to Oscar I's promise of military support for Denmark: still, it has been rightly said that 'the possibility of Scandinavian unity was great in 1848; hardly at any other time was the sentiment more fervent' (Jorgenson 1935, p. 164). Another, though more modest, Scandinavianist peak was essayed in 1863–4, with the renewed German threats to Schleswig-Holstein: Carl XV and IV (casting one eye on the acquisition of the throne of Denmark) promised Swedish-Norwegian military support to the Danes, just as his father, Oscar, had done in 1848 (Jorgenson 1935, p. 335). But, unlike 1848, there was now a much more awkward, and recent, prehistory of disagreement between Sweden and Norway, and the fall-out from Carl's actions was therefore different (Jorgenson 1935, p. 164). When war broke out both the Storting and the Swedish ministerial council each demurred, though for different reasons: the Norwegians required British (and French) military and diplomatic support, and specifically opposed any new constitutional link with Denmark, while the Swedes (who were prepared to countenance a 'federative' Scandinavia) rejected any binding military alliance or intervention (see e.g. Jorgenson 1935, p. 338). In essence, Scandinavianist sympathies came a poor second to Norwegian fears of a Swedish-dominated northern union, and to the Swedish desire to curb high-risk royal influence over foreign policy. In impetuously seeking a redefined, and a potentially grander union, Carl XV and IV had effectively subverted his existing united kingdoms.

Equally, Ireland's relationship with supranational institutions has often been decisively shaped by its relationship with the union, and with Britain. Constitutional nationalists were divided over the connection with the British empire, but many (like John Redmond) saw the evolving empire as a practical and attainable means of consolidating Irish interests, and of strengthening Ireland's standing in relation to Britain using language and institutions which were also generally acceptable and comprehensible to the British. Indeed, for a majority of Irish and Scots the European Economic Community and the European Union have fulfilled a related function—in so far as they have provided a forum beyond an English- or London-dominated United Kingdom and a potential counterbalance to unwanted political initiatives within the union state. Similarly, of course, a majority of the English people has come to view Europe as a constraint rather than a liberation. In these ways, therefore, Brexit stands in a tradition of divisive diplomatic or supranational questions which have sometimes threatened to undermine multinational union states.

In sum, union states comprise by definition different constituent polities with often profoundly different traditions of foreign and international engagement; and the corollary of this is that, while a properly calibrated foreign policy can serve to reinforce union, the temptation to take the unity of the union for granted through ill-conceived international initiatives has frequently proved hard to resist. Unity has often been consolidated through the identification of an obvious and mutually agreed external threat. But the consequences for union of pursuing the wrong war and the wrong enemy have been, or have threatened to be, truly disastrous.

6.7. The War Against Union and Empire, 1914–18

In developing further any discussion of foreign affairs, it should be remembered that war has been central to the formation, shaping, and termination of multinational union polities. Indeed, as will now be clear, one of the central contentions of this volume has been that the world war precipitated by the French revolution encouraged the creation of a succession of multinational union polities, beginning with (and often promoted by) the United Kingdom of Great Britain and Ireland. It will be recalled, too, that Viscount Castlereagh and his circle, mostly unionist Irishmen, were active in the propagation of union in the Netherlands and also in Sweden-Norway; and, more generally, that Britain was closely allied both to the newly centralized Austrian empire as well as to the United Kingdom of Portugal, Brazil, and the Algarves. Multinational union polities, as an elaboration and updating of the old composite monarchies, were the British response to the military challenge of the French republic, and the spiritual challenge of the French nation state.

War provided the circumstances for the nativity of the Dual Monarchy in 1867—and it shaped the circumstances of its demise in 1918: 'war unmade the Habsburg state' (Deak 2015, p. 264). The system of absolutist and centralized union rule associated with Baron Alexander von Bach (1813–93) was overturned on the battlefields of Magenta and Solferino; while the subsequent Austrian humiliation at the hands of the Prussians at Königgrätz/Sadowa in 1866 forced a comprehensive reshaping of the Habsburg empire. Oszkár Jászi was only one of many who firmly believed that the 'dualistic system' had been born out of Königgrätz (Jászi 1929, p. 106; see also section 3.5).

In each of these cases, war not only shaped the creation of unions, it also served to destabilize, reducing the possibility for flexibility, as well as calling into question the legitimacy of some of the central institutions of the union state. But in both the United Kingdom and in Austria-Hungary the Great War of 1914–18 arguably created newly toxic circumstances, solvents of union, rather than the final nails of a constitutional coffin. Indeed, this chapter focuses upon an examination of the centrifugal impact of global war on (primarily) these two great polities, and seeks to determine whether it had a transformative or merely a catalytic role in their ultimate fate as complex union states.

First, however, it should be said that British historians do not always fully recognize that the UK, though of course a victorious power, experienced through the war of 1914–18 similar disintegrative or centrifugal forces to those which helped to fracture some of its enemies, and in particular Austria-Hungary. The latter fell apart in 1918: but what might well be described as the 'first' United Kingdom, the state formed as a union between Britain and Ireland in 1800, also comprehensively broke down between 1919 and 1921. This meant the loss of around 22 per cent of its landed territory—proportionately more European land than lost by the defeated German empire.

Just as the most recent historiography on Austria-Hungary has tended to emphasize its viability even in 1914 (or indeed beyond, as late as the start of 1918), and to stress the devastating impact of war, so in fact the same (or similar) arguments may be made for the United Kingdom (see e.g. Bridge 1990, p. 380). But, while some historians of continental Europe (like Robert Gerwarth) have occasionally and rightly drawn the Irish revolution into wider discussions of 'when the First World War ended', on the whole British historians have tended (for different, though striking, reasons) to minimize or normalize the extent of the disruption and disintegration experienced by the UK state through Irish independence (1919–21). In this reading, the Irish war of independence happened in Ireland, and belongs to Irish history rather than British. A 'Whig', interpretation of British constitutional history lives on. Equally, for that matter, insular British and Irish historiographies live on.

What was the constitutional health of the United Kingdom (and the Dual Monarchy) before 1914? The history of Austria-Hungary, like that of the union of Great Britain and Ireland and the many other unions embraced by this work, has often been inflected—until very recently—through a teleology which emphasizes failure. But this has slowly changed within recent scholarship; and the overall direction of recent research on Austria-Hungary—and (and in a more limited fashion) on the United Kingdom of Great Britain and Ireland—has been to place greater stress on longevity and upon (therefore) at least the possibility of the survival of the two polities at the outbreak of war, in 1914 (Jackson 2013; Cole and Unowsky 2007; Judson 2016; cf. Steed 1919, p. 282). In each of these historiographies differing emphases have been placed upon the agency of the First World War within the story of failure: in each the emphasis has slowly but clearly shifted to seeking to understand the state's survival—and towards pushing back against narratives which offer a story of predetermined state failure.

With the Dual Monarchy, it is now argued widely that, while the nationalities questions were difficult, the overall condition of the empire in 1914 was far from terminal. The array of evidence for this proposition includes (as has already been discussed) the imaginative consociational settlement (or attempted settlement) of national disputes in Moravia (1905–6), Bukovina (1910), Budweis/Budějovice (1913), and Bohemia (1914), the economic consolidation of the empire, its sustained efforts towards administrative reform, and its relatively credible performance (in terms of mobilization, for example) at the start of the war (Deak 2015, pp. 260,

264; see sections 3.5, 5.4). Pieter Judson in particular has made an eloquent case for the virtues and robustness of the empire. Similarly, the British historian of central Europe, Alan Sked, has argued that, having survived the crises of the mid-19th century, the empire was 'in relatively good shape by 1914'—and that it was 'questions of foreign policy and dynastic honour or prestige' which had finally precipitated the empire's war (Sked 1989, p. 214). Steve Beller has argued that 'there is much that is laudable about the economic performance, the level of civilisation, the relative rule of law and the relative security which the Habsburg state had brought to central Europe by 1914', while acknowledging that there were also downsides to its performance (Beller 1996, p. 159). Historians now routinely make the point that the Dual Monarchy performed relatively well in terms of mobilizing and sustaining its war machine in the first years of the war; and that by 1917 (admittedly with considerable German help) it had attained many of its military goals. Even some contemporary, pre-war, English commentators (such as Wickham Steed) offered relatively upbeat assessments of the overall state of the imperial and royal armies (see e.g. Steed 1919, pp. 61–2).

Similarly, the case for the health of the Irish union centres on its longevity and flexibility and on the overall condition of Ireland in the years before the First World War (see Jackson 2013). In 1914 it is true that the powerful but minority unionist movement in the north-east of Ireland was energetically threatening the British government over the question of Irish devolution or home rule. It is also, of course, true that a powerful nationalist movement in Ireland had agitated against the British connection through much of the later 19th century. But those nationalists had very largely worked within the walls of Westminster; and from 1886 there had developed a relatively close working relationship between Irish nationalism and the British Liberal party (see e.g. Lubenow 1988). By 1914 nationalists were cooperating closely with Liberal ministers to deliver an agreed Irish settlement.

Thus, by 1914 mainstream Irish nationalism had effectively been contained and partly assimilated within British parliamentary culture for nearly 50 years. A modified version of the union, where there would be a British connection, Irish representation in London, and a sovereign British parliament together with a devolved and limited Irish assembly, looked set to be put in place through the medium of the third home rule bill. This modified version of union was influenced in turn by the shape and apparent success of other multinational union states both on continental Europe and in the British empire—states such as the Habsburg empire, or Canada, or the Union of South Africa (created in 1910), or even (at least in the 1880s and early 1890s) Sweden-Norway. While there was a small and energetic republican movement in Ireland before 1914, the British king, George V, had been well received during his coronation visit to Ireland in 1911. And even advanced separatists such as Pádraig Pearse embraced the appearance of a home rule measure in April 1912.

Linked with all this, there is a related and well-established case which emphasizes the sustained health of Irish constitutional nationalism—of the accommodationist movement which worked within the institutions of union, which sought its negotiated supersession within an imperial framework, and which supported the British war effort. It is reasonably clear that constitutional nationalism of this kind remained relatively secure until 1916–17, when the Easter Rising was fought, and when Sinn Féin was comprehensively reorganized under a new constitution and leadership. And there are surely parallels here with the accommodationist nationalisms of the Austro-Hungarian empire—which, until the war, sought to work within the (modified) parameters of the Dual Monarchy rather than wholly to overturn it (Jackson 2018b; Steed 1919, p. 122).

In short, it is clear that neither the Habsburg state nor the United Kingdom were in any form of terminal condition until well into the First World War. In and after 1917–18 the Dual Monarchy was weakened by military rule and by military and diplomatic setbacks, by massive food and other shortages, and by the death of the father of the Ausgleich of 1867, Franz Joseph: the 'nationalities question', which had been difficult but containable before the war, thrived in these collective circumstances. The United Kingdom was certainly victorious in 1918; but it, too, was weakened by the demands of the war. And the issue of Irish nationality, which had also been containable before 1914, was now becoming radicalized in the manner of the Habsburgs' Italian and Czech questions. By late 1918 the Dual Monarchy had collapsed; but in Ireland the general election of 1918, with the return of 73 separatists out of an Irish representation of 105, also signalled an impending crisis for the British union state. And on 21 January 1919—three days after the beginning of the Paris peace conference—the first shots of the Irish war of independence were fired.

If all this was indeed the case, however, then what *was* the utility of war for multinational unions and empires: why go to war? This question is posed, not to rehearse the detailed high-political and diplomatic background to the outbreak of war in August 1914, but rather to enquire briefly and more specifically about the relationship between conflict and the integrity of complex multinational polities. War and supranational armies occupy difficult positions within the historiography of both the United Kingdom and the Austro-Hungarian empire. On the one hand, they have been seen in each case as having a short-term integrative function, creating binding institutions and sometimes reinforcing unifying supranational identities. On the other hand, the experience of sustained large-scale conflict was thoroughly ambiguous; and there are clear senses in which warfare of this kind produced some apparent short-term 'benefits', while delivering ultimate destruction (see sections 4.4, 6.6).

It will be recalled that, for Linda Colley, the army and war were key constituents in the formation of Britishness in the 18th century, while for the Scots sociologist David McCrone 'war and the welfare state' supplied additional centripetal force in the 20th century (see Colley 1992; McCrone 1992; and see section 4.4). The First World War, and the British army, are generally regarded as forces promoting the consolidation of supranational—British and imperial—identities. Similarly, the joint Austro-Hungarian army and the longevity of its commander-in-chief, the monarch, Franz Joseph, have long been seen as key binding agents within the Dual Monarchy. Moreover, it will be further recalled that under the terms of the Ausgleich, Austria-Hungary had three common—shared—imperial ministries: foreign affairs, finance, and war. Foreign affairs, in particular, which was housed in the Ballhausplatz in Vienna, was home to (what have been seen as) 'supranational patriots', who pushed in the years immediately before the First World War for a more aggressive foreign policy precisely as a means of averting the disintegration and restoring the 'great power' status of the Dual Monarchy: these came to harmonize largely (if not uniformly) with the views of Conrad von Hötzendorf, the Chief of the General Staff, who 'argued repeatedly that the use of armed force alone could retard the forces of nationalism in the "multinational empire"; war was the only means of politics' (Herwig 1997, p. 9; see also e.g. Tunstall 2012, p. 118). Indeed, in one briskly direct argument, 'the Monarchy deliberately started a world war rather than compromise internally or externally on the south Slav question' (Sked 1989, p. 269; see also Bridge 1990, pp. 336–8; Herwig 1997, p. 18).

There is a (sometimes) underestimated parallel issue here relating to Ireland. The United Kingdom in 1914 was on the cusp of civil war on the basis of its own 'nationalities question'—Irish home rule. And it was with a palpable sense of relief that the prime minister, Asquith, turned to European politics in the summer of that year, and away from Ireland and the threat of civil conflict. Asquith and the Liberal cabinet of course did not go to war to escape the Irish question— that is to say, adapting Sked's formulation, they did *not* sign off on 'a world war rather than compromise internally or externally' on the Irish question. But it is certainly worth considering the extent to which war tacitly seemed to provide an opportunity for the reconstruction of national unity in the context of the Irish and other domestic troubles of the time (cf. Sked 1989, p. 269). Christopher Clark has eloquently described the pressures created by the Ulster crisis on the military and political classes, the extent to which war appeared to offer an alluring opportunity to sidestep home rule, and the resultant and astonishing '*union sacrée* that extended all the way from the unionists of all stripes to the Labour Party and even the Irish nationalists' (Clark 2013, p. 545).

Beyond government, many in both Ireland and the Dual Monarchy also saw opportunities for political gain through the conflict. As in Ireland, where Redmondites and unionists jockeyed to position themselves for the favour of the union government, so in Austria-Hungary nationalists saw the possibility of strategic advantage as a reward for their community's loyal support. Socialists saw, too, the possibility that deploying the support of the working classes for the war effort might bring further reform (Judson 2016, p. 385). War, therefore, appeared to offer new opportunities and new options for many across the empire, as indeed was also the case in the United Kingdom.

In short, in multinational unions like the United Kingdom or Austria-Hungary there was a critical group of union institutions clustered around the army and the monarch, titular commanders-in-chief of the army: the army and the crown, as supranational agencies in a multinational state, mattered relatively more here than in nation states—because with unions these agencies and institutions were relatively more significant as binding forces. As a corollary, it might be suggested that aggressive external strategies and warfare potentially mattered more in these polities as a means of unification. Martin Zückert has said (of the Habsburgs) that 'waging war in 1914 was also a potential attempt to integrate the polyethnic society by using military power. It was a way of escaping forward in order to stabilise the empire from the inside and to reduce external danger' (Leonhard and von Hirschhausen 2011, p. 502). The unspoken temptation of this *Flucht nach vorn* (flight to the front) certainly existed in some measure for the United Kingdom as well.

What was the reality of the impact of war on the different 'nationalities questions'? The war had the effect, not so much of creating the problems with union, as of radically concentrating them into one highly destructive constitutional amalgam. War also resolved those crucial ambiguities, and destroyed the wriggle-room, upon which multinational polities like the United Kingdom and Austria-Hungary had come to depend in terms of sustaining their longevity (Jackson 2013; Cornwall 2002, pp. 64ff.).

For a start, war brought the further marginalization of the small nations within multinational combatants like the United Kingdom or the Dual Monarchy. The demands of conducting the war meant that the concerns of the management of the union were relegated in both London and Vienna. The perennial tendency for the London government to overlook its geographical periphery was further encouraged, as the demands of the conflict pushed Irish issues ever further down the cabinet agenda. Yet the opportunities for enflaming the volatile national sensitivities of the Irish grew ever more, as did the distraction and tactlessness of (even basically friendly) British ministers. In the same way, the delicate diplomacy of the nationalities questions of the Habsburg state was relegated in favour of the pursuit of the war—especially in Cisleithania, where military rule was instituted (there never had been much by way of 'delicate diplomacy' regarding the nationalities in Transleithania).

War also brought an end to much, hitherto essential, flexibility and ambiguity. Hew Strachan has pithily remarked that, with war, 'government was more centralised, censorship more coordinated, the resources of the state more readily mobilised in Britain and France than in Germany' (in Butterwick-Pawlikowski et al. 2017, p. 50). With war came a disappearance of the necessary flexibility or ambiguity which had characterized much official responsiveness both in the United

Kingdom and the Dual Monarchy towards national unrest. The war, in short, brought a radical shock to popular expectations of the 'normal' functioning of the union state, whether in Austria-Hungary or in the United Kingdom (Cornwall 2002, pp. 8, 64; Cole 2014, p. 318). In particular, the war augmented the forces of centralization in both the United Kingdom and the Dual Monarchy (Deak 2015, p. 265).

Linked with this, the increased influence of the military and of their needs within British government delivered a set of decisions and policies which enflamed Irish separatist feeling. The liberal state was compromised through (for example) the draconian and wide-ranging Defence of the Realm Act, passed swiftly into law on 8 August 1914: unlike in Cisleithania (rebranded after 1915 as Austria), where the Reichsrat was suspended, the British parliament continued at least to sit, but the new legislation gave considerable powers to the Admiralty and the Army Council as well as instituting controls on the press and wider forms of censorship. In addition, conscription to military service was introduced in Britain in January 1916; and, while this was never extended to Ireland, the threat of its activation remained active virtually until the end of the war, serving as a recurrent and critical goad to nationalist anger. Moreover, military rule may not have been instituted explicitly and comprehensively throughout the United Kingdom, but it was certainly applied in Ireland—for example, in response to the separatists' insurgency during Easter week, April 1916. The subsequent martial law tribunals sentenced 15 of the insurgent leaders to death in a highly secretive and protracted manner which is still widely seen as a pivotal episode in the history of Ireland and the union.

In Cisleithania/Austria military dominance was associated with the continued suspension of the Reichsrat and of parliamentary government. Here the civilian authorities speedily accommodated themselves to an all-embracing military authority, with the concomitant suspension of free speech, freedom of association, and trial by jury. In Hungary (where civilian rule remained nominally in place) as well as in Austria, new wartime surveillance authorities were swiftly put in place to spy on the population. Military ascendancy was also associated with both repression as well as the consolidation of German interests in Cisleithania. Indeed, Peter Haslinger has observed that 'various forms of preemptive repression alienated [even those] groups that had cherished a critical loyalty towards the Habsburg dynasty thus far, and still had hopes for a reform of the empire...most of these repressive measures applied against south Slavs, Ukrainians and Jews' (Gerwarth and Manela 2014, p. 81; Cole 2014, pp. 317–18; Deak 2015, pp. 266–7).

More generally, the ferocious and bloody pressures created by the war activated a range of dormant or hitherto low-voltage national prejudices, especially within the governing nationalities of both the Dual Monarchy and the United Kingdom. The Habsburg navy (which was 34,000 strong in 1910) was chiefly recruited from (what German Austrians regarded as) the questionably loyal Dalmatian Croats and Italians of the Adriatric littoral (Deák 1990, pp. 194, 201). Moreover, as the war progressed, there were numerous (German) allegations of Czech and other (especially) Slav officers, and in some cases entire Slav units, going over to Austria-Hungary's enemies—just as there were instances of Slavs being targeted for their purported 'disloyalty' (Okey 2001, p. 379). Before 1917 a few Czechs, enrolled as 'the Czech companions', certainly fought in the Russian Third Army against Austria-Hungary and Germany: after 1917 a Czech Legion was raised from the prisoner-of-war camps in Russia and eventually reached a peak strength of around 40,000. But there is in fact little evidence to substantiate the most lurid tales of mass flight from the Habsburg forces; and the scholarly consensus is now that it became convenient for German and Czech nationalists—coming at the issue from different angles—each to embrace a mythology of Slavic disloyalty. For the German Austrians, especially those in the higher ranks of military command, such tales provided cover for the army's recurrent failures; but for the Czechs themselves, especially after 1917, these narratives could be woven into the foundation myths of their emergent nation state (Judson 2016, p. 407; Cole et al. 2011, pp. 199–220).

Just as there were Austrian suspicions of the Slavs, so with the United Kingdom war effort there were official suspicions of the loyalty of the Irish troops. And, as with the Slavs, so with the Irish, these suspicions were almost always exaggerated—fired, perhaps, by the *Staatsvolk* national prejudices of senior officers in each case; and indeed the vital point has been made that, just as unionists often ultimately lost faith in union, so it was actually 'more the ruling elite that lost faith in its peoples...than the other way round' (Cole 2014, p. 322). Republican separatists certainly sought help from Germany, and (as with Sir Roger Casement (1864–1916)) sometimes looked to recruit support from among those Irish prisoners of war in German hands; but the fruits of these efforts were in fact extremely meagre (it is thought that around 56 Irishmen fought with the Germans, as against the approximately 200,000 who fought in the British crown forces). However, as with the Czechs, so with Irish nationalists—the track-record of enormous national sacrifice within the context of an overarching imperial army jarred badly with the preferred birth narratives of the respective nation states. If Czech treason 'became a critical mythological component of the founding' of the newly minted Czechoslovakia in 1918–19, then Irish 'treason' (in the form of the 1916 rising) became the key component of the founding myths of modern Ireland (cf. Judson 2016, p. 407). In both cases the inconvenient truth was that patriots had fought and died bravely *within* (though not necessarily *for*) the armies of union and empire; but this could not be officially acknowledged by the Czechs or by the Irish for many years to come. Moreover, as in Austria-Hungary, so in Ireland, the story of the war came to be shaped around a narrative which was convenient for, and tacitly agreed by, both nationalists and loyalists (similar narratives were relevant in Finland at this time, given that Finns fought in Prussian regiments) (Kirby 2006, p. 157).

But the overall militarization of government represented, as Judson has remarked in relation to Austria-Hungary, 'a radical departure from the normal functioning of the Rechtsstaat', as well as the subversion of systems of governance which 'had tied together popular expectations and administrative responses' (Judson 2016, p. 393; Deak 2015, pp. 267–8). In short, whether in Austria-Hungary or in parts of the United Kingdom, the war came to threaten both the legitimacy of the state as well as a crisis of popular expectations. Linked with this last point, the war also brought an end to exceptionalism. The exceptionalism which was practised by the British state in Ireland before the war now largely ended. Treating Ireland as a special case within the union had come—by at least the end of the 19th century—to be an accepted stratagem of union government, and was expressed in a range of policies, from land reform (especially land purchase) through to home rule itself. But the war ended much of this—and reasonable Irish expectations of exceptional treatment (based securely on past ministerial performance) were rudely affronted between 1916 and 1918 by British governments' repeated (integrationist) efforts to extend military conscription to Ireland. In short, union government had demanded tactful exceptionalism: war governance demanded uniformity. In this distinction lay some of the origins of division and separation within both Austria-Hungary and the United Kingdom.

The uncertainty and protracted nature of war helped to destabilize the frameworks of the union state (though of course this weakening was not confined to unions alone). Defeat for the Habsburgs was, given issues of numbers, money, and technology (and military track-record) always a real possibility, but it was certainly not assured until as late as 1918 (Sked 1989, p. 187). István Deák has argued that, even in 1917, 'it seemed as if the country's war aims had been more or less accomplished: the defeat and humiliation of Serbia, Romania and Russia, and now even the near-defeat and humiliation of Italy' (Deák 1990, p. 192). By the same token, however, it is important to remember that, from the perspective of separatist nationalism in Ireland, the victory of the United Kingdom was by no means clear as late as the spring of 1918, given the initial dramatic successes of the Germans' *Kaiserschlacht* in the weeks following 21 March. For opponents of union and empire, the war offered sustained and tantalizing opportunities, even within the context of an ultimately victorious power.

War brought, too, an enhancement of the influence of diasporic nationalists—Irish, Czech, and south Slav—on the politics of the British and Habsburg empires (see section 6.6). In the context of war the role of national diasporas—or the communities of the irredenta—assumed a damaging significance for union and imperial states like Britain or Austria-Hungary. Irish communities in the United States of America helped to delay US entry into the war until 1917: they also supplied finance and other forms of support to Irish nationalists in Ireland. Equally, exiles, diasporas, and fellow nationals outside the boundaries of the Dual Monarchy helped to thwart its war effort and to undermine its integrity as the war progressed.

At the same time the conflict brought a clear and disproportionate weakening of some of the classes which had most effectively contributed to binding union and empire. With Austria-Hungary it has been calculated that already by the end of 1914 the Habsburg army had lost nearly half of its pre-war regular officers as casualties (both dead and wounded): 'other armies may have had similarly high losses during the first campaigns, but the Austro-Hungarian armed forces lost their military elite that was multilingual and had experience with the multinational structure of the empire' (Hirschhausen and Leonhard 2001, p. 512). The consequence of this carnage was that a generation of less experienced and more particularist officers took the place of this supranational cadre—a generation more likely to be nationalist rather than supranationalist, or Habsburg, in their loyalties. In a similar manner, the disproportionate casualties sustained by the supranational landed and aristocratic cadre of the British army, as well in particular by the Irish landed classes, constituted a disproportionate assault on a unionist military elite—and thus on the union state itself.

How did war shape national and supranational identities in union states? As the foregoing analysis will have made clear, the wider relationship between warfare and union states was complex; and a final brief comment on war and identity is therefore required. On the one hand, a clearly defined enemy—a discrete 'Other'—has functioned as a means of unification within such states, as with Linda Colley's thesis concerning the consolidation of Britain and Britishness as against Catholic France in the 18th century. In the 20th century, too, British identity has been repeatedly boosted through national mobilization in the context of foreign war. However, as the examples of the First and Second World Wars readily underline, there are complexities here. While wars have underpinned overarching union identities such as Britishness, albeit in complex ways, they have also commonly reinforced the constituent national identities of the union state—Irish, Scots, Welsh. And service in the First World War, together with participation in the subsequent peace conferences, certainly served to consolidate the national identities of the contributing dominion and imperial territories such as Canada (and Australia, India, and South Africa). The First World War, therefore not only delivered a stronger Britishness, but also a more robust Irish and Scottish set of identities. War simultaneously boosted Britain, its union, and its empire—but also undermined them.

Moreover, with the dominant nationalities, the *Staatsvölker*, of the union state, there were also tipping points where they effectively disinvested from union, and developed in ways which were inimical to it (see also section 6.4). In Austria-Hungary, for example, a robust German identity re-emerged during the First World War, especially within the dominant military cultures in the western, Cisleithanian, half of the empire. It seems clear that these contributed to the general weakening of trust and confidence in the empire which ultimately hastened its demise. Within the United Kingdom, it has long been recognized that once-ferocious

Conservative unionists had their passions defused, and to some extent turned from union, during the long and bloody years of the Great War. This ultimately helped to provide the political basis for Conservative acquiescence to the grant of dominion status to the insurgent 26 counties of the new Irish Free State in 1921–2.

What of the impact of war on the mutual obligations binding the union state and its citizens? In the end it has been suggested that 'war destroyed the empire of the Habsburgs over time by eroding any sense of mutual obligation between people and state: popular and dynastic patriotism withered away, calling into question the very raison d'être of empire' (Judson 2016, p. 441). In Austria-Hungary the state in the end could not even ensure an adequate food supply, aside from any question of the suspension of 'normal' civil rights. Maureen Healy, for example, has argued that:

> the collapse [of the empire] was even more deeply internal than previously imagined. The state was discredited not only in the eyes of national minorities in other parts of Austria or in the minds of weary troops at the front, as other histories have shown, but also in the markets, apartment houses, schoolyards, streets and the pubs of its own imperial capital.

Her emphasis is on the increasingly harsh conditions of life during the war, rather than the nationalities question: but, as she states, her 'study has found the roots of the collapse of the Habsburg state in the mundane and every day' (Healy 2004, p. 300). This same erosion of trust and obligation was central to the weakening and ultimate failure of the Irish union. In Ireland the state apparently reneged upon what were seen as central political obligations—the enactment of home rule—aside from any question of the suspension of civil rights (especially in 1916 and after), or the increasingly disrespectful treatment of Irish nationalists and their leadership. In short, while there was a general weakening of the moral authority of the state across Europe, this erosion was particularly corrosive in the context of multinational unions. Here the bonds of the constitutional compound were especially vulnerable—and here the solvent effects of war were especially great.

Returning, finally, to the opening observation of the chapter, the British were of course one of the victorious allied powers, while the Austro-Hungarians were not; and these central facts have naturally shaped much of the interpretation of the fall-out from war. Sharp contrasts between the condition of the defeated powers, like Austria-Hungary, and that of successful powers, like the United Kingdom, are commonly made; and (in many respects) they remain entirely reasonable. But was the contrast between the experience of Europe's multinational unions and empires and Britain really as fundamental as this kind of assessment would seem to suggest? It is worth reflecting further on the closely shared experience of victor and defeated: as Robert Gerwarth and Erez Manela have pointed out, 'the conflict had [also] dealt a substantial blow to those empires that emerged victorious'

(Gerwarth and Manela 2014, p. 4). In fact it has been underlined in the most recent scholarship that 'the Great War became not just a war for empire and between empires but also one...against empires' (Gerwarth and Manela 2014, p. 177). It is worth underlining that (what has been earlier called here) the 'first edition' or 'first version' of the United Kingdom—the United Kingdom of Great Britain and the entire island of Ireland—clearly failed between 1916 and 1921, when Irish independence was achieved. The proximate cause, or at any rate the critical context, illuminating the demise of the first union was of course the First World War.

Much recent historiographical discussion has focused on the extent to which the end of the war brought the replacement of large imperial (or, it is argued here, multinational union) polities—not by homogeneous nation states—but rather by smaller multinational union polities with different types of ethnic minority challenge. Austria-Hungary of course ultimately dissolved into the autonomous republics of Austria, Hungary, and Czechoslovakia and the kingdom of Yugoslavia— and ceded further territories to Italy (Trieste and the south Tirol), Romania (Transylvania), and to the second Polish republic (Galicia). Each of these successor states was complex and multinational, Czechoslovakia having substantial German as well as Hungarian and Ukrainian minorities. Similarly inter-war Romania possessed large Hungarian and German and Ukrainian minorities.

But the United Kingdom of Great Britain and Ireland was also redefined, if less catastrophically, as the United Kingdom of Great Britain and Northern Ireland, with (after 1922) the Irish Free State seceding: indeed the framers of the new state carefully examined the constitutions of numerous of the successor states to the Austro-Hungarian empire (Heffernan 2012, p. 224). The six counties of the northeast of Ireland became a self-governing province within the United Kingdom, but contained a mixed population of those who now emphasized their British and UK identities (around two-thirds) alongside those, mostly Catholic, who emphasized their Irishness. As in central and eastern Europe, so in the fragmenting United Kingdom of 1921–2, there was enforced displacement and movement of peoples—and sustained controversies over causation and the apportionment of blame.

Britain's status as a victor from the war meant that the secession of Ireland and the creation of a new Northern Ireland were *not* part of the peace settlement at Paris. But these events were no less directly linked to the experience of war than the reconfiguration of central Europe. And just as with this redrawing of continental frontiers, so Ireland's independence brought the creation of a new border between it and the United Kingdom. Again, Britain's status as a victor nation meant that this was not directly a part of the proceedings at Versailles, but the connections are clear enough. Just as the Treaty of Versailles made provision for border readjustments and commissions by plebiscite in Schleswig (February and March 1920), East Prussia (July 1920), and Silesia (March 1921), and just as the

Treaty of Saint Germain made provision for a commission and plebiscite in Carinthia (October 1920), so the contested nature of the frontier between the new Irish Free State and Northern Ireland was addressed by a boundary commission in 1924–5—though in the event not by any plebiscite (though this was certainly discussed). In general the tensions between the break-up of empire, national self-determination, and maximalist demands for historic frontiers (as with Czech nationalists in Bohemia) also played out in Ireland (Zách 2021, pp. 55ff.). Here there were tensions between separatist Irish nationalists and the British empire, and an Irish nationalist demand for the historic borders of the island of Ireland.

Much discussion on the fall-out from the war focuses on the idea of a continuing conflict: Gerwarth is only the most recent and most eloquent scholar to focus upon the idea of 'why the first world war failed to end'. This notion of a continuing conflict applies to the dismembered Austria-Hungary—but it is also extremely relevant to the United Kingdom of Great Britain and Ireland, and indeed to its colonial territories. In essence the consolidation of radical nationalism which characterized the later stages of the war for the Habsburg empire applied similarly within the United Kingdom and its empire, with Irish and an array of other (colonial) nationalisms, including Canadian, Australian, South African, and Indian, feeding into movements for either greater or complete autonomy and separation from London.

Irish independence from the United Kingdom, attained in 1921–2, had a complex influence on other freedom movements within the wider British empire. The guerrilla tactics of the Irish Republican Army, as well as the related political strategies of the separatist movement (Sinn Féin), were earnestly studied by nationalists in Egypt, India, Palestine, Cyprus, and Malaya. Equally, the official diplomatic pressure applied by Irish nationalists through the newly formed government of independent Ireland provided an inspiration and lead to other British dominions (such as Canada, South Africa, and Australia) for further powers of self-government—these culminating in a measure of co-equality, the Statute of Westminster (1931).

It is also possible to sustain comparisons at a more granular level. Germany and Austria's experience and export of the *Freikorps* phenomenon after 1919 have been seen as possessing a post-war British analogy in terms of the Black and Tans in Ireland (as well as the spectrum of Irish paramilitarism—the unionist and pro-state paramilitarism of the North). Moreover, the experience of the disputed frontier which was a fundamental part of the history of central and eastern Europe after 1918 was also part of the United Kingdom's experience—in terms of the border which emerged after 1920–1 between Northern Ireland and the Irish Free State. Here, religion was the key defining agent of national identity, rather than as with (say) Silesia, language. But there was indeed violence—and innovative comparative research has been undertaken into the ethnic violence of Silesia and south Ulster, suggesting some analogies, but also demonstrating that the Irish frontier, whatever its occasional horrors, was a relatively less traumatic shatter-zone (Wilson 2010).

In addition the story and memory of war in Europe were inflected through the political requirements of the successor states: Austro-Hungary's war was conventionally read in the light of the national stories of successor states such as Czechoslovakia. In a sense this was also true for the full story of the United Kingdom's war, in so far as critical aspects of that story reflected the preferred narratives of the successor states of the former United Kingdom of Great Britain and Ireland. Austria-Hungary's war story was reinterpreted as one of sustained military incompetence and of the systematic alienation and defiance of those disaffected national minorities (like the Czechs) within the imperial army. Both German Austrians, *Deutschösterreicher*, and the new governments of the successor states effectively collaborated in producing a narrative of the war which emphasized the 'nationality problem' of the Habsburg armies (von Hirschhausen and Leonhard 2001, pp. 508–9). Ireland's war story, influenced by the independent Irish state, was one of silence and neglect concerning the conflict—at least until the 1980s. The struggle against the British of 1916–21, when less than 600 Irish republican fighters died, was privileged over the struggle of Ireland with Britain between 1914 and 1918, when 35,000 Irish died in the ranks of the British army. For, if the proper action of Czech nationalists was to fight *against* the Austro-Hungarian empire rather than with it, then (from the point of view of independent Ireland) the proper action of Irish nationalists was to fight *against* the British empire rather with it.

Just as *Deutschösterreicher* tended to enhance their role and military virtues at the expense of the other nationalities of the imperial army, so those Irish who identified most closely with Britain—the Ulster unionists—embroidered their role and their military virtues at the expense of other Irish within the British army. Moreover, Austria-Hungary's war story embraced a version of *die Dolchstoßlegende*, the German 'stab-in-the-back myth'—with the idea that the hinterland, especially that of the nationalities, was a key explanation for the military and political failure. The unionists of the United Kingdom had (despite the British victory in 1918) their own *Dolchstoßlegende*—provided by the revolutionary nationalists who went to war against the British empire in Dublin during the Easter Rising of 1916.

The war toppled empire: it has been said that 'back in 1918 Lenin's and Wilson's talk of self-determination and the rights of small nations had inspired the enemies of empire everywhere...there was hardly a year in the interwar period when Paris or London was not involved in quelling some form of colonial unrest' (Gerwarth 2016, p. 267). In this sense, if the First World War came to be a war against empire, then there was little differentiation between victors and vanquished. The First World War overturned the Austro-Hungarian empire, but it also supplied some of the weaponry for the overturning of the British empire.

But the chemistry of multinational unions and multinational empires was linked; and England and Britain not only possessed a global empire, they also exercised a form of 'internal colonialism' in Ireland and—perhaps—Scotland (see Hechter 1975; Kumar 2003, p. 85). In other words, if the First World War came to be war against empire, then it also came to be a war which brought into question the stability of union states like the United Kingdom. A war against empire could, and often did, mean a war against union.

7
Untied Kingdoms
Past Politics and Present History

Now the map of Europe shows us that in cases like those of Hungary and Norway, a vigorous sense of nationality is compatible with effective organic union tempered by nationality.

(Gladstone 1892, p. 225)

A staunch Catholic, one of [Otto von Habsburg's] most famous interventions occurred when Ian Paisley heckled Pope John Paul II during a 1988 visit to the Strasbourg parliament. Snatching Paisley's banner reading 'John Paul II: Anti-Christ', von Habsburg helped eject Paisley from the chamber.

(*Irish Times*, 5 July 2011)

In a polity divided as to race, public opinion and power of resistance into a dozen entities, the triumph of a non-ethical standpoint of government is singularly facilitated...it must rise superior to the lower expediency represented by the line of least resistance and comprehend the perennial efficacy of the higher expediency represented by the principle of Justice.

(Steed 1919, pp. 295–6)

history is past politics; and politics present history

(E. A. Freeman, November 1880, quoted by Hesketh 2014, pp. 105–8)

it is not beyond the bounds of possibility that the history of the Austro-Hungarian empire, or of Spain's composite monarchy under the House of Austria, both of them relegated by historians of the nation state to the dust-heap of history, might still have something to say to a very different age.

(Sir John Elliott, in Elliott 2012, p. 79)

There was indisputably a proliferation of the notion and nomenclature of the 'united kingdom' during, and at the conclusion of, the conflict with Napoleonic France. Taking numerous case studies, this book has sought to offer some wide-ranging reflections on the nature of these different unions and united kingdoms in the 'long' 19th century and beyond. They were generally polities which had begun life as composite monarchies or as personal unions, and which had later developed into an array of different forms of multinational (and often specifically designated) 'united kingdom'. They were also polities which, aside from these resemblances, were otherwise linked by chronology, being created at roughly the same time, and often by the exigencies of British foreign and imperial policy.

The United Kingdom of Great Britain and Ireland, through especially its foreign secretary, Viscount Castlereagh (in office between 1812 and 1822) and his lieutenants, was central to both the origins and the preservation of this network; and indeed it will now be clear that one of the contentions of the book (given the influential role of Castlereagh and his circle) is that Britain may be said to have exported supranational union just as the French republic exported revolution and the nation state (see section 1.5, Figure 1.1). Much of Castlereagh's work was in turn shaped by strategic thinking inherited from his sometime political patron, William Pitt (see Figure 2.1). This of course is not to suggest that the British invented 'union', or even parliamentary union, or that they had exclusive rights over the concept. But it is to say that some of the key British and Irish architects of the United Kingdom emerged as staunch promoters and defenders of other union polities in the early 19th century—generally, as with the Irish union, with security and the French threat both firmly in mind. It is also to say that these architects of union were effectively using union to reinvent the institutions of the *ancien régime* for an age of revolution and beyond (Schultz 2001).

But there was also, ultimately, a reciprocity of influences and connections. Contemporary Britons—politicians, scholars, travellers—naturally saw rich and dense interlinkages connecting the different unions of 19th-century Europe and beyond; and from these they eventually came to identify exemplars or paradigms for the constitutional reform of the United Kingdom. The best known case of such a set of influences rests with W. E. Gladstone, as the epigraphs to this chapter illustrate; but Gladstone was merely the most prominent, and the most influential, of a much wider cohort who thought carefully about the reform of their own country (or indeed, more generally, about its merits and demerits) in comparative terms. The intercommunication of influences with these union polities across the long 19th century is truly striking, with (for example) Scotland at different times both influencing and being influenced by the politics of Irish nationhood, and Canada both receiving and bestowing influence from and on the unions of the United Kingdom.

In particular Irish nationalists and Irish unionists for long engaged with the history of the multinational union states of continental Europe and beyond, seeking both angels and demons, and both models as well as warnings. Irish Catholics on the whole warmly embraced Habsburg Europe, and sometimes sought refuge within its boundaries: Irish Protestants (some of whose ancestors had originally fled from Moravia and other crownlands) were more suspicious, and indeed there is an unremarked historical aptness in the fisticuffs exchanged in 1988 in the European parliament by Ian Paisley and Otto von Habsburg (and which were described at the head of the chapter). In short, the story of the unions of the United Kingdom has been closely associated with external exemplars and warnings; and, more generally, the story of these unions has always been associated with European analogy and comparison. It remains the case that the unions of the United Kingdom are intimately bound within European (and wider) politics. Unions and united kingdoms have been British and Irish—and also European; but they have been transnational and indeed transcontinental as well.

These unions, while sharing some familial similarities, had distinctive histories and cultures; and each has therefore been examined through the elucidation of separate case studies. But these individual stories, and the patient excavation of individual unions, reveal various overall similarities in terms of formation and survival and (sometimes) longevity; and they also point to some shared weaknesses, and some shared experiences of decline and demise. Pragmatic and contingent creations, these unions often lacked a visionary ideal: pragmatic and contingent, they were forged (like many subsequent federal unions) in the context of economic and military need (see e.g. Parent 2011 for the theme of security and voluntary union). The United Kingdom of Great Britain and Ireland (1801), the Austrian empire (1804), the United Kingdoms of Sweden-Norway (1814), the United Kingdom of the Netherlands (1815) were all created in the context of a world war, and against the backdrop of the struggle against revolutionary and Napoleonic France. An additional form of 'union' polity, the Grand Duchy of Finland, came into being at this time (1809): and indeed a further 'united kingdom', that of Portugal, Brazil, and the Algarves, was created and also decisively shaped in the light of the contingencies of the global conflict (1815).

When and why did these unions fail (cf. Hicks 1978; Buchanan 1991; Lehning 1998)? As has been discussed, the notion of failure is not always absolute; and to some extent the idea of a union's 'failure' (as with that of any form of state) is linked to questions of purpose, and ethics, and succession, no less than basic notions of longevity. These multinational unions often lacked 'the vision thing', but they rarely lacked purpose; and in some cases this purpose was triumphantly fulfilled—even though, in the long run, the union itself ultimately came apart. Moreover, the success of a union can scarcely be defined exclusively by its longevity, and especially if the latter was sustained by systematic and prolonged oppression (the 'dark arts' of union governance, discussed at length in section 4.11). Lastly, unions rarely had clear-cut, discrete endings; they were more often characterized by *rallentando* and reprise than by a curt finale. In other words, unions (like other polities) may be judged not only by the finality of their endings, but rather by the continuities and legacies which they bequeathed: they may have died, but moved on to an afterlife or reincarnation.

Moreover, any consideration of the longevity and ends of multinational union polities needs to embrace Oszkár Jászi's warning that simple binaries of centripetal and centrifugal influences rarely suffice as analytical tools (see Figure 5.2). As Jászi shrewdly observed in relation to the physics of destruction within the Dual Monarchy, 'almost all of the centripetal forces developed in their later course centrifugal tendencies in one direction or another' (Jászi 1929, p. 133).

With all these caveats firmly in view, some solvents of union may now be isolated and identified. For a start these polities uniformly lacked any compelling and binding narrative: indeed, in most cases their individual creation was vitiated by lasting allegations of corruption—and worse. The toxic allure of 'English gold' or the vanities of noble title or official patronage have been central elements of the popular accounts of the birth of union in both Scotland and Ireland. But the calculus of profit in Edinburgh and Dublin was matched by the 'Dutch arithmetic', the *arithmétique hollandaise*, of the Netherlands—the shady operations by which the constitution of the new United Kingdom of the Netherland was passed into law (Marteel 2018, p. 61).

Of course the pressure of cash operated not just at an individual or sectional level, but also with the nation itself, and indeed as an essential purpose of union: unions were frequently born because one of the component national partners required a bailout. In essence Scotland was assisted in 1706-7 through the English exchequer; and the northern Netherlands, heavily indebted at the end of the Napoleonic occupation, was rescued through its union with the south. In 1840 the indebted citizens of Upper Canada were supported through union with their more solvent compatriots in Lower Canada; and there was also a range of financial forces impelling the proponents of federal union, or 'confederation', in 1867.

Moreover, unions were often forged, not merely through financial or professional inducements, but in the context of the rattled sabres of the putative dominant partner: the Scots union was associated with English troop reinforcements, the Irish union followed the bloody suppression of the 1798 rising, the Swedish-Norwegian union followed military action by the Swedes, and the Canadian union followed the rebellions of 1837-8 (see e.g. Jorgenson 1935, pp. 17-18; Berg 2014, pp. 276-7). All of this seemed like a far cry from the upbeat (and carefully curated) tales of the birth of nation states—whether the portrayals of sturdy citizen-soldiers securing against-the-odds victories over the redcoats and their mercenary allies in the American colonies, or heroic accounts of the overturning of entrenched privilege and oppression during the French revolution, or the stories of uninterrupted gallantry and derring-do which ostensibly defined the *Risorgimento* and German unification (certainly in terms of liberal narratives such as those provided by G. M. Trevelyan) (Cannadine 1992). Haggling over a promotion in the peerage, or a job, or over the 'Equivalent', or over compensation for a parliamentary borough, scarcely occupied the same elevated territory in terms of vision or ideals.

'The vision thing' was often lacking, too, in the constitutional detail of these union states. The acts of union which created Great Britain and the United Kingdom, for example, were essentially canny business contracts which addressed costs and benefits, but which ultimately were not associated with any elaborate statement of overarching principle or idealism (nor were they designed to be). There *were* of course such elevating documents elsewhere within the diffuse British constitution, whether Magna Carta, or the Bill of Rights, or (in Scotland) the Claim of Right; but these tended to be expressions of liberty within the context of the individual nations of the union, and within a particular definition of the relationship between parliament and the crown. They were *not* statements of the purpose or usefulness of the union state and its essential structures. In the absence of a codified constitution, and given the contractual nature of the acts of union themselves, the United Kingdom was fundamentally a deal, but not an ideal. So, too, were most of the other union polities considered within this volume: they had a purpose, but not a vision.

Related to this point, unions often lacked, or failed to produce, an overarching or binding identity. The Dual Monarchy of course never generated an effective 'Austro-Hungarianness', and indeed there was never a single citizenship or single passports. This, too, was the case in Sweden-Norway, where citizens were either Norwegians or Swedes, but never Swedish-Norwegian: the Scandinavian movement of the mid-19th century might in theory have served to provide a form of unifying identity for the United Kingdoms, but in practice the fit was never right (it also embraced Denmark, Finland, and Iceland) and in any case it melted away after the 1860s (Jorgenson 1935; Hemstad 2010, 2018). In the United Kingdom, while there was a single citizenship, and a single passport, and while there *was* 'Britishness', this (with its emphases on Protestantism and Britain itself) did not effectively embrace Ireland or Irishness, and worked in different ways in different parts of the UK: there was never any overarching identity for the whole state (Henderson and Wyn Jones 2021, p. 195). In each of these different unions, however, there were some compensating dynastic loyalties—to the Houses of Habsburg, Bernadotte, Hanover, Saxe-Coburg and Gotha or (after 1917) Windsor. These could, and did, work to bind and to unify; but it was often an identity or a loyalty which was vulnerable to shifts both within the respective ruling houses, and in the credibility and standing of their representatives, especially the crowned heads.

This had a bearing on cultures of commemoration within complex multinational union polities. In almost all of the unions reviewed in this volume, unifying acts of public commemoration were rarely associated with the events or fact of union, but were instead often linked with the celebration of the monarch and of the royal dynasty (see e.g. Beller's discussion of Franz Joseph's diamond jubilee: Bucur and Wingfield 2001, pp. 68–9). Unlike nation states, there has rarely been a 'union day' in these polities, though there have been many proxies, including not just the ruling house and its festivals, but also (especially in the United Kingdom) commemorations of the different anniversaries associated with the First and Second World Wars. In Austria-Hungary there was no widespread celebration of the Ausgleich or of dualism; but there were instead various earnest commemorations of the anniversaries and other festive occasions associated with the House of Habsburg—and in particular the emperor-king Franz Joseph (see Figures 3.2, 3.3, 3.4). Equally, in the United Kingdom there have never been 'union days' for the creation of Great Britain, still less for the UK itself (in 1801); but there have instead been coronations, jubilees, royal birthdays, royal weddings, and royal funerals (see Figure 3.1). The lack of a developed public culture of commemoration in this area has meant that, at times of challenge, and in the absence of more compelling alternatives, unionists have sometimes been forced to resort to (what seem like, given the underdeveloped hinterland) shallow displays of flag-waving. And indeed, while (or, rather, because) the United Kingdom is of course much more than the House of Windsor, it may be that (from the point of view of the overall health of the polity) there has been too precariously great a state investment in the monarchy and its somewhat intermittent good behaviour.

Created in particular circumstances, and for particular purposes, these multinational unions were often susceptible to changed contingency and context (cf. Parent 2011, p. 15). Born in warfare, these unions ultimately proved vulnerable (for example) to the traumatic impact of global war in 1914–18, whether as vanquished powers (the Dual Monarchy) or even as victors (in the case of the United Kingdom). War proved uniquely damaging to the complex cultures of flexibility, negotiation, and arbitration which had otherwise been so successful in sustaining both the UK and Austria-Hungary up to 1914. Unions often depended for their survival upon malleability; and war tended to eliminate the wriggle-room necessary for such gymnastics.

Often originating (at least partly) in considerations of commercial well-being, these unions were also vulnerable to economic downturn. Sometimes this might be associated with the rigours of global conflict, and ultimately with basic issues of food and nurture, as with the internal collapse of Austria-Hungary in 1918. But it needs to be stressed that the relationship between unions and prosperity has never been straightforward—and that there has been a complex of influences and contingencies in play. It is true that economic cooperation and growth have generally, though not uniformly, been associated with the consolidation of union: it is routinely argued, for example, that the unionism of Scotland and of eastern Ulster was reinforced through successful integration within the booming industrial and imperial economy of 19th-century England. Equally, the growth of Scots nationalism has been loosely associated with the retreat of British industry and the escalation of Britain's economic woes in the last decades of the 20th century (and beyond). Yet, as has been argued, the strength of union was not simply a function of prosperity, but rather of perceptions of its equitable distribution. Moreover, prosperity was not an absolute; and the relativities of experience within complex union polities were also relevant to its integrity. By extension, perceptions (or the reality) of inequity, even in the context of relative prosperity, could be profoundly damaging. And a combination of relative economic downturn, allied with such inequities, could be catastrophic (as was the case with the Great Famine in Ireland). This compound was also in place, albeit in a very much less deadly form, in Scotland in the late 20th century, with its mixture of protracted economic difficulties, rapid deindustrialization, and strong perceptions of the 'theft' of Scottish oil reserves by incompetent union ministers (see e.g. Harvie 1994).

Unions were generally created in particular circumstances, the result of contingency and pragmatism; but they also sometimes acquired a subsequent purpose and rationale which could, in turn, be superseded. With the Habsburgs and their empire, this central binding purpose, this 'Austrian idea', was tied up for a time with the epic struggle in continental Europe between Christianity and Islam, and indeed between Catholic and Protestant states; but (as Masaryk observed) 'when the Islamic tide receded...the Hapburgs needed to find another saving sanction for themselves and their rule' (quoted in Steed 1937, p. 50). Their ultimate failure, in this thesis, was an inability to fully reinvent themselves as a 'federation of self-governing and well-governed peoples in the Danube Basin and in the Balkans...[and] as a symbol of freedom in Central and South Eastern Europe' (Steed 1937, p. 50).

Similarly, with the United Kingdom successive unions (in 1603 and 1707 and even in 1801) were bound with a practical endorsement of Protestantism; and from the start they were linked with the validation and consolidation of empire (Armitage 2000). The corollary of this has been that the retreat of Britishness and union in the United Kingdom have each been associated with the decline both of empire and of religious faith: secularization and de-colonization have combined, therefore, to subvert union (Nairn 1977; Devine 2016). Expressing this another way, the failure of each of these complex union polities has been closely associated with a failure (or relegation) of their acquired or desired purpose.

These were also often asymmetric unions dominated by one major partner, whose pre-eminence (and distinctiveness) was defined generally in terms of culture and politics, and often in terms of money and people. Britain and the northern Netherlands were Protestant, while Ireland and Belgium were Catholic: Sweden and England were seen as aristocratic, while Norway and (allegedly) Scotland were much less so. While asymmetry in other forms of (federal) union has sometimes been associated with diversity and strength, the pressure within each of the unions considered here was towards the cultural and political hegemony of the main nation: that is to say, asymmetry tended towards the extinguishing of diversity rather than its augmentation. English dominance within the United Kingdom and British dominance within the United Canadas, Dutch dominance within the United Netherlands (despite relative numerical weakness), Swedish dominance within the United Kingdoms of Sweden-Norway were all complemented by German Austrian dominance within the Austrian empire and Cisleithania, and by German and Hungarian dominance within the subsequent Dual Monarchy. In each case these cultural ascendancies were associated with national reaction—and indeed with the enflaming of the question of nationality: equally the dynamic expansion of the union state away from what had been its settled or agreed parameters tended to stimulate nationalist reaction.

Unions and empire, rather than being (as frequently depicted) the antithesis of nationalism, were instead closely interconnected with its shaping and calibration: by the same token, federalization has often been seen as a stimulus to nationalism (Lehning 1998, pp. 6, 111–50). Moreover, union states often worked best when they rested upon component polities which were themselves characterized by unity and a developed or mature patriotism. By way of contrast, unions fared less well when they comprised individual building blocks which were disunited or characterized by half-formed and evolving nationalisms: that is to say they fared less well with fissiparous building blocks which sought to achieve their own unity through defining the institutions of the union state as an alien Other. On a different, but related tack, there are even senses in which unions were often in essence failed nation states.

But nationalism, and the role of national difference (or its exaggeration), supply only one element of the story of union, and of its failures. Multinational union states often harboured significant communities who did not identify strongly with any single nation or ethnicity, but who were instead characterized primarily by a binding supranational dynastic (or other) bond: much has been made of this within recent Habsburg historiography, but there is a strong case for applying the concept elsewhere, and including within the unions of the United Kingdom. It may be that these 'non-national' communities of the Dual Monarchy (and of the United Kingdom) are to be identified with the hybridities associated with identity inside colonial frameworks (cf. Zahra 2008, 2010; Judson 2016). This would certainly make sense in terms of the conceptual overlap between notions of union and of empire—but ultimately the question may only be posed here, rather than resolved.

Often overlooked, but equally important, is the role of unionism in the failure of union—the influence and impact of those ostensible supporters of union (see also section 6.4). At one level this is the unremarkable story of unionists within dominant nationalities seeking at times to enforce their influence (sometimes, as has been discussed, oppressively) over their 'subordinate' partners. But—and linked with this previous point—unions have failed, or have been decisively weakened, because unionists have either grown pessimistic and lost interest (as in Sweden), or have (in some cases) actively undermined the ostensible object of their desire (as in Britain and Ireland). Centralizing elites within Cisleithania during the First World War helped to loosen the bonds of loyalty within the Monarchy through both their increasingly oppressive governance, *and* through a related lack of faith in the Monarchy's constituent nationalities ('it was more the ruling elite that lost faith in its peoples rather than the other way round': see e.g. Cole 2014, p. 322). In the United Kingdom before the war, unionists aggressively challenged some of the central binding institutions of the union state. Arguing in 1912–14 that home rule Liberals had unfairly changed the (uncodified) rules of the British constitutional 'game', unionists in Ireland and Britain looked set to subvert parliament, the army, and even the monarchy. That is to say, British and Irish unionists (like some Habsburg loyalists) effectively sought to uphold and define union through destruction: *ubi solitudinem faciunt, unionem appellant.*

At a more apocalyptic level of risk, there were also cases when defenders of union and empire, polities often originating in global conflict, sought to unify and sustain their complex homelands through considering the agency of foreign warfare (see section 6.7). This has tended to be associated with weakening (rather than broken) multinational powers for whom alternative options have appeared to be wanting: broken polities generally have not had the capacity to go to war. Throughout this work it has been stressed that Austria-Hungary for long retained some possibilities of internal self-renewal; but, still withal, 'the view that the Dual Monarchy was by 1914 in a critical state...which rendered some foreign action imperative as a diversion or as a solution, is not without a certain plausibility' (Bridge 1991, p. 336). An alternative, though closely related, perspective is that the Monarchy had sufficient internal strength to realistically contemplate warfare at this time, while not having sufficient internal strength to resist its lure (cf. Bridge 1991, p. 338). Contemporaries also thought that the parlous condition of the United Kingdom in the summer of 1914, with the looming possibility of conflict over Ulster, was one of the contexts for the decision to go to war on 4 August. Indeed Christopher Clark has (rightly) gone so far as to say that 'nowhere else in Europe, with the possible exception of Austria-Hungary, did domestic [Ulster and Irish] conditions exercise such direct pressure on the political outlook of the most senior military commanders' (Clark 2013, pp. 490, 545).

More recently, and connecting these historical themes with the contemporary, Brexit in Britain appears to have been (amongst much else) an expression of the partial disinvestment from union of its major, English, partner. It has certainly been true that the United Kingdom in the aftermath of devolution has brought distinctive Scots, Welsh, and Northern Irish parliamentary institutions, and a reinforcement of the relevant national identities; but the deficit in terms of the institutional expression of Englishness within the union polity has grown ever more stark (Henderson and Wyn Jones 2021, p. 206). It is of course the case that the United Kingdom, even with devolution, retains much of the infrastructure and even more of the mindset of a centralized union state; and it is true too that there have been some concessions to English national sensitivity (such as the 'English votes for English laws' initiative instituted in parliamentary procedure in

2015, though suspended in 2020: see e.g. Kenny 2014). But there is of course no exclusively English parliament and executive; and the United Kingdom parliament has in recent years provided a platform for apparently rebarbative (and expensive) Scots nationalists and apparently choleric and complaining (and expensive) unionists from Northern Ireland. There are grounds for believing that Brexit has been an assertion of English national identity in the context of an array of challenges, arising partly from the evident inequities of the devolution settlement, but also from continental Europe (Henderson and Wyn Jones 2021, pp. 195ff.). While it seems paradoxical that some English politicians should have denounced the supranational European union using the vocabulary of nationalism, while simultaneously defending the supranational British and Irish unions using the vocabulary of unionism, the paradox may be more apparent than real: they may be implicitly rejecting union *tout court* (see e.g. Henderson and Wyn Jones 2021, p. 215).

On the other hand, while some few unions (like the Netherlands, or Portugal, Brazil, and the Algarves) died young ('infant mortality' in Norman Davies's bleak typology), the majority survived to a venerable old age; and, yet again, some (like the United Kingdom and Canada) remain with us still, in however precarious a condition (see Davies 2011). Unions may have been uninspired and uninspiring in terms of their origins, they may have been unequal, and they may not have conformed to the expectations moulded by the proponents of the nation state; but they had some compensating strengths and virtues. How, then, may we explain the strength and longevity of the multinational union state, on the basis of the evidence surveyed within this work?

As has been noted, unions survived while their defining purposes remained alive and relevant. The United Kingdom, for example, was for long bound by a strong sense of English and British security requirements; and the potential threat posed by Ireland in this respect was a concern driving union in 1799–1800, powering unionist resistance to home rule, and preoccupying the negotiators of the Anglo-Irish Treaty and of Irish independence in 1921-2 (see e.g. Fraser 1912). Irish independence became politically possible for (certainly) British Conservatives, not only because it contained provision for unionists through partition, but also because it addressed the question of British security through the device of the so-called 'Treaty ports' (those naval and military bases around the Irish coastline which were retained by the British between 1922 and 1938)—and because, with the comprehensive defeat of Germany in 1918, the most obvious recent threat to British security had now evidently disappeared. Looking back to 1830, the disaggregation of the (united) kingdom of the Netherlands became possible with some shifts in the geopolitical landscape which had originally given it meaning; while the survival of the complex Habsburg empire in its various iterations was bolstered through its continuing usefulness to superpowers like Britain and Russia in terms of the European strategic balance.

These polities often possessed an inner sturdiness, anchored in buttressing institutions and agencies; and they often benefited from popular loyalty or at least popular passivity. As Wickham Steed said of the Dual Monarchy in 1913:

> In judging the affairs of the Hapsburg Monarchy, it is easy to underestimate its hidden powers of resistance, its secret vitality and the half-unconscious dynastic cohesion of its peoples. For these forces and qualities full allowance must always be made, even though the signs of their existence be overshadowed by symptoms of decrepitude and disintegration.   (Steed 1919, p. 282)

Steed's comment might equally be applied to the unions of the United Kingdom. Both were often malleable polities, which proved adaptable to the challenges and exigencies of threat and change: the semi-confessional incorporating union of Britain and Ireland developed substantially across the span of the long 19th century, abandoning its oppressive church establishment (in Ireland), gaining new electorates, and effectively shedding an old and deeply contested pattern of land ownership. Similarly, Austria-Hungary—and in particular Cisleithania—proved able to generate stimulating new strategies to answer the challenges of class and nationality, whether through expanding enfranchisement or though the new provincial settlements in Moravia and Galicia and elsewhere.

Moreover, by their nature, unions often produced cultures of negotiation and (at best) compromise (though this is not to say that their respective political classes systematically fostered such cultures). However, successful unions were often sustained conversations: unsuccessful unions tended to be dominant power monologues. In the United Province of Canada, as has been shown, there was something approaching a consociational settlement in place from the late 1840s, allowing a form of power-sharing between the two main language communities, English and French. The 90-year history of the United Kingdoms of Sweden-Norway was a history of detailed, sometimes fractious, but still relentless negotiation; and, while not entirely without threat, the dissolution of the union itself was achieved in a broadly peaceable and negotiated fashion. Austria-Hungary in its last two decades was characterized by protracted official and administrative negotiation and compromise; and even the notorious 'Badeni crisis' of 1897, which was marred by a breakdown of political civility and heightened national confrontation, has now been seen as stimulating much official self-reflection as well as a new era of 'reform and compromise'. In fact the whole era between Badeni and the outbreak of war in 1914, once seen as the prelude to state death, has now been convincingly reframed as one distinguished by sustained 'political discussion, participation in important debates, and, most of all, considerations of imperial reform' (Deak 2015, pp. 226. 235). The United Kingdom of Great Britain and Northern Ireland, despite some preferred Churchillian self-images emphasizing heroic intransigence, has still shown itself capable of generating and embracing creative ideas for negotiation and compromise, including (to take one key example) its contribution to the achievement of the Good Friday Agreement in 1998.

However, it is also true that the blunt majoritarian political cultures of Westminster and of other union polities have created some real challenges. In the end, both in the UK and the Dual Monarchy across the late 19th century, cultures of negotiation certainly developed—but primarily between nationalist protest and central government. In the Irish case (but not only so), this tended to encourage a focus and an emphasis on London at the expense of home—with the result that intercommunity tensions and fractiousness gathered pace in Ireland itself. Moreover, the political classes in both London and Vienna often proved to be relatively unresponsive, except in the particular contexts of intense brinkmanship and pressure: Wickham Steed tellingly noted in 1913 that 'an Austrian people need never despair as long as it can find means, in case of need, to frighten the government'; and the same painful lesson was taken on board both by contemporary Irish nationalists of all hues as well as by Ulster unionists (Steed 1919, p. 125). Indeed, there have also been critical moments in the history of the United Kingdom when these political cultures of negotiation and compromise have dramatically stalled—for example, immediately before and during the First World War (see section 6.7). As has been noted, global war has not been conducive to those cultures of flexibility and malleability on which union states have thrived. In the 21st century the debate in the United Kingdom over leaving the European Union produced a remarkable polarization and intolerance, reminiscent indeed of the chasm in British politics which opened up between 1912 and 1914 (see Jackson 2016).

Unions held together because they were able to generate institutions and identities which effectively embraced nationality. Unions often functioned like empires. Union government, like imperial government, was associated with favoured classes or indeed favoured nations, beyond the perceived *Staatsvölker* of the union: unions and empires survived because they ruled through division. If the English were the *Staatsvolk* of the United Kingdom, then the Scots effectively enjoyed a favoured nation status (certainly in terms of the attitudes of the governing elite); at the same time the Dual Monarchy was a complex layering of relatively advantaged nations, with the German Austrians and Hungarians at the top, but with Galician Poles and (at least in the theory of the *Nagodba*) Croats also featuring in the hierarchies of privilege (Markovits and Sysyn 1982, p. 91). For some of the reasons detailed earlier, the United Kingdom represented the patriotic feeling of the Scots and Welsh relatively more effectively than the Irish; and a key issue with the Irish union from the start was the extent to which distinctive national institutions, which in other parts of the United Kingdom might have served as bolsters of union, in fact promoted unpopular minority interests—and thus divergence (see sections 2.1, 2.2; and also Jackson 2013).

Like empires, unions survived because they became adept at managing dissent—including through military and extra-judicial intervention. Ireland under the union, like the crownlands of the Dual Monarchy under the Habsburgs, was characterized by a comparatively heavy police and military presence, and by intense surveillance. Ireland under the union, like the crownlands of the Dual Monarchy, was affected by recurrent protest, which was sometimes bloodily suppressed: each was characterized by extra-judicial action, in the Irish case with the periodic and regular suspension of normal legal procedure. In short, unions were often tainted by the dark arts of imperial rule: they were sustained by suppression and force (see section 4.11).

In all of the union polities under consideration the monarchy occupied a position of considerable strategic significance; and, while all of these unions conspicuously failed to generate a wholly binding nationalistic, or rather supranational, identity, they were often very closely associated with an effective dynastic loyalism or a wider imperialism. There was indeed no satisfactory United Kingdom identity; but perhaps to expect such an identity is to apply nationalist expectations within these alternative, supranational, environments. Moreover, if the UK and even Britishness fell short, then there was still a passion for monarchy and empire (and their associated institutions) which reached and influenced conservative Irish nationalists such as John Redmond. And even a complex and heterodox unionist such as the cosmopolitan Scot, F. S. Oliver, while unmoved and unenthused by notions of Britain and Britishness, was similarly captivated by monarchy and empire (see e.g. Oliver 1930–5, vol. 1, p. 42; Figure 5.4). In short, supranational unions were not nation states, and were not generally associated with unifying national identities. But they *were* bound by alternative, and often no less potent, loyalties to the ruling dynasty or to the ideals and institutions linked to the dynasty. And, beyond dynastic identity, there were the loyalties forged by those individuals and communities for whom self-preservation and self-interest were more active instincts than nation and nationalism (or indeed unionism and empire).

Failing unions, or ostensibly failing unions, have indeed shown themselves to be capable of reinvention; and federalism has often been investigated or applied as a central dimension of this process (see chapter 5). As has been seen, the parliamentary union of the United Canadas (1841–67) was successfully reconfigured (alongside some of the maritime provinces of British North America) with the new federal dominion of Canada in 1867. By the beginning of the 20th century reform of the Dual Monarchy was increasingly sought through various proposed forms of what amounted to federalization—the most pervasive of which was the notion of raising the unified Slav provinces into a trialism which would supersede the dualism of the Ausgleich. In the contemporary United Kingdom unionist intellectuals like F. S. Oliver, strongly impressed by the successes of American federation, thought that it might be possible to satisfy the appetites of Irish home rulers through the cake of a federated United Kingdom. But the history of federalism (at least in so far as it has been applied in the context of the British-Irish relationship) has been difficult: it has been been broached from a position of relative negotiating weakness by, successively, Irish nationalists (as in 1870) or Scots nationalists (in 1892–3) or Welsh nationalists (in 1913) (see e.g. Butt 1870; Mitchell 1893; John 1912; Griffith 1913). It has generally been considered by unionists (as in 1910–20, in an Irish context, or in the early 21st century in a Scots context) when the successive tides of nationalism have seemed to be well-nigh irresistible. Federalism, in the context of the 'Celtic' nationalisms, has thus been a difficult, though not necessarily an impossible, sell; but equally there is a sense in which it has constituted an effort to address issues of vision or faith through the devices of contract and legalism. In any event, in the past the federalist 'moment'—the occasion when unionist and nationalist strengths have been evenly balanced and thus the chances of a deal have been greatest—has never properly arisen. Unionists have only offered federalism when they have been too weak and when nationalism has been too strong for each realistically to pursue the notion. All this is not say that a federal reform is wholly unachievable; but it is to say both that the history of the issue highlights the difficulties, and that federalism (once achieved) is no panacea (for the latter see e.g. Lehning 1998, pp. 6, 111–50).

Unions have been sustained through many other institutional resources: Adolf Fischof's four armies—standing (military), sitting (bureaucratic), crawling (police), and kneeling (church) will be recalled from earlier in this account (see sections 4.4, 4.5, 4.11, 4.6). Imperial and royal armies, for example, have often served to provide unifying agencies for the different nations of complex states, though at the same time (as has been seen) it would be wrong to attempt any overly crude correlation. In general, however, armies and *some* forms of external conflict have served to bind unions such as the United Kingdom or the Dual Monarchy, while—conversely—the defeat, humiliation, subversion, or politicization of armies have all been disproportionately damaging. Also, since unions may be essentially parliamentary, parliaments can serve, as in the British case, as unifying agents; though the discrediting of the institution or of the parliamentary classes may do damage to union itself (again, as in the British—or Austrian—cases) (cf. Parent 2011, p. 20). An expanding state, with concomitant overarching bureaucracies and policing regimes, has often served to deepen the linkages between its peoples and the union itself; though dynamic unions of this kind may grow and strengthen while simultaneously invoking failure through disrupting established social frontiers and firing nationalist opposition. Lastly, churches—whether the Anglican or Catholic—have been deployed as unifying agents in unions such as the United Kingdom and Dual Monarchy respectively; though their successes in this regard have been, at best, incomplete (as the case of Ireland within the United Kingdom painfully illustrates). In all of these cases strongly centripetal institutions have the simultaneous capacity to act centrifugally.

Successful unions have also drawn upon considerable social capital. Aristocracies have often united complex multinational polities, most obviously in the British case through the widespread landholdings of the richest nobles; and, by extension, the decline of the landed classes from c.1870 onwards was associated with the greater vulnerability of union and the consolidation of national movements (see section 4.3). Equally, socialism and social democrats have often sought to defend the interests of the working classes through fully utilizing the resources of the union state—rather than permitting (say) supranational corporations to disadvantage working communities fragmented and weakened by national division. Again, the British Labour Party, though originally strongly home rule in its sympathies, looked to bolster the union state in the interests of working people for much of the mid and late 20th century. Class politics have thus, on the whole, served as union politics (though cf. Beneš 2016, esp. pp. 239–44). By extension, the decline of class politics, and the consolidation of neo-liberal individualism as well as of identity politics, appear to be associated with the loosening of union (see section 4.10).

Finally, mention has already been made of the transnational connectivity of unions: the extent to which the British and Irish looked beyond the shores of their own islands both in terms of 'exporting' union as well as identifying useful models of constitutional change. In fact this search for comparators has not only had a spatial, but also a temporal dimension: the history of unions has for long had a strongly didactic or applied quality. The Irish union, for example, was modelled on the perceived successes of its Scots predecessor, with numerous politicians and scholars (such as the Scots historian and politician, John Bruce (1744–1826)) carefully applying the lessons of 1707 in 1800 (Bruce 1799). As has been said, those Irish and British most closely involved with the attainment of the Irish union often helped to export the idea of union to continental Europe and indeed beyond. Lord Durham drew closely upon the history of the unions of the United Kingdom in addressing the challenges of provincial government in Canada in 1838–9; and the opponents of union in Canada often looked to the opponents of union in Ireland for inspiration (Coupland 1945, pp. 161–2; section 3.4).

By the the mid-1880s Gladstone was poring over the history of different unions, both in Europe and north America, in order to sketch a vision of a reformed, reconstituted but still fundamentally united kingdom. More generally, much Irish, Scottish, and British history was produced at this time, some of it directly encouraged by Gladstone himself, in order to inform and indeed direct debate on the most pressing constitutional issue of the day, Irish home rule. In particular the history of the Scottish union was once again disinterred by numerous scholars and politicians (such as Peter Hume Brown and A. V. Dicey) in order to better understand the pathology and prospects of its Irish counterpart (e.g. Hume Brown 1914; Dicey amd Rait 1920). A generation later, immediately after the First World War, Britain had re-emerged (as at the beginning of the 19th century) as a net exporter of the union model, with (for example) R. W. Seton-Watson applying the evidently beneficent lessons of the Scottish union to the successor states of the Dual Monarchy.

Other unions exercised an equally didactic allure at this time. Oszkár Jászi defined his exploration of the history and collapse of the Dual Monarchy as having a wider application and utility. This was a matter not simply of reflecting on the nature and viability of such union states, but also (and more generally) on international combinations like the League of Nations:

> the question is whether the [Habsburg] Danubian experiment was due to fail because it was an organic, almost a natural impossibility, or because it was only a consequence of factors depending on will and insight which could have been avoided by a more advanced statesmanship and more clear-sighted policy and better organised civic education. The answer to this question will determine almost *sub specie aeternitatis* the fate of all future experiments intending to unite various and antagonistic national wills into a harmonious international order protecting and supplementing the interest of each nation.   (Jászi 1929, p. 4)

Jászi's reflections and diagnoses clearly came too late (in 1929) for the purpose of curing the incontrovertibly defunct Austria-Hungary; but its history could (he believed) still highlight lessons for future supranational unions such as the League. In essence, a main point in his study was to warn contemporary and future 'experimenters' that the Dual Monarchy had failed not because of its own inherent contradictions, but rather because 'a more advanced statesmanship' was desperately wanting. In particular he mourned the lack of a proactive civic education concerning union, though the precise form and content of this remained largely unclear—and his prescription has generally been given short shrift.

But, at least in a particular sense, Jászi had a point. Despite its didactic heritage and its former vitality, and despite Jászi's reflections and warnings, it would seem that the history of union is currently at a discount within the United Kingdom. Successive British ministers appear, for example, to have relegated most of the complex history of their relationship with the union and with unionism: mention has already been made of David Cameron's historical amnesia at the time of the Scots independence referendum, in 2014 (see section 5.2). Since then, when forced to choose between their political and economic heritage (in the form of the unions of the United Kingdom) or a radical patriotism (in the form of a 'hard' Brexit), some British governments have—at enormous risk, whether to the integrity of the UK, the stability of the Irish settlement of 1998, or (not least) to their own unity and reputation—opted for the high-stakes game. As has been said, the pursuit of Brexit (whatever its wider merits and demerits, its opportunities and constraints) apparently signalled the simultaneous support and negation of the idea of union.

In December 1885 Gladstone famously ambushed the Scot, Arthur Balfour, President of the Local Government Board, urging on him and his Conservative ministerial colleagues the need to address the challenge of Irish government reform. This was followed by the suggestion that, if the Tories were minded to settle the 'whole question of the future Government of Ireland', they would have the full support of the Liberal party (Jackson 2004, p. 65: see e.g. Gladstone 1928, p. 396). It is important not to underestimate Gladstone's sometimes oleaginous self-righteousness, or the extent to which his morality and self-interest coincided (as with his profoundly problematic attitudes towards slavery and the slave trade): it is equally important not to underestimate the very deeply principled commitment of many Conservatives to the union (Quinault 2009). Still, in essence, the choice offered by Gladstone was between a consensual, cross-party reform of the union, which carried an immediate risk to both Conservative and Liberal unity, and a higher stakes power game wherein the stability of the constitution and of the union state became subject to party competition—'a pawn in the English political game' (O'Connor 1925, vol. 1, p. v).

With the lavish benefits of hindsight it is now clear that a (temporarily) united Conservative party chose to fight; and indeed it then proceeded to win the battle over home rule. But, as some of the more thoughtful of their number (including Balfour and Carson) eventually came to accept, they ultimately lost the war over the constitution and the union. Unsurprisingly, it has in fact almost always proved impossible to uphold union states by simultaneously subverting their essential institutions and structures.

Here again the deleterious impact of unionists no less than nationalists, together with the cost of rudely mishandling the fragile cultures of multinational united kingdoms, would each appear to provide ample material for current reflection. To that end, the chronicle of Britain and Europe's united kingdoms surely remains vital 'present history'.

Select Union Chronology

1296–1328	First Scottish 'war of independence'.
1302	July: Flemish victory over the French at Courtrai (battle of the Golden Spurs).
1332–57	Second Scottish 'war of independence'.
1397	June: Kalmar union binding Denmark, Norway, and Sweden.
1472	Creation of the Council of Wales.
1477	Burgundian Netherlands inherited by the Habsburgs.
1523–4	Sweden leaves the Kalmar union.
1535	(sometimes cited as 1536) Laws in Wales Act ('act of union').
1536	Denmark declares Norway to be an integral part of the Danish kingdom.
1542	Laws in Wales Act ('act of union'). Creation, by Henry VIII, of the crown and kingdom of Ireland.
1581	States General repudiates rule of Philip II over the Netherlands.
1585	August: Antwerp reconquered by the Spanish (Netherlands).
1603	March: union of the crowns of Scotland and England under James VI and I.
1620	November: battle of the White Mountain (Bohemia).
1648	January: Peace of Münster. October: Peace of Westphalia (and end of Thirty Years' War).
1649	January: execution of King Charles I. May: proclamation of the Commonwealth of England.
1660	May: accession of King Charles II and restoration of the Stuart monarchy in England.
1661	August: Sovereignty Act, Norway (introduction of absolutist rule, following Denmark).
1665	November: the Lex Regia in Denmark (royal absolutism consolidated).
1688–9	Revolution in England and parliamentary deposition of James VII and II.
1695–1700	The Darien venture of the Company of Scotland.
1700	Transfer of southern Netherlands from Spanish to Austrian rule.
1706	May: battle of Ramillies—and establishment of Dutch rule over southern Netherlands until the end of the war of the Spanish Succession.
1707	May: commencement of parliamentary union between England and Scotland.

1714	August: accession of George, elector of Hanover, to the British throne (and creation of personal union binding Britain and Hanover).
1715–16	Jacobite uprising, Scotland.
1745–6	Jacobite uprising, Scotland.
1763	February: Treaty of Paris and end of Seven Years' War.
1771	Norwegian Literary Society founded.
1772	August: first partition of Poland.
1774	June: Quebec Act (House of Commons, London).
1780	December: outbreak of fourth Anglo-Dutch war (to January 1783).
1781	October: Joseph II's Patent of Toleration (Austria).
1782	January: Joseph II's Edict of Tolerance (for Jews). July: amendment of Poynings's law by Yelverton's act (legislative independence, Ireland).
1783	April: passage of Renunciation act (legislative independence, Ireland).
1784	Bohemian Scientific Society founded (Prague, Bohemia).
1787	June: Prussian intervention in the Dutch republic.
1788	'Small revolution' in the Austrian Netherlands: unity with Dutch republic mooted.
1789	October: Austrian army defeated at Turnhout by Belgian insurgents. December: all of southern (Belgian) provinces freed. Rebel government (Committee of Breda) created.
1790	January: creation of United States of Belgium. February: death of the emperor Joseph II and accession of Leopold II. November: reoccupation of the southern provinces by the Austrian army.
1791	December: creation of Upper and Lower Canada through the Constitutional Act.
1792	November: French invasion of the Austrian Netherlands.
1793	January: second partition of Poland.
1794	June: French victory at Fleurus.
1795	January: French incursion into the Dutch republic, and creation of the Batavian republic. October: formal integration of southern Netherlands provinces into France. October: third partition of Poland.
1797	August: draft constitution for the Batavian republic rejected in a referendum.
1798	April: revised constitution for the Batavian republic accepted in referendum. May: outbreak of rebellion in Leinster (Ireland). June: coup d'état in the Batavian republic.
1799	March: first elections to new Dutch provincial assemblies (and end of old federal structure).

1800	May: introduction of a bill for union into the Irish parliament (Dublin).
	August: act of union (Ireland) receives royal assent.
1801	January: inauguration of the Irish union.
	September/October: conservative coup d'état in the Batavian republic.
1804	11 August: formal declaration of an Austrian empire by Francis I.
1806	Louis Bonaparte nominated as king of Holland.
1807	August: British bombardment of Copenhagen. Danes declare war on Britain.
	November: flight of Portuguese royal family from Lisbon.
1808	January: Brazilian ports opened to foreign vessels.
	February: Russia annexes Finland.
	March: arrival of Portuguese royal family at Rio de Janeiro.
1809	March–July: Porvoo diet and the establishment of the Grand Duchy (Principality) of Finland.
	May: Gustav IV Adolf deposed by the Swedish Riksdag and replaced by Carl XIII.
	September: Sweden ceded Finland to Russia.
1810	July: Louis Bonaparte abdicates and Holland united with France.
	October: Jean-Baptiste Bernadotte adopted as heir (Prince Carl Johan) by Carl XIII.
1811	Promulgation of *Allgemeines bürgerliches Gesetzbuch* (Austria).
1812	March: Castlereagh appointed Foreign Secretary (UK).
1813	March: Treaty of Stockholm.
	October: battle of Leipzig (battle of the Nations).
1814	January: Treaties of Kiel. Norway ceded to the Swedish crown.
	April: Storting meets at Eidsvoll and formulates a Norwegian constitution.
	July: Willem I accepts rule over the united Netherlands.
	August: Convention of Moss agreed between Norway and Sweden.
	October: Storting accepts union with Sweden.
	November: Storting 'elects and recognizes' Carl XIII as king Carl II of Norway.
1815	February: Swedish Riksdag confirms union with Norway.
	March: United Kingdom of the Netherlands proclaimed.
	June: battle of Waterloo.
	August: Act of Union between Sweden and Norway promulgated.
	August: constitution of the United Kingdom of the Netherlands agreed.
	December: formal promulgation of the United Kingdom of Portugal, Brazil, and the Algarves.
1816	March: death of Queen Maria of Portugal and accession of João VI (John VI).
1818	Bohemian National Museum founded.
	February: death of Carl XIII of Sweden-Norway and succession of Carl XIV Johan.
1819	September: language resolution in the Netherlands.

1821	Imposition of the northern Netherlands school model on the south. The Norwegian national flag designed and accepted. January: Cortes held in Lisbon. August/September: George IV visits Ireland.
1822	Amortization syndicate created (Netherlands). August: death of Castlereagh (Lord Londonderry) (UK). August: visit of George IV to Scotland. September: Brazilian independence declared, with Pedro I as constitutional emperor.
1824	Netherlands Trading Company founded.
1825	June: creation of Collegium Philosophicum, Leuven/Louvain.
1826	Death of João VI (John VI) of Portugal.
1827	July: Willem of the Netherlands secures a concordat with Rome.
1828–9	Petition movement, southern Netherlands.
1829	April: Catholic 'emancipation' in the United Kingdom.
1830	July: overthrow of the Bourbon monarchy, Paris. August: Provisional government declares Belgian independence. December: London conference on Belgium.
1831	April: abdication of Pedro I of Brazil. June: Eighteen Articles (secession settlement) proposed for Belgium. Willem's 10-day military campaign in Belgium.
1833	Armistice between the Netherlands and Belgium.
1834	*Afscheiding* within the Dutch Reformed Church.
1835	Publication of the Kalevala by Elias Lönrott: era of Finnish cultural nationalism.
1836	František Palecký's *History of Bohemia*.
1837	July: death of William IV, and end of personal union between Hanover and the UK. November: uprising in Lower and Upper Canada. December: Canadian republic declared by William Lyon Mackenzie.
1838	August: passage of Tithe Rent Charge Act, Ireland.
1839	Willem I accepts Belgian secession. February: Lord Durham's report on Canadian union laid before Commons. November: Newport (Chartist) rising.
1840	July: death of the earl of Durham: passage of the British North America/Union Act. July: foundation of the Loyal National Repeal Association (Ireland). October: abdication of Willem I of the Netherlands.
1841	February: inauguration of the Canadian union at Montreal.
1843	Great Disruption within the Church of Scotland.
1844	Nine men's constitutional proposal in the Netherlands. March: death of Carl XIV Johan of Sweden-Norway. Succession of Oscar I. October: Derrynane manifesto.

1845–51	Great Irish Famine/*An Gorta Mór*.
1848	February: revolution in Paris sparks off wider revolutionary unrest.
	March: abolition of *robota* in Bohemia. Outbreak of first Schleswig war (1848–52).
	March: Willem II unilaterally commissions new Dutch constitution.
	April: abolition of *robota* in Galicia.
	May: German national assembly meets in Frankfurt.
	June: General Alfred (Prince) Windisch-Grätz bombards Prague.
	September: emancipation measure of Vienna parliament.
	October: Vienna revolt suppressed by Windisch-Grätz.
1849	March: Kremsier constitution pre-empted by the March constitution.
	March/April: Hungary breaks with the Habsburgs, and Russian Army summoned.
	July: Baron Alexander von Bach Austrian Minister of the Interior (to August 1859).
	November: Prince Felix von Schwarzenberg Minister President of the Austrian empire (d. 1852).
1850–1	Creation of customs union between Austria and Hungary.
1853	April movement in the Netherlands against reintroduced Catholic hierarchy
	National Association for the Vindication of Scottish Rights.
	Abolition of serfdom in Hungary.
	October: war declared between Ottoman and Russian empires.
1854	March: France and Britain declare war on Russia (Crimean war).
1855	Concordat between Austrian empire and Catholic Church.
	Creation of Creditanstalt, Vienna.
1858-59	Federation considered in British North America.
1858	March: foundation of the Irish Republican (Fenian) Brotherhood (Ireland).
	July: Alexander Galt proposes federal union for British North America.
1859	June: disastrous Austrian campaign against Piedmont and France (Magenta and Solferino).
	July: death of Oscar I of Sweden-Norway and accession of Carl XV and IV.
1860	October: Austrian constitutional 'diploma'.
1861	February: February Patent (Austria).
	April: outbreak of civil war between the northern and southern US states.
	August: passive resistance in Hungary resumes after dissolution of the Diet.
1863	Alexander II calls the Finnish Diet and advances pro-Finnish policies.
1864	February-October: second Schleswig war (Denmark and German Confederation).
	September: Charlottestown conference on Canadian confederation.
	October: Quebec conference on Canadian confederation.
1865–7	Second joint Norwegian-Swedish committee on the union.
1865	December: Riksdag reform bill passed into law (henceforth bicameral parliament in Sweden).

1866–8	Devastating famine in Finland.
1866	April–June: Fenian raids on New Brunswick and Canada. July: battle of Königgrätz/Sadowa. August: Peace of Prague. December: London conference on Canadian confederation.
1867	February: Ausgleich (compromise) between Hungary and Austria (Cisleithania). March: passage of British North America Act (confederation). July: inauguration of the Dominion of Canada (Ontario, Quebec, New Brunswick, Nova Scotia). December: execution of the three Fenian 'Manchester Martyrs', England.
1868	September: Nagodba—subdualism and autonomy for Croatia-Slavonia within the kingdom of Hungary. Hungarian Nationalities Law enacted.
1869	July: disestablishment of the (Anglican) Church of Ireland.
1870	July: Manitoba and North West Territories join Dominion of Canada. August: passage of Gladstone's Irish land act. September: first meeting of Isaac Butt's Home Government Association.
1871	July: British Columbia joins Dominion of Canada. October: rejection of the Fundamental Articles by Franz Joseph (Cisleithania).
1872	Abolition of Norwegian statholdership. September: death of Carl XV and IV of Sweden-Norway and accession of Oscar II.
1873	May: economic crash, Austria-Hungary. July: Prince Edward Island joins Dominion of Canada.
1874	Trade treaty between Norway and Sweden.
1875	Completion of statue of Carl XIV Johan in Christiania, Norway. October: Scandinavian monetary union (with Norway's accession). October: Kálmán Tisza Minister President of Hungary (in office to March 1890).
1879	Teaching of Magyar compulsory in nursery schools in Transleithania. August: Eduard Count von Taaffe Minister President of Cisleithania (in office to November 1893).
1880	First official census of language in the Habsburg empire. Ministers now to be seated in Norway's Storting: Storting's power over constitution affirmed. May: foundation of *Deutscher Schulverein* in Austria-Hungary. May: Charles Stewart Parnell elected leader of the Irish Parliamentary Party.
1881	Teaching of Magyar compulsory in primary schools in Transleithania. March: assassination of Alexander II of Russia. August: passage of Gladstone's second Irish land act.
1882	October: foundation of the Irish National Land League.

1884	July: Christian Schweigaard (Conservative) resigns as Norwegian prime minister and is succeeded by Johan Sverdrup (Liberal). Principle of ministerial responsibility to legislature asserted.
1885	Swedish Riksdag asserts its control over foreign policy (and against royal authority). Creation of Scottish Office and Secretaryship for Scotland. August: institution of Princess's day holiday in the Netherlands.
1886	February: beginning of the *Doleantie* split within the Netherlands. April: introduction of the first home rule bill, Ireland. June: defeat for Gladstone's home rule bill. June: passage of Crofters' Holdings Act (Scotland). November: publication of A. V. Dicey, *England's Case Against Home Rule*.
1887	September: Mitchelstown massacre.
1888	August: Scottish Labour party created. August: provision for elected county councils, England and Wales.
1889	January: creation of Social Democratic Party, Austria (*Sozialdemokratische Arbeiterpartei Oesterreichs*). January: Crown Prince Rudolf's death at Mayerling, near Vienna. August: provision for elected county councils, Scotland.
1890	September: Thomas Ellis's call for a Welsh assembly at Bala.
1893	University of Wales founded. February: introduction of the second home rule bill (Ireland). September: defeat of the second home rule bill (Ireland).
1894	April: Irish TUC created.
1896	June: suffrage reforms enacted (Cisleithania)
1897	Ending of tariff alignment in Sweden-Norway. April: Count Kasimir Badeni's language ordinances (requiring bilingualism in official business in Bohemia). November: Badeni resigns (Cisleithania).
1898	Storting finally rejects the union flag in favour of a 'pure' Norwegian alternative. August: democratic local government instituted for Ireland.
1899–1905	First wave of russification in Finland ('first period of oppression').
1899	Badeni decrees revoked (Cisleithania). Scottish Workers' Representation Committee created. Austrian Social Democrats call for a federal Austria-Hungary. February: February manifesto advances russification policies in Finland. October: war in South Africa (to May 1902).
1901	January: Commonwealth of Australia inaugurated.
1902	Fourth (and final) Swedish-Norwegian committee on the union.
1903–6	Crisis over the use of German in the army in Hungary.
1903	August: final passage of George Wyndham's Land Act (Ireland).

1904	April: Élesd, Bihor, killings (33 Romanian deaths).
	June: assassination of Bobrikov, key promoter of russification in Finland.
1905	Serb-Croat coalition.
	Moravian compromise (Cisleithania).
	National Museum of Wales founded.
	January: revolution in Russia.
	March: creation of the Ulster Unionist Council.
	June: Storting declares Norwegian independence.
	August: union rejected by popular plebiscite in Norway (367,149 to 184).
	September: Saskatchewan and Alberta join the Dominion of Canada.
	September: Karlstad agreement on the termination of the Sweden-Norway union.
	October: Swedish-Norwegian union formally disestablished.
1906	Aurel Popovici, *Die Vereinigten Staaten von Gross Oesterreich*.
	April: Austrian trade war with Serbia (to March 1908).
	December: universal male suffrage, Austria (Cisleithania).
1907	Formation of the Welsh Department of the Board of Education.
	Otto Bauer, *Die Nationalitätenfrage und die Sozialdemokratie*.
	April/May: Imperial conference, London, grants Newfoundland dominion status.
	September: formation of Sinn Féin (merging of National Council and Sinn Féin League).
	October: Černová killings (14 Slovak protesters dead).
1908–14	Second wave of russification in Finland.
1908	Publication of R. W. Seton-Watson, *Racial Problems in Hungary*.
	October: Austro-Hungarian annexation of Bosnia.
	November: Baron Max von Beck's fall as Minister President of Cisleithania.
1909	Bukovina political settlement (Cisleithania).
1910	May: Union of South Africa inaugurated.
	November: Tonypandy riots (Wales).
1911	Publication of R. W.Seton-Watson's *Southern Slav Question*.
	Publication of R. W. Seton-Watson's *Corruption and Reform in Hungary*.
	July: investiture of Edward as Prince of Wales, Caernarfon Castle.
	August: Llanelli riots.
	August: Parliament Act (United Kingdom).
1912	April: introduction of third home rule bill, Ireland.
	May: Irish Labour Party founded by James Connolly, James Larkin, William O'Brien.
1914	Galician political settlement (Cisleithania).
	June: assassination of Franz Ferdinand in Sarajevo (Bosnia).
	June: second reading of bill for Scots home rule (UK).
	July: Bachelor's Walk massacre, Dublin.
	August: outbreak of First World War. Defence of the Realm Act (UK).
	September: third home rule bill on statute books, though suspended.

374 UNITED KINGDOMS

1915	March: eastern front defeats for Austria-Hungary, Lemberg and Premissil.
1916	April: Easter Rising, Ireland. May–July. Lloyd George negotiations on home rule and exclusion (Ireland). July: opening of the Somme offensive. November: death of Emperor-King Franz Joseph, and accession of Karl (Austria-Hungary).
1917	March (February Old Style): revolution in Russia and establishment of the Provisional Government. October: southern front victory for Austria-Hungary at Caporetto. October: Sinn Féin ard-fheis and revised constitution, Ireland (De Valera president). November (October Old Style): (Bolshevik) revolution in Russia. December: declaration of Finnish independence.
1918	January: Woodrow Wilson's Fourteen Points envision federalization of Habsburg empire. January–May: civil war in Finland. March: *Kaiserschlacht* on the western front: last major German offensive of the war. March: Treaty of Brest-Litovsk and end of war on eastern front. May: Kaisers Wilhelm and Karl meet at Spa, Belgium. June: Allies recognize Czech National Council as 'basis' for Czechoslovak government. October: Karl's Manifesto and offer of federalization. October: Czech republic declared at Prague. November: armistice. November: declaration of republic of German Austria. December: general election, United Kingdom: Sinn Féin victorious in Ireland. December: Kingdom of the Serbs, Croats, and Slovenes declared.
1919	January. Outbreak of war of independence (Ireland).
1920	February and March: plebiscites in Schleswig. February: Government of Ireland bill introduced (proposing partition). July: plebiscite in East Prussia. October: plebiscite in Carinthia (Austria). December: passage of the Government of Ireland Act.
1921	March: plebiscite in Silesia. June: opening of the Northern Ireland parliament by George V. December: Anglo-Irish Treaty signed.
1922	December: formal establishment of the Irish Free State/Saorstat Éireann.
1924	November: first meeting of the Irish Boundary Commission.
1925	August: creation of Plaid Cymru. December: tripartite agreement between Britain, Irish Free State, and N. Ireland on Irish border.
1929	Publication of Oszkár Jászi, *Dissolution of the Habsburg Monarchy*. October: kingdom of the Serbs, Croats, and Slovenes renamed as Yugoslavia.

SELECT UNION CHRONOLOGY

1934	February: Newfoundland's dominion status ends. April: merger of Scottish Party and National Party of Scotland to form the Scottish National Party.
1937	July: constitutional referendum (and general election), Ireland.
1938	March: German occupation of Austria (Anschluss).
1939	March: German occupation of Czech lands (Slovakia separate client state). September: outbreak of the Second World War.
1945	May: allied victory in Europe.
1947	May: Welsh Regional Council of the Labour party created.
1949	March: Newfoundland joins Canada as its tenth province. April: Ireland formally becomes a republic outside the British commonwealth.
1958	July: Empire Games at Cardiff.
1969	January: Czechoslovakia becomes a federal union. July: investiture of Prince Charles as Prince of Wales, Caernarfon Castle. August: rioting in Derry and Belfast and deployment of British troops on streets.
1972	March: prorogation of devolved Stormont government and parliament (N. Ireland).
1974	January: power-sharing executive takes office (N. Ireland). April: first conference of the new Welsh TUC.
1979	March: first referendum on Scottish devolution.
1985	November: Hillsborough (Anglo-Irish) Agreement signed.
1994	August: Provisional IRA announces 'complete cessation of hostilities' (N. Ireland).
1997	May: return of Labour party (under Tony Blair) to power (UK). September: devolution referenda in Scotland, Wales.
1998	April: signing of the Good Friday Agreement (N. Ireland).
2006	October: St Andrews Agreement (relating to N.Ireland).
2014	September: referendum on Scottish independence.
2016	June: referendum on the United Kingdom's membership of the European Union.
2020	January: Britain's 'exit day' and final departure from the EU.
2022	September: death of Queen Elizabeth II and accession of Charles III.
2023	February: publication of Windsor Framework (EU and UK government).

Bibliography (including Reference Lists)

Manuscript Sources

Archibald Acheson, second earl of Gosford papers, Public Record Office of Northern Ireland
Herbert Henry Asquith, first earl of Oxford and Asquith papers, Bodleian Library, Oxford
James Bryce, Viscount Bryce papers, Bodleian Library, Oxford
Edward Carson, Lord Carson of Duncairn papers, Public Record Office of Northern Ireland
Robert Dunlop papers, University of Manchester Library, Manchester
Walter Elliot papers, National Library of Scotland, Edinburgh
W. E. Gladstone papers, British Library, London
Frederick Hamilton-Temple-Blackwood, first marquess of Dufferin & Ava papers, Public Record Office of Northern Ireland
Harford Montgomery Hyde papers, Public Record Office of Northern Ireland
Arthur Berriedale Keith papers, University of Edinburgh
John George Lambton, first earl of Durham papers, University of Durham
Alexander Murray, Lord Murray of Elibank papers, National Library of Scotland, Edinburgh
John Murray (company) papers, National Library of Scotland, Edinburgh
Henry Petty-Fitzmaurice, fifth marquess of Lansdowne papers, British Library, London
Frederick Scott Oliver papers, National Library of Scotland, Edinburgh
Robert Stewart, second marquess of Londonderry (Viscount Castlereagh) papers, Public Record Office of Northern Ireland, Belfast
R. W. Seton-Watson papers, School of Slavonic and Eastern European Studies, University College, London
Henry Wickham Steed papers, British Library, London

Newspaper and Journal Sources

Dublin University Magazine
Freeman's Journal
Irish Independent
Irish Times
Morning Leader
Quebec Mercury
Saturday Review
The Economist
The Outlook

Printed Primary Sources

Adamson, Ian (1974), *The Cruthin: A History of the Ulster Land and People*. Newtownards: Nosmada Books.
Alden, Percy (ed.) (1909), *The Hungary of Today*. London: Eveleigh Nash.

378 BIBLIOGRAPHY (INCLUDING REFERENCE LISTS)

Alin, Oscar (1889–91), *Den svensk-norska unionen*. Stockholm: Norsted & Söners.
Alison, Archibald (1842), *History of Europe from the Commencement of the French Revolution in MDCCLXXXIX to the Restoration of the Bourbons in MDCCCXV*, 5th edition, 10 vols. London: William Blackwood.
Alison, Archibald (1861), *The Lives of Lord Castlereagh and Sir Charles Stewart*, 3 vols. London: William Blackwood.
Anderson, R. A. (1935), *With Horace Plunkett in Ireland*. London: Macmillan.
Andrassy, Count Julius (1908), *The Development of Hungarian Constitutional Liberty*. London: Kegan Paul, Trench, Trübner & Co.
Anon. [Sir Walter Scott] (1816), *Paul's Letters to his Kinsfolk*, 2nd edition (Edinburgh and London: Archibald Constable & Co.
Anon. ['A Resident'] (1830), *A Narrative of a Few Weeks in Brussels in 1830*. Brussels: Pratt & Barry.
Anon. [possibly Isaac Butt] (1835), 'The Belgic Revolution', *Dublin University Magazine*, 6/35 (Nov.).
Anon. [Baron Magnus F. F. Björnsterna] (1840), *On the Moral State and Political Union of Sweden and Norway in Answer to Mr Laing's Statement*. London: William Clowes.
Anon. [Librarian, Foreign Office] (1841), *British and Foreign State Papers, 1812–14*, vol. 1, pt 1, compiled by the librarian and keeper of papers at the Foreign Office. London: James Ridgway.
Anon. (1845), *Essays on the Repeal of the Union, to which the Association Prizes were Awarded; with a Supplemental Essay Recommended by the Judges*. Dublin: James Duffy.
Anon. ['An Englishman': Baron Henry de Worms] (1870), *The Austro-Hungarian Empire and the Policy of Count Beust: A Political Sketch of Men and Events from 1866 to 1870*. London: Chapman & Hall.
Anon./'Sixty one' [G. Hely-Hutchinson] (1874), *A Trip to Norway in 1873*. London: Bickers & Son.
Anon. [Eighty Club] (1907), *Hungary: Its People, Places and Politics: Visit of the Eighty Club in 1906*. London: T. Fisher Unwin.
Anon. [National Fund for Welsh Troops] (1915), *The Land of my Fathers: A Welsh Gift Book* London: Hodder & Stoughton.
Anon./'I.O.' [C. J. C. Street] (1921), *The Administration of Ireland, 1920*. London: Philip Allan.
Argyll, [John Campbell, ninth] Duke of (1907), *Passages from the Past*, 2 vols. London: Hutchinson.
Armitage, John (1836), *The History of Brazil from the Period of the Arrival of the Braganza Family in 1808 to the Abdication of Don Pedro I in 1831*, 2 vols. London: Smith, Elder & Co.
Bain, John (1906), *The New Reformation*. Edinburgh: Clark & Co.
Barclay of Ury, Captain [Robert] (1842), *Agricultural Tour of the United States and Upper Canada with Miscellaneous Notices*. Edinburgh: William Blackwood & Sons.
Barnes, John (1998), *Federal Britain: No Longer Unthinkable?* London: Centre for Policy Studies.
Barrow, John (1831), *A Family Tour through South Holland, up the Rhine, and across the Netherlands to Ostend*. London: John Murray.
Barry, Michael Joseph (1845), *First Prize Repeal Essay: Ireland, as she was, as she is, and as she shall be*. Dublin: James Duffy.
Barton, Dunbar Plunket (1914), *Bernadotte: The First Phase, 1763–99*. London: John Murray.
Barton, Dunbar Plunket (1921), *Bernadotte and Napoleon, 1763–1810*. London: John Murray.

Barton, Dunbar Plunket (1925), *Bernadotte: Prince and King, 1810-44*. London and Dublin: John Murray.
Barton, Dunbar Plunket (1929), *The Amazing Career of Bernadotte*. London: John Murray.
Bates, Jean Victor (1918), *Our Allies and Enemies in the Near East: With an Introduction by Right Hon. Sir Edward Carson*. New York: Dutton.
Bates, Jean Victor (1921), *Sir Edward Carson: Ulster Leader*. London: John Murray.
Baty, Thomas (1909), *International Law*. London: John Murray.
Bauer, Otto (1907), *Die Nationalitätenfrage und die Sozialdemokratie*. Vienna: Verlag der Wiener Volksbuchhandlung.
Biron, Sir Chartres (1936), *Without Prejudice: Impressions of Life and Law*. London: Faber & Faber.
Blackie, J. S. (1892), *The Union of 1707 and its Results: A Plea for Scottish Home Rule*. Glasgow: Morrison Brothers.
Bluntschli, Johann Kaspar (1965), *Lehre vom modernen Staat*, 3 vols, new edition. Aalen: Scientia Verlag.
Bornhak, Konrad (1896), *Einseitige Abhängigkeitsverhältnisse unter den modernen Staaten*. Leipzig: Duncker & Humblot.
Bosanquet, Bernard (1899), *The Philosophical Theory of the State*. London: Macmillan.
Boulger, Demetrius (1913), *The History of Belgium, 1815-65: Waterloo to the Death of Leopold I*. London: Isaac Pitman & Sons.
Boyd, John (1914), *Sir George Étienne Cartier Bart., His Life and Times: A Political History of Canada from 1814 to 1873*. Toronto: Macmillan Company of Canada.
Breton, William H. (1835), *Scandinavian Sketches, or a Tour in Norway*. London: Bohn.
Brown, Gordon (2014), *My Scotland, our Britain: A Future Worth Sharing*. London: Simon & Schuster.
Bruce, John (1799), *Report on the Events and Circumstances which Produced the Union of the Kingdoms of England and Scotland*, 2 vols. London: privately published.
Bryce, James (ed.) (1887), *Handbook of Home Rule: Being Articles on the Irish Question*. London: Kegan Paul, Trench & Co.
Bryce, James (1888), *The American Commonwealth*, 2 vols. London: Macmillan.
Bryce, James (1901), *Studies in History and Jurisprudence*, 2 vols. Oxford: Oxford University Press.
Bryce, James (1921), *Modern Democracies*, 2 vols. London: Macmillan.
Buckley, Kate (ed.) (1886), *Diary of a Tour in America by Rev M.B. Buckley of Cork, Ireland, a Special Missionary in North America and Canada in 1870 and 1871*. Dublin: Sealy, Bryers & Walker.
Burgess, J. W. (1899), *Political Science and Constitutional Law*. Boston: Columbia College.
Burgess, John (1886), 'The Recent Constitutional Crisis in Norway', *Political Science Quarterly*, 1/2, pp. 259-94.
Butenschøn, B. A. (ed.) (1968), *Travellers Discovering Norway in the Last Century: An Anthology*. Oslo: Dreyers.
Butt, Isaac (1860), *The History of Italy, from the Abdication of Napoleon I, with Introductory References to that of Earlier Times*, 2 vols. London: Chapman & Hall.
Butt, Isaac (1870), *Home Government for Ireland: Irish Federalism! Its Meaning, its Objects and its Hopes*. Dublin: Falconer.
Chambers, William (1839), *A Tour in Holland, the Countries on the Rhine and Belgium in the Autumn of 1838*. Edinburgh: Chambers.
Chappell, Edgar L (1943), *Wake up Wales! A Survey of Welsh Home Rule Activities*. London: Foyle's Welsh Co.

Cheng, Seymour Ching-Yuan (1931), *Schemes for the Federation of the British Empire*. New York: Columbia University Press.
Clarke, Edward Duncan (1819), *Travels in Various Countries of Europe, Asia and Africa. Part the Third: Scandinavia*, 2 vols. London: Cadell & Davies.
Clauss, Immanuel (1894), *Die Lehre von den Staatsdienstbarkeiten*. Tübingen: Laupp.
Conway, Derwent [Henry David Inglis] (1829), *A Personal Narrative of a Journey through Norway, Part of Sweden, and the Islands and States of Denmark*. Edinburgh: Constable.
Cooke, Edward (1798), *Arguments for and against an Union between Great Britain and Ireland Considered: To which is Prefixed, a Proposal on the Same Subject by Josiah Tucker D.D., Dean of Gloucester*, new edition. London: Stockdale.
Cooley, Thomas M. (1868), *A Treatise on the Constitutional Limitations which Rest upon the Legislative Power of the States of the American union*. Boston: Little Brown & Co.
Coupland, Reginald (1925), *The Quebec Act: A Study in Statesmanship*. Oxford: Oxford University Press.
Coupland, Reginald (1945), *The Durham Report*. Oxford: Oxford University Press.
Coupland, Sir Reginald (1954), *Welsh and Scottish Nationalism: A Study*. London: William Collins.
Crawford, William Sharman (1833), *The expediency and Necessity of A Local Legislative Body in Ireland: Supported by a Reference to Facts and Principles*. Newry: Examiner Office.
Daa, Ludvig Kristensen (1841), *Svensk-Norsk Haand-Ordbog*. Oslo: Guldberg & Dzwonkowski.
Daunt, William J O'Neill (1848), *Personal Recollections of the Late Daniel O'Connell MP*, 2 vols. London: Chapman & Hall.
De Kiewiet, C. W., and F. H. Underhill (eds) (1955), *Dufferin-Carnarvon Correspondence, 1874–1878*. Toronto: Champlain Society.
Dent, John Charles (1881), *The Last Forty Years: Canada since the Union of 1841*, 2 vols. Toronto: George Virtue.
Dicey, A.V. (1882), 'Home Rule from an English Point of View', *Contemporary Review*, 42 (July), 66–86.
Dicey, A. V. (1887), *England's Case Against Home Rule*, 3rd edition. London: John Murray.
Dicey, A. V. (1893), *A Leap into the Dark: Or our New Constitution*. London: John Murray.
Dicey, A. V. (1902), *Introduction to the Study of the Law of the Constitution*, 6th edition. London: Macmillan.
Dicey, A. V. (1911), *A Leap into the Dark: A Criticism of the Principles of Home Rule as Illustrated by the Bill of 1893*. London: John Murray.
Dicey, A. V. (1913), *A Fool's Paradise: Being a Constitutionalist's Criticism on the Home Rule Bill of 1912*. London: John Murray.
Dicey, A. V., and Robert S. Rait (1920), *Thoughts on the Union between England and Scotland*. London: Macmillan.
Dicey, Edward (1864), *The Schleswig-Holstein War*, 2 vols. London: Tinsley Brothers.
Dicey, Edward (1866), *The Battlefields of 1866*. London: Tinsley Brothers.
Dickinson-Berry, Frances May (1918), *Austria-Hungary and her Slav Subjects*. London: George Allen & Unwin.
Di Lampedusa, Giuseppe Tomasi (1960). *The Leopard*, first English translation. London: Collins & Harvill.
Drage, Geoffrey (1909), *Austria-Hungary*. London: John Murray.
Dufferin and Ava, Marquess of [Frederick Hamilton-Temple-Blackwood] (1903), *Letters from High Latitudes: Being Some Account of a Voyage in 1856 in the Schooner Yacht 'Foam' to Iceland, Jan Mayen and Spitzbergen*, 11th edition. London: John Murray.

Dufferin and Ava, Harriot Georgina Blackwood, Marchioness of (1891), *My Canadian Journal: Extracts from Letters Home Written while Lord Dufferin was Governor General of Canada*. London: John Murray.
Dunlop, Robert (1909), 'Truth and Fiction in Irish History', *Quarterly Review*, 210/419.
Dunraven, Earl of (1912), *The Finances of Ireland Before the Union and After*. London: John Murray.
Dunraven, Earl of (1922), *Past Times and Pastimes*, 2 vols. London: Hodder & Stoughton.
Edwards, H. J. W. (1938), *The Good Patch: A Study of the Rhondda Valley*. London: Jonathan Cape.
Edwards, [Sir] Owen Morgan (1901), *The Story of the Nations: Wales*. London: T. Fisher Unwin.
Edwards, [Sir] Owen Morgan (1906), *A Short History of Wales*. London: T. Fisher Unwin.
Elliott, J. H. (2012), *History in the Making*. New Haven and London: Yale University Press.
Ellis, T. E. (and Annie J. Ellis) (1912), *Speeches and Addresses by the Late T. E. Ellis*. Wrexham: Hughes & Sons.
Ensor, R. C. K. (1915), *Belgium*. London: Williams & Norgate.
Ferguson, Adam (1833), *Practical Notes Made during a Tour in Canada and a Portion of the United States in MDCCCXXXI*. Edinburgh: William Blackwood.
Ferguson, Adam (1834), *Practical Notes Made during a Second Visit to Canada in 1833*. Edinburgh: William Blackwood.
Fisher, Joseph R. (1899), *Finland and the Tsars, 1809–99*. London: Edward Arnold.
Foot, M. R. D., and Colin Matthew (eds) (1968–94), *The Gladstone Diaries: With Cabinet Minutes and Prime-Ministerial Correspondence*, 14 vols. Oxford: Oxford University Press.
Fraser, Major General Sir Thomas (1912), *The Military Danger of Home Rule for Ireland*. London: John Murray.
Freeman, Edward A. (1888), 'Irish Home Rule and its Analogies', *New Princeton Review*, 6/5 (Sept.), pp. 172–95.
Freeman, Edward A (1893), *History of Federal Government in Greece and Italy*, ed. J. B. Bury, 2nd edition. London: Macmillan.
Gannon, Patrick J (1918). 'Bohemia and its Ulster Question', *Studies: An Irish Quarterly Review*, 7/28 (Dec.), pp. 644–58.
Gareis, Karl (1883), *Allgemeines Staatsrecht*. Freiburg im Breisgau: J. C. B. Mohr.
Gayda, Virginio (1915), *Modern Austria: Her Racial and Social Problems*. London: T. Fisher Unwin.
Geyl, Pieter (1920), *Holland and Belgium, their Common History and their Relations: Three Lectures*. Leiden: Sijthoff.
Geyl, Pieter (1964), *History of the Low Countries: Episodes and Problems*. London: Macmillan.
Gierke, Otto (1863–81), *Das deutsche Genossenschaftsrecht*. Berlin: Weidmannsche Buchhandlung.
Gill, T. P. (1887), *The Home Rule Constitutions of the British Empire*. London: Irish Press Agency.
Gillespie, Paul (2014), *Scotland's Vote on Independence: The Implications for Ireland*. Dublin: Institute of International and European Affairs.
Gladstone, William Ewart (1892), *Special Aspects of the Irish Question: A Series of Reflections in and since 1886*. London: John Murray.
Gladstone, Viscount [Herbert] (1928), *After Thirty Years*. London: Macmillan.
Godkin, Revd James (1845), *Third Repeal Prize Essay: The Rights of Ireland*. Dublin: James Duffy.
Griffith, Arthur (1918), *The Resurrection of Hungary*, new edition Dublin: Whelan & Son.

Griffith, Gwilym O. (1913), *The New Wales: Some Aspects of National Idealism with a Plea for Welsh Home Rule*. Liverpool: Hugh Evans & Sons.
Hailsham, Lord (1978), *The Dilemma of Democracy: Diagnosis and Prescription*. London: William Collins.
Headlam, Maurice (1947), *Irish Reminiscences*. London: Robert Hale.
Heber, Amelia (1830), *The Life of Reginald Heber DD, Lord Bishop of Calcutta, with Selections from his Correspondence, Unpublished Poems, and Private Papers: Together with a Journal of his Tour in Norway, Sweden, Russia, Hungary and Germany and a History of the Cossaks*, 2 vols. London: John Murray.
Herbert, Sir Robert (1902), *Speeches on Canadian Affairs by Henry Howard Molyneux, Fourth Earl of Carnarvon*. London: John Murray.
Hodgson, Adam (1824), *Letters from North America Written during a Tour in the United States and Canada*, 2 vols. London: Hurst Robinson & Co.
Hume Brown, Peter (1914), *The Legislative Union of England and Scotland: The Ford Lectures Delivered in Hilary Term 1914*. Oxford: Clarendon Press.
Jászi, Oszkár (1929), *The Dissolution of the Habsburg Monarchy*. Chicago: Chicago University Press.
Jebb, Richard (1905), *Studies in Colonial Nationalism*. London: Edward Arnold.
Jellinek, Georg (1882), *Die Lehre von den Staatsverbindungen*. Vienna: Hölder
Jellinek, Georg (1896), *Über Staatsfragmente*. Heidelberg: Gustav Koester.
John, Edward T (1912), *Home Rule for Wales: Addresses to 'Young Wales'*. Bangor: Jarvis & Foster.
Joyce, James (1922), *Ulysses*. Paris: Shakespeare & Co.
Joynson-Hicks, William (preface) (1916), *Austro-Magyar Judicial Crimes: Persecutions of the Jugoslavs: Political Trials, 1908–16*. London: Howes & Co.
Keary, Charles Francis (1892), *Norway and the Norwegians*. London: Percival & Co.
Keith, Arthur Berriedale (1909), *Responsible Government in the Dominions*. London: Stevens & Sons.
Keith, Arthur Berriedale (1916), *Imperial Unity and the Dominions*. Oxford: Clarendon Press.
Keith, Arthur Berriedale (1940), *The Constitution of England from Queen Victoria to George VI*, 2 vols. London: Macmillan.
Kiernan, T. J. (1930), *History of the Financial Administration of Ireland to 1817*. London: P. S. King & Co.
Kirkpatrick, Frederick Alexander (1914), *Imperial Defence and Trade*. London: Royal Colonial Institute.
Knatchbull-Hugessen, C. M. (1908), *The Political Evolution of the Hungarian Nation*, 2 vols. London: National Review Office.
Laband, Paul (1964), *Staatsrecht des deutschen Reiches*, 4 vols, new edition. Aalen: Scientia Verlag.
Labilliere, Francis Peter de (1894), *Federal Britain: Unity and Federation of the Empire*. London: Sampson Low, Marston & Co.
Laing, Samuel (1836), *Journal of a Residence in Norway during the Years 1834, 1835 and 1836, Made with a View to Enquire into the Moral and Political Economy of that Country and the Condition of its Inhabitants*. London: Longman, Hurst, Rees, Orme, Brown, Green & Longman.
Laing, Samuel (1839), *A Tour in Sweden in 1838; Comprising Observations on the Moral, Political and Economical State of the Swedish Nation*. London: Longman, Orme, Brown, Green, & Longmans.
Laing, Samuel (1842), *Notes of a Traveller on the Social and Political State of France, Prussia, Switzerland, Italy and Other Parts of Europe during the Present Century*. London: Longman, Brown, Green & Longmans.

Latham, Robert Gordon (1840), *Norway and the Norwegians*, 2 vols. London: Richard Bentley.
Lecky, William Edward Hartpole (1908). *A History of England in the Eighteenth Century*, 8 vols. London: Longmans, Green & Co.
Leggo, William (1878), *The History of the Administration of the Right Honorable, Frederick Temple, Earl of Dufferin*. Montreal and Toronto: Lovell & G. Mercer Adam.
Londonderry, Charles William Vane, Third Marquess of (1838), *Recollections of a Tour in the North of Europe in 1836-7*, 2 vols. London: Richard Bentley.
Londonderry, Charles William Vane, Third Marquess of (1848-53), *Memoirs and Correspondence of Viscount Castlereagh, Second Marquess of Londonderry*, 12 vols. London: Henry Colburn & Co.
Londonderry, Edith, Marchioness of (1938), *Retrospect*. London: Frederick Müller.
Lorne, Marquess of (1884), *Memories of Canada and Scotland: Speeches and Verses*. Montreal: Dawson Bros.
Lucas, Sir Charles Prestwood (ed.) (1912), *Lord Durham's Report on the Affairs of British North America*, 3 vols. Oxford: Clarendon Press.
Luccock, John (1820), *Notes on Rio de Janeiro and the Southern Parts of Brazil Taken during a Residence of Ten Years in that Country from 1808 to 1818*. London: Samuel Leigh.
Lyall, Sir Alfred (1905), *The Life of the Marquis of Dufferin and Ava*, 2 vols. London: John Murray.
Lynd, Robert (1919). *Ireland: A Nation*. London: Grant Richards.
Macartney, Maxwell H. H. (1923), *Five Years of European Chaos*. London: Chapman & Hall.
Macgregor, John (1859), *Our Brothers and Cousins: A Summer Tour in Canada and the States*. London: Seeley, Jackson & Halliday.
Mackay, Charles (1859), *Life and Liberty in America: Sketches of a Tour in the United States and Canada in 1857-8*. New York: Harper & Bros.
Mackay, James Hutton (1911), *Religious Thought in Holland during the Nineteenth Century*. London: Hodder & Stoughton.
Maguire, Thomas (1838), *Doctrine de l'église catholique d'Irlande et de celle du Canada sur la révolte: Recueil de pièces constatant l'uniformité de cette doctrine dans les deux pays, et sa conformité avec celle de l'église universelle*. Quebec.
Mahaffy, Robert Pentland (1908), *Francis Joseph I, his Life and Times: An Essay in Politics*. London: Duckworth.
Maine, Sir Henry (1875), *Lectures on the Early History of Institutions*. London: John Murray.
Maxwell, John S. (1848), *The Czar, his Court and People, Including a Tour in Norway and Sweden*. London: Richard Bentley.
McGill, Alexander (1921), *The Independence of Iceland: A Parallel for Ireland*. Glasgow: P. J. O'Callaghan.
McKenna, Michael (1847), *Federalism Illustrated and the Integrity of the British Empire Demonstrated through a Repeal of the Act of Union with a Federal Constitution and an Irish Parliament*. Addressed to the *Rt Hon Lord Cloncurry*. Dublin: S. J. Machen.
Melding, David (2005), *Unionism in a Multinational State*. Barry: Cymdeithas Y Kymberiaid.
Melding, David (2007), *Wales and the Idea of Britain*. Penarth: Cymdeithas Y Kymberiaid.
Melding, David (2009), *Will Britain Survive beyond 2020?* Cardiff: Institute of Welsh Affairs.
Melding, David (2013), *The Reformed Union: Britain as a Federation*. Cardiff: Institute of Welsh Affairs.
Merriam, Charles Edward (1900), *History of the Theory of Sovereignty since Rousseau*. New York: Columbia University Press.
Meyer, Georg (1878), *Lehrbuch des deutschen Staatsrechts*. Leipzig: Duncker & Humblot.

Mitchell, James (1819), *A Tour through Belgium, Holland, along the Rhine, and through the North of France in the Summer of 1816: In which is Given an Account of the Civil and Ecclesiatical Polity and of the System of Education of the Kingdom of the Netherlands.* London: T. & J. Allman.

Mitchell, William (1892), *Home Rule for Scotland and Imperial Federation.* Edinburgh: Scottish Home Rule Association.

Mitchell, W[illiam] (1893), *Is Scotland to be Sold Again? Home Rule for Scotland.* Edinburgh: Scottish Home Rule Association.

Mogi, Sobei (1931), *The Problem of Federalism: A Study in the History of Political Theory*, 2 vols. London: George Allen & Unwin.

Moore, Thomas (1880), *A Tour through Canada in 1879, with Remarks on the Advantages it Offers to the British Farmer.* Dublin: Irish Farmer Office.

Morgan, J. Vrynwy (1908), *Welsh Political and Educational Leaders in the Victorian Era.* London: Nisbet.

Morgan, J. Vyrnwy (1916), *The War and Wales.* London: Chapman & Hall.

Morgan, J. Vyrnwy (1918), *Life of Viscount Rhondda.* London: H. R. Allenson.

Murray, Alice E. (1903), *A History of the Financial and Commercial Relations between England and Ireland from the Time of the Restoration.* London: P. S. King & Co.

Nansen, Fridtjof (1905), *Norway and the Union with Sweden.* London: Macmillan.

Naylor, R. A. (1887), *Letters on Sweden (1882) and Norway (1884).* Warrington: Private Circulation.

Nicholson, Ivor, and Lloyd Williams (eds) (n.d. [1919]), *Wales: Its Part in the War.* London: Hodder & Stoughton.

O'Brien, Georgina (ed.) (1916), *Reminiscences of the Rt Hon Lord O'Brien of Kilfenora.* London: Edward Arnold.

O'Brien, R. Barry (1901), *The Life of Lord Russell of Killowen.* London: Smith, Elder & Co.

O'Brien, R. Barry (ed.) (1910), *The Home Rule Speeches of John Redmond M.P.* London: T. Fisher Unwin.

O'Brien, R. Barry (1912), *Dublin Castle and the Irish People*, 2nd edition. London: Kegan Paul, Trench, Trubner & Co.

O'Connor, Rt Hon. Sir James (1925), *History of Ireland, 1798–1924*, 2 vols. London: Edward Arnold.

Oliver, Frederick Scott (1906), *Alexander Hamilton: An Essay on American Union.* London: Archibald Constable & Co.

Oliver, Frederick Scott ['Pacificus'] (1910), *Federalism and Home Rule.* London: John Murray.

Oliver, Frederick Scott (1913), *The Alternatives to Civil War.* London: John Murray.

Oliver, Frederick Scott (1914), *What Federalism is Not.* London: John Murray.

Oliver, Frederick Scott (1918), *The Irish Question: Federation or Secession.* New York: Civil Service Print Co.

Oliver, Frederick Scott (1930–5), *The Endless Adventure*, 3 vols. London: Macmillan.

O'Malley, Thaddeus (1873), *Home Rule on the Basis of Federalism.* Dublin: William Ridgeway.

Phillips, Walter Alison (1903), *Modern Europe 1815–99.* London: Rivingtons.

Phillips, Walter Alison (1914), *The Confederation of Europe: A Study of the European Alliance, 1813–23, as an Experiment in the International Organisation of Peace.* London: Longmans, Green & Co.

Phillips, Walter Alison (1926), *Revolution in Ireland, 1906–1923.* London: Longmans, Green & Co.

Pirenne, Henri (1899–1932), *Histoire de Belgique*, 7 vols. Brussels: Henri Lamertin.

Pirenne, Henri (1915), *Belgian Democracy: Its Early History*. Manchester: Manchester University Press.
Popovici, Aurel C. (1906), *Die Vereinigten Staaten von Groß-Österreich: Politische Studien zur Lösung der nationalen Fragen und Staatsrechtlichen Krisen in Österreich-Ungarn*. Leipzig: B.Elischer.
Porter, John Grey Vesey (n.d. [1843]), *Some Agricultural and Political Irish Questions Calmly Discussed*. London: Ridgway.
Porter, John Grey Vesey (1844), *Ireland*. London and Dublin: Ridgway, Fisher, Son & Co.; Keene.
Price, Edward (1853), *Norway and its Scenery, Comprising the Journal of a Tour: with Considerable Additions and a Road-Book for Tourists; with Hints to Anglers and Sportsmen*, ed. Thomas Price. London: Henry G.Bohn.
Pym, Francis, and Leon Brittan (1978), *The Conservative Party and Devolution*. London: Scottish Conservative Party.
Ramm, Agatha (ed.) (1962), *The Political Correspondence of Mr Gladstone and Lord Granville, 1876–1886*, 2 vols. Oxford: Clarendon Press.
Ramsay, George (1845), *Supplemental Repeal Essay: A Proposal for the Restoration of the Irish Parliament*. Dublin: John Duffy.
Redlich, Josef (1903), *Local Government in England*, tr. F. W. Hirst, 2 vols. London: Macmillan.
Redlich, Josef (1908), *The Procedure of the House of Commons: A Study of its History and Present Form*, 3 vols. London: Archibald Constable & Co.
Redlich, Josef (1910), *Das Wesen der österreichischen Kommunal-Verfassung*. Leipzig: Duncker & Humblot.
Redlich, Josef (1920–6), *Das österreichische Staats- und Reichsproblem*, 2 vols. Leipzig: der neue Geist Verlag/P. Reinhold.
Redlich, Josef (1925), *Österreichs Regierung und Verwaltung im Weltkrieg*. Vienna, and New Haven: Hölder-Pichler-Tempsky; Yale University Press
Redlich, Josef (1929), *Emperor Francis Joseph of Austria: A Biography*. London: Macmillan.
Redmond, John (1898), *Historical and Political Addresses*. London and Dublin: Sealy, Bryers & Walker.
Rees, William (1938), 'The Union of England and Wales, with a Transcript of the Act of Union', *Transactions of the Honourable Society of Cymmrodorion: Session 1937*. London: Cymmrodorion Society.
Rees, William (1938), *The Union of England and Wales*. London: Cymmrodorion Society.
Rehm, Hermann (1907), *Allgemeine Staatslehre*. Leipzig: G. J. Göschen
Reid, Andrew (1886), *Ireland: A Book of Light on the Irish Problem, Contributed in Union by a Number of Leading Irishmen and Englishmen*. London: Longmans, Green & Co.
Reid, Stuart (1906), *Life and Letters of the First Earl of Durham, 1792–1840*, 2 vols. London: Longman, Green & Co.
Renner, Karl (Rudolf Springer) (1902), *Der Kampf der österreichischen Nationen um den Staat*. Leipzig and Vienna: Deuticke.
Renner, Karl (Rudolf Springer) (1906), *Grundlagen und Entwicklungsziele der Österreichisch-Ungarischen Monarchie: Politische Studie über den Zusammenbruch der Privilegenparlamente und die Wahlreform in beiden Staaten, über die Reichsidee und ihre Zukunft*. Leipzig and Vienna: Deuticke.
Rhondda, Margaret Viscountess et al. ['His daughter and others'] (1921), *D. A. Thomas, Viscount Rhondda*. London: Longman, Green & Co.
Robinson, John Beverley (1840), *Canada and the Canada Bill: Being an Examination of the Proposed Measure for the Future Government of Canada: with an Introductory Chapter,*

Containing Some General Views Respecting the British Provinces in North America. London: J. Hatchard & Son.

Roebuck, John Arthur (1835), *The Canadas and their Grievances*. London.

Rowntree, B. Seebohm (1910), *Land and Labour: Lessons from Belgium*. London: Macmillan.

Saint George, George (1836), *A Saunter in Belgium in the Summer of 1835, with Traits Historical and Descriptive*. London: F. C. Westley.

Samuels, Arthur Warren (1912), *Home Rule Finance: An Examination of the Financial Bearings of the Government of Ireland Bill, 1912*. Dublin: Hodges, Figgis & Co.

Sanson, Joseph (1820), *Travels in Lower Canada, with the Author's Recollections of the Soil and Aspect; The Morals, Habits and Religious Institutions of that Country*. London: Richard Phillips & Co,

Seeley, John R. (1883), *The Expansion of England: Two Courses of Lectures*. London: Macmillan & Co.

Seton-Watson, R. W. (1898), *Scotland for ever, and Other Poems*. Edinburgh: David Douglas.

Seton-Watson, R. W. (Scotus viator) (1907), *The future of Austro-Hungary and the Attitude of the Great Powers*. London: Constable & Co.

Seton-Watson, R. W. ('Scotus viator') (1908), *Racial Problems in Hungary*. London: Constable & Co.

Seton-Watson, R. W. (1911a), *The Southern Slav Question and the Hapsburg Monarchy*. London: Constable & Co.

Seton-Watson, R. W. (1911b), *Corruption and Reform in Hungary: A Study of Electoral Practice*. London: Constable & Co.

Seton-Watson, R. W. (1912), *Absolutism in Croatia*. London: Constable & Co.

Seton-Watson, R.W. (1915), *The Future of Bohemia*. London: Nisbet & Co.

Seton-Watson, R. W. (1917), *The Rise of Nationality in the Balkans*. London: Constable & Co.

Seton-Watson, R. W. (1919), *Europe in the Melting-Pot*. London: Macmillan.

Seton-Watson, R. W. (1924), *The New Slovakia*. Prague: F. Borový.

Seton-Watson, R. W. (1937). *Britain in Europe, 1789–1914*. Cambridge: Cambridge University Press.

Shearman, Hugh (1950), *Finland: The Adventures of a Small Power*. London: Steven & Sons.

Shinn Jr., Ridgway F., and Richard A. Cosgrove (eds) (1996), *Constitutional Reflections: The Correspondence of Albert Venn Dicey and Arthur Berriedale Keith*. Lanham, MD, and London: University Press of America.

Shirreff, Patrick (1835), *A Tour through North America Together with a Comprehensive View of Canada and the United States as Adapted for Agricultural Emigration*. Edinburgh: Oliver & Boyd.

Sidgwick, Henry (1891), *The Elements of Politics*. London: Macmillan.

Sidgwick, Henry (1913), *The Development of European Polity*. London: Macmillan.

Smith, Goldwin (1904), *My Memory of Gladstone*. London: T. Fisher Unwin.

Southey, Robert (1810), *History of Brazil*, 3 vols. London: Longmans, Hurst, Rees & Orme.

Southey, Robert (1902), *Journal of a Tour in the Netherlands in the Autumn of 1815*. Boston and New York: Heinemann.

Spalding, Thomas Alfred (1896), *Federation and Empire*. London: H. Henry & Co.

Staunton, Alderman [Michael] (1845), *Second Repeal Prize Essay: Reasons for a Repeal of the Legislative Union between Great Britain and Ireland*. Dublin: James Duffy.

Steed, Henry Wickham (1914), *The Hapsburg Monarchy*, 3rd edition. London: Constable & Co.

Steed, Henry Wickham (1919), *The Hapsburg Monarchy*, new edition. London: Constable & Co.

Steed, Henry Wickham (1924), *Through Thirty Years, 1892–1922: A Personal Narrative*, 2 vols. London: Heinemann.

Steed, Henry Wickham (n.d. [1937]), *Doom of the Habsburgs*. London: Arrowsmith
Steed, Henry Wickham, Walter Alison Phillips, et al. (1914), *A Short History of Austria-Hungary and Poland*. London: Encyclopedia Britannica.
Stewart, George (1878), *Canada under the Administration of the Earl of Dufferin*. Toronto: Rose-Belford Publishing Co.
Street, Cecil John Charles (1922), *The Administration of Ireland, 1921*. London: Philip Allan.
Street, Cecil John Charles (1923), *Hungary and Democracy*. London: T. Fisher Unwin.
Street, Cecil John Charles (1924), *East of Prague*. London: Geoffrey Bles.
Street, Cecil John Charles (n.d. [1929]), *Slovakia, Past and Present*. London: Czech Society of Great Britain.
Talbot, Edward Allan (1824), *Five Years' Residence in the Canadas; Including a Tour through Part of the United States of America in the Year 1823*. London: Longman, Hurst, Rees, Orme, Brown & Green.
Tennant, Charles (1824), *A Journey through Parts of the Netherlands, Holland, Germany, Switzerland, Savoy and France in the Year 1821-22*, 2 vols. London: Longman, Hurst, Rees, Orme, Brown & Green.
Tennent, James Emerson (1841), *Belgium*, 2 vols. London: Richard Bentley.
Thomas, Ceinwen (1957), *Monmouthshire in Wales: The Facts: The Act of Union*. Gwent: Meibion.
Tocqueville, Alexis de (1856), *The Old Regime and the Revolution*. New York: Harper & Bros.
Tremenheere, Hugh Seymour (1852), *Notes on Public Subjects Made during a Tour in the United States and in Canada*. London: John Murray.
Trollope, William (1842), *Belgium since the Revolution of 1830: Comprising a Topographical and Antiquarian Description of the Country*. London: How & Parsons.
Vincent, J. E. (1896), *The Land Question in North Wales: Being a Brief Survey of the History, Origin, and Character of the Agrarian Agitation and of the Nature and Effect of the Proceedings of the Welsh Land Commission*. London: Longman, Green & Co.
Vincent, J. E. (1897), *The Land Question in South Wales: A Defence of the Landowners of South Wales and Monmouthshire*. London: Landowners' Association of South Wales & Monmouthshire.
Vinje, Aasmund Olafsen (1863), *A Norseman's Views of Britain and the British*. Edinburgh: William P. Nimmo.
Vosnjak, Bogumil (1918), *A Dying Empire: Central Europe, Pan-Germanism, and the Downfall of Austria-Hungary*. With a preface by T. P. O'Connor, MP. London: G. Allen & Unwin.
Waddie, Charles (1883), *The Treaty of Union*. Edinburgh: Waddie & Co.
Waddie, Charles (1891), *How Scotland Lost her Parliament, and What Came of it*. Edinburgh: Waddie & Co.
Waddie, Charles (1895), *The Federation of Greater Britain*. Edinburgh: Waddie & Co.
Waddie, Charles (1907), *The Bicentenary of the Union of the Scottish and English Parliaments: A Brief Historical Account of How it Affected the Welfare of Scotland*. Edinburgh: Waddie & Co.
Walpole, Spencer (1893), *The Land of Home Rule: An Essay on the History and Constitution of the Isle of Man*. London: Longmans, Green & Co.
Ward, Adolphus (1899), *Great Britain and Hanover: Some Aspects of the Personal Union*. Oxford: Clarendon Press.
Webster, Sir Charles (1925), *The Foreign Policy of Castlereagh, 1815-22*. London: G. Bell & Sons.
Webster, Sir Charles (1931), *The Foreign Policy of Castlereagh, 1812-15*. London: G. Bell & Sons.

Westerkamp, Justus B. (1892), *Staatenbund and Bundesstaat*. Leipzig: Brockhaus.
White, Arnold (1901), *Efficiency and Empire*. London: Methuen.
White, Charles (1835), *The Belgic Revolution of 1830*, 2 vols. London: Whitakker & Co.
White, Charles (ed. and tr.) (1838), *Belgium and the 24 Articles*. Brussels: A. Cauvin.
Wilde, Oscar (1894). *A Woman of No Importance*. London: John Lane.
Williams, William Llewellyn (1909), *The Union of England and Wales, Transactions of the Honourable Society of Cymmrodorion: Session 1907-8*. London: Cymmrodorion Society.
Willoughby, Westel W. (1896), *An Examination of the Nature of the State*. New York: Macmillan.
Willson, Thomas B. (1908), *Norway at Home*, London: Newnes.
Wilson, Daniel (1825), *Letters from an Absent Brother Containing Some Account of a Tour through Parts of the Netherlands, Switzerland, Northern Italy and France in the Summer of 1823*, 2 vols, 3rd enlarged edition. London: George Wilson.
Wollstonecraft, Mary (1889), *Letters Written during a Short Residence in Sweden, Norway and Denmark*. London: Cassell.
Yonge, Charles Duke (1868), *The Life and Administration of Robert Banks, Second Earl of Liverpool KG, Late First Lord of the Treasury*, 3 vols. London: Macmillan.

Secondary Sources

Aan de Wiel, Jérôme (2009), *The Irish Factor 1899-1919: Ireland's Strategic Importance for Foreign Powers*. Dublin: Irish Academic Press.
Aaron, Jane, and Sarah Prescott (2020), *Welsh Writing in English, 1536-1914: The First Four Hundred Years* (The Oxford Literary History of Wales, 3). Oxford: Oxford University Press.
Acemoglu, Daron, and James A. Robinson (2012), *Why Nations Fail: The Origins of Power, Prosperity and Poverty*. London: Profile Books.
Aerts, R. (2010), 'Civil Society or Democracy? A Dutch Paradox', *BMGN: Low Countries Historical Review*, 125/2-3, pp. 209-36.
Ajzenstat, Janet (1988), *The Political Thought of Lord Durham*. Montreal and Kingston: McGill-Queen's University Press.
Akenson, Donald Harman (1986), *The Orangeman: The Life and Times of Ogle Gowan*. Toronto: James Lorimer.
Alofsin, Anthony (2006), *When Buildings Speak: Architecture as Language in the Habsburg Empire and its Aftermath*. Chicago: Chicago University Press.
Anderson, Benedict (2006), *Imagined Communities: Reflections on the Origin and Spread of Nationalism*, new edition. London: Verso.
Andrén, Nils (1964), *Government and Politics in the Nordic Countries: Denmark, Finland, Iceland, Norway, Sweden*. Stockholm: Almqvist & Wiksell.
Arieta, Jon, and J. H. Elliott (2009), *Forms of Union: The British and Spanish Monarchies in the Seventeenth and Eighteenth Centuries*. Donostia: Eusko Ikaskuntza/Editorial S.A. Sociedad de Estudios Vascos.
Armitage, David (2000), *Ideological Origins of the British Empire*. Cambridge: Cambridge University Press.
Arnstein, Walter L (1996), 'Queen Victoria and the Challenge of Roman Catholicism', *The Historian*, 58/2 (Winter), pp. 295-314.
Asch, Ronald (ed.) (2014), *Hannover, Grossbritannien und Europa: Erfahrungsraum Personalunion, 1714-1837*. Göttingen: Wallstein.

Ash, Mitchell, and Jan Surman (eds) (2012), *The Nationalisation of Scientific Knowledge in the Habsburg Empire, 1848–1918*. Basingstoke: Palgrave Macmillan.

Aubel, Felix (1994), 'Welsh Conservatism, 1885–1935', Ph.D. thesis, University of Wales.

Aubel, Felix (1996), 'The Conservatives in Wales, 1880–1935', in Martin Francis and Ina Zweiniger-Bargielowska (eds), *The Conservatives and British Society*. Cardiff: University of Wales Press, pp. 96–110.

Badar-Zaar, Birgitta (2014), 'Rethinking Women's Suffrage in the Nineteenth Century: Local Government and the Entanglements of Property and Gender in the Austrian Half of the Habsburg Monarchy, Sweden and the United Kingdom', in Kelly Grotke and Markus Prutsch (eds), *Constitutionalism, Legitimacy and Power: Nineteenth Century Experiences*. Oxford: Oxford University Press, pp. 107–26.

Barman, Roderick (1988), *Brazil: The Forging of a Nation, 1798–1852*. Stanford: Stanford University Press.

Barman, Roderick (1999), *Citizen Emperor: Pedro II and the Making of Brazil*. Stanford: Stanford University Press.

Barry, G., E. Dal Lago, and R. Healy (eds) (2016), *Small Nations and Colonial Peripheries in World War One*. Boston: Brill/Humanities.

Bartkus, Viva Ona (1999), *The Dynamics of Secession*. Cambridge: Cambridge University Press.

Bartlett, Thomas (1979) 'The Townshend Viceroyalty, 1767–72', in Thomas Bartlett and David Hayton (eds), *Penal Era and Golden Age: Essays in Irish History, 1690–1800*. Belfast: Ulster Historical Foundation, pp. 88–112.

Barton, H. Arnold (1970), 'The Swedish Succession Crises of 1809 and 1810 and the Question of Scandinavian Union', *Scandinavian Studies*, 42, pp. 309–33.

Barton, H. Arnold (1986), *Scandinavia in the Revolutionary Era, 1760–1815*. Minneapolis: University of Minnesota Press.

Barton, H. Arnold (1998), *Northern Arcadia: Foreign Travelers in Scandinavia, 1765–1815*. Carbondale, IL: Southern Illinois University Press.

Barton, H. Arnold (2003), *Sweden and Visions of Norway: Politics and Culture, 1814–1905*. Carbondale, IL: Southern Illinois University Press.

Barton, H. Arnold (2006), 'Finland and Norway, 1808–1917', *Scandinavian Journal of History*, 31/3–4, pp. 221–36.

Baycroft, Timothy (2004), *Culture, Identity and Nationalism: French Flanders in the Nineteenth and Twentieth Centuries*. Woodbridge: Boydell.

Baycroft, Timothy, and Mark Hewitson (eds) (2006), *What is a Nation? Europe 1789–1914*. Oxford: Oxford University Press.

Bebbington, D. W. (1982), 'Religion and National Feeling in Nineteenth Century Wales and Scotland', in S. Mews (ed.), *Religion and National Identity*. Oxford: Blackwell/Ecclesiastical History Society, pp. 489–504.

Bell, Duncan (2011), *The Idea of Greater Britain: Empire and the Future of World Order, 1860–1900*. Princeton: Princeton University Press.

Bell, Duncan (2016), *Reordering the World: Essays on Liberalism and Empire*. Princeton: Princeton University Press.

Beller, Steven (1996), *Francis Joseph*. Harlow: Longman.

Beller, Steven (2018), *The Habsburg Monarchy, 1815–1918*. Cambridge: Cambridge University Press.

Beneš, Jakub S. (2017), *Workers and Nationalism: Czech and German Social Democracy in Habsburg Austria, 1890–1918*. Oxford: Oxford University Press.

Berg, Roald (2009), 'The Nineteenth Century Norwegian-Swedish Border: "Imagined Community" or "Pluralist Security System"', *Journal of Northern Studies*, 1, pp. 91–103.

Berg, Roald (2012), 'Norwegian Attitudes towards the British, 1814–1914', in H. Pharo and P. Salmon (eds), *Britain and Norway: Special Relationships*. Oslo: Akademika Vorlag, pp. 23–50.

Berg, Roald (2014), 'Denmark, Norway and Sweden in 1814: A Geopolitical and Contemporary Perspective', *Scandinavian Journal of History*, 39/3, pp. 1–22.

Berg, Roald (2019), 'Emotions in International Politics: Distrust of the British in Norwegian Public Life, 1814–1914', *Scandinavica*, 58/2, pp. 98–114.

Berg, Roald (2020), 'Norway's Foreign Politics during the Union with Sweden, 1814–1905', *Diplomacy and Statecraft*, 31/1 (Mar.), pp. 1–21.

Berg, Roald, and Eva Jakobsson (2006), 'Nature and Diplomacy: The Struggle over the Scandinavian Border Rivers in 1905', *Scandinavian Journal of History*, 31/3–4, pp. 270–89.

Berger, Stefan (2020), 'Comparative and Transnational History', in Stefan Berger, Heiko Feldner, and Kevin Passmore (eds), *Writing History: Theory and Practice*, 3rd edition. London: Bloomsbury, pp. 157–67.

Berger, Stefan, and Chris Lorenz (eds) (2008), *The Contested Nation: Ethnicity, Class, Religion and Gender in National Histories*. London: Palgrave Macmillan.

Berger, Stefan and Alexei Miller (eds) (2015), *Nationalizing Empires*. Budapest: Central European University Press.

Berger, Stefan, Mark Donovan, and Kevin Passmore (eds) (1998), *Writing National Histories: Western Europe since 1800*. London: Routledge.

Berger, Stefan, Linas Eriksonas, and Andrew Mycock (eds) (2008), *Narrating the Nation: Representations in History, Media and the Arts*. Oxford: Oxford University Press.

Bernard, Jean Paul (1983), *Les rébellions de 1837–1838: Les patriotes du Bas-Canada dans la mémoire collective et chez les historiens*. Montreal: Boréal Express.

Bew, John (2009), *The Glory of Being Britons: Civic Unionism in Nineteenth Century Belfast*. Dublin: Irish Academic Press.

Bew, John (2011), *Castlereagh: From Enlightenment to Tyranny*. London: Quercus.

Bew, Paul (1980), *C. S. Parnell*. Dublin: Gill & Macmillan.

Beyen, Marnix (2005), 'Belgium: A State that Failed to be Ethnic', in Linas Eriksonas and Leos Müller (eds), *Statehood before and beyond Ethnicity: Minor States in Northern and Eastern Europe, 1600–2000*. Brussels: Peter Lang.

Bhabha, Homi K. (ed.) (1990), *Nation and Narration*. London: Routledge.

Biagini, Eugenio (2007), *British Democracy and Irish Nationalism, 1876–1906*. Cambridge: Cambridge University Press.

Bielenberg, Andy (2009), *Ireland and the Industrial Revolution: The Impact of the Industrial Revolution on Irish Industry, 1801–1922*. London: Routledge.

Blackstock, Allan, and Frank O'Gorman (eds) (2014), *Loyalism and the Formation of the British World, 1775–1914*. Woodbridge: Boydell.

Blake, Raymond, Jeffrey Keshen, Norman Knowles, and Barbara Messamore (2017), *Conflict and Compromise: Pre-Confederation Canada*. Toronto: University of Toronto Press.

Blom, J. C. H., and E. Lamberts (eds) (2006), *History of the Low Countries*, new edition. New York and Oxford: Berghahn.

Boehmer, Elleke (1995), *Colonial and Postcolonial Literature*. Oxford: Oxford University Press.

Bogdanor, Vernon (2009), *The New British Constitution*. Oxford: Hart Publishing.

Bogdanor, Vernon (2022), *The Strange Survival of Liberal Britain: Politics and Power before the First World War*. London: Bloomsbury.

Bowen, H. V. (ed.) (2011), *Wales and the British Overseas Empire: Interactions and Influences, 1650–1830*. Manchester: Manchester University Press.

Bowman, William D. (1999), *Priest and Parish in Vienna, 1780-1880*. Boston: Brill Academic/Humanities Press.
Boyce, D. G., and J. Stubbs (1976), 'F. S. Oliver, Lord Selborne and Federalism', *Journal of Imperial and Commonwealth History*, 5/1, pp. 53-81.
Boyer, John (1986), 'The End of an Old Regime: Visions of Political Reform in Later Imperial Austria', *Journal of Modern History*, 58/1 (Mar.), pp. 159-93.
Boyer, John (1994), 'Religion and Political Development in Central Europe around 1900: A View from Vienna', *Austrian History Yearbook*, 25, pp. 13-57.
Boyer, John W. (1995), *Political Radicalism in Late Imperial Vienna: Origins of the Christian Social Movement*. Chicago: Chicago University Press.
Bradshaw, Brendan, and John Morrill (eds) (1996), *The British Problem c.1534-1707: State Formation in the Atlantic Archipelago*. London: Palgrave Macmillan.
Bradshaw, Brendan, and Peter Roberts (eds) (1997), *British Consciousness and Identity: The Making of Britain, 1533-1707*. Cambridge: Cambridge University Press.
Branch, Michael, Janet Hartley, and Antoni Maczak (eds) (1995), *Finland and Poland in the Russian Empire*. London: School of Slavonic and East European Studies (SSES Occasional Papers).
Bremner, G. A., and Jonathan Conlin (eds) (2015), *Making History: Edward Augustus Freeman and Victorian Cultural Politics*. Oxford: Oxford University Press.
Bridge, F. R. (1972), *Great Britain and Austria-Hungary, 1906-14: A Diplomatic History*. London: London School of Economics/Weidenfeld.
Bridge, F. R. (1990), *The Habsburg Monarchy among the Great Powers, 1815-1918*. Oxford: Bloomsbury/Berg Publishers.
Brockliss, Laurence, and David Eastwood (eds) (1997), *A Union of Multiple Identities: The British Isles, 1750-1850*. Manchester: Manchester University Press.
Brook, Nick (2018), *Terrorism and Nationalism in the United Kingdom: The Absence of Noise*. Basingstoke: Palgrave Macmillan.
Brooks, Simon (2017), *Why Wales Never was: The Failure of Welsh Nationalism*. Cardiff: University of Wales Press.
Brown, Douglas, Herman Bakvis, and Gerald Baier (2019), *Contested Federalism: Certainty and Ambiguity in the Canadian Federation*, 2nd edition. Oxford: Oxford University Press.
Brown, Michael (2016), *The Irish Enlightenment*. Cambridge MA: Harvard.
Brown, Stewart J. (2001), *The National Churches of England, Scotland and Ireland, 1801-46*. Oxford: Oxford University Press.
Brown, Stewart J. (2008), *Providence and Empire, 1815-1914*. Harlow: Longman.
Brown, Stewart J. (2017), 'The Established Churches, Church Growth and Secularisation in Imperial Britain, c.1830-1930', in D. N. Hempton and Hugh McLeod (eds), *Secularisation and Religious Innovation in the North Atlantic World*. Oxford: Oxford University Press, pp. 25-43.
Brown, Stewart J., and Michael Fry (eds) (1993), *Scotland in the Age of the Disruption*. Edinburgh: Edinburgh University Press.
Brubaker, Rogers (1996), *Nationalism Reframed: Nationhood and the National Question in the New Europe*. Cambridge: Cambridge University Press.
Brubaker, Rogers, Margit Feischmidt, Jon Fox, and Liana Grancea (2006), *Nationalist Politics and Everyday Ethnicity in a Transylvanian Town*. Princeton: Princeton University Press.
Brusatti, Alois (ed.) (1973), *Die Habsburgermonarchie, 1848-1918, Band 1: die wirtschaftliche Entwicklung*. Vienna: Verlag der österreichischen Akademie der Wissenschaften.
Bryden, John, Ottar Brox, and Lesley Riddoch (eds) (2015), *Northern Neighbours: Scotland and Norway since 1800*. Edinburgh: Edinburgh University Press.

Buchanan, Allen (1991), *Secession: The Morality of Political Divorce from Fort Sumter to Lithuania and Quebec*. Boulder, CO: Westview Press.
Buchanan, Allen (1997), 'Theories of Secession', *Philosophy and Public Affairs*, 26/1 (Jan.), pp. 31–61.
Buckner, Phillip A. (ed.) (2010), *Canada and the British Empire* (Oxford History of the British Empire, Companion Series). Oxford: Oxford University Press.
Buckner, Phillip A. (2003), 'Acheson, Archibald, 2nd Earl of Gosford', in *Dictionary of Canadian Biography*, vol. 7. Toronto: University of Toronto Press.
Buckner, Phillip A., and John G Reid (eds) (1994), *The Atlantic Region to Confederation: A History*. Toronto: University of Toronto Press.
Buckner, Phillip A. (1985), *The Transition to Responsible Government: British Policy in British North America, 1815–50*. Westport, CT: Greenwood.
Bucur, Maria, and Nancy M. Wingfield (eds) (2001), *Staging the Past: The Politics of Commemoration in Habsburg Central Europe, 1848 to the Present*. West Lafayette, IN: Purdue University Press.
Bugge, Peter (2017), 'Loyal in Word and Deed: The Czech National Movement and the Habsburg Monarchy in the Long Nineteenth Century', in Jana Osterkamp and Martin Schulze Wessel (eds), *Exploring Loyalty*. Göttingen: Vandenhoeck & Ruprecht.
Burgess, Michael (ed.) (1990), *Canadian Federalism: Past, Present and Future*. Leicester: Leicester University Press.
Burgess, Michael (1995), *The British Tradition of Federalism*. Leicester: Leicester University Press.
Burgess, Michael (2000), *Federalism and the European Union: The Building of Europe, 1950–2000*. London: Routledge.
Burgess, Michael (2006), *Comparative Federalism: Theory and Practice*. London: Routledge.
Burgess, Michael (2012), *In Search of the Federal Spirit: New Theoretical and Empirical Perspectives in Comparative Federalism*. Oxford: Oxford University Press.
Burgess, Michael, and Alain-G. Gagnon (2010), *Federal Democracies*. London: Routledge.
Burgess, Michael, and John Pinder (eds) (2007), *Multinational Federations*. London: Routledge.
Burns, Robin B. (2003), 'McGee, Thomas D'Arcy', in *Dictionary of Canadian Biography*, vol. 9. Toronto: University of Toronto Press.
Butterwick, Richard (ed.) (2001), *The Polish-Lithuanian Monarchy in European Context, c.1500–1795*. Basingstoke: Palgrave Macmillan.
Butterwick-Pawlikowski, Richard, Quincy Cloet, and Alex Dowdall (eds) (2017), *Breaking Empires, Making Nations? The First World War and the Reforging of Europe*. Warsaw: Collège d'Europe.
Cabestan, Jean-Pierre, and Pavković, Aleksandar (eds) (2012), *Secessionism and Separatism in Europe and Asia: To have a State of one's own*. London: Routledge.
Cameron, Ewen (1996), *Land for the People? Government and the Scottish Highlands, 1880–1925*. East Linton: Tuckwell.
Campbell, Fergus (2009), *The Irish Establishment, 1879–1914*. Oxford: Oxford University Press.
Cannadine, David (1990), *The Decline and Fall of the British Aristocracy*. New Haven: Yale University Press.
Cannadine, David (1992), *G. M. Trevelyan: A Life in History*. London: Harper Collins.
Caraway, David Todd (2003), 'Retreat from Liberalism: William I, the Freedom of the Press, Political Asylum, and the Foreign Relations of the United Kingdom of the Netherlands, 1814–1818', Ph.D. thesis, University of Delaware.

Careless, J. M. S. (1968), *The Union of the Canadas: The Growth of Canadian Institutions, 1841-1857*. Toronto: McClelland & Stewart.
Carey, Hilary (2008), *Empires of Religion*. Basingstoke and New York: Palgrave Macmillan.
Chomsky, Noam (2006), *Failed States: The Abuse of Power and the Assault on Democracy*. New York: Metropolitan Books.
Clark, Christopher (2006), *Iron Kingdom: The Rise and Downfall of Prussia, 1600-1947*. London: Allen Lane.
Clark, Christopher (2013), *The Sleepwalkers: How Europe Went to War in 1914*. London: Allen Lane.
Clark, Christopher, and Wolfram Kaiser (eds) (2003), *Culture Wars: Secular-Catholic Conflict in Nineteenth Century Europe*. Cambridge: Cambridge University Press.
Cohen, Deborah (2004), 'Comparative History: Buyer Beware', in Deborah Cohen and Maura O'Connor (eds), *Comparison and History: Europe in Cross-National Perspective*. New York: Routledge, pp. 57-70.
Cohen, Deborah and Maura O'Connor (eds) (2004), 'Comparative History, Cross-National History, Transnational History—Definitions', in Deborah Cohen and Maura O'Connor (eds), *Comparison and History: Europe in Cross-National Perspective*. New York: Routledge, pp. ix-xxiv.
Cohen, Gary (1981), *The Politics of Ethnic Survival: Germans in Prague, 1861-1914*. Princeton: Princeton University Press.
Cohen, Gary (1998), 'Neither Absolutism Nor Anarchy: New Narratives on Society and Government in Late Imperial Austria', *Austrian History Yearbook*, 29, pp. 37-61.
Cohen, Gary (2007), 'Nationalist Politics and the Dynamics of State and Civil Society in the Habsburg Monarchy, 1867-1914', *Central European History*, 40/2 (June), pp. 241-78.
Cole, Laurence (2000), *'Für Gott, Kaiser und Vaterland': Nationale Identität der deutschsprachigen Bevölkerung Tirols, 1860-1914*. Frankfurt: Campus Verlag.
Cole, Laurence (ed.) (2007), *Different Paths to the Nation: Regional and National Identities in Central Europe and Italy, 1830-70*. Basingstoke: Palgrave Macmillan.
Cole, Laurence (2014), *Military Culture and Popular Patriotism in Late Imperial Austria*. Oxford: Oxford University Press.
Cole, Laurence, Christa Hämmerle, and Martin Scheutz (eds) (2011), *Glanz-Gewalt-Gehorsam: Militär und Gesellschaft in der Habsburgermonarchie (1800 bis 1918)*, Essen: Klartext.
Cole, Laurence, and Daniel Unowsky (eds) (2007), *The Limits of Loyalty: Imperial Symbolism, Popular Allegiances, and State Patriotism in the Late Habsburg Monarchy*. Oxford and New York: Berghahn.
Colley, Linda (1992), *Britons: Forging the Nation, 1707-1837*. New Haven: Yale University Press.
Colley, Linda (2014a), 'Empires of Writing: Britain, America and Constitutions, 1776-1848', *Law and History Review*, 32/2 (May), pp. 237-66.
Colley, Linda (2014b), *Acts of Union, Acts of Disunion*. London: Profile Books.
Colley, Linda (2021), *The Gun, the Ship and the Pen: Warfare, Constitutions and the Making of the Modern World*. London: Profile Books.
Congleton, Roger (2011), *Perfecting Parliament: Constitutional Reform, Liberalism and the Rise of Western Democracy*. Cambridge: Cambridge University Press.
Connelly, John (2020), *From Peoples into Nations: A History of Eastern Europe*. Princeton: Princeton University Press.
Conway, Martin (2012), *The Sorrows of Belgium: Liberation and Political Reconstruction, 1944-47*. Oxford: Oxford University Press.
Conway, Stephen (2011), *Britain, Ireland and Continental Europe in the Eighteenth Century: Similarities, Connections, Identities*. Oxford: Oxford University Press.

Cookson, J. E. (1997), *The British Armed Nation, 1793–1815*. Oxford: Oxford University Press.
Cornell, Paul (1967), *The Alignment of Political Groups in Canada, 1841–67*. Toronto: University of Toronto Press.
Cornwall, Mark (ed.) (1990), *The Last Years of Austria-Hungary: Essays in Political and Military History 1908–1918*. Exeter: University of Exeter Press.
Cornwall, Mark (2000), *The Undermining of Austria-Hungary: The Battle for Hearts and Minds*. Basingstoke: Palgrave Macmillan.
Cornwall, Mark (ed.) (2002), *The Last Years of Austria-Hungary: A Multinational Experiment in Early 20th Century Europe*, new edition. Liverpool: Liverpool University Press.
Cornwall, Mark (2015), 'Traitors and the Meanings of Treason in Austria-Hungary's Great War', *Transactions of the Royal Historical Society*, 25, pp. 113–34.
Cornwall, Mark (2017), 'Loyalty and Treason in Late Habsburg Croatia: A Violent Discourse before the Great War', in Martin Schulze-Wessel and Jana Osterkamp (eds), *Exploring Loyalty*. Göttingen: Vandenhoeck & Ruprecht.
Cornwall, Mark, and R. J. W. Evans (eds) (2007), *Czechoslovakia in a Nationalist and Fascist Europe, 1918–48*. Oxford: Oxford University Press.
Cornwall, Mark, and Murray Frame (eds) (2001), *Scotland and the Slavs: Cultures in Contact 1500–2000*. Newtownville: Oriental Research Partners.
Cornwall, Mark, and John Paul Newman (eds) (2016), *Sacrifice and Rebirth: The Legacy of the Last Habsburg War*. New York: Berghahn.
Cosgrove, Richard A. (1978), 'The Relevance of Irish History? The Gladstone-Dicey Debate about Home Rule, 1886–7', *Eire-Ireland*, 13/4, pp. 6–21.
Cosgrove, Richard A. (1980), *The Rule of Law: Albert Venn Dicey, Victorian Jurist*. Chapel Hill, NC: University of North Carolina Press.
Cragoe, Matthew (1995), 'Conscience or Coercion? Clerical Influence at the General Election of 1868 in Wales', *Past and Present*, 149/1 (Nov.), pp. 140–69.
Cragoe, Matthew (1996), *An Anglican Aristocracy: The Moral Economy of the Landed Estate in Carmarthenshire, 1832–95*. Oxford: Oxford University Press.
Cragoe, Matthew (1998a), 'The Anatomy of an Eviction Campaign: The General Election of 1868 in Wales and its Aftermath', *Rural History*, 9/2, pp. 177–93.
Cragoe, Matthew (1998b), 'Welsh Electioneering and the Purpose of Parliament: "From Radicalism to Nationalism" Reconsidered', *Parliamentary History*, 17/1, pp. 113–30.
Cragoe, Matthew (2000a), 'George Osborne Morgan, Henry Richard and the Politics of Religion in Wales, 1868–74', *Parliamentary History*, 19/1 (Jan.), pp. 118–30.
Cragoe, Matthew (2000b), 'Conscience or Coercion? Clerical Influence at the General Election of 1868 in Wales: Reply', *Past and Present*, 169/1, pp. 205–13.
Cragoe, Matthew (2004), *Culture, Politics and National Identity in Wales, 1832–86*. Oxford: Oxford University Press.
Cragoe, Matthew (2010), '"A Contemptible Mimic of the Irish": The Land Question in Victorian Wales', in Matthew Cragoe and Paul Readman (eds), *The Land Question in Britain, 1750–1950*. Basingstoke: Palgrave Macmillan, pp. 92–108.
Cragoe, Matthew, and Paul Readman (eds) (2010), *The Land Question in Britain, 1750–1850*. Basingstoke: Palgrave Macmillan.
Creighton, Donald G. (1956), *The Empire of the St Lawrence: A Study in Commerce and Politics*. Toronto: Macmillan Canada.
Creighton, Donald G. (1964), *The Road to Confederation: The Emergence of Canada, 1863–67*. Toronto: Macmillan Canada.
Cronne, H. A., T. W. Moody, and D. B. Quinn (eds) (1949), *Essays in British and Irish history in honour of James Eadie Todd*. London: Frederick Muller.

Crossick, Geoffrey (1978), *An Artisan Elite in Victorian Society: Kentish Town, 1840–80*. London: Croom Helm.
Cullen, Ruairí (2017), 'Contention and Innovation: The Medieval Period in Late Nineteenth and Early Twentieth Century Irish Historiography', Ph.D. thesis, Queen's University, Belfast.
Curran, Declan, Lubomyr Luciuk, and Andrew Newby (eds) (2015), *Famines in European Economic History: The Last Great European Famines Reconsidered*. London and New York: Routledge.
Curtis, L. Perry (1963), *Coercion and Conciliation in Ireland, 1880–92: A Study in Conservative Unionism*. Princeton: Princeton University Press.
Curtis, L. Perry (1971), *Apes and Angels: The Irishman in Victorian Caricature*. Washington, DC: Smithsonian Institution Press.
d'Ancona, Matthew (ed.) (2009), *Being British: The Search for the Values that Bind the Nation*. London: Mainstream Publishing.
Daley, Robert Charles (1986), 'Edmund Bailey O'Callaghan: Irish *Patriote*', Ph.D. thesis, Concordia University, Montreal.
Dal Lago, E., R. Healy, and G. Barry (eds) (2016), *1916 in Global Context: An Anti-Imperial Moment*. London: Routledge.
Dann, Uriel (1991), *Great Britain and Hanover, 1740–69*. Leicester: Leicester University Press.
Davies, John (1992), 'Wales and Ireland Compared', *Planet*, 95 (Oct.–Nov.).
Davies, John (1993), *A History of Wales*. London: Allen Lane.
Davies, John E. (2020), *The Changing Fortunes of a British Aristocratic Family, 1689–1976: The Campbells of Cawdor and their Welsh Estates*. Woodbridge: Boydell.
Davies, Norman (1999), *The Isles: A History*. Oxford: Oxford University Press.
Davies, Norman (2011), *Vanished Kingdoms: The History of Half-Forgotten Europe*. London: Allen Lane.
Davies, Russell (2015), *People, Places and Passion: A Social History of Wales and the Welsh, 1870–1945*. Cardiff: University of Wales Press.
Deák, Iztván (1990), *Beyond Nationalism: A Social and Political History of the Habsburg Officer Corps, 1848–1918*. Oxford: Oxford University Press.
Deak, John (2014), 'The Great War and the Forgotten Realm: The Habsburg Monarchy and the First World War', *Journal of Modern History*, 86/2, pp. 336–80.
Deak, John (2015), *Forging a Multinational State: State Making in Imperial Austria from the Enlightenment to the First World War*. Stanford, CA: Stanford University Press.
Deak, John, and Jonathan E Gumz (2017), 'How to Break a State: The Habsburg Empire's Internal War, 1914–18', *American Historical Review*, 122/4, pp. 1105–36.
De Meeüs, Adrien (1962), *History of the Belgians*. London: Thames & Hudson.
Derry, T. K. (1973), *A History of Modern Norway, 1814–1972*. Oxford: Clarendon Press.
Deseure, Brecht (2016), 'National Sovereignty in the Belgian Constitution of 1831: On the Meaning(s) of Article 25', in Ulrike Müssig (ed.), *Reconsidering Constitutional Formation/ National Sovereignty* (Studies in the History of Law and Justice, 6). Cham: Springer.
Deutsch, Karl (1966), *Nationalism and Social Communication: An Enquiry into the Foundations of Nationality*, 2nd edition. Cambridge, MA: MIT Press.
Devine, T. M. (ed.) (1990), *Conflict and Stability in Scottish Society, 1750–1850*. Edinburgh: John Donald.
Devine, T. M. (1999), *The Scottish Nation, 1700–2000*. London: Allen Lane.
Devine, T. M. (2016), *Independence or Union? Scotland's Past and Scotland's Present*. London: Allen Lane.
Devine, T. M. (2018), *The Scottish Clearances: A History of the Dispossessed*. London: Allen Lane.

Diamond, Jared (2005), *Collapse: How Societies Choose to Fail or Survive*. London: Allen Lane.
Donaldson, Gordon (1990), *A Northern Commonwealth: Scotland and Norway*. Edinburgh: Saltire Society.
Duchacek, Ivo D. (1970), *Comparative Federalism: The Territorial Dimension of Politics*. New York: Holt, Rinehart & Winston.
Ducharme, Michel (2006), 'Closing the Last Chapter of the American Revolution: The 1837–8 Rebellions in Upper and Lower Canada', *Proceedings of the American Antiquarian Society*, 116/2, pp. 413–30.
Ducharme, Michel (2014), *The Idea of Liberty in Canada during the Age of Atlantic Revolutions, 1776–1838*. Montreal and Kingston: McGill-Queen's University Press.
Duffy, Joe (2015), *Children of the Rising: The Untold Story of the Young Lives Lost during Easter 1916*. Dublin: Hachette Books Ireland.
Dunthorne, Hugh, and Michael Wintle (eds) (2013), *The Historical Imagination in 19th Century Britain and the Low Countries*. Leiden: Brill.
Eddie, Scott (2008), 'Economic Policy and Economic Development in Austria-Hungary, 1867–1913', in Peter Mathias and Sidney Pollard (eds), *Cambridge Economic History of Europe from the Decline of the Roman Empire, Volume 8: The Industrial Economies*. Cambridge: Cambridge University Press, pp. 814–86.
Edwards, Andrew (2004), 'Answering the Challenge of Nationalism: Goronwy Roberts and the Appeal of the Labour Party in North-West Wales during the 1950s', *Welsh History Review*, 22/1 (June), pp. 126–57.
Edwards, Andrew (2011), *Labour's Crisis: Plaid Cymru, the Conservatives and the Decline of the Labour Party in North-West Wales, 1960–74*. Cardiff: University of Wales Press.
Edwards, Owen Dudley (2022), *Our Nation and Nationalisms*. Edinburgh: Luath Press.
Edwards, Owen Dudley, Gwynfor Evans, Ioan Rhys and Hugh MacDiarmid (eds) (1968), *Celtic Nationalism*. London: Routledge & Kegan Paul.
Elcock, Howard, and Michael Keating (eds) (1998), *Remaking the Union: Devolution and British Politics in the 1990s*. London: Frank Cass.
Elliott, J. H. (1992), 'A Europe of Composite Monarchies', *Past and Present*, 137/1 (Nov.), pp. 48–71.
Elliott, J. H. (2018), *Scots and Catalans: Union and Disunion*. New Haven: Yale University Press.
Ellis, John S. (1996), 'The Prince and the Dragon: Welsh National Identity and the 1911 Investiture of the Prince of Wales', *Welsh History Review*, 18/2, pp. 272–94.
Ellis, John S. (1998), 'Reconciling the Celt: British National Identity, Empire and the 1911 Investiture of the Prince of Wales', *Journal of British Studies*, 37/4 (Oct.), pp. 391–418.
Ellis, John S. (2008), *Investiture: Royal Ceremony and National Identity in Wales, 1911–1969*. Cardiff: University of Wales Press.
Elstad, Hallgeir (2015), 'Religion and Patriotism in 1814 Norway', *Kirchliche Zeitgeschichte*, 28/1, pp. 98–105.
Elviken, Andreas (1931), 'The Genesis of Norwegian Nationalism', *Journal of Modern History*, 3, pp. 365–91.
Engels, David (2013), *Le déclin: La crise de l'Union européenne et la chute de la république romaine*. Paris: Éditions du Toucan: L'Artilleur.
English, Richard (2006), *Irish Freedom: The History of Irish Nationalism*. London: Macmillan.
English, Richard (2011), *Is there an English Nationalism?* London: Institute for Public Policy Research.
English, Richard, and Michael Kenny (eds) (1999), *Rethinking British Decline*. Basingstoke: Palgrave Macmillan.

English, Richard, and Charles Townshend (eds) (1998), *The State: Historical and Political Dimensions*. London: Routledge.
Engman, Max, and David Kirby (eds) (1989), *Finland: People, Nation, State*. London: Hurst.
Evans, A. (2016), '"A Lingering Diminuendo?": The Conference on Devolution, 1920', *Parliamentary History*, 35/3, pp. 315-35.
Evans, A. (2017), '"Too Old a Country...Too Long Accustomed to Regard her Life as One and Indivisible": England and the Speaker's Conference on Devolution', *Contemporary British History*, 31/3, pp. 366-83.
Evans, Ellen L. (1999), *The Cross and the Ballot: Catholic Political Parties in Germany, Switzerland, Austria, Belgium and the Netherlands, 1785-1985*. Boston: Brill/Humanities.
Evans, Neil (1991), 'Internal Colonialism? Colonization, Economic Development and Political Mobilization in Wales, Scotland and Ireland', in Graham Day and Gareth Rees (eds), *Regions, Nations and European Integration: Remaking the Celtic Periphery*. Cardiff: University of Wales Press, pp. 235-64.
Evans, Neil (2004), '"When Men and Mountains Meet": Historians' Explanations of the History of Wales', *Welsh History Review*, 22/2, pp. 222-51.
Evans, Neil (2015), '"A World Empire, Sea-Girt": The British Empire, State and Nations, 1780-1914', in Alexei Miller and Stefan Berger (eds), *Nationalizing Empires*. Budapest: Central European University Press, pp. 31-98.
Evans, Neil, and Huw Pryce (eds) (2017), *Writing a Small Nation's Past: Wales in Comparative Perspective, 1850-1950*. London and New York: Routledge.
Evans, R. J. W. (1998), 'Language and Society in the Nineteenth Century: Some Central-European Comparisons', in Geraint H. Jenkins (ed.), *Language and Community in the Nineteenth Century*. Cardiff: University of Wales Press, pp. 397-424.
Evans, R. J. W. (2006), *Austria, Hungary and the Habsburgs: Essays on Central Europe, c.1683-1867*. Oxford: Oxford University Press.
Evans, R. J. W. (2010), 'Nonconformity and Nation: The Welsh Case', *Welsh History Review*, 25/2 (Dec.), pp. 231-8.
Evans, R. J. W. (2020), 'Remembering the Fall of the Habsburg Monarchy One Hundred Years on: Three Master Interpretations', *Austrian History Yearbook*, 51, 269-91.
Fair, John D. (1999), 'F. S. Oliver, Alexander Hamilton and the "American Plan" for Resolving Britain's Constitutional Crises, 1903-21', *Twentieth Century British History*, 10/1, pp. 1-26.
Ferguson, William (1977), *Scotland's Relations with England: A Survey to 1707*. Edinburgh: John Donald.
Ferguson, William (1994), '+Gordon Donaldson, 1913-93', *Proceedings of the British Academy*, 84, pp. 265-79.
Ferrari, Giuseppe Franco (ed.) (2015), *Two Centuries of Norwegian Constitution: Between Tradition and Innovation*. The Hague: Eleven International.
Finlay, Richard (2002), 'Queen Victoria and the Cult of Scottish Monarchy', in E. J. Cowan and Richard Finlay (eds), *Scottish History: The Power of the Past*. Edinburgh: Edinburgh University Press, pp. 209-24.
Finlay, Richard (2005), 'Scotland and the Monarchy in the Twentieth Century', in William Miller (ed.), *Anglo-Scottish Relations from 1900 to Devolution and Beyond*. Oxford: Oxford University Press.
Fishman, J. S. (1998), *Diplomacy and Revolution: The London Conference of 1830 and the Belgian Revolution*. Amsterdam: CHEV.
Fitzgerald, John (1995), 'The Nationless State: The Search for a Nation in Modern Chinese Nationalism', *Australian Journal of Chinese Affairs*, 33 (Jan.), pp. 75-104.

Fitzmaurice, Andrew (2014), *Sovereignty, Property and Empire, 1500–2000*. Cambridge: Cambridge University Press.

Fitzpatrick, David (1977), *Politics and Irish Life, 1913–21: Provincial Experience of War and Revolution*. Dublin: Gill & Macmillan.

Fjågesund, Peter, and Ruth Symes (2003), *The Northern Utopia: British Perceptions of Norway in the Nineteenth Century*. Amsterdam and New York: Brill.

Fletcher, Ian C. (1997), '"This Zeal for Lawlessness": A. V. Dicey, *The Law of the Constitution*, and the Challenge of Popular Politics, 1885–1915', *Parliamentary History*, 16/3, pp. 309–29.

Fletcher, Ian C. (2000), '"Women of the Nations Unite!" Transnational Suffragism in the United Kingdom, 1912–1914', in Ian C Fletcher, Philippa Levine, and Laura E. Nym Mayhall (eds), *Women's Suffrage in the British Empire: Citizenship, Nation and Race*. London: Routledge, pp. 103–20.

Ford, Trowbridge (1970), 'Dicey as a Political Journalist', *Political Studies*, 18/2, pp. 220–35.

Ford, Trowbridge (1973), 'Dicey's Conversion to Unionism', *Irish Historical Studies*, 18/72, pp. 552–82.

Ford, Trowbridge (1985), *Albert Venn Dicey: The Man and his Times*. Chichester: Barry Rose.

Forsyth, Murray (1981), *Unions of States: The Theory and Practice of Confederation*. Leicester: Leicester University Press.

Forsyth, Murray (ed.) (1989), *Federalism and Nationalism*. Leicester: Leicester University Press.

Francis, Martin, and Ina Zweiniger-Bargielowska (eds) (1996), *The Conservatives and British Society, 1880–1990*. Cardiff: University of Wales Press.

Franck, Thomas (ed.) (1968), *Why Federations Fail: An Inquiry into the Requisites for Successful Federalism*. New York and London: New York University Press.

Franck, Thomas (2008), 'The Centripede and the Centrifuge: Principles for the Centralisation and Decentralisation of Governance' in Tomer Broude and Yuval Shany (eds), *The Shifting Allocation of Authority in International Law: Considering Sovereignty, Supremacy and Subsidiarity*. London: Bloomsbury, pp. 19–32.

Fraser, T. G. (1984), *Partition in Ireland, India and Palestine: Theory and Practice*. London: Macmillan.

Frost, Robert (2015), *The Oxford History of Poland-Lithuania*, vol. 1. *The Making of the Polish-Lithuanian Union, 1385–1569*. Oxford: Oxford University Press.

Fry, Michael (2004), *The Dundas Despotism*, new edition. Edinburgh: Edinburgh University Press.

Frydenlund, Bård (2015), 'British Agents in Norway in 1814: The Norwegian Independence and Constitution of 1814', *Scandinavica*, 54/1, 30–47.

Gailey, Andrew (1987), *Ireland and the Death of Kindness: The Experience of Constructive Unionism, 1890–1905*. Cork: Cork University Press.

Gailey, Andrew (2016), *The Lost Imperialist: Lord Dufferin, Memory and Mythmaking in an Age of Celebrity*. London: John Murray.

Gammelgaard, Karen, and Eirik Holmoyvik (eds) (2014), *Writing Democracy: The Norwegian Constitution 1813–2014*. New York: Berghahn.

Gammerl, Benno (2010), *Untertanen, Staatsbürger und Andere: der Umgang mit ethnischer Heterogenität im Britischen Weltreich und im Habsburgerreich 1867–1918*. Göttingen: Vandenhoeck & Ruprecht.

Gammerl, Benno (2018), *Subjects, Citizens and Others: Administering Ethnic Heterogeneity in the British and Habsburg Empires, 1867–1918*. New York: Berghahn.

Garside, Patricia, and Michael Hebbert (eds) (1989), *British Regionalism, 1900–2000*. London and New York: Bloomsbury/Mansell.

Garver, Bruce M (1978), *The Young Czech Party 1874-1901 and the Emergence of a Multiparty System*. London and New Haven: Yale University Press.
Garvin, Tom (1987), *Nationalist Revolutionaries in Ireland, 1858-1928*. Oxford: Oxford University Press.
Garvin, Tom (1996), *1922: The Birth of Irish Democracy*. Dublin: Gill and Macmillan.
Gellner, Ernest (1983), *Nations and Nationalism: New Perspectives on the Past*. Oxford: Blackwell.
Geoghegan, Patrick M. (1999), *The Irish Act of Union: A Study in High Politics, 1798-1801*. Dublin: Gill & Macmillan.
Geppert, Dominik, and Robert Gerwarth (eds) (2008), *Wilhelmine Germany and Edwardian Britain: Essays on Cultural Affinity*. Oxford: Oxford University Press.
Geppert, Dominik, William Mulligan and Andreas Rose (eds) (2015), *The Wars Before the Great War: Conflict and International Politics Before the Outbreak of the First World War*. Oxford: Oxford University Press.
Gerö, Andras (1995), *Modern Hungarian Society in the Making: The Unfinished Experience*. Budapest and New York: Central European University Press.
Gerwarth, Robert (2016), *The Vanquished: Why the First World War Failed to End*. London: Allen Lane.
Gerwarth, Robert, and John Horne (eds) (2012), *War in Peace: Paramilitary Violence in Europe after the Great War*. Oxford: Oxford: Oxford University Press.
Gerwarth, Robert, and Erez Manela (eds) (2014), *Empires at War, 1911-23*. Oxford: Oxford University Press.
Glassheim, Eagle (2005), *Noble Nationalists: The Transformation of the Bohemian Aristocracy*. Cambridge, MA: Harvard University Press.
Glassheim, Eagle (2016), *Cleansing the Czech Borderlands: Migration, Environment and Health in the Former Sudetenland*. Pittsburgh: University of Pittsburgh Press.
Glassl, Horst (1977), *Nationale Autonomie im Vielvölkerstaat: der mährische Ausgleich*. Munich: Sudetendeutsche Stiftung.
Glenny, Misha (1999), *The Balkans: Nationalism, War and the Great Powers, 1804-1999*. London: Granta.
Glenthøj, Rasmus, and Morten Nordhagen Ottosen (2014), *Experiences of War and Nationality in Denmark and Norway, 1807-15*. Basingstoke: Palgrave Macmillan.
Godsey, William D. (1999), *Aristocratic Redoubt: The Austro-Hungarian Foreign Office on the Eve of the First World War*. West Lafayette, IN: Purdue University Press.
Godsey, William D. (2004), *Nobles and Nation in Central Europe: Free Imperial Knights in the Age of Revolution, 1750-1850*. Cambridge: Cambridge University Press.
Golden, J. J. (2013), 'The Protestant Influence on the Origins of Irish Home Rule, 1861-1871', *English Historical Review*, 128/535, pp. 1483-1516.
Good, David (1984), *The Economic Rise of the Habsburg Empire, 1750-1914*. Berkeley, CA: University of California Press.
Götz, N., and Hackmann, J. (eds) (2003), *Civil Society in the Baltic Sea Region*. Aldershot and Burlington, VT: Ashgate.
Gray, R. Q. (1976), *The Labour Aristocracy in Victorian Edinburgh*. Oxford: Oxford University Press.
Greenwood, F. Murray, and James H. Lambert (2003), 'Sewell, Jonathan', in *Dictionary of Canadian Biography*, vol. 7. Toronto: University of Toronto Press.
Greer, Allan (1993), *The Patriots and the People: The Rebellion of 1837 in Rural Lower Canada*. Toronto: University of Toronto Press.
Greer, Allan (1995), '1837-8: Rebellion Reconsidered', *Canadian Historical Review*, 76/1, pp. 1-18.

Greer, Allan, and Ian Radforth (eds) (1992), *Colonial Leviathan: State Formation in Mid-Nineteenth Century Canada*. Toronto: University of Toronto Press.

Griffith, Wil (2006), 'Devolutionist Tendencies in Wales, 1885–1914', in Duncan Tanner, Chris Williams, W. P. Griffith, and Andrew Edwards (eds), *Debating Nationhood and Governance in Britain, 1885–1939: Perspectives from the Four Nations*. Manchester: Manchester University Press, pp. 89–117.

Grigg, Russell (2018), '"You should Love your Country and should Ever Strive to be Worthy of your Fatherland": Identity, British Values and St David's Day in Elementary Schools in Wales, c.1885–1920', *Welsh History Review*, 29/1 (June), pp. 99–125.

Grob-Fitzgibbon, Benjamin (2015), 'The Curious Case of the Vanishing Debate over Irish Home Rule: The Dominion of Canada, Irish Home Rule and Canadian Historiography', *American Review of Canadian studies*, 45/1, pp. 113–28.

Grotke, Kelly L., and Markus J. Prutsch (eds) (2014), *Constitutionalism, Legitimacy and Power: Nineteenth Century Experiences*. Oxford: Oxford University Press.

Guelke, Adrian (1988), *Northern Ireland: The International Perspective*. Dublin: Gill & Macmillan.

Guldi, Jo (2012), *Roads to Power: Britain Invents the Infrastructure State*. Cambridge, MA: Harvard University Press.

Gumz, Jonathan (2009), *The Resurrection and Collapse of Empire in Habsburg Serbia, 1914–18*. Cambridge: Cambridge University Press.

Gwynedd Jones, Ieuan (1981), *Explorations and Explanations: Essays in the Social History of Victorian Wales*. Llandysul: Gomer.

Gwynedd Jones, Ieuan (1987), *Communities: Essays in the Social History of Victorian Wales*. Llandysul: Gomer.

Hackmann, J. (2012), *Vereinskultur und Zivilgesellschaft in Nordosteuropa: regionale Spezifik und europäische Zusammenhänge*. Vienna: Böhlau Verlag.

Haesly, Richard (2018), Review of Simon Brooks, 'Why Wales Never was', *Nations and Nationalism*, 24/4 (Oct.), pp. 1215–17.

Hajdarpasic, Edin (2015), *Whose Bosnia? Nationalism and Political Imagination in the Balkans, 1890–1914*. Ithaca, NY: Cornell University Press.

Hálfdanarson, Gudmundur (1995), 'Social Distinctions and National Unity: On the Politics of Nationalism in Nineteenth Century Iceland', *History of European Ideas*, 21/6 (Nov.), pp. 763–79.

Hálfdanarson, Gudmundur (2000), 'Iceland: A Peaceful Secession', *Scandinavian Journal of History*, 25/1–2 (June), pp. 87–100.

Hálfdanarson, Gudmundur (2006), 'Severing the Ties: Iceland's Journey from a Union with Denmark to a Nation State', *Scandinavian Journal of History*, 31/3–4, pp. 237–54.

Hanak, Harry (1962), *Great Britain and Austria-Hungary during the First World War: A Study in the Formation of Public Opinion*. Oxford: Oxford University Press.

Hannig, Alma (2013), *Franz Ferdinand: Die Biographie*. Vienna: Amalthea Verlag.

Harris, Bob (2014), *A Tale of Three Cities: The Life and Times of Lord Daer, 1763–94*. Edinburgh: Edinburgh University Press.

Harris, C. A. (2004), 'Sir Edward Thornton, Count of Cassilhas in the Portuguese Nobility (1766–1852)', revised H. C. G. Matthew, in H. C. G. Matthew and Brian Harrison (eds), *Oxford Dictionary of National Biography*. Oxford: Oxford University Press.

Harris, J. (ed.) (2003), *Civil Society in British History: Ideas, Identities, Institutions*. Oxford: Oxford University Press.

Harrison, Brian (1982), *Peaceable Kingdom: Stability and Change in Modern Britain*. Oxford: Oxford University Press.

Harrison, Brian (1996), *The Transformation of British Politics, 1860–1995.* Oxford: Oxford University Press.
Hart, Marjolein t, Joost Jonker, and Jan Luiten van Zanden (eds) (2010), *A Financial History of the Netherlands.* Cambridge: Cambridge University Press.
Harvie, Christopher (1976a), *The Lights of Liberalism: University Liberals and the Challenge of Democracy, 1860–86.* London: Penguin.
Harvie, Christopher (1976b), 'Ideology and Home Rule: James Bryce, A. V. Dicey and Ireland, 1880–87', *English Historical Review,* 91/159, pp. 298–314.
Harvie, Christopher (1994), *Fool's Gold: The Story of North Sea Oil.* London: Hamish Hamilton.
Harvie, Christopher (2008), *A Floating Commonwealth: Politics, Culture and Technology on Britain's Atlantic Coast, 1860–1930.* Oxford: Oxford University Press.
Haslinger, Peter (1993), *Arad, November 1918: Oszkár Jászi und die Rumänen in Ungarn 1900–1918.* Vienna: Böhlau Verlag.
Haslinger, Peter (1994), *Der ungarische Revisionismus und das Burgenland 1922–1932* Frankfurt: Peter Lang.
Haslinger, Peter (1996), *Hundert Jahre Nachbarschaft: die Beziehungen zwischen Österreich und Ungarn 1895–1994.* Frankfurt: Peter Lang.
Haslinger, Peter (2009), *Nation und Territorium im tschechischen politischen Diskurs, 1880–1938.* Munich: Oldenbourg Verlag.
Haslinger, Peter, and Joachim von Puttkamer (eds) (2007), *Staat, Loyalität und Minderheiten in Ostmittel- und Sudosteuropa 1918–1941.* Munich: Oldenbourg Verlag.
Hayton, David, James Kelly, and John Bergin (eds) (2010), *The Eighteenth Century Composite State: Representative Institutions in Ireland and Europe, 1689–1800.* Basingstoke: Palgrave Macmillan.
Hayward, Will (2022), *Independent Nation: Should Wales Leave the UK?* London: Biteback.
Healy, Maureen (2004), *Vienna and the Fall of the Habsburg Empire: Total War and Everyday Life in World War One.* Cambridge: Cambridge University Press.
Healy, Róisín (2003), *The Jesuit Specter in Imperial Germany, Studies in Central European Histories.* Boston: Brill.
Healy, Róisín (2017), *Poland in the Irish Nationalist Imagination: Anti-Colonialism within Europe.* London: Palgrave Macmillan.
Healy, Róisín (ed.) (2019), *Mobility in the Russian, Central and East European Past.* London: Routledge.
Healy, Róisín, and E. Dal Lago (eds) (2014), *The Shadow of Colonialism on Europe's Modern Past, 1860–1960.* London: Palgrave Macmillan.
Heard, Andrew (1991), *Canadian Constitutional Conventions: The Marriage of Law and Politics.* Oxford: Oxford University Press.
Hechter, Michael (1975), *Internal Colonialism: The Celtic Fringe in British National Development, 1536–1966.* London: Routledge Kegan Paul.
Heffernan, Brian (ed.) (2012), *Life on the Fringe? Ireland and Europe, 1800–1922.* Dublin: Irish Academic Press.
Heimann, Mary (2011), *Czechoslovakia: The State that Failed.* New Haven: Yale University Press.
Heindl, Waltraud (2013), *Josephinische Mandarine: Bürokratie und Beamte in Österreich,* vol. 2.: *1848–1914.* Vienna: Böhlau Verlag.
Helmedach, Andreas (2002), *Das Verkehrssytem als Modernisierungsfaktor: Strassen, Post, Fuhrwesen und Reisen nach Triest und Fiume vom Beginn des 18. Jahrhunderts bis zum Eisenbahnzeitalter.* Munich: Oldenbourg Verlag.

Hempton, David, and Hugh McLeod (eds) (2017), *Secularisation and Religious Innovation in the North Atlantic World*. Oxford: Oxford University Press.

Hemstad, Ruth (2010), 'Scandinavianism, Nordic Cooperation and "Nordic Democracy"', in Jussi Kurunmäki and Johan Strang (eds), *Rhetorics of Nordic Democracy*. Helsinki: Finnish Literature Society, pp. 179–93.

Hemstad, Ruth (ed.) (2014), *'Like a Herd of Cattle': Parliamentary and Public Debates Regarding the Cession of Norway, 1813–14*. Oslo: Akademisk Publisering.

Hemstad, Ruth (2015), 'Madame de Staël and the War of Opinion Regarding the Cession of Norway, 1814–15', *Scandinavica*, 54/1, pp. 100–20.

Hemstad, Ruth (2018), 'Scandinavianism: Mapping the Rise of a New Concept', *Contributions to the History of Concepts*, 12/1 (Summer), pp. 1–21.

Hemstad, Ruth (2019), 'The United Kingdoms of Norway and Sweden and the United Kingdom of the Netherlands, 1814–30: Comparative Perspectives on the Politics of Amalgamation and Nation Building', *Scandinavica*, 58/2, pp. 76–97.

Henderson, Ailsa (2007), *Hierarchies of Belonging: National Identity in Scotland and Quebec*. Montreal: McGill-Queen's University Press.

Henderson, Ailsa, and Richard Wyn Jones (2021), *Englishness: The Force Transforming Britain*. Oxford: Oxford University Press.

Henderson, Diana (1989), *Highland Soldier, 1820–1920: A Social Study of the Highland Regiments*. Edinburgh: John Donald.

Hennessy, Peter (2015), *The Kingdom to Come: Thoughts on the Union Before and After the Scottish Referendum*. London: Haus.

Henshaw, Victoria (2014), *Scotland and the British Army, 1700–50: Defending the Union*. London: Bloomsbury.

Herwig, Holger H. (1997), *The First World War: Germany and Austria-Hungary, 1914–18*. London: Edward Arnold.

Hesketh, Ian (2014), 'History is Past Politics; and Politics is Present History: Who Said it?', *Notes and Queries*, 61, pp. 105–8.

Hicks, Ursula (1978), *Federalism, Failure and Success: A Comparative Study*. London: Macmillan.

Hilson, Mary (2017), '"A Model Co-Operative Country": Irish–Finnish Contacts at the Turn of the Twentieth Century', *Irish Historical Studies*, 41/160 (Nov.), pp. 221–37.

Hilson, Mary, and Andrew Newby (2015), 'The Nordic Welfare Model in Norway and Scotland', in John Bryden, Ottar Brox, and Lesley Riddoch (eds), *Northern Neighbours: Scotland and Norway since 1800*. Edinburgh: Edinburgh University Press, pp. 211–29.

Hilton, Boyd (2006), *'A Mad, Bad and Dangerous People': England 1783–1846*. Oxford: Oxford University Press.

Hirschhausen, Ulrike von (2009), 'From Imperial Inclusion to National Exclusion: Citizenship in the Habsburg Monarchy and in Austria, 1867–1923', *European Review of History/Revue Européene d'Histoire*, 16/4 (Aug.), pp. 551–73.

Hirschhausen, Ulrike von, and Jörn Leonhard (2001), *Nationalismen in Europa: West- und Osteuropa im Vergleich*. Göttingen: Wallstein Verlag.

Hodgkin, Katharine, and Susannah Radstone (eds) (2003), *Memory, History, Nation: Contested Pasts*. London: Routledge.

Hoffmann, S. L. (2006), *Civil Society, 1750–1914: Studies in European History*. Basingstoke: Palgrave Macmillan.

Holmøyvik, Eirik (2005), 'The Theory of Sovereignty and the Swedish-Norwegian Union of 1814', *Journal of the History of International Law*, 7, pp. 137–56.

Honings, R., Rutten, G., and Kalmthout, T. V. (eds) (2018), *Language, Literature and the Construction of a Dutch National Identity (1780–1830)*. Amsterdam: Amsterdam University Press.

Hoppen, K. Theodore (1984), *Elections, Politics and Society in Ireland, 1832-85*. Oxford: Oxford University Press.
Hoppen, K. Theodore (2016), *Governing Hibernia: British Politicians and Ireland, 1800-1921*. Oxford: Oxford University Press.
Hoppit, Julian (2017), *Britain's Political Economies: Parliament and Economic Life, 1660-1800*. Cambridge: Cambridge University Press.
Houston, Cecil J., and William J. Smyth (1980), *The Sash Canada Wore: A Historical Geography of the Orange Order in Canada*. Toronto: University of Toronto Press.
Howe, Stephen (2002), *Ireland and Empire: Colonial Legacies in Irish History and Culture*. Oxford: Oxford University Press.
Howell, David W. (1993), 'A "Less Obtrusive and Exacting" Nationality: Welsh Ethnic Mobilisation in Rural Communities, 1850-1920', in David Howell et al. (eds), *Roots of Rural Ethnic Mobilisation*. New York: European Science Foundation/New York University Press, pp. 51-98.
Howell, David W. (2013), 'The Land Question in 19th Century Wales, Ireland and Scotland: A Comparative Study', *Agricultural History Review*, 61/1, pp. 83-110.
Hroch, Miroslav (2000), *Social Conditions of National Revival in Europe: A Comparative Analysis of the Social Composition of Patriotic Groups among the Smaller European Nations*. New York: Columbia University Press.
Hroch, Miroslav (2015), *European Nations: Explaining their Formation*. London and New York: Verso.
Hughes, Brian (2016), *Defying the IRA: Intimidation, Coercion and Communities during the Irish Revolution*. Liverpool: Liverpool University Press.
Hutchinson, John (1987), *The Dynamics of Cultural Nationalism: The Gaelic Revival and the Creation of the Irish Nation State*. London: Allen & Unwin.
Hyde, H. Montgomery (1933), *The Rise of Castlereagh*. London: Macmillan.
Hyde, H. Montgomery (1953), *Carson: The Life of Sir Edward Carson*. London: Heinemann.
Hyde, H. Montgomery (1959), *The Strange Death of Lord Castlereagh*. London: Heinemann.
Ihalainen, Pasi, Michael Bregnsbo, Karin Sennefelt, and Patrik Winton (eds) (2011), *Scandinavia in the Age of Revolution: Nordic Political Cultures, 1740-1820*. London: Routledge.
Ingrao, Charles (1994), *The Habsburg Monarchy, 1618-1815*. Cambridge: Cambridge University Press.
Jackson, Alvin (1989), *The Ulster Party: Irish Unionists in the House of Commons, 1884-1911*. Oxford: Oxford University Press.
Jackson, Alvin (1995), *Colonel Edward Saunderson: Land and Loyalty in Victorian Ireland*. Oxford: Oxford University Press.
Jackson, Alvin (1997), 'British Ireland: What if Home Rule had been Enacted in 1912', in Niall Ferguson (ed.), *Virtual History: Alternatives and Counterfactuals*. London: Picador paperback, pp. 175-227.
Jackson, Alvin (2004), *Home Rule: An Irish History, 1800-2000*. London: Phoenix Paperbacks.
Jackson, Alvin (2010), *Ireland 1798-1998: War, Peace and Beyond*, 2nd edition. London: Blackwell Wiley.
Jackson, Alvin (2013), *The Two Unions: Ireland, Scotland and the Survival of the United Kingdom, 1707-2007*. Oxford: Oxford University Press.
Jackson, Alvin (2016), 'Shamrock and Saltire: Irish Home Rule, Independence and the Scottish Referendum, 1914-2014', in Senia Paseta (ed.), *Uncertain Futures: Essays about the Irish Past for Roy Foster*. Oxford: Oxford University Press, pp. 257-69.
Jackson, Alvin (ed.) (2017a), *Oxford Handbook of Modern Irish history*. Oxford: Oxford University Press.

Jackson, Alvin (2017b), 'Foreword, Ireland and Finland: Mr Gladstone, National and Transnational Historiographies', *Irish Historical Studies*, 41/60 (Nov.), pp. 163–5.
Jackson, Alvin (2018a), 'The Failure of British and Irish Federalism, c.1800–1950', in Robert Schütze and Stephen Tierney (eds), *The United Kingdom and the Federal Idea*. London: Bloomsbury, pp. 44–60.
Jackson, Alvin (2018b), *Judging Redmond and Carson: Comparative Irish Lives*. Dublin: Royal Irish Academy.
Jackson, Alvin (2019), 'Union States, Civil Society and National Symbols in the Nineteenth Century: Comparing United Kingdoms', *Scandinavica*, 58/2, pp. 58–75.
Jackson, Alvin (2022), 'Why did Wales Stay in the Union in the Early Twentieth Century?' in Bruce Kinzer, Molly Kramer and Richard Trainor (eds), *Reform and its Complexities in Modern Britain: Essays Inspired by Sir Brian Harrison*. Oxford: Oxford University Press, pp. 248–80.
Jackson, Ben (2020), *The Case for Scottish Independence: A History of Nationalist Political Thought in Modern Scotland*. Cambridge: Cambridge University Press.
Jackson, Daniel (2009), *Popular Opposition to Home Rule in Edwardian Britain*. Liverpool: Liverpool University Press.
Jalland, Patricia (1979), 'United Kingdom Devolution 1910–14: Political Panacea or Tactical Diversion', *English Historical Review*, 94/373, pp. 757–85.
Jalland, Patricia (1980), *The Liberals and Ireland: The Ulster Question in British Politics to 1914*. Hassocks: Harvester.
Jansson, Torkel (2016), 'Scandinavia between the Congress of Vienna and the Paris Commune', in E. I. Kouri and J. E. Olesen (eds), *The Cambridge History of Scandinavia*, vol. 2. *1520–1870*. Cambridge: Cambridge University Press, pp. 685–90.
Jarrett, M. (2013), *The Congress of Vienna and its Legacy: War and Great Power Diplomacy after Napoleon*. London and New York: I. B. Tauris.
Jenks, W.A. (1950), *The Austrian Electoral Reform of 1907*. New York: Columbia University Press.
Jenks, W. A. (1965), *Austria under the Iron Ring*. Charlottesville, VA: University Press of Virginia.
Johnnes, Martin (2011), 'Wales, History and Britishness', *Welsh History Review*, 25/4, pp. 596–61.
Jones, Aled, and Bill Jones (2003), 'The Welsh World and the British Empire, c.1851–1939: An Exploration', *Journal of Imperial and Commonwealth History*, 31/2, pp. 57–81.
Jones, Bill (1999), 'Banqueting at a Moveable Feast: Wales, 1870–1914', in Gareth Elwyn Jones and Dai Smith (eds), *The People of Wales*. Llandysul: Gomer, pp. 145–78.
Jones, J. Graham (1987), 'E. T. John and Welsh Home Rule, 1910–1914', *Welsh History Review*, 13/4, pp. 453–67.
Jones, J. Graham (1997), 'Michael Davitt, David Lloyd George and T. E. Ellis: The Welsh Experience, 1886', *Welsh History Review*, 18/3, pp. 450–82.
Jones, Wyn (1986), *Thomas Edward Ellis, 1859–99*. Cardiff: University of Wales Press.
Jorgenson, Theodore (1935), *Norway's Relations to Scandinavian Unionism, 1815–71*. Northfield, MN: St Olaf College Press.
Joyce, Patrick (2013), *The State of Freedom: A Social History of the British State since 1800*. Cambridge: Cambridge University Press.
Judge, Jane (2016), 'Nation and State in the Belgian Revolution, 1787–1790', Ph.D. thesis, University of Edinburgh.
Judson, Pieter (1996), *Exclusive Revolutionaries: Liberal Politics, Social Experience and National Identity in the Austrian Empire, 1848–1914*. Ann Arbor: University of Michigan Press.

Judson, Pieter (2006), *Guardians of the Nation? Activists on the Language Frontiers of Imperial Austria*. Cambridge, MA: Harvard University Press.
Judson, Pieter (2016), *The Habsburg Empire: A New History*. Cambridge, MA: Harvard University Press.
Judson, Pieter (2017), '"Where our Commonality is Necessary...": Rethinking the End of the Habsburg Monarchy', *Austrian History Yearbook*, 48 (Apr.), pp. 1–21.
Judson, Pieter, and Marsha Rozenblit (eds) (2005), *Constructing Nationalities in East Central Europe*. New York and Oxford: Berghahn.
Jupp, Peter J. (2004), 'Edward Cooke (1755–1820)', in H. C. G. Matthew and Brian Harrison (eds), *Oxford Dictionary of National Biography*. Oxford: Oxford University Press.
Jutikkala, Eino, and Kauko Pirinen (1979), *A History of Finland*, revised edition. London: Heinemann.
Kabdebo, Thomas (2001), *Ireland and Hungary: A Study in Parallels*. Dublin: Four Courts Press.
Kalberg, Stephen (1987), 'The Origins and Expansion of Kulturpessimismus: The Relationship between Public and Private Spheres in Early Twentieth Century Germany', *Sociological Theory*, 5/2, pp. 150–64.
Kann, Robert A. (1974), *A History of the Habsburg Empire: 1526–1918*. Berkeley, CA: University of California Press.
Kappeler, Andreas (1992), *The Formation of National Elites* (Comparative Studies on Governments and Non-Dominant Ethnic Groups in Europe, 1850–1940). New York: New York University Press.
Karlsson, G. (2000), *History of Iceland*. Minneapolis: University of Minnesota Press.
Kearney, Hugh (1989), *The British Isles: A History of Four Nations*. Cambridge: Cambridge University Press.
Kearney, Hugh (2007), *Ireland: Contested Ideas of Nationalism and History*. New York: New York University Press.
Keating, Michael (1988), *State and Regional Nationalism: Territorial Politics and the European State*. Hassocks: Harvester Wheatsheaf.
Keating, Michael (1999), 'Asymmetrical Government: Multinational States in an Integrating Government', *Publius*, 29/1 (Winter), pp. 71–86.
Keating, Michael (2001), *Nations against the State: The New Politics of Nationalism in Quebec, Catalonia and Scotland*, new edition. Basingstoke: Palgrave Macmillan.
Keating, Michael (2009), *The Independence of Scotland: Self-Government and the Shifting Politics of Union*. Oxford: Oxford University Press.
Keating, Michael (2010), 'The Strange Death of Unionist Scotland', *Government and Opposition*, 45/2, pp. 365–85.
Keating, Michael (2021), *State and Nation in the United Kingdom*. Oxford: Oxford University Press.
Keating, Michael, and David Bleiman (1979), *Labour and Scottish Nationalism*. London: Macmillan.
Kelly, T. Mills (2003), 'Last Best Chance or Last Gasp? The Compromise of 1905 and Czech Politics in Moravia', *Austrian History Yearbook*, 34, pp. 279–301.
Kendle, John (1968), 'The Round Table Movement and "Home Rule All Round"', *Historical Journal*, 11/2, pp. 332–53.
Kendle, John (1971), 'Federalism and the Irish Problem in 1918', *History*, 56/187, pp. 207–30.
Kendle, John (1989), *Ireland and the Federal Solution: The Debate over the United Kingdom Constitution, 1870–1921*. Montreal and Kingston: McGill-Queen's University Press.
Kendle, John (1997), *Federal Britain: A History*. London: Routledge.

Kennedy, James (2015), *Liberal Nationalisms: Empire, State and Civil Society in Scotland and Quebec*. Montreal: McGill-Queen's University Press.
Kennedy, James C. (2017), *A Concise History of the Netherlands*. Cambridge: Cambridge University Press.
Kenny, Michael (2014), *The Politics of English Nationhood*. Oxford: Oxford University Press.
Kidd, Colin (1993), *Subverting Scotland's Past: Scottish Whig Historians and the Creation of an Anglo-British Identity, 1689–1830*. Cambridge: Cambridge University Press.
Kidd, Colin (2008), *Union and Unionisms: Political Thought in Scotland, 1500–2000*. Cambridge: Cambridge University Press.
King, Jeremy (2002), *Budweisers into Czechs and Germans? A Local History of Bohemian Politics, 1848–1948*. Princeton: Princeton University Press.
King, Preston (1982), *Federalism and Federation: Ideologies and Institution*. London: Croom Helm.
Kinzer, Bruce, Molly Kramer and Richard Trainor (eds) (2022), *Reform and its Complexities in Modern Britain: Essays inspired by Sir Brian Harrison*. Oxford: Oxford University Press.
Kirby, David (1995), *The Baltic World, 1772–1993: Europe's Northern Periphery in an Age of Change*. London: Longman.
Kirby, David (2006), *A Concise History of Finland*. Cambridge: Cambridge University Press.
Kirby, James (2019), 'A. V. Dicey and English Constitutionalism', *History of European Ideas*, 45/1, pp. 33–46.
Kirchner Reill, Dominique (2012), *Nationalists Who Feared the Nation: Adriatic Multinationalism in Habsburg Dalmatia, Trieste und Venice*. Stanford, CA: Stanford University Press.
Kirk, James (1996), *Her Majesty's Historiographer: Gordon Donaldson, 1913–93*. Edinburgh: Edinburgh University Press.
Kirkwood, Patrick (2019), 'Alexander Hamilton and the Early Republic in Edwardian Imperial Thought', *Britain and the World*, 12/1, pp. 28–50.
Kissane, Bill (2000), 'Nineteenth Century Nationalism in Finland and Ireland: A Comparative Analysis', *Nationalism and Ethnic Politics*, 6/2, pp. 25–42.
Kissinger, Henry (1957), *A World Restored: Metternich, Castlereagh and the Problem of Peace, 1812–1822*. Boston: Houghton Mifflin Co.
Klinge, Matti (2000), *A Brief History of Finland*, 3rd edition. Helsinki: Otava.
Knaplund, Paul (ed.) (1952), *British Views on Norwegian-Swedish Problems, 1880–1895: Selections from the Diplomatic Correspondence*. Oslo: Norsk Historisk Kjeldeskriftinstitutt.
Knaplund, Paul (1970), *Gladstone's Foreign Policy*. London: Frank Cass.
Knapp, Vincent (1988), *Austrian Social Democracy, 1889–1914*. Washington, DC: University Press of America.
Kocka, Jürgen (2003), 'Comparison and Beyond', *History and Theory*, 42/1 (Feb.), pp. 39–44.
Koenigsberger, H.G. (1978), 'Monarchies and Parliaments in Early Modern Europe: Dominium Regale or Dominium Politicum et Regale', *Theory and Society*, 5/1, pp. 191–217*.
Kohr, Leopold (2001), *The Breakdown of Nations*, new edition. London: Green Books.
Komlos, John (1983), *The Habsburg Monarchy as a Customs Union: Economic Development in Austria-Hungary in the Nineteenth Century*. Princeton: Princeton University Press.
Kořalka, Jiří (1991), *Tschechen im Habsburgerreich und in Europa 1815–1914*. Vienna: Oldenbourg Verlag.
Kořalka, Jiří (2007), *František Palacký*. Vienna: Austrian Academy of Sciences.
Kossman, E. H. (1978), *The Low Countries, 1770–1940*. Oxford: Oxford University Press.

Kouri, E., and Jens E. Olesen (eds) (2016), *The Cambridge History of Scandinavia*, vol. 2. *1520–1870*. Cambridge: Cambridge University Press.
Kożuchowski, Adam (2013), *The Afterlife of Austria-Hungary: The Image of the Habsburg Monarchy in Inter-war Europe*. Pittsburgh: University of Pittsburgh.
Krikorian, Jacqueline, David Cameron, Marcel Martel, Andrew McDougall, and Robert Vipond (eds) (2017), *Roads to Confederation: The Making of Canada, 1867*, 2 vols. Toronto: University of Toronto Press.
Kronenbitter, Günther (2003), *'Krieg im Frieden': Die Führung der k.u.k. Armee und die Grossmachtpolitik Österreich-Ungarns 1906–14*. Munich: Oldenbourg Verlag.
Krueger, Rita (2009), *Czech, German and Noble: Status and National Identity in Habsburg Bohemia*. Oxford and New York: Berghahn.
Kumar, Krishan (2003), *The Making of English National Identity*. Cambridge: Cambridge University Press.
Kuzmany, Börries (2013), 'Der Galizische Ausgleich als Beispiel moderner Nationalitätenpolitik?', in E. Haid, S. Weismann, and B. Wöller (eds), *Galizien: Peripherie der Moderne—Moderne der Peripherie*. Marburg: Herder Institut.
Kuzmany, Börries (2016), 'Habsburg Austria: Experiments in Non-Territorial Autonomy', *Ethnopolitics*, 15/1 (Jan.), pp. 43–65.
Kuzuchowski, Adam (2013), *The Afterlife of Austria-Hungary: The Image of the Habsburg Monarchy in Inter-War Europe*. Pittsburgh: University of Pittsburgh Press.
Kwan, Jonathan (2013), *Liberalism and the Habsburg Monarchy, 1861–1895*. Basingstoke: Palgrave Macmillan.
Lane-Poole, Stanley (2004), 'John Philip Morier (1778–1853), revised H. C. G. Matthew, in H. C. G. Matthew and Brian Harrison (eds), *Oxford Dictionary of National Biography*. Oxford: Oxford University Press.
Langholm, Sivert (2016), 'Norway: The Emergence of the Nation State', in E. I. Kouri and J. E. Olesen (eds), *The Cambridge History of Scandinavia*, vol. 2. *1520–1870*. Cambridge: Cambridge University Press, pp. 962–74.
Lant, Jeffrey (1980), *Insubstantial Pageant: Ceremony and Confusion at Queen Victoria's Court*. London: Hamish Hamilton.
LaSelva, Samuel (1996), *The Moral Foundations of Canadian Federalism: Paradoxes, Achievements and Tragedies of Nationhood*. Montreal: McGill-Queen's University Press.
Lavin, Deborah (1996), *From Empire to International Commonwealth: A Biography of Lionel Curtis*. Oxford: Oxford University Press.
Leerssen, Joep (2018), *National Thought in Europe. A Cultural History*, 3rd edition. Amsterdam: Amsterdam University Press.
Leerssen, Joep, and Karl Ulrich Syndram (eds) (1992), *Europa Provincia Mundi: Essays in Comparative Literature and European Studies Offered to Hugo Dyserinck on the Occasion of his Sixty-Fifth Birthday*. Amsterdam: Rodopi.
Lehning, Percy (ed.) (1998), *Theories of Secession*. London: Routledge.
Leonhard, Jörn, und Ulrike von Hirschhausen (2009), *Empires und Nationalstaaten im 19. Jahrhundert*. Göttingen: Vandenhoeck & Ruprecht.
Leonhard, Jörn, and Ulrike von Hirschhausen (eds) (2011), *Comparing Empires: Encounters and Transfers in the Long Nineteenth Century*. Göttingen: Vandenhoeck & Ruprecht.
Leiren, T. I. (1975), 'Norwegian Independence and British Opinion, January to August 1814', *Scandinavian Studies*, 47/3, pp. 364–82.
Leisse, Olaf (2012), *Untergang des österreichischen Imperiums: Otto Bauer und der Nationalitätenfrage in der Habsburger Monarchie*. Marburg: Tectum Verlag.
Leslie, John (1991) 'Der Ausgleich in der Bukowina von 1910: zur österreichischen Nationalitätenpolitik vor dem ersten Weltkrieg', in Emil Brix, Thomas Fröschl, and Josef

Leidenfrost (eds), *Geschichte zwischen Freiheit und Ordnung: Gerald Stourzh zum 60. Geburtstag*. Graz and Vienna: Verlag Styria, pp. 113–44.

Levine, Phillipa (2014), 'Is Comparative History Possible?', *History and Theory*, 53/3, pp. 331–47.

Lindgren, Raymond (1959), *Norway-Sweden: Union, Disunion and Scandinavian Integration*. Princeton: Princeton University Press.

Lindström, Fredrik (2008), *Empire and Identity: Biographies of the Austrian State Problem in the Late Habsburg Empire*. West Lafayette, IN: Purdue University Press.

Lino, Dylan (2016), 'Albert Venn Dicey and the Constitutional Theory of Empire', *Oxford Journal of Legal Studies*, 36/4, pp. 751–80.

Lino, Dylan (2018), 'The Rule of Law and the Rule of Empire: A. V. Dicey in Imperial Context', *Modern Law Review*, 81/5, pp. 739–64.

Litván, György (2006), *A Twentieth Century Prophet: Oscar Jászi, 1875–1957*. Budapest: Central European University Press.

Livesey, James (2009), *Civil Society and Empire: Ireland and Scotland in the Eighteenth Century Atlantic World*. New Haven: Yale University Press.

Lloyd Jones, Naomi (2014), 'Liberalism, Scottish Nationalism and the Home Rule Crisis, 1886–93', *English Historical Review*, 129/539 (Aug.), pp. 862–87.

Lloyd Jones, Naomi (2015), 'Liberal Unionism and Political Representation in Wales, c.1886–1893', *Historical Research*, 88/214 (Aug.), pp. 482–507.

Lloyd Jones, Naomi, and Maggie Scull (eds) (2018), *Four Nations Approaches to Modern British History: A (Dis)United Kingdom?* London: Palgrave Macmillan.

Lok, M. (2017), 'The United Kingdom of the Netherlands (1815–1830): A Case of Failed European Nation Building?', in F. Démier and E. Musiani (eds), *Les nations européennes entre histoire et mémoire, xixe–xxe siècles*. Paris: Presses Universitaires de Paris Nanterre, pp. 37–43.

Loughlin, James (1986), *Gladstone, Home Rule and the Ulster Question, 1882–93*. Dublin: Gill & Macmillan.

Loughlin, James (2007), *The British Monarchy and Ireland: 1800 to the Present*. Cambridge: Cambridge University Press.

Loughlin, James (2013), 'Royal Agency and State Integration: Ireland, Wales and Scotland in a Monarchical Context, 1840s–1921', *Journal of Imperial and Commonwealth History*, 41–3, pp. 1–26.

Lownie, Andrew (1995), *John Buchan: The Presbyterian Cavalier*. London: Constable.

Lubenow, W. C. (1988), *Parliamentary Politics and the Home Rule Crisis: The British House of Commons in 1886*. Oxford: Oxford University Press.

Lucas, Colin (1990), 'Great Britain and the Union of Norway and Sweden', *Scandinavian Journal of History*, 15/3–4, pp. 269–78.

Macartney, Carlisle Aylmer (1934), *National States and National Minorities*. Oxford: Oxford University Press.

Macartney, Carlisle Aylmer (1968), *The Habsburg Empire, 1790–1918*. London: Weidenfeld & Nicolson.

McBride, Ian (2009), *Eighteenth Century Ireland: The Isle of Slaves*. Dublin: Gill & Macmillan.

McCartney, Donal (1973), 'The Political Use of History in the Work of Arthur Griffith', *Journal of Contemporary History*, 8/1, pp. 3–19.

McCrone, David (1992), *Understanding Scotland: The Sociology of a Stateless Nation*. London: Routledge.

McDowell, R.B. (1964), *The Irish Administration, 1801-1914*. Routledge, Kegan, Paul: London.

Macedo, Stephen, and Allen Buchanan (eds) (2003), *Secession and Self-Determination: Nomos XLV*. New York: New York University Press.
McGarry, Fearghal (2017), *The Rising: Ireland, Easter 1916*, updated edition. Oxford: Oxford University Press.
McGaughey, Jane G.V. (2020), *Violent Loyalties: Manliness, Migration and the Irish in the Canadas, 1798–1841*. Liverpool: Liverpool University Press.
McGee, Owen (2016), *Arthur Griffith*. Dublin: Merrion Press.
MacInnes, Allan, and Douglas Hamilton (eds) (2014), *Jacobitism, Enlightenment and Empire, 1680–1820*. London: Pickering & Chatto.
MacInnes, Allan, Kieran German, and Leslie Graham (eds) (2014), *Living with Jacobitism, 1690–1788: The Three Kingdoms and Beyond*. London: Pickering & Chatto.
Mackillop, Andrew, and Micheál Ó Siochrú (eds) (2008), *Forging the State: European State Formation and the Anglo-Scottish Union of 1707*. Dundee: Dundee University Press.
McKibbin, Ross (1990), *Ideologies of Class: Social Relations in Britain, 1880–1950*. Oxford: Oxford University Press.
McLean, Iain (2010), *What's Wrong with the British Constitution?* Oxford: Oxford University Press.
McLean, Iain, and Alistair McMillan (2005), *State of the Union: Unionism and the Alternatives in the United Kingdom since 1707*. Oxford: Oxford University Press.
McLeod, Hugh (1996), *Poverty and Piety: Working Class Religion in Berlin, London and New York, 1870–1914*. New York and London: Holmes and Meier.
McLeod, Hugh (1999), *Religion and the People of Western Europe, 1789–1989*. Oxford: Oxford University Press.
McLeod, Hugh (2000), *Secularisation in Western Europe, 1848–1914*. Basingstoke and New York: Palgrave Macmillan.
McLeod, Hugh, and Werner Usdorf (eds) (2003), *Decline of Christendom in western Europe, 1750–2000*. Cambridge: Cambridge University Press.
McMahon, Richard, and Andrew Newby (2017), 'Introduction—Ireland and Finland, 1860–1930: Comparative and Transnational Histories', *Irish Historical Studies*, 41/160 (Nov.), pp. 166–79.
Maguire, Martin (2008), *The civil service and the Revolution in Ireland, 1912–38: 'Shaking the Blood-Stained Hand of Mr Collins'*. Manchester: Manchester University Press.
Manchester, Alan K. (1933), *British Preeminence in Brazil: Its Rise and Decline*. Chapel Hill, NC: University of North Carolina Press.
Markovits, Andrei S., and Frank E. Sysyn (eds) (1982), *Nationbuilding and the Politics of Nationalism*. Cambridge, MA: Harvard University Press.
Marteel, Stefaan (2007), 'Constitutional Thought under the Union of the Netherlands: The "Fundamental Law" of 1814–15 in the Political and Intellectual Context of the Restoration', *Parliaments, Estates and Representation*, 27/1, pp. 77–94.
Marteel, Stefaan (2018), *The Intellectual Origins of the Belgian Revolution: Political Thought and Disunity in the Kingdom of the Netherlands, 1815–30*. London: Palgrave Macmillan.
Martin, Ged (1972), *The Durham Report and British Policy*. Cambridge: Cambridge University Press.
Martin, Ged (ed.) (1990), *The Causes of Canadian Confederation*. Fredericton: Acadiensis Press.
Martin, Ged (1995), *Britain and the Origins of Canadian Confederation, 1837–67*. Vancouver: University of British Columbia Press.
Martin, Ged (1999), 'Canada from 1815', in Andrew Porter (ed.), *The Oxford History of the British Empire*, vol.3. *The Nineteenth Century*. Oxford: Oxford University Press.

Martin, Ged (2013), *Sir John A. MacDonald: Canada's First Prime Minister*. Toronto: University of Toronto Press.

Masson, Ursula (1998-9), 'Divided Loyalties: Women's Suffrage and Party Politics in South Wales 1912-1915', *Llafur*, 7/3-4, pp. 113-26.

Masson, Ursula (2000), '"Political Conditions in Wales are Quite Different...": Party Politics and Votes for Women in Wales, 1912-15', *Women's History Review*, 9/2, pp. 369-88.

Masson, Ursula (2010), *'For Women, for Wales, and for Liberalism': Women in Liberal Politics in Wales, 1880-1914*. Cardiff: University of Wales Press.

Matthews, Gethin (2017), '"For Freedom and Justice": Responses of Chapels in the Swansea Area to the First World War', *Welsh History Review*, 28/4 (Dec.), pp. 676-710.

Matthews, I. M. (2000), 'Conscience or Coercion? Clerical Influence at the General Election of 1868 in Wales', *Past and Present*, 169, pp. 194-204.

Matthews, Wade (2013), *The New Left, National Identity and the Break-up of Britain*. Leiden: Brill.

Maye, Brian (1997), *Arthur Griffith*. Dublin: Griffith College Publications.

Mayne, Richard, and John Pinder (1990), *Federal Union, the Pioneers: A History of Federal Union*. London: Macmillan.

Mecham, Mike (2019), *William Walker: Social Activist*. Dublin: Umiskin Press.

Meekison, J. Peter (ed.) (1977), *Canadian Federalism: Myth or Reality*. Toronto: University of Toronto Press.

Megner, Karl (1986), *Beamte: wirtschafts—und sozialgeschichtliche Aspekte des k.k. Beamtentums*. Vienna: Verlag der Österreichischen Akademie der Wissenschaften.

Mestad, Ola (2015), 'The Most Awkward and Embarrassing Question: British Treaty Obligations, the Role of the Law of Nations and the Establishment of the Swedish Norwegian union in 1814', *Scandinavica*, 54/1, pp. 48-64.

Mestad, Ola, and Dag Michalsen (2005), *Rett, nasjon, union: Den svensk-norske unionens rettslige historie, 1814-1905*. Oslo: Universitetsforlaget.

Michalsen, Dag (2014) 'The Norwegian Constitution of 1814 between European Restoration and Liberal Nationalism', in Kelly L Grotke and Markus J. Prutsch (eds), *Constitutionalism, Legitimacy and Power: Nineteenth Century Experiences*. Oxford: Oxford University Press, pp. 211-24.

Michalsen, Dag (2016), 'Rechtsstaatlichkeit and the Norwegian Constitution, 1814-2014', in Peter-Christian Müller-Graff, Hans Petter Graver, and Ola Mestad (eds), *European Law and National Constitutions* (Deutsch-Norwegisches Forum des Rechts). Berlin: Berliner Wissenschafts-Verlag.

Miller, David (1995), *On Nationality*. Oxford: Oxford University Press.

Miller, Manjari Chatterjee (2021), *Why Nations Rise*. Oxford: Oxford University Press.

Mitchell, James (2010a), 'The Westminster Model and the State of Unions', *Parliamentary Affairs*, 63/1 (Jan.), pp. 85-8.

Mitchell, James (2010b), 'The Narcissism of Small Difference: Scotland and Westminster', *Parliamentary Affairs*, 63/1 (Jan.), pp. 98-116.

Mitchell, James (2014), *The Scottish Question*. Oxford: Oxford University Press.

Mitchell, James, Lynn Bennie, and Rob Johns (2011), *The Scottish National Party: Transition to Power*. Oxford: Oxford University Press.

Mitchison, Rosalind (ed.) (1980), *The Roots of Nationalism: Studies in Northern Europe*. Edinburgh: John Donald.

Mohr, Thomas (2016), 'Imperial Federation, 1900-39: A Precedent for British Legal Relations with the European Union?', *Comparative Legal History*, 4/2, pp. 131-61.

Mohr, Thomas (2017), 'The Impact of Canadian Confederation in Ireland', in M. Marcel and J. Krikorian (eds), *Globalizing Canadian Confederation*. Toronto: University of Toronto, pp. 178–93.
Mohr, Thomas (2019), 'Irish Home Rule and Constitutional Reform in the British Empire, 1885–1914', *Revue Française de Civilisation Britannique*, 24/2, pp. 161–77.
Mokyr, Joel (1977), *Industrialisation in the Low Countries, 1795–1850*. New Haven: Yale University Press.
Moore, Bob, and Henk van Nierop (eds) (2003), *Colonial Empires Compared: Britain and the Netherlands, 1750–1850*. Aldershot: Ashgate.
Moore, Margaret (ed.) (1998), *National Self-Determination and Secession*. Oxford: Oxford University Press.
Morgan, K. O. (1969), 'The Liberal Unionists in Wales', *National Library of Wales Journal*, 16/2, pp. 163–71.
Morgan, K. O. (1980), *Wales in British Politics, 1868–1922*, 3rd edition. Cardiff: University of Wales Press.
Morgan, K. O. (1981), *Rebirth of a Nation: Wales, 1880–1980*. Oxford: Oxford University Press.
Morgan, K. O. (1995), *Modern Wales: Politics, Places and People*. Cardiff: University of Wales Press.
Morgan, K. O. (2014), *Revolution to Devolution: Reflections on Welsh Democracy*. Cardiff: University of Wales Press.
Morgan, William John (ed.) (1973), *The Welsh Dilemma: Some Essays on Nationalism in Wales*. Llandybie: Christopher Davies.
Morton, Graeme, Boudien de Vries, and R. J. Morris (eds) (2006), *Civil Society, Associations and Urban Places: Class, Nation and Culture in Nineteenth Century Europe*. Aldershot and Burlington, VT: Ashgate.
Morton, Graeme (1999), *Unionist Nationalism: Governing Urban Scotland, 1830–1860*. East Linton: Tuckwell.
Morton, W. L. (1999), *The Critical Years: The Union of British North America, 1857–73*. Don Mills, Ontario: Oxford University Press.
Motyl, Alexander J. (2001), *Imperial Ends: The Decay, Collapse and Revival of Empires*. New York: Columbia University Press.
Muenger, Elizabeth (1991), *The British Military Dilemma in Ireland: Occupation Politics, 1886–1914*. Dublin: Gill and Macmillan.
Mulholland, Marc (2012), *Bourgeois Liberty and the Politics of Fear: From Absolutism to Neo-conservatism*. Oxford: Oxford University Press.
Müller, Frank Lorenz, and Heidi Mehrkens (eds) (2016), *Royal Heirs and the Uses of Soft Power in Nineteenth Century Europe*. London: Palgrave Macmillan.
Mulvagh, Conor (2016), *The Irish Parliamentary Party at Westminster, 1900–18*. Manchester: Manchester University Press.
Murad, Anatol (1968), *Franz Joseph I of Austria and his Empire*. New York: Twayne Publishers.
Murdoch, Alexander (1980), *The People Above: Politics and Administration in Mid-Eighteenth Century Scotland*. Edinburgh: John Donald.
Murphy, James (2001), *Abject Loyalty: Nationalism and Monarchy in Ireland during the Reign of Queen Victoria*. Washington, DC: Catholic University of America Press.
Nairn, Tom (1977), *The Break-up of Britain: Crisis and Neo-nationalism*. London: New Left Books.
Nairn, Tom (1990), *The Enchanted Glass: Britain and its Monarchy*, new edition. London: Picador.

Nairn, Tom (2002), *Pariah: Misfortunes of the British Kingdom*. London: Verso.

Nemes, Robert (2003), 'The Uncivil Origins of Civil Marriage: Hungary', in Christopher Clark and Wolfram Kaiser (eds), *Culture Wars: Secular-Catholic Conflict in Nineteenth Century Europe*. Cambridge: Cambridge University Press, pp. 313–35.

Neumann, Iver B. (2000), 'State and Nation in the Nineteenth Century: Recent Research on the Norwegian Case', *Scandinavian Journal of History*, 25/3, pp. 239–60.

Newby, Andrew (2009), '"In Building a Nation Few Better Examples can be Found": Norden and the Scottish Parliament', *Scandinavian Journal of History*, 34/3, pp. 307–29.

Newby, Andrew (2010), 'A Swedish View of Scott's Scotland: Carl Graffman's Skottska Vuer', *History Scotland*, 10/3, pp. 25–30.

Newby, Andrew (2013a), '"One Valhalla of the Free": Scandinavia, Britain and Northern Identity in the Mid-Nineteenth Century', in J Harvard and P Stadius (eds), *Communicating the North: Media Structures and Images in the Making of the Nordic Region: The Nordic Experience*, vol. 3. Farnham: Ashgate, pp. 147–69.

Newby, Andrew (2013b), 'Scottish Anti-Catholicism in a British and European Context: The "North Pole Mission" and Victorian Scotland', in Y M Werner and J Harvard (eds), *Anti-Catholicism in a Comparative and Transnational Perspective: European Studies*, 31, pp. 237–51.

Newby, Andrew (2014a), '"Rather Peculiar Claims upon our Sympathies": Britain and Famine in Finland, 1856–68', in M. Corporaal, C. Cusack, L. Janssen, and R. van den Beuken (eds), *Global Legacies of the Great Irish Famine: Transnational and Interdisciplinary Perspectives* (Reimagining Ireland, vol. 60). Oxford and Bern: Peter Lang.

Newby, Andrew (2014b), '"The Cold Northern Land of Suomi": Michael Davitt and Finnish Nationalism', *Journal of Irish and Scottish Studies*, 6/1, pp. 73–92.

Newby, Andrew (2014c), '"Neither do These Tenants or their Children Emigrate!" Famine and Transatlantic Emigration from Finland in the Nineteenth Century', *Atlantic Studies*, 11/3, pp. 383–402.

Newby, Andrew (2014d), '"On their Behalf No Agitator Raises his Voice"—The Irish Distressed Ladies Fund: Gender, Politics and Urban Philanthropy in Victorian Ireland', in N. Koefoed, Å. Karlsson Sjögren, and K. Cowman (eds), *Gender in Urban Europe: Sites of Political Activity and Citizenship, 1750–1900*. London: Routledge, pp. 178–93.

Newby, Andrew (2015), '"Acting in their Appropriate and Wanted Sphere": The Society of Friends and Famine in Ireland and Finland, c. 1845–68', in Patrick Fitzgerald, Christine Kinealy, and Gerard Moran (eds), *Irish Hunger and Migration: Myth, Memory and Memorialization*. Quinnipiac, CT: Quinnipiac University Press.

Newby, Andrew (2016), '"Os Selve Alene": A Norwegian Account of the Easter Rising', *Studia Celtica Fennica*, 13, pp. 33–46.

Newby, Andrew (2017), '"Black Spots on the Map of Europe": Ireland and Finland as Oppressed Nationalities, c.1860–1910', *Irish Historical Studies*, 41/160 (Nov.), pp. 180–99.

Newby, Andrew (2018), 'A Swedish View of Galway in 1893: Hulo Vallentin's Letters from Home-Rule Land', *Journal of the Galway Archaeological and Historical Society*, 70, pp. 1–16.

Newby, Andrew (2019), '"A True Friend of Scandinavia": Michael Davitt's Northern Travels of 1904', in F. Barber, H. Hansson, and S. Dybris McQuaid (eds), *Ireland and the North*. Oxford and Bern: Peter Lang, pp. 121–47.

Newby, Andrew and Richard McMahon (2017), 'Select Document: John Hampden Jackson, "Finland and Ireland: Assorted Comparisons"' (1937), *Irish Historical Studies*, 41/160 (Nov.), pp. 256–70.

Newby, Andrew, and Timo Myllyntaus (2015), '"The Terrible Visitation": Famine in Finland and Ireland 1845–68—Towards an Agenda for Comparative Irish-Finnish Famine Studies', in Declan Curran, Lubomyr Luciuk, and Andrew Newby (eds), *Famines in European Economic History: The Last Great European Famines Reconsidered.* London and New York: Taylor & Francis, pp. 145-65.

Niemi, Marjaana (2017), 'Breaking from and Building on the Past: Helsinki and Dublin after Independence', *Irish Historical Studies*, 41/160 (Nov.), pp. 238-55.

Noel, S. J. R. (1974), 'Consociational Democracy and Canadian Federation', in Kenneth McRae (ed.), *Consociational Democracy: Political Accommodation in Segmented Societies*. Toronto: University of Toronto Press, pp. 262-68.

Noel, S. J. R. (1993), 'Canadian Responses to Ethnic Conflict: Consociationalism, Federalism and Control', in John McGarry and Brendan O'Leary (eds), *The Politics of Ethnic Conflict Regulation*. London: Routledge, pp. 41-61.

Nolte, Hans-Heinrich (1997), *Europäische innere Peripherien im 20. Jahrhundert*. Stuttgart: Franz Steiner.

Nordlund, Karl (1905), *The Swedish-Norwegian Union Crisis: A History with Documents*. Upsala and Stockholm: Almqvist & Wiksell.

Norgate, Gerald Le Grys (2004a), 'Richard Charles Francis Christian Meade, Third Earl of Clanwilliam (1795-1879)', revised H. C. G. Matthew, in H. C. G. Matthew and Brian Harrison (eds), *Oxford Dictionary of National Biography*. Oxford: Oxford University Press.

Norgate, Gerald Le Grys (2004b), 'Percy Clinton Sydney Smythe, Sixth Viscount Strangford (1780-1855), revised H. C. G. Matthew, in H. C. G. Matthew and Brian Harrison (eds), *Oxford Dictionary of National Biography*. Oxford: Oxford University Press.

Norgate, Gerald Le Grys (2004c), 'Richard le Poer Trench, Second Earl of Clancarty (1767-1837), revised H. C. G. Matthew, in H. C. G. Matthew and Brian Harrison (eds), *Oxford Dictionary of National Biography*. Oxford: Oxford University Press.

Nurmi, K (2012), 'Imagining the Nation in Irish and Finnish Popular Culture in the Early Nineteenth and Twentieth Centuries', in Brian Heffernan (ed.), *Life on the Fringe? Ireland and Europe, 1800-1922*. Dublin: Irish Academic Press.

Ó Cadhla, Stiofán (2006), *Civilizing Ireland: Ordnance Survey, 1824-42: Ethnography, Cartography, Translation*. Dublin: Irish Academic Press.

O'Callaghan, Margaret (1994), *British High Politics and Nationalist Ireland: Criminality, Land and the Law under Forster and Balfour*. Cork: Cork University Press.

O'Halpin, Eunan (1987), *Decline of the Union: British Government in Ireland, 1892-1920*. Dublin: Gill & Macmillan.

Ó hAnnracháin, Tadhg (2015), *Catholic Europe 1592-1648: Centre and Peripheries*. Oxford: Oxford University Press.

O'Leary, Brendan (2019), *A Treatise on Northern Ireland*, 3 vols. Oxford: Oxford University Press.

O'Leary, Paul (1999), 'Religion, Nationality and Politics: Disestablishment in Ireland and Wales 1868-1914', In J. R. Guy and W. G. Neely (eds), *Contrasts and Comparisons: Studies in Irish and Welsh Church History*. Powys and Keady: Welsh Religious Historical Society, Church of Ireland Historical Society.

O'Leary, Paul (2000), *Immigration and Integration: The Irish in Wales, 1798-1922*. Cardiff: University of Wales Press.

O'Leary, Paul (2016), 'States of Union: Modern Scotland and British History', *Twentieth Century British History*, 27/1 (Mar.), pp. 124-43.

O'Leary, Paul (2017), 'Wales and the First World War', *Welsh History Review*, 28/4, pp. 591-617.

Okey, Robin (1991), 'Education and Nationhood in Wales, 1850-1940', in Janusz Tomiak et al. (eds), *Schooling, Educational Policy and Ethnic Identity*, vol. 1. Aldershot and New York: Dartmouth/New York University Press, pp. 35-62.

Okey, Robin (2001), *The Habsburg Empire, c.1765-1918: From Enlightenment to Eclipse*. Basingstoke: Palgrave Macmillan.
Okey, Robin (2007), *Taming Balkan Nationalism: The Habsburg 'Civilising Mission' in Bosnia, 1878-1914*. Oxford: Oxford University Press.
Okey, Robin (2010), 'Wales and Eastern Europe: Small Nations in Comparison', in T. M. Charles-Edwards and R. J. W. Evans (eds), *Wales and the Wider World: Welsh History in an International Context*. Donington: Shaun Tyas, pp. 184-217.
Okey, Robin (2015), 'Lesser-Used Languages and Linguistic Minorities in Europe since 1918: An Overview', in Geraint H. Jenkins (ed.), *Let's Do our Best for the Ancient Tongue: The Welsh Language in the Twentieth Century*. Cardiff: University of Wales Press, pp. 627-56.
Ormsby, William (1969), *The Emergence of the Federal Concept in Canada, 1839-45*. Toronto: University of Toronto Press.
Osmond, John (ed.) (1985), *The National Question Again: Welsh Political Identity in the 1980s*. Llandysul: Gomer.
Ouellet, Fernand (1980), *Lower Canada 1791-1840: Social Change and Nationalism*. Toronto: University of Toronto Press.
Palmer, Stanley (1988), *Police and Protest in England and Ireland, 1780-1850*. Cambridge: Cambridge University Press.
Parent, Joseph M. (2011), *Uniting States: Voluntary Union in World Politics*. Oxford: Oxford University Press.
Paterson, Lindsay (1994), *The Autonomy of modern Scotland*. Edinburgh: Edinburgh University Press.
Pearson, Raymond (1983), *National Minorities in Eastern Europe, 1848-1945*. London and Basingstoke: Palgrave Macmillan.
Pentland, Gordon (2015), 'Edward Heath, the Declaration of Perth, and the Scottish Conservative and Unionist Party, 1966-1970', *Twentieth Century British History*, 26/2 (June), pp. 249-73.
Péporté, Pit, et al. (2010), *Inventing Luxembourg: Representations of the Past, Space and Language from the Nineteenth to the Twenty-First Centuries*. Leiden: Brill.
Péter, László (1984), 'R. W. Seton-Watson's Changing Views on the National Question of the Habsburg Monarchy and the European Balance of Power', *Slavonic and East European Review*, 82/3 (July), pp. 655-79.
Peterson, Scott, and Iain McLean (2007), 'Of Wheat, the Church in Wales and the West Lothian Question', *Welsh History Review*, 23/3 (June), pp. 151-74.
Petterson, Lars (2016), 'Sweden: The Emergence of the Nation State', in E. I. Kouri and J. E. Olesen (eds), *The Cambridge History of Scandinavia*, vol. 2. *1520-1870*. Cambridge: Cambridge University Press, pp. 975-91.
Philip, Alan Butt (1975), *The Welsh Question: Nationalism in Welsh Politics*. Cardiff: University of Wales Press.
Pittock, Murray (ed.) (2006), *The Reception of Sir Walter Scott in Europe*. London: Bloomsbury.
Poggi, Gianfranco (1978), *The Development of the Modern State: A Sociological Introduction*. London: Hutchinson.
Poggi, Gianfranco (1990), *The State: Its Nature, Development and Prospects*. Stanford, CA: Stanford University Press.
Polasky, Janet L. (1984), *Revolution in Brussels, 1787-1793*. Brussels: Académie Royale de Belgique.
Pollard, Michael (2005), 'Sunset or Dawn? F. S. Oliver's "Endless Adventure" in History and Politics, 1921-34', *History*, 90/3, pp. 387-410.

Polvinen, Tuomo (1995), *Imperial Borderland: Bobrikov and the Attempted Russification of Finland, 1898-1904*. Durham, NC: Duke University Press.
Porter, Andrew (2004), *Religion versus Empire? British Protestant Missionaries and Overseas Expansion, 1700-1914*. Manchester: Manchester University Press.
Pribram, Alfred Francis (1951), *Austria-Hungary and Great Britain, 1908-14*, tr. Ian F. D. Morrow. Oxford: Oxford University Press.
Prokopovych, Markian (2008), *Habsburg Lemburg: Architecture, Public Space and Politics in the Galician Capital, 1772-1914*. West Lafayette, IN: Purdue University Press.
Pryce, W. T. R. (2007), 'Region or National Territory? Regionalism and the iIea of the Country of Wales, c.1927-98', *Welsh History Review*, 23/2 (Feb.), pp. 99-152.
Puttkamer, Joachim von (2003), *Schulalltag und nationale Integration in Ungarn, Slowaken, Rumänen und Siebenbürger Sachsen in der Auseinandersetzung mit der ungarischen Staatsidee, 1867-1914*. Munich: Oldenbourg.
Quinault, Roland (2009), 'Gladstone and Slavery', *Historical Journal*, 52/2, pp. 363-83.
Rauchensteiner, Manfred (2013), *Der erste Weltkrieg und das Ende der Habsburgermonarchie*. Vienna: Böhlau.
Redvaldsen, David (2014), 'Great Britain and the Norwegian Constitution of 1814', *Journal of Parliaments, Estates and Representation*, 34/2, pp. 182-202.
Redvaldsen, David (2016), 'The Role of Britain in Late Modern Norwegian History', *Britain and the World*, 9/1 (Mar.), pp. 10-31.
Reid, Colin (2014), '"An Experiment in Constructive Unionism": Isaac Butt, Home Rule and Federalist Political Thought during the 1870s', *English Historical Review*, 129/537, pp. 332-61.
Reifowitz, Ian (2003), *Imagining an Austrian Nation: Joseph Samuel Block and the Search for a Supraethnic Austrian Identity, 1845-1919*. Boulder, CO: East European Monographs.
Rembold, Elfie (2000), '"Home Rule All Round": Experiments in Regionalising Great Britain, 1886-1914', in Peter Catterall, Wolfram Kaiser, and Ulrike Walton-Jordan (eds), *Reforming the Constitution: Debates in Twentieth-Century Britain*. London: Routledge, pp. 201-24.
Rexheuser, Rex (ed.) (2005), *Die Personalunionen von Sachsen-Polen (1697-1763) und Hannover-England (1714-1837): Ein Vergleich*. Wiesbaden: Harrassowitz Verlag.
Roberts, Michael (1953-8), *Gustavus Adolphus: A History of Sweden, 1611-1632*, 2 vols. London: Longmans.
Roberts, Michael (1968), *The Early Vasas: A History of Sweden, 1523-1611*. Cambridge: Cambridge University Press.
Roberts, Michael (1986), *The Age of Liberty: Sweden, 1719-1772*. Cambridge: Cambridge University Press.
Robinson, D. H. (2020), *Natural and Necessary Unions: Britain, Europe and the Scottish Question*. Oxford: Oxford University Press.
Rosenthal, Lawrence, and Vesna Rodic (eds) (2014), *The New Nationalism and the First World War*. Basingstoke: Palgrave Macmillan.
Rosland, Sissel (2017), 'The Rise and Fall of the Norwegian Example as an Argument for Irish Self-Government', *Nordic Irish Studies*, 16, pp. 123-40.
Rothenberg, Gunther (1999), *The Army of Francis Joseph*. West Lafayette, IN: Purdue University Press.
Rowland Hughes, Dewi (2006), *Cymru Fydd*. Cardiff: University of Wales Press.
Rozenblit, Marsha (2004), *Reconstructing a National Identity: The Jews of Habsburg Austria during World War 1*. Oxford: Oxford University Press.
Ryerson, Stanley (1973), *Unequal Union: Roots of Crisis in the Canadas, 1815-73*. Toronto: University of Toronto Press.

Sas, N. C. F. van (1985), *Onze natuurlijkste bondgenoot: Nederland, Engeland en Europa, 1813-1831*. Groningen: Wolters-Noordhof

Saunders, Robert E. (2003), 'Robinson, Sir John Beverley', in *Dictionary of Canadian Biography*, vol. 9. Toronto: University of Toronto Press.

Sayers, Melanie (2011), 'Philip Kerr and the Irish Question', Ph.D. thesis, University of Edinburgh.

Schöpflin, George (1999), *Nations, Identity, Power: The New Politics of Europe*. New York: New York University Press.

Schultz, Kirsten (2001), *Tropical Versailles: Empire, Monarchy and the Portuguese Royal Court in Rio de Janeiro, 1808-21*. London: Routledge.

Scott, F. D. (1935), *Bernadotte and the Fall of Napoleon*. Cambridge, MA: Harvard University Press.

Searle, G. R. (1971), *The Quest for National Efficiency: A Study in British Politics and Political Thought, 1899-1914*. Oxford: Basil Blackwell.

Seip, Anne-Lise (1995), 'Nation-Building within the Union: Class and Culture in the Norwegian Nation-State in the Nineteenth Century', *Scandinavian Journal of History*, 20/1, pp. 35-50.

Seton-Watson, Hugh, and Christopher (1981), *The Making of a New Europe: R. W. Seton-Watson and the Last Years of Austria-Hungary*. London: Methuen.

Shannon, Richard (1999), *Gladstone: Heroic Minister, 1865-1898*. London: Allen Lane.

Shedel, James (1990), 'Emperor, Church and People: Religion and Dynastic Loyalty during the Golden Jubilee of Franz Joseph', *Catholic Historical Review*, 76/1, pp. 71-92.

Sigurdsson, D. L. (2004), 'A Parallel Much Closer: The 1918 Act of Union', *Irish Historical Studies*, 34/133 (May), pp. 79-92.

Simms, Brendan, and Torsten Riotte (eds) (2007), *The Hanoverian Dimension to British History, 1714-1837*. Cambridge: Cambridge University Press.

Simms, J. G., *Colonial Nationalism, 1698-1776*. Cork: Mercier Press.

Sked, Alan (1989), *The Decline and Fall of the Habsburg Empire, 1815-1918*. London: Longman.

Sked, Alan (2014), 'Austria-Hungary and the First World War', *Histoire@politique: Culture, Politique, Société*, 1/22, pp. 16-49.

Sondhaus, Lawrence (2000), *Franz Conrad von Hötzendorf: Architect of the Apocalypse*. Boston: Brill/Humanities Press.

Sparks, Mary (2014), *The Development of Austro-Hungarian Sarajevo, 1878-1918: An Urban History*. London: Bloomsbury.

Spiers, Edward (1996), 'Army Organisation and Society in the Nineteenth Century', in Thomas Bartlett and Keith Jeffery (eds), *A Military History of Ireland*. Cambridge: Cambridge University Press, pp. 335-57.

Stagg, Frank Noel (1956), *East Norway and its Frontier*. London: George Allen & Unwin.

Stanbridge, Karen (2003), *Toleration and State Institutions: British Policy towards Catholics in Eighteenth Century Ireland and Quebec*. Lanham, MD: Lexington Books.

Stead, Peter (1980), 'The Language of Edwardian Politics', in David Smith (ed.), *A People and a Proletariat*. London: Pluto Press, pp. 148-65.

Stephens, H. M. (2004),'William Vesey Fitzgerald, Second Baron Fitzgerald and Vesey (1783-1843)', revised by Peter Gray, in H. C. G. Matthew and Brian Harrison (eds), *Oxford Dictionary of National Biography*. Oxford: Oxford University Press.

Stevenson, Garth (2006), *Parallel Paths: The Development of Nationalism in Ireland and Quebec*. Montreal: McGill-Queen's University Press.

Stevenson, Garth (2009), *Unfulfilled Union: Canadian Federalism and National Unity*, 5th edition. Montreal: McGill-Queen's University Press.

Stone, Norman (1975), *The Eastern Front, 1914–17*. London: Hodder & Stoughton.
Stourzh, Gerald (2007), *From Vienna to Chicago and Back: Essays on Intellectual History and Political Thought in Europe and America*. Chicago: Chicago University Press.
Stourzh, Gerald (2011), 'Die dualistische Reichsstruktur, Österreichsbegriff und Österreichsbewusstsein, 1867–1918', in *Der Umfang der österreichischen Geschichte: ausgewähtle Studien, 1990–2010*. Vienna: Böhlau Verlag.
Stråth, Bo (2005), *Union och demokrati: De förenade rikena Sverige och Norge 1814–1905*. Nora: Bokförlaget Nya Doxa.
Sugar, Peter F., et al. (eds) (1990), *A History of Hungary*. London: I. B. Tauris.
Suodenjoki, Sami (2017), 'Mobilising for Land, Nation and Class Interests: Agrarian Agitation in Finland and Ireland, 1879–1918', *Irish Historical Studies*, 41/160 (Nov.), pp. 200–20.
Tangeraas, L. (1983), 'Castlereagh, Bernadotte and Norway', *Scandinavian Journal of History*, 8/1–4, pp. 193–223.
Tanner, Duncan, Chris Williams, and Deian Hopkin (eds) (2000), *The Labour Party in Wales, 1900–2000*. Cardiff: University of Wales Press.
Tarlton, Charles D. (1965), 'Symmetry and Asymmetry as Elements of Federalism: A Theoretical Speculation', *Journal of Politics*, 27/4, pp. 861–74.
Taylor, A. J. P. (1948), *The Habsburg Monarchy, 1809–1918: A History of the Austrian Empire and Austria-Hungary*. London: Hamish Hamilton.
Taylor, Simon J. (2003), 'Disestablished Establishment: High and Earthed Establishment in the Church in Wales', *Journal of Contemporary Religion*, 18/2, pp. 227–40.
Thomas, Geraint (2013), 'The Conservative Party and Welsh Politics in the Inter-War Years', *English Historical Review*, 128/533 (Aug.), pp. 877–913.
Thompson, Frank (2001), *The End of Liberal Ulster: Land Agitation and Land Reform, 1868–86*. Belfast: Ulster Historical Foundation.
Thorne, Roland (2004), 'Robert Stewart, Viscount Castlereagh and Second Marquess of Londonderry (1769-1822)', in H. C. G. Matthew and Brian Harrison (eds), *Oxford Dictionary of National Biography*. Oxford: Oxford University Press.
Thornley, David (1964), *Isaac Butt and Home Rule*. London: MacGibbon & Kee.
Tilly, Charles (1984), *Big Structures, Large Processes, Huge Comparisons*. New York: Russell Sage Foundation.
Todorova, Maria (1997), *Imagining the Balkans*. New York: Oxford University Press.
Tollebeek, Jo (1998), 'Historical Representation and the Nation-State in Romantic Belgium, 1830–50', *Journal of the History of Ideas*, 59/2, pp. 329–53.
Tollebeek, Jo (2015), 'The Use of History in Belgium and the Netherlands, 1945–65: Presentism and Historicism in the Work of Jan Romein, Pieter Geyl and Leopold Flam', *Dutch Crossing*, 39/1 (Mar.), pp. 54–73.
Torrance, David (2009), *We in Scotland: Thatcherism in a Cold Climate*. Edinburgh: Birlinn.
Torrance, David (2014), *Britain Rebooted: Scotland in a Federal Union*. Edinburgh: Luath Press.
Torrance, David (2020), *'Standing up for Scotland': Nationalist Unionism and Scottish Party Politics, 1884–2014*. Edinburgh: Edinburgh University Press.
Townend, Paul (2016), *The Road to Home Rule: Anti-Imperialism and the Irish Nationalist Movement*. Madison, WI: University of Wisconsin Press.
Tulloch, Hugh (1980), 'A. V. Dicey and the Irish Question, 1870–1922', *Irish Jurist*, 15/1, pp. 137–65.
Tunstall, Graydon (2012), 'Austria-Hungary', in Richard Hamilton and Holger Herwig (eds), *The Origins of World War I*, Cambridge: Cambridge University Press.

Turner, Michael (2006), 'Radical Agitation and the Canada Question in British Politics, 1837-41', *Historical Research: The Bulletin of the Institute of Historical Research*, 79/203, pp. 90-114.
Tyler, J. E. (1938), *The Struggle for Imperial Unity, 1868-95*. London: Royal Empire Society/ Longmans, Green & Co.
Unowsky, Daniel (2005), *The Pomp and Politics of Patriotism: Imperial Celebrations in Habsburg Austria, 1848-1916*. West Lafayette, IN: Purdue University Press.
Upton, L. F. S. (2003), 'Smith, William (1728-93)', in *Dictionary of Canadian Biography*, vol. 4. Toronto: University of Toronto Press.
Valeriano, Brandon, and John Van Benthuysen (2012), 'When States Die: Geographic and Territorial Pathways to State Death', *Third World Quarterly*, 33/7, pp. 1165-89.
Van den Bossche, Geert (2001), *Enlightened Innovation and the Ancient Constitution: The Intellectual Justifications of Revolution in Brabant, 1787-1790*. Brussels: Koninklijke Vlaamse Academie van België voor Wetenschappen en Kunsten.
Van der Burg, Martijn (2010), 'Transforming the Dutch Republic into the Kingdom of Holland: The Netherlands between Republicanism and Monarchy, 1795-1815', *European Review of History*, 17/2, pp. 151-70.
Viaene, Vincent (2001), *Belgium and the Holy See from Gregory XVI to Pius IX (1831-59)*. Leuven: Leuven University Press.
Vick, B. E. (2014), *The Congress of Vienna: Power and Politics after Napoleon*. Cambridge, MA, and London: Harvard University Press.
Vincent, John (1977), 'Gladstone and Ireland', *Proceedings of the British Academy*, 63, pp. 193-238.
Walchester, Kathryn (2014), *Gamle Norge and Nineteenth Century British Women Travellers in Norway*. London: Anthem Press.
Walker, Brian (1989), *Ulster Politics: The Formative Years, 1868-86*. Belfast: Ulster Historical Foundation.
Walker, Graham (2005), *A History of the Ulster Unionist Party: Protest, Pragmatism and Pessimism*. Manchester: Manchester University Press.
Walker, Graham (2016), *The Labour Party in Scotland: Religion, the Union and the Irish Dimension*. London: Palgrave Macmillan.
Wallace, Ryland (1991), *Organise! Organise! Organise! A Study of Reform Agitations in Wales, 1840-1886*. Cardiff: University of Wales Press.
Wandruska, Adam, and Peter Urbanitsch (eds) (1975), *Die Habsburgermonarchie, 1848-1918*, vol. 2. *Verwaltung und Rechtswesen*. Vienna: Verlag der österreichischen Akademie der Wissenschaften.
Wank, Solomon (2009), *In the Twilight of Empire: Count Alois Lexa von Aehrenthal (1854-1912), Imperial Habsburg Patriot and Statesman*, vol. 1. *The Making of an Imperial Habsburg Statesman*. Vienna: Böhlau Verlag.
Ward, Paul (1998), *Red Flag and Union Jack: Englishness, Patriotism and the British Left, 1881-1924*. Woodbridge: Boydell.
Ward, Paul (2005), *Unionism in the United Kingdom, 1918-74*. Basingstoke: Palgrave Macmillan.
Ward, Paul (2011), *Huw T. Edwards and Welsh Socialism*. Cardiff: University of Wales Press.
Ward-Smith, Gabrielle (2001), 'Baldwin and Scotland: More than Englishness', *Journal of Contemporary British History*, 15/1, pp. 61-82.
Watkin, T. G. (1992), 'Disestablishment, Self-Determination and the Constitutional Development of the Church in Wales', in Norman Doe (ed.), *Essays in Canon Law: A Study of the Church in Wales*. Cardiff: University of Wales Press.

Watson, Alexander (2014), *Ring of Steel: Germany and Austria-Hungary at War, 1914–18*. London: Allen Lane.
Watson, Alexander (2019), *The Fortress: The Great Siege of Przemýsl*. London: Allen Lane.
Weber, Eugen Joseph (1979), *Peasants into Frenchman: The Modernisation of Rural France, 1870–1914*. London: Chatto & Windus.
Weill, Rivka (2003), 'Dicey was Not Diceyan', *Cambridge Law Journal*, 62/2 (July), pp. 474–94.
Wheare, Kenneth C. (1947), *Federal Government*. Oxford: Oxford University Press.
Wheatley, Michael (2001), 'John Redmond and Federalism in 1910', *Irish Historical Studies*, 32/127 (May), pp. 343–64.
Whiteside, Andrew (1975), *The Socialism of Fools: Georg Ritter von Schönerer and Austrian Pan-Germanism*. Berkeley, CA: University of California Press.
Wielenga, Friso (2015), *A History of the Netherlands, from the Sixteenth Century to the Present Day*, tr. Lynne Richards. London: Bloomsbury.
Wilkie, James (1991), 'Schottlands Weg in die britische Union', in Emil Brix, Thomas Fröschl, and Josef Leidenfrost (eds), *Geschichte zwischen Freiheit und Ordnung: Gerald Stourzh zum 60. Geburtstag*. Graz and Vienna: Verlag Styria, pp. 319–37.
Williams, Chris (1997), 'Democracy and Nationalism in Wales: The Lib-Lab Enigma', in R. Stradling et al. (eds), *Conflict and Coexistence: Nationalism and Democracy in Modern Europe*. Cardiff: University of Wales Press, pp. 107–31.
Williams, Emyr W. (1990), 'Liberalism in Wales and the Politics of Welsh Home Rule 1886–1910', *Bulletin of the Board of Celtic Studies*, 37, pp. 191–207.
Williams, Glanmor (2007), *The Welsh Church from Reformation to Disestablishment, 1603–1920*. Cardiff: University of Wales Press.
Williams, Gwyn Alf (1982), *The Welsh in their History*. London: Croom Helm.
Williams, Rowan (2019), 'How the Welsh Fought back', *New Statesman*, 26 June.
Williamson, Samuel R. (1991), *Austria-Hungary and the Origins of the First World War*. London: Macmillan.
Wilson, David (2008–11), *Thomas D'Arcy McGee*, 2 vols. Toronto: McGill-Queen's University Press.
Wilson, David (2009), *Irish Nationalism in Canada*. Montreal and Kingston: McGill-Queen's University Press.
Wilson, Timothy (2010), *Frontiers of Violence: Conflict and Identity in Ulster and Upper Silesia, 1918–1922*. Oxford: Oxford University Press.
Wingfield, Nancy M. (ed.) (2003), *Creating the Other: Ethnic Conflict and Nationalism in Habsburg Central Europe*. New York and Oxford: Berghahn.
Wingfield, Nancy (2007), *Flag Wars and Stone Saints: How the Bohemian Lands Became Czech*. Cambridge: Cambridge University Press.
Wintle, Michael (1987), *Pillars of Piety: Religion in the Netherlands in the Nineteenth Century*. Hull: Hull University Press.
Wintle, Michael (2000), *An Economic and Social History of the Netherlands, 1800–1920*. Cambridge: Cambridge University Press.
Witte, Els, and Harry van Velthoven (1999), *Language and Politics: The Belgian Case Study in Historical Perspective*. Brussels: VUB University Press.
Wold, Atle (2015), *Scotland and the French Revolutionary War, 1792–1802*. Edinburgh: Edinburgh University Press.
Wolff, Larry (1994), *Imagining Eastern Europe: The Map of Civilisation on the Mind of the Enlightenment*. Stanford, CA: Stanford University Press.

Wolff, Larry (2010), *The Idea of Galicia: History and Fantasy in Habsburg Political Culture*. Stanford, CA: Stanford University Press.

Wolffe, John (ed.) (2013), *Protestant-Catholic Conflict from the Reformation to the 21st Century: The Dynamics of Religious Difference*. Basingstoke: Palgrave Macmillan.

Worthington, David (2012), *British and Irish Experiences and Impressions of Central Europe, c.1560–1688*. Farnham: Ashgate.

Wright, Frank (1988), *Northern Ireland: A Comparative Analysis*. Dublin: Gill & Macmillan.

Wright, H. R. C. (2013), *Free Trade and Protection in the Netherlands, 1816–30*. Cambridge: Cambridge University Press.

Wright, Martin (2016), *Wales and Socialism: Political Culture and National Identity before the Great War*. Cardiff: University of Wales Press.

Zách, Lili (2014), 'Ireland, Czechoslovakia and the Question of Small Nations in the Context of Ireland's Wartime Neutrality', in Aidan O'Malley and Eve Patten (eds), *Ireland, West to East: Irish Cultural Connections with Central and Eastern Europe*. Bern: Peter Lang.

Zách, Lili (2020), '"The First of the Small Nations": The Significance of Central European States in Irish Nationalist Political Rhetoric, 1918–22', *Irish Historical Studies*, 44/165 (May), pp. 25–40.

Zách, Lili (2021), *Imagining Ireland Abroad, 1904–45: Conceiving the Nation, Identity and Borders in Central Europe*. London: Palgrave Macmillan.

Zahra, Tara (2006), '"Each Nation Cares Only for its own": Empire, Nation and Child Welfare Activism in the Bohemian Lands, 1900–18', *American Historical Review*, 111/5 (Dec.), pp. 1378–1402.

Zahra, Tara (2008), *National Indifference and the Battle for Children in the Bohemian Lands, 1900–48*. Ithaca, NY: Cornell University Press.

Zahra, Tara (2010), 'Imagined Non-Communities: National Indifference as a Category of Analysis', *Slavic Review*, 69/1 (Spring), pp. 93–119.

Index

Note: Figures are indicated by an italic '*f*' following the page numbers.

For the benefit of digital users, indexed terms that span two pages (e.g., 52–53) may, on occasion, appear on only one of those pages.

Aasen, Ivar 315
Abdul Hamid II, Sultan of the Ottoman
    Empire 192
Acemoglu, Daron 294–5
Acheson, Archibald *see* Gosford, 2nd Earl of
Adler, Victor 229–30
Aehrenthal, Alois Lexa, Graf von 152–3, 190
Åkerhielm, Gustaf, Baron 117–18
Alexander I, King of Yugoslavia 160
Alexander I, Tsar of Russia 218
Alexander II, Tsar of Russia 195, 218
Algarves *see* United Kingdom of Portugal, Brazil,
    and the Algarves
Amortisatie Syndicaat/Amortization
    Syndicate 95–6
Anckarsvärd, Carl, Count 237
Anderson, R. A. 114
Andrássy, Gyula, Count 143–4, 311–12
Anker, Carsten 25
Apponyi, Albert, Count 14, 182
Argyll, Dukes of 234
Argyll, Archibald Campbell, 10th Earl
    (and 1st Duke of) 234
Argyll, George Campbell, 8th Duke of 32
Argyll, John Campbell, 9th Duke of
    see Lorne, Lord
aristocracy and elites 174–80, 363
    Austria-Hungary 137, 146, 174–8, 190
    and colonial nationalism 175
    and government 179–80
    and monarchy 174–9
    Netherlands 179–80
    Norway 179–80
    as proportion of population 176
    subverting unions 179–80
    and supranationalism 174–5, 178–9
    Sweden 111, 114, 179–80
    UK 44–5, 68–9, 74, 178–9, 363
    uniting unions 178
    waning power and influence 177–9
armies 180–5
    Austria-Hungary 138, 154–6, 164, 182–5,
        191, 362

and compulsory military service 183–4, 186
national armies vs. union armies 182–3
as multi-ethnic institutions 183, 185
Netherlands 185
Sweden-Norway 106–7, 182–3, 318–19
UK *see* British army
uniting unions 182
and supranationalism 183–5
Armitage, David 11
Armitage, John 209
Asquith, H. H. (1st Earl of Oxford & Asquith)
    250, 259–60, 338
associationalism 210–12, 214–15
Athelstan, King of England 41
Austria-Hungary (Dual Monarchy) 2, 4–5, 7,
    11–12, 56, 134–58, 303
    Agram/Zagreb treason trials (1909) 153, 243
    and aristocracy 137, 146, 174–8, 190
    army 138, 154–6, 164, 182–5, 191, 362
    as asymmetrical union 103–4
    Ausgleich ('compromise'; 1867) 13–14, 31,
        103, 136, 143–4, 157–8, 181, 207, 240, 247,
        256, 280, 302–3, 311–12
    Badeni crisis (1897) 150–1, 207–8, 359–60
    banking 221–2
    Bosnia, annexation of 8, 153, 201–2
    Budweis/České Budějovice 323–6, 335–6
    Bukovina compromise (1910) 148, 152,
        321–3, 335–6, 359
    bureaucracy 185–92
    and cartography 238–9
    and Catholicism 135, 137, 174–5, 183, 192,
        195–7, 199–200, 304
    and centralization 137–8, 166–7, 189–90
    and civic education 312–13
    and coat of arms 153, 327
    comparison with Ireland 138, 140–2, 149
    comparison with UK 13–14, 135–6,
        138, 140–1
    as composite monarchy 305
    as confederation 247
    and consociationalism/power-sharing 151,
        335–6

Austria-Hungary (Dual Monarchy) (*cont.*)
  and Croats 146–8, 153, 236–7
  and Czechs 149–51, 189
  dissolution (1918) 43–4, 157–8, 297–9, 321, 344–5, 364
  divide and rule strategy 235–7
  economic effects of union 223–4, 227
  electoral system 208–9
  and emigration 331–2
  ethnic, linguistic, and religious diversity 135, 141, 144, 201, 324, 332
  ethnic stereotyping 237
  February Patent (1861) 142–3
  and federalism (trialism) 12–13, 144–5, 149–50, 157, 266, 279–86, 361–2
  and First World War 153–6, 170, 181–2, 184–5, 335–7, 339–43, 347, 357
  and foreign policy 142, 153–4, 190–1, 332, 337–8
  Fundamental Articles (1871) 149–50, 235–6, 281
  Galician compromise (1914) 148, 152, 321–3, 335–6, 359
  and German identity 138, 318, 343–4
  and German language 135, 137–8, 140–2, 150–2, 179–80, 185–6, 201–2, 223
  historiography of 17–18
  imperial architecture 217
  kaiserlich und königlich identity 186–7, 190, 312
  Kremsier constitution (1849) 139–40, 280–1, 313
  and *Kulturpessimismus* 316–17
  longevity factors 164–5, 182, 359
  and magyarization 145–6, 236, 321
  Manifesto (imperial federalist initiative; October 1918) 157
  as model for UK 7, 29–32, 144, 146–8
  and monarchy 166–70, 199–200, 240
  and monument building 197–8, 217, 299
  Moravian compromise (1905) 148, 151–2, 321–3, 335–6, 359
  Nagodba ('agreement'; 1868) 145–8, 236–7, 259–60, 283–4
  and national differences 145, 321–3
  and national identity, lacking 141, 164, 353, 355
  and nationalism 15–16, 18
  nationality self-determined 151–2, 229–30
  and parliament 207–9
  as 'prison of nations' 17–18
  and Protestantism 196–8
  railways 146, 221–2
  and reform 240, 242
  and religion 195–8
  as 'relic of earlier age' 13–15

  and repression 242–3
  and revolt (1848) 139–42, 167
  and rural and peasant communities 141–2, 221, 323
  and Serbia 146–8, 153–4, 227
  and Social Democratic Party 229–31
  and state consciousness, lack of 312–14
  successor states 11, 17–18, 136, 160, 345, 347
  and supranational loyalty 16, 138, 164, 174–5, 183–4, 356
  as trade and customs union 221
  UK as model 136
  unionism, constructive 146–8
Austrian Netherlands *see* southern Netherlands
Aylmer, Matthew Whitworth-Aylmer, 5th Lord 127

Bach, Alexander, Freiherr von 139–41, 221–2, 334
Bachelor's Walk massacre (1914) 241–2
Badeni, Kasimir, Graf von 150–1, 359–60
Bagot, Sir Charles 132–3
Baldwin, Robert 132–3
Baldwin, Stanley (1st Earl Baldwin of Bewdley) 52–3
Balfour, Arthur (1st Earl of Balfour) 52–3, 179, 239–40, 242, 365
Balfour, Gerald (2nd Earl of Balfour) 179, 239–40, 242
banking and currency *see under* economy
Battle of Courtrai/Kortrijk (1302) 94–5, 302
Battle of Fleurus (1794) 93
Battle of Magenta (1859) 103–4, 142, 334
Battle of Nancy (1477) 91–2
Battle of Ramillies (1706) 92–3
Battle of Sadowa/Königgrätz (1866) 103–4, 136, 143, 302–4, 334
Battle of Solferino (1859) 103–4, 142, 334
Battle of Waterloo (1815) 94, 173
Battle of Zborov (1917) 155–6
Bauer, Otto 151–2, 229–30, 282
Beck, Max, Freiherr von 151, 207–8
Belcredi, Richard, Graf von 281
Belgium 249
  and class 228
  and economy 232
  home rule 1
  independence 98–9, 160
  and monarchy 166
  and nationalism 324
  see also United Kingdom of the Netherlands; United States of Belgium
Belleau, Sir Narcisse-Fortunat 172–3
Beller, Steven 143–4, 322, 335–6
Beneš, Jakub 230

Berchtold, Leopold, Graf 191, 281–2
Bernadotte, Carl Johan *see* Carl XIV Johan, King of Sweden and Norway
Beust, Friedrich, Graf von 281
Bhabha, Homi 11
Biron, Sir Chartres 86
Bjørnson, Bjørnsterne 115, 231, 315, 331
Björnsterna, Magnus, Count 30
Black, Jeremy 329
Blackstone, William 206
Blair, Tony 52, 308–9
Bloomfield, Benjamin Bloomfield, 1st Lord 27
Bocskai, István, Prince of Transylvania 196
Bogdanor, Vernon 301
Bonar Law, Andrew 52–3
Bonde, Knut 237
Bosnia-Herzegovina 8, 153, 201–2
Boström, Erik 119, 330–1
Brazil 27–8; *see also* United Kingdom of Portugal, Brazil, and the Algarves
Brexit 53, 181–2, 219, 250, 267, 288, 319–20, 329, 333, 357–8, 360, 364
British army 138, 182–3
  and First World War 184–5, 343
  and Ireland 49–50, 75–7, 183, 185
  and Scotland 52–4, 75–7, 183
  and union identity 337–8
  and Wales 75–7
British North America 121–2, 125–6, 232, 271–3
Brockliss, Laurence 1
Broglie, Maurice-Jean de, Bishop 98, 203
Brooks, Simon 55, 81
Brown, George 270, 274
Brown, Gordon 52, 132, 250–1, 308
Brown, Michael 213
Brown, S. J. (Jay) 192–3
Bruce, James *see* Elgin, 8th Earl of
Bruce, John 363
Bruck, Karl Ludwig von 141–2
Bryce, James (1st Viscount Bryce) 3, 31, 249
Buchan, John *see* Tweedsmuir, Lord
Bulwer-Lytton, Sir Edward (1st Lord Lytton) 272
bureaucracy 185–92
  Austria-Hungary 185–92
  and centralization 189–90
  and state growth 188–90
  subverting unions 191
  Sweden-Norway 186–7, 191
  UK 186–90
  unions having separate administrations 186–7
Burgess, Michael 192–3, 248, 251, 262, 287
Burgundy, Dukes of 91–2, 94
Butt, Isaac 9–10, 22, 30, 206–7, 251–2, 255, 258–9, 266

Calvinism 62–3, 71–3, 91–2, 97, 197, 201–3; *see also* Protestantism
Cameron, David 250, 364
Campbell, Menzies 250
Canada 2, 4, 160
  and Catholicism 123
  comparison with Ireland 123
  confederation (1867) 12–13, 121–2, 247, 255, 274–5, 285, 287, 361–2
  Irish and Scottish influence 276–7
  as model for UK 258–9, 277
  Ninety Two Resolutions (1834) 126–8
  Quebec Act (1774) 123, 125–6, 129–30, 172–3, 193
  see also United Province of Canada (United Canadas)
Canning, George 28
Carey, Hilary 192
Carl XII, King of Sweden 215
Carl XIII, King of Sweden (Carl II of Norway) 327–8
Carl XIV Johan, King of Sweden (Carl III Johan of Norway) 25, 88*f*, 110–12, 174, 237, 327–8
  monuments to 218
  popularity 113
  portraits of 112
  Sweden-Norway union 14, 24–5, 104–5
  union as security 25–6
  visit to Norway 113
Carl XV, King of Sweden (Carl IV of Norway) 114, 174, 333
Carleton, Sir Guy (1st Lord Dorchester) 123
Carnarvon, Henry Herbert, 4th Earl of 122
Carnegie, Andrew 32
Carson, Edward (Lord Carson of Duncairn) 49, 86, 267, 316
Cartier, Sir George-Étienne 132, 172–3, 269–71, 274
Casement, Sir Roger 341
Castlereagh, Robert Stewart, Viscount (later 2nd Marquess of Londonderry) 6, 28–9, 34*f*, 93, 228, 350
  and Austria-Hungary 134–5, 138–9, 158–9
  British union 19–21
  Dutch–Belgian union 21–3, 94
  Swedish–Norwegian union 25–7
Catholic Church, Catholicism 46–7, 54, 92, 95, 97–100
  Austria-Hungary 135, 137, 174–5, 183, 192, 195–7, 199–200, 304
  Canada 122–4, 172–3, 193, 277–8
  Ireland 122–3, 133–4, 193, 197, 204, 234–5, 277–8, 350–1
  Netherlands 97–100, 194, 201–4
  UK 22–3, 69, 123, 193, 204

Catholic emancipation (1829) 22–3
Cecil, Robert *see* Salisbury, 3rd Marquess of
Černová massacre (1907) 242–3
Chamberlain, Joseph 31
Charles VI, Holy Roman Emperor 136
Charles the Bold, Duke of Burgundy 91–2
Choiseul, Étienne François, Duc de 27–8
Chomsky, Noam 294–5
Christian II, King of Denmark 102
Churchill, Lord Randolph 86, 316
Churchill, Winston 52–3, 76–7
church and religion 192–205
    Austria-Hungary 195–202
    Finland 194–5, 204
    Netherlands 97–100, 194, 201–3
    role of monarchs within 195
    Russia 194–5
    state churches and union 204
    Sweden-Norway 105, 193–4, 200–1, 204
    UK 54, 71–3, 79, 193, 195–8
    see also Catholic Church, Catholicism; Protestantism
civil society and civic space 210–19
    and associationalism 210–12, 214–15
    Austria-Hungary 217
    Ireland 212–13, 215–18
    and monarchy 217
    and national differences 216
    Netherlands 213
    Scotland 211–12, 215–16
    Sweden-Norway 213–16, 218–19
    and unionist nationalism 212
    and unions 211–13, 218
Clam-Martinic, Heinrich, Graf von 282
Clancarty, Richard Trench, 2nd Earl of 19–21, 23, 35*f*, 94, 179–80
Clanwilliam, Richard Meade, 3rd Earl of 22
Clark, Christopher 192, 338, 357
class *see under* unions; *see also* aristocracy and elites
Clint, George 87*f*
Cole, Laurence 183–4
Colley, Linda 46, 62–3, 182, 206, 256–7, 288, 337–8, 343
Collins, Michael 188–9
colonialism 11–12, 15, 58–9, 121–2; *see also* empires
composite monarchy *see under* monarchy
Congress of Vienna (1815) 23, 27–8
Connolly, James 65, 67–8
Conrad von Hötzendorf, Franz, Graf 154–6, 337–8
Conservatism and Conservative party 47, 51–3, 81–3, 85

Constantine II, King of Scotland 41
Constitution Reform Group 250
Conway, Derwent *see* Inglis, H. D.
Conway, Martin 324
Cooke, Edward 19–21, 25, 28–9, 38*f*
Cornwall, Mark 157–8
Coupland, Sir Reginald 1, 55, 70–3, 123–4, 129
Cragoe, Matthew 175
Craig, Sir James Henry 125
Crawford, William Sharman 257, 266
Creditanstalt (bank) 221–2
Crimean war 142, 222
Croats and Croatia 145–8, 153, 236–7, 250, 259–60, 283
Cromwell, Oliver 62, 124–5
Cromwell, Thomas (1st Earl of Essex) 68–9
Curtis, Lionel 252, 260–1
Cymru Fydd (Young Wales) 55, 60–2, 79
Czechs and Czechoslovakia 150–1, 157–8, 160, 298–300, 345
    Czech Brigade 155–6
    and Fundamental Articles (1871) 149–50
    national monuments 197–8, 299
    and Russian army 340–1
Czörnig, Karl Freiherr von 238–9

Daa, Ludvig Kristensen 315
Dalhousie, George Ramsay 9th Earl of 125
Dalrymple, James *see* Stair, Viscount
Dance, George 34*f*
Davidson, Ruth (Baroness) 53
Davidson, Peter 171
Davies, Norman 294–7
Davis, Thomas 60
Deák, Ferenc 145, 311–12
Deák, István 177–8, 183–4, 342
Deane, Seamus 15
Denmark
    composite monarchy 5
    League of Armed Neutrality 24
    and Scandinavianism 314–15, 332
    and Schleswig-Holstein 315, 333
    union with Norway (1661) 102
    union with Sweden and Norway (1397) 102
Dewar, Donald 52
Diamond, Jared 295
Dicey, A. V. 7, 12–13, 144, 247, 254–6, 259–60, 263–6, 268, 287, 291*f*, 363–4
Dilke, Sir Charles 253–4
Dorchester, Lord *see* Carleton, Sir Guy
Douglas, Ludvig, Count 117–18
Douglas-Home, Alec (Baron Home of the Hirsel and 14th Earl of Home) 52–3
Dual Monarchy *see* Austria-Hungary

Dufferin, Frederick Hamilton-Temple-Blackwood, 1st Earl (later 1st Marquess) of 112, 122, 276–7
Dundas, Henry *see* Melville, Viscount
Durham, John Lambton, 1st Earl of 122, 125, 129–31, 270, 275, 363
Dutch Reformed Church 72–3, 97, 194, 202–3
Dutch republic 92–3
Duyse, Prudens van 302

Eastwood, David 1
economy
    banking and currency 44–5, 105, 141–2, 211, 219–22, 300
    and common language 223
    taxation and debt 95, 98, 106, 137, 219–20, 224–7, 260, 301–2, 307–8, 352
    trade and tariffs 219–21, 224, 232
    and unions 187, 219–20, 223–4, 226–8, 232–3, 354–5
Edward VII, King of the United Kingdom 48–9, 74–5, 171–2, 327–8
Edward VIII, King of the United Kingdom 75
Edwards, H. J. W. 78–9
Edwards, Huw 228–9
Edwards, Sir Owen William Morgan 57
Eighty Club 33
Elgin, James Bruce, 8th Earl of 132–3, 276–7
Elizabeth II, Queen of the United Kingdom 53–4, 169–70, 199, 244*f*, 327–8
Elliot, Walter 42, 85
Elliott, Sir John 8, 56–7, 248, 349
Ellis, Thomas Edward 57, 60–2, 73–4, 79–81
Élesd massacre (1904) 242–3
empires 4, 10–11, 15, 56, 234;
    see also colonialism
England
    and Anglicanism 204
    attitudes towards Irish 238
    attitudes towards Scots 238
    and Brexit 329, 357–8
    and British army 183
    as colonizer 41–2, 58–9
    as composite monarchy 5, 9–10, 42–3
    formation of kingdom 41
    migration and settlement 58–9
    unions a response to external threats 19, 59–60, 180–1, 301
    union with Scotland (1707) 14, 20–1, 42–3, 181, 286–7
    union with Wales 40, 56–7
Eötvös, József 145
European Union (EU) 17–18, 53, 219, 333
Evans, R. J. W. (Robert) 55–6, 71–3, 81

federalism 9–10, 149–50, 285–8
    Austria-Hungary 12–13, 144–5, 149–50, 157, 266, 279–86, 361–2
    Canada 255, 268–79, 361–2
    historiography 247–50
    UK 247, 250–68, 285–7, 361–2
    and unions 3, 12–13, 247, 285, 288, 361–2
    USA 12, 248–9, 256, 361–2
Fellner and Helmer (architects) 217
Ferdinand I, Emperor of Austria 167
Ferdinand II, Emperor of Austria 195–6
Ferenc II Rákóczi, Prince of Transylvania 196
Ferguson, Adam 211
Finland, Grand Duchy of 2, 6, 24–5
    bureaucracy 186–7
    comparison with Ireland 194–5
    creation of (1809) 303
    dissolution (1917) 43–4
    and First World War 341
    imperial architecture 218
    as model for the UK 31–2
    and religion 194–5, 204
    and russification 202
First World War 337–48
    and Austria-Hungary 153–6, 170, 181–2, 335–7, 339–43, 347, 357
    and conscription 184–5
    and Russia 340–1
    and Sweden-Norway 331
    and UK 47–9, 77, 331, 334–5, 338–41, 343–5, 357
    and unions 300, 334–5, 339
    and USA 342
Fischer, Jacques 31–2
Fischof, Adolf 185–6, 192, 362
Fisher, Warren 187–8
FitzAlan, Edmund FitzAlan-Howard, 1st Viscount 278
Fitzgerald and Vesey, William Vesey Fitzgerald, 2nd Lord 27
Fitzpatrick, David 325
Fitzwilliam, William Fitzwilliam, 4th Earl 126
France 164
    centralized nation state as French export 6, 350
    and Dutch republic, occupation of 93–4
    as threat to Britain 19–21, 23, 25–6, 28–9, 93, 104–5, 334
Francis II, Holy Roman Emperor (Francis I, Emperor of Austria) 136–8, 303
Franck, Thomas 295–6
Frank, Josip 224
Franz Ferdinand, Archduke 160, 169–70, 280–2

Franz Joseph I, Emperor of Austria 162*f*, 167–9, 174, 327–8, 337, 353–4
  and aristocracy 176–7
  and Ausgleich 143–4, 168–9, 281–2
  as binding agent 164, 167–9
  and foreign affairs 142
  and Fundamental Articles 281
  golden jubilee (1898) 169, 200
  and Hungary, dislike for 169–70
  and Kremsier constitution 281
  piety 199–200
  portraits 168, 217
  and Social Democrats 230–1
  suspension of February Patent 143
Franzos, Karl 304
Frederick III, King of Denmark and Norway 102
Free Imperial Knights of the Holy Roman Empire 174–5
Freeman, E. A. 7, 255, 262–3, 268, 349
Friedjung, Heinrich 243
Friel, Brian 238–9
Frost, Robert 248

Galligan, Brian 249, 295–6
Galt, Alexander 270
Garibaldi, Giuseppe 215
Gayda, Virginio 185–6
Geer, Louis de 116–17
George III, King of the United Kingdom 123, 170–1
George IV, King of the United Kingdom 113, 170–1
George V, King of the United Kingdom 48–9, 171–2, 245*f*, 336
George VI, King of the United Kingdom 245*f*
Gérard, François 88*f*
Germany 5–6, 61–2, 255–6
Gerwarth, Robert 335, 344–6
Geyl, Pieter 96–7
Gibbons, Luke 15
Gillespie, Paul 250
Gladstone, William Ewart 32–3, 86, 349–50, 363–5
  and Austria-Hungary 144, 241–2, 259–60, 271–2
  and Canada 32, 259–60, 277
  and Church of Ireland 46–7
  and federalism 12–13
  on home rule 1, 33, 47, 181–2
  and Sweden-Norway 30–3, 241–2
Goschen, George (1st Viscount Goschen) 225–6, 307–8
Gosford, Archibald Acheson, 2nd Earl of 127–8
Gourlay, Robert 270

Gove, Michael 52–3
Grant, Ulysses S. 273
Granville, Granville Leveson-Gower, 2nd Earl 31
Grey, Charles Grey, 2nd Earl 25
Griffith, Arthur 136, 144
Griffith, Gwilym 62, 79–80
Grönberg, Alexander 31–2
Gustavus Vasa, King of Sweden 102

Haakon VII, King of Norway 114–15, 119
Habsburg, Otto von 349–51
Habsburg dynasty 113, 166–70
  and Catholicism 137, 167–9, 174–5, 196, 199–200
  and dynastic loyalty 16, 61, 75, 167
  and Netherlands 90–2
  Pragmatic Sanction (1713) 136
  see also Austria-Hungary (Dual Monarchy)
Hagerup, Francis 119
Hain, Peter 250
Hamilton, Alexander 123, 252
Hamilton-Temple-Blackwood, Frederick *see* Dufferin, 1st Earl (later 1st Marquess) of
Hanover, House of 43–4, 75, 170–1, 178–9
Hanover, Kingdom of 5, 10, 42–3, 329
Harcourt, William 316
Hardie, Keir 66
Harrison, Brian 65–6
Harvie, Christopher 55
Haslinger, Peter 340
Headlam, Maurice 187–8
Healy, Maureen 344
Healy, T. M. 47
Heath, Edward 52–3
Hechter, Michael 12, 15, 41–2
Hegel, Georg Wilhelm Friedrich 13
Helsinki
  Church of St Nicholas 195
  imperial monuments 218
Henry VII, King of England 73–4
Henry VIII, King of England and Ireland 5, 57
Hirschhausen, Ulrike von 10–11, 192
Hjärne, Harald 118, 318–19
Hlinka, Andrej 242–3
Hodges, Charles Howard 89*f*
Hoffmann, Stefan Ludwig 213
Hohenwart, Karl, Graf von 149–50, 281
Home Government Association (Ireland) 258–9
home rule *see under* United Kingdom of Great Britain and Ireland
Hoppen, K. Theodore 70–1, 140–1, 325
Hoppner, John 87*f*
Hoyos, Alexander, Graf von 190

INDEX 427

Hughes, Brian 325–6
Hume, Joseph 127
Hume Brown, Peter 363–4
Hus, Jan 197–8, 299

Ibsen, Sigurd 119
Imperial Federation League 253–4
India, and British rule 11
Inglis, H. D. (Derwent Conway) 112
Ireland 16
  and agrarian insurgency 69–70
  Anglo-Irish Treaty (1921) 14, 50–1, 181–2, 298, 319
  aristocracy and elites 44–5, 47, 65, 68–70, 74, 175, 178–9, 234–5
  attitudes towards English 238
  and British army 49–50, 75–7, 183, 185
  Bureau of Military History 16, 325
  bureaucracy 188–90
  Catholic emancipation 22–3, 46–7, 196–7
  Catholicism 46–7, 49, 54, 71–3, 79, 122–3, 133–4, 193, 197, 204, 234–5, 277–8, 350–1
  Church of Ireland 46–7, 69–70, 197
  and civil society 212–13, 217–18
  and coercion acts 240–1
  and colonialism 11, 15, 41–2, 58–9
  comparison with Austria-Hungary 138, 140–2, 149
  comparison with Croats 236–7
  comparison with Bosnia 201–2
  comparison with Canada 122–4, 126, 128–30, 133–4, 277–8
  comparison with Finland 194–5
  comparison with the Netherlands 22–3, 106
  comparison with Norway 103
  comparison with Sweden-Norway 111, 116–17, 120–1
  comparison with Wales 60
  composite monarchy 5, 9–10
  Criminal Law and Procedure (Ireland) Act (1887) 240–1
  Curragh incident (March 1914) 49–50
  currency 300
  as Dominion 252–3
  Easter Rising (April 1916) 47–8, 244, 337, 340–1, 347
  economic effects of union 78–9, 106, 141–2, 225–6, 308
  education, expansion of 141–2
  and emigration 331–2
  and empire 78–80
  and English language 188–9, 223
  and evangelicalism 79
  and exceptionalism 48, 342
  and federalism 254–61, 266–7, 285–6
  and First World War 47–9, 331, 334–5, 341, 347
  and fiscal union 219–20
  Great Famine 59–60, 69, 106, 225–6, 304–5, 354–5
  home rule 1, 9–10, 16–17, 29–31, 39, 47–50, 260, 286, 309, 316, 319, 336
  industrial unrest 65
  and ethnic characterization and stereotypes 60, 237–8
  Irish Church Act (1869) 46–7, 239, 241–2
  Irish language revival 103
  and Labour party 67–8
  land reform and land purchase 69–70, 179, 239–42
  and Liberalism 81
  and Manchester Martyrs 241–2
  and monarchy 171–2, 217
  and monument building 299
  and nationalism 48–51, 55, 60, 63, 65, 77–8, 103, 197, 336, 350–1
  police and military 300
  and Presbyterianism 128
  and Protestant ascendancy 45, 47, 54, 63, 126, 133–4, 140–1, 212, 234–5
  and Protestantism 58, 69, 84, 197, 350–1
  Royal Irish Constabulary 47–8, 276–7
  rural communities and farmers 60, 69–70, 141, 239–40, 309
  and southern Netherlands, connections with 92
  Tithe Rent Charge Act (1838) 46–7, 69–70
  and Ulster 269
  and Ulster unionists 50, 78–9, 207, 347
  and union (1801) 19–21, 43–5, 103, 124–5, 129, 181–2, 219, 301, 352
  and union, break with 298, 345
  and union, influence in 309
  and unionism 49, 83, 207, 226, 232–3, 316, 350–1, 356–7
  union challenged 43–4, 47–51, 257
  union as sometimes flexible 134
  uprising (1798) 19, 103–4, 128–9
  and violence 241–2, 361
Irish Citizen Army 65
Irish Free State 160–1, 297, 300, 343–6
Irish National Land League 50
Irish Ordnance Survey 238–9
Irish Reform Association 260–1
Irish Republican Army (IRA) 50–1, 325–6, 346
Irish Republican Brotherhood 43–4, 50
Irish Transport and General Workers' Union 65
Irish Volunteers 49–50

Irish War of Independence 337
Italy
   enlarged after the fall of Austria-Hungary 160, 345
   and First World War 155
   formation of 152–3

Jansson, Torkel 214
Jászi, Oszkár 3, 223, 290f, 314
   on aristocracy and elites 177, 227
   on Ausgleich 145–6, 334
   on Austria-Hungary as failure 164, 284, 297–8, 317, 321
   on Austria-Hungary as model for future unions 306, 364
   on bureaucracy 185–6
   on Catholic Church 192
   on centripetal and centrifugal forces 18–19, 48–9, 135, 164–5, 174, 249, 352
   on civic education 297–8, 312–13
   on Franz Joseph 167
   on repression 146
   on social cohesion 304
   on 'well-tempered dissatisfaction' 236
Jay, John 256
Jellinek, Georg 8, 289f
João VI (John VI), King of Portugal 27–8, 175–6
John, E. T. 62, 261, 264–5
John Paul II, Pope 200, 349
Johnson, Andrew 273
Johnson, Boris 86, 250
Johnston, Thomas (Tom) 52
Joseph II, Holy Roman Emperor 136–8, 166–7, 303
   and Austrian Netherlands 92–3, 98–100
   bureaucracy 187–8
   creation of peers 176
   monuments to 197–8, 217
   religious toleration 196–7
Joyce, James 199
Judson, Pieter 15–16, 18, 174, 183–4, 298, 306, 323–5, 335–6, 342

Kaiser, Wolfram 192
Karl I, Emperor of Austria 156–8, 162f, 163f, 168–9, 200, 245f, 246f, 282, 327–8
Kendle, John 219, 262–4, 308–9
Kerr, Philip see Lothian, Marquess of
Khuen-Héderváry, Károly, Count 146–8, 199–200, 242
King, Jeremy 323–4
Kjéllen, Rudolf 118, 305, 318–19
Koenigsberger, H. G. 8
Koerber, Ernest von 149, 189–90, 207–8, 236, 242

Kohr, Leopold 294–5
Kossuth, Lajos 280
Krueger, Rita 175
Kumar, Krishan 41–2, 311–12
Kuyper, Abraham 72–3

Labilliere, Francis de 253–4
Labour party 51–2, 66–8, 85, 228–31, 363
LaFontaine, Sir Louis-Hippolyte 127, 132–3, 172–3
Lagerheim, Alfred 119
Laing, Samuel 25, 105, 109, 112–13, 199, 214–15, 327
Lalor, James Lintan 239–40
Lambton, John George see Durham, 1st Earl of
Larkin, James 67–8
Latham, R. G. 112–13
Leerssen, Joep 94, 101, 302
Leonhard, Jörn 10–11, 192
Liberalism 80–1
Liberal Unionism 81–2
Lincoln, Abraham 273
Lindgren, Raymond 105–6, 109–10
Lisgar, John Young, 1st Lord 276–7
Liverpool, Robert Banks Jenkinson, 2nd Earl of 25
Livesey, James 45, 211
Lloyd George, David (1st Earl Lloyd George) 63–4, 77, 79
Lodge, Richard 315–16
Londonderry, 2nd Marquess of see Castlereagh, Viscount
Londonderry, 3rd Marquess of see Stewart, Charles
London Protocol (1814) 23
Lorne, Lord, John Campbell (later 9th Duke of Argyll) 32, 276–7
Lothian, Philip Kerr, 11th Marquess of 253, 261
Louis Bonaparte, King of Holland 93
Lutheranism 197, 200–1, 204
Luxembourg, Grand Duchy of 5

McCabe, James 325–6
MacCannell, Daniel 171
McCrone, David 182, 337–8
Macdonald, Sir John A. 122, 269–72, 274–5
Macdonald, John Sandfield 269–70
MacDonald, Ramsay 66
McGee, Thomas D'Arcy 276
Mackenzie, William Lyon 128–9
McKibbin, Ross 65–6
Mackillop, Andrew 43
McLeod, Hugh 192
Macmillan, Harold (1st Earl of Stockton) 52–3
Manela, Erez 344–5

Manners-Sutton, Sir John (later 3rd Viscount Canterbury) 272
Mannix, Daniel, Monsignor (later Archbishop) 245*f*
Margutti, Albert Freiherr von 168–9
Maria Theresa, Holy Roman Empress 136–7, 176
Marr, Andrew 250
Marteel, Stefaan 95
Mary, Queen of the United Kingdom 245*f*
Masaryk, Tomáš 194–5, 197–8, 355
Maximilian I, Holy Roman Emperor 91–2
Maximilian, Emperor of Mexico 273
May, Theresa 250
Meade, Richard *see* Clanwilliam, 3rd Earl of
Méan, François Antoine de, Archbishop 99–100
Mechelin, Leo 194–5
Melding, David 81–3, 85–6, 250
Meltzer, Fredrik 327
Melville, Henry Dundas, 1st Viscount 234
Metternich, Klemens, Prinz von 138–9
Michalsen, Dag 109, 111
Michelsen, Christian 119, 330–1
Miliband, Ed 250
Mitchell, William 255, 258, 264–5
Mitchelstown massacre (1887) 241–2
monarchy 166–74
   and aristocracy 174–5, 177–9
   and civil society 217
   and commemorative events 115, 162*f*, 169–71, 200, 353–4
   composite 5, 13–14, 43, 305, 327–8
   and dynastic loyalty 75, 112–13, 138, 167, 169, 199–200, 353, 361
   and established church 199–200, 205
   and nomenclature 327–8
   as religious mediators 195
   and royal tours 112–13
   unifying role 166–8, 174, 205, 361
Monck, Charles Monck, 4th Viscount 122, 276–7
Morgan, K. O. (Lord Morgan) 55, 69
Morier, John Philip 26–7
Morris, R. J. 210
Morton, Graeme 212
Moyard, Major 101
Muir, Edwin 71–3
Mulgrave, George Phipps, Lord (later 2nd Marquess of Normanby) 272
Munch, Peter Andreas 315
Murray, John 265–6
Musil, Robert 311–12

Nairn, Tom 311–12
Nansen, Fridtjof 104, 113, 115–16, 119, 216, 220
Napoleon I, Emperor of the French 23, 25

nationalism 15–16, 18, 60
   and economic prosperity 227–8
   and religion 197
   supranationalism 164
   and unions 101–3, 320, 328, 356
National Association of the Vindication of Scottish Rights 212
National Service League 184–5
Nederlandsche Handel-Maatschappij (NHM)/ Netherlands Trading Company 95–6, 100
Nelson, Fraser 52–3
Nelson, Robert 129
Nemes, Robert 197
Newcastle, Henry Pelham-Clinton, 5th Duke of 272
Nicholas I, Tsar of Russia 195
Nicholas II, Tsar of Russia 202
Nicholson, Ivor 66–7
Nielsen, Yngvar 118
Northern Ireland 13, 39, 261–2, 311–12, 345
   and Brexit 329
   and Catholic population 160–1, 298–9
   Civil Authorities (Special Powers) Act (1922) 240–1
   and devolved parliament (1921–72) 52
   and power-sharing 133
   and separatist republicanism 16–17
Norway
   and aristocracy 179–80
   army 182–3
   attitudes towards Swedes 238
   British naval blockade (1807–14) 102–3
   and civil society 214, 219
   comparison with Ireland 103
   composite monarchy 5, 14
   home rule 1
   League of Armed Neutrality 24
   and monarchy 112–15
   and monuments 218
   and nationalism 110
   national revival 102–3
   and Scandinavianism 332
   and unionism 108, 115–16
   union symbolism 216
   union with Denmark 102
   union with Denmark and Sweden 102
   union with Sweden, opposition to 25–7

O'Brien, Peter (1st Lord O'Brien of Kilfenora) 240–1
O'Brien, William 47, 65, 67–8, 240–1, 299
O'Callaghan, Edmund Bailey 127–30
O'Connell, Daniel 171–2, 299
   and Canada 127, 131, 277–8
   and English language 223

O'Connell, Daniel (*cont.*)
  and federalism 254-5, 258
  and land reform 69-70
  on Sweden-Norway 30
  and Westminster parliament 206-7
O Griffith, Gwilyn 261
Okey, Robin 55-6, 187-8, 201-2, 313
Oliver, F. S. 9-10, 251-5, 260-1, 267, 292*f*, 311, 361-2
O'Malley, Thaddeus 30, 254-7, 259
Orange, House of 42, 91, 94, 173, 194
Orange Order 121-2, 128, 278
Orthodox Church 195, 202, 204
Oscar I, King of Sweden and of Norway 114, 216, 327
Oscar II, King of Sweden and of Norway 112-14, 117-18, 231, 330-1
Ó Siochrú, Micheál 43
Ottoman empire 153, 192

Paelinck, Joseph 35*f*
Paine, Thomas 206, 256-7
Paisley, Ian (Lord Bannside) 349-51
Palacký, František 139, 197, 280, 284-5
Papineau, Louis-Joseph 126-8
parliament 205-10
  as corrupt 208-9
  subverting unions 207-9
  threatened by military 209
  uniting unions 206-7, 209
Parnell, Charles Stewart 12-13, 30, 65, 78, 206-7, 299, 309
Patterson, Arthur 31
Pearse, Pádraig 336
Philip II, King of Spain, Portugal, Naples and Sicily 91-2
Phillips, Thomas 76-7
Phipps, George *see* Mulgrave, Lord
Pigott, Richard 243
Pirenne, Henri 100
Pitt, William 19-21, 28, 87*f*, 124-5, 130-1, 350
Plaid Cymru 83, 228-9, 294-5
Pocock, J. G. A. 17
Popovici, Aurel 280-1, 284-5
Porter, Andrew 192
Porter, John Grey Vesey 257-8
Portugal 27-8; *see also* United Kingdom of Portugal, Brazil, and the Algarves
Presbyterianism 54, 65-6, 69, 71-3, 85, 128, 204
Princip, Gavrilo 153
Protestantism
  Austria-Hungary 196-8
  Canada 124
  Finland 194-5
  Ireland 350-1
  Netherlands 22, 194, 202-4
  Sweden-Norway 193-4
  UK 22-3, 58, 62-3, 69, 71-3, 79, 84-5, 193, 195-7, 199, 204, 304, 355
  See also Calvinism; Lutheranism; nonconformism; Presbyterianism

Quebec 123-4, 193, 195, 203, 253, 274-5, 277-8, 287
Quebec Act (1774) 123, 125-6, 129-30, 172-3, 193

railways 96, 107-9, 141-2, 146, 186, 201-2, 221-2, 271, 274-5
Ramsay, George *see* Dalhousie, 9th Earl of
Redlich, Josef 136, 152-3, 189, 304
Redmond, John 47, 49, 60-1, 65, 77-8, 144, 171-2, 206-7, 217, 277-8, 333, 361
Rees, William 56, 73-4
Renner, Karl 151-2, 229-30, 282
Rhodes, Cecil 78
rifle club movement 215
Roberts, Frederick Roberts, 1st Earl 184-5
Robinson, James 294-5
Robinson, John Beverley 125
Roebuck, J. A. 127, 270
Romania 160
Ross, William (Willie) 52
Rozenblit, Marsha 323-5
Rudolf, Crown Prince 238-9
Rudolf of Habsburg 199-200
Russell, Sir Charles (1st Lord Russell of Killowen) 81
Russell, Lord John (1st Earl Russell) 126-7
Russia 25-6
  and Finland 31-2, 181-2, 194-5, 202
  and First World War 340-1
  Napoleon's invasion of 25
  October Revolution (1917) 155
  Sweden, threat to 24-5, 28-9

Salisbury, Robert Gascoyne-Cecil, 3rd Marquess of 179, 317-18
Salisbury, Robert Gascoyne-Cecil, 7th Marquess of 250
Salmond, Alex 50-1, 227-8
Saunderson, Edward 47
Scandinavianism 108, 215, 314-15, 332, 353
Schäffle, Albert 149-50
Schimmelpenninck, Rutger Jan 93
Schönborn, Franziskus, Graf von, Cardinal Archbishop 200
Schönerer, Georg Ritter von 152-3, 197

Schwarzenberg, Felix von, Prince 139–40, 281
Scotland
   aristocracy and elites 44–5, 68–9, 179, 234
   and Brexit 329
   and British army 52–4, 75–7, 183
   bureaucracy 190
   and Catholicism 69
   Church of Scotland (Kirk) 54
   and civil society 211–12, 218
   comparison with Canada 131–2
   composite monarchy 5, 9–10, 42
   coronation tour of George IV (1822) 113, 171
   Crofters' Holdings Act (1886) 46, 69–70
   Darien colony 226
   and devolution 13, 52
   and Dutch republic, connections with 92
   economic effects of union 51, 78–9, 106, 226–7, 307–8, 352, 354–5
   and empire 78
   and ethnic characterization and stereotypes 60, 237–8
   and federalism 286
   and fiscal union 219–20
   formation of kingdom 41
   home rule 16–17, 29, 39, 46, 259–60, 286, 309
   and Labour party 52, 66–8, 85
   as model for Canada 123, 130–1, 275
   and monarchy 53–4, 171, 217
   and nationalism 50–1, 54–5, 63, 73, 227–8
   political influence 43, 52–3, 308
   and Presbyterianism 54, 65–6, 69, 71–3, 85, 204
   and Protestantism 62–3, 69, 72–3
   Royal Regiment of Scotland 53–4
   and rural communities 46, 69
   and Scottish Office (1885) 46, 186–7
   union (1707) 14, 20–1, 42–4, 54, 57–8, 124–5, 181, 219, 286–7, 301, 352
   union challenged 51–3
   and unionism 52–3
   and unionist nationalism/nationalist unionism 44, 63, 212
Scott, Sir Walter 61, 91–2, 94, 171, 173, 302
Scottish Home Rule Association 255, 258, 264–5
Scottish National Party (SNP) 16–17, 46, 53–4
security *see under* unions
Seely, Sir John 253–4
Selborne, William Palmer, 2nd Earl of 260–1
Serbs and Serbia 146–8, 153–4, 157–8, 160, 227
Seton-Watson, Christopher 196, 313–14
Seton-Watson, Hugh 196, 313–14
Seton-Watson, R. W. 7, 136, 144–5, 153, 208–9, 224, 236–7, 243, 264–5, 282–4, 293*f*, 321, 326–7, 363–4

Seward, William Henry 272–3
Sewell, Jonathan 125, 270
Simms, Brendan 329
Sinn Féin 283–4, 337, 346
Sked, Alan 153–4, 335–6
Smith, Abram 129
Smith, F. E. (1st Earl of Birkenhead) 86, 316
Smith, Sir Sidney 28
Smith, William 125, 270
Smythe, Percy *see* Strangford, Viscount
socialism 228–31; *see also* Labour party
Société Générale 100
South Africa 75–6, 79–80, 252, 255 *see also* South African War; Union of South Africa
South African War (second Boer War) 75–6, 79, 184–5, 317–18, 331
southern Netherlands 92, 94, 137
Southey, Robert 95, 173
Sozialdemokratische Arbeiterpartei Österreichs (Social Democratic (Workers') Party of Austria) 229–31
Spalding, Thomas 253–4
Springer, Rudolf *see* Renner, Karl
Stair, James Dalrymple, 1st Viscount 44
Stang, Frederik 115
Steed, Henry Wickham 144–5, 164–5, 167, 182, 189, 195–6, 207–8, 242, 313, 321, 349, 359–60
Steen, Johannes 116–18
Stewart, Charles (3rd Marquess of Londonderry) 19–21, 37*f*
Stewart, Robert *see* Castlereagh, Viscount
Strachan, Hew 339–40
Strangford, Percy Smythe, 6th Viscount 19–20, 22, 27–8, 36*f*
Street, C. J. C. 242–3
Stuart, Charles Edward ('Bonnie Prince Charlie'; 'the Young Pretender') 171
Stuart, Henry, Cardinal York 171
Stuart, James Francis Edward ('the Old Pretender') 171
Supilo, Frano 136
Sverdrup, Johan 231
Sweden
   aristocracy 111, 114, 176, 179–80, 214–15
   attitudes towards Norwegians 238
   civil society 214–15
   composite monarchy 5, 14
   conflict with Russia 24–5
   and nationalism 108–9, 118
   rifle club movement 215
   union with Denmark and Norway (1397) 102
   union with Norway, disinvestment in 318–19
Switzerland 249, 255–6
symbolism, union *see under* unions

Taaffe, Eduard, Graf von 148–9, 222, 236
Taché, Sir Étienne-Pascal 172–3, 274
Talbot, Lord Edmund *see* FitzAlan, Viscount
Tarlton, Charles 249, 295–6
taxation and debt *see under* economy
Tennent, James Emerson 90–1, 97–8
Thatcher, Margaret (Baroness) 51–3
Thököly, Imre, Prince of Upper Hungary and of Transylvania 196
Thomas, D. A. 64
Thomas, David 66–7
Thornton, Edward 27
Tisza, István, Count 168–9, 209
Tisza, Kálmán 145
Tocqueville, Comte de 157
Tone, Wolfe 78
Townshend, George, 3rd Viscount (later 1st Marquess) 234–5
trade and tariffs *see under* economy
Treaty of Chaumont (1814) 23
Treaty of Karlstad (1905) 107
Treaty of Kiel (1814) 25, 102
Treaty of Malmö (1524) 102
Treaty of Paris (1814) 23, 122–3
Treaty of St Germain (1919) 345–6
Treaty of Stockholm (1813) 25–6
Treaty of Tilsit (1807) 24–5
Treaty of Versailles (1919) 345–6
Trench, Richard Le Poer *see* Clancarty, 2nd Earl of
Trevelyan, G.M. 352
Tucker, Josiah 20–1
Tudor dynasty 73–4
Tweedsmuir, John Buchan, 1st Lord 276–7

Ulster Provisional Government 207
Ulster unionists 50, 78–9, 207, 347
Ulster Volunteer Force 207
Ulster Volunteers 49–50
unions
  age of 2, 6, 28
  as 'antique survivals' 305
  asymmetrical 101, 103–4, 233–4, 306–10, 355–6
  as British export 6–7, 19–29, 122, 129–30, 350, 363
  and centralization 189–90, 296
  and class 228–33
  and commemoration 353–4
  as common in Europe 56
  and communication systems, importance of 107
  and composite monarchies 5, 13–14
  constructive unionism 233, 239, 241–2
  created by force 181–2
  and differences 326–7
  divide and rule strategy 234–9
  and early modern state formation 43
  and economy 187, 219–20, 223–4, 226–8, 232–3, 354–5
  and emigration and diasporas 331–2
  and empires 4, 11, 15, 234
  and external threats 19, 59–60, 180–2, 272–3, 301, 351
  and failure 294–7, 351
  and federalism 3, 12–13, 247, 285, 288, 361–2
  and flexibility/malleability 3, 10, 12–14, 239, 359–60
  and foreign affairs 328–34
  and irredenta 332
  and *Kulturpessimismus* 311, 316–17
  and longevity 14–19, 351
  and modernity 306
  and nationalism 101–3, 320, 328, 356
  and reform 239–42
  and reverse asymmetry ('tyranny of the weak') 309–10
  and security 180–5
  and socialism 228–31
  and successor states 159–61
  and supranational identity 174, 185, 356
  and supranational security 181–2
  supranational unions 306, 333, 361
  symmetrical 295–6
  types of union 56–7
  and union symbolism 215–16, 327–8
  and unionism 215, 356–7
  and violence and repression 196–7, 240–4
  and 'vision thing', lacking 301, 351, 353
  and war 181–2, 191–2, 337–9, 343, 354, 357
Union of South Africa 252, 298, 336; *see also* South Africa; South African War
United Empire Loyalists 122–3
United Irishmen, Society of 126
United Kingdom of Denmark-Norway 255–6
United Kingdom of Great Britain and Ireland (1801–1922; UK) 2, 4–5, 10, 39
  Anglo-Irish Treaty (1921) 14, 50–1, 181–2, 298, 319, 345
  aristocracy and elites 44–5, 68–9, 74, 174–6, 178–9, 228–9, 363
  army *see* British army
  Austria-Hungary as model 7, 29–32, 144, 146–8
  and British history 17
  Britishness and national identity 16, 61–2, 164, 303–4, 311–12, 320, 353
  bureaucracy 186–90

Canada as model 29–32, 258–9, 277
and cartography 238–9
and Catholic emancipation 22–3
and Catholicism 69, 123, 193, 204
Church of England and Ireland 193, 198
Church of Scotland 193
and civil society 211–13, 218
and coercion acts 240–1
and colonialism 11, 15
comparison with Austria-Hungary 135–6, 138, 140–1
as composite monarchy 43, 305
and Conservative party (Tories) 47, 51–3, 81–3, 85
and constitution, unwritten 206
creation of (1800–1) 19–21, 28–9, 44–5, 103–5, 181–2, 198
Defence of the Realm Act (1914) 47–8, 340
and devolution 13, 16–17, 52
dissolution (1921–2) 47–8, 159–61, 334–5, 344–5
economic basis of union 219, 231–2, 352
economic effects of union 51, 58–9, 83, 106, 223, 225–7
as empire 11, 49, 78–80, 84
and English language 223
ethnic, religious, and linguistic diversity 135
and ethnic characterization and stereotypes 60, 237–8
and failure 47–8, 298
and federalism 247, 250–68, 285–7, 361–2
and First World War 47–9, 77, 155–6, 331, 334–5, 338–41, 343–5, 357
as fiscal union 219–20, 307–8
and foreign policy 329, 331
and home rule 1, 7, 9–10, 29, 33, 46–7, 49, 250, 259–62, 319
industrial unrest 64–5
influence of European models 29–33
Jacobite revolts 43–4
and *Kulturpessimismus* 317–18
and Labour party 51–2, 66–8, 85, 228–31, 363
and land ownership 47, 50, 60, 68–71, 84, 179
middle-classes aligned with union 64
and military oppression 76–7
as model for Austria-Hungary 136
and monarchy 73–5, 113, 166, 170–3, 199, 361
and nationalism 13, 15–17, 39
and parliament 50, 206–7, 209
as parliamentary union 43, 50
and postal addresses 326–7
and Protestantism 22–3, 58, 62–3, 71–3, 79, 84–5, 193, 195–7, 199, 204, 304, 355

as 'relic of earlier age' 13–15
and religion 54, 71–3, 198
and religion, evangelical 79
ruling classes aligned with union 44–5, 68
and rural communities 46, 60, 69–71, 84, 141, 239–40, 309
and supranational identity 324–5, 356
and supranational loyalism 16, 138
Sweden-Norway as model 29–33, 109, 255–6
as trade and customs union 219–20
union as asymmetrical 103–4, 307–9
union as British export 6–7, 19–29, 122, 129–30, 350, 363
union as 'corrupt' 198, 301, 352
union as flexible 45–7, 309–10, 359
union as incomplete 44–6
union as lacking vision 353
union providing security 19–21, 39, 59–60, 181–2, 358
and unionism 13, 51–3, 83, 207, 232–3, 315–16, 320
and unionism, constructive 239
union symbolism 215–16
US as model 259
working-class alignment with union 65–6, 228–9
see also England; Ireland; Scotland; Wales
United Kingdom of Great Britain and Northern Ireland (1922–) 13, 16–17, 52–3, 160–1, 345, 359–60
Austria-Hungary as model 148
and Brexit 53, 181–2, 219, 250, 267, 288, 319–20, 329, 333, 357–8, 360, 364
and Conservative party 53, 83
Good Friday Agreement (1998) 13, 359–60
Scotland Act (1978) 46–7
union providing security 181
United Kingdom of the Netherlands 2, 4, 6, 21, 90–102, 255–6
and aristocracy 179–80
and *arithmétique hollandaise* 95, 198–9, 301–2, 352
and army 185
as asymmetric union 94–5, 98, 101–4, 224–5
as bulwark against France 28–9, 93–4, 104–5
and Calvinism 97, 201–3
and Catholicism 97–100, 194, 201–4
comparison with Canada 95
comparison with Ireland 22–3, 106
as composite monarchy 5, 166
creation of (1814–15) 22–4, 90–1, 95, 103, 198–9, 301–2
dissolution (1830–31) 43–4, 98–101, 159–60, 297

United Kingdom of the Netherlands (*cont.*)
   and Dutch language 96–8
   and Dutch Reformed church 194, 202–3
   economic effects of union 95–6, 100, 224–5, 352
   infrastructure projects 96
   and monarchy 100–1, 173
   and nationalism 100
   and parliament 4–5
   and Protestantism 22, 194, 202–4
   religion and lack of state church 97–100, 194, 201–3
   and vision, lack of 100–1
United Kingdom of Portugal, Brazil, and the Algarves 2, 6, 27
   and aristocracy 175–6
   and Cortes 205–6, 209
   creation of (1815) 27–8, 198–9, 303
   dissolution (1822) 43–4, 297
   and trade relations 221
United Kingdoms of Sweden-Norway 2, 4–6, 14, 102–21
   and aristocracy 111, 114, 176, 179–80
   as asymmetrical union 103–4
   Bodø affair (1818–21) 116
   as bulwark against France 28–9, 104–5
   as bulwark against Russia 28–9, 104–5, 181–2
   bureaucracy 186–7, 191
   Church of Norway; Church of Sweden 105, 193–4, 200–1, 204
   and civil society 213–15, 219
   comparison with Ireland 111, 116, 120–1
   comparison with Scotland 131–2
   creation of (1814–15) 24–7, 102, 181, 198–9, 302
   dissolution (1905) 18, 107, 119–20, 297
   Eidsvoll constitution (1814) 102–3, 108, 113, 193–4
   and emigration 331–2
   and federalism 285
   and First World War 331
   and flags and coats of arms 216, 327
   and foreign policy 115–17, 120, 191, 329–31, 333
   and infrastructure 107, 222
   as model for UK 29–33, 109, 255–6
   and monarchy 105, 111–14, 120, 166, 174
   and nationalism 108–9, 118
   and national identity, lacking 353
   and politics 105, 231
   and rural communities 117–18, 187, 231
   and Scandinavianism 108, 332–3
   separate economies 105–6
   separate military 106–7, 182–3, 318–19
   separate postal systems 107–8
   Swedish disinvestment from union 318–19
   as trade and customs arrangement 101–2, 220
   union as flexible 111
   union providing security 25–6, 181–2
   and unionism 108, 215, 232–3, 315
United Province of Canada (United Canadas) 2, 4–5, 9, 12–13, 43–4, 121–34
   as asymmetrical union 131, 269
   and Catholicism 122–4, 172–3, 193, 277–8
   'château clique' 126
   Code civil du Bas-Canada 134
   and colonialism 121–2
   comparison with Ireland 122–4, 126, 128–30, 133–4, 277–8
   comparison with the Netherlands 95
   and consociationalism/power-sharing 133, 209, 359–60
   creation (1841) 121–2, 124, 129–31, 219, 269
   dissolution (1867) 121–2
   economic basis of union 124–6, 219, 352
   economic effects of union 131–2
   'family compact' 126
   and federation movement (1858–9) 270–2, 274
   and Fenian threat 273–4
   as model for UK 29–32
   and monarchy 172–3
   and parliament 209
   and Protestantism 124
   Scotland as model 123, 130–1, 275
   and seigneurial system 179
   UK as model 129–30
   union as flexible 134
   and US threat 272–4
   see also Canada
United States of America 9, 12–13, 29–31
   as asymmetrical union 307
   civil war 271–4
   constitution 206, 254–7
   and federalism 12, 248–9, 256, 361–2
   and First World War 342
   and immigrants 331–2
   as model for UK 259
   possible union with British North America 271–3
United States of Belgium (1790) 92–3
Unowsky, Daniel 169

Van Buren, Martin 129–30
Victoria, Queen of the United Kingdom 48–9, 61, 74–5, 162*f*, 170–2, 174, 199
Vincent, J. E. 60

Wales
   aristocracy and elites 68–71, 175
   and Brexit 329

and colonialism 58–9
comparison with Ireland 60
composite monarchy 9–10
and Conservatism 81–3
and demeaning stereotypes 60
and devolution 13
economic effects of union 58–9, 78–9
and empire 78–80
and ethnic characterization and stereotypes 60
and evangelicalism 79
and the *Gwerin* 61, 64–5
and home rule 29, 39, 79–80, 84, 261
investiture of Prince of Wales (1911) 64, 75, 170–1
and Labour party 66–8, 85, 228–9
and Liberalism 80–1, 85–6
and miners' strikes 64
and monarchy 171
and nationalism 55, 60, 70–1, 73
National Library of Wales 63–4
National Museum of Wales 63–4
and nonconformism 63–4, 71–3, 77–9, 85
and Protestantism 58, 62–3, 72–3, 85
and rural communities 60, 70–1, 84
union as annexation 56–7, 59–60, 83–4
and unionism 80–1, 83
union with England 40, 55–86
University of Wales 63–4
Welsh Language Act (1993) 83
Welsh Office (1964–5) 58, 82–3
Walker, William 67–8
Walsh, William, Archbishop 245*f*
Ward, Paul 228–9
Webster, Sir Charles 22
Wedel Jarlsberg, Johan Casper Herman, Count 108

Weinmann, F. L. 7
Welsh National League 264–5
Wesselényi, Miklós, Baron 280
White, Arnold 184–5
White, Charles 91–2, 94, 99–100
Wielenga, Friso 99–100
Wilhelm II, Emperor of Germany 117–18, 157
Wilkie, James 140–1
Willem I, King of the Netherlands (Willem Frederik, Prince of Orange) 23–4, 89*f*, 91–2, 94–8, 100–1, 173, 202–3, 224–5
Willem II, King of the Netherlands 94, 173
William IV, King of the United Kingdom 327–8
William of Orange, King of England, Scotland, and Ireland 42
Williams, Gwyn Alf 61, 78–9
Williams, John, Revd 77–8
Williams, Llewellyn 73–4
Williams, Lloyd 66–7
Williams, Rowan, Archbishop 73
Williams, William Llewellyn 57
Wilson, Woodrow 157
Wingfield, Nancy 60
Worms, Henry de, Baron 134–5
Wyndham, George 47, 316–18

Young, John *see* Lisgar, 1st Lord
Young Ireland 266, 276
Young Scots' Society 55
Young Wales *see* Cymru Fydd
Yugoslavia 157–8, 298–9, 345

Zahra, Tara 15
Zita, Empress of Austria 200, 245*f*, 246*f*
Zückert, Martin 339